Enterprise Software Architecture and Design

Entities, Services, and Resources

Dominic Duggan

A JOHN WILEY & SONS, INC., PUBLICATION

For general information on our other products and services please contact our Customer Care Department within the U.S. at 877-762-2974 or, outside the U.S. at 317-572-3993 or fax 317-572-4002.

Wiley also publishes its books in a variety of electronic formats. Some content that appears in print, however, may not be available in electronic format.

Library of Congress Cataloging-in-Publication Data:

Duggan, Dominic.
   Enterprises software architecture and design: entities, services, and resources applications / Dominic Duggan.
      p. cm.—(Quantitative software engineering series; 10)
   ISBN 978-0-470-56545-2 (hardback)
1.   Enterprise Software Architecture and Design (Computer science) I. Title.
TK5105.5828.D84 2012
004.6′54—dc23

                                                    2011031403

Printed in the United States of America.

10 9 8 7 6 5 4 3 2 1

To My Father

Contents in Brief

Contents

List of Figures

Acknowledgements

Thanks to Larry Bernstein for suggesting this book, and for his friendship.
Thanks to my students for their enthusiasm.
Thanks to my family for their support and encouragement.

D. D.

1

Introduction

Communications protocol development has tended to follow two paths. One path has emphasized integration with the current language model. The other path has emphasized solving the problems inherent in distributed computing. Both are necessary, and successful advances in distributed computing synthesize elements from both camps.

Waldo et al. [1]

This book is about *programming-in-the-large*, a term coined by DeRemer and Kron [2] to distinguish the assembly of large applications from components, from the task of implementing those components themselves. Many of the principles of programming-in-the-large were earlier elucidated by Parnas in two articles [3, 4]. It is striking how many of the key ideas of programming-in-the-large that remain relevant today were in Parnas' seminal work.

In the 1980s, with the rise of local area networks (LANs) and object-oriented programming, distributed software buses appeared as solutions to the growing complexity of networked heterogeneous software systems. The synthesis of these trends saw the emergence of the Common Object Request Broker Architecture (CORBA) in the late 1980s. Long before then, industries such as banking and air travel had developed on-line networked transactional systems that are still in heavy use today. CORBA, as originally envisaged, was to be the glue for allowing those legacy systems to be incorporated into modern applications. The use of systems such as CORBA, and particularly of transaction processing monitors, as the backbone for enterprise middlewares has, indeed, been a success story in enterprise software environments. Unfortunately, and perhaps predictably, the challenge of heterogeneity remained, as a heterogeneous collection of software buses emerged for application deployment.

Enterprise Software Architecture and Design: Entities, Services, and Resources,
First Edition. Dominic Duggan.
© 2012 John Wiley & Sons, Inc. Published 2012 by John Wiley & Sons, Inc.

In the 1990s, a true sea change happened with the advent of the World Wide Web. Besides making the uniform resource locator (URL) a part of the daily culture, the spectacular success of the Web has required enterprises to consider how their business model can adapt to this newly popular communication medium. The first Netscape browser included support for the hypertext transfer protocol (HTTP) for the Web, but also supported the safe execution of dynamically downloaded Java applets in the Web browser. It also had support for the CORBA communication protocol to enable those applets to connect back to the server through sophisticated inter-object request broker protocols. Clearly, the thinking here was that a simple protocol, such as the Web protocol, should just be an entry point into the more sophisticated realm of distributed enterprise applications built on modern middleware.

The vision of ubiquitous distributed object systems connecting the world together did not materialize. It became impossible to ignore the significance of location that distributed object systems were supposed to mask. No amount of middleware layering can hide the fact that there is a network connecting the points together, and that network has effects such as latency and failures that cannot be masked from applications. At the same time, the Web protocols that were supposed to be just an entry point into more sophisticated protocols showed amazing staying power, while frustration grew with the complexity of the more "sophisticated" approaches. Most importantly, connecting applications across enterprise boundaries remains a difficult problem, perhaps inevitably so because market forces push against a standardized solution to the problem.

The first decade of the 21st century saw the rise of Web services, an alternative approach to distributed object systems for providing and consuming software services outside the enterprise. Rather than run over proprietary protocol stacks, Web services were proposed to operate over the same Web protocol that had been such a spectacular success for business-to-consumer e-commerce. Although business-to-business e-commerce over reliable messaging systems has been in use for many years, the clear trend has been to vastly increase the scale of this inter-operation by making use of the Web protocol stack. Enterprises must learn to leverage the Internet for rapid and agile application development by continually striving for the optimum mix of in-house expertise and outsourced software services. Thus, service-oriented architecture (SOA) emerged: partly driven by the enabling technology of Web services, partly building on work in component-based development for programming-in-the-large, and partly seeking to align the information technology (IT) architecture with the business goals of the enterprise.

The experience of the WS-* standardization effort has been an interesting one. Developers in the field resisted adoption of the WS-* stack, essentially citing the end-to-end argument underlying the original design of the Internet to decry the complexity of the various layers in the stack. The controversy has had an evident effect. Despite early enthusiasm for simple object access protocol (SOAP)- and Web services description language (WSDL)-based Web services, many companies have pulled back and are instead adopting so-called RESTful (representational state transfer) Web services. As an indication of the "zeitgeist", one IT writer went so far as to declare the SOAP protocol stack to be the worst technology of the last decade [5].

Yet, despite the fact that difficult challenges remain, there is room for optimism. For all of its flaws, asynchronous JavaScript and XML (AJAX) has clearly moved the ball forward in terms of building responsive networked applications where code is easily deployed to where it needs to be executed—essentially anywhere on the planet. As we shall see in Chapter 5, this trend looks likely to intensify. Meanwhile, tools such as jQuery have emerged to tame the complexities of clumsier tools such as the Document Object Model (DOM), while RESTful Web services have emerged as a backlash against the complexity of SOAP-based Web services. If there is a lesson here, it may, perhaps, be in E. F. Schumacher's famous admonition: "Small is beautiful" [6]. Just because a multi-billion dollar industry is pushing a technology, does not necessarily mean developers will be forced to use it, and there is room for the individual with key insight and the transforming idea to make a difference.

However, platforms such as the SOAP stack have at least had a real motivation. Architects and developers tend to have opposing ideas on the subject of SOAP versus REST. REST, or some derivative of REST, may be argued to be the best approach for building applications over the internet, where challenges such as latency and independent failures are unavoidable. Nevertheless, the issues of enterprise collaboration and inter-operation that motivated SOAP and WSDL, however imperfect those solutions were, are not going away. Indeed, the move to cloud computing, which increasingly means outsourcing IT to third parties, ensures that these issues will intensify in importance for enterprises. The criticality of IT in the lives of consumers will also intensify as aging populations rely on healthcare systems that make increasing use of IT for efficiency, cost savings and personalized healthcare. Similarly, IT will play a crucial role in solving challenges with population pressure and resource usage that challenge all of mankind. For example, Bill Gates has made the case for improved healthcare outcomes as critical to reducing family size in developing countries; IT is a key component in delivering on these improved outcomes.

The intention of this book is to cover the principles underlying the enterprise software systems that are going to play an increasing part in the lives of organizations of all kinds and of individuals. Some of the issues that SOA claims to address have been with us for decades. It is instructive, therefore, while discussing the problems and proposed solutions, to also ensure that there is agreement on the definition of the principles. However the book must also be relevant and discuss current approaches. Part of the challenge is that, following the battles of the last decade, it is not clear what role technologies such as Java Enterprise Edition (Java EE) and Windows Communication Foundation (WCF), so central to the adoption of SOA, will play in future enterprise systems. Therefore, this book emphasizes principles in a discussion of some of the current practices, with a critical eye towards how the current approaches succeed or fail to live up to those principles, with passing speculation about how matters may be improved.

In this text the focus is on data modeling and software architecture, particularly SOA. SOA clearly dominates the discussion. This is not intended to denigrate any of the alternative architectural styles, but SOA brings many traditional issues in software engineering to the forefront in enterprise software architecture, and it has ambitious goals for aligning IT strategy with business goals. Domain-driven design is essentially object-oriented design, and it is principally discussed in order to counterpoint it with SOA. There is reason to believe that domain-driven architecture will play a more prominent role in enterprise software architecture, as experience with mobile code progresses. Resource-oriented architecture (ROA) is certainly the technology of choice for many developers, but it is not clear how well it will address the needs of application architects attempting to deal with the issues in enterprise applications. Many of the issues in software architecture highlighted by SOA will also eventually need to be addressed by ROA.

As noted by Waldo et al., the development of enterprise applications has broadly followed two courses: the "systems" approach, in which developers have focused on the algorithmic problems to be solved in building distributed systems, and the "programming environment" approach, which has attempted to develop suitable tools for enterprise application development. The success of the former has been substantially greater than the latter, where the retreat from SOAP-based to REST-based Web services can be viewed as the most recent failure to develop an acceptable programming model. Much of the focus of the systems approach has been on the proper algorithms and protocols for providing reliability and, increasingly, security for enterprise applications. The use of these tools in application development is still a challenge. Computer scientists, sometimes express surprise when they learn of the importance of these tools in the infrastructure of the cloud.

Service developers wrestle with the problems of network security and independent failures every day—even if the solutions are sometimes flawed because of imperfect understanding of the problems and solutions. While the last several decades have seen attempts to build middleware platforms that encapsulate the use of these tools, isolating application developers from the problems with distributed applications, the REST philosophy challenges the assumptions underlying this approach, at least for applications that run over the Web, based on an end-to-end argument that focuses responsibility for dealing with the issues on the application rather than the system. This is a basic rejection of three decades of distributed programming platforms, and challenges the research and developer community to develop the appropriate abstractions that make this effort scalable. Certainly, the application developer must have the appropriate tools provided in programming frameworks. However, even with these tools, the developer still has the responsibility of using and deploying these tools in their application. This approach is in opposition to the traditional middleware approach, which purports to allow developers to build applications without regard to distribution and rely on the middleware to handle the distribution aspects.

The material in this text comes primarily from two teaching courses: first, and primarily, a course on software architecture for enterprise applications; secondly, a course in distributed systems, with an evolving focus on cloud computing. The focus of the software architecture course, and of this text, is on software design and development, including data and process modeling, and design principles. The software architecture course involves hands-on development of an enterprise application, demonstrating aspects of the software architectures considered in this text, using current tools. This approach is highly recommended in order to keep the material "real". However it is also recommended that students be provided with copious tutorials and hands-on guidance, for dealing with "nitty-gritty" details that should not distract from the overall enterprise application perspective. The distributed systems and cloud computing course involves more advanced assignments and programming techniques, that complements the enterprise applications course. For example, the material on failure models (Sect. 2.3), data replication (Sect. 6.9) and distributed protocols (App. B) is covered there, with this volume used as a recommended reference. In these courses, the author has chosen to emphasize REST-based Web services. A related course, in enterprise and cloud computing, has more time to consider SOAP-based Web services from the enterprise perspective, as well as the use of tools such as Hadoop and Cassandra for large-scale cloud-based data processing.

This tension between the "systems" and "programming environment" aspects of the material is reflected in two appendices to this volume. The first appendix reviews the concept of time in distributed systems, a fundamental consideration in the design of any distributed application. Some other aspects of distributed systems, in particular dealing with failures and replication, are also considered in other parts of the text and may be omitted in a course focusing on software architecture. The student wishing to gain a deep appreciation of the issues in enterprise software architecture will hopefully see these aspects addressed in a complementary distributed programming course. A more in-depth consideration of these topics could be addressed by supplementing the summary material in this text with some of the classic research papers from the literature. In any case, any developer of enterprise applications must have at least a basic understanding of the principles of distributed systems, hence the decision to include an introduction to distributed system concepts in this text.

The second appendix provides an introduction to the Haskell functional programming language. Concepts from Haskell are used in several examples in the text, for example when discussing component-based software re-use. Haskell provides an elegant language for describing abstractions, and Sect. 5.4 considers its use in defining embedded domain-specific languages. Sect. 7.6 considers the use of Haskell in verifying client-side conformance with RESTful business protocols, again making use of Haskell's rich support for defining programming abstractions. Finally, there is also a school of thought that the future of RESTful programming is as some form of functional programming. It remains to be seen if this will be the case but, in any case, this provides additional motivation for providing a Haskell tutorial in a text on enterprise software applications.

There is much that is not considered in this volume; a second volume will consider these other issues. Service-oriented architecture is, boiled down to its essence, two things: abstract data types and asychronous communication. In this volume, only the first of these is considered; the other requires further elucidation, particularly in relation to event-driven architecture (EDA). There are also important issues with distributed agreement that there has not been space to fully address. So-called orchestration and choreography of enterprise applications is an important and intellectually interesting topic that will be addressed in the sequel. We also consider the role of the cloud in enterprise applications in more depth in the sequel volume. Finally, security and privacy are obviously important concerns for enterprise applications, particularly when those applications run in the cloud, and we also consider these issues in the sequel volume.

REFERENCES

1. Waldo J., Wyant G., Wollrath A., and Kendall S. A note on distributed computing. Technical report, Sun Microsystems Laboratories, 1994.
2. DeRemer F. and Kron H. H. Programming-in-the-large versus programming-in-the-small. *IEEE Transactions on Software Engineering*, 1976;2:80–86.
3. Parnas D. On the criteria to be used in decomposing systems into modules. *Communications of the ACM*, 1972;15:1053–1058.
4. Parnas D. A technique for software module specification. *Communications of the ACM*, 1972;15:330–336.
5. Turner J. The best and worst tech of the decade, December 2009.
6. Schumacher E.F. Small is beautiful: Economics as if people mattered. Hartley and Marks Publishers; 2000.

2

Middleware

For general purposes, RPC has been a failure. Because the purpose was to mask the fact that the RPC was remote and you can't do that. I've been involved in a number of the projects, and I've become clearly convinced that the sum contribution of our RPC efforts was negative.
Butler Lampson [1]

2.1   ENTERPRISE INFORMATION SYSTEMS

The most important resource in an enterprise is information. The history of *enterprise information systems* (EISs) is one of providing access to, and supporting processing of, that information. A standard way of conceptualizing the architecture of an EIS is in three tiers:

1. At the *resource tier*, the resource management logic provides access to the enterprise asset that the enterprise information system is organized around. This is typically a database or a legacy resource, for example Customer Information Control System (CICS) applications for transaction processing.

2. At the *application tier*, the business or application logic leverages that resource to support an enterprise application. For example, this may be an e-commerce application that utilizes a back end database to record transactions.

3. At the client or *presentation tier*, the presentation logic is the interface between the application and its clients, where the latter may be users or other applications.

Enterprise Software Architecture and Design: Entities, Services, and Resources,
First Edition. Dominic Duggan.
© 2012 John Wiley & Sons, Inc. Published 2012 by John Wiley & Sons, Inc.

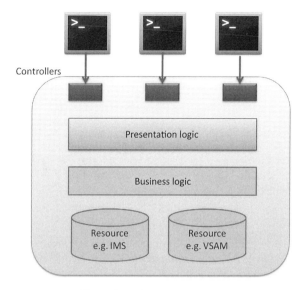

Figure 2.1 *Single-tier systems*

Early enterprise applications ran on mainframe computers and all three tiers were, to a large extent, centralized on the mainframe: data in files or databases, application logic written in COBOL or PL/1, and presentation logic based on 3270 terminals ("green screens"). This is depicted in Fig. 2.1. The classic exemplar of such *single-tier systems* is CICS, still the most widely used software system in the world, with over 20 billion CICS transactions occurring *daily* at the time of writing. The continuing ubiquity of CICS underlies the widespread deployment of a COBOL code base, with 90% of financial transactions and 70% of transactions generally occurring in the context of COBOL applications. Figure 2.1 depicts a single-tier system, as exemplified by CICS. CICS is essentially an operating system in its own right, providing facilities for transaction processing that were missing in early batch operating systems. CICS applications reflect the above three-tier architecture for enterprise information systems. The presentation logic is defined using the Basic Mapping System (BMS), which provides a language for specifying how forms are laid out on terminal screens and how form data are mapped into application language data structures. Business logic is typically written in COBOL or PL/1 augmented with CICS macros in a "pseudo-conversational" style where software routines are invoked in response to users submitting completing forms, defining an implicit work flow for transactional applications. Users of the system log into the CICS system running on the mainframe, with CICS providing lightweight processes for such end-users within the CICS process, and navigate through screen-based forms posted by business logic routines. Data storage is typically based on database-management systems (DBMS), such as the IMS hierarchical DBMS or the DB2 relational DBMS, or record-based file systems, such as Virtual Storage Access System (VSAM). Such legacy systems represent a significant part of the enterprise resources that modern enterprise information systems encapsulate.

Single-tier systems are not automatically inferior to other systems. In fact, there are advantages to keeping all components on one platform: fast and secure access between processes (via in-memory communication mediated by the operating system kernel rather than over the network), centralized administration, and efficient power utilization based on being able to shift computing resources from lightly-loaded to heavily-loaded applications. Such factors are driving a move to virtualized server architectures in the world of Windows/Unix servers, where many of the lessons of the past are being re-learned (as discussed in Sect. 6.9.1). Modern server platforms bear a remarkable resemblance to the mainframes of the past, particularly in the virtualization of resources and centralized management. Interfaces are typically Web-based with rich interactive interfaces, rather than based on 3270 terminals and Virtual Terminal Access Method (VTAM). Nowadays, mainframes themselves support server operating systems, such as Linux and OpenSolaris and middleware systems, such as Java EE, leveraging the mainframe support for highly scalable virtualization and impressive input-output performance.

Two-tier systems or *client-server systems* emerged in the 1980s with the advent of the personal desktop computer. Desktop computers and workstations with bitmap graphics provided platforms for much richer user interface experiences than earlier terminal-based systems as indicated in Fig. 2.2. The adoption of these interfaces was facilitated by the deployment, out of research laboratories, of LAN and distributed systems technologies, such as Ethernet and remote procedure call. One of the most important developments with client server systems, from the point of view of enterprise applications, is that of the *application program interface* (API). Obviously, APIs were already well known from operating systems and from systems

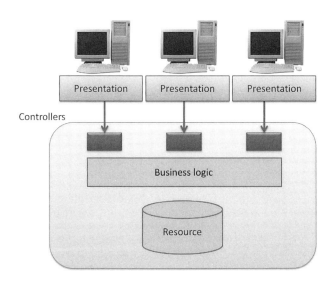

Figure 2.2 *Two-tier (client-server) systems*

software, such as DBMSs and transaction processing monitors, with programmatic interfaces. As we will see, client-server systems crucially rely on explicit interfaces or service contracts between clients and servers to make clear the relative rights and responsibilities of the parties in a distributed enterprise application. The importance of such interfaces is demonstrated by the provision in many distributed programming environments of domain-specific languages—so-called interface description languages (IDLs)—for describing those contracts.

Client-server systems retain some of the advantages of single-tier systems. They maintain some level of centralized administration and maintenance on the server while off-loading much of the interface to clients. They are vulnerable to issues that are always present in distributed applications, particularly that of *independent failures*: unless provision is made for replicating critical parts of the system, failure in some components may ripple out to affect other components, leading to a web of vulnerability. This is exacerbated as clients need to interact with multiple services to achieve their goals. Each service provides its own interface or API to clients and it is left to the client to correctly combine these separate interfaces. Assuming that the interfaces include support for fault tolerance over unreliable networks, for example for managing database transactions and replicated servers, the coordination of these mechanisms becomes a non-trivial responsibility for clients. This leads to the phenomenon of "fat clients", which are historically considered undesirable. We consider fat clients again when we consider domain-driven architecture in Sect. 5.6[1].

Three-tier systems factor out some, or all, of the business logic in enterprise information systems into an explicit middle tier; the software layer that supports this is often referred to as *middleware* (see Fig. 2.3). A middleware system is intended to provide the "glue" that binds together disparate clients and resources in a distributed EIS. As with client-server systems, APIs are critical for describing and communicating data; such systems provide an IDL for specifying interfaces. Middleware systems provide discovery services for locating services for clients and a "wire protocol" that all users of the middleware system can use to exchange data. Middleware systems also provide critical infrastructure for coordinating applications in a reliable manner, particularly via reliable message queues and the coordination of distributed database transactions. Modern middleware systems may also support *load balancing*, directing client requests to the least heavily loaded in a pool of server instances, and transparent rollover of clients from failed resource managers and server to backup servers. There are many examples of middleware systems,

---

[1]Fat clients should be distinguished from *rich internet applications* (RIA), as supported by systems such as AJAX, Flex and Silverlight. The latter systems are generally intended to improve the user experience with Web-based applications, providing highly interactive interfaces based on dynamically downloading user interface code from the Web server to the client Web browser. There is no reason that such an approach should not also allow downloading of parts of the middleware to the client. This has, in fact, happened with companies replacing SOAP-based interfaces to their Web services with AJAX code that is downloaded to the client and calls back to their Web services using proprietary interfaces. However, there are issues with ceding control and coordination of enterprise resources to untrusted client hosts. In the above systems, Web service calls are used to retrieve data from the server, but there is otherwise no reservation of resources on the server.

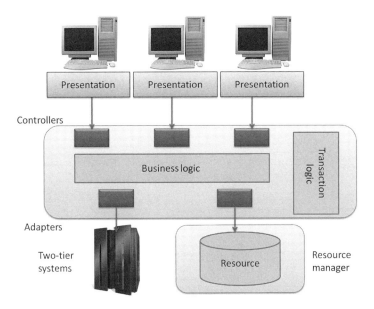

Figure 2.3 *Three-tier systems*

such as CICS, Encina, Tuxedo, CORBA, Java EE, and WCF. Middleware systems provide support for integrating local business logic into the global logic of the system itself. For example, Java EE allows business logic to be expressed as method code in *Enterprise Java Beans* (EJBs), and the latter are then deployed as server objects in the Java EE application server.

Middleware systems connect disparate forms of clients and resources and allow the logic for managing such connections to be defined as part of the application logic in the middleware, rather than making it the responsibility of the clients. Some of these back-end resources may themselves be two-tier systems for whom the application logic in the middleware is itself now a client. This may happen, for example, if the resource manager is a DBMS where application logic is defined using *stored procedures* in the DBMS. Another example is a legacy CICS application that has been modified to support access via HTTP or message queuing, rather than terminal-based forms. *N-tier systems* refer to three-tier systems where the back-end resources may themselves be three-tier systems, or where the presentation logic is split with some on the server (via a Web server) and some on the client (via a Web browser, possibly supporting rich Internet applications).

A typical picture of a modern enterprise information system then, as depicted in Fig. 2.4, is a cluster of Web servers, accessible through the enterprise firewall, that are connected via the internal enterprise network to a cluster of application servers that implement application logic. With n-tier systems, these Web servers may be deployed in Web containers on the application servers. The Web servers may be outside the enterprise firewall, in a so-called perimeter network, or *demilitarized zone* (DMZ), defined by a second firewall between the Web server cluster and the

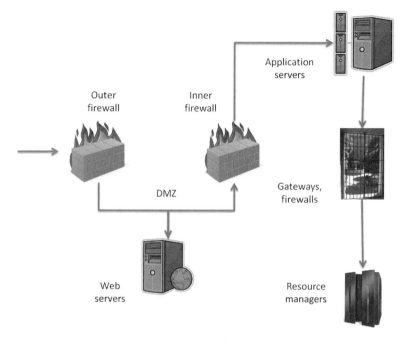

Figure 2.4   *Enterprise network*

internal network. The inner firewall only allows communication to the internal network from the external cluster, so any attack on the network requires compromising the latter machines. The application servers are connected via gateways and inner firewalls to internal resource managers, such as database servers, file servers, and wrapped two-tier systems.

Although this appears to assume physical distribution of the resources, it is well to note that much, or all, of this arrangement can be virtualized in mainframe architectures (by which term we include modern virtualized servers). Communication within the enterprise is made more secure and more efficient by performing it between the memories of virtual machines running on the same physical machine, communicating over virtual, rather than physical, LANs. It may still be desirable to have the point of the entry, the Web cluster, in the DMZ. Furthermore, the hypervisor on the mainframe now becomes a critical component for maintaining the integrity of the system.

2.2   COMMUNICATION

As we have seen, components of an enterprise information system are typically distributed over networks, be the distribution physical or virtual. Portions of this distribution will always be physical, for example for clients or resources that are outside enterprise boundaries, in cases where latency and network reliability dictates geographic constraints on where components are located, or where the scale of the enterprise resources is too large for a single virtualized server. We now consider issues in how communication can be structured between those distributed components.

Networks are essentially like postal networks that have varying reliability; the Internet results from connecting together a collection of such regional postal networks. Machines are like apartment blocks connected by these postal networks. Residents of these apartment blocks communicate by sending postcards (*packets*). Both sender and destination are identified by the addresses of their respective apartment buildings (IP addresses) and their apartment numbers Transmission Control Protocl (TCP) or User Datagram Protocol (UDP) port numbers, depending on the protocol used for process-to-process communication. Just as with postal networks, packets may get lost in the system. If this happens, the Internet leaves it to the original sender of a message (with some cooperation from the receiver) to detect that the message was lost and resend it.

The latter is one of most important decisions made in the design of the Internet and is worth dwelling on for a few moments. Given that data being transferred from sender to receiver must be routed through a sequence of intermediate hosts, where does the responsibility for coping with failures lie? One alternative is to perform error detection and correction point-to-point: a node waits for acknowledgement from the next node when it sends a data frame and resends the data in the absence of such an acknowledgement. The *end-to-end argument* in system design [2] is that such an approach is not justified by a cost-benefit analysis: the cost of point-to-point or link-level error correction is not justified by the benefit because the probability of link failures is small. Indeed, most packet loss in the Internet is caused by overloaded routers dropping packets because of a lack of buffer space, rather than link failures. Therefore, the Internet is designed for packet loss as the exception rather than the norm, with packet loss and re-transmission handled at the endpoints of a communication rather than in the intermediate nodes (Fig. 2.5). The end-to-end argument has become a general organizing principle in distributed systems, although one must be careful not to misapply it in circumstances where the underlying assumptions do not hold. For example, wireless communication may well exhibit sufficient link failures to justify a point-to-point approach to error recovery.

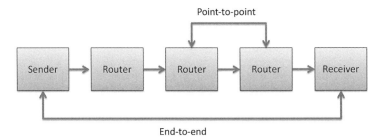

Figure 2.5 *End-to-end versus point-to-point error correction*

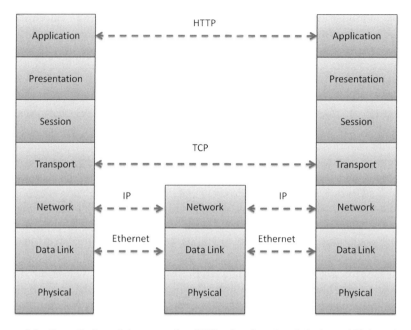

Figure 2.6   *Open Systems Interconnection (OSI) network protocol stacks and Web protocols*

Parties communicating in a network must have an underlying language that they share; this language is termed a *network protocol*. An example of protocol stacks is provided in Fig. 2.6. For example, Web browsers and Web servers are parties that need to communicate over the Internet and HTTP is the protocol that they use. This protocol specifies lines of text that the browser sends to the server and lines of text that the server returns in response. Some of these lines of text are protocol headers that identify, for example, the resource on the server being requested. Other lines correspond to application data. In order to communicate, the browser and server must, in addition, have a means of communicating these lines of text between each other. They must therefore make use of an underlying service layer that performs this communication. This lower layer uses TCP, the Internet protocol for reliable process-to-process communication, to provide this communication: the parties establish a TCP connection and then read and write to each other as though they were communicating through the file system. TCP realizes this communication by breaking up the data stream into a sequence of packets using end-to-end mechanisms between sender and ultimate receiver to ensure that packets are delivered at the receiver reliably and in the right order. The TCP packets must somehow be routed to their destination and TCP relies on another service layer below it. This next layer uses IP to route packets (IP packets containing TCP packets as payload) along a path through the network, much as mail is forwarded in a physical postal network. Specific machines called *routers* provide the function of postal sorting offices, forwarding packets to the next router on the path to their eventual destination. IP requires the ability for a machine to communicate with its neighboring machines, and protocols such as Ethernet (IEEE 802.3) or WiFi (IEEE 802.11) are used to realize these lower service layers. Figure 2.6 depicts a router between the two parties that are communicating. Only the lower layers of the protocol stack are involved in intermediate routing.

In conclusion, we see that communication is realized in networks by building higher level protocols (such as HTTP) on top of lower level protocols (TCP). The combination of such a collection of protocols is referred to as a *protocol stack*. For example, the protocol stack for the Web is based on HTTP over TCP/IP networks. A classic model for categorizing layers in network protocol stacks is the seven-layer OSI model, where, for example, HTTP is an application layer protocol, TCP a transport layer protocol and IP is at the network layer. Protocols such as HTTP and Simple Mail Transfer Protocol (SMTP) are sometimes referred to as "transports" for Web services. To be more accurate, we will refer to them as *transfer protocols* as they typically run over the TCP transport protocol and are intended to exchange request and response messages over a reliable transport.

In practice, the reality is somewhat more complicated than this as a result of phenomena such as *tunneling* of protocols through other protocols. An analogy to explain tunneling is that of driving a car from London to Paris. One route is through the Channel Tunnel, which requires the driver to vacate the car while it is transported through the tunnel on a train. Similarly, an IP packet transmitted from London to Paris may be transmitted as the payload of a packet in the wide area network (WAN) protocol connecting the two cities, e.g., Asynchronous Transfer Mode (ATM). Another example is communicating over a virtual private network (VPN): applications on the VPN may very well believe that they are communicating over a TCP/IP connection, but the reality is that the IP packets are payloads in a tunnel constructed using IPsec, IP and other protocols, such as Point-to-Point Protocol (PPP) over Ethernet.

Enterprise applications that communicate over such networks must use some API supported by the network. Typically, this API is based on *message-passing*. We can abstract the various forms of API into a small set of operations:

1. a `send` operation for sending a message
2. a `receive` operation for receiving a message
3. optionally, a `reply` operation for replying to a message.

The `send` operation transmits a message over the network to the destination machine, where it is buffered until the receiver is ready to process the message. The `receive` operation retrieves a message from the message buffer and returns it to the application. Typically, the `receive` operation is *blocking*: the receiver thread of control is suspended by the run-time system (it is said to block), waiting for a message to arrive if there is no message buffered by the communication system. Once a message arrives, it is buffered and the receiver thread is scheduled to resume execution. There may be an optional non-blocking variant of the `receive` operation that allows the receive to poll the message buffer. Where it is provided, the `reply` operation is always non-blocking: the receiver acknowledges receipt of a message, perhaps returning the result of performing a request represented by that message, and carries on with its next task.

   The important distinction in these message-passing operations is in the blocking behavior of the send operation, as summarized in Fig. 2.7. With *synchronous message passing*, the sender thread blocks until a reply or acknowledgement is received from the other party. With *asynchronous message passing*, the send operation does not block. Rather, the operation returns "immediately" and the sender continues with the next task. This is the *"send and forget"* model of communication that is realized by the UDP protocol that is an alternative transport protocol to TCP. This is useful for sending notifications or heartbeat messages, for example. If the message is lost, another such message will be sent shortly. In practice, senders may want some assurance that their message was successfully transmitted to the receiver and some communication stacks will block the send operation until an implicit acknowlededgment is received from the receiver (re-transmitting the message transparently to the application if the acknowledgement is not received in a timely fashion). To avoid blocking because of this wait for an acknowledgement, the message may be buffered in the communication system so that the send operation does, indeed, unblock immediately while the communication system continues to work to deliver the message to the destination. An example of this is the TCP stack, which uses a sliding window protocol with an array of buffers to pipeline the sending of packets in a transport connection. If the sender becomes too prolific with sending messages, buffer space may become exhausted and, at that point, the send operation must either fail or start blocking. The latter may be a useful approach to flow-control, preventing the sender from overwhelming a slow receiver with messages.

   The alternative to asynchronous message-passing is always to have the send operation be a blocking operation. In formal systems, such as Hoare's Communicating Sequential Processes (CSP) and Milner's Calculus of Communicating Systems (CCS) [3, 4], the sending operation blocks until the receiver is ready to receive. The semantics of these formal systems focus on the resulting synchronization point as the basis for reasoning about the correctness of distributed systems. In practice, a synchronous send operation is normally designed to block until an explicit response is received from the receiver, assuming that the original message that was sent was a request for some service. The motivation is to allow the programmer to think of message passing as a form of procedure call, which programmers are comfortable reasoning about. A procedure call into a library is essentially a service request, with the caller suspending execution until the service call returns with a result. A blocking send operation allows a client to request a service of a remote server in a similar fashion, suspending execution until a response message is returned from the server. This form of communication is often referred to as *remote procedure call.*

   There must be some way for the receiver to explicate which service request they are responding to. This has sometimes been provided with an explicit reply operation (that does not block). In Business Process Execution Language (BPEL), a language designed for composing Web services, there is support for correlating response messages with their corresponding request messages. In remote procedure

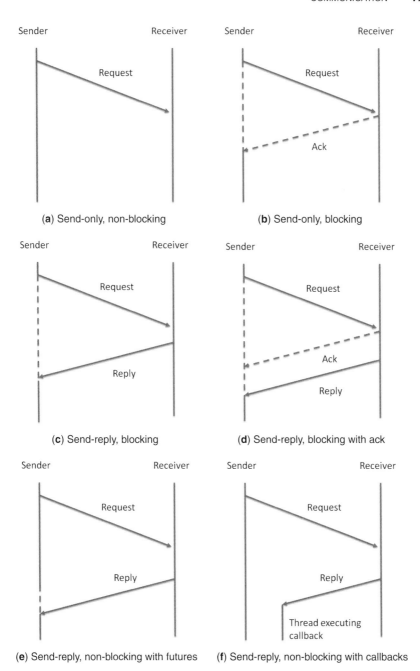

Figure 2.7 *Message-passing semantics*

call stacks that are based on blocking message passing, a server routine generated by a compiler takes care of correlating a server response to a client request and uses lower-level protocols, such as TCP or UDP, to implement the communication.

We will consider remote procedure call in more detail later in this chapter. For now, we note some variants on this abstraction that support *asynchronous remote procedure call*. One of these variants, called *futures* or *promises* [5–7], provides non-blocking semantics for the send operation when a response is expected. Rather than a response, the send operation returns (implicitly, as in languages such as Multilisp, or explicitly, as in the java.util.concurrent.Future API in Java) a placeholder for the response value. The sending process continues with its normal processing until it needs the response value. Once the response value is returned, it is placed by the communication system in the placeholder and a flag set. When the sending process tries to access the response value, it is forced to block if the response has not yet been received. This form of asynchronous message-passing is intended, as with synchronous message-passing, to promote a useful reasoning model for application developers while mitigating some of the latency issues with blocking message passing.

Another variant on asynchronous message passing, again where the sender requires a response from the receiver, is the use of the CALLBACK pattern. A callback is a closure (a function pointer with state, e.g., a delegate in C#) or an object with a designated method that is registered with a software system. The callback is triggered (the function called or a designated callback method invoked) on the occurrence of an event that is detected by the software system. For example, a graphical user interface (GUI) may allow callbacks to be registered with text windows and buttons, to notify the application when buttons are pressed or text is entered. The callbacks typically write into variables shared with the application. Similarly, an API for message-passing may provide a variant of the send operation that does not block and return a result value, but rather takes a callback as an extra argument:

```
// Synchronous RPC API
interface IServer { int send (int arg); }
```

```
// Asynchronous RPC API
interface IReply { void reply (int output); }
interface IServer { void send (int input, IReply callback); }
```

The send operation does not block and the sender proceeds with further processing. The callback is saved by the communication system and is invoked when the response message is received from the receiver. The execution of the callback proceeds in a thread of control separate from that of the sender and the two threads may need to synchronize (for example, using mutex locks and condition variables) if the sender thread requires the result of the remote request. Asynchronous message-passing based on callbacks is realized in several middleware systems, including CORBA, and is a common pattern in BPEL programs. An example of the definition of a service interface using callbacks in WSDL is provided in Fig. 4.23 in Sect. 4.4.2.

This relatively simple picture is complicated by the realities of network communication. Deutsch and Gosling [8] identified eight fallacies of distributed computing that many implementors assume of enterprise systems:

1. *The network is reliable:* Although LANs are fairly reliable, servers may still experience software failures and routers may drop packets as a result of buffer exhaustion. Even Web service standards, such as WS-ReliableMessaging only consider the failure of message loss and it is left up to applications to deal with persisting data through node (server) failures. We consider issues with host failure in the next section and issues with providing reliable communication in the context of host failures in Sect. 2.4.

2. *Latency is zero: Latency* is the time taken for an empty message to be sent to a destination and a response returned. Although latency is low on a LAN, the speed of light is a physical limitation on reducing latency over WANs. For example, one can expect latencies of 80 ms on ping messages across the Atlantic, between New York and London. New cables are being laid across the Atlantic that are intended to reduce this latency to 60 ms for high frequency financial trading. While some of this latency is caused by factors such as routing, peering and the communication stack, it is physically impossible to reduce it below 30 ms because of the absolute limit of the speed of light. As latency puts a lower bound on the time it takes to acknowledge receipt of a packet, this suggests that packet size be maximized in order to maximize throughput over wide area communication. One way to achieve this is with *sliding window protocols*, allowing packets to be sent asynchronously as long as there is enough space to buffer the packets (in case they need to be re-transmitted). As receipt of packets is acknowledged, buffer space is freed up on the sender, allowing more packets to be transmitted, as depicted in Fig. 2.8(**a**). This is an example of *pipeline parallelism*, where several packets are in transit concurrently but at different stages in the "pipeline" between sender and receiver, as depicted in Fig. 2.8(**b**).

3. *Bandwidth is infinite:* As packet loss is handled end-to-end, this places a limit on bandwidth. For example, with a round-trip latency of 40 ms for transcontinental communication and a packet loss rate of 0.1%, with a *maximum*

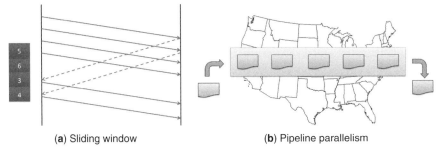

(**a**) Sliding window   (**b**) Pipeline parallelism

Figure 2.8 *Sliding window protocols for pipeline parallelism*

transmission unit (MTU) size of 1500 bytes (the standard for Ethernet v2), throughput is limited to 6.5 Mbps. With a MTU size of 9000 bytes (so-called Jumbo frames, available on special purpose networks), throughput can be increased to about 40 Mbps. However, there is a limit to the ability to increase packet sizes. Although sliding window protocols may side-step some of these limitations, the fundamental point is that, even with high overall potential bandwidth in network links, the limitations imposed by end-to-end failure handling mean that developers should assume some limitations on the bandwidth available for an application.

4. *The network is secure:* Enterprise security is traditionally based on "perimeter defenses", relying on firewalls to protect the internal enterprise network from outside attackers. This model is increasingly outdated, as collaborations between enterprises blur the distinction between trusted and untrusted parts of the network. Rather than allowing defenses to stop at the perimeter defined by the firewall, enterprises should practice *defense in depth*, using internal firewalls to define *enclaves* within the enterprise network, and securing internal communications using, for example, Secure Sockets Layer (SSL) or Transport Layer Security (TLS). Furthermore, all services should validate their inputs to prevent attacks such as buffer overflow attacks, even if those services are only available behind the firewall.

5. *Topology does not change:* Applications should not make assumptions about the location of critical infrastructure components, such as single sign-on and authorization servers. A standard way to decouple applications from the location of services is to reference the services using their Domain Name System (DNS) name rather than their IP address, but this does not protect applications if the DNS name changes—a common problem with broken Web links. We consider a more general solution to this issue in Sect. 6.11.3. The IP protocol uses a flexible routing strategy based on making routing decisions on a per-hop basis; and the WS-Addressing standard adopts this approach for addressing endpoints in SOAP-based communications. The IP protocol assumes that hosts are stationary during communication, and Mobile IP has been developed as an extension of IP that circumvents this assumption. We consider Mobile IP further in Sect. 6.11.3. In enterprise middleware, message brokers and enterprise service buses similarly decouple applications from routing decisions using publish-subscribe semantics that automatically route packets to all intended recipients.

6. *There is one administrator:* Even within an enterprise, there may be separate administrators for databases, Web servers, the network, Linux hosts, Windows hosts, and the mainframe. Once an application crosses enterprise boundaries, which is increasingly the norm with cloud computing, the situation becomes even more complicated, and provisioning resources and diagnosing faults may involve the cooperation of multiple IT departments. Software upgrades now involve coordination between several parties, likely in several organizations, in order to ensure version compatibility across software bases and applications.

7. *Transport cost is zero:* Protocol stacks incur significant overhead for remote communication. Some of this cost is in marshalling and unmarshalling data, converting it for transmission over the network and back again, as will be explained in Sect. 2.4 when we discuss remote procedure call. Using XML as an external representation for program data certainly exacerbates this issue and, despite the appeal of "self-describing data", many applications will choose more efficient binary alternatives or lighter-weight text alternatives, such as JavaScript Object Notation (JSON), to be discussed in Sect. 4.5. Significant costs are associated with the copying of data between buffers in the various layers of the protocol stack. Various techniques have been developed over the years to alleviate this overhead, as discussed in Sect. 6.6.4.

8. *The network is homogeneous:* CORBA was developed as a "software bus" layer over heterogeneous networked systems. Inevitably, heterogeneity crept back into networked applications, e.g., between CORBA and Distributed Component Object Model (DCOM) systems. SOAP-based Web services were intended to bridge this heterogeneity but, again, heterogeneity has crept into implementations of the SOAP-based protocol stack with incompatibilities between the Java EE and WCF implementations. We consider these issues further in Sect. 6.7.2.

2.3 SYSTEM AND FAILURE MODELS

Failures remain a hard problem in building distributed and enterprise applications. In this section, we consider some of the failure models that have been considered in distributed systems research. Before discussing failure models, we need to be explicit about our system models. Two extremes of system models have been described in the literature:

1. *Asynchronous system models* assume no upper bound on the time taken to deliver a message across the network, no upper bound on the difference in processing speeds on different hosts, and no upper bound on relative drift of physical clocks on different hosts. The import of these assumptions is that time becomes a wholly local phenomenon, with applications unable to reply on a global notion of time for coordination, as depicted in Fig. 2.9(**a**).

2. *Synchronous system models* assume much tighter constraints on relative execution speeds, assuming that message delivery delays, host processing speeds and relative clock drift are all bounded from above. This assumes a tightly coordinated execution model for processes on different hosts, essentially allowing algorithms and protocols to be defined in terms of message "rounds", as depicted in Fig. 2.9(**b**).

In practice, both models are extremes. The asynchronous model makes no assumptions whatsoever about the network environment. It may be possible, in practice, to make reasonable assumptions about upper bounds on communication delays, for example if the parties that are communicating are on the same LAN.

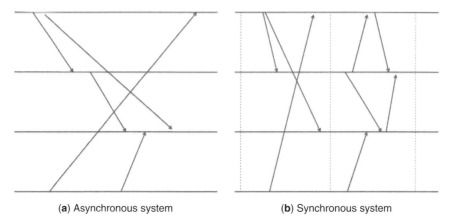

(**a**) Asynchronous system   (**b**) Synchronous system

Figure 2.9   *System models*

The synchronous model makes unrealistically strong assumptions about the level of coordination between the hosts. Such assumptions may be warranted on a multi-processor machine, but not over a network. On the other hand, as explained in Appendix B, a technique that is often used for developing a distributed algorithm is to assume some notion of global time in developing an initial algorithm and then to adapt the algorithm to the absence of global time using, for example logical time. An intermediate model between these two extremes is that of *partial synchrony* [9]. This model assumes that clocks are synchronized within some upper bound and that there are approximate bounds on message delivery time. This effectively justifies the use of timeouts to make decisions about the state of remote hosts, although applications are not required to know what the upper bounds are. There is still the challenge of distinguishing crashes from network partitions.

Figure 2.10 describes a typical architecture for a load-balancing Web service. Clients are, via a DNS mapping that maps the server domain to several IP addresses, directed to one of several load balancers. This ensures that the service is still available if one of the load balancers fails. The load balancers distribute client requests among application servers running on a server cluster in such a way as to spread the load among the servers. This distribution is possible because Web service invocations are state-less on the application servers. Any state modifications are done on the back-end database. This scales for business-to-consumer e-commerce because most consumer activity consists of searching the business inventory. With some allowances for stale data, this content can be replicated across the application servers. Therefore, a client request can be forwarded by a load balancer to any of the available servers and, in particular, to the most lightly loaded server. The back-end database is only involved in updates that must be immediately visible on all application servers, such as changes to the customer account, additions to or deletions from the shopping cart, etc.

If client state is cached on the application server, then this picture becomes complicated. An example of where this may be necessary is where a client is

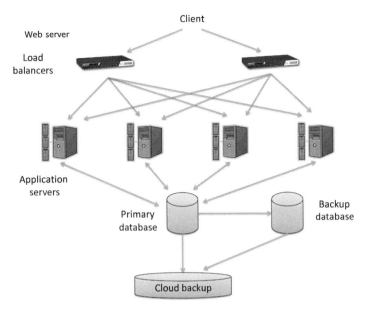

Figure 2.10 *Architecture for a load-balancing Web service*

required to log in before using the Web site. Once the client has authenticated and logged in, the Web server may save a cookie on the client, identifying the state for the log-in session that is cached on the server[2]. Redirection of a client's requests by the load-balancing front-ends may favor the same application server each time, to avail of caching of client state on that server. Alternatively, the session state may be saved on a separate session server in the cluster or on a back-end database server. Caching on a session server avoids over-burdening a back-end database with state maintenance. Caching on the Web server avoids having to retrieve client state, such as the contents of a shopping basket, from a database upon every client request. This preference for directing client requests to a particular application server is referred to as *affinity* in load-balancing clusters. In practice, a shopping cart is accessed relatively infrequently, so it may be sufficient to only store a small amount of information, including the client identity, in the session state. There is a tension here between the performance gain from distributing the client request load across the application servers versus the gain from having client state cached on one particular server.

While this architecture distributes the processing load over several application servers, failure of the back-end database server may be an issue. Therefore, the architecture includes a "hot standby" server that is intended to take over if the primary fails. The database server logs its updates at the standby server with some frequency. If the primary fails, the standby takes over as a new primary server.

---

[2]The notion of session state in a Web server is not without controversy. We consider issues of state-ful versus state-less Web services in Sect. 6.10, and the RESTful approach in Sect. 7.5.

There may be a delay in this process while the standby completes the performance of the update operations that were logged by the primary. There is also a window of vulnerability where the primary may crash before it has had a chance to finish logging the most recent updates at the standby. The standby will take over as primary without seeing these updates, but eventually its own updates will have to be reconciled with missed primary updates. For example, a bank customer's account may go into overdraft because the standby, unaware of a withdrawal operation done on the primary, allows a second withdrawal operation on the original balance. Once detected during reconciliation, this can be handled by sending the customer a letter requesting their cooperation in correcting the mistake. Any potential damage is limited by a cap on how much a customer may withdraw per day.

The distributed systems community has identified several classes of processor or host failures in a networked system:

1. *Fail-stop failures* make very strong assumptions about failures. Processors can only fail by crashing and, moreover, other processors can deterministically test if the processor has failed. We consider the implementation of this strong failure model below.

2. *Network partitions* allow hosts to be isolated from each other on separate subnets, perhaps because of the failure of an intermediate router. The danger of network partitions is that protocols that rely on failure detection based on communication failures may make the wrong decision about the failure of remote hosts, because those hosts are still active but isolated from the current node. Pessimistic techniques, such as quorum consensus, discussed in Sect. 6.9.2, prevent pathologies in such a scenario by allowing no more than one collection of active hosts to make progress while the network is partitioned. Other techniques allow the collections of hosts to make progress and reconcile their separate states when they are reconnected.

3. *Crash failures* again assume that machines only fail by no longer responding to other machines. However, in this model it is not possible to distinguish between a machine that has crashed and a machine that is slow to respond. This model is perhaps closer to the physical reality of the Internet, but it is also one for which some classic impossibility results are well known.

4. *Byzantine failures* allow for machines that fail in arbitrary manners. This includes crash failures, but also includes machines that continue to respond after failing, producing invalid results whose invalidity may be difficult to detect. The distinction is sometimes made between malicious and non-malicious Byzantine failures: the latter assumes that all Byzantine failures are independent, while the former applies the Byzantine failure model to situations where malicious attackers have compromised some of the processes.

The fail-stop model assumes that failures can always be reliably detected and diagnosed. In practice, *failure detection*, the problem of accurately determining if a site has failed, is one of the hard problems in programming distributed systems. For example, a "hot standby" server must only take over as primary if it correctly

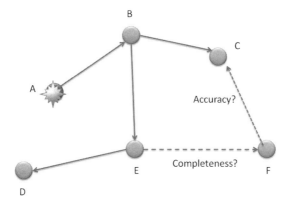

Figure 2.11   *Failure detectors*

determines that the original primary has failed. If the standby takes on the role of primary while the original primary is still running, the result will be chaos for clients of the system. Sometimes primary and standby may share a disk drive with a token, and only the server with possession of the token is allowed to be the primary. If the standby believes the primary has failed, it takes the token, effectively disabling the primary if in fact it is still active.

More generally, nodes in a server cluster may exchange periodic *heartbeat messages* to confirm that they are still active. Each node maintains a list of the nodes that it believes are still active, and expects heartbeat messages from other nodes to confirm they are still active. Various strategies may be used to disseminate heartbeat information, on the basis of which judgements are made about the health of nodes in the system. Alternatively, a failure detection system may pro-actively ping processes, and report these as failed if they do not respond in a timely fashion. As the lack of receipt of a heartbeat message or a response to a ping is an unreliable indication of failure, some detectors will first put a node that did not respond on a "suspect's list", essentially giving it a grace period during which another detector may report that the site is still active before declaring that it has failed. Nevertheless, the correctness of these detectors can only be probabilistic in an asynchronous system and they may produce false positives.

A failure detection system is *complete* if every correct node is eventually informed of the failure of a node. In the example given in Fig. 2.11, the system is not complete if node F does not learn of the failed node. This is actually the concept of *strong completeness*. A weaker notion of *weak completeness* only requires that a correct node eventually learns of the failed node. Strong completeness can be constructed from weak completeness: once a failed process is detected by a correct process, it informs the other processes. The difference between strong and weak completeness is that the latter only considers *detection*, while strong completeness also requires *dissemination*.

However, the decision that a neighboring node has failed, based on a lack of timely responsiveness, is at best an imperfect indication of a failure. A failure detector that always reports all sites as failed satisfies the strong completeness property.

A failure detector is *accurate* if every decision made that a node has failed is correct. This is the notion of *strong accuracy*. Weaker notions include *weak accuracy* (some correct process is never suspected of having failed) and *eventual weak accuracy* (there is a time after which some correct process is not suspected by any other correct process). Eventual accuracy allows detectors to make mistakes, as long as they eventually recognize that they have made mistakes and correct their outputs. In the eventually weak case, there is at least one correct process that is (after some period of confusion) never suspected by the other correct processes. Such a process is a candidate for a coordinator process, that may be used by protocols to demonstrate the use of failure detectors in solving distributed problems[3].

Failure detection is not an end in itself, but rather a potentially useful tool in solving other distributed problems. Some of the key problems that have been identified in distributed systems include the following:

1. *Global consensus* requires that a collection of processors, given an initial input, come to an agreement on an eventual output from each of those processors [10]. In its simplest manifestation, the input to each processor may be either true or false, and all processors must agree to output the same value, whether it be true or false. A trivial solution is to simply say that all processors output the same value, say true, no matter the input. To avoid trivial solutions, the problem statement also requires *validity*: the output value that is eventually chosen must appear as one of the inputs to the processes. Finally, a third property that is required of any solution to global consensus is that it must eventually terminate. Protocols that potentially run forever are not satisfactory.

2. *Atomic commitment* originates as a problem from distributed databases and requires that the parties reach agreement on whether or not to make their database updates permanent, i.e., to commit, or abort, their updates. As with consensus, we assume that every process has an initial input value, true or false (the local decision whether or not to commit), and that the processes must agree on a final output value. The formal properties required of a non-blocking solution to atomic commitment are: (i) no two processes can decide different output values (Agreement); (ii) every correct (i.e., non-crashed) process must eventually decide on its output value (Termination); (iii) the value true can only be decided if all processes propose true (Commit validity); and, (iv) the value false can only be decided if some process crashes or votes for the output value false (Abort validity).

3. The consensus problem considers crash failures in an asynchronous system where failure detection is difficult to distinguish from delayed communication. *Byzantine agreement* [11] considers the same objective of reaching

---

[3]The protocol for building strong completeness from weak completeness must be careful to preserve accuracy in the case where failure detection is only eventually accurate. This can be done by having processes listen for suspected processes that may announce they are still alive. In the eventually weak case, the process that is eventually not suspected can subsequently inform the correct nodes that it has not failed.

agreement on an output value among several processes but assumes the weaker failure model of Byzantine failures: a failed processor may produce no further output, or may produce incorrect output that cannot be distinguished from correct output. The name of the problem comes from considering the problem of a collection of generals, each one commanding an army of the Byzantine empire[4]. The challenge is to coordinate the attacks of several such armies on a (presumably Ottoman) foe so that all armies attack the foe at the same time. Unfortunately, some of the generals may be disloyal and may be conspiring to split the Byzantine forces so that some will attack at different times and be defeated. An inessential modification that is sometimes made is to assume a single general (a leader process) is coordinating the attacks of several lieutenant generals. The Byzantine failures hypothesis includes the possibility that the general himself is disloyal and is lying to his lieutenants about the plans to attack. The two conditions of the Byzantine agreement problem are, then: (i) all loyal lieutenants ("correct processes") obey the same order; and, (ii) if the commanding general is loyal (the leader process is correct), then every loyal lieutenant obeys the order that he sends. If the general is lying, then the lieutenants are free to ignore his orders and decide for themselves whether or not to attack.

4. *Leader election* requires the selection of a leader process from a collection of processes in the presence of process failures. Exactly one process must be chosen as the leader and all other processes must be informed of the outcome. Solutions to this problem are often used as subroutines in other protocols.

5. Several other problems, such as mutual exclusion, termination detection, deadlock detection and distributed garbage collection are considered in Appendix B.

A solution to these, or any other, problems in distributed systems are required to satisfy two types of properties:

1. A *safety property* essentially requires that an algorithm does not reach an "incorrect" state or produce an "incorrect" result. The agreement and validity conditions for global consensus are examples of safety properties. We may allow a distributed algorithm to temporarily "go wrong", provided it eventually corrects itself. The notion of weak accuracy for failure detectors is an example of such a safety property. Therefore, the most general notion

---

[4]The Byzantine Empire was descended from the Eastern Roman Empire and survived long after the Western Roman Empire officially ended in 476 CE. The Eastern Empire was based in Constantinople in Asia Minor, originally named Byzantium and renamed after the Emperor Constantine made it the administrative center of the eastern part of the Empire in 324 CE. The Byzantine Empire officially ended with the sack of Constantinople by the Ottoman Empire in 1453 CE. Constantinople is now modern Istanbul, the capital city of Turkey. What has this to do with the distributed agreement problem? Apparently nothing. Although it is tempting to assume that the problem name was chosen to reflect the infamous palace intrigues of the Byzantine Empire, in fact the "Byzantine" nationality for the generals in the statement of the problem was chosen so as not to offend any current nationalities.

of *violation* of a safety property is one such that, if the property is violated in an execution E of the algorithm, then there is another execution E' that is the same as E up to the point where the property is violated; thereafter the safety property continues to be violated in E'. So, a safety property requires a *guarantee* that, if the property is temporarily violated, it will eventually be re-established by the algorithm.

2. A *liveness property* requires that an algorithm does eventually make progress and achieve a desirable state, such as to produce a result of some form. The requirement that a solution to global consensus terminates is an example of a liveness property. *Non-blocking atomic commitment* refers to the atomic commitment problem with the termination property which requires, for example, that the protocol cannot block indefinitiely on a host failure. *Two-phase commit* (2PC), the most widely used protocol for atomic commitment, fails to satisfy this liveness property, as it relies on a leader process that is a single point of failure. Similarly, Byzantine agreement requires that a solution to the problem terminate. If we assume a synchronous system for Byzantine agreement, then the failure of the commanding general to send any messages can be classified as a failure of the leader process and, in this case, the "correct" lieutenants are free to make their own decision without the general's input.

In a classic result in the theory of distributed systems, Fischer, Lynch and Patterson (FLP) [10] demonstrated that global consensus is provably impossible in the presence of processor crashes in the asynchronous system model. These network assumptions are somewhat compatible with the characteristics of wide-area communication over the Internet. It is perhaps no surprise that other related problems, such as atomic commitment, can be shown to also be impossible in an asynchronous distributed system. An interesting point about the FLP impossibility result is that it only relies on the *potential* for a failure—in this case the loss of a message. If a solution to global consensus existed that satisfied both the safety and liveness properties specified for the problem, then the system would need to make progress despite the delay of critical messages. The impossibility proof demonstrates that this forces the system to reconfigure itself to deal with the potentially lost message, and the message can subsequently be delivered when that message is no longer critical. By repeating this strategy ad infinitum, an adversary can keep forcing the protocol to reconfigure itself and prevent it from reaching a solution state. This contradicts the liveness property required for a solution to global consensus, demonstrating the impossibility of achieving a solution to the problem as stated.

The theory of *unreliable failure detectors* [12] sheds further light on these results. Consider strengthening the assumption of asynchrony by allowing "oracles" that report whether or not other hosts on the network have failed. The theory of unreliable failure detectors distinguishes several forms of oracles based on the relative reliability of their results. One extreme is the *perfect failure detector*, that is both strongly complete and strongly accurate. This detector reports all hosts that have failed and never makes mistakes. The *eventually strong failure detector* is strongly complete and eventually weakly accurate. With this failure detector, every crashed host is eventually detected by all correct processes and at least one correct (running) node is eventually not suspected of being crashed by any detectors (although detectors are allowed to make mistakes about this host as long as they eventually correct themselves). There is also an *eventually weak failure detector* that is weakly complete and eventually weak accurate but, as we have noted, strong completeness can be constructed from weak completeness.

With the eventually strong failure detector, consensus can be achieved, provided that less than half of the nodes fail. The processes execute an unlimited number of "rounds", with a rotating coordinator chosen based on the round number in each round. The coordinator in a round broadcasts a request to all nodes for their values and collects these values in the acknowledgements that are returned, as depicted in Fig. 2.12. The coordinator combines these input values into a single output value and outputs this value once it has received a response from a majority of the nodes. A node that (perhaps inaccurately) suspects the coordinator moves on to the next round in the protocol, incrementing its own internal counter identifying the round. For termination, it still sends the "failed" coordinator a negative acknowledgement in case its failure detection was inaccurate; the coordinator finishes this round once it has heard from a majority of the nodes. Eventually weak accuracy requires that at least one correct process is eventually not suspected by the other processes and, among these candidate coordinators, one will eventually receive positive acknowledgements from the majority of the processes (as the failed processes are always in the minority) in one of its rounds. This coordinator then broadcasts the output value to all of the nodes in a reliable broadcast that will be received by all correct nodes.

Figure 2.13 summarizes what this tells us about consensus and failure detection. *Reliable broadcast* requires that if a process broadcasts a message to all other processes in a collection, then eventually every process in that group receives the broadcast. Appendix B.3.4 considers some approaches to implementing reliable broadcast that make no assumptions about time in the underlying network and are applicable in an asynchronous system. This is an example of a problem that can

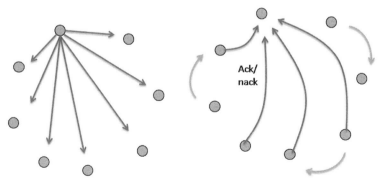

(**a**) Round i: coordinator broadcasts   (**b**) Round i: participants ack or nack

Figure 2.12   *Consensus with unreliable failure detector*

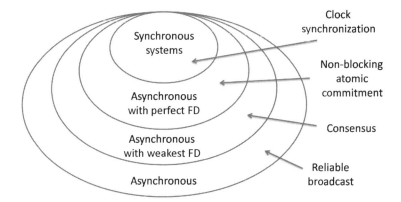

Figure 2.13 *Failure detectors and distributed problems*

be solved using just the assumption of asynchrony. We consider several other such problems in Appendix B.

On the other hand, as consensus is possible with the eventually weak failure detector, this implies that even this "weakest" detector is impossible to implement in an asynchronous system because of the FLP result. The non-blocking atomic commitment problem is not solvable with the weakest failure detector as the surviving hosts must synchronize their decision with the crashed hosts; however, it can be solved using the perfect failure detector. *Three-phase commit* (3PC) [13] is an example of a protocol that can achieve non-blocking atomic commitment in the fail-stop model. Finally, clock synchronization requires the very strong assumption of synchrony, going beyond the usefulness of failure detectors for solving distributed problems.

There are several approaches that one may take in light of these impossibility results. One approach is to use randomized consensus protocols that "flip a coin" at certain steps in the protocol and, as a result, may not achieve the correct result. However, they do achieve the correct result with high probability [14]. Although correctness is not guaranteed, the possibility of an error in the protocol is sufficiently remote that it should not be of practical concern. Another approach is taken by the Paxos algorithm [15]: although there is a worst-case scenario where the algorithm may run forever as two or more processes compete to be the "leader" of a group of processes, the probability of this outcome is, again, sufficiently remote that it is not of practical concern. The partial synchrony approach may be used to achieve consensus, provided a bound is put on the number of processes that may fail. A more radical approach is to replace the problem of failure detection with that of *group membership*: if a process is suspected by some other process of having failed, it is "evicted" from the process group and must re-enter the group as a new member of the process group whether it actually failed or not. This approach avoids the latency issues associated with approaches that seek to achieve consensus of one of its related properties. However, it trades performance for weaker correctness guarantees. Failure detectors have an application in such process group systems as group membership can accommodate false positives. We consider some of the solutions to achieving agreement in more depth in Chapter 10 in the sequel volume, as some of these solutions are in use in the cloud infrastructure.

Although potentially useful in clusters or in an enterprise middleware, these approaches are tightly coupled and may not scale well up to large numbers of nodes or wide area inter-enterprise contexts. Therefore, geographically distributed, inter-enterprise business-to-business services are fundamentally asynchronous: the purpose of a Web service call may just be to insert a request message in the service provider's request message queue. When the response is returned from the service provider, it is inserted into the requester's reply message queue[5]. This interaction pattern can be expressed using the callback pattern described in Sect. 2.2. Another example is provided in terms of a WSDL interface for asynchronous service invocation in Sect. 4.4.2 (e.g., Fig. 4.23). The service requester sends a service request message to the service provider and includes in that request the uniform resource identifier (URI) for a callback service that the provider can use to communicate the reply. Along with the service façade pattern, this is a heavily used pattern in SOA interactions. It is also the basis for the AJAX programming model, although the intention there is to provide a responsive user interface for a highly interactive Web application.

We have focused on crash failures and the challenge of dealing with these failures in asynchronous systems where it is difficult to distinguish host failures from delayed messages. We conclude this section by considering Byzantine failures and, in particular, the problem of Byzantine agreement that originated the consideration of these forms of failures. We assume a synchronous system, so that protocols may be specified in terms of rounds of messages exchanged between the parties. Messages that are expected, but not received, within a round are considered as a form of Byzantine failure on the part of the process that should have sent the message. Consider a scenario where three generals are trying to reach agreement on their battle plans and no more than one general can be disloyal. General A may know he is loyal, but there is the possibility that General B or C is not. One may conclude that the two loyal generals can out-vote the one traitor, but the difficulty is that the disloyal general may lie to the other generals about what he is saying to his colleagues. It can, indeed, be shown that with just three generals, it is not possible to overcome a single traitor and, in general, it is not possible to overcome up to f Byzantine failures without at least $3f+1$ generals[6]. Essentially, the loyal generals need to form a super-majority to out-vote the traitor in their midst.

This lower bound can be relaxed if we strengthen the capabilities of the generals [11]. Assume that the Byzantine Empire had the technology to digitally sign messages to ensure that the contents of the messages could not be forged or tampered with—a capability presumably lost during the Sack in 1453. Furthermore, we assume, without loss of generality, an overall commanding general and his lieutenant generals. Finally, we assume that no more than f processes exhibit

---

[5]Even achieving reliable message delivery with node failures is an example of consensus.
[6]This is the reason that space shuttles flew with four on-board computers.

Byzantine failures (are disloyal). For non-vacuous solutions, we require at least $f+2$ processes, but this is the only lower bound on the number of processes. The following protocol provides a solution to the Byzantine agreement problem:

1. In the first round, the general broadcasts a signed message (either `true` or `false`, to attack or not to attack) to all of his lieutenants.

2. In the ith round of the protocol, each loyal commander (some subset of the general and his lieutenants) considers any messages with $i-1$ signatures received in the previous round. He records any *orders* received in messages signed by the general. The commander then adds his own signature to each of the *messages* with $i-1$ signatures and broadcasts the result to all other processes. This step of the protocol is repeated f times for a total of $f+1$ rounds.

3. After the last round, each loyal commander considers the set of orders that he has recorded, signed by the general. If this set is empty or has more than one (i.e., contradictory) order then the general is disloyal and the loyal commander chooses the default decision, e.g., not to attack. If the set of orders signed by the general is a singleton, then the loyal commander executes that order.

Figure 2.14(**a**) provides an example of the protocol where the the general, process A, and the lieutenant, process B, are disloyal ($f = 2$) and trying to get loyal lieutenants C and D to reach decisions. Lieutenant A only sends its order (to attack) to process B in the first round. Lieutenant B adds its signature to this message and forwards the result to lieutenant D in the second round. In the third and final round, lieutenant D adds its signature to the message and broadcasts the result to all other lieutenants, including the other loyal lieutenant, C. Both C and D receive the order to attack and execute that order.

The errors in the previous example were errors of omission. In the example in Fig 2.14(**b**), the disloyal general sends contradictory orders. It sends an attack order to B and an order not to attack to loyal lieutenant C. In the second round, C adds its signature to the order not to attack and broadcasts this order to all other lieutenants, including the other loyal lieutenant D. If disloyal lieutenant B forwards the contradictory order (to attack) to D, then in the third, and final, round D adds its signatures to both of these contradictory orders and broadcasts them to all lieutenants, including all loyal lieutenants. As both C and D receive contradictory orders from A, they know the general is disloyal and they both choose the default action (e.g., do not attack).

Why does the algorithm work? If the general is loyal, then in the first round it broadcasts the same signed order to all of its lieutenants. At that point, all of the lieutenants know their orders, but they do not know if they can trust the general yet. Therefore, the algorithm must run for another f rounds. The scenario the protocol is preventing is one where a disloyal general issues contradictory orders to different loyal lieutenants without the latter realizing it. The additional rounds in the protocol give the loyal lieutenants the opportunity to re-broadcast any orders

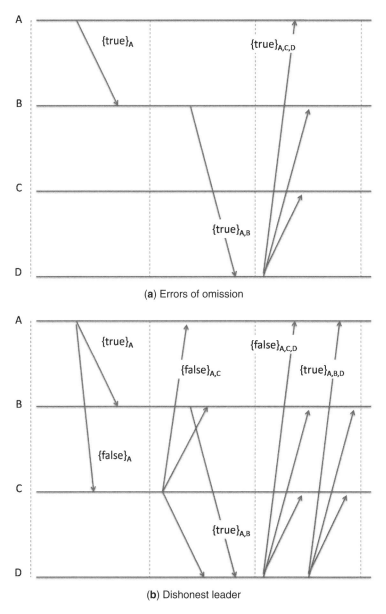

(a) Errors of omission

(b) Dishonest leader

Figure 2.14 *Byzantine Agreement protocol*

they have received, signed by the general, to all of the other loyal lieutenants. The general may try to delay the lieutenants sharing their contradictory orders by relaying those orders through other disloyal lieutenants. This is the significance of the requirement that, by the end of the protocol, messages that are exchanged must have $f+1$ distinct signatures. This ensures that messages that have been relayed from the general must have been relayed through at least one loyal lieutenant, as at least one of the signatures on the message was added by a loyal lieutenant. As a loyal lieutenant will broadcast any orders it receives from the general to all other loyal lieutenants, this ensures that all loyal lieutenants see all other loyal lieutenants' orders by the end of the protocol, even if the contractory orders are only exchanged in the last round of the protocol, as in Fig. 2.14(**b**) on the facing page.

Although digital signatures significantly weaken the lower bounds for Byzantine agreement, this is still an extremely expensive protocol. If all processes are correct, then $O(n^2)$ messages are exchanged in each round, where n is the number of processes. This protocol assumes a synchronous system, which is a very strong, perhaps unrealisitically strong, assumption for a networked system. On the other hand, protocols for Byzantine agreement have been developed for asynchronous systems. We consider some of these protocols in Chapter 10 in the sequel volume.

2.4   REMOTE PROCEDURE CALL

Remote procedure call (RPC) was described in a classic paper by Birrell and Nelson [16]. RPC is a form of synchronous message passing, motivated by the analogy between:

1. a caller into a library service routine suspending its execution until the library routine returns, and
2. a client of a remote service suspending its execution until a remote service request message is acknowledged by a reply message.

An RPC system is an entire programming environment designed to take this analogy as far as possible. For example, an application, using the local file system, calls into an API that includes operations like open, read, write and close. Using RPC, an application is able to use a file system on a remote server in a broadly similar fashion. The application does not need to distinguish between the use of local and remote resources, and programming distributed (client-server) systems is no different from programming with local libraries. This is the rationale for the original design of the Network File System (NFS) developed by Sun Microsystems, using Sun RPC (now ONC RPC) as the communication primitive.

In reality, as the quote at the beginning of this chapter suggests and as discussed in Sect. 2.3, matters are more complicated.

An RPC system (implicitly or explicitly) defines a domain-specific language for describing server interfaces to clients. This *IDL* is particularly useful in multi-language environments, providing a lingua franca for describing contracts between clients and servers where they may be implemented in different languages. This was part of the original motivation for CORBA, providing access to legacy COBOL applications as remote server objects accessed by new clients written, for example, in C++. The following example of the CORBA IDL describes an interface for bank accounts, including operations for depositing and withdrawing money. Note the last operation, which has been tagged as a oneway operation that does not require acknowledgement (and may not be reliably delivered):

```
module Bank {
 interface Account {
  // The account owner and balance.
  read-only attribute string name;
  read-only attribute CashAmount balance;

  // Operations available on the account.
  void deposit (in float amount);
  void withdraw (in float amount);
  oneway void notice(in string text);
 };
};
```

An RPC system provides an *IDL compiler* that generates language-specific type specifications from an interface description. This is depicted in Fig. 2.15. For example, a CORBA IDL compiler might generate a C header file and a COBOL copybook from an interface description to be used to ensure that a C client and a COBOL server are making the same assumptions about operations and data formats. The IDL compiler also generates client and server *stub operations*. These operations are used at run-time to mask the network communication from the application. The client stub is linked in with the client code and serves as a proxy for the server operation that is implemented in a separate process, presumably on a separate machine. The client application calls into the client stub as though it were an implementation of the server operation on the client machine (Fig. 2.16).

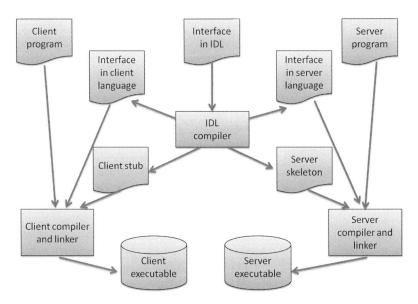

Figure 2.15 *Compiling and linking client stubs and server skeletons*

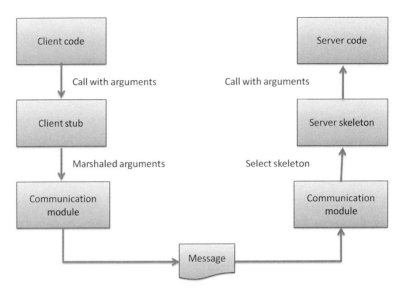

Figure 2.16   *Invoking services via stubs*

The stub takes the arguments passed into the operation and *marshals* them into the payload of a message that is then sent as a request message to the server. The client stub then blocks while waiting for a reply message to be received from the server. At the server, the request message is received and delivered to the server stub (sometimes referred to as a *skeleton*). The latter *unmarshals* the original arguments from the message into program variables, then performs an upcall into the actual server operation on that machine. When the server operation returns to the skeleton with its result, the latter is marshaled into a reply message that the skeleton sends back to the client. The client stub unblocks when the reply message is received: it unmarshals the reply data from the message payload and returns back to the client, passing back result data to the client in a language-specific manner.

As messages may be lost, the RPC system may include protocols for acknowledging successful transmission of requests, with a request automatically re-transmitted if an acknowledgement is not received within a certain period of time. This is an example of the RELIABLE MESSAGING pattern, in support of composability of software services. It is possible that a request is successfully performed but the reply message is lost, leading to a potential re-execution of the request on the server. If requests should not be executed more than once, requests can be tagged with request identifiers, so the server-side RPC system can detect and ignore duplicate requests. These sequence numbers require that client and server share state, requiring the establishment of a connection between the two to initialize this shared state. Alternatively, the communication may be performed over a TCP transport connection. If the server crashes, the connection is broken as it is too expensive to store the shared state in persistent storage. There are several variations on such protocols. For example, large messages may be transmitted using a "blast" protocol that sends the message as several packets, with a single acknowledgement message that identifies those packets that were successfully received. This protocol reduces the latency and improves the responsiveness of RPC calls involving large messages. The NFS v4 protocol supports *compound RPC operations*: rather than issuing individual RPC requests in sequence, with a request acknowledged before the next request is issued, the requests may be batched and sent together, with a single acknowledgement at the end of the batched RPC operation, as illustrated in Fig. 2.17. The motivation is to reduce latency on the client, which will become problematic over a WAN where clients may be some distance from the server.

RPC systems provide various other services for building client-server systems. A name server provides a way for clients to discover the location of the services they need, for example doing a name-based lookup. Clients must make some assumptions about the location of the name server, for example by connecting to it on some standard port. However, they are released from having to make assumptions about the locations of the other services, which greatly facilitates flexible system configuration. This is an example of loose coupling of clients to service—a theme to which we will be returning at several points in this book. In a procedural RPC system, the client *binds* to the server by performing a name server look-up and obtains a *handle*—a data structure with the information required by the RPC operations to locate and interact with the server (Fig. 2.18). This handle is an extra argument to the RPC operations, so the remote interface is not quite the same as the

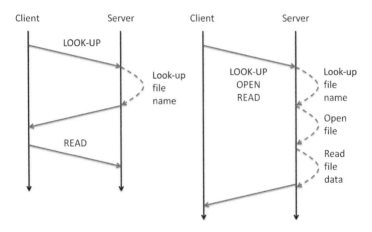

Figure 2.17 *Compound RPC*

Figure 2.18 *Service discovery*

local interface for the operations. Object-oriented RPC or *remote method invocation* (RMI) encapsulates this handle and any other state information that is required for remote interaction in the state of a *proxy object*. The object's interface may or may not distinguish it from local objects. For example, Java RMI requires that all proxy objects implement the java.rmi.Remote interface (ensuring that such objects are marshaled "by reference" as network links), and that their method signatures throw the java.rmi.RemoteException exception:

```
public interface IHello extends java.rmi.Remote {
  public String hello (String name) throws java.rmi.RemoteException;
}
public class Hello implements IHello extends java.rmi.UnicastRemoteObject {
  public String hello (String name) throws java.rmi.RemoteException {
    return "Hello, " + name;
  }
}
```

The fact of network communication is no longer transparent with Java RMI interfaces. The method signatures, through the throws clauses, reflects that invoking methods on a proxy object may result in network failures. Java EE EJBs do not carry these restrictions on their interfaces and EJBs may be Plain Old Java Objects (POJOs). This is because the application server may handle network failures using transactional RPC, as discussed below. However, it is still the responsibility of the application to handle these failures when they are reported back to the client.

Servers typically provide access to a stateful resource such as a database. Traditionally, databases are stored on disk, where access times may be characterized as glacial compared with the speed of modern processors. For reasons of processor utilization and responsiveness, servers therefore handle requests from different clients in parallel, with one client request being processed while another is blocked waiting for completion of an input-output request. Therefore, RPC systems often provide lightweight thread libraries to support the creation and synchronization of multiple threads of control in the server process. Other services that may be provided by an RPC system include a distributed file system and an authentication server for building secure applications.

In the presence of possible server failures, we can consider several possible semantics for reliable RPC:

1. *At least once semantics:* The client continues resending the request message until it receives a response.
2. *At most once semantics:* The client gives up if it does not receive a response.
3. *Exactly once semantics:* The client request is performed exactly once on the server.

Consider trying to provide a reliable remote printer service in the presence of crash failures. An example RPC protocol stack may wait, at the client, for an acknowledgement from the server. We have seen that clients may re-transmit

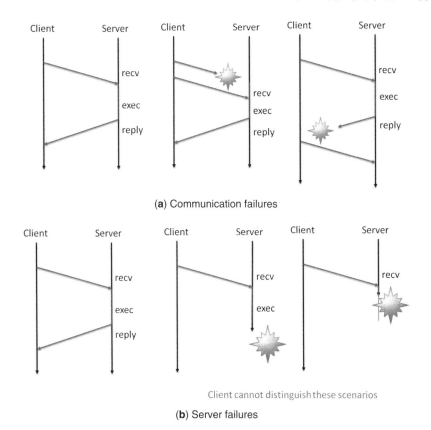

(a) Communication failures

Client cannot distinguish these scenarios

(b) Server failures

Figure 2.19 *Failure scenarios with RPC*

requests if not acknowledged, as depicted in Fig. 2.19(a). Duplicate requests can be filtered out by sharing state between the client and server (sequence numbers that are used to tag request messages). However, receiving a client request at the server does not automatically mean that the request is executed. The server has the choice of sending the acknowledgement before or after the print request is performed. A server failure can happen before the request is received, after the request is finished, or at any point between, including between performing the request and sending an acknowledgement, as depicted in Fig. 2.19(b).

If the server always sends the acknowledegment before performing the operation, then there is the danger that it crashes after sending the acknowledgement but before it has a chance to actually perform the operation. In that case, the client will incorrectly deduce that the operation has been successfully performed. On the other hand, if the server always sends the acknowledgment after performing the operation, then there is the danger that it crashes after performing the operation but before it has a chance to send the acknowledgement. In that case, the client will time-out waiting for an acknowledgement from the server (or the server notifies the client on reboot that it has recovered from a crash) and incorrectly deduce that

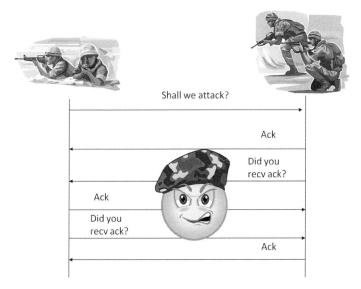

Figure 2.20 *Limitations of using acknowledgements for coordination*

the operation has not been performed. It will re-issue the request to the server and, if successful, the latter will perform the operation a second time.

One may wonder if, with a little more ingenuity, one could provide an exactly-once semantics for RPC. The answer is that, in the absence of further assumptions, it is not possible, and the problem is with achieving global consensus between parties in an asynchronous system. Consider just the challenges with communication failures, where messages may be lost. By analogy, consider attempting to coordinate the attacks of two allied armies, say Red and Blue, both situated on hills overlooking an enemy encampment. Clouds between the hills obscure the armies' views of each other, so they rely on messengers that must make their way through the enemy camps from one hilltop to another. We assume the enemy can only stop the messengers and cannot insert forged messages into the communication. If the Red commander decides to attack, she sends a message to this effect to the Blue commander. However she cannot attack until she receives an acknowledgement, otherwise there is the danger of the Red army attacking on its own and being defeated. The Blue commander, on receipt of the message, can acknowledge it, but now she also must know that that acknowledgement was received before she knows that it is safe to proceed. This is depicted in Fig. 2.20. In general, there is no finite protocol to reach agreement in this scenario. Take any hypothetical protocol that does, minimize the number of messages exchanged in the protocol, and now omit one of the messages in the resulting protocol. If the result is still a successful execution of the protocol, then that contradicts the minimality of the protocol in the first instance. More generally, as we have seen, consensus is not achievable in an asynchronous system.

In the domain of enterprise information systems, there are instances where it may be possible to avoid some of the issues with implementing reliable RPC. In particular, at-least-once semantics is the same as exactly-once-semantics if the operation is *idempotent*: the result of the operation is the same whether it is performed just once or many times. For example, if an update operation just performs a "blind write", replacing data with new data, then the operation can be treated as idempotent. On other hand, an update operation that involves inserting into a data collection in general cannot be treated as idempotent.

A challenge that arises with middleware systems is one where there are several databases being modified by an enterprise application. For example, a sales application may need to update both an inventory database (to reflect goods sold) and a customer database (with customer billing information). If one of these operations succeeds while the other fails, the enterprise information system will be left in an inconsistent state (a customer billed for inventory not shipped, or inventory shipped without billing the customer). *Transactional RPC* allows several request operations to be grouped for application purposes into a *transaction*, with the property that a transaction is failure atomic: either all of the request operations succeed, or the transaction fails and the affected databases are rolled back to a state as though none of the operations were performed. Transactions are important for enterprise applications, both for reliability and for concurrency control, and we will be considering transactions and transactional RPC in depth in Chapter 9 in the sequel volume. Middleware support for transactions is represented by a *transaction processing monitor* (TPM), which is responsible for the transaction logic (see Fig. 2.2) that coordinates the decision of whether a transaction operating on several databases should succeed or fail. All of the aforesaid issues with achieving global consensus in distributed systems apply.

For LAN applications, such as NFS, RPC systems have been broadly successful. For example, NFS has been successfully deployed in academic and commercial environments. This distributed file system exposes an API to client machines that is somewhat similar to the local Unix file system API, including operations for reading and writing files on the remote server. Operations on the remote file system are implemented in an analogous manner to system calls into the local kernel for local file operations. The original implementation of NFS used Sun RPC to realize communication between client and server, with the RPC compiler generating client-side stubs for the NFS client that operates in the client operating system kernel. There are subtle differences between the local and remote APIs. For example, in the original NFS design, servers were always stateless and had no memory of client interactions. This was done to make recovery from server failure relatively easy as there was no server state to be restored[7]. As a result, the read and write operations then explicitly specified the position in the file where reading and writing, respectively, should commence, whereas local read and write operations in the Unix API assume that the kernel keeps track of the current position in the file. However,

---

[7]Since NFS version 4, the NFS protocol has been stateful in order to conform with the locking semantics of the Windows file system.

these differences are to do with the semantics of the NFS application itself, which was designed to be stateless, rather than with the use of RPC. The semantics of Sun RPC is weak and does not guarantee at-least-once nor at-most-once semantics. Nevertheless, this does not appear to be a problem in practice, presumably because of the fact that NFS is usually deployed over LANs, where network failures are relatively infrequent. Server failures are a different issue.

2.5 MESSAGE-ORIENTED MIDDLEWARE

Although RPC has been used successfully in client-server applications over LANs, for wide-area and particularly inter-enterprise application, reliable *message-oriented middleware* (MOM) has seen broader acceptance. Several reasons can be cited, but at root the issue is one of *loose coupling* versus *tight coupling*. Consider a lumber yard performing an RPC request to a distributor of building products for a request for quote on a particular kind of molding. The distributor may, in turn, perform service requests to various lumber mills for price and delivery schedules for the requested product. Assuming these service requests are implemented as RPC, the lumber yard and the distributor are blocked waiting for responses from lumber mills. These RPC calls are "live" in the sense that the call stacks at the lumber yard and distributor are blocked but taking up machine resources in machine memory while they await responses. Suppose the distributor now experiences a server failure. The lumber yard will eventually interpret a lack of response from the distributor as a failure. The service calls to the lumber mills are *orphan service calls* and must eventually be detected as such and terminated by the lumber mills. This may happen, for example, when the distributor host eventually recovers, generates a new *epoch identifier*, and attaches that epoch identifier to all subsequent service calls. The epoch identifier informs the lumber mill servers that any service calls corresponding to earlier epochs are stale.

   This example scenario is possible to implement, but the logic quickly becomes complicated and fragile. Furthermore, it requires enterprises to provision resources for outside parties, and management of these resources in the presence of failures and limited trust is a challenge. The advantage of RPC for building distributed applications is that the call stack manages much of the context for the developer. For example, the distributor may contact a list of lumber mills in order. As each response is received, it contacts the next lumber mill in the list. This can be implemented very simply in RPC as a loop over a list of lumber mills with an RPC call on each iteration. As the call to a lumber mill finishes, control returns to the loop in the distributor, which iterates to perform the next service call. The call stack saves the context of the call, to be resumed when a result is returned from a lumber mill. This simplicity comes at the cost of provisioning resources on the machines involved in the interaction, and dealing with failures. Remote failures can be mapped to the throwing of exceptions, as is done by Java RMI for network failures. However, orphan RPC calls, as a result of the failure of the machine making the service call, do not have a natural counterpart in sequential programming.

The apparent remote failure may not be actual as a result of the unreliability of failure detectors in asynchronous networks. If a remote failure can be mapped to an exception, then the receiver of that exception now has the responsibility of coping with the apparent failure, either by retrying the service call when the server recovers, or backing out of the interaction entirely. Coordinating the failure recovery is usually a considerable challenge. We have seen that transactional RPC has been developed to support the latter, coordinating the undoing of a collection of related update operations in the event of a failure at one of the participating machines. Undoing the entire transaction may not be possible, or even desirable.

MOM provides reliable asynchronous message-passing operations for parties that need to collaborate. The send operation specifies a queue to which a message should be sent. An acknowledgement delivered from the receiver to the sender middleware informs the latter that the message has been received and saved on disk. The sender is now guaranteed that the message has been reliably delivered to the receiver and will survive future failures of the receiver host. If the sender expects an eventual reply message, that will be realized by the receiver using the same reliable message-passing operations to send a reply message to the sender reply queue. In typical APIs for such queues, parties expecting messages on certain queues may use a blocking receive operation, or they may register callbacks that are executed by middleware threads when messages are received. An example of the latter is the use of message-driven beans in Java EE that implement the interface required for callback objects that respond to the receipt of messages in Java Messaging Service (JMS) queues. JMS itself was originally intended as a Java API for third-party messaging systems such as IBM MQSeries, although open source implementations of JMS are now available.

Consider the earlier example of a lumber yard's service request to its distributor which, in turn, causes the propagation of requests to lumber mills. Consider, for example, if the lumber yard has successfully sent the service request to the distributor. What this means is that the lumber yard has received an acknowledgement of receipt of the request, guaranteeing that the message has been reliably saved at the latter. If the distributor fails, the message should survive the failure (unless failure has been catastrophic and messages cannot be recovered from the message database or the log of received messages). The lumber yard now waits for receipt of a reply message, perhaps by registering a callback on the reply queue.

The latter scenario, involving reliable asynchronous message queues, is a better match with the physical reality of inter-enterprise communication. Business processes at each partner enterprise will typically be considerably longer in duration than the basic, system-level operations supported by RPC. This is especially true if human-level intervention is required at some stage in the processing, for example for approval of a quote in supply chain management. Communication is over the Web, or at least the Internet, involving higher latencies and a higher probability of communication and host failures. Reliable asynchronous messaging decouples the service requester and provider from each other, reducing the length of the window during which they may be affected by such failures. If one of the sites fails, they should transition to recovery without the other party ever being aware of the failure. A useful analogy here is between person-to-person email communication versus telephone communication. The latter decouples the parties and allows them to communicate in an asynchronous fashion, allowing for example a busy party to handle the request when they have time. Telephone conversations provide faster responsiveness, but at the cost of both parties needing to be involved in the conversation at the same time.

The disadvantage of the reliable message-passing approach is that it provides a lower-level programming abstraction than RPC and, therefore, the application is left with the responsibility of maintaining application state across communications. For example, the distributor process saves its context on the RPC call stack while invoking a lumber mill service. That context is restored upon return from the service call back to the distributor. If the distributor is in the middle of a loop where it is cycling through a list of lumber mills, issuing service calls in sequence, that information is saved implicitly as part of the RPC abstraction (on the call stack). The cost of this higher level of abstraction is that the application has, to some extent, lost control over failure handling. With asynchronous message passing, an application that is cycling through a list of lumber mills must explicitly save that context (e.g. the lumber mills that remain to be contacted) when it sends a request message and starts waiting for a reply message. This is more work for the application but, on the other hand, gives the application greater autonomy and control over error-handling. This is, fundamentally, the source of Lampson's criticism of RPC cited at the beginning of this chapter.

We have described *decoupling* of the communicating parties as the advantage of asynchronous message-passing. There are other aspects to decoupling, for example how the parties address each other. One way for a party to bind to the message queue of another is to explicitly specify an address for the latter, such as a TCP/IP address for network communication, or a file path for file-based communication. This strongly couples the parties to each others' addresses. The parties can be decoupled by having them refer to each others' message queues indirectly through a naming and directory service, as is done with RPC environments. For example, in the Java EE environment, reference by business objects to JMS queues is done by the Java Naming and Directory Interface (JNDI), a standard Java API for referencing all forms of naming systems. A JMS queue is allocated at deploy time by the server administrator, bound to a queue name, and business objects use that queue name to look up, and obtain, a reference to the queue at run-time. The latter is typically specified by the programmer using dependency injection[8]:

```
@Resource(name = "jms/RequestMessages")
Queue requests;
```

The @Resource annotation specifies that the variable declared below it should be instantiated (by the container that runs the application) with an object obtained by

---

[8]We explain dependency injection in more depth in Sect. 6.5.4 and in Sect. 6.10.1.

performing a lookup on the local JNDI name `"jms/RequestMessages"`. We provide further details on how to bind this logical name in Sect. 6.11.2, when we consider JNDI in more detail. All the operations on the queue are transactional and are committed or aborted atomically, along with any database updates that are part of the same transaction. Dependency injection can be used to obtain a reference to a session context that can be used to manually abort the transaction.

We have seen that naming provides one level of decoupling between parties communicating via message queues. There is another form of decoupling with message queues—one that significantly extends their semantics. So far, we have assumed unicast communication from one party to another. *Publish-subscribe systems* support flexible communication patterns where a message is broadcast to a group of receivers. Rather than specifying the group of recipients explicitly, senders are, again, decoupled from receivers by having the recipients specified by a name—referred to as a topic. The recipients who eventually receive the broadcast message are those that have indicated interest in receiving the message by registering their interest with the middleware. The recipients are said to have *subscribed* to the topic and the broadcasting of a message to the recipients is referred to as *publishing* on that topic. It is the responsibility of the middleware to ensure that all recipients that have subscribed to a particular topic receive the messages that are published on that topic. The part of the system that performs this routing logic is referred to as a *message broker*, as depicted in Fig. 2.21.

The decoupling provided by message brokers and publish-subscribe systems leads to modular systems to which components can be added or removed without modifying the other components. This is because the routing logic has been

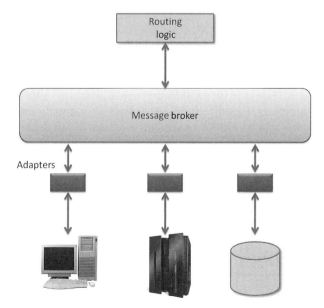

Figure 2.21 Message brokers

lifted from the individual components and placed in the message broker, and the routing of messages determined by the subscriptions of components to particular "channels." A further extension of this semantics is to enrich the message broker with *work flow semantics*. The message broker is now responsible, not just for routing messages to subscribers of their topics, but also for containing application logic that enforces the exchange of messages involved in a particular use case. For example, receipt of a customer order gives rise to an inventory check for availability, as well as a customer credit check. Assuming both messages give rise to positive responses, a message to arrange shipping of the goods is dispatched and the finance department is contacted to bill the customer. A record of the transaction is sent to the product planning department for the purposes of sales forecasting. Support for expressing this work flow logic may be provided by a tool with a graphical language for describing such flows of control, either as an additional product or integrated into the message broker.

Because of their high cost, the use of such tools for *enterprise application integration* (EAI) is normally the province of large enterprises. The need to define application logic in a vendor-specific language such as a work flow language is also regarded as a barrier to entry of the use of such systems. Work in *business process modeling* (BPM) has been addressing some of these issues, defining industry standards such as WS-BPEL and Business Process Modeling Notation (BPMN). The remaining issue of integrating middleware platforms is addressed in the next section.

2.6   WEB SERVICES AND SERVICE-ORIENTED ARCHITECTURE (SOA)

Software as a service (SaaS) has emerged as a useful paradigm for software distribution, leveraging the availability of the Web as a medium for providing external access to services. Classical software distribution models assume that software is licensed to customers, who then install that software on their own hosts. Licensing includes technical support from the software vendor, working with the customer's own IT support to resolve any issues. The SaaS distribution model hosts the software as an application on the vendor's machines. The customer accesses the software remotely, essentially via RPC to the vendor machines. Rather than paying license fees for the right to install the software on their own machines, customers are now metered by the vendor based on their usage of resources to run the application on the vendor machines. Internet services such as Yahoo and Google provide various software services to users and businesses, including email, calendars, document editing and so on. In the business-to-business (B2B) e-commerce world, early examples of the SaaS model emerged in the *customer relationship management* (CRM) field. Google Apps is a prominent example of a SaaS model, providing various business office applications as online services rather than as licensed software.

Although these applications are available to end-users via the Web, for B2B business-to-business purposes it is also necessary to be able to provide programmatic access to these services. For example, this would allow scheduling software to access on-line calendars to determine the schedules of participants for whom a meeting is being arranged. Web services were developed to address the shortcomings of using middleware, such as CORBA, for this purpose.

In the last two sections, we have seen various ways in which middleware platforms can connect separate applications via network communication. These middleware platforms have their own disadvantages. Originally designed for LANs and intra-enterprise applications, the extension of these platforms for inter-enterprise applications is not straightforward. The CORBA platform, for example, was developed as a "software bus" to overcome the heterogeneity of a multitude of hardware and software platforms within an enterprise. CORBA specifies its own IDL in order to describe server interfaces in a language-independent fashion. Each domain in the enterprise is represented by an *object request broker* (ORB) that facilitates communication among parties within that domain. For cross-domain communication, CORBA specifies inter-ORB protocols, such as the Internet Inter-ORB Protocol (IIOP) for transmitting messages over the TCP/IP stack. However, extending this to inter-enterprise communication is challenging. For example, enterprise networks are protected by firewalls that limit external communication. A standard solution to dealing with firewalls is tunneling traffic, such as IIOP traffic through the HTTP Web protocol. This requires the provision of gateways within the enterprises to place request and response messages in HTTP payloads. This process is clumsy and does not address issues such as naming and discovery, and control of coordination protocols, for example for transaction completion. It also runs counter to end-to-end approaches to security, such as encryption of the HTTP messages based on keys negotiated by the parties involved in the communication.

All of this assumes that the parties involved in the communication are using the same version of the CORBA middleware. In fact, there may be interoperability issues between different implementations of the CORBA protocol stack, let alone between CORBA and Microsoft protocol stacks. Although vendors have developed products that provide gateways between these protocols, their deployment tends to be sensitive to configuration errors, and they are not interoperable with each other.

Industry-specific solutions to application integration have been developed. Ariba and CommerceOne were early contenders in the field of Web-based procurement services. Such solutions, based on relying on a trusted third party for coordination, have met with limited success [17]. Industry standards to support such integration include UN/EDIFACT, ebXML and RosettaNet [18–20], of which the latter two are XML-based. In the retail field, Walmart Corporation requires the use of Electronic Data Interchange for Administration, Commerce and Transport (EDIFACT) standards among its suppliers, establishing a form of enforced integration through industry dominance. In the healthcare industry, Health Level 7 (HL7) and Universal Data Element Framework (UDEF) are standards for the interchange of clinical and healthcare data. In some cases (e.g. ebXML), these frameworks specify message exchanges for particular use cases, but applications in general must still define their own communication patterns once they go beyond these use cases.

Web services (in the sense of the WS-* protocol stack defined by the World Wide Web Consortium) were originally developed with these integration issues in mind [21]. In its original manifestation, Web services can be viewed as an RPC stack defined with the HTTP Web protocol as its transfer protocol. The standard defines an IDL, the WSDL description language for Web service interfaces, as well as a wire message format, SOAP. A standard binding specifies how messages are encoded as payloads in HTTP messages. This is intended to be an open framework in the sense that it can be extended, as necessary, for particular applications. Web services distinguish between the "abstract" interface of a service, as specified by the operations that are provided by that service, and the "concrete" binding of that service to a particular transfer protocol, transport, and network address. Although the default concrete binding specifies the sending of SOAP messages as payload in HTTP requests and responses, other bindings can be defined, e.g. SMTP, sending messages as emails, and bare HTTP messages (without the use of SOAP).

In the original vision of Web services, use of the software services provided by an enterprise is no longer limited by compatibility with that enterprise's middleware. Web services are used to encapsulate the software services, abstracting away from details of the enterprise middleware. Outside parties perform Web service calls over the Web protocol stack, exchanging SOAP messages with XML payloads. The design of SOAP is perhaps surprising for what it prescribes and does not prescribe. Whereas most messaging formats specify the provision of addressing information in message headers, SOAP leaves this specification to a separate standard, WS-Addressing. Other issues, such as reliable message delivery and signing and encryption for security are similarly left to other standards. On the other hand, SOAP lays out, in some detail, the mechanics of message header processing by intermediate application nodes, as well as the handling of application faults, such as authentication failure. It therefore envisions scenarios such as application-level tunneling and routing of messages, as well as value-added services at "edge" nodes in an interaction. Because of its reliance on XML over HTTP and the overhead associated with XML-based message formats, the level of communication in Web services is intended to be much more coarse-grained than in classical RPC stacks. While the style of interaction was originally envisioned as an "RPC style" [21], that has now been completely superseded by a "document style," although the terms "RPC style" and "document style" refer to the encoding of request information in messages, rather than the style of the underlying message-passing (synchronous or asynchronous). We explain these terms in Sect. 4.4.1.

If the intention of Web services is to provide a basis for inter-enterprise application integration, that is vendor-neutral and middleware-neutral, then this requires specification of how to represent many details of interaction supported by traditional middleware. This has led to a proliferation of standards, e.g., WS-Addressing for end-to-end message routing, WS-ReliableMessaging and WS-Transaction for reliability, WS-Security and WS-Policy for security, as well as WS-BPEL for business process automation. The complexity introduced by these standards, and to some extent already present in the SOAP and WSDL languages themselves, has led to a backlash in much of the software community. The necessity of being able to invoke software services programmatically over the Web is still recognized as essential for inter-enterprise applications. Reaction against the complexity of the

WS-* stack has led to widespread adoption of so-called "RESTful" Web services. Java EE, for example, supports JAX-RS, a standard API for implementing RESTful Web services in Java that is an alternative to JAX-WS, the earlier standard for defining SOAP-based Web services in Java. Many APIs originally developed as SOAP-based Web services, for example providing programmatic access to Yahoo and Google services, have been replaced by RESTful interfaces. We consider the REST paradigm, and what it means for Web services to be RESTful, in much more detail in Chap. 7.

We began this section by discussing the concept of SaaS. Service-oriented architecture advocates that SaaS be an organizing principle for the enterprise software base. This involves de-emphasizing monolithic application-specific software projects and instead focusing on building an enterprise "software inventory." The units of this inventory are the software components that have been identified as making up the software assets of the company. These assets are represented as software services, with explicit interfaces and invocable via the enterprise middleware. In a SOA, business applications that were once monolithic, as in Fig. 2.22(**a**), are now the result of composing a collection of these software assets, invoking them as services through explicit interfaces where needed, as in Fig. 2.22, perhaps using a specialized work flow language, such as WS-BPEL or BPMN.

The advantages of SOA are readily apparent. By identifying the useful services provided by the software base, cutting across application boundaries, redundancy can be reduced (e.g., merging software services that were developed in isolation for separate applications). Invoking services through their APIs allows one implementation to be replaced by another, allowing systems to be upgraded on a component-by-component basis. Exposing back-end software functionality as services provides access to this functionality to departments that previously had no such access, enabling more flexible sharing of resources, such as data stores encapsulated as services. The modular structure of SOA supports "agile" application development, allowing new applications to be developed quickly by re-using existing software assets as services, with the novelty in the code being the implementation of software services for newly identified required services, as well as composition logic that binds together the services in the new application. The notion of efficient software development based on re-using existing software assets is at least as old as the notion of software libraries. What is different with the current advocacy of SOA is the scale of the unit of re-use, as well as the distribution of the software assets. Rather than libraries for data structures and algorithms, or for system resources such as files and threads, the focus of SOA is on business assets modularized as software services. The value proposition for SOA is based on aligning the enterprise software architecture with the long term business needs of the enterprise in an increasingly competitive environment.

At the simplest level of SOA, these business assets may be data logic (e.g. a customer databases) or business logic (e.g. the logic for writing insurance policies). These business assets are invocable as software services over a software bus, now termed an *enterprise service bus* (ESB), implemented over middleware (Fig. 2.23).

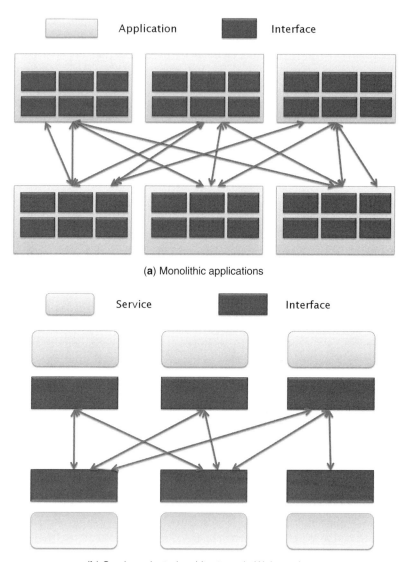

(a) Monolithic applications

(b) Service-oriented architecture via Web services

Figure 2.22   *Service-oriented architecture*

If the middleware supports invocation of service across enterprise boundaries, as was the original motivation for WS-* Web services, then SOA supports inter-enterprise collaboration on a completely new scale, allowing an enterprise to combine services of other enterprises, as well as its own, to develop new end-user applications. With inter-enterprise collaboration now the norm, rather than the exception, in enterprise software projects, SOA may be regarded as essential for modern enterprise software applications.

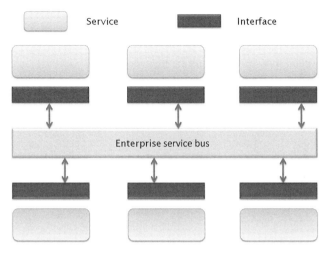

Figure 2.23 *SOA via Web services and enterprise service bus*

On the other hand, the promise of SOA also faces considerable challenges. We have already seen the mixed success so far with Web services, which have attempted to deal with the engineering issues of providing access to software services across diverse middleware platforms. Providing access to data and business logic that previously existed only as back-end functions, poses huge challenges in terms of protecting business intelligence. There may be legislative requirements, such as privacy laws in the healthcare industry that place severe restrictions on the usage of certain data, such as patient clinical information. Simple access control, itself already a challenge in the decentralized inter-enterprise setting, is not sufficient: there must also be mechanisms for controlling and auditing the usage of information once access has been granted. Security and privacy issues lie not only with the provider of software services, but also with the requester. The provider of a service based on composing several third-party services may want to protect customer information from those third parties, if only to avoid those parties stealing their customer base. It is no surprise that SOA governance is a major issue in the management of software services.

There are well-known challenges with so-called software-intensive systems of systems that are relevant to SOA. For example, apparently independent services may access shared resources and inadequate provision for specifying and handling this may give rise to phenomena such as deadlock. *Deadlock* is a phenomenon from concurrent programming, where different processes can no longer make progress because they are blocked waiting for resources to be released by the other. For example, two processes, P and Q, may wish to have exclusive access to records A and B in a database. Suppose P obtains an exclusive lock on A, then Q obtains an exclusive lock on B, then P attempts to obtain a lock on B while Q attempts to obtain an exclusive lock on A. At this point, the two processes are deadlocked, waiting for the other to release its lock before they can make further progress.

Deadlock detection and recovery are difficult issues, with known techniques developed in the field of operating systems (e.g. the Banker's algorithm) and distributed systems (e.g., snapshot protocols, discussed in Appendix B) to address them. In practice, deadlock may be dealt with by human operators noticing that parts of the system are no longer responding and terminating the associated processes.

Deadlock may arise in integrated enterprise systems as separate services attempt to obtain exclusive access to underlying resources that they implicity share through the integration. This suggests that the notion of service interfaces needs to be somewhat richer than the rather elementary properties specified in classic IDLs, expressing invariants that may need to expose the use of underlying resources. Quality of service is another important facet of service interfaces. The Ariadne 5 rocket failure was caused by one of the most famous software bugs in history: an upgraded accelerometer overloaded the primary and backup inertial guidance systems, causing the rocket to veer off course until it was forced to self-destruct [22]. There was no violation of explicit component interfaces because these interfaces did not consider quality of service. Business applications are typically focused on business flows rather than real-time and reactive processing, and the Ariadne 5 incident is an example of the type of tight coupling that SOA seeks to avoid. Nevertheless, other aspects of quality of service, such as failure resilience, may well be important aspects of a software service. We conclude that, although SOA may be of tremendous benefit to business software applications, there are considerable challenges to implementing SOA in a safe and secure fashion.

2.7   CLOUD COMPUTING

One may be forgiven for interpreting cloud computing as a return to single tier systems, so it is perhaps fitting that we consider cloud computing at the conclusion of this chapter. In some sense, our introductory overview of middleware and enterprise software architecture has brought us full circle. We consider cloud computing in more detail in Chapter 10 in the sequel volume.

Cloud computing envisions a "virtual mainframe" composed of computing services, perhaps servers in a data center, or data centers themselves connected by high-speed, high-bandwidth networks, accessible by end-users and their applications over the Internet, perhaps via Web services. Cloud computing can be seen as an enabler of SaaS, but it also goes beyond SaaS in specifying how the infrastructure for SaaS is provided and how that infrastructure is utilized.

We have already discussed the paradigm of SaaS, providing software applications (or their building blocks) as services accessible via some form of middleware, such as Web services. The service-oriented paradigm has also been applied in other ways for Web-based application development:

1. *Platform as a Service* (PaaS) refers to middleware systems that are hosted on service provider machines, rather than on those of the application provider. An example of a PaaS system is Google AppEngine. AppEngine provides

an application server architecture for developing three-tier Web applications. Developers specify their business logic using the AppEngine SDK (written in languages such as Python and Java), create an application identifier, and then use this identifier to upload their application to the Google servers. Data storage is based on the BigTable service [23], part of the middleware infrastructure that underlies Google application services. The application then runs at a well-defined URL (based on the application identifier), executing business logic in response to Web service requests. The cost of using Google AppEngine is the necessity of using the AppEngine APIs for communication and data storage. The advantage is that scalability and reliability are provided automatically by Google server management, for example automatically increasing the number of server instances during periods of peak customer demand. Another example of PaaS is Microsoft Azure. It allows the deployment of applications using. NET libraries and the Common Language Runtime (CLR) in the cloud.

2. *Infrastructure as a service* (IaaS) refers to a lower level approach to providing a platform for Web services. Rather than requiring application developers to commit to a particular API, such as Java EE, .NET or Google AppEngine, this approach allows developers to customize their own server machine, including the operating system (e.g., Linux, or Solaris or Windows), data storage (e.g., MySql or SQL Server) and middleware (e.g., Apache Tomcat, Weblogic or Ruby on Rails). The developer builds their software stack of choice in a virtual machine image. This latter image is then uploaded to a physical server that replicates the virtual server image as appropriate and assigns each running virtual machine its own network address. This is the service provided by Amazon Elastic Compute Cloud (Amazon EC2): virtual machine images are constructed as Amazon machine images (AMIs) which are loaded into Amazon Simple Storage Service (S3), a Web-based data store that we consider in Sect. 7.3. EC2 then deploys virtual machine images based on how the system is configured by the developer. The greater generality of the EC2 approach comes with a price: the infrastructure is not able to provide the same level of automatic scalability as with systems such as Google AppEngine. Instead, it is the developer's responsibility to monitor performance characteristics, such as current demand and configure more resources in response to spikes in application demand. This may be done with the use of third-party products to automate this scaling, for example specialized to configurations involving specific middleware and databases.

Both PaaS and IaaS come under the rubric of *utility computing*, i.e., providing access to computing resources on an on-demand basis. Users of utility computing are billed based on usage of resources such as CPU cycles and disk and network bandwidth usage. Utility computing may be appropriate for providers of software as services as an economically attractive alternative to building their own computing resources. Google AppEngine, Microsoft Azure, and Amazon EC2 are all examples of utility computing, making different design decisions in the trade-off of generality and flexibility versus automated support for scalability and reliability. Following Arbrust et al. [24], we interpret the term "cloud computing" to refer to the combination of utility computing and SaaS, i.e., both the provision of software services as Web services over the Internet and the use of utility computing of some variety as a platform for the provisioning of those software services. An analogy is made with on-demand pay-per-view television, consisting of on-demand video (SaaS) and electrical power underlying that end-user application (utility computing).

What is the motivation for cloud computing? One vision for cloud computing is exemplified by Google Apps: to enable the outsourcing of IT operations such as email and document editing to third parties. The economic argument for such outsourcing is based on several factors:

1. Economies of scale in building computer and networking environments, on the order of a seven-fold reduction in unit costs for large-scale systems as opposed to medium-scale systems [24].

2. Utility providers may be service providers, such as Amazon, Google, and Yahoo, with off-peak resources that they can share with other service providers at little extra cost beyond an administrative infrastructure.

3. Flexibility in choosing the location of physical resources, e.g., locating data centers where cheap hydroelectric power is available.

4. Being able to dynamically increase the provisioning of computing resources in response to spikes in customer demand and, just as importantly, releasing those resources during periods of low demand. This is similar to the motivation for virtualizing server machines: rather than wasting resources (including electrical power) over-provisioning for peak periods of demand, they instead rely on a heterogeneous collection of services with demand spikes occurring in different cycles. This allows for a more efficient utilization of resources, shifting them from less-loaded to more-loaded services as demand fluctuates.

There are, on the other hand, significant challenges with cloud computing. There are obvious security and privacy issues with uploading proprietary or sensitive information to third party servers. Can one trust the utility provider to respect the confidentiality of the data and to provide adequate safeguards to protect that data against other software services running on that server? For example, there is some question as to whether storing student grades, or even enrollment information, "in the cloud" is in violation of the Family Educational Rights and Privacy Act (FERPA) in the USA. Other challenges include automatic scaling of resources, scalable storage, lock-in to proprietary data formats and APIs, and performance predictability.

There is one class of applications that has emerged as a very successful application of cloud computing: batch processing of large data sets based on frameworks for automatic parallelization of the processing over a cluster of virtual server instances. An example of such a framework is the MapReduce system, originally developed for internal applications by Google and subsequently developed as the open source Hadoop system. This provides a functional programming model for describing processing of large data sets. The MapReduce/Hadoop system automatically parallelizes the processing, scheduling processing on nodes in a server cluster that minimizes data movement across the network, and automatically handling server failures during the batch processing. Parallelization is important for responsiveness, allowing processing to be done in hours that may otherwise take weeks. The user of MapReduce can provision computing resources "in the cloud," upload code and data, and download the resulting data when processing is finished. The use of utility computing to provision server resources is surely justified in this instance, as servers are only required for the duration of particular batch jobs[9].

2.8 NAMING AND DISCOVERY

We conclude this chapter with a discussion of naming and discovery in distributed and enterprise applications. We have already seen examples of the importance of naming, both in RPC and MOM systems: by identifying the recipient of a message based on a name rather than a network address, the sender and receiver are decoupled in their logic. The sender of a message (or invoker of a service call) specifies an application name for the intended recipient; the naming system translates that to the address of the recipient. The resulting *location transparency* enables greater flexibility in configuring the system, allowing components' network locations to be chosen and updated to maximize quality of service, and supporting application-level dynamic reconfiguration based on installing new components and modifying the name to address translation (or, indeed, the address to route translation in the case of mobile hosts). Although publish-subscribe systems can be viewed as filtering messages based on their topics, they may also be viewed as a further generalization of naming systems, where routing of messages is based on who has subscribed to particular topics. There are many examples where naming places a critical role in the infrastructure of the Internet. DNS provides a mapping from application-level domain names to IP addresses. The former is an important abstraction for building Web and Internet applications, while the latter is necessary for finding a route to a machine on the Internet. Arguably, the greatest contribution of the World Wide Web has been the invention of uniform resource identifiers (URIs) and URLs that allow resources to be identified anywhere on the Web. The domain name is the most important part of any URL, hence the importance of DNS for the Web.

The WS-* Web services stack assumes concrete bindings for Web service interfaces that include an *endpoint URL*. The latter specifies a transfer protocol, a machine name or IP address and port number, and a *context root*, analogous to a file path on the server machine. The machine address and port number identify a Web service dispatcher, such as a SOAP router and the context root identifies

---

[9]On the other hand, when the National Security Agency decided to use the techniques of MapReduce to perform penetration analysis for military sites, it chose to build its own private "cloud", for obvious reasons.

the service being invoked. The WS-Addressing standard allows application-level routing of SOAP messages, layering such addressing of address information in SOAP headers over the SOAP specification itself, where the latter prescribes the responsibility of intermediate hosts for processing such headers.

However, the reality of name look-up in the Internet is more complicated and demonstrates that there is still room for further development in the naming and addressing of enterprise Web services. A particular example is the phenomenon of caching of Web content in *content distribution networks* (CDNs), such as the Akamai network [25]. For a fee, the latter provides regional caches for content providers, particularly for graphic images that may otherwise cause slow download times for Web pages (and irritated Web site users). A download by a user of a Web page causes the browser to issue download requests for the images referenced in that Web page. As these images are referenced by URLs, DNS look-ups are used to determine the machines from which the images should be downloaded. Here, Akamai plays a "trick": the Web page is pre-processed by the customer to rewrite the URLs so that image requests are redirected to Akamai servers with additional information added to the URL for Akamai purposes. Having been diverted to Akamai servers, a further "trick" is played by rewriting DNS entries to direct download requests for content to the regional Akamai caching servers that are geographically closest to the user performing the download.

Content distribution networks are an example of servers remote-controlling their clients, directing clients to particular server instances based on routing and network load. It also demonstrates that a "name" identifying a resource or a service can have several different levels of interpretation. Originally, a DNS name identified a machine at the application level on the Internet, and the IP address provided a route to that machine at the network level. The Akamai example of a CDN demonstrates that, in some instances at least, a name identifies an abstract resource, which may then be mapped to a specific (application-level) resource instance, which is then mapped to an IP address for a route to that machine. We further consider the issue of naming and discovery for services in Sect. 6.11.3.

2.9 FURTHER READING

Tanenbaum [26] provides a comprehensive discussion of issues in computer networks. Birrell and Nelson [16] provided one of the earliest descriptions of the implementation of RPC, for the Courier system developed at Xerox PARC. Birman [5] and Coulouris et al. [28] discuss various aspects of the design and implementation of distributed systems. Alonso et al. [29] provide an overview of WS-* Web services in the context of middleware and the shortcomings that Web services were intended to address. Armbrust et al. [24] provide the rationale for cloud computing presented here, as the combination of SaaS and utility computing, and also consider the economics of relying on the cloud for IT services.

REFERENCES

1. Lampson B. Gold and fool's gold: Successes, failures, and futures in computer systems research. In: USENIX Conference, 2006.

2. Saltzer JH, Reed DP, and Clark DD. End-to-end arguments in system design. In: Proceedings of the Second International Conference on Distributed Computing Systems; 1981: 509–512.

3. Milner R. Communication and Concurrency. Prentice-Hall; Englewood Cliffs, NJ, 1989.

4. Hoare CAR. Communicating Sequential Processes. Prentice-Hall; Englewood Cliffs, NJ, 1985.

5. Friedman D, Wise D. The impact of applicative programming on multiprocessing. In: International Conference on Parallel Processing; 1976: 263–272.

6. Baker H, Hewitt C. The incremental garbage collection of processes. In: *Proceedings of the Symposium on Artifical Intelligence Programming Languages*. Vol. 12 of SIGPLAN Notices, 1977.

7. Liskov B, Shrira L. Promises: Linguistic support for efficient asynchronous procedure calls in distributed systems. In: Proceedings of the SIGPLAN '88 Conference on Programming Language Design and Implementation; 1988: 260–267.

8. Rotem-Gal-Oz A. Fallacies of distributed computing explained. Sun Microsystems white paper; 2006.

9. Dwork C, Lynch N, Stockmeyer L. Consensus in the presence of partial synchrony. Journal of the ACM 1988; 35: 288–323.

10. Fischer MJ, Lunch N, Paterson M. Impossibility of distributed consensus with one faulty process. Journal of the ACM 1985; 32: 374–382.

11. Lamport L, Pease M, Shostak R. The byzantine generals problem. ACM Transactions on Programming Languages and Systems 1982; 4: 382–401.

12. Chandra TD, Hadzilacos V, Toueg S. The weakest failure detector for solving consensus. Journal of the ACM 1996; 43: 685–722.

13. Skeen D. Crash Recovery in a Distributed Database System. PhD thesis, University of California at Berkeley; June 1982.

14. Aspnes J. Randomized protocols for asynchronous consensus. Distributed Computing 2003; 16: 165–175.

15. Lamport L. Paxos made simple. ACM SIGACT News (Distributed Computing Column) 2001; 32: 51–58.

16. Birrell AD, Nelson BJ. Implementing remote procedure call. ACM Transactions on Computer Systems 1984; 2: 39–59.

17. Hamm S. From hot to scorched at commerce one. Business Week, February 3, 2003. Available at: http://www.businessweek.com/magazine/content/03_05/b3818110.htm.

18. Un/edifact: United nations electronic data interchange for administration, commerce and transport. Available at: http://www.unece.org/trade/untdid/texts/unredi.htm. ISO standard ISO 9735.

19. Rebstock M, Fengel J, Paulheim H. Ontologies-Based Business Integration. Chapter Case Study: Designing ebXML—The Work of UN/CEFACT. Springer-Verlag; 2008.

20. Rosetta net. Available at: http://www.rosettanet.org.

21. Box D. A young person's guide to the simple object access protocol: Soap increases interoperability across platforms and languages. MSDN Magazine, March 2000. Available at: http://msdn.microsoft.com/en~us/magazine/bb985060.aspx.

22. Nuseibeh B. Ariane 5: Who dunnit? IEEE Software 1997; 14.

23. Chang F, Dean J, Ghemawat S, Hsieh WC, Wallach DA, Burrows M, Chandra T, Fikes A, Gruber RE. Bigtable: A distributed storage system for structured data. In: OSDI'06. USENIX, 2006: 205–218.

24. Armbrust M, Fox A, Griffith R, Joseph AD, Katz RH, Konwinski A, Lee G, Patterson DA, Rabkin A, Stoica I, Zaharia M. Above the clouds: A berkeley view of cloud computing. Technical Report UCB/EECS-2009-28. University of California–Berkeley, February 2009.

25. Mahajan R. How akamai works. Available at: http://research.microsoft.com/en-us/um/people/ratul/akamai.html.

26. Tanenbaum A. Computer Networks, 4th edn. Prentice-Hall; Englewood Cliffs, NJ, 2002.

27. Birman K. Reliable Distributed Systems: Technologies, Web Services and Applications. Springer Verlag; Berlin, Germany, 2005.

28. Coulouris G, Dollimore J, Kindberg T, Blair G. Distributed Systems: Concepts and Design, 5th edn. Addison-Wesley; Boston, MA, 2011.

29. Alonso G, Casati F, Kuno H, Machiraju V. Web Services. Springer; Berlin, Germany, 2004.

3

Data Modeling

We have seen that an important aspect of enterprise application integration is the ability to integrate data representations. Several industry-specific standards have been developed for this purpose, such as UN/EDIFACT, ebXML, RosettaNet, HL7 and UDEF. Many of these standards are XML-based, and the use of XML as a basis for defining such data representation languages has been a trend for some time. XML itself is based on Standard Generalized Markup Language (SGML), a predecessor of HTML. Like SGML, XML is an open family of languages in the sense that developers define their own application-specific dialects. For this purpose, it is necessary to have a way of specifying what it means for a document to be well-formed in one of these dialects. One may refer to this specification as the *business rules* for well-formed data. Making these rules explicit is an important part of specifying the data contract between parties that intend to collaborate and share data.

Natural language is one way of specifying these business rules, but more formal description languages can support automatic checking of the well-formedness of documents. Two ways of specifying the well-formed documents in an XML dialect are Data Type Definitions (DTDs) and XML Schemas. Relax NG is another language for specifying well-formed XML documents, that we do not consider here. DTDs are a legacy of the origins of XML in SGML, while XML Schemas use a much richer language for specifying document structure. Nevertheless, the latter is also more verbose and heavyweight than the former, and it does well to consider using DTDs where the descriptions are succinct and the use of XML relatively light.

We will, in this chapter, examine the facilities that XML Schemas provide for defining business rules for well-formed data. We first give an overview of data modeling from the perspective of Entity-Relationship (E-R) diagrams and Unified Modeling Language (UML) class diagrams [1, 2]. The former is a popular tool for conceptual modeling in database applications, while the latter is a standard formalism for specifying the static structure of object-oriented software applications. We

Enterprise Software Architecture and Design: Entities, Services, and Resources,
First Edition. Dominic Duggan.
© 2012 John Wiley & Sons, Inc. Published 2012 by John Wiley & Sons, Inc.

look at UML support for specifying processes and dynamic behaviors in Chapter 13 in the sequel. There is much overlap in the E-R and UML formalisms and our intention is only to place data modeling using XML schemas in context. Therefore, our treatment of E-R and UML provides a high level summary, emphasizing the concepts they have in common. The reader wishing to learn more can consult many fine texts.

3.1 ENTITIES AND RELATIONSHIPS

3.1.1 Concepts and Entities

We are concerned with the modeling of concepts and instances of those concepts within a particular domain. One form of concept describes a collection of instances of interest. For example, as depicted in Fig. 3.1, the concept of interest is that of an animal. An instance of this concept is an actual animal, such as the tiger named Sher Kahn.

There are many approaches to conceptual modeling in disciplines such as philosophy and epistemology. Most approaches to conceptual modeling take the approach of *classification*: determining a set of defining properties for the objects of interest and classifying objects according to which defining properties they satisfy. Different concepts in the domain are distinguished by their properties. Other approaches in epistemology and cognitive science include *prototypical approaches* (based on prototypical instances of concepts that can be matched probabilistically with purported instances to judge the latter's match with the concept) and *exemplar-based approaches* (based on sets of exemplar instances that define the concept). We assume the classification approach hence forth. With this approach, we construct a representation of the concept of interest in the model based on a classification of the properties that any instance of that concept is expected to satisfy in the model. We refer to this representation of the concept as an *entity type*, *class* or *class type*.

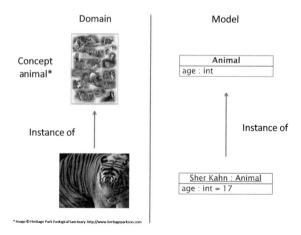

Figure 3.1 *Concepts and models*

We refer to an instance of the entity type in the model as an *entity*, *instance* or *object*. The *extension of an entity type* is the collection of instances of that entity type in the model.

Entity types are represented in E-R and UML modeling by rectangles labeled by the names of those entity types. In UML class diagrams, entities (objects, instances) are represented by rectangles labeled by the underlined names of the entities. A UML instance may be annotated with its class. In Fig. 3.1, we use UML notation for the entity type Animal that represents the concept of an animal, and for the entity Sher Kahn that is an instance of that entity type in the model.

3.1.2   Attributes and Relationships

An entity typically has *attributes*. Attributes are named and have types and those types denote the range of possible values that an attribute can hold. Attributes are similar to fields or data members in objects in object-oriented languages such as C++, Java, and C#. Attributes may have visibility properties (public, private and protected), reflecting the eventual realization of the model in a language such as C++, Java, or C#. In Fig. 3.1, all instances of Animal have an attribute age that can take integer values and that is publicly visible. One typically assumes a collection of *data types* that describe the primitive values that attributes may be bound to. These values are sometimes said to be of *simple type*. For example, XML Schemas define a broad range of data types, including strings, numbers, dates, and so on. In an instance in UML, attributes may be bound to values in classes and instances. This is reflected in Fig. 3.1, where the tiger named Sher Kahn has an age attribute bound to 17.

Concepts that describe collections of instances are one example of what we seek from conceptual modeling. Another form of concept of interest is that of *relationships* between instances. The concept of a relationship is represented by a *relationship type* in the E-R model, and a relationship in the model is an instance of such a relationship type (representing an instance of the relationship in the domain). UML refers to relationship types (class-level) as associations and to relationships (instance-level) as links. Entities typically denote instances in the domain that are named by nouns, whereas relationships are typically associated with verbs[1].

The simplest case is that of binary relationships, relating just two entities. For example, an Animal entity may be related to a Person entity by an is-pet-of relationship. A binary relationship type between two entity types is represented by a line connecting the rectangles representing those entity types. This line may be labeled at either end with the *role* that each respective entity plays in such a relationship. For example, for the is-pet-of relationship between Animal and Person, an Animal entity plays the role of pet in the relationship, while a Person entity plays the role of owner.

One already sees the potential for ambiguity: when should one choose to represent a relationship between entities as an E-R relationship and when should one

---

[1]Nevertheless, it is also possible to treat a relationship as a noun through the process of reification, as we shall see.

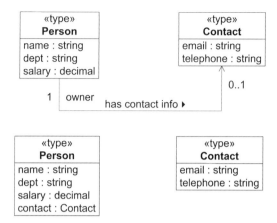

Figure 3.2 *Relationships versus attributes in UML*

choose to represent it using an attribute? For example, if we define an entity type for personal contact information, as in Fig. 3.2, when would it be acceptable to define the entity type Person to contain an attribute named contact which can bind to instances of the entity type Contact. As the example suggests, attributes attach a notion of "ownership" to the relationship: the Person with the contact attribute dominates the relationship with the corresponding contact entity. In general, it is recommended that entity types defined in the model should only be referenced through relationships [2]. If the concepts of Person and Contact are represented in the same model, then references by the former to the latter should be done using relationships.

In the relational data model [3], which is often the target of E-R data modeling, entity types are interpreted by *tables*[2]. Such a table has a column for each of the attributes defined for the entity type. Each entity corresponds to a row in the table. The value for a given row and column denotes the corresponding entity's binding for the attribute associated with that column. Values are taken from simple types defined by built-in data types, where each column is defined to only hold values of the data type specified for the corresponding attribute. Therefore, the relational data model suggests that use of attributes should be reserved for values of simple types, and never for complex data representing other entities.

In a table in a relational database, certain columns are designated as those that uniquely identify each row. For example, in a table of student data, students may be identified by student identifiers. Such a uniquely-identifying column is termed a *primary key*. If there is no natural column, or collection of columns, that can serve as a primary key, such a column may be added to the database design, with the values in each row generated by the database system itself and guaranteed to be unique for each row. Entities in one table may reference entities in another table by their primary key. For example, students may reference their faculty advisors

---

[2]The table is the *extension* or *interpretation* of the entity type in a particular database.

by their faculty identifiers. The latter reference to a primary key in another table is termed a *foreign key*. In the example in Fig. 3.3, the id column in the Contact table is both a primary key for the Contact entities and a foreign key referencing the corresponding entity in the Person table. Foreign keys are the mechanism for representing relationships in relational databases, and XML schemas include support for specifying primary and foreign keys in XML documents. An *extension* or *interpretation* of an n-ary relationship type in a database can be represented by an n-ary table, sometimes referred to as a "join table", with a foreign key for each of the n entity types in the relationship type. Each row in this table represents a relationship in the relationship type.

XML Schemas allow deep structure in documents. For example, an element for a Person may contain a child element for that person's contact information, as depicted in Fig. 3.3. Relational database systems that are engineered to store XML content as complex data may flatten out such nested XML documents to "flat" structures (rows in tables), effectively by lifting nested elements out of the document structure and putting that nested content in its own table, and using foreign keys to maintain the relationship with the original table. The example in Fig. 3.3 is the result of this form of transformation. In the original XML document, contact information is embedded as a child element in a personnel document for a Person. In the mapping to a relational database, the contact information is extracted into a separate table having the same primary key as the original. Another strategy may "unbox" the contact information so that its content is added as extra columns to the Person table, eschewing the need for a separate Contact table. This process of flattening XML content to relational form is sometimes referred to as *shredding* of XML data in database systems.

Performing this flattening at the level of conceptual modeling as part of design, rather than internally in the database system as part of storage, has some repercussions. It can result in a clumsy design with namespace pollution because all elements must be declared at the top level of the schema. This has repercussions for encapsulating importation hierarchies in XML schemas, as we will see in Sect. 3.6. The benefit of automating the flattening of XML documents within a database system that stores the document is that the developer is free to define rich document structure where effectively anonymous entities are nested within other entities. Related considerations have led to database systems being extended with support for storing various kinds of complex user-defined types, particularly for object relational and XML databases, as we will see.

If the relational data model suggests that attributes should be reserved for values of simple type, it should be observed that, at least conceptually, attributes could be eliminated entirely, replacing them with relationships. For example, one could define an entity type for each data type and define instances for each of the values of the data type. The number 17 is then the name of an entity and the fact that Sher Kahn is 17 years old is denoted by a relationship between him and the entity named 17. UML class diagrams include a *stereotype*[3] <<Type>> that

---

[3]Stereotypes are annotations on UML classes (entity types). Such a stereotype on a class specifies that instances of that class are used to extend instances of the "meta-schema" for UML itself.

```
<Person>
    <Id>123456</Id>
    <Name>John Smith</Name>
    <Department>Finance</Department>
    <Salary>50</Salary>
    <Contact>
        <Email>js@email.com</Email>
        <Telephone>555-6789</Telephone>
    </Contact>
</Person>
<Person>
    <Id>654321</Id>
    <Name>Jane Doe</Name>
    <Department>Marketing</Department>
    <Salary>39</Salary>
    <Contact>
        <Email>jd@email.com</Email>
        <Telephone>555-1234</Telephone>
    </Contact>
</Person>
```

(**a**) XML data

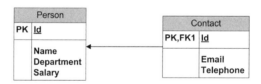

Person:

Id	Name	Department	Salary
123456	John Smith	Finance	50
654321	Jane Doe	Marketing	39

Contact:

Id	Email	Telephone
123456	js@email.com	555-6789
654321	jd@email.com	555-1234

(**b**) Representation in relational model

Figure 3.3 *Storing XML data in relational form*

can be associated with an entity type, denoting that it is the entity type for values of the data type identified by the name of the entity type. The Object Role Model methodology eschews attributes entirely, relying, instead, on relationships to represent such properties [4]. Nevertheless, attributes are found to be practically useful in E-R and UML modeling, essentially providing an immediate and obvious implementation of a relationship. In turn, this provides some economy in the model specification.

3.1.3 Properties of Relationship Types

Relationship types typically have *cardinality constraints*, dictating the number of instances of the respective entity sets that are related by a relationship of that type. For example, the relationship between Person and Contact in Fig. 3.2 is *one-to-one*, assuming that a person has no more than one set of contact information. In this relationship, the Person entity plays the role of the owner of the contact information, while the Contact entity plays the role of the contact information itself, info. The 0..1 annotation for the info role specifies that a person may have no contact information associated with them (but contact information always has an associated person).

UML also allows arrowheads as annotations on associations. These arrowheads play no role in the relationships themselves, but are UML notation for specifying *navigability*. For example, the arrowhead on the Contact end of the relationship in Fig. 3.2 signifies that it is possible to navigate from a Person instance to the corresponding Contact instance. These navigability annotations effectively specify where instance implementations should store pointers to related instances. As our concern is data modeling rather than code design, we omit navigability annotations from UML diagrams from this point forward. For brevity, we also omit the <<type>> stereotype annotation from class (entity type) declarations, although they should be understood as being implicit as we are modeling data design rather than implementations.

Other cardinality constraints of interest specify *one-to-many*, *many-to-one* and *many-to-many* relationships. Figure 3.4 gives an example of these relationships. Each faculty member advises several students, but each student has a single faculty advisor (and exactly one). This is an example of a relationship that is one-to-many

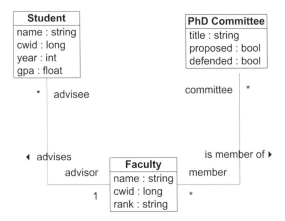

Figure 3.4 *One-to-many and many-to-many relationships*

from faculty members to students. This is reflected by the cardinality annotation of 1 on the advisor role, and * on the advisee role. On the other hand, a faculty member may serve on several PhD committees, and PhD committees are required to have several committee members. Therefore, this is an example of a relationship that is many-to-many, reflected by the * annotation on both roles of the relationship.

We have only considered binary relationships, relating exactly two entities. More generally[4], a relationship may involve n entities for any $n > 0$. Figure 3.5(**a**) provides an example of a quaternary relationship type whose instances relate four entities: a course, a campus where that course is taught, the faculty member teaching the course, and a student enrolled in the course. Such a relationship type is realized by instances of the form:

> Prof. Jones teaches MA 115 to Joe Bloggs at the Madison campus.
>
> Prof. Jones teaches HUM 371 to Jane Doe at the Teaneck campus.
>
> Prof. Jones teaches MA 115 to Jane Doe at the Madison campus.

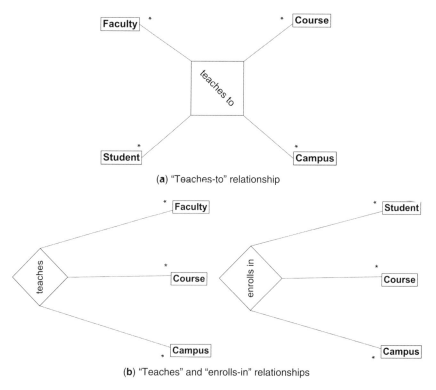

(**a**) "Teaches-to" relationship

(**b**) "Teaches" and "enrolls-in" relationships

Figure 3.5   *n-ary relationships*

---

[4]A relationship type with arity $n = 1$ is effectively a unary predicate and is synonymous with an entity type.

If we assume that each course has exactly one instructor for each campus where it is taught, then this model will contain a great deal of duplication. In the above example, the fact that Professor Jones teaches MA 115 at the Madison campus is repeated for every statement about the students enrolled in the course at that campus. Figure 3.5(**b**) decomposes the original quaternary relationship type into two ternary relationship types. One relationship type represents the teaching of a course at a campus by an instructor, while the other relationship type represents the enrollment of a student in a course at a campus. We can decompose the above relationships into the following instances:

> Prof. Jones teaches MA 115 at the Madison campus.
>
> Prof. Jones teaches HUM 371 at the Teaneck campus.
>
> Joe Bloggs enrolls in MA 115 at the Madison campus.
>
> Jane Doe enrolls in HUM 371 at the Teaneck campus.
>
> Jane Doe enrolls in MA 115 at the Madison campus.

This model no longer duplicates the information about which courses each faculty member teaches.

In general, relationship types in a conceptual model should always be *elementary* in the sense that there is no decomposition of any n-ary relationship type R into relationship types $R_1, \ldots, R_k$ of arity $n_1, \ldots, n_k$, respectively, for some $k, n_1, \ldots, n_k$, such that:

- the extensions of the relationship types $R_1, \ldots, R_k$ refer to the same collection of entities as the extension of the original relationship type R;
- the arities of the latter relationship types are strictly less than that of the former, $n_i < n$ for all $i = 1, \ldots, k$;
- relationships in (the extension of) R can be represented instead using relationships in (the extensions of) $R_1, \ldots, R_k$.

The original quaternary relationship type in Fig. 3.5(**a**) on the facing page is non-elementary (*composite*), as the decomposition into the ternary relationship types in Fig. 3.5(**b**) demonstrates. The reason can be explained in terms of *functional dependencies*. A functional dependency relates sequences of entity types in a relationship type, and is written in the form:

$$a_1, \ldots, a_m \rightarrow b_1, \ldots, b_n$$

for some *m,n* where $a_1, \ldots, a_m, b_1, \ldots, b_n$ are distinct entity types. Such a statement asserts that instances of $a_1, \ldots, a_m$ uniquely identify the identities of the entities $b_1, \ldots, b_n$. For example, the statement that justified the above decomposition was that:

```
Course, Campus → Faculty.
```

In other words, a course and a campus uniquely identify the instructor (once teaching assignments are determined). In the decomposition, teaching assignments are recorded in the `teaches` relationship type and the redundant mention of the instructor in the `teaches-to` relationship type is dropped, resulting in the simpler `enrolls-in` relationship type.

Another form of dependency that can lead to non-elementary relationship types is *multi-valued dependencies*. Whereas functional dependencies mean that a certain sequence of entities determines (the identities of) another sequence of entities, with multi-valued dependencies the former sequence of entities determines a *set* of other sequences of entities. Extending the example above, let us say that any course can have several textbooks. Textbook information for courses is recorded using the ternary `has-text` relationship type described in Fig. 3.6 (**a**). For example:

CS600 uses AHU83 at Madison campus.

CS600 uses AHU74 at Madison campus.

CS600 uses AHU83 at Teaneck campus.

CS600 uses AHU74 at Teaneck campus.

In these instances, there is some duplication in the listing of textbook information, because the two sections of CS600 at the different campuses are using the same two texts. However, suppose a new policy is instituted that different sections of the same course offered at different campuses *must* coordinate so that they use the

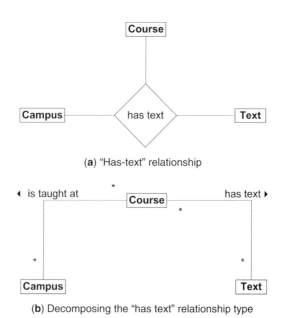

(**a**) "Has-text" relationship

(**b**) Decomposing the "has text" relationship type

Figure 3.6 *n-ary relationships*

same texts. The fact that a course can have more than one textbook is important, as it means there is no functional dependency, Course $\nrightarrow$ Text, even under the new policy: there may be more than one text for a course. However, the above redundancy will appear whenever a course is offered at both campuses. In general, the problem is that there is a multi-valued dependency:

$$\text{Course} \twoheadrightarrow \text{Text } | \text{ Campus}.$$

This dependency denotes that each instance of Course will, in general, define a set of textbooks; the content of this set is independent of the campus where the course is offered. Defining the textbook information in the ternary has-text relationship type leads to unnecessary duplication. The solution is to break this ternary relationship type into two binary relationship types, as in Fig. 3.6(**b**).

3.1.4 Special Relationship Types

For many-to-many relationships, there may be situations where the designer would like to associate additional information with a relationship—information that is not specific to any of the entities involved in the relationship. For the example of PhD Committee introduced in Fig. 3.4, a member of a committee may have a specific role, such as committee chair or external examiner. For the example of student enrollment in a class in Fig. 3.5(**b**), a student will expect to have a grade associated with the class at the end of the semester.

Effectively, we need a way of treating a relationship (an instance of a relationship type) as an entity, so that we may associate further information with the relationship. This process is termed *reification* of the relationship to an entity. In E-R modeling, reification is termed *aggregation*. UML static modeling provides *association classes* for this purpose. Figure 3.7(**a**) defines an association class that reifies committee membership, recording information about the role a committee member plays on the committee. Figure 3.7(**b**) defines an association class that reifies enrollment in a course, recording the student grade and any instructor comments about that student's performance.

If the modeling language provides no support for reification, then it can be implemented by the modeler by introducing entities that explicitly represent relationships and relating an entity representing a relationship to the n entities involved in the original relationship by n new relationships. This is also how any n-ary relationship can be replaced by n binary relationships. Resource Description Framework (RDF) which we consider in Chapter 14 in the sequel, therefore assumes only binary relationships, relying on the modeler to perform this reduction to binary relationships before modeling the relationships in RDF[5].

Conceptual modeling languages also recognize some pre-defined relationship types. In particular, two relationships that receive attention are the *part-of* and *is-a* relationship types. UML recognizes two variations on the "part-of" relationship type. The *aggregation* relationship type[6] relates an entity type to another entity

---

[5]Although RDF has support for reification, it only supports reifying binary relationships.
[6]This is not to be confused with E-R aggregation, which is a form of reification.

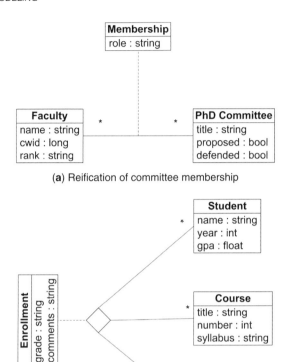

(**a**) Reification of committee membership

(**b**) Reification of course enrollment

Figure 3.7   *Reification with association classes*

type of which it constitutes a component. Figure 3.8 gives an example of a digital single lens reflex (DSLR) camera entity type which is related to its components (memory card, camera body, lens and flash) by the aggregation relationship type.

The *composition* relationship type is a stronger form of the "parts-of" relationship type, where the lifetime of the component entity is determined by the lifetime of the entity of which it constitutes a component. Figure 3.9 provides an example where the lifetime of the radio determines the lifetime of its component entities (analog-to-digital converter, digital-to-analog converter, modulator, etc). It is assumed that the components of the radio are discarded with the radio at the end of its lifetime. In the case of the DSLR, the components may be re-used in other instances of DSLR at the end of the lifetime of the original DSLR. For example, if the camera body is replaced, the lens, memory card and flash may be re-used with a replacement camera body.

The "is-a" relationship is particularly important. It constitutes a central organizing principle for almost all bodies of knowledge. Consider, for example, the use

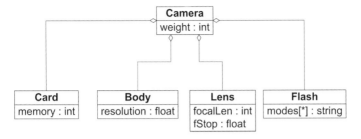

Figure 3.8 *Aggregation*

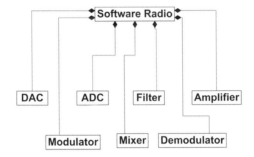

Figure 3.9 *Composition*

of cladistics and cladograms for organizing species of organisms into hierarchies based on shared inherited characteristics. E-R modeling considers two relationship types for the "is-a" relationship. *Generalization* is a "bottom-up" relationship from more specific to more general entities and is intended to generalize from a collection of specific concepts to a more general concept that encompasses the former. In this sense, the collection of entity types that is generalized from is intended to be exhaustive. For example, Fig. 3.10 defines the entity type Community for entities that make up the personnel of a university community. This entity type generalizes from students, faculty, and administrative staff that consistitutes an exhaustive list of the form of personnel that make up said community. The general entity type in a generalization hierarchy may satisfy either or both of the following properties:

1. *Completeness:* All instances of the specific entity types are also instances of the general entity type.
2. *Disjointness:* No entity belongs to more than one of the specific entity types.

A generalization that satisfies both of these properties is referred to as a *partition*. Disjointness may be violated by the example given in Fig. 3.10 if students work in an administrative capacity (we assume teaching and research assistants are exempt). Furthermore, if we wish to satisfy disjointness, we must decide that deans and provosts are either faculty or administrative staff, but not both.

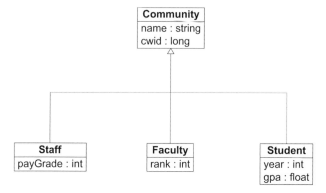

Figure 3.10 *Generalization*

The E-R relationship type of *specialization* is intended to be a "top-down" relationship type from more general to more specific instance types. We depict it graphically in the UML fashion, with the arrow pointing from the more specific to the more general[7]. Principally, specialization differs from generalization in the fact that the set of alternatives is no longer assumed to be closed. Figure 3.11 depicts a specialization hierarchy for content types, from the most general concept of `Content` to more general concepts, such as `Book`, `Music` and `Film`. There are further specializations, such as of `Book` to `E-Book` and `AudioBook`, and of `Film` to `InteractiveFilm` based on BD-Live for Blu-Ray. These are not intended to be exhaustive lists of the possible specializations. For example, we have omitted `Podcasts` from the list of specializations of `MediaContent`. Indeed, trying to exhaustively list all content types appears a hopeless, and pointless, exercise, given the rate at which new media types emerge. Instead, the intention is that this hierarchy is "open" to the addition of further entity types to the hierarchy, whereas the list of entity types for `Community` in the previous example is "closed".

Programmatically, this distinction is significant: if a hierarchy is based on generalization, then a program processing an entity of the general type may reason by cases on what the specific entity type is for the instance. If the hierarchy is based on specialization, then there is a danger that reasoning by cases is non-exhaustive. This is a motivation for object-oriented programming, that factors reasoning by cases into the data objects themselves. This has implications for software architecture, as we will see in Chapters 5 and 6 when we consider domain-driven architecture and SOA.

On the other hand, all more specific entities, related by specialization or generalization to a more general entity type, share the attributes associated with that "parent" entity type. For example, all instances of `Media` have `title` and `genre` attributes, so an application may list or search a media catalogue based on these attributes alone without needing to consider the media types of the instances.

---

[7]This relationship type is referred to as "generalization" in UML. We use the E-R terminology of "specialization".

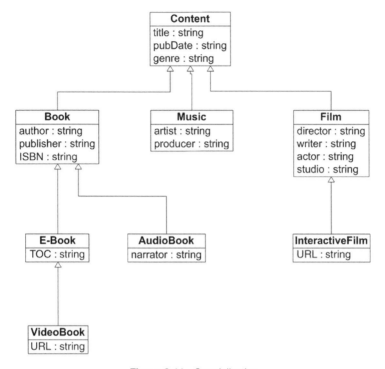

Figure 3.11 *Specialization*

We conclude by noting that, underlying the conceptual modeling languages summarized here, there are well-known logical languages for explaining the same concepts. First order logic (FOL) [5] provides a language for describing entities and relationships between those entities. In FOL, *terms* are formal names for entities. These names may be atomic (as they are in languages such as Datalog [6]) or composite. *Predicates* are verbs for making "statements" about entities and relating entities. A unary predicate makes a statement about a single entity and can be used to define entity types. For example, "Aristotle was a philosopher" uses the predicate "X was a philosopher" to classify the entity named "Aristotle." The statement "Plato taught Aristotle" uses a binary predicate to relate (the entity named) Aristotle to another entity (named "Plato"). *Entailment* relates one property to another. For example, we may assert that all entities who were taught by Plato were philosophers with the entailment:

(Plato taught X) entails (X was a philosopher).

Logic is a formal language for making statements about entities and relationships between those entities. The intention is that there is some interpretation that is intended for the entities and relationship types named in the logical statements. Set theory is used to describe such interpretations. An *interpretation* assumes a domain of instances or *elements*, for example the set of people who lived in Athens in the fourth century BC. The interpretation gives a meaning to every term (name) as an element in the domain. It interprets every unary predicate (property) as a set of elements; these are the instances that satisfy the property in the interpretation. It interprets every n-ary predicate, for $n > 1$, as a *relation*, i.e., a boolean-valued function mapping from n arguments to `true` or `false`[8]. A statement is true in the interpretation if the relation for that statement maps the translations of the corresponding terms to `true`. For example, if the interpretation of the predicate "X `taught` Y" is the boolean-valued function F, then the statement "`Plato taught Aristotle`" is true (in the interpretation) if $F(Plato, Aristotle) = $ `true`. Logical entailment in FOL is interpreted as subset inclusion. For example, let *PlatosStudents* be the set of people in Athens who were taught by Plato, and let *Philosophers* be the set of philosophers. The logical statements may assert that the property "`Plato taught` X" entails the property "X `was a philosopher.`" In the interpretation, this is represented by the subset inclusion *PlatosStudents* $\subseteq$ *Philosopher*.

If logic and set theory naturally generalize all the modeling languages we have considered, the latter are still useful for the idioms and concepts they provide the concept modeler with. Logic may be considered as the "assembly language" underlying languages for conceptual modeling. There are also some aspects of modeling languages that defy simple explanations. For example, null values are a problematic aspect of the relational data model. We conclude with the following summary of some of the terminologies used by the various approaches:

Concept	E-R	UML	Logic	Set theory
Noun concept	Entity type	Class (type)	(Unary) Predicate	Set
Verb concept	Relationship type	Association	(n-ary) Predicate	Relation
Noun instance	Entity	Object	Term	Element
Verb instance	Relationship	Link	Statement	Tuple
Is-a verb	Specialization	Generalization	Entailment	Subset
Reification	Aggregation	Assoc class		

3.2 XML SCHEMAS

XML is a general format for storing and transmitting data—storing *metadata* with the data that may facilitate processing of the data. XHTML, an XML dialect that is intended to replace HTML, is intended for displaying data in Web browsers but the applications of XML representations are open-ended. The following document provides an example:

---

[8]More specifically, a relation R is a set of n-tuples and its *characteristic function* is a boolean-valued function F_R such that $F_R(x_1, \ldots, x_n) = $ `true` if and only if $(x_1, \ldots, x_k) \in R$.

```
<book category="Computers">
  <author>
    <firstName>Mark</first-name>
    <lastName>Hansen</last-name>
  </author>
  <title>SOA Using Java Web Services</title>
  <ISBN>…</ISBN>
  <publication>2007</publication>
</book>
```

The metadata in this document is given by the *tags* `<book>`, `<author>`, etc. If `<title>` is an opening tag, then `</title>` is the corresponding closing tag. An *element* is composed of an opening and closing tag and the content between those tags. For example, the above document contains a single `<title>` element, with content "SOA Using Java Web Services." An element may have *attributes* that are bound to values. For example, the `<book>` element has a single attribute named category that has the value "Computers".

Content may be simple or complex. *Simple content* consists solely of string data, without any attributes or nested elements. The content of the `<title>` element is simple. *Complex content* contains nested elements called "child" elements, and/or attributes. The `<author>` element contains two child elements, a `<firstName>` and a `<lastName>` element. Both of the latter have simple content, but the `<author>` element has complex content. The root element `<book>` obviously has complex content; the category attribute is part of that content.

DTDs precede XML Schemas, and provide a simpler and more lightweight tool for specifying well-formed documents. DTDs specify the structure of elements' content using a collection of rules, for example:

```
<!ELEMENT firstName (PCDATA) >
<!ELEMENT lastName (PCDATA) >
<!ELEMENT author (firstName, lastName) >
…
<!ELEMENT book (author+, title, ISBN, publication) >
<!ATTLIST book category CDATA #REQUIRED >
```

This specifies that the `<firstName>` and `<lastName>` elements consist of parsed data. An `<author>` element consists of a `<firstName>` element followed by a `<lastName>` element. A `<book>` element must have one or more authors, as well as a title, ISBN and publication date. It has a single required attribute category that has a value of type CDATA (character data). Although useful for relatively simple data specifications, DTDs do not support namespaces, which remains a serious deficiency.

The purpose of XML Schemas is to support the *specification* of a particular XML dialect suited to an application, and *validation* of XML instance documents in that application. Validation refers to ensuring that instance documents are well-formed relative to the specification of the particular application dialect. The example above may be used in a book inventory application. This application will want to ensure that any documents it exchanges with other parties (clients and servers) will be well-formed. This validation check is best performed at the boundaries where the application interacts with other parties. XML Schemas provide a language for specifying *types* for XML documents. A document validator can then automatically verify that a document has a specified type.

Some example schemas are provided in Fig. 3.12. An XML schema specifies:

1. A *vocabulary* defined by the elements and attributes that it declares for a document.
2. A *structure* defined by rules that specify the form of the content of the elements and attributes.

```
<?xml version="1.0" encoding="UTF-8"?>
<schema xmlns="http://www.w3.org/2001/XMLSchema"
        targetNamespace="http://www.example.org/content"
        xmlns:tns="http://www.example.org/content"
        elementFormDefault="qualified">

 <element name="content">
   <complexType>
     <sequence>
       <element name="title" type="string"/>
       <element name="pubDate" type="date"/>
       <element name="genre" type="string" minOccurs="0"
                               maxOccurs="unbounded"/>

       …
     </sequence>
   </complexType>
 </element>
</schema>
```

(a) XML schema with element declarations

```
<?xml version="1.0" encoding="UTF-8"?>
<schema xmlns="http://www.w3.org/2001/XMLSchema"
        targetNamespace="http://www.example.org/content"
        xmlns:tns="http://www.example.org/content"
        elementFormDefault="qualified">

 <element name="content" type="tns:contentType" />
 <complexType name="contentType">
   <sequence>
     <element name="title" type="string"/>
     <element name="pubDate" type="date"/>
     <element name="genre" type="string" minOccurs="0"
                             maxOccurs="unbounded"/>

     …
   </sequence>
 </complexType>
</schema>
```

(b) XML schema with type definitions

Figure 3.12   *XML schemas with element declarations and type definitions*

As applications may use more than one document type and, therefore, more than one XML schema, there is a danger of confusion because of overlapping vocabularies in different schemas. Every XML schema specifies a *namespace* that is a unique identifier for that schema. Every use of the schema uses the namespace to disambiguate the use of the vocabulary for that schema. Namespaces use the syntax of URIs. The example schema in Fig. 3.12 (**a**) introduces a namespace http://www.example.org/content. This is termed the *target namespace* for the XML schema declaration.

The schema in Fig. 3.12 (**a**) introduces an *element declaration* for a new element named <content>. The content of this element is declared to contain three forms of child elements (other content elided):

1. the <title> element with content type string;
2. the <pubDate> element with content type date;
3. the <genre> element with content type string.

The date type is a refinement of the string type. Both are pre-defined simple types in XML schema. This schema introduces a vocabulary that contains four new element names: <content>, <title>, <pubDate> and <genre>. These element names are associated in client applications with the namespace defined by these schema. In an instance of this element, there must be exactly one <title> and one <pubDate> element. However, there may be any number of <genre> elements, as given by the minOccurs="0" and maxOccurs="unbounded" attribute specifications for this element. All element declarations have default specifications of minOccurs="1" and maxOccurs="1" for these attributes that specify how many times an element may repeat in the content.

The schema in Fig. 3.12(**b**) is a variant on the former declaration. It defines the same namespace and vocabulary. However, in this case the definition of the content type for the <content> element is lifted out to a separate *type definition*, named contentType. While element names appear in instance documents, type names exist only in the space of XML schemas. The motivation for type definitions is to support the building of re-usable design libraries, based on type definitions that can be re-used in different applications to define common content type for different elements.

The declaration of the <content> element in Fig. 3.12(**b**) refers to the content-Type type definition to specify the former's content type. Because of this, some of the declarations and definitions in the schema (i.e., the <content> element declaration) make reference to other declarations and definitions (i.e., contentType). In fact, there are two vocabularies being used in this schema declaration:

1. The vocabulary identified with the target namespace http://www.example. org/content because of the reference in the <content> element declaration to the contentType type definition.
2. The vocabulary of XML Schemas itself, which defines element names such as <schema>, <element>, <complextype>, etc., as well as attribute names, such as name, type, targetNamespace, etc.

Namespaces are used to keep these vocabularies separate, to avoid confusion. The attribute definition:

```
<schema … xmlns:tns="http://www.example.org/content" … >
```

introduces `tns` as a qualifier for the namespace `http://www.example.org/content`. This qualifier is used as a prefix to unambiguously refer to the declarations and definitions of the schema associated with the latter namespace. For example, the declaration of the `<content>` element qualifies its reference to the `contentType` type definition by prefixing the reference with this namespace qualifier:

```
<element name="content"  type="tns:contentType" >
```

On the other hand, the references to the vocabulary of XML schemas itself is unqualified. This is enabled by the declaration of a *default namespace*, as specified by the declaration:

```
<schema xmlns="http://www.w3.org/2001/XMLSchema" … >
```

The default namespace is that of XML Schemas itself. Therefore, any unqualified element or type name used in this schema must be specified in the schema for XML Schemas itself.

It is at the discretion of the schema designer to decide which of several schemas being used in a schema specification should be declared to be the default namespace. In this example, one could alternatively make the target namespace be the default:

```
<schema … xmlns:xsd="http://www.w3.org/2001/XMLSchema"
         xmlns="http://www.example.org/content" … >
```

This specification declares `xsd` as a local qualifier for the namespace of XML schemas. In this case, the `<content>` element would be declared as:

```
<xsd:element name="content"  type="contentType" >
```

The references to the vocabulary of XML Schemas must now be qualified, whereas the reference to the `contentType` type definition is unqualified as it is in the vocabulary associated with the default namespace (in this case, the target namespace).

Figure 3.13 provides an example instance document for either of the schemas declared in Fig. 3.12. This instance document uses two namespaces:

1. The namespace defined by the aforesaid schema declaration and referenced by the namespace qualifier m. Element names `<content>`, `<title>`, `<pubDate>` and `<genre>` are qualified by this namespace.
2. The namespace defined for XML schema instances, with the namespace qualifier `xsi`. This namespace defines the attribute `xsi:schemaLocation`, that specifies the namespace for the schema of the document itself and the location of the document containing that schema specification `Catalog.xsd`. Although this attribute is required for an instance document, validators are not required

```
<?xml version="1.0" encoding="UTF-8"?>
<m:content xmlns:m="http://www.example.org/content"
   xmlns:xsi="http://www.w3.org/2001/XMLSchema-instance"
   xsi:schemaLocation="http://www.example.org/content Catalog.xsd" >
  <m:title>Lawrence of Arabia</m:title>
  <m:pubDate>1963-01-30</m:pubDate>
  <m:genre>Drama</m:genre>
  <m:genre>History</m:genre>

  …
</m:content>
```

Figure 3.13   *Instance document*

to accept the location provided for the schema specification for obvious security reasons.

3.3   DEFINING NEW TYPES

There are two forms of type definitions in XML schemas:

1. Simple-type definitions specify new named types for simple content, i.e., refined string types.
2. Complex-type definitions specify new named types for complex content, i.e., content that may contain elements and attributes.

3.3.1   Defining Simple Types

The general form of a *simple type definition* is:

```
<simpleType name=name>
  <restriction base=source>
    <facet value=value/>
    <facet value= value/>

    …
  </restriction>
</simpleType>
```

A simple-type definition refines an existing string type. Pre-defined string types include string, boolean (containing two literals, "true" and "false"), number (that contains other number types, such as integer and float), decimal, date, time, dateTime (that includes both date and time), gYear (for a year in the Gregorian calendar), anyURI (for both absolute and relative URIs), and so on.

Facets are used to specify the restrictions on the original simple type:

1. A facet may specify a restriction on the length of string values, or a maximum or minimum length.
2. A facet may specify an upper or lower bound on a range of number values, inclusive or exclusive of the bound.

```
<simpleType name="telephoneType">
  <restriction base="string">
    <length value="12"/>
    <pattern value="\d3-\d3-\d4"/>
  </restriction>
</simpleType>
```

(a) Telephone number

```
<simpleType name="ageType">
  <restriction base="integer">
    <minInclusive value="0"/>
    <maxExclusive value="125"/>
  </restriction>
</simpleType>
```

(b) Allowable age

```
<simpleType name="genreType">
  <restriction base="string">
    <enumeration value="Drama"/>
    <enumeration value="History"/>
    <enumeration value="Comedy"/>
    <enumeration value="Mystery"/>
    <enumeration value="SciFi"/>
    <enumeration value="Art"/>
    <enumeration value="Blues"/>
    <enumeration value="Classical"/>
    <enumeration value="Rock and Roll"/>
  </restriction>
</simpleType>
```

(c) Genre

Figure 3.14 Examples of datatype definitions

3. A facet may specify an enumeration of string literals for the possible values of the new type.
4. A facet may specify a pattern for possible values.

Figure 3.14(**a**) gives an example of a pattern for telephone numbers, including area and exchange codes. Figure 3.14(**a**) provides a specification for allowable ages in an application (allowable ages are defined here as 0 to 65 years, inclusive). Finally, Fig. 3.14(**c**) defines a type that is an enumeration of genres for various content types. If the examples in Fig. 3.12 are modified to use the genre datatype rather than the pre-defined string type for the <genre> element[9], then the application will have more precise typing and checking of applications that use the <content> element.

---

[9]There is no confusion in using the same name for an element and a type as XML Schema tools are able to determine which name is intended from the context. Similarly, the same name may be used for an attribute and an element.

```
<simpleType name="bookGenres">
   <restriction base="string">
     <enumeration value="Drama"/>
     <enumeration value="Art"/>
     <enumeration value="Mystery"/>
     <enumeration value="History"/>
   </restriction>
</simpleType>
<simpleType name="filmGenres">
   <restriction base="string">
     <enumeration value="Drama"/>
     <enumeration value="SciFi"/>
     <enumeration value="Comedy"/>
   </restriction>
</simpleType>
<simpleType name="musicGenres">
   <restriction base="string">
     <enumeration value="Blues"/>
     <enumeration value="Classical"/>
     <enumeration value="Rock and Roll"/>
   </restriction>
</simpleType>

<simpleType name="genreType">
   <union memberTypes="tns:bookGenres
                       tns:filmGenres
                       tns:musicGenres"/>
</simpleType>
```

(a) Genres by category

```
<simpleType name="telephoneList">
    <list itemType="tns:telephoneType"/>
</simpleType>
<element name="contact">
  <complexType> <sequence>
    <element name="email" type="string"/>
    <element name="telephone" type="tns:telephoneList"/>
  </sequence> </complexType>
</element>
```

(b) List of telephone numbers

Figure 3.15 *Examples of compound datatype definitions*

Two forms of compound datatype definitions are allowed. Both are demonstrated in Fig. 3.15. In Fig. 3.15(**a**), we see that a new datatype can be defined as the union of the set of values that inhabit a collection of other data types. In this example, the definition of the genre datatype from Fig. 3.14(**c**) is broken up into genres for film, books, and music. The original definition of genre is then reconstructed by forming the union of these component genres.

In Fig. 3.14(**a**), we considered the definition of a datatype for telephone numbers. In Fig. 3.15(**b**), this is used in the definition of the type of list of telephone numbers. Entries in such a list are separated by white space. This telephone list type is then used in the declaration of an element for contact information. You are invited to specify a pattern datatype for well-formed email addresses.

3.3.2   Defining Complex Types

We have seen examples of *complex-type definitions*, for example in Fig. 3.12. That example demonstrates that a complex content type may be defined as a sequence of elements, where some of the elements may be repeated if their `maxOccurs` attribute value is specified to be greater than one. Specifying a `minOccurs` attribute value of zero for an element means that the element is optional in the content. It is also possible to specify that the content is a *union* of the component elements rather than a sequence, using the `<choice>` element of XML Schemas. An example is provided in Fig. 3.16. For a `<content>` element, we add to the generic attributes (title, publication date and genres) the type-specific content, specified as a `<choice>` element. This last part of the content of the `<content>` element will either be a `<film>`, `<book>`, or `<music>` element in an instance document. Exactly one of these

```
<?xml version="1.0" encoding="UTF-8"?>
<schema xmlns="http://www.w3.org/2001/XMLSchema"
        targetNamespace="http://www.example.org/content"
        xmlns:tns="http://www.example.org/content"
        elementFormDefault="qualified">

   <element name="catalog">
      <element name="content" type="tns:contentType"
         minOccurs="0" maxOccurs="unbounded"/>
   </element>
   <complexType name="contentType">
      <sequence>
         <element name="title" type="string"/>
         <element name="pubDate" type="date"/>
         <element name="genre" type="tns:genreType"
                minOccurs="0" maxOccurs="unbounded"/>
         <choice>
             <element name="film" type="tns:filmType"/>
             <element name="book" type="tns:bookType"/>
             <element name="music" type="tns:musicType"/>
         </choice>
      </sequence>
   </complexType>
   <simpleType name="genreType"> … </simpleType>
   <complexType name="filmType"> … </complexType>
   <complexType name="bookType"> … </complexType>
   <complexType name="musicType"> … </complexType>
</schema>
```

Figure 3.16   *Schema with choice element*

```
<?xml version="1.0" encoding="UTF-8"?>
<m:catalog xmlns:m="http://www.example.org/content"
  xmlns:xsi="http://www.w3.org/2001/XMLSchema-instance"
  xsi:schemaLocation="http://www.example.org/content Catalog.xsd">
  <m:content>
    <m:title>Lawrence of Arabia</m:title>
    <m:pubDate>1963-01-30</m:pubDate>
    <m:genre>Drama</m:genre>
    <m:genre>History</m:genre>
    <m:film> <m:director>David Lean</m:director> … </m:film>
  </m:content>
  <m:content>
    <m:title>Janson's History of Art</m:title>
    <m:pubDate>2006-02-16</m:pubDate>
    <m:genre>Art</m:genre>
    <m:genre>History</m:genre>
    <m:book> <m:author>Penelope Davies</m:author> …… </m:book>
  </m:content>
  <m:content>
    <m:title>Beethoven: Symphonies Nos. 7 & 8</m:title>
    <m:pubDate>1990-11-10</m:pubDate>
    <m:genre>Classical</m:genre>
    <m:music> … </m:music>
  </m:content>
</m:catalog>
```

Figure 3.17   *Instance document for schema in Fig. 3.16*

elements must appear in the content rather than the sequence of all three, as would be the case had the content been specified as a `<sequence>` element rather than a `<choice>` element. In the example in Fig. 3.17, three instances are provided in a parent element called `<catalog>` (added to the schema). Each instance has generic content (title, publication date, and genres[10]), with type-specific content provided by a `<film>` and `<book>` element, respectively.

Element declarations and complex-type definitions may include attribute declarations. Figure 3.18(**a**) provides an example of the specification of a `category` attribute for the `<content>` element. The attribute can take one of three values: "Fiction", "Non-fiction", and "Faction" (the latter corresponds to dramatized "non-fiction"). Figure 3.18(**b**) demonstrates that attributes may be associated with simple content in a type definition. The result is a new complex type that is derived from the original simple (data) type. In this case, the new complex type `titleType` has a simple content type (the simple `string` type), but adds the `lang` attribute that associates a language with the title of the content. Finally, Fig. 3.18(**c**) demonstrates an element that has no content beyond that provided by attributes. The element is intended to be for art associated with the content, such as cover art for a book or album cover, or for a film poster. The complex type for the element specifies an

---

[10]Note that the genres for this entry, now taken from the enumerated data type `genreType` defined in the schema, must be qualified by the namespace in the instance document.

```
<simpleType name="categoryType">
  <restriction base="string">
    <enumeration value="Fiction"/>
    <enumeration value="Faction"/>
    <enumeration value="Non-fiction"/>
  </restriction>
</simpleType>
<complexType name="contentType">
  <sequence>
    <element name="title" type="string"/>
    <element name="pubDate" type="date"/>
    <element name="genre" type="tns:genreType"
            minOccurs="0" maxOccurs="unbounded"/>
    <choice> … </choice>
  </sequence>
  <attribute name="category" type="tns:categoryType" use="required"/>
</complexType>
```

(a) Category attribute

```
<simpleType name="langType">
  <restriction base="string">
    <enumeration value="en"/>
    <enumeration value="fr"/>
    <enumeration value="ga"/>
  </restriction>
</simpleType>
<complexType name="excerptType">
  <simpleContent>
    <extension base="string">
      <attribute name="lang" type="tns:langType" default="en"/>
    </extension>
  </simpleContent>
</complexType>
<element name="excerpt" type="tns:excerptType"/>
```

(b) Attribute for simple content

```
<complexType name="artType">
  <attribute name="src" type="anyURI"/>
  <attribute name="alt" type="string" default="[Art]"/>
</complexType>
<element name="art" type="tns:artType"/>
```

(c) Art element

Figure 3.18   *Declaration of attributes*

empty content, but provides a URL for the art as an attribute, as well as an `alt` attribute for text to be provided if no art is available to be linked to.

The examples involving attributes raise the question of when information should be specified in attributes, as opposed to when it should be specified in the content. The explanations on this point are, on balance, unsatisfying. The general rule is that attributes should be reserved for metadata, while the data are stored as content. What is the dividing line between data and metadata? For Web pages, metadata is understood to refer to information that is not displayed in Web browsers. For example, the URL identifying an image, defined as an attribute of the `<img>` element, is not displayed. Rather, the image itself is displayed. This explanation is obviously unsatisfactory for general XML data, which are intended for more general applications than presentation in a Web browser. For example, it does not provide an adequate explanation for why the URI for cover art is specified as an attribute rather than as content type in Fig. 3.18(**c**). For the `category` example in Fig. 3.18(**a**), there is no reason why categories should not be stored as content rather than as attributes, in a similar manner to genres.

In file systems, metadata refers to file name, file owner, access permissions, dates created and last modified, and indexes for fast retrieval, etc. The data are then the actual file contents. It appears difficult to apply this model to the separation of metadata and data in XML documents. Much of the above metadata is represented in the storage medium, such as a file system or database system, rather than the XML document itself. Even if one chooses to incorporate this metadata directly into XML documents themselves, for example representing access permissions and indexes as attributes, one faces the obstacle that attributes themselves can only be bound to values of simple type. This arbitrary restriction rules out representing many forms of metadata as attributes, so it must, instead, be represented as content. Otherwise, the metadata must be represented outside the document itself in the underlying storage container.

The example in Fig. 3.18(**b**), where title elements have an attribute that identifies the language of the title, suggests an example where the value of an attribute may guide the processing of the content. For example, content might be filtered or automatically translated based on the value of this attribute. Other explanations suggest a demarcation between information in the document for the benefit of the provider (e.g., information for inventory purposes) and that intended for the end-user. Presumably, these explanations are intended to generalize the distinction described above between information displayed in a Web browser and that which guides the display. This appears to be the metaphor that offers the best guidelines for when to use attributes, although one should be aware that these guidelines will have to be ignored in circumstances when the metadata cannot be represented as simple content.

3.4   DERIVED TYPES

We saw in the previous section that the `<choice>` element could be used when some of the content could be any one of several different alternative content types. The use of the `<choice>` element is effectively a form of generalization, as explained in 3.1.4 and shown in Fig 3.10. Generalization assumes a single entity type T that generalizes k entity types $T_1, \ldots, T_k$, recording those characteristics that all of the latter entity types have in common. In the schema shown in Fig. 3.16, we effectively factored out the common content (title, publication date, and genre) into a prefix of the element content and used a choice element to abstract from the attributes that the different content types did not share.

Admittedly, this was a poor example of generalization. The latter concept (as defined in 3.1.4) normally assumes that all possible specializations of the general concept are known, as generalization is performed "bottom-up." This is the rationale for the completeness condition for the entity type defined by generalization. The example of generalization in Fig. 3.10 provided a better example, where all of the specializations (for the roles in a university community) are known and stable. A `<choice>` element modeling this latter example would contain three child elements for the cases where an entity represented students, faculty, or administrative staff.

A better mechanism for modeling a scenario, such as diverse content types for various types of media, is the relationship of *specialization* discussed in Sect. 3.1.4. A specialization hierarchy for the `<content>` element type was presented in Fig. 3.11. The salient difference between generalization and specialization hierarchies is that, for the latter, the "root" entity type must be able to encompass the addition of new specializations (e.g., podcasts) without invalidating the hierarchy. In this section, we consider support in XML Schemas for specialization.

Specialization proceeds from the more general concept to the more specific. In Fig. 3.11, the root of the hierarchy is the general concept of content type, named `<content>`. Specializations of this entity type include book, film, and music content. These entity types may be specialized further. For example, even if we restrict our attention to digital media, book content type can be specialized to e-books or audio books.

Specialization is supported in XML Schemas through the mechanism of *type derivation*. When deriving a new type by derivation (a.k.a. specialization), we refer to the original type as the *parent* or *base* type, and we refer to the specialized type as the *child* or *derived* type.

3.4.1 Derived Simple Types

We have already seen several examples of derived simple types in Fig 3.14: `telephoneType` and `genreType` (specializing the `string` type), and `ageType` (specializing the `integer` type). Every datatype definition specifies a content type. A derived type constitutes a *subtype* of the parent type.

Recall that the "extension" of an entity type is the set of instances in an interpretation of that type. If T_1 is a subtype of T_2, sometimes denoted $(T_1 \leq T_2)$, then we require, for semantic correctness, that the extension of T_1 in the interpretation is a subset of the extension of T_2. Figure 3.19 demonstrates the subset inclusions among (extensions of) derived simple types. The encompassing circle contains all possible string values for the XML `string` type. The `telephoneType` definition specifies, using a pattern, string values for valid telephone numbers. The `genreType` definition specifies, using an enumeration, a set of string values for possible genres for content. The `ageType` definition specifies a set of string values, those representing integer values between 0 and 125 inclusive; it restricts the XML `integer` type, which, in turn, restricts the `string` type. All three of these derived types defines a subset of the original type. If we restrict one of these further, then we obtain a smaller subset contained within the original set of values. For example:

```
<simpleType name="workingAgeType">
  <restriction base="tns:ageType">
    <minInclusive value="16"/>
    <maxExclusive value="67"/>
  </restriction>
</simpleType>
```

This defines a set of values that is a subset of those defined by the `ageType` definition, depicted in Fig. 3.19.

3.4.2 Derived Complex Types

XML Schemas provides several mechanisms for defining derived complex types:

1. *Derivation by extension:* A complex type may be derived from an existing complex type by adding elements and/or attributes to the former. This is analogous to the use of "subclassing" in object-oriented languages to define a new class that is a subtype of the base class.

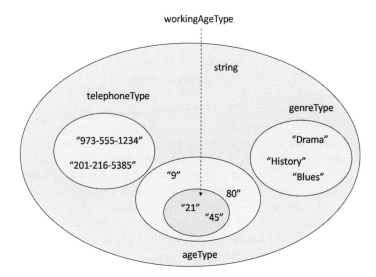

Figure 3.19 *Inclusion among simple subtypes*

2. *Derivation by restriction:* As we have seen, a complex type may consist of simple content but with one or more attributes that distinguish the type itself from a simple type. If a new simple type is derived from the original simple content type by restriction, then this can be used to define a new complex type that derives from the original complex type definition, by restricting the underlying simple content type.

We first consider derivation by extension for complex types. Figure 3.20 provides a fragment of the specialization hierarchy for content type described in Fig. 3.11. The root of this specialization hierarchy is given by a base type: `contentType`. We specify that this type is *abstract* (by specifying `abstract="true"`) to denote that it cannot be the precise content type for an element. Rather, actual element content type must be based on a type derived from this. Several types are derived from `contentType` by extending this type with additional elements: `bookType` and `filmType`, with `audioBookType` derived from `bookType` by further derivation.

As demonstrated in Fig. 3.19, the derivation of a simple type from another type by restriction always yields a subtype, one for which the set of values for the derived type is a subset of those for the supertype. For example, `workingAgeType` is a subtype of `ageType`, which, in turn, is a subtype of `string`. The derivation of a complex type by extension also yields a subtype. For example, `bookType` is a subtype of `contentType` and `audioBookType` is a subset of `bookType`. Because of this subtyping, content of type `audioBookType` may be used wherever content of type `contentType` is specified, for example as the content in a `<content>` element. This is referred to as *type substitutability* for XML Schemas.

To understand the justification for type substitutability, recall that we assume that concepts, and therefore entity types representing sets of entities, are defined by their properties. Complex types define entity types for the (complex) content of elements in documents. A simple type of `string` allows any simple content in an element. Similarly, a complex type with an empty definition can be extended with any complex content, and therefore allows any complex content in an element. The complex type `contentType` defines a subset of the set of all complex content by requiring `<title>`, `<pubDate>`, and `<genre>` elements (in that order). The complex type `bookType` defines a further subset of the `contentType` complex content by adding the further requirement that the content include `<author>`, `<publisher>`, and `<isbn>` elements. The complex type `filmType` defines another subset of the `contentType` complex content by instead adding the requirement that the content include `<director>` and `<writer>` elements. This is depicted in Fig. 3.21. In this way, each extension of a complex type adds more constraints on the possible complex content defined by a complex type, and therefore defines a subset of the complex content allowed by the based (extended) type.

One issue that needs to be addressed in an instance document for the schema in Fig. 3.20 is that the content for a `<content>` element may be (and, in fact, must be because `contentType` is declared to be abstract) of a derived type. Therefore, that content may contain additional content beyond that specified in the definition of `contentType`. Tools for processing the content must know exactly what the

```
<schema xmlns="http://www.w3.org/2001/XMLSchema"
        targetNamespace="http://www.example.org/content"
        xmlns:tns="http://www.example.org/content"
        elementFormDefault="qualified">
  <element name="catalog">
    <complexType> <sequence>
        <element name="content" type="tns:contentType"
          maxOccurs="unbounded"/>
    </sequence> </complexType>
  </element>
  <simpleType name="genreType"> … </simpleType>
  <complexType name="contentType" abstract="true">
    <sequence>
      <element name="title" type="string"/>
      <element name="pubDate" type="date"/>
      <element name="genre" type="tns:genreType"
                           maxOccurs="unbounded"/>
    </sequence>
  </complexType>
  <complexType name="bookType">
    <complexContent> <extension base="tns:contentType" >
      <sequence>
        <element name="author" type="string"/>
        <element name="publisher" type="string"/>
        <element name="isbn" type="string"/>
      </sequence>
    </extension> </complexContent>
  </complexType>
  <complexType name="audioBookType">
    <complexContent> <extension base="tns:bookType" >
      <sequence>
        <element name="narrator" type="string"/>
      </sequence>
    </extension>
  </complexContent> </complexType>
  <complexType name="filmType">
    <complexContent> <extension base="tns:contentType" >
      <sequence>
        <element name="director" type="string"/>
        <element name="writer" type="string"/>
      </sequence>
    </extension> </complexContent>
  </complexType>
  </schema>
```

Figure 3.20 *Derived complex types*

content type is. The XML Schema instance specification includes a `type` attribute that may be used for this purpose. An example instance document is provided in Fig. 3.22. The instance document contains two `<content>` elements. Each element has a `type` attribute that precisely specifies the (derived) content type for the elements (`filmType` and `audioBookType`, respectively).

```
<?xml version="1.0" encoding="UTF-8"?>
<m:catalog xmlns:m="http://www.example.org/content"
          xmlns:xsi="http://www.w3.org/2001/XMLSchema-instance"
          xsi:schemaLocation="http://www.example.org/content
                              Catalog.xsd">
  <m:content xsi:type="m:filmType">
    <m:title>Lawrence of Arabia</m:title>
    <m:pubDate>1963-01-30</m:pubDate>
    <m:genre>Drama</m:genre>
    <m:genre>History</m:genre>
    <m:director>David Lean</m:director>
    <m:writer>Robert Bolt</m:writer>
  </m:content>
  <m:content xsi:type="m:audioBookType">
    <m:title>Desolation Island</m:title>
    <m:pubDate>2001-09-01</m:pubDate>
    <m:genre>Drama</m:genre>
    <m:genre>History</m:genre>
    <m:author>Patrick O'Brian</m:author>
    <m:publisher>Recorded Books</m:publisher>
    <m:isbn>978-1402502248</m:isbn>
    <m:narrator>Patrick Tull</m:narrator>
  </m:content>
</m:catalog>
```

Figure 3.21   *Example instance for schema of Fig. 3.20*

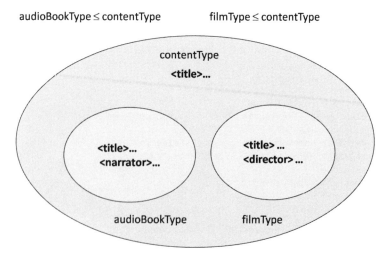

Figure 3.22   *Inclusion among complex subtypes*

We have seen subtyping of content type based on restriction of simple types and extension of complex types. Wherever content of a particular type is specified, content of any subtype of that type may be provided instead. *Element substitution* extends this subtyping from content to elements. A *head element* defines a *substition group*, and any elements that are declared to be in that substitution group may be provided where the head element is specified. The constraint that must be specified is that the content type of any element in the substitution group must be a subtype of that for the head element. For example:

```
<element name="foo" type="fooType"/>
<element name="bar" substitutionGroup="foo" type="barType"/>
<element name="baz" substitutionGroup="foo" type="bazType"/>
```

The element <foo> is the head element of a substitution group that includes <bar> and <baz>. The constraint that XML Schemas impose is that the content types barType and bazType must be subtypes of fooType. In other words, any consumer of a <foo> element will be satisfied with a <bar> or <baz> element instead, because the content of either of the latter two will include the content required of a <foo> element.

Figure 3.23 (**a**) provides the definition[11] of substitution groups based on the derived complex type definitions in Fig. 3.20. There are two substitution groups: one defined with head element <content> and content type contentType that contains <book> and <film> elements. The <book> element itself defines a substitution group that contains, in this example, the element <audioBook>. As an <audioBook> element is substitutable for a <book> element, and the latter is substitutable for a <content> element, an <audioBook> element is substitutable for a <content> element. Indeed, because the head element <content> is declared to be abstract, there can be no such elements in instance documents. Elements must instead be in the substitution group defined by <content>. An example is provided in Fig. 3.21. As the exact content type of each entry in the catalog is now specified by the element tags, there is no longer any need for the xsi:type attribute. The two derivation hierarchies, for type substitutability and element substitution, both based on derivation of complex types, are summarized in Fig. 3.24.

An example of a complex type with simple content was provided in Fig. 3.18 (**b**). That type defined a simple content type of string for text excerpts, but was complex because it also included an attribute that specified the language of the excerpt. Figure 3.25 extends this example to demonstrate the derivation of a new complex type based on a restriction of an underlying simple content type. The derivation hierarchy is provided in Fig 3.26, and the type definitions are provided in Fig. 3.25. A new excerpt simple type, shortExcerptContent, is defined as a restriction of the string type as a content type for "short" excerpts of no more than 160 Latin characters (so they will fit in text messages).

---

[11]The "root" element <content> is declared as a global element so that it can be referenced in other element declarations as the head element of a substitution group. The ref="tns:content" attribute declaration in the body of the <catalog> element allows that global element declaration to be referenced as the content element for the catalog.

```
<element name="content" type="tns:contentType" abstract="true"/>
<element name="book" substitutionGroup="tns:content"
                      type="tns:bookType"/>
<element name="audioBook" substitutionGroup="tns:book"
                          type="tns:audioBookType"/>
<element name="film" substitutionGroup="tns:content"
                     type="tns:filmType"/>
<element name="catalog">
  <complexType>
    <sequence>
      <element ref="tns:content" maxOccurs="unbounded"/>
    </sequence>
  </complexType>
</element>
```

(a) Declaration of substitution group

```
<?xml version="1.0" encoding="UTF-8"?>
<m:catalog xmlns:m="http://www.example.org/content"
  xmlns:xsi="http://www.w3.org/2001/XMLSchema-instance"
  xsi:schemaLocation="http://www.example.org/content Catalog.xsd">
  <m:film>
    <m:title>Lawrence of Arabia</m:title>
    <m:pubDate>1963-01-30</m:pubDate>
    <m:genre>Drama</m:genre>
    <m:genre>History</m:genre>
    <m:director>David Lean</m:director>
    <m:writer>Robert Bolt</m:writer>
  </m:film>
  <m:audioBook>
    <m:title>Desolation Island</m:title>
    <m:pubDate>2001-09-01</m:pubDate>
    <m:genre>Drama</m:genre>
    <m:genre>History</m:genre>
    <m:author>Patrick O'Brian</m:author>
    <m:publisher>Recorded Books</m:publisher>
    <m:isbn>978-1402502248</m:isbn>
    <m:narrator>Patrick Tull</m:narrator>
  </m:audioBook>
</m:catalog>
```

(b) Instance document

Figure 3.23 *Element substitution*

The complex type derivation that is based on this refinement of the content type is done in two stages. In the first stage, a second attribute is added to the complex type, a `len` attribute that specifies if the content is `short` or `long`. We call this intermediate complex type the `taggedExcerptType`. In the second stage, this type with `lang` and `len` attributes is refined by incorporating the restricted content type `shortExcerptContent`.

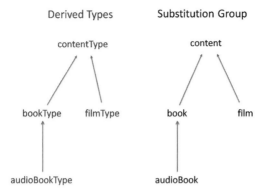

Figure 3.24 *Type substitutability and element substitution*

```
<simpleType name="lenType">
  <restriction base="string">
    <enumeration value="short"/>
    <enumeration value="long"/>
  </restriction>
</simpleType>
<complexType name="taggedExcerptType">
  <simpleContent>
    < extension base="tns:excerptType" >
      <attribute name="len" type="tns:lenType" default="long"/>
    </extension>
  </simpleContent>
</complexType>
<simpleType name="shortExcerptContent">
  <restriction base="string">
    <maxLength value="160"/>
  </restriction>
</simpleType>
<complexType name="shortExcerptType">
  <simpleContent>
    < restriction base="tns:taggedExcerptType" >
      <simpleType>
        <restriction base="tns:shortExcerptContent"/>
      </simpleType>
    </restriction>
  </simpleContent>
</complexType>
<element name="excerpt" type="tns:taggedExcerptType"/>
```

Figure 3.25 *Derived complex type based on derived simple content type*

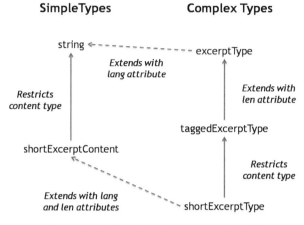

Figure 3.26 *Derivation hierarchy for Fig. 3.25*

3.5 DOCUMENT HIERARCHIES

In this section, we consider the issue of organizing schemas into multiple documents. In general, XML Schemas provide two mechanisms for structuring schemas composed of several documents:

1. The `include` construct envisions that the definition of a single namespace is broken up into several documents. This construct allows the definition of that namespace to be combined into a single document that is referenced by instance documents and other schemas that use the declarations and definitions of that namespace.

2. The `import` construct envisions that a namespace definition uses the declarations and definitions of other namespaces. This construct allows the definition of a new namespace to make reference to those existing namespaces.

Figure 3.27 provides an example of a schema broken into several documents and combined using `include`. This schema is for information about vintage fighter aircraft. Figure 3.27(**a**) provides the part of the schema for mechanical information, while Fig. 3.27(**b**) provides the part of the schema for armaments information. Both documents share the same target namespace. These schemas are combined in the final definition of the target namespace in Fig. 3.27(**c**). In all three examples, the target namespace is the same, denoting that we have broken the definition of a single namespace into several fragments that are combined in Fig 3.27(**c**). Figure 3.28 provides an example of an instance document for the combined namespace.

The `import` construct is used when combining existing schemas in the definition of a new schema. The existing schemas and the new schema all define *distinct* namespaces. This is in contrast with the `include` construct, which combines definitions in separate files for a *single* namespace. In this example, information about feature films comes in two forms: credits for the making of the film itself, and

```
<schema xmlns="http://www.w3.org/2001/XMLSchema"
    targetNamespace="http://www.example.org/fighter"
    xmlns:tns="http://www.example.org/fighter"
    elementFormDefault="qualified">
 <complexType name="mechanicalType"> <sequence>
    <element name="engine" type="string"/>
    <element name="fuelDelivery" type="string"/>
 </sequence> </complexType>
</schema>
```

(a) Schema for mechanical specifications

```
<schema xmlns="http://www.w3.org/2001/XMLSchema"
    targetNamespace="http://www.example.org/fighter"
    xmlns:tns="http://www.example.org/fighter"
    elementFormDefault="qualified">
  <complexType name="armamentType"> <sequence>
    <element name="machineGun" type="string"/>
    <element name="cannon" type="string"/>
  </sequence> </complexType>
</schema>
```

(b) Schema for armaments specifications

```
<schema xmlns="http://www.w3.org/2001/XMLSchema"
    targetNamespace="http://www.example.org/fighter"
    xmlns:tns="http://www.example.org/fighter"
    elementFormDefault="qualified">
  <include schemaLocation="Mechanical.xsd"/>
  <include schemaLocation="Armaments.xsd"/>
  <element name="fighter">
    <complexType> <sequence>
      <element name="name" type="string"/>
      <element name="mechanical" type="tns:mechanicalType"/>
      <element name="armaments" type="tns:armamentType"/>
    </sequence> </complexType>
  </element>
</schema>
```

(c) Combined aircraft schema

Figure 3.27   *Example of including schemas*

information about a specific media version of the film (e.g., for a particular disk transfer). We assume the existence of two namespaces for the latter categories of information: `http://www.imdb.com/credits` and `http://www.dvdtalk.com/format`, respectively. Figure 3.29(**a**) provides the definition of content type for feature film credits (director, writer, etc.), while Figure 3.29(**b**) provides the definition of content type for media-specific film information (aspect ratio, encoding technique, etc). Figure 3.30(**a**) gives the definition of a schema that imports both of these schemas in the definition of a new schema that combines filmmaker credits and format information for films. Figure 3.30(**b**) gives an example instance document.

```
<?xml version="1.0" encoding="UTF-8"?>
<m:fighter xmlns:m="http://www.example.org/fighter"
    xmlns:xsi="http://www.w3.org/2001/XMLSchema-instance"
    xsi:schemaLocation="http://www.example.org/fighter Fighter.xsd">
  <m:name>Spitfire</m:name>
  <m:mechanical>
    <m:engine>Rolls Royce Merlin PV-12</m:engine>
    <m:fuelDelivery>R.A.E. restrictor</m:fuelDelivery>
  </m:mechanical>
  <m:armaments>
    <m:machineGun>Browning M2</m:machineGun>
    <m:cannon>Hispano-Suiza HS.404</m:cannon>
  </m:armaments>
</m:fighter>
```

Figure 3.28   *Example instance for schema in Fig. 3.27*

```
<schema xmlns="http://www.w3.org/2001/XMLSchema"
    targetNamespace="http://www.imdb.com/credits"
    xmlns:tns="http://www.imdb.com/credits"
    elementFormDefault="qualified">
  <complexType name="creditType">
    <sequence>
      <element name="director" type="string"/>
      <element name="writer" type="string"/>
    </sequence>
  </complexType>
</schema>
```

(a) Schema for film credits

```
<schema xmlns="http://www.w3.org/2001/XMLSchema"
    targetNamespace="http://www.dvdtalk.com/format"
    xmlns:tns="http://www.dvdtalk.com/format"
    elementFormDefault="qualified">
  <complexType name="formatType">
    <sequence>
      <element name="aspect" type="string"/>
      <element name="encoding" type="string"/>
    </sequence>
  </complexType>
</schema>
```

(b) Schema for film format

Figure 3.29   *Example schemas to be imported*

It will be observed that, in the instance document, the elements imported from the other namespaces must be explicitly qualified (e.g., `<imdb:director>` and `<dvd:aspect>`). This is because of the attribute declaration in the schema:

```
<schema … elementFormDefault="qualified">
```

```
<xsd:schema xmlns="http://www.w3.org/2001/XMLSchema"
      targetNamespace="http://www.example.org/film"
      xmlns:tns="http://www.example.org/film"
      xmlns:imdb="http://www.imdb.com/credits"
      xmlns:dvd="http://www.dvdtalk.com/format"
      elementFormDefault="qualified">
   <import namespace="http://www.imdb.com/credits"
           schemaLocation="Credits.xsd"/>
   <import namespace="http://www.dvdtalk.com/format"
           schemaLocation="Format.xsd"/>
   <element name="catalog">
     <complexType>
       <sequence>
         <element name="film" maxOccurs="unbounded">
           <complexType"> <sequence>
             <element name="credits" type="imdb:creditType"/>
             <element name="format" type="dvd:formatType"/>
           </sequence> </complexType>
         </element>
       </sequence>
     </complexType>
   </element>
</schema>
```

(a) Schema importing other schemas

```
<?xml version="1.0" encoding="UTF-8"?>
<m:catalog xmlns:m="http://www.example.org/film"
    xmlns:imdb="http://www.imdb.com/credits"
    xmlns:dvd="http://www.dvdtalk.com/format"
    xmlns:xsi="http://www.w3.org/2001/XMLSchema-instance"
    xsi:schemaLocation="http://www.example.org/film Film.xsd" >
  <m:film>
    <m:credits>
      <imdb:director>David Lean</imdb:director>
      <imdb:writer>Robert Bolt</imdb:writer>
    </m:credits>
    <m:format>
      <dvd:aspect>anamorphic</dvd:aspect>
      <dvd:encoding>AC-3</dvd:encoding>
    </m:format>
  </m:film>
</m:catalog>
```

(b) Example instance for schema in Fig. 3.30 (a)

Figure 3.30 *Importing schemas*

   Say that an element declared in a schema is *global* if the declaration is not nested within another element declaration or a type definition—otherwise an element is declared *locally*. In the schema in Fig. 3.30(**a**), the `<catalog>` element is declared globally, while the `<film>`, `<credits>`, and `<format>` elements are declared locally. By declaring `elementFormDefault="qualified"` in the schema, we require that all elements be fully qualified with their namespaces in instance documents. Hence, in the example in Fig. 3.30(**b**), the elements imported from the credits and format namespaces must be qualified in the instance document.

This qualification is troubling for obvious reasons. Every instance document based on the schema reflects the import hierarchy described in Fig. 3.30 (**a**), effectively exposing the design history of the schema. Any changes in the import hierarchy threaten to invalidate an existing corpus of instance documents.

Declaring `elementFormDefault="unqualified"` in all schema specifications weakens the above requirement for instance documents, only requiring global elements in the instance document to be qualified with their namespace. An example instance document for the film information schema, suitably modified, is presented in Fig. 3.31. The problem with this approach is the danger of name conflicts in the imported namespaces once elements are no longer qualified by their namespaces. This is fundamentally a weakness in the definition of XML Schemas, viz. the inability to rename elements in imported schemas.

3.6 RELATIONSHIP TYPES IN XML SCHEMAS

We have seen how "is-a" and "part-of" relationships may be represented in XML Schemas. We conclude by considering the representation of more general application-specific relationship types.

The example of personal contact information in Fig. 3.3 demonstrated how one-to-one relations can be represented in XML Schemas, with a person's contact information embedded within that person's personal information. One-to-many relationships can be represented in a similar manner. For example, Fig. 3.32 demonstrates how the one-to-many relationship type between advisors and students, depicted graphically in Fig. 3.4, can be represented using embedding. Students are

```
<?xml version="1.0" encoding="UTF-8"?>
<m:catalog xmlns:m="http://www.example.org/film"
   xmlns:xsi="http://www.w3.org/2001/XMLSchema-instance"
   xsi:schemaLocation="http://www.example.org/film Film.xsd">
  <film>
    <credits>
      <director>David Lean</director>
      <writer>Robert Bolt</writer>
    </credits>
    <format>
      <aspect>anamorphic</aspect>
      <encoding>AC-3</encoding>
    </format>
  </film>
</m:catalog>
```

Figure 3.31 *Example instance for schema in Fig. 3.30 (a) with* `elementFormDefault="unqualified"`

```
<schema xmlns="http://www.w3.org/2001/XMLSchema"
    targetNamespace="http://www.example.org/academic"
    xmlns:tns="http://www.example.org/academic"
    elementFormDefault="qualified">
  <element name="community">
    <complexType> <sequence>
      <element name="faculty" maxOccurs="unbounded">
        <complexType> <sequence>
          <element name="cwid" type="integer"/>
          <element name="name" type="string"/>
          <element name="student" maxOccurs="unbounded">
            <complexType> <sequence>
              <element name="cwid" type="integer"/>
              <element name="name" type="string"/>
              <element name="gpa" type="float"/>
            </sequence> </complexType>
          </element>
        </sequence> </complexType>
      </element>
    </sequence> </complexType>
  </element>
</schema>
```

Figure 3.32 *Representing one-to-many using embedding*

listed by advisor, embedded within the information for their advisor. Both students and faculty are identified by their campus-wide identification (ID) number (<cwid>).

Embedding does not extend to many-to-many relationships. Consider the example of PhD membership from Fig. 3.3. Embedding would require that information about PhD committees be embedded within faculty information while, at the same time, faculty information would be embedded within PhD committee membership, which is clearly impossible. Instead, what can be done is to embed *references* to the respective entities within their XML descriptions. An example schema is provided in Fig 3.33. Each faculty member is identified by their campus-wide ID, while each committee is identified by the campus-wide ID of the corresponding student. We assume that no-one attempts to pursue two PhD degrees simultaneously.

As we have seen in Fig. 3.3, in the relational data model, relationships between entities are represented using primary and foreign keys. Entities are identified by their primary keys and are referenced in other entities by their primary keys. The latter key references are termed foreign keys. XML Schemas provide a way of annotating schemas with information about primary and foreign keys, as demonstrated in Fig. 3.33. The <key> element is used to declare a primary key, using XPath references to identify the part of the XML content that holds the primary key. We explain XPath in Sect. 4.2. the <key> declaration for the faculty primary key identifies the <cwid> element in the <faculty> element as the key value. The <keyref> declaration for the faculty foreign key in the committee information

```
<schema xmlns="http://www.w3.org/2001/XMLSchema"
  targetNamespace="http://www.example.org/academic"
  xmlns:tns="http://www.example.org/academic"
  elementFormDefault="qualified">
  <element name="community" type="tns:communityType">
   <key name="facultyPrimaryKey">
    <selector xpath="./tns:faculty"/>
    <field xpath="tns:cwid"/>
   </key>
   <keyref name="facultyForeignKey" refer="facultyPrimaryKey">
    <selector xpath="./tns:committee"/>
    <field xpath="tns:member"/>
   </keyref>
   <key name="cmtePrimaryKey">
    <selector xpath="./tns:committee"/>
    <field xpath="tns:studentid"/>
   </key>
   <keyref name="cmteForeignKey" refer="cmtePrimaryKey">
    <selector xpath="./tns:faculty"/>
    <field xpath="tns:cmte"/>
   </keyref>
  </element>

 <complexType name="communityType">
  <sequence>
    <element name="faculty" maxoccurs="unbounded">
    <complexType> <sequence>
     <element name="cwid" type="long"/>
     <element name="name" type="string"/>
     <element name="advisee" type="long" maxOccurs="unbounded"/>
     <element name="cmte" type="long" maxOccurs="unbounded"/>
    </sequence> </complexType>
   </element>
   ...
   <element name="committee" maxoccurs="unbounded">
    <complexType> <sequence>
     <element name="studentid" type="long"/>
     <element name="member" type="long" maxOccurs="unbounded"/>
    </sequence> </complexType>
   </element>
  </sequence>
 </complexType>
</schema>
```

Figure 3.33   *Representing many-to-many relationship types using keys*

identifies each `<member>` element in the `<committee>` element as a foreign key reference to a faculty primary key.

3.7   METASCHEMAS AND METAMODELS

We have provided examples of both schemas and instance documents when discussing XML Schemas. A schema defines a namespace and a vocabulary for describing data. An instance document is written using the vocabulary defined by this schema. A validator essentially reads the schema as a declarative program that is used to check that an instance document is well-formed according to the business rules specified by the schema. The schema is said to define metadata that describes the data.

The specification of well-formed XML Schemas is, itself, defined as an XML Schema—one that defines the namespace http://www.w3.org/2001/XMLSchema. The latter is an example of the general concept of a *meta-schema*, i.e., a schema that describes the metadata. This is depicted in Fig. 3.34. An XML editor can validate an instance document using the corresponding schema. An XML Schema editor is a special case of such an editor that validates documents against the schema of XML Schemas.

Meta-modeling is a well-known concept in conceptual modeling, as well as in logic and set theory. We have seen that in conceptual modeling, entity types are defined using classifying properties that categorize entities. An entity type itself can be viewed as an entity at the meta-level. An example is provided in Fig. 3.35. In Fig. 3.11, Book, Music, and Film were defined as entity types for certain forms of content. Each of these entity types specialized the general content type of Content, which specified content information shared by all of the specialized entity types. In Fig. 3.35 we describe Book, Music, and Film as *entities*, rather than *entity types*. The "meta-entity type" for these entity types is the type MediaType, which defines a "meta-attribute" defining the standards organizations for the different forms of media. For example, this might be the Motion Picture Association of America (MPAA) for feature films, the Recording Industry Association of America (RIAA) for musical content, and Publishers International for books. Each of the three meta-entities specifies its own value for this attribute.

Meta-modeling is well known in object-oriented design via the concepts of *meta-objects* and *meta-classes*. For example, every object in Java is an example of an

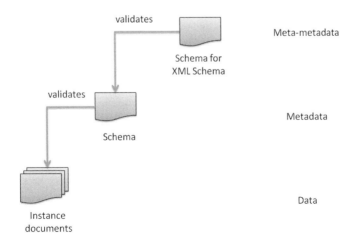

Figure 3.34 *Schemas and meta-schemas*

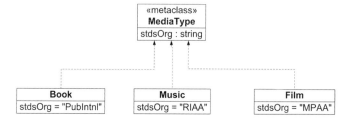

Figure 3.35   *Meta-entities for media types*

entity, and its class an example of an entity type. Any string is an object of class String. The object String.class denotes the meta-object for this class, that contains run-time system operations for obtaining informaton about the class and creating objects of the class. Each such meta-object itself has a class, the class Class of meta-objects. This latter is an example of a meta-class.

The UML modeling language also has support for meta-modeling. UML itself is defined using a meta-model that provides semantics for the UML constructs. Stereotypes provide limited support for extending this meta-model in application-specific ways, extending meta-classes such as Entity and Association (for entity types and relationship types, respectively) with extra attributes that are useful for modeling purposes in a particular domain.

3.8   FURTHER READING

Codd [3] introduced the relational data model that underlies most modern database systems. Chen [1] introduced the entity-relationship model for requirements engineering for database applications. UML, as its name suggests, is the unification of several modeling languages that werc originally developed for requirements analysis and design for object-oriented software [2]. UML was standardized by the Object Management Group (OMG), the organization that also standardized the CORBA framework mentioned in Chapter 2. Another conceptual modeling language is the Object Role Model [4]. Olivé [7] provides a tutorial on concept modeling using FOL with examples in UML and E-R; we adopt his terminology and notation.

REFERENCES

1. Chen PPS. The entity-relationship model: Towards a unified view of data. ACM Transactions on Database Systems 1976;1:9–36.

2. Rumbaugh J, Jacobson I, Booch G. The Unified Modeling Language Reference Manual. Boston, MA: Addison-Wesley; 2005.

3. Codd EF. A relational model of data for large shared data banks. *Communications of the ACM* 1970;13:377–387.

4. Halpin T. Information Modeling and relational databases: From conceptual analysis to logical design. Waltham, MA: Morgan Kaufmann; 2001.

5. Enderton H. A Mathematical Introduction to Logic, 2nd edn. Waltham, MA: Academic Press; 2001.

6. Gallaire H, Minker J, editors. Logic and Data Bases. In: Advances in Data Base Theory. New York: Plenum Press; 1978.

7. Olive A. Conceptual Modeling of Information Systems. Berlin: Springer; 2007.

4

Data Processing

"The details of this technology can be ignored for the purposes of this discussion." This perspective is dangerous because it essentially denies two important facts: that technologies can differ from each other in salient ways, and that they can change over time. Losing sight of either of these can lead to confusion, or worse.

Andrew MacAfee [1]

4.1 PROCESSING XML DATA

In processing XML data, applications have several choices for how to represent the data. These choices reflect both architectural design choices and the nature of the data and the resources available to programs that process that data. Broadly, the approaches to processing XML data can be categorized as follows:

1. *Tree processing:* XML data are loaded and parsed into a tree data structure in computer memory. Application programs can navigate this tree by following links and can modify nodes in the tree, e.g., to add or remove child nodes. This is the typical approach to processing XML data, e.g., when the data represent a configuration file setting some deployment parameters for an application. A popular approach to tree processing is the DOM, which is the basis for client-side processing of Web pages in AJAX. The processing model for DOM is depicted in Fig. 4.1(**a**).

2. *Schema binding:* a variant on the tree processing approach is to compile an XML schema to a collection of classes (one class per XML element) and then build an XML document as a tree structure constructed of objects. An example of this approach is the Java Architecture for XML Binding (JAXB), as depicted in Fig. 4.1(**b**), which is part of Java support for Web services

Enterprise Software Architecture and Design: Entities, Services, and Resources,
First Edition. Dominic Duggan.

development. Whereas DOM provides special node types and operations for navigating through the subtrees of a node, JAXB represents nodes as objects whose classes are compiled from XML schema elements and where subtrees are represented as object references in the fields of a node object.

3. *Stream processing:* if the XML data are too large to fit in memory, an alternative model is to never try to build a tree representation of it but, instead, to process the XML data as they are being read from a file. For example, the XML data may represent hundreds of megabytes or gigabytes of transaction processing data that need to be analyzed. This is a good candidate for an application of parallel data processing using MapReduce. The XML data may represent a "live stream" that must be processed efficiently in real time; building a tree data structure for every item in the data stream may be unnecessary and expensive. Two popular approaches to doing this are Simple API for XML (SAX) and Streaming API for XML (StAX), as depicted in Fig. 4.1(**c**).

The DOM approach favors faster development and supports in-memory update of the XML document. These updates can be saved by rewriting the document to external storage. The schema binding approach also supports update and, in addition, facilitates greater reliability by relating application program data types to the data model. The SAX approach supports high-performance XML processing, based on processing the data as they are parsed. However, it has the disadvantage that it only supports sequential access to the XML data and does not support update. It is also a lower-level approach than the other alternatives: the application program sees the individual elements, attributes and items of content, but the structure of the document must be inferred from this. For example, SAX could be used to define a DOM tree-builder, although this would obviously be incompatible with the motivation for using SAX in the first place. Nevertheless, sequential read-access to data describes a very large proportion of XML applications and performance is important, particularly with the growing ubiquity of mobile devices.

We describe these approaches in more detail in the following subsections.

4.1.1   Tree Processing

The DOM is a library for building documents as trees in computer memory. Figure 4.2 provides an example representation of a document as a tree structure, based on the schema in Fig. 3.16 with the addition of a category attribute. DOM defines several forms of node interfaces, such as:

Document   Element   NamedNodeMap   Text

Creation of a DOM tree begins with the creation of a document node. Content nodes, such as element nodes and attribute nodes are created using operations of

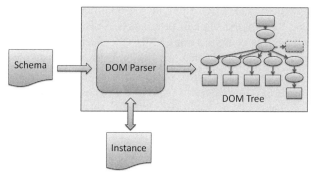

(**a**) Tree processing

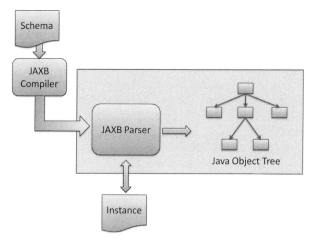

(**b**) Schema binding

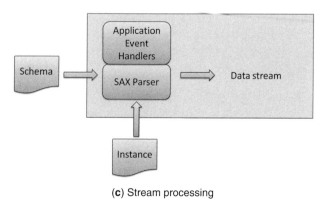

(**c**) Stream processing

Figure 4.1   *Processing XML data*

```
<?xml version="1.0"encoding="UTF-8"?>
<c:catalog xmlns:c="http://www.example.org/catalog"
  xmlns:xsi="http://www.w3.org/2001/XMLSchema-instance"
  xsi:schemaLocation="http://www.example.org/catalog Catalog.xsd">
  <c:content category="Faction">
    <c:title>Lawrence of Arabia</c:title>
    <c:pubDate>1963-01-30</c:pubDate>
    <c:genre>Drama</c:genre>
    <c:genre>History</c:genre>
    <c:film>
      <c:director>David Lean</c:director>
    </c:film>
  </c:content>
</c:catalog>
```

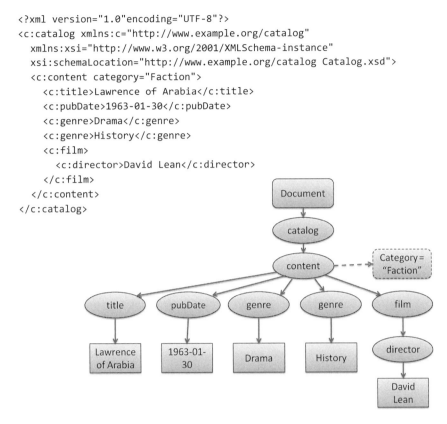

Figure 4.2   *Document object model*

this document node and added as descendants of the document root node. Fields are available in a root node for navigating the tree under that node, including checking the type of a node, navigating a list of the child nodes for a node (as a NodeList object representing a sequence of nodes), and navigating a list of the attributes and their values for a DOM element node (as a NamedNodeMap object representing a list of name-value pairs).

DOM defines Element and Attr interfaces for accessing a node of the appropriate DOM node type at a higher level of abstraction than the Node interface. The Element interface includes operations for accessing and setting attribute values, removing attributes, and accessing child elements by name. A node with the Attr interface represents an attribute in a DOM document not directly represented in the DOM tree, but accessible from the name-value map for the attributes of an element node. For example, the following code unparses a DOM tree of the form described in Fig. 4.2:

```
import javax.xml.parsers.DocumentBuilderFactory;
import javax.xml.parsers.DocumentBuilder;
import org.w3c.dom.Document;
```

```
final JAXP_PREFIX = "http://java.sun.com/xml/jaxp/properties/";
final String SCHEMA_LANGUAGE = JAXP_PREFIX + "schemaLanguage";
final String SCHEMA_SOURCE = JAXP_PREFIX + "schemaSource";
final String W3C_SCHEMA = "http://www.w3.org/2001/XMLSchema";
DocumentBuilderFactory factory = DocumentBuilderFactory.newInstance();
// Turn on validation, and enable use of namespaces.
factory.setValidating(true);
factory.setNamespaceAware(true);
factory.setAttribute(SCHEMA_LANGUAGE, W3C_SCHEMA);
// Override any schema location def in the instance document.
factory.setAttribute(SCHEMA_SOURCE, …);
DocumentBuilder builder = factory.newDocumentBuilder();
// Load and parse an XML document.
Document doc = builder.parse(…);
```

This example uses the DOM parser provided by the JAXP library that supports both DOM and SAX. The document builder factory produces parser objects. The factory is configured to be aware of XML namespaces and to perform validation. The language for XML schemas is defined to be that of World Wide Web Consortium (W3C) schemas and the factory is configured to use a particular schema for validating instance documents. This latter step overrides any schema location declarations in instance documents that are parsed. Finally, a parser is created and used to parse an XML document. A reference to the resulting DOM tree is stored in the local variable doc.

The following example illustrates the processing of a DOM tree, in this case displaying a list of the titles stored in the catalog:

```
// Display a list of titles from the catalog.
Element catalog = doc.getDocumentElement();
NodeList items = catalog.getELementsByTagName("content");
for (int i=0; i < items.getLength(); i++) {
    Node titleNode = items.item(i).getFirstChild();
    System.out.println("Title:"+titleNode.getFirstChild().nodeValue());
}
```

The Document node at the root of the DOM tree has a convenience method for returning the tree for the content root element—in this case a <catalog> element. The code computes a list of all <content> elements that are children of this root element. The first child element of each content element is a <title> element. Each of these elements has a child node of DOM type Text and the nodeValue method returns the string value of this leaf node.

This example demonstrates some of the drawbacks of DOM. The API is fragile to programmer errors as there is no way to automatically check the code against the document schema. For example, if the last line prints titleNode.nodeValue(), this will attempt to print the value of the node for the <title> element, which is null in DOM. The correct code prints the value of the Text child node that contains the simple content for the <title> element. Although careful design and testing can avoid, or correct, these potential mistakes, schemas inevitably evolve and the challenge is to ensure that code that performs unchecked DOM processing of instance documents remains compatible with the evolved schemas. For example, if the schema is altered so that the <title> element is no longer the first child element of the <content> element, the code will no longer be correct if it continues to assume that the <title> element can be obtained via a call to the getFirstChild() method. For that reason, DOM is best used as a technology for relatively small applications, e.g., reading and editing configuration files, or as an underlying implementation layer for content-based processing, as it is used by jQuery (discussed in Sect. 4.5).

4.1.2 Schema Binding

The schema binding approach is similar to DOM in that XML documents are parsed into object trees in computer memory. On the other hand, the classes for this object tree are generated by a compiler from the XML schema, with a class generated for each element. This makes a direct connection between the data model for the XML document and the data types used in the program that accesses it.

Figure 4.3 gives part of a schema definition that could be used to validate the catalog example from the previous subsection. A datatype definition for categoryType may be found for example in Fig. 3.18(**a**) in Chapter 3. A datatype definition for genreType may be found in Fig. 3.15(**a**) in Chapter 3. Figure 4.4 gives some of the class definitions compiled from the schema using the JAXB compiler. The Java code is annotated with information for validation purposes, such as that the <title> and <pubDate> elements are required for content of type contentType. The pubDate field is represented in memory by an object of type XMLGregorianCalendar, but marshalled as a value of the built-in XML type date.

There is some loss of precision in the Java representation. The type of the category attribute, an enumeration of constants, is translated as an enumeration type in Java. On the other hand, the <genre> element has as its XML value the union of a collection of enumerations, but Java does not have the notion of a union of enumeration types, so a genre is simply represented in the ContentType class as a string. The <choice> element in the content of <info> is translated as three fields, although in any content object, no more than one of these fields can be non-null. In general, there is no perfect match between XML schemas and the Java type system. For this reason, JAXB specifies annotations that may be used to direct marshalling and unmarshalling between XML data and program data. We provide examples of this below, as well as an alternative approach using JIBX.

The following piece of code parses a document to an object of the Catalog class, using a JAXB unmarshaller object. The latter is initialized with the Java package name that was specified when binding the schema so that the unmarshaller knows where to find the classes using the class loader:

```
JAXBContext jcontext = JAXBContext.newInstance("org.example.www");
Unmarshaller unmarshaller = jcontext.createUnmarshaller();
unmarshaller.setValidating(true);
Catalog catalog = (Catalog) unmarshaller.unmarshal(…);
```

```
<schema targetNamespace="http://www.example.org/catalog"
    xmlns:tns="http://www.example.org/catalog"
    xmlns="http://www.w3.org/2001/XMLSchema">
    …
    <element name="catalog">
        <complexType>
         <sequence>
           <element name="content" type="tns:contentType" minOccurs="0"
             maxOccurs="unbounded" />
         </sequence>
        </complexType>
    </element>

    <complexType name="contentType">
      <sequence>
        <element name="title" type="string" />
        <element name="pubDate" type="date" />
        <element name="genre" type="tns:genreType"
          minOccurs="0" maxOccurs="unbounded" />
        <element name="info">
          <choice>
            <element name="film">
              <complexType> <sequence>
                <element name="director" type="string"
                  maxOccurs="unbounded"/>
              </sequence> </complexType>
            </element>
            <element name="book"> … </element>
            <element name="radio"> … </element>
          </choice>
        </element>
      </sequence>
      <attribute name="category" type="tns:categoryType"
                          use="required"/>
    </complexType>
</schema>
```

Figure 4.3   *Catalog schema*

Binding a schema also generates an object factory class that can be used to construct an XML document in memory which is then marshalled out to a file on disk:

```
ObjectFactory factory = new ObjectFactory();
Catalog catalog = factory.createCatalog();
ContentType content = factory.createContentType();
content.setTitle("Laurence of Arabia"); …
catalog.getContent().add(content);
Validator validator = jcontext.createValidator();
validator.validate(catalog);
Marshaller marshaller = jcontext.createMarshaller();
marshaller.marshal(catalog, …);
```

The object factory provides methods for constructing objects of the classes generated from the schema binding. The set methods for the fields are used to

```
@XmlRootElement(name = "catalog")
public class Catalog {
  @XmlElement(required = true)
  protected List<ContentType> content;
  // Add item to catalog: catalog.getContent().add(item)
  public List<ContentType> getContent() { return content; }
}

public class ContentType {
  @XmlElement(required = true)
  protected String title;
  @XmlElement(required = true)
  @XmlSchemaType(name = "date")
  protected XMLGregorianCalendar pubDate;
  protected List<String> genre;
  @XmlElement(required = true)
  protected ContentType.Info info;
  @XmlAttribute(required = true)
  protected CategoryType category;
  public String getTitle() { return title; }
  public void setTitle(String value) { this.title = value; }
  public List<String> getGenre() { return this.genre; }
  …
  public static class Info {
    protected ContentType.Info.Film film;
    protected ContentType.Info.Book book;
    protected ContentType.Info.Music music;
    public static class Film { … }
    …
  };
}
```

Figure 4.4   *JAXB mapping for schema*

build the document tree. For content of a list type, an element of this list is added to the underlying Java list object. The object tree resulting from these operations is validated before being marshalled to a file on disk. The Java input-output stack allows other forms of output streams for marshalling, including streaming the output into the input to a DOM or SAX parser.

JAXB also supports customization of unmarshalling and marshalling using application-specific content in an annotation element in the schema. The following is an example:

```
<annotation>
  <appinfo>
    <jaxb:globalBindings>
      <jaxb:javaType name="java.util.Date" xmlType="date"
        parseMethod="org.example.DateAdapter.parseDate"
        parseMethod="org.example.DateAdapter.printDate"/>
    </jaxb:globalBindings>
  </appinfo>
</annotation>
```

The `<jaxb:globalBindings>` element specifies customizations at the global scope level: all definitions and declarations in the schema, as well as in schemas included or imported by the schema. Other scopes include the target namespace alone (schema scope), elements that reference a specified definition or declaration (definition scope), and a specific element (component scope).

The custom unmarshalling and marshalling elements are defined as static methods of the DateAdapter class, which is defined as follows:

```
import java.util.Calendar;
import java.util.Date;
import java.util.GregorianCalendar;
import java.xml.bind.DatatypeConverter;

public class DateAdapter {
  public static Date parseDate(String s) {
    return DatatypeConverter.parseDate(s).getTime();
  }
  public static String printDate (Date dt) {
    Calendar calendar = new GregorianCalendar();
    calendar.setTime(dt);
    return DatatypeConverter.printDate(calendar);
  }
}
```

Other customizations of global binding include for example setting the `choiceContentProperty` of the `globalBindings` element to true, which causes an interface to be generated for the `<choice>` element rather than simply mapping each subelement of the choice element to a class.

The DOM model is intended to be simple to implement. It therefore pushes some of the complexity of interpreting the data content of a document element onto the application. For example the XHTML fragment:

```
<p>This is a <strong>bold</strong> paragraph.</p>
```

is parsed to a DOM node with three child nodes. The first and third nodes are `Text` nodes, while the second is an element node. This is referred to as *mixed content*. To retrieve the data content of this node, the application must navigate to the `Text` nodes and invoke their `nodeValue()` methods. As we have seen, `nodeValue()` for an element node is `null`. Schema binding is geared to the situation where document trees do not have mixed content, simplifying navigation and yielding more compact trees.

Schema modifications require re-compilation of the Java classes, with the possibility of compiler errors in the clients of those classes. This is better at least than the situation with DOM, where errors caused by schema modification may lie undetected in client application programs.

As will be discussed in Sect. 6.6, a frequent situation in the development of a Web service is a mismatch between the data format that a developer has designed their program to process, and the default data format generated from a schema for the data. A common solution is to write translation code that receives the data parsed to the default format and then tranlates it to the format expected by the program. This translation routine could be written using any of the approaches described in this section, including external stylesheets, as discussed below. However, this is a very inefficient way to proceed. A great deal of the computing cycles consumed by enterprise software are doing exactly this kind of data translation. A more efficient alternative is to customize marshalling and unmarshalling of data so that the result of schema binding is compatible with the data format that the program expects.

JIBX [2] is a high performance alternative to JAXB. Whereas JAXB provides annotations for Java programs and XML schemas, that may be used to customize the default mapping between XML data and Java, JIBX provides the description of the relationship between Java and XML data representations separate from either of the latter two languages. This approach provides greater flexibility for customizing the representation of data in Java and XML, with the respective representations related by *mapping rules* in JIBX. These mapping rules may, in turn, specify customization of the default marshalling and unmarshalling strategies for XML data. JAXB also allows mapping rules to be defined to modify the marshalling and unmarshalling of data, in a separate binding file, although the JIBX language for these rules is more flexible.

Figure 4.5 provides an alternative Java representation for the schema in Fig. 4.3. This representation uses different field names and data types for some of the fields. A JIBX binding file, to map between XML data and this Java format, is provided in Fig. 4.6. A `<mapping>` element describes the translation between an element and a Java class, where the `name` attribute identifies the element. The example maps the `<catalog>` element to the `ContentDB` class. The content of this element, a sequence of `<content>` elements, is mapped to a Java list of `Content` objects.

The second mapping relates the `<content>` element to the `Content` class. For example, the `<title>` element is mapped to a field in the object named `title` and with type `java.lang.String`. The `<genre>` sequence is mapped to an array of strings. The `<info>` element is mapped to a field `detail` of the abstract type `Detail`. The mapping rules for `<film>` and `<book>` elements relate them to concrete subclasses of `Detail`, so the `detail` field may be instantiated with either a `Film` or `Book` object, if either of these two elements are unmarshalled.

Another example is provided in Fig. 4.7, demonstrating that the XML data and Java representation may have different structures. Figure 4.7(**c**) provides a Java representation that matches the structure of the XML data in Fig. 4.7(**a**). By omitting the `field` attribute in the definition of the mapping for the `<telephones>` element, we obtain the unboxed representation in Fig. 4.7(**d**).

```
public class ContentDB {
  private List<Content> contentList;
}
public class Content {
  private String name;
  private Date published;
  private String[] genre;
  private Category category;
  private Detail detail;
}
public enum Category {
  public static Category valueOf(String s) {…}
}
public abstract class Detail { }
public class Film extends Detail {
  public String[] director;
}
public class Book extends Detail {
  public String[] author;
}
```

Figure 4.5 *Alternative schema representation*

This approach has its limitations. For example, suppose we redefine the Java representation for content items as follows:

```
public abstract class Info {
  …
  private Category category;
}
public class Film extends Info { … }
public class Book extends Info { … }
```

where we "unbox" the detail field and merge its fields with the Info class. This form of unboxing is supported by schema binding tools such as Castor and JIBX, but it is not possible to define mapping rules that allow instances of the schema to be parsed to this representation. The problem is with the schema, which, in this case, would require arbitrary look-ahead during parsing in order to determine what the mapped type of a content element is. To fix this problem, the only option is to re-factor the original schema, or to parse the input and then transform the result.

Sosnoski [3] provides some performance figures for various XML processing tools. The use of introspection during marshalling and the use of push parsing (using SAX) both incur performance penalties for various tools. JIBX modifies class files to insert data conversion routines, obviating the need for introspection, and relies on pull parsing rather than push parsing. Both of the latter parsing techniques are described in the next section.

4.1.3 Stream Processing

Both of the previous approaches were based on the parsing of XML documents into trees in memory. The schema binding approach is usually more space efficient

```
<binding>
   <mapping name="catalog" class="ContentDB">
     <collection field="contentList" item-type="Content"/>
   </mapping>

   <mapping name="content" class="Content">
     <value name="title" field="name"/>
     <value name="pubDate" field="published" type="java.util.Date"/>
     <collection field="genre">
       <value name="genre"/>
     </collection>
     <value value-style="attribute" name="category"
       field="category" type="Category"/>
     <structure name="info" field="detail" type="Detail"/>
   </mapping>

   <mapping name="film" class="Film">
     <collection name="director" field="director">
   </mapping>

   <mapping name="book" class="Book">
     <collection name="author" field="author">
   </mapping>
</binding>
```

Figure 4.6   *JIBX mapping rules*

[3] as it generates more compact trees than DOM trees, and is certainly more reliable as it relates the data model of the document to the data types used in the program. The final approach we describe is very different: rather than building a data structure representing a document in memory, the document is processed as it is being parsed. This approach is not as flexible as the others: XML data can only be accessed sequentially, rather than in any random order, and cannot be updated. Nevertheless, this form of access is sufficient for many applications and it may yield a more scalable approach than the previous approaches as it does not require the building of a tree representation of the XML document in memory. A widely used example of this is SAX [4]. A similar processing model is used by the native XML parsing support in International Organization for Standardization (ISO) COBOL [5]. We consider SAX in this section. SAX is a push-based parsing model—we consider the pull-based StAX programming model [6] later in this section. The pull-based model supports more efficient execution as the program only calls the parser when it needs the next input token rather than buffering tokens, as sometimes happens with SAX parsing [3].

Rather than *tree-based*, as with the previous approaches, data processing is *event-based* in the SAX stream processing model. The application registers callbacks with the parser. These callbacks are invoked at significant points during the parsing of the input to perform application processing of the input, as depicted in Fig. 4.8. For example, one callback is called whenever parsing of an element begins and another is invoked when parsing of an element completes. Similarly,

```
<contact>
  <name>Boris Karloff</name>
  <e-mail>boris@karloff.name</e-mail>
  <telephones>
    <cell>201-555-1234</cell>
    <work>201-555-6789</cell>
  </telephones>
</contact>
```

(**a**) XML data

```
<binding>
 <mapping name="contact" class="Contact">
   <value name="name" field="name"/>
   <value name="e-mail" field="email"/>
   <structure name="telephones" [ field="phones" ]>
     <value name="cell" field="cell"/>
     <value name="work" field="work"/>
   </structure>
 </mapping>
</binding>
```

(**b**) JIBX mapping

```
public class Contact {
  public String name;
  public String email;
  public Telephones phones;
}
public class Telephones {
  public String cell;
  public String work;
}
```

```
public class Contact {
    public String name;
    public String mail;
    public String cell;
    public String work;
}
```

(**c**) Boxed representation   (**d**) Unboxed representation

Figure 4.7   *Boxed and unboxed representations with JIBX*

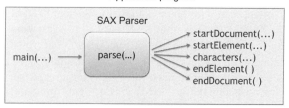

Figure 4.8   *SAX architecture*

there are callbacks for the beginning and completion of the parsing of the document as a whole. A callback is also called for processing of character data. The SAX specification does not specify at what point in the recognition of character data this callback should be invoked. Therefore, it is the responsibility of the application to buffer the content within an element for processing when the closing tag is encountered.

The interface for SAX callbacks is specified as the ContentHandler interface. Default null implementations for the callbacks are provided by the DefaultHandler class; an implementation can extend this to provide non-null implementations where required:

```java
public class ContentPrinter implements ContentHandler
                        extends DefaultHandler {
 private String contentTag = "";
 private boolean parsingElement = false;
 private StringBuffer content = new StringBuffer();
 public ContentPrinter (String tag) { contentTag = tag; }
 public void startElement(String namespaceURI, String localName,
     String qName, Attributes atts) throws SAXException {
  if (localName.equals(contentTag)) {
    parsingElement = true;
  }
 }
 public void characters(char[] chars, int startIndex, int endIndex) {
   content.append(chars,startIndex,endIndex-startIndex);
 }
 public void endElement(String namespaceURI, String localName,
     String qName) throws SAXException {
  if (parsingElement && localName.equals(contentTag)) {
    System.out.println("Title: " + content);
    content.setLength(0);
    parsingElement = false;
  }
 }
}
```

A validating SAX parser is created by using the factory pattern, as before:

```java
SAXParserFactory factory = SAXParserFactory.newInstance();
factory.setNamespaceAware(true);
factory.setValidating(true);
SAXParser parser = factory.newSAXParser();
parser.setProperty(SCHEMA_LANGUAGE, W3C_SCHEMA);
```

The application must register an "XML reader" with the parser as a callback. More accurately, the callback is an XML stream reader, processing the events that correspond to a tokenization of an XML document into tags and blocks of characters. The parser processes XML data as they are parsed by invoking the content handler callback registered with the reader:

```
XMLReader reader = parser.getXMLReader();
reader.setContentHandler(new ContentPrinter());
reader.parse(…);
```

The event-based SAX architecture is an example of a *push-based stream pro-cessing model:* content is pushed to application event handlers as the input XML data are parsed. As mentioned earlier, an alternative model is a *pull-based stream processing model:* again, the application processes the XML data serially as a stream of tokens but, in this case, the main thread is in the application and reading of the input data only advances as the application requests the next token in the input stream. This provides greater flexibility than the push-based model, allowing, for example, the application to process several input streams in parallel (perhaps merging those streams). An example of the pull-based model is StAX [6].

The StAX architecture has two variants: cursor-based and iterator-based. The *cursor-based* model provides a cursor for navigating a "virtual" XML tree top-down and left-to-right. The XML tree is "virtual" in the sense that it is not explicitly built. Nevertheless, the cursor provides access to each element and text node in such a tree in the order in which they would appear in a traversal:

```
public interface XMLStreamReader {
    public int next() throws XMLStreamException;
    public boolean hasNext() throws XMLStreamException;
    public String getText();
    public String getLocalName();
    String getAttributeLocalName(int index);
    String getAttributeValue(int index);
    String getAttributeValue(String namespaceUri, String localName);
    String getNamespaceURI(int index);
    …
}
```

The interface provides operations for obtaining the text (if the cursor is posi-tioned over simple content) or the element name (if the cursor is positioned over an element) corresponding to the current event. There are also operations, for example, for indexed access to attributes and namespaces associated with the current ele-ment. The next() method is used to advance to the next event in the stream, or the next node in the virtual XML tree, in a manner analogous to iterators for iterating over the elements of a collection data structure.

The *iterator-based* model reports attributes and namespaces as events in the stream, rather than the indexed access provided by the cursor model. Each of these events has an interface that specializes XMLEvent interface. There are interfaces such as StartElement, EndElement, Characters, Attribute and Namespace:

```
public interface XMLEventReader extends java.util.Iterator {
    public Object next();
    public boolean hasNext();
    public XMLEvent nextEvent() throws XMLStreamException;
    …
}
```

The iterator-based model is appropriate for defining *transducers*, i.e., stream processors that generate new output streams. These can be used to define XML data processor "stacks" based on layering each processor over the output of the processor beneath it. Both the XMLStreamReader and XMLEventReader interfaces have analogous output interfaces.

4.1.4 External Processing

A final alternative we consider for programmatic processing of XML is to delegate this processing to an external processor. An example in this regard is the Extensible Stylesheet Language Transformations (XSLT) language for defining *stylesheet transformations* that transfrom XML documents. Stylesheets are not to be confused with cascading style sheets (CSS) that are used to customize the default presentation logic in HTML documents. XSLT stylesheets are intended to decouple the structure of data from their presentation. Data are stored in XML documents whose schemas reflect the underlying data models, while XSLT stylesheets provide templates for how those documents should be presented as HTML documents for viewing. However, the stylesheet model is very general, and templates may be written that define transformations between arbitrary XML schemas. XHTML is just one example of a possible target schema for the result of a transformation.

Figure 4.9 provides an example of a XSLT stylesheet. This stylesheet generates an HTML document from an XML document cataloging film information. An example input and output are provided in Fig. 4.9(**b**). A stylesheet consists of several matching rules called templates. Each template matches some part of an XML document and generates a new fragment of XML based on that, where parts of the former are copied to the latter. The example in Fig. 4.9(**a**) defines two templates. The first template matches the root of the input document and generates the beginning and ending html and body tags for the output HTML document. The <apply-templates> element is an XSLT command to apply processing to the content of the root element. The second template matches a <catalog> element and generates a HTML table in the output. It loops over any <content> elements that are children the <catalog> element and generates a row in the HTML table for each entry in the catalog. The cell entries in each row are taken from the category attribute, the title of the film, and the name of the director. The specification of elements and attributes in the input document is specified using XPath syntax. We explain XPath in Sect. 4.2.

Stylesheets may be invoked programmatically using the JAXP libraries, for example:

```
import org.w3c.dom.Document;
import javax.xml.transform.dom.DOMSource;
import javax.xml.transform.stream.StreamSource;
import javax.xml.transform.stream.StreamResult;
import javax.xml.parsers.DocumentBuilderFactory;

DocumentBuilderFactory factory = DocumentBuilderFactory.newInstance();
//factory.setNamespaceAware(true);
```

```
//factory.setValidating(true);
DocumentBuilder builder = factory.newDocumentBuilder();
Document document = builder.parse(dataFile);
DOMSource source = new DOMSource(document);
StreamSource stylesource = new StreamSource(stylesheetFile);
Transformer transformer = factory.newTransformer(stylesource);
StreamResult result = new StreamResult(System.out);
transformer.transform(source, result);
```

In this case, there are two input XML documents: the data to be processed, and the stylesheet to perform the processing. The data are parsed into an in-memory DOM tree and wrapped as source for a transformation. The transformation itself is generated using a transformer factory, with input read from a stylesheet file.

```
<?xml version="1.0"?>
<xsl:transform xmlns:xls="http://www.w3.org.1999/XSL/Transform"
     version="1.0">
 <xsl:template match="/">
   <html><body> <xsl:apply-templates/> </body></html>
 </xsl:template>
 <xsl:template match="catalog">
   <table border="1">
     <xsl:for-each select="content">
       <tr>
         <td><xsl:value-of select="@category"/></td>
         <td><xsl:value-of select="title"/></td>
         <td><xsl:value-of select="film/director"/></td>
       </tr>
     </xsl:for-each>
   </table>
 </xsl:template>
</xsl:transform>
```

(**a**) Style sheet

```
<catalog >
  <content category="Faction">
    <title>Lawrence of Arabia</title>
    <film><director>
      David Lean
    </director></film>
  </content>
  <content category="Fiction">
    <title>Cavalcade</title>
    <film><director>
      Frank Lloyd
    </director></film>
  </content>
</catalog>
```

```
<html><body>
  <table border="1">
    <tr>
      <td>Faction</td>
      <td>Lawrence of Arabia</td>
      <td>David Lean</td>
    </tr>
    <tr>
      <td>Fiction</td>
      <td>Cavalcade</td>
      <td>Frank Lloyd</td>
    </tr>
  </table>
</body></html>
```

(**b**) Source XML document

(**c**) Result HTML document

Figure 4.9   *XSLT example*

The output stream is to standard output. The `transform()` method applies the style sheet to the input DOM tree.

In the above example, the input is parsed as a DOM tree, to which a transformation is then applied. The output could also be to a DOM tree, for example for presenting the result in a document editor window. Input and output may also be defined using SAX. In the former case, the transformer defines the event handlers for the event stream that results from SAX parsing. In the latter case, the transformer itself generates SAX events as it produces the output of the transformation.

Stylesheets have capabilities that go beyond this simple example. For example, XLST stylesheets support imperative update-in-place, so that a document is modified, rather than generating a new document in order to perform updates. Obviously, in this case, the input must be a DOM tree.

As we have seen with the above example, XSLT stylesheets are closely tied to the XPath query syntax for navigating XML documents. The intention is that such stylesheet transformations define the interfaces where data is exchanged between different parts of an enterprise information system. XSLT can provide different presentation logics for different clients of the system: XHTML for Web browser access, and XSL Formatting Objects (FO) for generating Portable Document Format (PDF) documents, for example. Stylesheets may define transformations between departments with different data models for data that they share, or between different enterprises that exchange documents for collaboration or e-commerce. Stylesheets may also define filtering of data as they are transmitted between these different parts of the enterprise architecture. We summarize these different places where XSLT may be used for defining filters in Fig. 4.10.

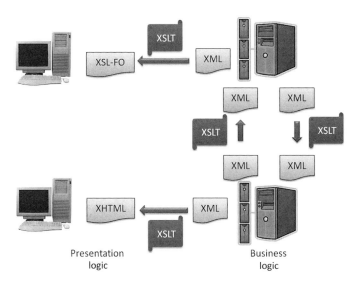

Figure 4.10 *XSLT in enterprise architecture*

An alternative technology for providing the "glue" logic between parts of the enterprise information system is the XQuery language, which we describe in the next section.

4.2   QUERY LANGUAGES AND XQUERY

XPath is a path-based query language for XML data defined as part of the XSL stylesheet suite of standards for processing XML. We have already reviewed XSLT, another part of this suite, that specifies transformations based on matching XML data against templates and producing a new document with parts extracted from the original document. In this section, we review XQuery, a query language that allows both the querying and transforming of XML data. XQuery uses XPath to specify parts of XML documents, but builds upon XPath to provide a richer query language.

XQuery is based on a data model where XML data are represented as trees of nodes. Each node is distinct, even if two distinct nodes have identical content. There are several kinds of nodes: document, namespace, element, attribute, text, comment, and processing instruction. The data model also contains atomic values. An item is either a node or an atomic value. A sequence is a series of items. The result of a query is always a sequence.

XQuery provides two functions for inputting XML data: `doc()` reads an XML document from a file, while `collection()` is used to access a collection of documents in a database. XQuery then uses XPath expressions to select portions of the input document or collection of documents. The result of the XPath expression is a sequence of tree nodes.

XPath provides a path-based syntax for specifying sequences of nodes in XML data, similar to the syntax for specifying paths in the file system in Unix and Windows. A path is evaluated as a query from left to right, where the steps in the query evaluation are separated by the / element.

1. The root of every document is a document node. This node is not visible in the textual presentation of an XML document, but it is part of the XQuery data model. The path expression denoted by the / symbol evaluates to the document node at the root of the XML tree.

2. Any element name used as a search term evaluates to the sequence of nodes that are children of the current node that are element nodes with matching names. For example, `content` evaluates to all `<content>` elements that are children of the current node. The expression `/catalog` evaluates to all `<catalog>` element nodes that are children of the document node.

3. The expression `/catalog/content` evaluates to all `<content>` element nodes that are children of the `<catalog>` element nodes selected by the expression `/catalog`. The expression `/catalog/content/film` evaluates to all `<film>` element nodes that are children of the nodes selected by `/catalog/content`.

4. There are special path expressions: the expression . evaluates to the current node, the expression .. evaluates to the parent of the current node, and the expression // evaluates to all nodes in the document nested beneath the current node. For example, /catalog// evaluates to all nodes beneath the <catalog> element nodes selected by the path expression /catalog. The expression /catalog//film evaluates to all <film> element nodes that are nested, at any depth, below the <catalog> nodes selected by the expression /catalog.

5. Attributes are referenced using the @ operator in front of an attribute name. For example, the expression /catalog/content/@category evaluates to all category attribute nodes that are children of the <content> element nodes selected by the expression /catalog/content.

6. There are also functions that in path expressions evaluate to other forms of tree nodes. For example, text() evaluates to text nodes that are children of the currently selected nodes. The expression /catalog/content/title/text() evaluates to a sequence of text nodes, each one a child of a <title> node in the sequence resulting from the query /catalog/content/title.

An XPath expression always evaluates to a sequence of items, as there may be more than one result in a search. Furthermore, an XPath expression denoting an element evaluates to a sequence of element nodes satisfying that query, rather than the text nodes that are children of those nodes that represent the content of the elements. For example, on the XML document in Fig. 4.11, the query /catalog/content//director returns the sequence of elements:

```
<c:director>David Lean</c:director>
<c:director>Frank LLoyd</c:director>
<c:director>Orson Welles</c:director>
```

To return a sequence of director names, without the element tags, use the text() function. The query:

```
                /catalog/content//director/text()
```

evaluates to the sequence of strings ("David Lean", "Frank LLoyd", "Orson Welles"), for example.

Any step in a query may include a boolean expression, enclosed in square brackets:

1. Any number in square brackets denotes a subscript. The expression /catalog/content/film/director[1] denotes the first director credited with each film in the catalog. Note that this is not the same as the first film director listed in the catalog. The expression /catalog/content/film/director[last()] denotes the last director credited with each film. The expression //film/director[last()-1] denotes the second-to-last film director, and so on. In general, it is possible in XQuery

```
<?xml version="1.0" encoding="UTF-8"?>
<c:catalog xmlns:c="http://www.example.org/catalog"
  xmlns:xsi="http://www.w3.org/2001/XMLSchema-instance"
  xsi:schemaLocation="http://www.example.org/catalog Catalog.xsd"
  elementFormDefault="qualified">
<c:content category="Faction">
  <c:title>Lawrence of Arabia</c:title>
  <c:pubDate>1963-01-30</c:pubDate>
  <c:genre>Drama</c:genre>
  <c:genre>History</c:genre>
  <c:info><c:film> <c:director>David Lean</c:director>
                ... </c:film></c:info>
</c:content>
<c:content category="Non-Fiction">
  <c:title>Janson's History of Art</c:title>
  <c:pubDate>2006-02-16</c:pubDate>
  <c:genre>History</c:genre>
  <c:genre>Art</c:genre>
  <c:info><c:book> <c:author>Penelope Davies</c:author>
                ... </c:book></c:info>
</c:content>
<c:content category="Fiction">
  <c:title>Cavalcade</c:title>
  <c:pubDate>1933-04-15</c:pubDate>
  <c:genre>Drama</c:genre>
  <c:info><c:film> <c:director>Frank LLoyd</c:director>
                ... </c:film></c:info>
</c:content>
<c:content category="Fiction">
  <c:title>War of the Worlds</c:title>
  <c:pubDate>1938-10-30</c:pubDate>
  <c:genre>Science Fiction</c:genre>
  <c:info><c:radio> <c:director>Orson Welles</c:director>
                ... </c:radio></c:info>
</c:content>
<c:content category="Fiction">
  <c:title>The Illuminatus! Trilogy</c:title>
  <c:pubDate>1983-12-01</c:pubDate>
  <c:genre>Fantasy</c:genre>
  <c:genre>Drama</c:genre>
  <c:info><c:book> <c:author>Robert Shea</c:author>
              <c:author>Robert Anton Wilson</c:author>
  </c:book></c:info>
</c:content>
</c:catalog>
```

Figure 4.11 *Catalog example*

to test if a node precedes or follows another in the "document order" that orders nodes from top to bottom and from left to right.

2. Other predicates are built from comparison operations and boolean operators provided by XPath. For example, the expression

```
/catalog/content[
    date-greater-than(pubDate,xs:date("1950-12-31"))]
```

evaluates to all content published since 1950 and the expression

```
/catalog/content[
    date-greater-than(pubDate,xs:date("1950-12-31"))]/title
```

evaluates to the title nodes for all content published since 1950.

3. Attributes may also be referenced in XPath expressions. The path expression `//content[@category="Fiction"]` evaluates to the sequence of content nodes for which the `category` attribute is set to "`Fiction`".

4. The XPath function `position()` computes the position of the current node in the sequence of nodes it occurs in below its parent node. Then, the expression `/catalog/content[position()<3]` returns the first two `<content>` elements.

The XQuery query language builds on XPath, using XPath expressions to denote parts of XML documents and providing a functional query language for searching and transforming XML data. The language is functional in the sense that it is side-effect free; this is done in order to simplify query optimization. Nevertheless, support for in-place update has been added to XQuery, allowing the specification of modifications in place of an underlying XML database. As with XPath, every expression in XQuery evaluates to a sequence of items, where an item is a node in an XML tree or else an atomic value. In addition, XQuery allows the creation of new markup that may wrap the results of a query. So, similarly to XSLT, XQuery provides the ability to define transformations between XML documents.

The primitive expressions include XPath expressions and literals. The constructs for defining compound expressions are often described in terms of the XQuery FLWOR (For, Let, Where, Order by, Return):

1. The `for` construct iterates through the elements of a sequence defined by an XPath expression. An iterator variable is bound for each value in the sequence. Nested loops are defined by allowing muliple sequences in the `for`, or defining nested `for` loops.

2. The `let` construct binds new local variables and evaluates a query expression in the context of those local declarations. Such variables are only visible in the scope of the `let` construct, and those declarations are discarded when the result of the `let` body is returned. They are given an initial value when they are introduced and this value cannot be modified. The language does not provide an assignment operator.

3. The `where` construct adds a boolean condition that filters the sequence of items defined by an expression.

4. The `order by` construct orders the results of a query based on the value of an XPath expression relative to the original XML tree or forest.

5. The `return` construct allows the return of a query result from a `for` or `let`.

One of the more gratifying aspects of XQuery is that, unlike many other XML-based domain specific languages, such as XSLT or WS-BPEL, XQuery provides a reasonable syntax. A separate XML-based syntax for XQuery is intended to be only viewed by XML processing tools, as it should be.

The reader may have wondered how to relate namespaces in XML instance documents to the use of namespaces in queries. XQuery resolves this issue by allowing a module containing XQuery code to import a namespace, for example:

```
import schema namespace n = "http://www.example.org/catalog"
at "Catalog.xsd";
```

The prefix n: can be used in the program to qualify elements and attributes with their namespace. As with XML Schemas, one can also define a default namespace in an XQuery program:

```
declare default element namespace "http://www.example.org/xquery/result"
```

The following simple query evaluates to the sequence of <title> elements for the document in Fig. 4.11:

```
for $t in doc("catalog.xml")/n:catalog/n:content/n:title
   return $t
```

Consider a variant where we wish each <title> element to be wrapped in a <content> element. XQuery supports the creation of new markup in the results of queries:

```
for $t in doc("catalog.xml")/n:catalog/n:content/n:title
   return <content> $t </content>
```

In fact, this expression returns a sequence of four identical elements, each one of the form <content> $t </content>. What has happened here? If we describe XML data as *static content* and XQuery code as *dynamic content*, then the error is that the reference to the query variable $t is nested in the element constructor for the <content> element in the query result. All content for this element is assumed to be static, whereas the intention is to combine static content (the <content> element constructor) and dynamic content (the value of the $t variable). The element constructor denotes a way to embed static content in dynamic XQuery code, but this example requires a facility for embedding dynamic content in static content. This is provided by the bracket construct { } in XQuery. For example, the following code returns a sequence of <title> elements nested in <content> elements, each one with a content title taken from the document:

```
for $t in doc("catalog.xml")/n:catalog/n:content/n:title
   return <content> { $t } </content>
```

The following expression wraps a <catalog> element around this sequence of results. Again, the bracketing construct is needed to embed the query result in the document being returned:

```
<catalog> {
  for $t in doc("catalog.xml")/n:catalog/n:content/n:title
  return <content> { $t } </content>
} </catalog>
```

The following variant on the query copies the `category` attribute from the original content. In this case, the XPath expression for the `for` construct evaluates to the `<content>` nodes, and the `category` attribute and `<title>` child nodes are selected using further XPath expressions:

```
declare namespace k = "http://www.example.org/titles";
<k:titles> {
  for $c in doc("catalog.xml")/n:catalog/n:content
  return
    <k:title category="{$c/@category}">
      { $c/n:title/text() }
    </k:title>
} </k:titles>
```

This produces, as its content, the document:

```
<?xml version="1.0" encoding="UTF-8"?>
<k:titles xmlns:k="http://www.example.org/titles">
 <k:title category="Faction">Lawrence of Arabia</k:title>
 <k:title category="Non-Fiction">Janson's History of Art</k:title>
 <k:title category="Fiction">Cavalcade</k:title>
 <k:title category="Fiction">War of the Worlds</k:title>
 <k:title category="Fiction">The Illuminatus! Trilogy</k:title>
</k:titles>
```

Note that this example includes nested brackets: the bracketed expression `{$c/n:title/text()}` within the bracket expression for the query as a whole, for example. The value of the attribute is also denoted as dynamic content within a bracket: `{$c/@category}`. The fact that this expression is embedded in quotes is immaterial: the quotes are just part of the static content.

XQuery provides an alternative syntax for element constructors, one that allows element names to be computed dynamically. For example, an equivalent formulation of the expression above is provided by:

```
element k:titles
  { for $c in doc("catalog.xml")/n:catalog/n:content
    return element k:title
              { attribute category { $c/@category },
                 $c/n:title/text() }
  }
```

Now suppose we have a function `translateTo` that translates strings to the language given the language code as a second argument, we may define:

```
element
  { translateTo("titles", "ga") }
```

```
{
  for $c in doc("catalog.xml")/n:catalog/n:content
    return element { translateTo("title", "ga") }
           { attribute category { $c/@category },
             $c/n:title/text() }
}
```

The result is the following document:

```
<?xml version="1.0" encoding="UTF-8"?>
<k:graid xmlns:k="http://www.example.org/titles">
    <k:teideal category="Faction">Lawrence of Arabia</k:teideal>
    …
</k:graid>
```

The where clause filters items from the result of a query. For example:

```
<k:titles> {
    for $c in doc("catalog.xml")/n:catalog/n:content
    return
      <k:title category="{$c/@category}">
      { $c/n:title/text() }
      </k:title>
    where $c//director = "Orson Welles"
} </k:titles>
```

This produces as its content the document:

```
<?xml version="1.0" encoding="UTF-8"?>
<k:titles xmlns:k="http://www.example.org/titles">
    <k:title category="Fiction">War of the Worlds</k:title>
</k:titles>
```

There is a subtlety: the binary = equality operation is a *general comparison operation*, defined for sequences of items and is true if at least one item in the left sequence matches at least one item in the right sequence. To understand why this is so, consider the following example:

```
for $c in doc("catalog.xml")/n:catalog/n:content
   return $c
   where $c//author = "Robert Anton Wilson"
```

For this query to succeed and return "The Illuminatus! Trilogy", the comparison must succeed even though the left-hand sequence contains two authors. Because of the semantics of general comparison, sequence equality is intransitive in XQuery: it may be the case that we have X = Y and Y = Z, but we do not have X = Z. The eq operation is defined for *value comparison*, comparing simple values instead of sequences of values and there are analogous operations for inequality (ne, lt, le, gt, ge). On the other hand, value comparison raises an error when applied to a sequence.

Two important operations whose definition XQuery supports are *join* and *document inversion*. Join is familiar to SQL programmers. Conceptually, it forms the Cartesian product of two tables, where each row in the result is the concatenation

```
<schema targetNamespace="http://www.example.org/review"
    xmlns:tns="http://www.example.org/review"
    xmlns="http://www.w3.org/2001/XMLSchema">
  …
  <element name="reviews">
    <complexType>
      <sequence>
       <element name="review" type="tns:reviewType" minOccurs="0"
         maxOccurs="unbounded" />
      </sequence>
    </complexType>
  </element>

  <complexType name="reviewType">
    <sequence>
      <element name="title" type="string" />
      <element name="pubDate" type="date" />
      <element name="reviewer" type="string"/>
      <element name="eval" type="string"/>
    </sequence>
    <attribute name="lang" type="language" use="required"/>
  </complexType>
</schema>
```

Figure 4.12   *Review schema*

of a row from each of the argument tables, and then filters out the rows that are not equal on certain columns. In XQuery, the "rows" in a table are defined by a sequence of elements and columns are defined by child elements of these elements. For example, suppose we store a list of reviews for content items in a separate document. Each content item is identified by title and publication date. We will assume that it is unlikely for a film and content tie-in, such as a book or game, to be published on exactly the same date. Each review is stored separately, including the reviewer identity and the review itself. An example review database is provided in Fig. 4.13.

A query that joins these two databases is provided by:

```
import schema namespace r = "http://www.example.org/review"
  at "Review.xsd";
<imdb> {
    for $c in doc("catalog.xml")/n:catalog/n:content,
        $r in doc("reviews.xml")/r:reviews/r:review
    where $c/title = $r/title and $c/pubDate = $r/pubDate
    return
    <info>
      <title> { $c/title/text() } </title>
      <pubDate> { $c/pubDate/text() } </pubDate>
      <director> { $c/info/film/director/text()} </director>
      <reviewer> { $r/reviewer/text() } </reviewer>
      <eval lang="{$r/@lang}"> { $r/eval/text() } </eval>
    </info>
} </imdb>
```

```
<?xml version="1.0" encoding="UTF-8"?>
<r:reviews xmlns:r="http://www.example.org/review"
    xmlns:xsi="http://www.w3.org/2001/XMLSchema-instance"
    xsi:schemaLocation="http://www.example.org/review Review.xsd"
    elementFormDefault="qualified">
  <r:review lang="en">
    <r:title>Lawrence of Arabia</r:title>
    <r:pubDate>1963-01-30</r:pubDate>
    <r:reviewer>A Reviewer</r:reviewer>
    <r:eval>When you pan and scan LOR, you lose the desert.</r:eval>
  </r:review>
  <r:review lang="ga">
    <r:title>Lawrence of Arabia</r:title>
    <r:pubDate>1963-01-30</r:pubDate>
    <r:reviewer>M. Dwyer</r:reviewer>
    <r:eval>Taim in ngra leis an priomhscannan seo.</r:eval>
  </r:review>
  <r:review lang="en">
    <r:title>Janson's History of Art</r:title>
    <r:pubDate>2006-02-16</r:pubDate>
    <r:reviewer>Art Student</r:reviewer>
    <r:eval>A fun textbook.</r:eval>
  </r:review>
  <r:review lang="en">
    <r:title>Cavalcade</r:title>
    <r:pubDate>1933-04-15</r:pubDate>
    <r:reviewer>Pauline Kael</r:reviewer>
    <r:eval>An orgy of British self-congratulation.</r:eval>
  </r:review>
  <r:review lang="en">
    <r:title>The Illuminatus! Trilogy</r:title>
    <r:pubDate>1983-12-01</r:pubDate>
    <r:reviewer>A Reviewer</r:reviewer>
    <r:eval>I have seen the fnords.</r:eval>
  </r:review>
</r:reviews>
```

Figure 4.13   *Review database*

There is an issue with this result: it will fail for books as there is no child element for a director. Instead, the relevant field is for an author. We can generalize from the domain of feature films (and radio broadcasts) to define a field for "auteur." To do this, we define a user function that maps from the media-specific part of a content record to an "auteur" value. Here is a user-defined function in XQuery:

```
declare function local:toAuteur ($info as element(n:info))
  as element(auteur)*  {
  for $n in $info/node() return
    typeswitch ($n)
      case $f as element(n:film)
        return
          for $d in $f/n:director
          return element auteur { $d/text() }
```

```
      case $f as element(n:book) return …
      case $f as element(n:radio) return …
      default return { }
  };
```

The function is named `local:toAuteur`, where `local:` is a namespace prefix for user defined functions in the current XQuery namespace, and takes a single parameter `$info` which is required to be an `<info>` element from the namespace for the catalog. XQuery provides a construct for examining the type of a node in the XML tree, for example to determine the specific element name of a node where the specific name is obscured by a choice element or substitution group. The `toAuteur` function uses the `typeswitch` construct to examine the specific content type of the child element of the `<info>` element, which is a choice of three possible element names. Each of these elements is defined in the `contentType` type definition in Fig. 4.3. The function returns `<auteur>` elements for each director or author associated with the content. The modified query is as follows:

```
import schema namespace r = "http://www.example.org/review"
  at "Review.xsd";
<imdb> {
  for $c in doc("catalog.xml")/n:catalog/n:content,
      $r in doc("reviews.xml")/r:reviews/r:review
    where $c/n:title = $r/r:title and $c/n:pubDate = $r/r:pubDate
    return
      <info>
        <title> { $c/n:title/text() } </title>
        <pubDate> { $c/n:pubDate/text() } </pubDate>
        { local:toAuteur($c/n:info)) }
        <reviewer> { $r/r:reviewer/text() } </reviewer>
        <eval lang="{$r/@lang}"> { $r/r:eval/text() } </eval>
      </info>
} </imdb>
```

This produces a result document of the form:

```
<imdb>
  <info>
    <title>Lawrence of Arabia</title>
    <pubDate>1963-01-30</pubDate>
    <auteur>David Lean</auteur>
    <reviewer>A Reviewer</reviewer>
    <eval lang="en">
      When you pan and scan LOR, you lose the desert.
    </eval>
  </info>
  <info>
    <title>Lawrence of Arabia</title>
    <pubDate>1963-01-30</pubDate>
    <auteur>David Lean</auteur>
    <reviewer>M. Dwyer</reviewer>
    <eval lang="ga">
      Taim in ngra leis an priomhscannan seo.
```

```
    </eval>
  </info>
  …
</imdb>
```

The reviews for books (and radio broadcasts) are now included in the result of the join, which is agnostic regarding the form of the media content. This result may not be what is desired, as each content record is repeated for each review. The following variation on the join query organizes the reviews together under the media item for which they are a review:

```
import schema namespace r = "http://www.example.org/review"
 at "Review.xsd";
<imdb> {
  for $c in doc("catalog.xml")/n:catalog/n:content
  return
  <info>
    <title> { $c/n:title/text() } </title>
    <pubDate> { $c/n:pubDate/text() } </pubDate>
    { local:toAuteur($c/n:info) }
    <reviews>
    { for $r in doc("reviews.xml")/r:reviews/r:review
      where $c/n:title = $r/r:title and $c/n:pubDate = $r/r:pubDate return
      <review>
        <reviewer> { $r/r:reviewer/text() } </reviewer>
        <eval lang="{$r/@lang}"> { $r/r:eval/text() } </eval>
      </review>
    }
    </reviews>
  </info>
} </imdb>
```

The result of this query is the following:

```
<imdb>
  <info>
    <title>Lawrence of Arabia</title>
    <pubDate>1963-01-30</pubDate>
    <auteur>David Lean</auteur>
    <reviews>
      <review>
        <reviewer>A Reviewer</reviewer>
        <eval lang="en">
          When you pan and scan LOR, you lose the desert.
        </eval>
      </review>
      <review>
        <reviewer>M. Dwyer</reviewer>
        <eval lang="ga">
          Taim in ngra leis an priomhscannan seo.
        </eval>
      </review>
    </reviews>
```

```
  </info>
  ...
</imdb>
```

Our final example from XQuery is document inversion: to reorganize a document so that what was a nested element becomes a top-level element. In the previous example, the reviews are organized by media item. The following query inverts the document structure so that reviews are organized by reviewer:

```
import schema namespace r = "http://www.example.org/review"
  at "Review.xsd";
<reviewers> {
  for $r in
    distinct-values(doc("Fig-4-13.xml")/r:reviews/r:review/r:reviewer)
  return
    <info>
      <reviewer> { string($r) } </reviewer>
      <reviews>
      { for $rr in doc("Fig-4-13.xml")/r:reviews/r:review
        where $r = $rr/r:reviewer
        return
        <review>
          <title> { $rr/r:title/text() } </title>
          <pubDate> { $rr/r:pubDate/text() } </pubDate>
          <eval> { $rr/r:eval/text() } </eval>
        </review>
      }
      </reviews>
    </info>
} </reviewers>
```

Evaluating this query produces the following result:

```
<reviewers>
  <info>
    <reviewer>A Reviewer</reviewer>
      <reviews>
        <review>
          <title>Lawrence of Arabia</title>
          <pubDate>1963-01-30</pubDate>
          <eval>When you pan and scan, you lose the desert.</eval>
        </review>
        <review>
          <title>The Illuminatus! Trilogy</title>
          <pubDate>1983-12-01</pubDate>
          <eval>I have seen the fnords.</eval>
        </review>
      </reviews>
  </info>
  ...
</reviewers>
```

Figure 4.14 provides an overview of where XQuery may be used in the enterprise architecture. It may be used, for example, at the interface between the business logic

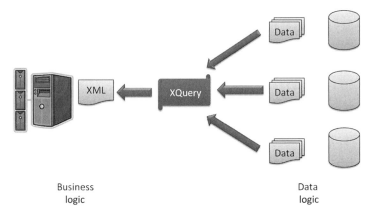

Business
logic

Data
logic

Figure 4.14 *Synthesis of documents using XQuery*

and data logic layers, synthesizing document data from data sources in back-end resources. The XQuery code is defined as part of the business logic and executed on the database. This is in opposition to XSLT, which is intended to be executed on XML data in the business tier. If the application server includes a caching native XML database, the XQuery code may be executed on that. In the next section, we consider how XML data may be represented in back-end databases, and also describe SQL/XML, an extension of SQL that allows XML data to be returned from SQL queries on a relational database.

4.3   XML DATABASES

Native XML databases have been defined, for example, by using the DOM object model and storing documents as DOM trees in an object-oriented database. Nevertheless, relational databases are still the storage medium of choice for enterprise information systems, and provide facilities such as transactional execution, backup and recovery, replication for high availability, and distributed access and access control, that would be expensive to replicate for other forms of storage media. Many relational DBMSs have been extended with support for storing XML data. Several alternatives are then available to the system designer, who must weigh the trade-off between flexibility and performance in choosing which storage option to choose for XML data in an application.

There are broadly three ways to represent XML content in relational databases:

1. "Shredding" of XML data into relational tables.
2. Storage as (large) strings.
3. Native XML storage (where supported).

A fourth alternative is to represent an XML document as a graph, stored as node and edge records in a database. Each node record represents a node in the original XML document, given an explicit node identifier, and edge records represent parent-child relationships in the document. This is a very general scheme, but one to be avoided in general. It is extremely difficult to define integrity constraints over this relationship, let alone to define queries over the data. Even if low-level SQL queries against this representation can be automatically generated from higher-level queries expressed, for example in XQuery, the optimization of such queries will be challenging given that the database system has essentially no static information about the overall structure of the documents (beyond what it can infer from this low-level representation).

In the remainder of this section, we examine each of the three approaches listed above. Before we do this, however, it is worth noting that native XML databases may still play an important role in an enterprise architecture. For example, a native XML database may provide an *in-memory database* (IMDB) in the application server that caches data retrieved from a relational database resource as XML documents, as depicted in Fig. 4.15. XML-specific queries may be applied to this cached data within the application server, even if the database is a legacy system that does not natively support XML data.

On the other hand, doing this has important implications for systems that are replicated for high availability. If we recall the example shown in Fig. 2.10 and the accompanying discussion in Fig. 2.4, load balancing depends on being able to direct each client request to any of the available application servers. Caching client data on the application server interferes with the ability to do this. An alternative is to factor the caching database out to a separate "session server" still in the server cluster, but separate from the application servers. We discuss these issues in more depth in Sect. 6.10.

4.3.1   Storage as Relational Tables

This strategy is available when the XML data are highly structured with a "fixed" schema. A relational table is created for each form of element, with each occurrence of the element stored as a row in the table. Simple content for an element is stored

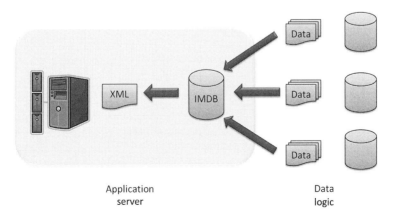

Figure 4.15   *In-memory native XML database in application server*

as an attribute in the corresponding row. Attributes of an element are also stored as columns in the table. Primary keys are generated for each table, and parent and child elements reference each other in the relational table representation using foreign keys. An example of this is provided in Fig. 3.3. Modifications of this scheme include flattening some of the elements nested in an element, moving the columns for these elements into the table for the parent element. This can be done if the nested elements do not recur in the document. The example schema in Fig. 4.3 can be represented using the relational schema with tables:

```
catalog (id, title, pub_date, film_id, book_id, radio_id)
catalog_genre (id, genre_id)
genre (genre_id, genre_name)
film (film_id, director, …)
```

There are three foreign keys, one for each form of content, for each catalog record, with the assumption that exactly one will be non-null. The many-to-many relationship between catalog entries and genres is given by the `catalog_genre` table.

At the interface between database and application server, the results of relational queries can be converted to XML by adding a root element to the overall result, and adding elements to each record in the rowset result and each of the column values within a row. Where nested structure is required in the result, relational query languages include support for defining this nested content. SQL/XML is an extension of the SQL relational query language with support for specifying XML content in the result of a query. For example:

```
select xmlelement (name "content",
    xmlattributes(category),
    xmlelement (name "id", id),
    xmlelement (name "title", title),
    xmlelement (name "pubDate", pub_date),
    xmlagg (
        select xmlelement (name "genre", genre_name) from genre
            where catalog.id = catalog_genre.id
            and catalog_genre.genre_id = genre.genre_id),
        xmlelement (name "info",
          select xmlelement (name "film",
            xmlelement ("director", director))
            from film where catalog.film_id = film.film_id))
from catalog
```

This example constructs a sequence of <content> elements, one for each row in the `catalog` database table. The `xmlelement` function constructs the element and the `xmlattributes` function defines a `category` attribute in this element from the `category` column in the `catalog` table. There are child elements for <title> and <pubDate> using the values from the corresponding columns in the table. The `film` element has (in this example) a single child element, the <director> element, defined by following the foreign key to the `film` table stored in the `catalog` record. Finally, the `xmlagg` function adds a forest of elements into the child elements for the <content> element, each one corresponding to a genre defined for this catalog record, and obtained from the intermediate table catalog_genre defining the relationship between content and genres.

This is a somewhat involved query to write but, in general, we expect such queries to be generated automatically by tools that map XML schemas into storage schemes for relational databases. In the reverse direction, XML data that is sent to be stored in the database is shredded into component tables and, again, this is boilerplate code that should be generated automatically by data conversion tools.

4.3.2 Storage as Large Strings

Rather than shredding an XML document to relational tables, another alternative is to store it as an atomic value—a large object of characters (*clob*) or a large object of bytes (*blob*). This alternative avoids the overhead of decomposing XML data into tables for storage and reconstituting it as the result of a query. This alternative, or native XML storage, may be necessary if the XML data has irregular storage, making it difficult to define a mapping to a relational schema. It may also be necessary if, potentially, documents have a recursive structure. For example, whereas a technical article may have a fixed depth (section/subsection/paragraph), a document describing the decomposition of machine parts into subparts may have arbitrary depth, as any part may have zero or more subparts.

This storage alternative may be mandated by contractual or regulatory constraints on the storage of some XML content. For example, it may be required to store exact copies of legal documents or stock transaction orders. String storage does not support contextual searching of XML data. To facilitate such searching, such strings may be parsed to XML documents as part of executing a query, or native XML copies may be redundantly stored in the database.

4.3.3 Native XML Storage

Many DBMSs include support for native storage of XML data. A type is added for objects of type XML. XML values may be stored as columns in tables containing other forms of data, or they may be stored in separate tables (accessed via a foreign key in the main table) if the size of an XML value slows down access to simpler values in a record. Unlike the string storage alternative, the DBMS understands the structure of the XML data and supports queries, expressed in languages such as XQuery, on such data. If a schema can be associated with an XML data-type column, this can be used to extend conformance checking of data with the database schema and can be used as input to query optimization to improve performance based on statically known information about the structure of the data.

SQL queries are used as normal to retrieve data from the database, but such queries can include XQuery queries for the XML part of the data. The latter queries parse XML data at run-time. The execution of these queries may be accelerated by defining indexes on the XML data, reducing the search space before any XML data is parsed. On the other hand, maintenance of these fine-grained XML indexes may slow down data modification.

Another design consideration for native XML storage is that locking for concurrency control purposes is typically at the level of rows in a table. Therefore, storing an entire XML document as a cell in a row means that the entire document is locked when the row is locked. Finer granularity locking requires that the document be shredded into relational tables. On the other hand, native storage avoids the overhead of shredding XML data to relational tables and reconstituting the XML data in a query result. The decision of which option to use is a design decision for the data modeler. In practise, a hybrid scheme, where some of the XML data is decomposed into relations and some is stored as values of XML data type, may be most appropriate to an application.

4.4   WEB SERVICES

The final application of XML that we will review is its use in Web services. This application is visible in everyday Web usage via AJAX-driven Web applications that execute on the client side and invoke server-side processing via Web services. However, the driving motivation for Web services has always been machine-machine interaction (as opposed to human-machine interaction for Web applications) for the purposes of B2B e-commerce. In this section, we will focus on the protocol stack for Web services standardized by the W3C. We consider RESTful Web services in Chapter 7.

We have discussed the motivation for Web services in Sect. 2.6 in Chapter 2. To recap, Web services as originally envisioned were intended to be a platform for remote procedure call deployed over the World Wide Web protocol stack (running HTTP over the TCP/IP stack, with request and response messages exchanged as XML documents). The tight coupling required for RPC and RMI is antithetical to the nature of the Internet, which can have high latency and is subject to lost traffic as a result of congestion. A more natural fit with B2B e-commerce is an asynchronous transfer of business documents. The latter document-style interaction has prevailed over the RPC-style interaction in actual Web service applications. In the realm of SOAP-based Web services, "document style" and "RPC style" only refer to the data format of the request and response messages. We explain these terms in Sect. 4.4.1. SOAP is agnostic as to whether communication is synchronous or asynchronous. That is left to the underlying transfer protocol specified in the binding. Other forms of semantics, such as transactional semantics, or cryptographic authentication and confidentiality, are provided by other protocols that may be layered on top of SOAP.

The intended set of interactions in SOAP-based Web services is provided in Fig. 4.16. A *service provider* publishes a service by registering it at a local discovery service. The protocol for service discovery formalized as part of Web services is termed Universal Description Discovery and Integration (UDDI). A *service requestor* interrogates the UDDI service to discover a service based on criteria that it provides. The critera are specific to the application area or the industry. The result of discovery is a list of t-models for the relevant services returned to the service requester. The latter provides information about the services matching the

Figure 4.16 *Interactions in SOAP-based Web services*

discovery criteria, including, in particular, interfaces for the services. The preferred language for describing these services is WSDL, which we describe in Sect. 4.4.2. We describe UDDI, and its failure as a Web service standard, in Sect. 6.11.1.

Figure 4.17 describes the WS-* Web services protocol stack. As can be seen, at the base of the stack is a standard for message format and processing based on the XML language SOAP. UDDI and WSDL provide a layer for service description above this. WSDL describes concrete interfaces in terms of SOAP messages that are exchanged, while UDDI assumes service discovery based on Web services. However, as of WSDL 2.0, service designers and implementors have the option of defining Web services without the use of SOAP, as reflected by the option of just using XML for message contents (we discuss this more fully in Chapter 7.) We consider the details of Web services, particularly SOAP, WSDL, and WS-Policy, in the following sections.

4.4.1   SOAP: (not so) Simple Object Access Protocol

Middleware standards such as CORBA and DCOM specify wire formats for messages to deal with the heterogeneity of distributed systems. All data to be transmitted must be marshalled to the binary format expected by the middleware before being sent as a message. One of the issues with this is that binary data formats, particulary proprietary formats, famously create problems as systems evolve into legacy systems and need to interface to newer systems. This was part of the motivation for XML for data storage: a self-describing data format facilitates the development of interface tools, such as filters and transformers. Another issue is that binary data formats push the problems of heterogeneous systems from the network up to the middleware. For example, interfacing CORBA

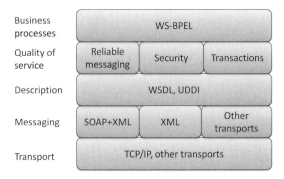

Figure 4.17 *Web services stack*

to DCOM, or even just interfacing different CORBA systems for enterprises, is usually a challenge.

The wire format for messages in SOAP has two layers: an *abstract layer*, where messages are described as XML documents, and a *binding layer*, where the formatting of these documents on a transfer protocol are defined. The binding for SOAP over HTTP defines two bindings: a *literal encoding*, where messages are marshalled as XML documents, and a *SOAP encoding* that provides rules for preserving data sharing during marshalling. The Message Transmission Optimization Mechanism (MTOM) supports the optimization of SOAP transmission for certain forms of content, particularly large binary content. MTOM provides the Abstract SOAP Transmission Optimization feature which, for example, provides for the transmission of SOAP messages as Multipurpose Internet Mail Extension (MIME) attachments over the HTTP protocol.

Figure 4.18 describes the structure of a SOAP message at the abstract layer. A *SOAP envelope* consists of zero or more header blocks followed by the SOAP body. Figure 4.19 provides an example of a SOAP request message. This XML document has as its root element the SOAP <envelope> element. It includes child

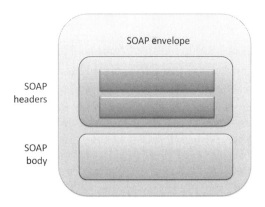

Figure 4.18 *Structure of a SOAP message*

```
<?xml version='1.0' ?>
<env:Envelope xmlns:env="http://www.w3.org/2003/05/soap-envelope">
  <env:Header>
    <wsse:Security
        env:role="http://www.w3.org/2003/05/soap-envelope/role/
                      ultimateReceiver"
        env:mustUnderstand="true"
        xmlns:wsse="http://docs.oasis-open.org/wss/2004/01/…">
      <sig:Signature
        xmlns:sig="http://www.w3.org/2000/09/xmldsig#">
        <sig:SignedInfo> … </sig:SignedInfo> …
        <sig:KeyInfo> … </sig:KeyInfo>
      </sig:Signature>
    </wsse:Security>
  </env:Header>
  <env:Body>
    <p:purchaseOrderRequest xmlns:p="http://www.example.org/soap-po">
      <p:ref>uuid:2349f80b-4f25-4880-aaea-67c7f09280a3</p:ref>
      <p:items>
        <p:item>
          <p:title>Lawrence of Arabia</p:title>
          <p:qty>100</p:qty>
        </p:item>
      </p:items>
      <p:amount> … </p:amount>
      <p:billTo> … </p:billTo>
      <p:shipTo> … </p:shipTo>
    </p:purchaseOrderRequest>
  </env:Body>
</env:Envelope>
```

Figure 4.19   *SOAP request*

elements for the header and the body, respectively, of the message. The request message contains purchase order information being communicated to a supplier for the purchase of some items identified in the <items> field of the payload. The namespace for the payload is completely defined by the application.

This request message has one header block for authenticating request messages. The namespace for the element of this header block, <wsse:Security>, uses the namespace for the WS-Security standard for SOAP message security, reflecting that the header block contains a message signature for end-to-end authentication. The header block includes signature information (the DSA signature of a SHA-1 hash of the message body, suitably encoded as a content string), and key information (an encoding of an X509 certificate that provides the public key for authentication, signed by a certification authority).

The root element for this header block includes two attributes that are part of the SOAP namespace. The intention is that there may be several intermediary points that a SOAP message may pass through before it reaches its ultimate destination. For each header block, the role attribute defines the points along the path from source to destination at which the header block should be processed. In the example in Fig. 4.19, the signature is intended to be authenticated by the final destination of the message, hence the `role` attribute for this header block specifies `ulti-mateReceiver`. This is the default value for the attribute. Other possible values are: (1) next (any intermediary should be able to process this header block, although once processed the header block is removed from the message before forwarding, unless processing reinserts it); (2) none (no SOAP node should process the header block, although it may be read as part of processing other header blocks); and, (3) application-defined roles (e.g., an application might define a role for logging purposes).

Associated with the `role` attribute is the `mustUnderstand` attribute, which mandates processing by any SOAP node that matches the role specification. SOAP fault-handling includes support for reporting a failure by a SOAP node to process a header block that it was mandated to process. Whether that failure is signalled back to the original sender depends, in general, on the underlying transfer protocol. If the `mustUnderstand` flag is false and a SOAP node does not process it, it is still required that the header block be removed before forwarding. SOAP provides a `relay` attribute to disable this and allow an unprocessed header block to be forwarded with the message. Therefore setting the `role` attribute to next, the `mustUnderstand` attribute to `false` and the `relay` attribute to `true` ensures that every intermediate SOAP node, and the ultimate destination, get the opportunity to inspect the header block, until it is eventually processed.

As we have seen, the payload for the request message is a `<purchaseOrderRe-quest>` element defined in the `http://www.example.org/soap-po` namespace. This is an example of the *document style* of SOAP message. The "document" style refers to the fact that the structure of the payload is defined completely by the application. An alternative is the *RPC style*, defined by the SOAP standard, that requires that the payload contain a single root element, whose name identifies the operation to be invoked remotely. Each of the child elements identifies a parameter to this operation. For example, the RPC style version of the above request message is given by:

```xml
<?xml version='1.0' ?>
<env:Envelope xmlns:env="http://www.w3.org/2003/05/soap-envelope">
  <env:Header> … </env:Header>
  <env:Body>
    <purchaseOrderRequest xmlns:p="http://www.example.org/soap-po">
      <ref>uuid:2349f80b-4f25-4880-aaea-67c7f09280a3</ref>
      <items>
        <p:item
          env:encodingStyle="http://www.w3.org/2003/05/soap-encoding">
          <p:title>Lawrence of Arabia</p:title>
          <p:qty>100</p:qty></p:item>
      </items>
      <amount> … </amount>
      <billTo> … </billTo>
      <shipTo> … </shipTo>
    </purchaseOrderRequest>
```

```
  </env:Body>
</env:Envelope>
```

The root element of the payload (identifying the operation) and its child elements (identifying the parameters) are no longer defined in the payload namespace, but are part of the structure of the message and distinguished from the data the message is transmitting. This complicates validation of the payload against a schema,[1] which is one of the reasons that the RPC style is now rarely used. This example also demonstrates the use of the optional SOAP encoding style for the `<p:item>` element. The SOAP standard provides complicated rules for marshalling elements where SOAP encoding is specified for sub-elements of a SOAP message.

Figure 4.20 provides a SOAP response to the request in Fig. 4.19. The fact that this is a response to a purchase order request message is suggested by the name of the payload root element, but SOAP itself leaves such considerations to the application. Both the request and response messages include the reference identifier for the original purchase order and this may be used to correlate the response message with the request message that it is in response to. This is not required by SOAP, as this correlation between request and response may instead be done at the transfer protocol layer.

The HTTP Web protocol includes the POST operation for uploading a document to a Web server and receiving a response document in return. This is a natural mechanism for exchanging request and response messages, such as above. However, the Web architecture mandates the use of the GET operation where the intention is to query a Web application without modifying the state of the application. The search parameters should be encoded as a query string as part of the argument to GET. The SOAP standard includes the specification of *message exchange patterns (MEPs)* that guide the binding of SOAP transmission to particular transfer protocols:

1. The *request-response* SOAP MEP denotes the sending of a response message and the receipt of a response message in return.

2. The *response-only* SOAP MEP denotes the receipt of a message without the sending of a prior request message.

```
<?xml version='1.0' ?>
<env:Envelope xmlns:env="http://www.w3.org/2003/05/soap-envelope">
  <env:Header> … </env:Header>
  <env:Body>
    <p:purchaseOrderResponse xmlns:p="http://www.example.org/soap-po">
      <p:ref>uuid:2349f80b-4f25-4880-aaea-67c7f09280a3</p:ref>
      <p:ourRef> … </p:ourRef>
      <p:dateReceived> 2011-02-14 </p:dateReceived>
    </p:purchaseOrderResponse>
  </env:Body>
</env:Envelope>
```

Figure 4.20 *SOAP response*

---
[1]The SOAP standard predates the XML Schema standard.

For the HTTP binding, the request-response MEP is bound to the usage of the POST operation in the transfer protocol, while the response MEP is bound to the usage of the GET operation. In the latter case, an XML request message is encoded in the query string for the GET operation and an XML response message is returned as the document downloaded from the server. The SOAP binding also provides the *Web method feature* to specify the HTTP operation to be used in a Web transfer protocol for SOAP messages. This may be used to specify bindings for additional application-defined MEPs, or to override the default choices for the standard SOAP MEPs.

Fault handling is also an important part of the SOAP architecture. Figure 4.21 provides a fault message for the request message in Fig. 4.19. This fault message may be returned as a result of an authentication failure at the receiver. The payload element is defined as part of the SOAP namespace. The fault code identifies the party responsible for the failure (sender or receiver). A subcode provides application-specific information, including a code (for automatic handling) and an explanation (for manual handling). The WS-Security standard defines the code and fault string in Fig. 4.21 for SOAP fault handling. SOAP does not mandate the return of a fault message to the original sender. Implementing such a return may be difficult for some transfer protocols. Recall that SOAP does not assume synchronous communication. It may be undesirable in some cases to require the return of a fault message to the sender. For example, reporting authentication failure may provide an opportunity for denial of service attacks. For the case of a message communicated point-to-point via HTTP using GET or POST, the fault message can be returned as part of the Web server response.

As can be seen, SOAP provides a great deal of machinery for enterprise message exchange, including provision for intermediate processing and for fault handling. To

```
<?xml version='1.0' ?>
<env:Envelope xmlns:env="http://www.w3.org/2003/05/soap-envelope">
  <env:Header> </env:Header>
  <env:Body>
    <env:Fault
      xmlns:wsse="http://docs.oasis-open.org/wss/2004/01/...">
      <env:Code><env:Value>env:Sender</env:Value></env:Code>
      <env:Subcode>
        <env:Value>wsse:FailedCheck</env:Value>
      </env:Subcode>
      <env:Reason>
        <env:Text xml:lang="en-US">
          The signature or decryption was invalid
        </env:Text>
      </env:Reason>
    </env:Fault>
  </env:Body>
</env:Envelope>
```

Figure 4.21   *SOAP fault*

appreciate some of the motivation for this, one should be aware that the envisioned scenario for SOAP processing is a potentially quite complicated intra-enterprise or inter-enterprise messaging network, composed of message processing nodes such as filters, content-based routers, etc. We review some of the choices in this design space in Chapter 8 in the sequel. This basic message-passing framework is the basis for a rich stack of protocols for performing Web services, as illustrated in Fig. 4.17, including:

1. WS-Addressing for providing addressing information for senders and receivers.
2. WS-ReliableMessaging for providing reliable message-passing. Although the default transfer protocol for SOAP is over the HTTP/TCP stack, messages may be lost because of the failure of intermediate nodes during the processing of these messages in application-level message networks.
3. WS-Security for end-to-end authentication and encryption.
4. WS-Policy for requiring certain run-time mechanisms in message passing, such as transactions or encryption.
5. WS-Coordination for obtaining global agreement among distributed partners.
6. WS-Transaction for reliable distributed database update.
7. WS-BPEL for automated business processing that makes use of the facilities provided by the Web services protocol stack.

4.4.2 WSDL: Web Services Description Language

As can be guessed from Fig. 4.16, the Web services framework has taken much of its original inspiration from RPC stacks for LANs. Besides the messaging format, the other critical component of an RPC system is the language for describing service interfaces. Without well-defined interfaces, any development of services is not sustainable, as service interfaces evolve and grow in complexity. WSDL is the interface definition language standardized for SOAP-based Web services. The widely implemented version 1.1 of WSDL was never more than a Web Services Consortium note. The eventual W3C standard, WSDL 2.0, repairs some unnecessary complexity in WSDL 1.1 and provides support for RESTful Web services (discussed in Chapter 7). Adoption of WSDL 2.0 has been slow as a result of an existing installed base of WSDL 1.1 interfaces. Nevertheless, we use WSDL 2.0 as an example of an XML-based interface definition language as it corrects several problems with WSDL 1.1.

The structure of a WSDL interface description is provided in Fig. 4.22. A WSDL document is split into two parts: the *abstract part* describes a service interface in the abstract in the sense of the operations that a service provides, while the *concrete part* describes concretely how the service can be invoked over a network. In turn, the abstract part is has two components:

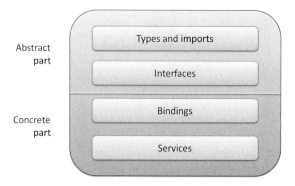

Figure 4.22 *Components of a WSDL interface description*

1. The *types* part of the document declares namespaces and imports, and includes schemas where necessary, and provides local type definitions and element declarations.

2. The *interface* part declares the operations that the service interface provides. Each operation has a specification of request and response messages. The interface specification also declares fault messages for which, as we have seen, SOAP provides special handling.

The concrete part, in turn, has two parts:

1. The *binding* part declares the transfer protocols that can be used for communication with the service. This includes the specification of how messages are marshalled and unmarshalled on the transport. An interface may have several bindings.

2. The *service* part specifies the actual network addresses of the services, typically as endpoint URLs for SOAP routers.

The separation of the abstract and concrete parts reflects the fact that a Web service may be offered over several different transfer protocol s, e.g., HTTP and Wireless Application Protocol (WAP). The separation of the binding and service parts reflects that a service endpoint may be defined dynamically, for example for callbacks in an asynchronous interaction.

We use the reviews service depicted in Fig. 4.23 as an example to demonstrate WSDL. The service provides two operations:

1. The getReviews operation returns a list of all reviews for a particular content item, as identified by a title and publication date. This is an obvious example of a synchronous operation involving the exchange of request and response messages.

2. The postReview operation adds a review to the database at the server. We assume that reviews are reviewed before being accepted, for example to check

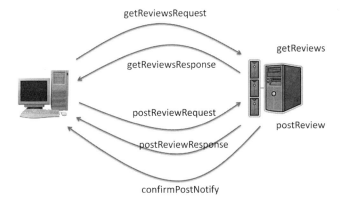

Figure 4.23 *Message exchanges with reviews service*

for appropriate language. This is an example of an asynchronous interaction: the reviewer gets an acknowledgement as an immediate response with a review identifier. Subsequently, the service calls back to the client, to confirm that that review has been accepted, by sending the `confirmPostNotify` message. To keep the example small, we assume that objectionable reviews are quietly discarded.

Figure 4.24 provides the abstract part of this service interface, providing only the details for the `getReviews` operation first of all. We consider the concrete part of this interface, and the details for the `postReview` operation, below. In Fig. 4.24, the `<type>` element defines a key type to specify items of content in messages (based on title and publication date). It also declares elements for request and response messages: the request message content type is defined to be the key type and the response message content type is a list of `<review>` elements.

It should be noted in this example that there are two target namespaces:

1. The target namespace for the schema is "`http://www.example.org/wsdl/reviews/schemas`". This is the name-space for types defined and elements declared in the `<type>` part of the WSDL document.
2. The target namespace for the WSDL document as a whole is "`http://www.example.org/wsdl/reviews`". This is the namespace for interfaces, operations, bindings and services defined in the WSDL specification.

The interface part of a WSDL document defines the signatures for a collection of operations that make up the service. In this example, there are two operations in `reviewsInterface`: `getReviews` and `postReview`. The `postReview` operation is elided in Fig. 4.24.

The abstract specification of an operation details the messages that are associated with invoking that service operation. The `getReviews` operation has two messages associated with it: a request message that specifies content by title and publication

```
<description
  xmlns="http://www.w3.org/ns/wsdl"
  xmlns:wsdlx= "http://www.w3.org/ns/wsdl-extensions"
  targetNamespace= "http://www.example.org/wsdl/reviews"
  xmlns:tns= "http://www.example.org/wsdl/reviews"
  xmlns:k="http://www.example.org/wsdl/reviews/schemas"
  xmlns:r="http://www.example.org/reviews">

<types>
  <xs:schema
    xmlns:xs="http://www.w3.org/2001/XMLSchema"
    targetNamespace="http://www.example.org/wsdl/reviews/schemas"
    xmlns:k="http://www.example.org/wsdl/reviews/schemas">

  <xs:import namespace="http://www.example.org/reviews"
    schemaLocation="Review.xsd"/>
  <xs:complexType name="keyType">
    <xs:sequence>
      <xs:element name="title" type="xs:string"/>
      <xs:element name="pubDate" type="xs:date"/>
    </xs:sequence>
  </xs:complexType>
  <xs:element name="getReviewsRequest" type="k:keyType"/>
  <xs:element name="getReviewsResponse">
    <xs:complexType> <xs:sequence>
      <xs:element name="review" type="r:reviewType"
          maxOccurs="unbounded"/>
    </xs:sequence> </xs:complexType>
  </xs:element>
  <xs:element name="invalidDataError" type="xs:string"/>
  </xs:schema>
</types>
<interface name="reviewsInterface">
 <fault name="invalidDataFault" element="k:invalidDataError"/>

 <operation name="getReviews"
    pattern="http://www.w3.org/ns/wsdl/in-out"
    style="http://www.w3.org/ns/wsdl/style/iri"
    wsdlx:safe = "true">
    <input messageLabel="In" element="k:getReviewsRequest"/>
    <output messageLabel="Out" element="k:getReviewsResponse"/>
    <outfault ref="tns:invalidDataFault" messageLabel="Out"/>
 </operation> …
 …
 </interface>
 …
</description>
```

Figure 4.24   *Reviews service: abstract part*

date; and a response message that includes a list of reviews. The content type for each review is described using the `reviewType` complex type defined earlier in Fig. 4.12.

WSDL requires that this abstract specification include a *WSDL MEP*. This is not to be confused with the SOAP MEP, where SOAP is one possible transfer protocol that may be used in the binding. WSDL specifies several possible patterns for the exchange of messages; additional patterns may be defined by applications. The pre-defined WSDL MEPs are `In-Only`, `Robust In-Only`, and `In-Out`. In addition, MEPs for `In-Optional-Out`, `Out-Only`, `Robust Out-Only`, `Out-In`, and `Out-Optional-In` are defined as non-normative extensions, and applications are free to define their own MEPs. These pre-defined MEPs are distinguished by whether the client or the service initiates the communication. For example, an `In-Only` MEP corre-sponds to a message sent to the service without any expectation of a response. An `Out-Only` MEP corresponds to a notification sent from the service without, necessarily, any prior input from the client. An `In-Out` MEP corresponds to a request message from the client triggering a response message from the service. This does not necessarily entail synchronous communication, as understood by tra-ditional middleware. Both messages might be exchanged via asynchronous message queues.

A further distinction is made based on whether a message can trigger a fault. A subtle distinction is made here between faults that *replace* messages and faults that *trigger* messages. For example, the `In-Out` pattern allows a fault message to replace any message after the first message in the pattern; and these fault messages may be specified in the WSDL specification. Recall that, in this case, faults refer to application faults, such as authentication failure, credit card verification failure, etc., rather than to system failures. Thus, applications are free to build some robustness into protocols by reporting intermediate failures. In contrast, the `Robust In-Only` pattern allows a message to trigger a fault and then *requires* that fault message to be delivered back to the sender of the message. This is a strong requirement that, in many cases, may not be possible to achieve.

Once the MEP is defined for an operation, the interface must specify the mes-sages for each role in that MEP. Each of these messages has a payload defined as an XML Schema element. In addition, fault messages may be specified to replace these messages. In the example in Fig. 4.24, the `In-Out` pattern is specified for the `getReviews` operation. The message for the role of input message (`messageLa-bel="In"`) has as its payload a `<getReviewsRequest>` element, while the message for the role of output message (`messageLabel="Out"`) has as its payload a `<getRe-viewsResponse>` element.[2] In addition, the payload for the fault message replacing the latter is defined to include an `<invalidDataError>` element. This is done using a

---

[2]It may appear redundant to specify `In` and `Out` attributes for `<input>` and `<output>` elements, respectively. The *message label* is differentiated from the *message direction* (input or output). The rationale is that applications may define patterns where there may be multiple messages involved, so the message labels would distinguish the messages in such patterns. If the `messageLabel` attributes are omitted, their values default to those shown.

named fault message, `invalidDataFault`, that is declared as a child of the `<inter-face>` element. Fault messages are declared outside operation declarations to allow their re-use across different operations.

In addition to specifying a MEP, an operation declaration also may optionally declare a *style*. These styles place additional constraints on the form of the elements that make up messages for the operation. The pre-defined styles are:

1. International Resource Identification (IRI): it must be possible to marshall the contents of a message as a URL, including a query string. This is for situations where a message is transmitted over HTTP using the `GET` method. The Web architecture requires the `GET` method for operations that are queries. The query parameters are encoded as a query string with the URI for such a call, hence the IRI restriction.
2. Remote Procedure Call (RPC): the message content must have a root element identifying an operation to be invoked and child elements for the arguments to that operation. This restriction is to facilitate marshalling RPC calls in programming languages to Web service invocations.
3. Multi-part: this places constraints on the data so it can be transmitted using XForms.

The attribute `wsdlx:safe` is an extension that allows the service designer to flag that the operation is *safe* in the sense that it does not change the state of the Web server. This has implications for the transfer protocol. Over HTTP, the fact that the operation is stateless requires that it be implemented using the `GET` Web method to be compatible with Web architecture. In turn, this information that the operation is stateless, is useful for Web caches and proxies, which may return a previously cached query result, and for load balancers for Web clusters.

Figure 4.25 gives a concrete binding for the abstract interface provided in Fig. 4.24. We add two additional namespaces to the WSDL specification:

1. The `wsoap:` namespace identifies the namespace for the SOAP 1.2 binding for WSDL. In turn, this binding defines several attributes that can be used to customize the binding for the `reviews` service.
2. The `soap:` namespace identifies the namespace for SOAP 1.2 envelopes.

The `type` attribute for the `<binding>` element defines the message format for the messages that implement the operations defined in the interface. In this case, this attribute specifies SOAP 1.2 as the message format. The `wsoap:protocol` attribute from the WSDL/SOAP binding defines the particular transfer protocol to be used. In this case, the binding specifies that SOAP messages will be transferred over HTTP.

The concrete binding for the `getReviews` operation is customized in several ways by the binding. The `wsoap:mep` attribute specifies the SOAP MEP to use for this operation—in this case the `SOAP-response` MEP. This is realized in the

```
<?xml version="1.0" encoding="utf-8" ?>
<description
    xmlns="http://www.w3.org/ns/wsdl"
    xmlns:wsdlx="http://www.w3.org/ns/wsdl-extensions"
    targetNamespace="http://www.example.org/wsdl/reviews"
    xmlns:tns="http://www.example.org/wsdl/reviews"
    xmlns:k="http://www.example.org/wsdl/reviews/schemas"
    xmlns:r="http://www.example.org/reviews"
    xmlns:wsoap="http://www.w3.org/ns/wsdl/soap"
    xmlns:soap="http://www.w3.org/2003/05/soap-envelope">
    ...
  <binding name="reviewsSOAPBinding" interface="tns:reviewsInterface"
    type="http://www.w3.org/ns/wsdl/soap"
    wsoap:protocol=
        "http://www.w3.org/2003/05/soap/bindings/HTTP/">
    <operation ref="tns:getReviews"
      wsoap:mep=
        "http://www.w3.org/2003/05/soap/mep/soap-response"/>
    <fault ref="tns:invalidDataFault" wsoap:code="soap:Sender"/>
  </binding>
  <service name="reviewsService" interface="tns:reviewsInterface">
    <endpoint name="reviewsEndpoint"
      binding="tns:reviewsSOAPBinding"
      address ="http://www.example.org/wsdl/reviews/soap/"/>
  </service>
    ...
</description>
```

Figure 4.25 *Reviews service: concrete part*

SOAP/HTTP binding by the GET method. The input message is encoded as the query string to the GET method, hence the necessity in the interface to specify the iri "style" for the operation. The output message is encoded as a SOAP document in the HTTP response from the server; the <fault> element specializes fault handling; and the wsoap:code attribute indicates which fault code triggers the sending of this fault message. In this case, if the receiver indicates a SOAP fault code of Sender, the invalidDataFault message is returned as part of the payload for a SOAP fault message in the HTTP response.

After all of this customization of the binding, the service is relatively straight-forward: it simply identifies the endpoint URL for the service.

We now consider the operation for posting a review. The interesting part of this operation is the use of a callback operation, provided by the client and called by the service, to confirm acceptance of a review posting. The WSDL specification for this callback operation is provided in Fig. 4.26. There is a single operation, confirmPost, with a WSDL MEP of In-Only, reflecting that the service does not expect an acknowledgement. In our example, we provide a SOAP/HTTP binding for this interface; however, the SMTP transfer protocol (sending the confirmation via e-mail) is a plausible alternative. The SOAP MEP for the SOAP/HTTP binding is defined to be request-response: the server uses the HTTP POST method to transmit the confirmation message to the client and the HTTP response message is empty.

```xml
<?xml version="1.0" encoding="utf-8" ?>
<description
    xmlns="http://www.w3.org/ns/wsdl"
    xmlns:wsoap="http://www.w3.org/ns/wsdl/soap"
    targetNamespace=
        "http://www.example.org/wsdl/reviews/confirmPost"
    xmlns:tns= "http://www.example.org/wsdl/reviews/confirmPost"
    xmlns:cp=
        "http://www.example.org/wsdl/reviews/confirmPost/schemas" >
  <types>
    <xs:schema
        xmlns:xs="http://www.w3.org/2001/XMLSchema"
        targetNamespace=
          "http://www.example.org/wsdl/reviews/confirmPost/schemas"
        xmlns:cp=
          "http://www.example.org/wsdl/reviews/confirmPost/schemas">

      <xs:complexType name="confirmPostType">
        <xs:sequence>
          <xs:element name="postid" type="xs:string"/>
        </xs:sequence>
      </xs:complexType>
      <xs:element name="confirmPostNotify" type="k:confirmPostType"/>
    </xs:schema>
  </types>
  <interface name="confirmPostInterface" >
    <operation name="confirmPost"
        pattern="http://www.w3.org/ns/wsdl/in-only">
      <input messageLabel="In" element="k:confirmPostNotify" />
      <outfault ref="tns:invalidDataFault" messageLabel="Out"/>
    </operation>
  </interface>
  <binding name="confirmPostSOAPBinding"
      interface="tns:confirmPostInterface"
      type="http://www.w3.org/ns/wsdl/soap"
      wsoap:protocol=
          "http://www.w3.org/2003/05/soap/bindings/HTTP/">
    <operation ref="tns:confirmPost"
      wsoap:mep=
          "http://www.w3.org/2003/05/soap/mep/request-response"/>
  </binding>
</description>
```

Figure 4.26   *Reviews service: specification for posting callback*

The important point to note about the example in Fig. 4.26 is that the WSDL specification describes every part of the callback service *except the endpoint URL*. This is obviously because the endpoint must be dynamically specified by each client as they call into the original service to post a review. This dynamic binding to a service address is the reason that WSDL separates the endpoint URL into a distinct part of the service specification, separate from the transfer protocol and binding.

The part of the original server WSDL specification that describes the `postReview` operation (at least the abstract part) is given in Fig. 4.27. The `postReview` operation is described in the interface part of the specification. This operation uses the `In-Out` WSDL MEP, with request and response message payloads described in the `types` part of the document. The response simply returns a response identifier generated by the service that the client can use to correlate this request with the later confirmation of post approval. The request includes a review, using the `reviewType` complex type earlier defined in Fig. 4.12.

```xml
<?xml version="1.0" encoding="utf-8"?>
<description
    xmlns="http://www.w3.org/ns/wsdl"
    xmlns:wsdlx= "http://www.w3.org/ns/wsdl-extensions"
    xmlns:wsdli="http://www.w3.org/ns/wsdl-instance"
    targetNamespace= "http://www.example.org/wsdl/reviews"
    xmlns:tns= "http://www.example.org/wsdl/reviews"
    xmlns:k="http://www.example.org/wsdl/reviews/schemas"
    xmlns:r="http://www.example.org/schemas/reviews"
    xmlns:cp="http://www.example.org/wsdl/reviews/confirmPost"
<?xml version="1.0" encoding="utf-8"?>
  <types>
    <xs:schema …
     wsdli:wsdlLocation=
         "http://www.example.org/wsdl/reviews/confirmPost
         ConfirmPost.wsdl" >
     <xs:simpleType
         name="confirmPostSOAPType"
         wsdlx:binding="cp:confirmPostSOAPBinding">
       <xs:restriction base="xs:anyURI"/>
     </xs:simpleType>
     <xs:complexType name="postReviewType">
       <xs:sequence>
         <xs:element name="review" type="r:reviewType"/>
         <xs:element name="callback" type="k:confirmPostSOAPType"/>
       </xs:sequence>
     </xs:complexType>
     <xs:element name="postReviewRequest" type="k:postReviewType"/>
     <xs:element name="postReviewResponse" type="xs:string">
    </xs:schema>
  </types>
  <interface name="reviewsInterface" > …
    <operation name="postReview"
        pattern="http://www.w3.org/ns/wsdl/in-out">
      <input messageLabel="In" element="k:postReviewRequest" />
      <input messageLabel="Out" element="k:postReviewResponse" />
      <outfault ref="tns:invalidDataFault" messageLabel="Out"/>
    </operation>
  </interface>
  …
</description>
```

Figure 4.27 *Review posting service: abstract part*

How is a callback operation communicated to a server? In distributed object systems, a network pointer to a client callback object is included in a client request to the server. The server then communicates back to the client by performing an RMI on the callback proxy. In Web services, services are identified by their endpoint URL. Therefore, the client should include an endpoint URL for the callback service in its request to post a review.

This is not hard to do: XML schemas already include a built-in datatype anyURI. However, we would like to link this URL to the binding for the service that the reviews server expects to find there when it calls back. An extension in WSDL 2.0 supports this, as shown in Fig. 4.27. The type for the post confirmation callback is specified as a simple type, a restriction of anyURI. In addition, the wsdlx:binding attribute (an extension of core WSDL 2.0) annotates this type with a reference to the binding for the callback service, confirmPostSOAPBinding. The latter binding is specified in the callback service description in Fig. 4.26. This binding is in the namespace of the WSDL namespace for the callback service, but we need to specify the location of the document for this service description. This is done using the wsdli:wsdlLocation attribute that specifies the document that defines this namespace. The namespace wsdli: is another extension of WSDL 2.0 that allows information about WSDL instance documents to be included.

It should be noted that there is an anomaly with the way that WSDL supports the declaration of a callback service interface. As we have seen, WSDL specifications are composed of abstract and concrete parts. The former describes the abstract service interface, while the latter describes the details of how to communicate with the service. However, the wsdlx:binding specification for the concrete binding for the callback service is defined in the abstract part of the request service specification. What if one wants to specify a SOAP-based callback service for a SOAP-based request service, and a REST-based callback service for a REST-based request service? The WSDL wsdlx:binding specification only allows a single binding to be specified for the callback service, and that concrete binding is declared in the abstract part of the service request specification.

We omit the concrete part of the postReview operation, as it does not contribute much new of note.

The Web services protocol stack builds upon XML, SOAP, and WSDL, as we have seen. RESTful Web services have emerged in opposition to the complexity of the WS-* protocol stack. REST advocates question the usefulness of the SOAP standard given its complexity. In response, WSDL 2.0 includes some support for defining RESTful Web services, without the use of SOAP, as we discuss in Chapter 7.

The criticism of the SOAP stack is based on the complexity of the Web services stack. Even XML is considered too heavyweight and clumsy by many developers for such platforms. In Sect. 4.5, we consider a lightweight alternative to XML that jettisons not just the WS-* stack, but most of the XML stack as well.

4.4.3   Web Service Policy

The purpose of WSDL is, in the tradition of interface definition languages, to hide the heterogeneity of intra-enterprise and inter-enterprise applications. Like all IDLs, it defines a type system to which the cooperating parties must somehow conform their data, and places contracts between these parties that enable interoperation at the level of being able to use each others' functionality remotely. No large distributed software system can survive without this basic sanity check on the different participants collaborating in an application.

However, compatible data formats and service contracts, in the sense of the service operations and their inputs and outputs, does not tell the whole story. The whole point of the SOAP and WSDL framework is to provide a foundation for building various forms of Web service protocol stacks, incorporating functionality such as secure and reliable communication, and transactional resource updates. To ensure safe and reliable collaborations, there should be a mechanism for checking that the parties are using the same run-time quality of service mechanisms for their interactions. There may also be security issues associated with ensuring appropriate use of the Web service protocol stack. For example, it may be required that any communication with outside parties be encrypted, either using TLS for the transport, or using the message-level security techniques of WS-Security. Can some of this compliance with enterprise communication policies be specified declaratively and then checked automatically during the course of Web service executions?

WS-Policy defines a framework for *defining* assertions about requirements for compliance with enterprise communication policies. It defines metadata that can be used to generate code to support policy compliance, including performing run-time checking that messages are being exchanged in compliance with policy.

The relevant parts of WS-Policy and related policy specification languages are as follows:

1. Various policy languages are defined that provide assertions about compliance with policies that applications are required to follow. For example, WS-SecurityPolicy defines assertions that require the use of secure channels for certain kinds of communication. WS-Addressing Metadata defines assertions that require the use of addressing information in SOAP headers.

2. WS-Policy itself defines operations for combining policy assertions, including choosing all of the policy assertions in a list, or choosing exactly one policy assertion from a list.

3. WS-Policy also provides a way for binding a policy or policies in a WSDL description, so that any data exchanged in messages that pass through the corresponding endpoint are governed by those policies.

We first consider support for defining policies. The following is an example of a SOAP message with SOAP headers that make use of upper level protocols in the WS-* stack:

```
<soap:Envelope>
  <soap:Header>
    <wsa:To>http://www.example.org/finance</wsa:To>
    <wsa:Action>
        http://www.example.org/ConfirmAuthorization
    </wsa:Action>
  </soap:Header>
  <soap:Body>…</soap:Body>
</soap:Envelope>
```

The `<wsa:To>` and `<wsa:Action>` elements are taken from the WS-Addressing namespace. These specify the intended recipient of a message and the service to be invoked at that recipient. In this case, the operation is to authorize a financial transaction. The following is an example of a policy expression that *requires* the use of WS-Addressing by other parties that wish to communicate with a service, or offers the capability to use WS-Addressing for clients that wish to use it in communications with the service:

```
<Policy>
  <wsam:Addressing>…</wsam:Addressing>
</Policy>
```

The `<Policy>` element is defined in the WS-Policy namespace and is used to construct policy expressions. The child element `<wsam:Addressing>` is defined in the WS-Addressing Metadata namespace. It is used to provide a *policy assertion* stating that WS-Addressing should be used for communications with this service. The last act we need to perform is to associate this policy expression with a binding for the service:

```
<wsdl:binding name="FinanceBindingWithWSA" type="tns:FinanceInterface">
  <Policy>
    <wsam:Addressing>…</wsam:Addressing>
  </Policy>
  …
</wsdl:binding>
```

By attaching this policy expression to the WSDL binding, we enrich the interaction that clients have with this service by requiring that they use WS-Addressing. As compliance with this policy can only be checked by monitoring the messages that are exchanged at run-time, the enforcement of this policy requires the insertion of policy-checking code into the run-time. In general, any policy assertion requires the *policy developer* to implement code that performs this checking and incorporate it in the WS-* stack. Thereafter, *service developers* can choose to use that policy assertion, if they please, in their WSDL service descriptions in the bindings. If they do choose to attach these policies to their bindings, then the policy developer's policy compliance checking code is incorporated into that service developer's protocol stack.

We now enrich the semantics of messages exchanged with additional semantics, namely the provision of security metadata with messages:

```
<soap:Envelope>
  <soap:Header>
    <wss:Security soap:mustUnderstand="true">
     <wsu:Timestamp wsu:Id="_0">
      <wsu:Created>…</u:Created>
      <wsu:Expires>…</u:Expires>
     </wsu:Timestamp>
    </wss:Security>
    <wsa:To>http://www.example.org/finance</wsa:To>
    <wsa:Action>
        http://www.example.org/ConfirmAuthorization
    </wsa:Action>
  </soap:Header>
  <soap:Body>…</soap:Body>
</soap:Envelope>
```

The security timestamps in the message are intended to prevent replay attacks by an attacker that records such messages between clients and the service, and subsequently re-transmits those messages attempting to act like a legitimate client. The `<wss:Security>` element is defined in the WS-Security namespace, while the `<wsu:Timestamp>` element is defined in the Web Services Security namespace. The following policy expression contains two policy assertions.

```
<Policy>
  <All>
    <wsam:Addressing>…</wsam:Addressing>
    <sp:TransportBinding>…</sp:TransportBinding>
  </All>
</Policy>
```

The `<All>` element defined in the WS-Policy namespace is a Boolean connective for policy assertions, declaring that all of the policy assertions that are its child elements must be satisfied for the policy to be satisfied by a chain of communications with a server. Again, one assertion specifies the use of WS-Addressing. The other, `<sp:TransportBinding>`, specifies the use of transport-level security (i.e., SSL or TLS) for all communications. This latter assertion is defined in the WS-SecurityPolicy namespace.

An alternative to transport-level security is message-level security, where the payloads of the SOAP messages are encrypted for secure communication. We can define another policy that allows either transport-level or message-level security to be used for communications:

```
<Policy>
  <All>
    <wsam:Addressing>…</wsam:Addressing>
    <ExactlyOne>
      <sp:TransportBinding>…</sp:TransportBinding>
      <sp:AsymmetricBinding>…</sp:AsymmetricBinding>
    </ExactlyOne>
  </All>
</Policy>
```

The element `<sp:AsymmetricBinding>` is another policy assertion defined in the WS-SecurityPolicy namespace, asserting that message-level security is used for communications. The element `<ExactlyOne>` is another Boolean connective for policy assertions defined in WS-Policy that requires that exactly one of its child assertions be satisfied by service communications. The resulting policy expression is essentially the specification for policy compliance-checking code that can be automatically generated from the policy specification and inserted in the communication stack for the service attaching this policy expression to its binding.

Policy expression may be nested, as policy specifiers provide more detailed specifications of the protocols that services and their clients must follow. For example, the following policy assertion for transport-level security provides more details about how transport-level security must be provided. The `<sp:TransportToken>` nested policy assertion specifies the form of the security token—in this case the Hypertext Transfer Protocol Secure (HTTPS) token. The `<sp:AlgorithmSuite>` nested assertion requires the use of the `Basic256Rsa15` algorithm in the transport-level security:

```
<sp:TransportBinding>
  <Policy>
    <sp:TransportToken>
      <Policy>
        <sp:HttpsToken><wsp:Policy/></sp:HttpsToken>
      </Policy>
    </sp:TransportToken>
    <sp:AlgorithmSuite>
      <Policy>
        <sp:Basic256Rsa15/>
      </Policy>
    </sp:AlgorithmSuite>
    …
  </Policy>
</sp:TransportBinding>
```

The policy developer may organize policy assertions using policy expressions with expression identifiers, and the service developer may then reference these policy expressions and the corresponding assertions in their service bindings:

```
<Policy wsu:Id="addressing">
  <wsam:Addressing>…</wsam:Addressing>
</Policy>
<Policy wsu:Id="security">
  <ExactlyOne>
    <sp:TransportBinding>…</sp:TransportBinding>
    <sp:AsymmetricBinding>…</sp:AsymmetricBinding>
  </ExactlyOne>
</Policy>
<wsdl:binding name="SecureBinding" type="tns:FinanceInterface">
  <PolicyReference URI="#security"/>
  <wsdl:operation name="ConfirmAuthorization">…</wsdl:operation>
  …
</wsdl:binding>
<wsdl:service name="FinanceService">
```

```
<wsdl:port name="FinanceDataPort" binding="tns:SecureBinding">
  <PolicyReference URI="#addressing"/>
  …
</wsdl:port>
</wsdl:service>
```

In this case, two policies are defined: one requiring the use of WS-Addressing (named `"addressing"`), the other requiring the use of exactly one of transport-level security or message-level security (called `"security"`). The `wsu:Id` attribute attaches a name to each of the two policies as URIs. The binding attaches the security policy and the service endpoint attaches the addressing policy. Note that it would be possible to specify another service endpoint that did not attach the addressing policy, in which case only the security policy would need to be complied with, in communications on that service endpoint.

To conclude our introduction to policy compliance checking with WS-Policy, policies may also be defined as optional or ignorable, or both. An *optional* policy is offered to clients that wish to avail of it. For example, a service may offer an optimized MIME serialization transmission protocol for messages. A policy is *ignorable* if it has no impact on clients' use of the service, and is only offered for informational purposes. An example is an ignorable policy assertion that the service site is logging communications.

4.5 PRESENTATION LAYER: JSON AND JQUERY

Most modern business-to-customer e-commerce Web sites are driven by AJAX. A Javascript program in the client Web browser manipulates the DOM tree for the Web page being presented to the client. The content being displayed is based on XML data that is exchanged asychonrously by background threads that run Web service requests against the Web server. Decoupling the user interface from the exchange of data with the Web server improves responsiveness and provides a smoother user experience. It also allows some tasks, such as input validation, to be performed on the client.

Although the "X" in AJAX stands for XML, an increasing number of such applications are eschewing XML for a simpler data notation. JSON is based on a subset of the Javascript language and provides a relatively compact notation for self-describing data. JSON is a language for describing values:

1. Basic values are numbers, strings, booleans and the special value `null`.
2. An *array* in JSON is a sequence of values. It is denoted in JSON by opening and closing square brackets, with commas separating the values. For example, here is a list of three genres: `["Drama", "History", "Fiction"]`.
3. An *object* in JSON is essentially an XML element, but without the pointless complications that XML adds. An object is a collection of fields, or name-value pairs, enclosed in brackets and separated by commas. Each field is denoted by a pair of a string and a value separated by a colon. For

example, here is an object containing a title and a publication date: { "title" : "Lawrence of Arabia", "pubDate" : "1963-01-30" }.

That essentially completes the description of JSON, with the exception of details about characters and numbers. An illustrative example of JSON-represented data is presented in Fig. 4.28(**a**). We offer some observations based on this example:

- JSON eschews the use of attributes altogether. The category attribute is represented in the JSON representation as a field. We are not aware of anyone missing the use of attributes in JSON.

- Typed XML supports heterogeneous forms of data, using elements, and with element names acting as tags to distinguish the different forms. In the catalog example, information specific to content types is denoted by the element names film, book, and radio. JSON requires the explicit addition of such tags, as is done with the "type" field in the example in Fig. 4.28. The *value* of this field plays the role of the film, book, and radio element *names* in the XML version of this data.

- JSON does not provide namespaces to disambiguate field names (or tags). It does not provide a type system such as XML Schema for typing JSON data. JSON does not even support XML DTDs, as explained below.

```
[
  {"id" : "B0016K40KY", "category" : "Faction",
   "title" : "Lawrence of Arabia", "pubDate" : "1963-01-30",
   "genres" : [ "Drame", "History" ],
   "info" : { "type" : "film", "director" : [ "David Lean" ], … }
  },
  {"id" : "0131934554", "category" : "Non-Fiction",
   "title" : "Janson's History of Art",
   "pubDate" : "2006-02-16",
   "genres" : [ "History", "Art" ],
   "info" : { "type" : "book", "author" : [ "Penelope Davies" ], … }
  },
  …
]
```

(**a**) JSON example

```
<!ELEMENT catalog [ item ] >
<!ELEMENT item { "id" : PCDATA, "category" : PCDATA,
  "title" : PCDATA, "pubDate" : PCDATA,
  "genres" : [ PCDATA ], "info" : (film | book | radio) }
>
<!ELEMENT film { "type" : PCDATA, "director" : [ PCDATA ] } >
<!ELEMENT book { "type" : PCDATA, "author" : [ PCDATA ] } >
<!ELEMENT radio { "type" : PCDATA, "director" : [ PCDATA ] } >
```

(**b**) JTD example

Figure 4.28   *JSON and JTD example*

JSON is a compelling alternative for the developer of Web applications that are clients of Web services. For example, here is a Javascript script that performs a Web service call and provides with that call a callback function:

```
<script type="text/javascript">
  function getCatalog() {
    val url = "http://www.example.org/json/catalog";
    new Ajax.Request (url, { method: "get", parameters: …,
                     onComplete: callback });
  }
  function callback(request) {
    rawText = request.responseText;
    jsonContent = eval("(" + rawText + ")");
    for (i=0; i<jsonContent.catalog.item.length; i++) {
      … jsonContent.catalog.item[i].title …
    }
  }
</script>
```

The callback function, when invoked with the response from the Web server, extracts the JSON content data and then parses that as a Javascript object. Parsing is done by the primitive `eval` function that takes a string and compiles that into Javascript code.[3] At that point, the content is immediately available as Javascript objects. The developer completely avoids the complexities of working with DOM, such as incompatibilities between DOM implementations. On the other hand, given that JSON is a subset of Javascript that does not include executable code, it is odd that marshalling of string data to JSON is done using a dangerous operation such as `eval`. The eval operation should be considered a "nuclear option," as it allows malicious code to be injected into the AJAX code by allowing an attacker to provide data that includes executable Javascript code. A safer alternative would be to provide a JAXB-like or JIBX-like interface for marshalling data to and from JSON objects that would fail if the data went beyond the subset of Javascript specified by JSON.

It will be seen that the approach of parsing JSON data into Javascript objects is related to schema binding for XML. The difference is that, unlike languages such as Java and C#, Javascript is a *prototype-based language* rather than a class-based language. Objects are created without having to define a class in advance; design re-use is obtained by "cloning" prototype objects. Therefore, it is unnecessary to compile a description of the data into classes. The objects are created directly from the data itself.

JSON avoids much of the complexity associated with XML, but at the cost of not having a type system for specifying and verifying safe data handling. To elaborate, consider a hypothetical adaptation of DTD to JSON. We will call this language JTD. It has:

---

[3]This should be familiar to any LISP or Scheme developer. The `eval` function is a mechanism for reflecting data into programs, and JSON and XML are essentially languages of S-expressions, as McCarthy suggested for LISP in 1958 [7].

1. The primitive type PCDATA for text data.

2. A sequence type for JSON "objects." Unlike DTD, the elements in the sequence are named and the sequence is enclosed in brackets {…}..

3. An iteration type for JSON "arrays," similar to the * quantifier in DTD. We denote the iteration type by square brackets […].

4. A union type, denoted by a sequence of types separated by vertical bars.

In summary, we have this comparison between DTD types and JTD types:

	DTD	JTD
Sequence/object	$(T_1, \ldots, T_k)$	$\{n_1 : T_1, \ldots, n_k : T_k\}$
Iteration/array	T^*	$[T]$
Union	$(T_1 \mid \ldots \mid T_k)$	$(T_1 \mid \ldots \mid T_k)$

Figure 4.28(**b**) gives a type specification in this hypothetical language for the catalog example in Fig. 4.28(**a**). However, there is a difficulty with this specification. When validating JSON data with respect to the specification, there is no way for the validator to know whether the info field is a film, book, or radio broadcast. The validator can try all possibilities, but this leads to an exponential blow-up, or worse, in the complexity of type-checking. There is a run-time clue as to which case is intended: the type field carries a run-time type tag. However, the validator does not know this, as it is not expressed in the type system.

This can be fixed by, for example, adding a *tagged union* to JSON and adding a corresponding *tagged union type* to JTD.[4] The tagged union explicitly represents a tag value with each of a set of possible alternative values and the tagged union type reflects the content type associated with each alternative. The tagged union and tagged union types look synctactically like JSON objects and JTD object types, respectively, except we use a bracketed expression {|…|} for both. We adapt the JTD type specification in Fig. 4.28(**b**) to use a tagged union type:

```
<!ELEMENT item
  {
    "id" : PCDATA,
    "category" : PCDATA,
    "title" : PCDATA,
    "pubDate" : PCDATA,
    "genres" : { PCDATA },
    "info" : {| "film" : film
```

[4]Alternatively, we may require that *every* JSON object starts with a special field that is intended to represent a type tag. This would be more compatible with the object-oriented nature of Javascript. However, this approach leads to some complications, so we consider the tagged union type approach for simplicity. There is also a pleasing symmetry with the "tagged product type" that JTD object types represent.

```
      | "book" : book
      | "radio" : radio
      |}
  }
>
```

The instance data is also modified to use tagged unions. For example, an individual catalog item is given by:

```
{ "id" : "B0016K40KY",
  "category" : "Faction",
  "title" : "Lawrence of Arabia",
  "pubDate" : "1963-01-30",
  "genres" : [ "Drame", "History" ],
  "info" : {| "film", "director" : [ "David Lean" ] |}
}
```

JTD is an exercise in adapting a simple type system (DTDs) to JSON. Tagged union types are, of course, very similar to choice elements in XML Schemas. If one instead tags objects with a type tag, one obtains an approach similar to that of element substitution in XML schemas. This approach still has the problem that it requires tags to be globally unique. An obvious approach to avoiding this is to qualify tags with globally unique prefixes to disambiguate them. This is, of course, the point of XML Schema namespaces. For safety and reliability in enterprise systems, some form of static validation of exchanged data is essential. If a simpler form of content language eventually replaces XML, perhaps descended from JSON, it will still require some of the mechanisms developed for XML Schemas, including type inheritance for design re-use. On the other hand, it will hopefully avoid some of the complications that XML inherits from its legacy as a document markup language.

The growing importance of JSON data in communicating with RESTful Web services has also drawn attention to the manipulation of JSON data in Java and C# programs. For example, the JSONObject class provides a Java representation for JSON collections of name-value pairs, while the JSONarray class provides a Java representation for JSON arrays. JAXB extensions in JAX-RS implementations allow data to be communicated either as XML or as JSON, supporting some level of interoperability between XML and JSON. A server may offer to return content of either XML or JSON media type, and the service client can then choose which of these two media types it prefers. Figure 4.29(**a**) provides a JAXB-annotated class. In particular, the email field is given a namespace different from the rest of the content. Figure 4.29(**b**) provides an instance of XML data that is consistent with these annotations and Fig. 4.29(**c**) provides this instance's representation in JSON, using the *Jackson encoding* [8]. The Jackson encoding emphasizes simplicity, for example by omitting the root element. However, it does not handle namespaces, such as the <email> element which is in a separate namespace from the rest of the document. Figure 4.29(**d**) provides a representation of the same data in JSON using the *Jettison mapped encoding*. In this case, the root element is preserved and the namespace of the email element is recorded using a dot-notation on the corresponding name, "w.email". Finally, the *Badgerfish* encoding [9] uses a more

```
@XmlRootElement(namespace = "http://www.example.org/xsd/contacts")
public class Contact {
  @XmlAttribute(name = "class") public String _class;
  @XmlElement protected String name;
  @XmlElement(namespace = "http://www.example.org/xsd/web")
  protected String email;
  @XmlElement protected List<TelephoneType> telephones;
}
public class TelephoneType {
  @XmlElement protected String telephone;
}
```

(**a**) JAXB class

```
<contact xmlns="http://www.example.org/xsd/contacts"
         xmlns:w="http://www.example.org/xsd/web"
         class="personal">
  <name>Boris Karloff</name>
  <w:email>boris@karloff.name</w:email>
  <telephones>  <telephone>201-555-1234</telephone>
                <telephone>201-555-6789</telephone>
  </telephones>
</contact>
```

(**b**) XML data

```
{ "@class" : "personal",
  "name" : "Boris Karloff",
  "email": "boris@karloff.name",
  "telephones" : [ "201-555-1234", "201-555-6789" ] }
```

(**c**) Jackson notation

```
{ "contact" :
 {"@class" : "personal",
  "name" : "Boris Karloff",
  "w.email": "boris@karloff.name",
  "telephones" : [ { "telephone" : "201-555-1234",
                     "telephone" : "201-555-6789" } ] }
 }
```

(**d**) Jettison mapped notation

```
{ "contact" :
 {"@xmlns" : { "$" : "…", "w" : "…" },
  "@class" : "personal",
  "name" : { "$" : "Boris Karloff" },
  "w.email": { "$" : "boris@karloff.name" },
  "telephones" : [ { "telephone" :{ "$":"201-555-1234" },
                     "telephone" :{ "$":"201-555-6789"  } }] }
}
```

(**e**) Badgerfish notation

Figure 4.29   *Representing XML data in JSON*

complicated encoding of XML in JSON that is intended to encode all of the original XML infoset in JSON. For example, the text content of an element is encoded in JSON as the value of a property "$"; this allows simple content to be annotated with attributes. The default namespace URI is encoded in the property @xmlns.$, and other namespaces are encoded as other subproperties of the @xmlns property. The actual name of the namespace qualifiers can be configured in a framework that implements the Badgerfish encoding, such as the Jettison implementation used in the Jersey reference implementation for JAX-RS.

Although JSON is being used for exchanging data between AJAX clients and the Web server, the Web page itself is still represented in the Web browser as an XML DOM tree. However, a welcome development in AJAX programming is the jQuery library, which provides a declarative API for matching parts of the DOM tree and performing operations on the tree. Elements of the DOM tree are selected using an operation of the form selector. This replaces the Javascript native selecting functions getElementById and getElementsByName, and provides a far superior API.

Figure 4.30 provides some examples of selectors in jQuery. For manipulating the presentation of the DOM tree in the Web browser, jQuery allows information about CSS properties of DOM elements to be queried and modified, using the .css(property) and .css(property,value) functions, respectively. For example, the following code changes the presentation of all hyperlinks in the DOM tree:

```
var allHyperlinks = $("a");
allHyperlinks.css('font-style','italic');
allHyperlinks.css('font-weight','bold');
```

More typically in jQuery, these operations are strung together:

```
$("a").css('font-style','italic').css('font-weight','bold');
```

Similarly, there are operations for querying and setting attributes (.attr()), adding CSS classes to, and removing CSS classes from, elements (.addClass()

Selector	Description
$("a")	Selects all <a> elements in the document.
$(".important")	Selects all elements with the CSS class important
$("a.important")	Selects all <a> elements with the CSS class "important".
$("&abstract")	Selects the element with the identity abstract
$("p[title]")	Selects <p> elements that contain a title attribute.
$("input[type = 'text']")	Selects <input> elements whose type attribute equals "text".
$("p:contains('Hello')")	Selects <p> elements that contain the text Hello.
$(h1:has(a))	Selects <h1> elements that contain a <a> element.

Figure 4.30 *Examples of jQuery selectors*

and `.removeClass()`, respectively), adding a CSS class if it is not already present, and removing it otherwise (`.toggleClass()`), getting and setting the text value of an element (`.text()`), and so on.

REFERENCES

1. MacAfee A. Yes, it is about the technology. Forbes Magazine; March 2010. Available at: http://www.forbes.com/2010/03/25/enterprise-computers-software-technolo%gy-cio-network-mcafee.html.

2. Sosnoski DM. JIBX: Binding XML to Java code. Available at: jibx.sourcforge.net.

3. Sosnoski D. XML and Java technologies: Data binding, Part 2: Performance. IBM DeveloperWorks; January 2003. Available at: http://www.ibm.com/developerworks/xml/library/x-databdopt2/.

4. Megginson D, Brownell D. SAX: Simple API for XML. Available at: http://www.saxproject.org/.

5. Ross T, Tindall N. XML, COBOL and application modernization. In: SHARE Conference. Tampa, FL; 2007. Available at: https://www-304.ibm.com/support/docview.wss?uid=swg27004198&aid=1.

6. Fry C, Slominski A, Saloranta T. StAX: Streaming API for XML. Available at: http://stax.codehaus.org.

7. McCarthy J. An algebraic language for the manipulation of symbolic expressions. Technical Report AI Memo No. 1, MIT Artificial Intelligence Laboratory; September 1958.

8. Saloranta T, Eastey M, Heaton R, Brown P. Jackson JSON preprocessor. Available at: http://jackson.codehaus.org.

9. Sklar D. Badgerfish. Available at: http://www.sklar.com/badgerfish.

5

Domain-Driven Architecture

"In general, just avoid to use the term fat client in meetings, sessions, and architectural descriptions. It is good neither for your project nor your career."

—Adam Bien [1]

5.1 SOFTWARE ARCHITECTURE

Software architecture is a term for which there are many definitions, but none that are universally accepted. The lack of a precise definition may be an inevitable result of the fact that it is trying to describe a concept that is germane to all software systems of non-trivial size. A software architecture defines the "structure" of a software system. This structural description at least considers the components of the system, the interfaces that those components offer to external parties, and the relationships between those components. Studies of software architecture go back to pioneering work by Dijsktra on a layered software architecture for operating systems [2], and work by Parnas on decomposing software systems into components [3].

The intention of making software architecture explicit is to gain a handle on the complexity of software systems, essentially by providing an overall "blueprint" of the system. Preferably, this blueprint is more than simply a diagram of circles and arrows on a white board. More substantively, a software architecture captures the non-functional properties of the software system, including the dependencies

Enterprise Software Architecture and Design: Entities, Services, and Resources,
First Edition. Dominic Duggan.

between the components. Functional properties are specified at a lower level than the architectural description.[1]

Software architecture may be contrasted with *system architecture*. The latter describes the components of a hardware/software system, in terms of nodes in a networked system, and control and data flow paths between those nodes. An example is the enterprise network described in Fig. 2.4 in Chapter 2. Software architecture, on the other hand, is end-to-end, focusing on the interactions between the software components, regardless of their physical location. Indeed, location transparency is often cited as one aspect of the loose coupling that is essential for SOA.

In this chapter, we focus on domain-driven architecture—a popular technique for designing distributed enterprise software systems. We introduced SOA in Chapter 2, and we consider it in much more detail in the next chapter; we consider ROA in Chapter 7. Sometimes, a concept is best understood in terms of its antithesis and so we consider domain-driven architecture to provide a counterpoint to both service-oriented and resource-oriented architecture.

In Chapter 8 in the sequel volume, we consider EDA, an architecture for enterprise software systems that emphasizes rapid response to new events of interest to the enterprise. EDA complements, rather than competes with, SOA (and ROA), and the two architectural styles may very well be combined in an actual architectural design. In the context of EDA, we also consider design patterns for message networks that may be used to support asynchronous communication in enterprise applications, both for EDA and for SOA applications.

5.2 DOMAIN-DRIVEN DESIGN

Domain-driven architecture is motivated by the rationale of domain-driven design. The latter is essentially object-oriented software design. The problem that domain-driven design seeks to avoid is the problem of a knowledge gap between requirements analysis and software design. The former, *requirements analysis*, involves domain experts in the analysis of an application domain and the formulation of the requirements for a software solution. The latter, *software design*, involves software architects and developers in the design, development and testing of a software application that satisfies those requirements. The "knowledge gap" happens when the architects and developers are divorced from the original business domain analysis and only see the result of this analysis. The domain model will have resulted from meetings and dialogue with domain experts, with much information communicated but not necessarily all of it distilled into the resulting domain model. The developer team may find ambiguities and inconsistencies in the domain model as they develop a software solution. This leads to inefficiencies where the domain experts may need to be re-consulted by the domain analysts, or worse, mistakes

---

[1]Obviously, there may be several levels in the description of a software system, so the dichotomy between functional and non-functional properties may not be as clear-cut as this simplistic description suggests.

and miscommunications creep into the design as the developers make incorrect assumptions to fill in the gaps or resolve the inconsistencies in the domain model. Laribee [4] makes the analogy with Plato's "Cave of Shadows", where the inhabitants of the cave can only view the shadows on the cave walls of the forms of the "real world" outside. According to this analogy, the developers are the people living in the cave, only able to guess at the true domain concepts as reflected in the domain model they are provided with.

Domain-driven design (DDD) emphasizes *model-driven design* that involves both analysts and developers simultaneously in domain analysis and software design. Developers are involved in the domain analysis, meeting with the domain experts. They then translate the knowledge gained from this analysis directly into software abstractions. Here, it is helpful to recall that Simula-67, the first object-oriented language, was designed as a simulation language for software modeling of real-world systems [5]. It is, therefore, no surprise, and a testament to the insights of Dahl and Nygard, that the essence of DDD is identifying classes of objects and the relationships between those classes. Objects represent domain entities identified as a result of the domain analysis: the corresponding model is a realization directly in a software design of the domain knowledge resulting from that analysis. Unlike agile software development, the objective is to model domain concepts as object-oriented software abstractions, rather than to provide early executable code realizations from requirements analysis. The resulting software design is recognized as the domain model—the code itself is a realization of that model. Any changes to this design are, in turn, recognized as modifications to the model resulting from the domain analysis, which may require clarification and confirmation from domain experts. Recognizing this fact helps to prevent the development of a gap between model and design, as may happen if the approach is to somehow relate model to design by a complex mapping process.

An important principle of DDD is that of *ubiquitous language*. Involving developers in the domain analysis with domain experts raises obvious communication challenges: the two communities will typically have very different technical vocabularies. Yet, eventually, the developer must become familiar with the domain concepts and so the domain analysis and software-based model design must be couched in the vocabulary of the domain. Consider, for example, the design of a health information system. A developer will, no doubt, guess that physicians and patients are important abstractions in this domain. Subsequent dialogue may reveal that the class of physicians should be broadened more generally to "providers", that include other classes of healthcare providers, such as home care providers and nurse practitioners. Furthermore, patient "encounters" are an important association between patients and providers. Particular types of encounters highlight specific roles for providers. For example, a procedure performed on a patient (such as a pharmacologic or radiologic procedure, physiotherapy, or a surgical procedure) will require a supervising physician and, optionally, a separate performing provider. A hospital stay will involve a referring physician, an admitting physician, and an authorizing physician for authorizing the patient release. All of these encounters will involve standardized forms: patient admission forms, referral and requisition forms, consent forms, daily flow sheets, physicians' orders, laboratory mount sheets, narcotic control forms, and so on. These and other aspects of the domain become part of the shared vocabulary, as reflected in the resulting software model.

As the language of the model emerges from the domain analysis, the various forms of *entities* in the model are also revealed. The entities are the core of the model in DDD and drive every other aspect of the design. They should, therefore, be identified early in the model design process. The most important distinguishing characteristic of an entity is its *identity*. The latter is not an implementation-dependent attribute, such as the memory address of an object or the network address for a remote object reference. Rather, identity should be based on domain-specific attributes, such as a patient medical record number in the case of a health information system. We have already seen data modeling involving entities and relationships in Chapter 3. However, another distinguishing aspect of DDD is to identify how these entities act on each other and make these actions an integral part of the behavior specification for the entities. This behavioral aspect of entity modeling distinguishes it from simple data modeling, and the association of behavior with entities in the domain model distinguishes it from service-oriented approaches. For example, a flow sheet may be represented by an entity (identified by patient and date). An operation for recording patient observations determines, based on patient physical data such as age and weight, if the observations indicate potential cause for concern:

```
class Patient {
  Age age;
  Weight weight;
  FlowSheet currentFlowSheet () { … }
  boolean dangerSigns (BloodPressure bp, Temperature temp) {
    return …;
  }
}
class FlowSheet {
  Patient patient;
  Station station;
  void recordObs (Time time, BloodPressure bp, Temperature temp){
    … record the observations …
    if (patient.dangerSigns(bp,temp))
      station.alert(time,patient);
  }
}
```

The latter is an example of another pattern from DDD: the association of *constraints* with entities, with dynamic checks during operations that the constraints are not violated. The isolation of constraint-checking in the `dangerSigns` method is an example of this pattern.

Not all values in the domain need to be modeled as entities. For example, a consent form will need to be recorded to demonstrate compliance with regulatory requirements, but it itself is not a part of the domain with internal state that interacts with other parts of the domain. Such objects are referred to as VALUE OBJECTS. They should be immutable so they may be copied and distributed among participants without raising consistency issues. Such objects are related to, but not quite the same as, transfer objects or data transfer objects [6]. DTOs are simple container objects that hold data without business logic, and are heavily used in service oriented applications. We consider DTOs in more detail in Sect. 6.1.

A standard objective of the model design is to minimize coupling between the entities, in order to facilitate subsequent maintenance. AGGREGATE ROOTS is a pattern that organizes entitites into hierarchies for access purposes. Access to an entity lower in the hierarchy is achieved by navigating from the entity at the root. Besides decoupling inter-entity dependencies, this can have other beneficial results. For example, it facilitates "lazy loading" of subordinate entities from a database, removing such entities from memory when they are no longer in use and logging accesses to these entities. The latter is an extremely important aspect of data processing in enterprise application domains such as financial or health information systems, where regulatory regimes place requirements on logging and reporting of access to individuals' personal data. In terms of the example above, the domain model may be organized so that access to a patient's current flow sheet is always directed through the entity node for that patient. One can certainly update a flowsheet through the sequence of accesses:

```
patient.currentFlowSheet().recordObs(…);
```

However, the pattern of aggregate roots instead requires that access to the flow sheet is always directed through the patient entity:

```
class Patient {
  …
  void recordObs (Time time, BloodPressure bp, Temperature temp){
    this.currentFlowSheet().recordObs(time,bp,temp);
  }
}
patient.recordObs(…);
```

Entities are typically persistent, which requires the presence of a database for storage. However, the support infrastructure for an application should not be part of the domain model, which is intended to provide software abstractions for the real-world agents in an application. If operations such as database queries become part of the model, then the domain logic may also move out of the entity behaviors and into these query operations, violating a fundamental precept of DDD. Providing a general query facility also offers an opportunity to bypass aggregate roots and retrieve subordinate entities directly from the database. The REPOSITORY pattern is intended to encapsulate the details of database access, both retrieval and update. For the example of a health information system, the repository may provide a facility for retrieving individual patients, or patients satisfying a particular criteria, e.g., referred to a particular clinic, or in a particular hospital ward, and diagnosed with a particular health condition. As depicted in Fig. 5.1, the repository interface refers only to entity types in the domain model, while internally it uses infrastructure-specific code for retrieving objects from the database or reconstituting objects based

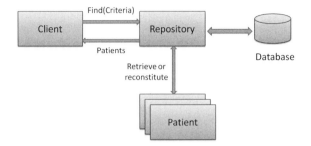

Figure 5.1 *Repository pattern*

on data retrieved from the database, and for performing database updates based on in-memory modifications to entity objects.

The repository pattern is related to the FACTORY pattern for creating new entities. It is also related to the pattern of the ANTI-CORRUPTION LAYER. The latter is intended to interface a domain-driven model to legacy systems and external models, and isolate the encapsulated domain logic of the former from the "corrupting influence" of the external model. An anti-corruption layer is structured as a service. In the parlance of DDD, if entities correspond to nouns, then services correspond to verbs that do not naturally fit with any particular domain entity. If domain logic is organized around objects representing entities in the domain, then *domain services* correspond to the use cases for the domain that may involve several peer entities. A service may also be used to provide cross-cutting functionality, such as authentication, logging, transactions and input-output, that does not properly belong to the domain model, but rather to the infrastructure supporting the domain.

In the structuring of an anti-corruption layer as a service, the external interface abstracts the legacy system and prevents aspects of the external model from leaking into the domain model, as depicted in Fig. 5.2. Each application service in the anti-corruption layer is structured as a facade, whose role is to encapsulate an underlying legacy system and expose a limited interface that only provides the functionality necessary for the clients of the domain model. Each such facade uses an adapter to mediate between the interface it needs from the external model and the actual interface that is provided. The TRANSLATOR pattern provides lower level intermediaries for conversion between the data types used by the external model and those used by the domain model. In some situations, where the external model provides a complex and tightly coupled interface, it may be useful to define an overall facade that mediates between the other facades and the interface of the external model. We provide further discussion of wrapping legacy systems, in the context of SOA in Sect. 6.6.

For an enterprise application of any reasonable size, a monolithic domain model will be a challenge for implementation and maintenance, for example for refactoring as part of the design and implementation process. It is important that the model be decomposed into submodels. Each submodel should be small enough to be the focus of a single team, with a clearly defined boundary separating it from other submodels. A submodel is not synonymous with a software module. A submodel

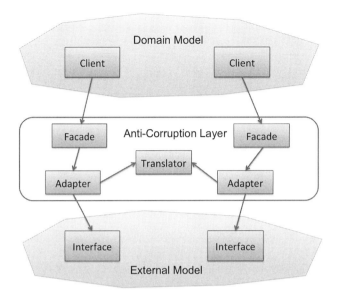

Figure 5.2 *Anti-corruption layer*

provides a logical frame for modeling part of the domain in relative isolation from other parts of the domain. It is defined by a BOUNDED CONTEXT that delimits the scope of the submodel in terms of its associated entities and ubiquitous language. The bounded context defines those part of the model that a team may work on independently, and what parts may be related to other parts of the model. Software modules provide a further logical refinement of each submodel, exhibiting "maximal cohesion and minimal coupling." This means that each module should exhibit maximal interactions among the entities of the module, while minimizing the interactions between entities in different modules. A good modular decomposition of a software system results in most execution being internal to modules, while minimizing the communication between modules. In the worst case, this still requires $O(N^2)$ communication channels among the N modules in one submodel. The CONTINUOUS INTEGRATION pattern establishes best practices for updating the model as a result of refined domain analysis, merging changes in the model into the code base and vice versa, and using regular automated builds and tests (perhaps done on an overnight basis) to ensure compatibility among the modules, and consistency with related domain submodels.

In practice there will be overlap in the concepts described by different submodels. A CONTEXT MAP is a graphical description of the domain submodels and the relationships between them. In particular the context map captures aspects of related entities that are described in different submodels. For example, Fig. 5.3 provides a context map for a clinical information system. There is a patient treatment submodel, that describes patient treatment, including drug treatment and radiology. Each treatment has a supervising health provider. Another submodel of the system involves patient billing, and so by necessity it must also model the concepts of

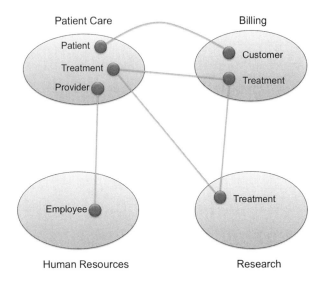

Figure 5.3 *Context map*

patients and treatments. However the billing submodel describes different facets of these entities. For example, health insurance, credit worthiness and billing addresses are the important aspects of patient entities in this submodel, while cost for billing purposes is a predominant aspect of treatments that is modeled. Another submodel describes the research department, which records information about treatments to assess health outcomes and perform epidemiological analyses. The focus in this submodel is on aggregating information about treatments and their outcomes. Another submodel describes the payroll department, which also models aspects of providers, including payroll, benefits and qualifications. The context map summarizes these submodels and the relationships between them, to ensure that aspects of related entities are modeled in a consistent fashion. For example, in the clinical information system described by the context map in Fig. 5.3, information about a patient treatment should be communicated to the billing and research departments. The billing department will need to relate this information to a patient's billing record, while the research department will need to relate the treatment information to the data warehouse it maintains about treatments and outcomes.

There are several design patterns in DDD that are intended to preserve consistency of related domain models. Some of these, such as the anti-corruption layer pattern, establish boundaries to ensure that a submodel is protected from interference by legacy systems and their contexts. Other patterns describe organizational patterns for cooperation among teams working on related submodels. For example, the SHARED KERNEL submodel designates an intersection of two contexts that the corresponding teams for the submodels share and work on together. This ensures interoperability in the software they develop, and avoids redundant duplication of efforts. The CUSTOMER-SUPPLIER pattern may be applicable where the kind of coordination required for the shared kernel pattern is not possible, but where two teams at least have the same management. With this pattern, one team is designated as the customer and the other as the supplier. The customer provides requirements to the supplier, and the supplier develops an implementation to the interface provided by the customer. Constant automated testing can be used to check the conformance of the supplier modules with the customer requirements. The CONFORMIST pattern assumes that the supplier will not work to the customer requirements, but the customer still finds it advantageous to use the supplier modules. The customer may create adapters to isolate its domain model from changes to the supplier model, similar to the anti-corruption layer. The SEPARATE WAYS pattern assumes that the submodels are naturally independent, so that the domain modeling for each proceeds in isolation from each other.

5.3 APPLICATION FRAMEWORKS

As a specific example of a design that is domain-driven (in the general sense of the term), we consider an example of an application framework from the financial engineering community [7]. *Application frameworks* are the approach currently favored in the object-oriented programming community for supporting re-use of software design and implementation [8]. A framework is intended to identify key abstractions that are useful for the implementation of a class of applications, as well as default implementations for a large part of those abstractions. Many of these abstractions will be based on the choice of domain-agnostic and domain-specific design patterns to communicate the structure and use of the framework to the application developer. Design time and run-time configuration engines provide the composition logic for building an application from the framework, incorporating code provided by the developer that "completes" the partial application defined by the framework.

For example, among many possible examples of this type, ASP.NET provides a framework for developing Web applications. This framework is structured as an interactive development environment for building GUIs. The presentation logic is specified using the HTML markup language, cascading style sheets, and a domain-specific ASP.NET markup language for specifying Web controls (widgets), among other purposes. Interactive Web applications are based on the use of "code-behind" logic, specified as callback event handlers associated with Web controls, that react (on the server) to user inputs. An ASP.NET Web page is translated into an object that is rendered by the ASP.NET engine, a resource in the Web server, into pure HTML by translating Web controls into HTML. On a "postback" of the Web page to the server, application-defined event handlers associated with the Web page process the user input and modify the properties of the Web controls in the ASP.NET page before it is re-rendered again into HTML. The framework provides many other capabilities, including data source and data controls for connecting to back-end databases and presenting the results of queries, supporting the definition of user interfaces for form-based editing of database records, providing default implementations for user authentication and authorization in terms of security controls, and so on.

ASP.NET is an example of a *top-down* framework approach. A proprietary application framework, developed by a third party, is used by an organization to develop applications relatively quickly by re-using existing design abstractions and their implementation. While used in many domains, this approach has potential pitfalls that the prospective framework user should be aware of. Although the use of a framework bypasses the need to develop much of the standard logic and infrastructure for an application, there is also a learning curve associated with becoming proficient with the framework's design and use. There is the danger of code bloat as a result of the inclusion of extraneous framework code with the application. Finally, there is the danger of technological lock-in, as applications become tightly coupled to the run-time system support and, more importantly, the organizing principles of a particular framework.

The *bottom-up* framework approach is based on an enterprise encoding the domain knowledge it has already learned and putting that knowledge into the form of a framework so it can be used to develop new applications in the same domain. The main obstacle with this approach is the time that must be taken to encapsulate knowledge from the domain model in a framework design and the time taken to implement those abstractions.

There are several potential benefits ascribed to the use of frameworks [8, 9]:

1. *Modularity:* Frameworks should provide stable interfaces that encapsulate implementation details and decouple client classes from implementation changes. Components within the framework, both those provided with the framework and those provided by the client, should be decoupled by binding to each other indirectly, through abstract classes or interfaces.

2. *Reusability:* The stable interfaces provided by frameworks should be amenable to re-use in multiple applications. In the case of bottom-up framework development, periodic re-evaluation and, where necessary, adapation of the framework design is essential. Without this periodic review, there is the danger of "architectural drift", as the flaws of the original design become more apparent over time.

3. *Extensibility:* Frameworks should provide "hooks" to allow the incorporation of client code into the framework. We consider strategies for incorporating client code into a framework below.

4. *Inversion of Control*: With traditional subroutine and class libraries, an application will typically import functionality from those libraries, e.g., using an I/O library to access the file system or the network. The imported library is a passive party in this composition, with the application responsible for spawning the threads for the computation. In the case of application frameworks, including application servers such as Java EE and WCF, it is typically the framework that is the active party. The framework is started as a program and calls into the client logic as part of its processing. The traditional control stack of the client calling the library is inverted. We consider context and dependency injection, a particularly important form of inversion of control, in Sect. 6.10.1.

As an example of the bottom-up approach to framework development, we consider below a case study from the domain of financial engineering—that of the ET++SwapsManager application framework [7]. This framework was developed as an exercise in incrementally developing an application framework designed around patterns learned from domain analysis and organized according to the precepts of object-oriented programming (and, unknown to the developers at the time, DDD).

Financial markets, when they function correctly, provide an avenue for an enterprise to secure funding. Such funding may be secured using various possible sources, including bank loans, equity securities (through the issuance of stocks), and debt securities (through the issuance of bonds). Funds are provided on the expectation of a return in the form of interest paid or participation in revenues (or losses). A *financial instrument* provides a source of funding to the enterprise that includes, with that funding, various instrumented aspects of the risk profile. Examples of the latter include the amount of interest to be paid, the payment schedule, exposure to market and currency fluctuations, and so on. A standard instrument is one for which a market exists for buyers and sellers of that instrument, and that market determines the current price for instances of the instrument. For new instruments, a price is determined for the instrument based on the *time value of money*, the equivalent value today of a future cash flow from that instrument. The assumption is that money received today is better than money received in the future. Money received in the future, e.g., via the redemption of a bond, must be discounted in value because of the risk that, e.g., that the bond holder will default. The value of a new instrument is estimated based on a *discount function* that performs an estimate based on the prices of instruments quoted in various financial markets. This is based on a portfolio of deals for various instruments (a *deal* is an instance of an instrument).

A simple example is an *interest rate swap*. Party B wishes to borrow money and, although it can obtain a better interest rate if the rate is floating, it prefers the security of a fixed rate loan. Party A, perhaps because of its size, can obtain funding at a more advantageous fixed rate. Therefore, Parties A and B "swap" their fixed- and floating-rate loans at a rate of interest that compensates A while still leaving the deal attractive to B. The two sides of the swap deal are referred to as *swap legs*. At the conclusion of the swap, both A and B should have equal value under prevailing market conditions. Otherwise, a compensation payment may be necessary. The value of a swap is based on its present value according to a discount function. In trading, however, the price of the swap is based on the interest rate (for the fixed leg) or the spread (for the floating rate leg). The trader in instruments manages the allocation of their portfolio across swaps in order to avoid exposure to imbalances.

The key issue in pricing an instrument is the time-value of money that determines the comparability of cash flows at different dates. This is used to calculate the present value of a projected future cash flow. In the ET++SwapsManager framework, two key abstractions in modeling this are the *instrument* and the *discount function manager*:

1. An instrument is an entity that generates projected cash flows over time, calculates the present values of those cash flows, calculates the price of a

swap, and constructs payment dates. Two key pieces of business logic for an instrument are delegated to subordinate entities, according to the STRATEGY pattern[2]: a *cash flow generator* entity abstracts the generation of cash flows, while a *pricer* entity abstracts the pricing of an investment.

2. A discount function manager incorporates pricing information from public markets (for a given market mix), calculates the discount factor for a given standard instrument in an instrument-specific calculation. The manager uses zero-coupon pricing to compute the discount factor of the instrument at different interest rates for the different kinds of markets. The logic for calculating a particular kind of rate, i.e., for a particular market, such as money markets, futures markets, swap markets, etc., is again encapsulated using the strategy pattern in a *calculation strategy*.

Figure 5.4 illustrates two ways that a framework might incorporate application logic. In Fig. 5.4 (a), the framework is defined as a *white box*. The hooks for client code, in this case the calculator strategies, are defined as abstract *hook methods* in the framework. The user of the framework provides implementations for these abstract methods via inheritance and instantiates the resulting class to create a discount function manager.

The white box approach to framework instantiation has its advantages and its disadvantages. By organizing the configuration logic into inheritance hierarchies, as done here with the DFManagerImpl and DFManager classes, the initialization logic is simplified for the framework user. On the other hand, this is also a disadvantage: relating the configuration logic to the implementation hierarchies is inflexible and will be difficult to change. Furthermore, the implementor of the DFManagerImpl client code must reason about internal framework details, such as an internal list of strategies and how it is initialized.

Figure 5.4 (b) illustrates a *black box* initialization for the framework. In this case, the client-supplied calculator strategies are provided to the framework as components required to satisfy the interface defined for a calculator strategy. The client now initializes the framework by installing instances for this interface in the discount function manager using a loader method provided by the framework, for example. This approach provides greater flexibility, as initialization logic is no longer tied to the inheritance structure of the framework. The client no longer has to reason about the internal structure of the discount function manager. They only have to provide algorithmic logic as calculation strategies, with the selection logic centralized in the manager. This is an application of *separation of concerns*, decomposing parts of the domain logic into separate components which overlap in their functionality as little as possible. However, it is now the responsibility of the framework client to properly follow the protocol for creating and installing calculator strategies.

---

[2]The strategy pattern describes the factoring of a business algorithm into a separate entity that the primary entity delegates to when it needs to execute that algorithm. This late binding of the algorithm provides flexibility in the choice of the algorithm at run-time.

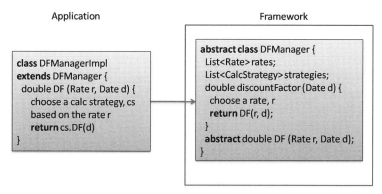

(**a**) White box framework

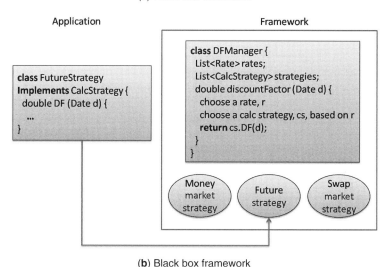

(**b**) Black box framework

Figure 5.4 *Instantiating a framework*

As an example of the use of these mechanisms, consider the calculation of cash flows for the fixed-swap leg of the interest rate swap application. This application is based on the principal of the loan, the fixed interest rate, and the accrual basis associated with the instrument (the number of days per year that interest accrues). The swap-leg parent provides logic for calculating accrual factors and payment dates. The cash-flow generator loops through these dates, computing a result list of cash-flows to be returned to the parent. This encoding of the algorithm is close to a textbook description.

This framework forms the basis for a GUI for domain experts, providing those experts with GUI tools to create new instances of instruments, and to edit data for those instruments, such as principal, interest rate, etc. A trader can create scenarios by directly manipulating the yield curve for an instrument seeing how cash-flows on both sides of an instrument are affected by interest rate changes.

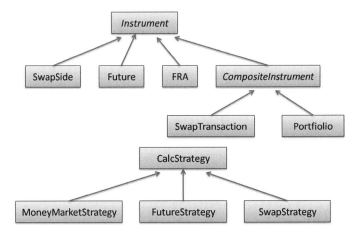

Figure 5.5 *Interfaces for financial instruments*

Once an instrument has been added to a portfolio, the framework can be used to analyze the aggregate effect of the instrument on that portfolio. The key to this domain-specific GUI environment is the set of interfaces that are used to organize the domain abstractions. Some of these interfaces, and the specialization hierarchies that relate them, are provided in Fig. 5.5.

5.4   DOMAIN-SPECIFIC LANGUAGES (DSLs)

An approach strongly related to the application framework approach to codifying domain knowledge is the use of domain specific languages (DSLs) [10]. In general, a DSL is a way of efficiently encoding domain-specific client logic at a level of abstraction that should match that of the domain expert[3]. Programs in such languages may be executed directly, or an application program generator may compile a DSL program into conventional high level code that then links to a library or a framework for execution. For example, the Risla[4] DSL was developed in the domain of financial engineering to accelerate the development of new financial instruments by domain experts from several weeks to a few days [11]. The principal purpose of Risla is to capture the logic for generating the cash-flows for a deal, an instance of a financial instrument. This information is used by the financial administration part of the enterprise to process the use of financial instruments, as well as the management information system department to evaluate the risk to the enterprise of particular financial instruments and deals.

An example of a Risla description of an instrument is provided in Fig. 5.6. Risla is an object-oriented language, organized around the description of financial instruments (called "products" in Risla). As with ET++SwapsManager, financial

[3]DSLs themselves are not new. Report Program Generator (RPG) was developed for report processing on mainframes in 1959.
[4]Risla is a Dutch-English acronym: Rente (interest) Informatie Systeem LAnguage.

```
product LOAN
declaration
   contract  data
      PAMOUNT  : amount                      %% Principal  Amount
      STARTDATE : date                       %% Starting  date
      MATURDATE : date                       %% Maturity  data
      INTRATE  : int-rate                    %% Interest rate
      RDMLIST  := [] : cashflow-list         %% List of redemptions.
   information
      PAF : cashflow-list                    %% Principal Amount Flow
      IAF : cashflow-list                    %% Interest Amount Flow
   registration
      %% Register  one  redemption.
      RDM(AMOUNT  : amount,  DATE : date)
   local
      %% Final  Principal  Amount
      FPA(CHFLLIST  : cashflow-list)  : amount
      %% Final  redemption
      FRDM  : cashflow
   error  checks
      "Wrong  term  dates"  in case  of STARTDATE  >= MATURDATE
      "Negative  amount"  in case  of PAMOUNT  < 0.0
implementation
   local
      define  FPA as IBD(CHFLLIST,  -/-PAMOUNT,  MATURDATE)
      define  FRDM as <-/-FPA(RDMLIST),  MATURDATE>
   information
      define  PAF as [<-/-PAMOUNT,  STARTDATE>]  >> RDMLIST>>[FRDM]
      define  IAF as [< -/-CIA( BL(RDMLIST,  <-/-PAMOUNT,
                                   <STARTDATE,  MATURDATE>>),
                             INTRATE ), MATURDATE >]
   registration
      define  RDM as
         error  checks
            "Date  not  in interval"  in case  of (DATUM < STARTDATE)
                                     or (DATUM >= MATURDATE)
            "Negative  amount"        in case  of AMOUNT <= 0.0
            "Amount  too  big"        in case  of
               FPA(RDMLIST  >> [<AMOUNT,  DATE>])  > 0.0
         RDMLIST  := RDMLIST  >> [<AMOUNT,  DATE>]
```

Figure 5.6 *Risla loan program [11]*

instruments are defined in Risla as classes. When two parties enter into a deal by agreeing on a contract, the class for the corresponding instrument is instantiated to an object whose internal state records the state of the deal. For example, the declaration of the loan instrument in Fig. 5.6 includes instance variables for the principal amount and the list of redemptions registered so far. The loan description also specifies properties of the deal, i.e., the flow of principal amounts (PAF) and the flow of interest amounts (IAF), that are useful information for the rest of the enterprise, as mentioned. The implementation section provides the implementation details, including the business logic for computing these cash flows. For example, the PAF is the concatenation of the negative of the original principal amount, the list of cash flows for the redemptions, and the final redemption value of the deal. The business logic includes the invocation of library operations on cash flows and balances, such as Initial Balance on Date (IBD) and Calculate Interest Amount (CIA). The Risla compiler generates COBOL code from Risla programs. COBOL is chosen as the target language to simplify interoperability with the existing base of financial software.

Risla exemplifies a case where the purpose of the DSL is to provide a domain-specific linguistic framework that domain experts and developers can use to communicate requirements for new software services. The syntax of the DSL is almost irrelevant[5]. The critical factor in the DSL design is the proper choice of domain abstractions and the semantics of the language constructs for combining and manipulating them.

DSLs can be viewed as a representation of domain knowledge in the enterprise. Done properly, the constructs and semantics of the DSL will be carefully chosen to reflect the result of a deep understanding of the domain. This will require some significant investment in domain analysis, preferably involving the collaboration of both domain experts and developers with some breadth of experience in different programming paradigms. Having invested in domain analysis, the developers will now face the task of building an implementation of the language. Although its semantics should be considerably simpler than a general-purpose language like Java or C#, there is still some investment to be made in tools for parsing, analysis, compilation, and interpretation. Some of this development effort can be short-circuited by developing an *embedded domain specific language*, i.e., an embedding of the DSL into an existing language. Much of the front-end parsing and analysis for the DSL is then provided gratis by the embedding language. An embedded DSL program may be directly evaluated in the embedding language, or a program generator may translate it to a lower level language, as is done with Risla.

In the remainder of this section, we consider a case study of an embedded DSL, again taken from the domain of financial engineering. Specifically, we consider a language for financial contracts embedded in the Haskell functional language.[6] We refer to this language as Haskell Contracts [12]. The constructs that it provides are summarized in Fig. 5.7. In that summary, we use the precise descriptions of the operations' semantics provided by the language designers.

An example of a financial contract is a contract C that provides, on 31 December 2012, the right to choose between:

---

[5]Unless a grave mistake is made, such as basing the syntax on XML.
[6]Haskell is described in more detail in Appendix A. We summarize the parts of Haskell that are necessary to understand the examples in this section. The declaration e :: T specifies that the expression e is a program expression with type T. If that expression is evaluated as a program, then if the evaluation completes it will result in a value of type T. If e :: $T_1 \rightarrow T_2$, then e is a function from the domain T_1 to the range T_2. If e :: $T_1 \rightarrow T_2 \rightarrow T_3$, then e is a function of two parameters from the domain T_1 and the domain T_2 to the range T_3. The application of a function f to arguments e_1 and e_2 is written simply using juxtaposition, i.e., as (f e_1 e_2). Parentheses are only used to remove syntactic ambiguity.

```
zero :: Contract
```
"zero is a contract that may be acquired at any time. It has no rights and no obligations, and has an infinite horizon."

```
one :: Currency → Contract
```
"(one k) is a contract that immediately pays the holder one unit of the currency k. The contract has an infinite horizon"

```
give :: Contract → Contract
```
"To acquire (give c) is to acquire all of c's rights as obligations and vice versa. For a bilateral contract q between parties A and B, A acquiring q implies that B acquires (give q)".

```
and :: Contract → Contract → Contract
```
"If you acquire (c1 'and' c2) then you immediately acquire both c1 (unless it has expired) and c2 (unless it has expired). The composite contract expires when both c1 and c2 expire".

```
or :: Contract → Contract → Contract
```
"If you acquire (c1 'and' c2) then you immediately acquire either c1 or c2 (but not both). If either has expired, that one cannot be chosen. When both have expired, the compound contract expires".

```
truncate :: Date → Contract → Contract
```
"(truncate t c) is exactly like c except that it expires at the earlier of t and the horizon of c. Notice that truncate limits only the possible *acquisition date* of c; it does not truncate c's rights and obligations, which may extend well beyond t".

```
then :: Contract → Contract → Contract
```
"If you acquire (c1 'then' c2) and c1 has not expired, then you acquire c1. If c1 has expired, but c2 has not, then you acquire c2. The compound contract expires when both c1 and c2 expire".

```
scale :: Observation → Contract → Contract
```
"If you acquire (scale o c), then you acquire c at the same moment, except that all the rights and obligations of c are multiplied by the value of the observables o at the moment of acquisition".

```
get :: Contract → Contract
```
"If you acquire (get c) then you must acquire c at c's expiry date. The compound contract expires at the same moment that c expires".

```
anytime :: Contract → Contract
```
"If you acquire (anytime c) you must acquire c, but you can do so at any time between the acquisition of (anytime c) and the expiry of c. The compound contract expires when c does".

Figure 5.7 *Primitives for Haskell contracts [12]*

- Both of:
  1. Receive $75 on 31 August 2015.
  2. Pay $100 on 30 June 2015.
- An option, to be exercised by 31 January 2013, to choose both of:
  1. Receive $80 on 31 August 2016.
  2. Pay $100 on 30 June 2018.

The *horizon*, or *expiry date*, of the contract is the date by which it must be acquired. The expiry date of the example is 31 December 2012. This contract includes an *option*, a subcontract of rights and obligations, that is optionally exercisable by 31 January 2013. Note that the horizon of the option extends beyond that of the parent contract. The *acquisition date* for a contract is the date on which it is acquired by a client. A contract should be acquired by its expiry date in order for its rights and obligations to accrue.

An example of a contract is a zero discount bond, that provides to the holder the right to redeem the bond for a certain amount (e.g., $100) at the specified date[7]:

```
zcb :: Date → Double → Currency → Contract
zcb "31 December, 2012" 100 USD
```

However, rather than build instruments such as this into the language design, Haskell Contracts provides a more primitive set of operations for specifying contracts. The one constructor builds a primitive contract that only specifies a single unit of currency, with no expiry date (an infinite horizon). Thus, (one USD) is a contract that can be acquired at any time and immediately bestows the benefit of $1 on the holder of the contract.

We place an expiry date on this instrument using the truncate constructor. This operation trims what may have been an infinite horizon to the specified expiry date:

```
truncate :: Date → Contract → Contract
truncate "31 December, 2012" (one USD)
```

We now have a bond with a redemption value of $1 that must be acquired by 31 December 2012, if we wish to redeem its benefit. We acquire the bond using the get operation:

```
get :: Contract → Contract
get (truncate "31 December, 2012" (one USD))
```

With the application of this operation, we commit to acquiring the contract at its acquisition date. Finally, we need a scaling operation to scale from a $1 bond value to the more interesting value. The scaleK operation is definable in terms of the other operations in Fig. 5.7:

```
scaleK :: Double → Contract → Contract
scaleK 100 (get (truncate "31 December, 2012" (one USD)))
```

This scaling operation is not primitive because there is an open-ended set of criteria besides constant values that may be used to scale the value of a contract. For example, the redemption value of an instrument may be based on the London Interbank Offered Rate (LIBOR) at a specified date. Haskell Contracts abstracts this set of time-varying quantities using the Observation data type[8]. Both contracts

---

[7]To simplify the exposition, we assume that the type Date is synonymous with String.
[8]Haskell Contracts actually uses a parameterized type (Obs T) where T is the type of the value that is time-varying.

and observations have values, but the value of an observation is objective in the sense that both parties to a contract can agree on its value. The konst constructor builds a constant observation, whose value never changes. Then we have:

```
scale :: Observation → Contract → Contract
scale (konst 100) (get (truncate "31 December, 2012" (one USD)))
```

In general, programming languages provide some basic mechanisms for combining control flows, such as seqential composition ("do s_1 followed by s_2"), parallel composition ("do s_1 and s_2 in parallel"), and choice ("do either s_1 or s_2 based on some criteria"). Haskell Contracts provide the then operation for sequential composition, the and operation for parallel composition, and the or operation for choosing among contracts. The and operation combines the benefits and obligations of two contracts. A contract is assumed to be under the control of the contract holder in the sense that the holder makes the decisions with respect to the choices in the contract. The give operation allows this perspective to be reversed in a contract so that the choices of the counter-party can be specified as part of the contract. For example, the following contract specifies a choice of c1 or c2 for the holder of the contract, and a choice of c3 or c4 for the counter-party[9]:

```
(c1 'or' c2) 'and' give (c3 'or' c4)
```

However, a key observation in the design of Haskell Contracts is that there are two notions of choice in contracts: there is the choice of *what* (in the sense of which contract should be chosen), and there is the choice of *when* (in the sense of when a contract is acquired). The anytime operation provides flexibility in when a contract is acquired. If a contract (anytime c) has expiry date T_2 and c has expiry date T_2, then the subcontract c can be acquired at any date between T_1 and T_2. For example, a so-called *European option* allows a choice of acquiring (or not) an underlying contract at a certain date:

```
get (truncate "31 December, 2012" ((zcb "6 June, 2014" 100 USD)
                                    'or' zero))
```

The (_ 'or' zero) part of the contract specifies that the zero coupon bond may not be acquired at all, using the zero constructor that incurs no rights or obligations. A decision must be made by 31 December 2012. If a decision is made to acquire, the bond is acquired on 31 December 2012 and is redeemed on 6 June 2014.

The operations in Fig. 5.7 define the constructors for an abstract syntax tree. To specify a semantics for the language, we must define an evaluator for programs in the language. In this case, an evaluator should compute the current value of a contract and this, in turn, will depend on assumptions about future values, such as foreign exchange rates, stock prices, and interest rates. The evalation is in terms of an abstract semantics of adapted stochastic processes, aka *value processes*, where a value process is a partial function from time to a random variable. Intuitively, if

---

[9]The syntax (c1 'or' c2) denotes the infix application of the or constructor, while (c1 'and' c2) denotes the infix application of the and constructor.

the value v is represented by a value process p, then $p(t)$ describes the possible values for p at time t. Both observables and contracts are translated to value processes that denote their values in a specific concurrency as random variables. Besides providing a vehicle to implementation, this abstract semantics provides a framework for reasoning about equality of contracts, based on their underlying abstract value processes.

This abstract semantics is reliant for its definition on certain primitive operations. For determining the value of a contract, denoted in currency k_1 (e.g., US dollars), in terms of currency k_2 (e.g., Euros), we need a process for translating one currency's value process to that of the other. This exchange rate process will necessarily rely on an underlying mathematical model of the evolution of exchange rates. For a value that is paid out in the future, its present value must be discounted with respect to future interest rates so, again, a mathematical model of the evolution of interest rates must be incorporated into the definition of a discounting function for value processes. The final step in implementing Haskell Contracts is an evaluation scheme for value processes. Any arbitrage scheme from the financial literature will suffice, e.g., the Ho and Lee lattice model [13].

Haskell Contracts is an example of a DSL design resulting from deep domain analysis, where the result of that analysis is a language that domain experts can use thereafter to communicate in a high-level fashion with developers. It is useful for prototyping where prototype programs execute directly in the metalanguage (in this case, Haskell), and where these programs may communicate through a variety of techniques with a software base of financial processing software implemented in lower level languages. Contract programs themselves may serve as specifications for instruments to be implemented by developers in more efficient languages, such as C++. More ambitiously, a program generator may try to generate these efficient implementations automatically from the DSL, although the higher the level of the DSL, the more sophisticated the compiler will need to be to produce code that is competitive in terms of performance with hand-written code.

Where is re-usability in this discussion of DSLs? *Cognitive distance* is defined (necessarily somewhat imprecisely) as "the amount of intellectual effort that must be expended by software developers in order to take a software system from one stage of development to another" [14]. Krueger [14] cites a reduction in cognitive distance as a critical requirement for any methodology that claims to promote software re-usability. On that basis, he rates application generators as the most promising software development paradigm for re-usable software abstractions. The rationale is that existing implementations may be adapted to new applications by working at the level of the domain model, making modifications to the domain-level solution, and eventually generating a new application from the modified domain model.

At least, that is the theory. In practice, it may be inevitable that DSL-generated applications will need to be customized and, at that point, the original DSL becomes little more than a historical artifact. It is certainly preferable if the generation of the application code from the DSL program can be reversed, so that changes to the application code are automatically propagated to the original DSL code. This is possible, for example, with the Eclipse Modeling Facility (EMF), that provides an implementation of model-driven architecture. However, that tool is very narrowly focused on the generation of platform-dependent data models, such as Java classes and interfaces, from platform-independent data models specified as UML class diagrams. EMF also illustrates another issue with program generators: the code produced by such generators can be fairly complex—inappropriately so for small applications.

Another concern with DSLs is their support for re-using domain logic: here there are two issues to be considered. First, does the DSL itself provide support for re-using designs and implementations? Whether it does or not will depend on language support for such re-use, such as parameterization, subtyping, and inheritance. As the design of these language features is normally outside the scope of the domain expert, and is the subject of decades of programming language research, this provides an additional motivation for embedding the DSL in an executable metalanguage such as Java, C#, or Haskell. Whether the metalanguage support for re-usability can be leveraged by the DSL will depend on the metalanguage and form of the embedding.

Second, the facility for re-using DSLs themselves should be considered. If DSLs become ubiquitous in the interfaces of domain-specific application frameworks, then the design and implementation of these DSLs appears to be a daunting task unless there is scope for re-using experience across the development of these DSLs. The easiest approach is to resort to a domain-agnostic scripting language, which at least has the benefit of a small fingerprint for its run-time system. A more ambitious approach would consider re-use applied at the level of language design and implementation. For example, the language implementation can be organized as a collection of classes for the abstract syntax tree constructors, where each class encapsulates evaluation and/or compilation logic for that type of node in an abstract syntax tree[10]. Inheritance can be used to define a new language by adding new constructors to an existing language.

Always deriving new DSLs from existing DSLs can quickly lead to "DSL bloat", as DSLs carry along unnecessary features re-used from the "parent" language. A more useful facility would be some form of *mixin-based inheritance*. Originating in the Common Lisp Object System (CLOS), *mixins* represent the "delta" that is used to specialize a base class to a subclass during inheritance [15, 16]. By decoupling mixins from classes, one obtains a framework where a mixin itself may be re-used in the extension of several classes. Classes themselves may become a secondary concern, depending on the mixin model. Implementation re-use is now realized through *mixin combination*—a more fundamental concept than inheritance—effectively, a form of multiple implementation inheritance, but more low level and therefore more flexible (and with better-defined semantics). Using this approach, one can imagine an application framework for developing new DSLs based on mixin combination[11],

---

[10]Further clarification of the "constructors versus observers" view of data types is provided in Sect. 6.1 in the next chapter.

[11]An alternative approach, that of *monad transformers*, supports the modular definition of language implementation stacks using parameterization [17].

where a DSL with certain features is obtained "off the shelf" by combining those features, provided as mixins in the framework [18, 19].

5.5   AN EXAMPLE API FOR PERSISTENT DOMAIN OBJECTS

We saw in Sect. 5.2 that encapsulating domain logic in domain objects is a fundamental precept of the DDD methodology. Long-term storage of application state is an important consideration in DDD. The repository pattern is used to save domain objects, with their state, in databases. In object-oriented middleware systems, a persistent entity object is often referred to as a PERSISTENT DOMAIN OBJECT (PDO), while the repository pattern is often referred to as the DATA ACCESS OBJECT (DAO). The Java Persistence Architecture (JPA), part of the Java EE framework for building enterprise applications, provides *entity beans* to model PDOs, and the `EntityManager` interface is essentially an interface for generic DAOs implemented by providers of database engines. A class for entity objects is identified by the `@Entity` annotation. The intention is that an entity object denotes a record in a database table. As long as it is "attached" via an entity manager, the values of the object fields in memory are synchronized with the cell values for the corresponding record in the database.

For example, Fig. 5.8(**a**) provides a class diagram with classes for patients, physicians, and flow sheets. We also factor patient addresses out of the patient class into a separate class for address value objects. We assume that patients are identified by record numbers, and physicians are identified by national provider identifier (NPI). Addresses and flow sheet lines are value objects and are not required to have identity (although, in practice, a flow sheet line could be uniquely identified by patient, date, and time). There is a one-to-one relationship between patients and their addresses, a one-to-many relationship from patients to flow sheets (one sheet per day that they are under observation), and a many-to-many relationship between patients and the physicians that examine them or meet with them. We assume that the patient-address relationship is unidirectional, the patient-flow-sheet relationship is bidirectional (we may want to navigate to a patient's overall information from one of that patient's flow sheets), and the patient-physician relationship is bidirectional.

Figure 5.8(**b**) provides an entity-relationship diagram corresponding to the class diagram in Fig. 5.8(**a**). This diagram reflects the introduction of system-generated primary keys to represent database identity for records for flow sheets, flow sheet lines, and addresses. The one-to-one relationship between patients and addresses is represented by an address foreign key in a patient record. The one-to-many relationship between patient and flow sheet is represented by a patient foreign key in a flow sheet record. In database terms, the flow sheet entity (the "many" part of the relationship) is said to be the "owner" of the relationship. The many-to-many relationship between patient and physician is represented by a join table, with each patient and physician foreign key pair representing an instance of the relationship.

Figure 5.9 provides an example of an *object-relation mapping* (ORM), relating a class declaration for in-memory objects to a database schema that describes the organization of tables and records in the database on disk. This example provides

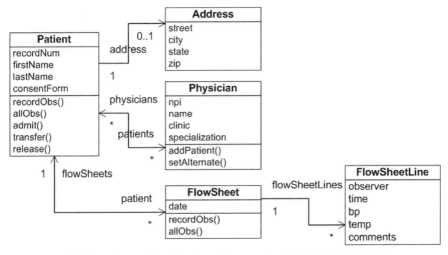

(a) Class diagram for patients, addresses, physicians and flow sheets

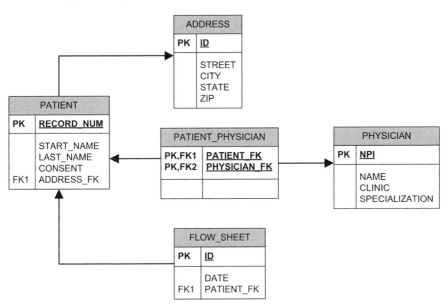

(b) Entity diagram for patients, addresses, physicians and flow sheets

Figure 5.8   *Patient entities and relationships*

a class for patient entities, using JPA annotations to describe the binding of such entities to a database schema. This class for patient entities is declared to be an in-memory realization of the database table called PATIENT. Parts of the latter table are cached in memory as Patient objects, with modifications to those objects flushed to the database on disk. The values of the firstName and lastName properties are taken from the FIRST_NAME and LAST_NAME columns, respectively, in the PATIENT

```
@Entity
@Table(name = "PATIENT")
public class Patient implements Serializable {
  private long recordNum;
  private String firstName;
  private String lastName;
  @id(name = "RECORD_NUM")
  @GeneratedValue
  public int getRecordNum() { return this.recordNum; }
  public void setRecordNum(int r) { this.recordNum = r; }

  @Column(name="FIRST_NAME")
  public String getFirstName() { return this.firstName; }
  public void setFirstName(String firstName) {
    this.firstName = firstName;
  }
  @Column(name="LAST_NAME")
  public String getLastName() { return this.lastName; }
  public void setLastName(String lastName) {
    this.lastName = lastName;
  }
  @Lob
  private byte[] consentForm;

  @OneToOne(fetch = FetchType.LAZY)
  @JoinColumn(name = "ADDRESS_FK", nullable = true)
  private Address address;

  @OneToMany(cascade = CascadeType.ALL, mappedBy = "patient")
  @OrderBy("date ASC")
  private List<FlowSheet> flowsheets;

  @ManyToMany(mappedBy = "patient")
  private Set<Physician> physicians;
  …
}
```

Figure 5.9   *Entity class for patient*

table. The RECORD_NUM field, for the patient record number, is the identifying primary key in the database. The values for this field are generated by the DBMS using a generation strategy chosen by the database system (the default strategy specification is AUTO).

Each patient record includes a scanned image of the signed patient consent form. This field is annotated to represent the fact that it is a large binary object using the @Lob annotation. This is an example of the forms of metadata that can be associated with data objects in enterprise systems. In this case, the database system can use the information provided by the metadata to choose an appropriate storage strategy, such as storing consent form values separately from patient records and not loading them immediately when loading patient records.

The one-to-one relationship between patient and address is represented in the patient object by the `address` field. The `@JoinColumn` annotation provides information about the foreign key in the patient record. In this case, the column annotation names the foreign key column in the underlying database and allows null values for when a patient's address is unknown. The `@OneToOne` annotation provides an example of a specification for fetching the address information from the database. A specification of `EAGER` would require that a patient's address information be retrieved at the same time as the patient record itself. In this case, the `LAZY` specification allows the database system to load the address information "lazily", if it so chooses. The choice of a *fetching strategy* may be important for efficient performance. An eager strategy performs any input-output and join operations all at once, at the cost of potentially loading much unneeded data and filling memory. A lazy strategy only loads parts of the database as needed, but incurs some input-output cost on each loading operation. The default strategy is eager for one-to-one and many-to-one relationships, and lazy otherwise. The declaration of the `Address` class is provided in Fig. 5.10(**a**).

The one-to-many relationship between patient and flow sheet is represented in the patient object by the `flowsheets` field, which is a reference to a list of flow sheets. The `@OrderBy` annotation specifies that the flowsheet records are accessed in ascending order by date, justifying the use of a list data structure for the flowsheets for a patient. There is no column in the patient database table for flow sheets, as the flow sheets for a patient are retrieved using a database query. To support this query, there must be either be a table to represent the relationship, with foreign keys to reference the patient and flowsheet tables, or else there must be a foreign key column in the flow sheet table that references the patient table. For the case of a bidirectional one-to-many relationship, there must be a backward reference from a child entity to the parent entity. The field in the flow sheet object, corresponding to this backward reference, is specified by the `mappedBy` attribute for the `@OneToMany` attribute in the `Patient` class. This annotation identifies the field that "owns" the relationship, in this case the `patient` field in the flow sheet class. Note that here the terminology for ownership reflects database terminology. In programming terms, the `flowsheets` field is a reference to a collection of flow sheets and the patient entity is a "parent" entity for those sheets: if the patient entity is deleted, the corresponding flow sheets are also deleted. However, in database terms, each flow sheet entity contains a foreign key that is used to reference the parent patient entity, and this foreign key in the subordinate entity "owns" the relationship.

The `FlowSheet` class is declared in Fig. 5.10(**b**). The `@ManyToOne` annotation on the `patient` field in the flow sheet class reflects the `@OneToMany` annotation in the patient class. The `@JoinColumn` annotation, which is always in the field that "owns" the relationship, specifies the database column for the foreign key, and in this case prevents null values being stored for this key in the database: every flow sheet is required to have an identifiable patient.

The `@ManyToMany` annotation on the `physicians` field in the `Patient` class specifies a many-to-many relationship between patients and the physicians who examine

```
@Entity
@Table(name = "ADDRESS")
public class Address implements Serializable {
  @Id @GeneratedValue
  private long id;
  private Street street;
  private City city;
  private State state;
  private Zip zip;
}
```

(a) Address class

```
@Entity
@Table(name = "FLOW_SHEET")
public class FlowSheet implements Serializable {
  @Id @GeneratedValue
  private long id;
  @Temporal(TemporalType.DATE)
  private Date date;
  @OneToMany(mappedBy="flowsheet")
  @OrderBy
  private List<FlowSheetLine> lines;
  …
  @ManyToOne
  @JoinColumn(name = "PATIENT_FK", nullable = false)
  private Patient patient;
}
```

(b) Flow sheet class

```
@Entity
@Table(name = "PHYSICIAN")
public class Physician implements Serializable {
  @Id
  @Column(name = "NPI")
  private long npi;
  …
  @ManyToMany
  @JoinTable(name = "PATIENT_PHYSICIAN",
    joinColumns = @JoinColumn (name = "PATIENT_FK",
                              referencedColumn = "RECORD_NUM"),
    inverseJoinColumns = @JoinColumn (name = "PHYSICIAN_FK",
                                     referencedColumn = "NPI"))
  private Collection<Patient> patients;
}
```

(c) Physician class

Figure 5.10 *Auxiliary class declarations*

them or consult with them. A many-to-many relationship is always represented by a join table, as reflected in Fig. 5.8(**b**). The details of this join table, if the defaults are insufficient, are specified in the class that "owns" the relationship (in database terms). For a many-to-many relationship, either entity can own the relationship, and the mappedBy attribute in the "non-owning" or "inverse" entity identifies the owning entity and field. In Fig. 5.9, the mappedBy attribute of the @ManyToMany annotation identifies the patient field of the Physician entity as that which owns this relationship. Therefore, information about the join table for the relationship is defined in the class declaration for the latter, in Fig. 5.10(**c**).

Note that there is no automatic maintenance of the relationship fields in the Java entity objects. It is up to the application developer to maintain the relationships between entities. For example, if a new flowsheet is added to a patient entity, the insertion code should also set the reference to the patient object in the flowsheet, and vice versa.

The fundamental concept in managing entity objects in JPA is that of the *persistence context*. This refers to a collection of persistent entities that are managed as a unit within a program. For a given entity identity, there should not be duplicate instances of that entity within a persistence context. The API for managing a persistence context is provided by the EntityManager interface, as described in Fig. 5.11. An *entity manager* has operations for storing ("persisting") entities in a database, retrieving entities from a database, updating the values of an entity's fields in the database, and so on. A given persistence context may have several entity managers. An entity manager may be considered as a generic DAO implementation, or it may be used in the definition of a domain-specific DAO. An example of the latter is provided in Fig. 5.12. Technically, this example is a violation of DDD, as the latter distinguishes between factories for creating objects and repositories for storing and retrieving objects. We provide an operation for creating patient entities in Fig. 5.12 as the primary key is generated by the database when a patient entity is persisted to the database.

A *persistence unit* is a named deployment descriptor that forms a bridge between a persistence context and a database. For a standalone application, it specifies

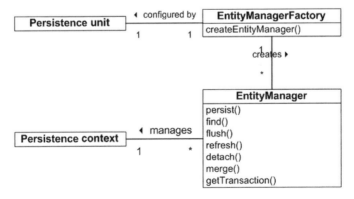

Figure 5.11 *API for Java persistence architecture*

```
@Entity
@NamedQuery(name = "findByName",
          query = "select p from Patient p where "
              + "p.firstName = :first and p.lastName = :last")
public class Patient { … }

public class PatientDAO {
   protected EntityManager em;

   public PatientDAO(EntityManager em) { this.em = em; }

   public Patient create(String first, String last, byte[] consent) {
     Patient patient = new Patient ();
     patient.setFirstName(first);
     patient.setLastName(last);
     patient.setConsentForm(consent);
     em.persist(patient);
     return patient;
   }
   public Patient retrieve(long id) {
     return em.find(Patient.class, id);
   }
   public List<Patient>
   findByName(String firstName, String lastName, int max) {
     Query query = em.createNamedQuery("findByName")
                 .setParameter("first", firstName)
                 .setParameter("last", lastName)
                 .setMaxResults(max)
     return (List<Patient>) query.getResultList();
   }
   public void delete(long id) {
     Patient patient = em.find(Patient.class, id);
     if (patient != null) em.remove(patient);
   }

   void beginTransaction() {
     em.getTransaction().begin();
   }
   void endTransaction() {
     em.getTransaction().commit();
   } }
```

Figure 5.12 *Data access object*

information, such as the database driver, authentication credentials, classes for
entity objects that are stored in the persistence context, information on physically
connecting to the database, and so on. In a container-managed application, the
persistence unit specifies a data source that is configured by the administrator of
the container. The *persistence provider* provides vendor-specific implementations
for such classes as the entity manager, queries, etc. The persistence unit configures
the implementation to use this implementation with a particular database. In a
situation where the persistence context is application-managed, as in a standalone

application, the entity manager factory provides an implementation for the entity manager, given the specification (by name) of a persistence unit. The `Persistence` class provides a bootstrap method for creating an entity manager factory:

```
EntityManagerFactory emf = Persistence.createEntityManagerFactory();
EntityManager em = emf.createEntityManager("PatientPU");
PatientDAO repository = new PatientDAO(em);
```

In the case where the persistence context is managed by a container, for example in a servlet or in an EJB in an application server, we rely on *dependency injection* for the actual instantiation of the entity manager. Dependency injection, introduced with an example in Sect. 2.5, is a pattern for resolving the dependencies of a software component based on criteria specified declaratively in the component. It is a form of inversion of control, introduced in Sect. 5.3, where initialization of a component is done by the container that the component executes in, rather than in the component itself. In the following example, the criteria are specified in the annotation on the program variable intended to hold a reference to an entity manager:

```
@PersistenceContext(unitName = "persistence/PatientDB")
EntityManager em;
```

The `@PersistenceContext` annotation specifies a dependency of this program on obtaining a reference to an entity manager. The specific persistence context to be managed, and therefore the class of the entity manager, are identified in the persistence unit descriptor identified by the `unitName` attribute, in this case bound to the local JNDI name `"persistence/PatientDB"`. A container such as an application server uses this annotation to bind the entity manager variable appropriately and ensures that this entity manager is propagated as the transaction context itself is propagated across method calls.

What if a domain object itself needs a reference to a DAO? For example, a patient object should have a reference to a DAO for flowsheet objects. This field should be annotated as a transient field, meaning that the flowsheet DAO is not stored in the database. How is the field initialized in a patient object? The problem is that en entity manager object for the flowsheet DAO cannot be obtained via dependency injection in an entity object. Dependency injection must be used in a service bean, as explained in the next chapter. Instead, a callback method is provided in the patient object, to set the flowsheets DAO in the patient object:

```
@Entity public class Patient {
  …
  @Transient FlowsheetDAO flowsheetDAO;
  public void setFlowsheetDAO(FlowsheetDAO fsdao) {
    this.flowsheetDAO = fsdao;
  }
}
```

This callback is invoked by the DAO for patient objects, when a patient object is persisted to the database or when it is retrieved from the database, for example:

```
public class PatientDAO { …
  private EntityManager em;
  public Patient retrieve(long id) {
    Patient patient = em.find(Patient.class, id);
    patient.setFlowsheetDAO(new FlowsheetDAO(em));
    return patient;
  }
}
```

The entity manager provides various operations for interfacing entity objects with a database, as demonstrated by some of the operations in Fig. 5.11. The persist operation stores an entity into the database and remove deletes the entity. The find operation retrieves an entity given a primary key. There is also support for more general queries. The Java Persistence Query Language (JPQL) language is a variant of SQL, with a dot-notation for object fields that allows either static (named) or dynamic queries to be executed in programs. The example in Fig. 5.12 uses a named query to support an operation for searching for patients with given first and last names.

There are also operations for synchronizing the contents of the database with the state of the persistence context in memory (flush), and in the other direction, for synchronizing the state of an in-memory object with the state of the corresponding entity in the database (refresh). The latter effectively rolls back any changes made to the object by the application, to the state when the object was originally retrieved from the database. When are the changes to an object made permanent in the database? As with all enterprise applications, database operations and therefore operations on entity objects are transactional. We introduced transactions in Sect. 2.4, and we discuss them in more depth in Chapter 9 in the sequel volume.

For now, it suffices to understand that:

1. All updates on a persistence context occur in the context of a transaction that groups those updates.
2. The updates are made permanent on the database when the transaction *commits*.
3. Alternatively, a transaction may *abort* and, in that case, all updates are rolled back so that the database is left unaffected by any of the update operations in that transaction.

If the persistence context is application-managed, then the client of the entity manager is responsible for managing the commit or abort of the underlying transaction:

```
EntityManager patientEM = emf.createEntityManager("PatientPU");
EntityTransaction tx = patientEM.getTransaction();
tx.begin();
patientEM.persist(patient);
…
tx.commit();
```

If, as part of application processing, another persistence context and entity manager are required, and commit or abort of that transaction need to be coordinated with the commit or abort of the transaction for the original entity manager, then these transactions are joined:

```
EntityManager physicianEM = emf.createEntityManager("PhysicianPU");
physicianEM.joinTransaction(patientEM.getTransaction());
…
patientEM.getTransaction().commit();
```

If the persistence context is container-managed by an application client or application server, then much of this management of transactions is done automatically, with annotations available to provide some application-specific configuration, such as when service calls spawn new transactions or re-use transactions from a calling service. If an application wishes to manually abort a transaction, it can do so by using dependency injection to inject an instance of the *session context*, which provides access to various parts of the execution context, including the transaction manager, security context, and local JNDI namespace:

```
@Resource SessionContext session;
session.setRollbackOnly();
```

A final aspect of this persistence API to discuss is the notion of *attached* and *detached* objects. An attached object is under the control of an entity manager as long as it is part of the persistence context managed by the entity manager. The detach method allows an entity object to be removed from a persistence context. After removal, the object is still available for application processing, including updates, but those updates are not synchronized with the database. If, at some point later, the application wishes the changes on a detached object to be synchronized with the database, the merge method for the entity manager does exactly this, adding the entity object back into the persistence context. This has an important application in architectures for DDD that make use of such an infrastructure, as we will see.

5.6 DOMAIN-DRIVEN ARCHITECTURE

In this section, we consider an architecture for DDD. We use *robustness diagrams* as a framework for motivating the architecture. Robustness diagrams are proposed by Rosenberg and Scott [20] as a bridge in UML modeling between requirements analysis and the software design, as illustrated in Fig. 5.13. *Boundary objects* represent the boundary between the actor and the system. They may, for example, be part of a user interface, or a servlet in a Web server. *Controller objects* are where the use case logic initially resides as a result of the requirements analysis. *Entity objects* in robustness diagrams are intended, at least initially, to be simple create, read, update and delete (CRUD) objects in a design, typically representing resource databases. As a DDD progresses, application logic should move from the

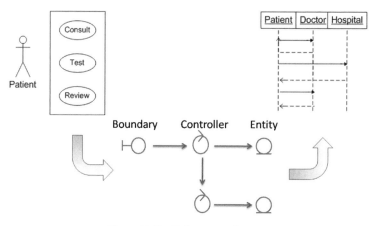

Figure 5.13   *Robustness diagram*

controller objects to the entity objects. By the conclusion of the design process, only that part of the use case logic that cannot be located in entity objects should remain in controller objects. In this way, controller objects may even become superfluous in the design and be eliminated altogether.

Boundary objects and entity objects remain. With the domain logic bound to the entity objects, the role of the boundary objects is largely to manage the interactions between the entity objects and the clients of the application. The typical design pattern for this role in multi-tier applications is the service façade pattern, which we consider in more detail in the next chapter. The façade pattern encapsulates and abstracts a collection of objects and services, forwarding clients requests to the underlying objects and, in some cases, providing the logic for synthesizing higher-level services from the underlying services. In DDD, this is formulated as the LAYERED ARCHITECTURE pattern for encapsulating complexity.

Consider the example of the ET++SwapsManager application framework in 5.3. What is the role of the service façade in such a framework? A typical application of façades is in layering, abstracting from lower level layers and providing a higher level API to clients. What does this mean in the context of the swaps manager framework? The entity objects provided in the framework are already at the right level of abstraction for the clients. Each entity object models a useful domain abstraction. There is no point in adding an extra level of abstraction for abstraction's sake.

Bien [1] proposes the GATEWAY pattern[12] as an alternative to the service facade pattern in this situation. The role of the gateway is not to abstract from the underlying entity objects, but to deliberately expose those entity objects to the client for direct interaction. The gateway loads entity objects for the client and the client invokes entity methods directly to execute domain logic. For example, the following provides a sample simplified API for a swaps manager gateway:

---

[12]This is not to be confused with Fowler's gateway pattern [21], where the latter is a client-specific encapsulation and abstraction of the logic for accessing a resource.

```
@Remote
public interface ISwapsManagerGateway {
  public Instrument[] getInstruments();
  public Deal getDeal(long key);
  // Transaction management
  public void commit();
  public void rollback();
  public void closeGateway();
}
@Remote
public interface Instrument {
  public Deal createDeal(String party, String counterParty);
}
@Remote
public interface Deal {
  public long getKey();
  public void addRedemption (Date date, float amount);
  public List<CashFlow> partyFlow();
  public List<CashFlow> counterPartyFlow();
}
```

The Instrument objects are factory objects; each object has the logic for creating an instance of the corresponding financial instrument. The gateway also provides a method for retrieving an existing instance of a deal by specifying the database key that identifies that instance.

Figure 5.14 provides a domain-driven architecture organized around entity objects (implemented as PDOs) made available to clients by a gateway. Although some controller logic may remain with intermediate services, the precepts of DDD dictate that most domain logic should reside in the entity objects. Domain logic that may remain in services includes logic that depends equally on several entities, as well as cross-cutting functionality, such as logging, authentication, etc.

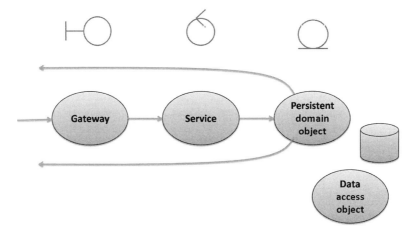

Figure 5.14 *Domain-driven architecture*

However, in this architecture, the services are secondary to the domain logic in the entity objects and the gateway that provides access to those entity objects.

In addition to loading entity objects for interaction with the client, the gateway is also responsible for transaction management. The interaction of the client with the database should be transactional in the sense that all update operations performed during a session with the client belong to a conceptual whole. In a typical Web service interaction, a client invokes a Web service call in a stateless façade operation. The latter operation initiates a transaction and all updates to entity objects are done in the context of this transaction. The termination of the service call completes the transaction and flushes updates to the database. The implication of this is that intermediate updates are tentative; if a service call terminates abnormally, the updates must be discarded.

With the gateway pattern, there is no longer a façade service operation upon which to hang the initiation and finalization of an encompassing transaction. The methods of the gateway provide references to entity objects to the client and the client interacts directly with these entities by invoking the business logic in the entity methods. In contrast with the service façade, there is no single encompassing operation whose invocation begins the transaction and whose completion terminates the transaction. At some point, the client will choose to either commit all changes to the database, or to discard the changes in the user interface (UI) and roll back the state of the UI to the last commit point. A variant on this, depending on the underlying transactional support, is to have the commit operation establish a *savepoint*, committing the updates of the transaction up to that point, so that a later rollback only rolls the database state back to the savepoint.

The responsibility for handling these transactional semantics rests with the gateway. This is reflected in the interface above by providing two operations in the gateway for managing a transaction. The `commit` operation completes a transaction and in the process makes any updates on entity objects permanent and flushes those updates to the database. The `rollback` operation aborts the transaction, discards updates to entity objects, and rolls their state back to the point at which the transaction started. To support these operations, the gateway will need to manage the entity objects that the client loads and updates, keeping track of the updates that should be flushed to the database if the transaction commits. We consider some strategies for doing this below.

Figure 5.15 provides an example realization of the abstract architecture in Fig. 5.14. The gateway uses a DAO to retrieve entity objects from the database, and the client references those PDOs as proxy entity objects. All operations on domain objects are performed on the server, invoked on the client via the proxies. As it is responsible for managing the lifetime of these PDOs across client calls, the gateway object is a stateful object on the server, with a proxy on the client. The easiest way to implement this state management is for the gateway to keep track of the aggregate roots for the domain data structures that have been retrieved, as well as the DAO that is used to load them. The gateway manages the transaction through the DAO, using its operations for committing and rolling back transactional

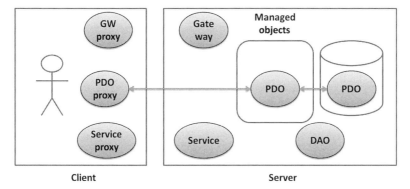

Figure 5.15 *Domain-driven architecture with proxy PDOs*

changes as requested by the client. As all retrieved entity objects are only referenced by the client through proxies, the entities remain managed PDOs throughout
an interaction session. This is the key to relying on the DAO for managing updates
on the database.

The architecture in Fig. 5.15 is a tightly-coupled one. The stateful gateway
object, and the pool of managed PDOs retrieved by the corresponding DAO from
the database, represent the state that is shared with the client across client calls to
domain logic in entity object methods. The entity object methods that are made
available in proxies should at least have a coarse granularity, otherwise they give
rise to fine-grained interactions with clients across the network. Such fine-grained
conversations will not scale because of the latency of the network communication
and the overhead of communication stacks. The entity interfaces will, at least, not
be CRUD interfaces, according to the tenets of DDD. Nevertheless, the domain
logic, in isolation, may reveal entity interfaces that are inappropriate for network
proxies owing to their granularity.

There are several solutions to this granularity issue. One solution is to use
façades to offer clients a more coarsely grained interface for operating on entity
objects. As clients should be discouraged from invoking the underlying fine-grained
logic in the entity objects, the interfaces for the latter are trimmed by removing this
functionality as far as clients are concerned. This leads us away from the principles
of DDD and towards SOA, which we consider in the next chapter.

Another alternative to avoid fine-grained interactions between clients and entities
over the network is to move the entity objects to the client. This is illustrated in
Fig. 5.16. Recall, for example, that the JPA interface for the entity manager includes
detach and merge operations on PDOs. The detach operation removes a PDO from
the pool of managed objects so the entity manager is no longer responsible for
synchronizing updates on that object's fields with the state of the corresponding
record or records on the database. The merge operation re-attaches a detached
object, re-inserting it into the pool of managed objects, and merging its state with
the state on the database. Using this approach, a protocol for removing fine-grained
interactions between a client and an entity object takes the following steps:

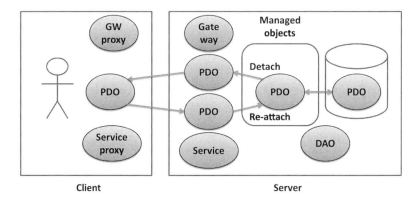

Figure 5.16 *Domain-driven architecture with detached PDOs*

1. Detach the object from the managed pool, serialize its state, transmit this state to the client, and reconstitute the entity object on the client after de-serializing its state. This logic can be a implemented as a simple downloading operation provided by the gateway.

2. Interact with the entity object on the client machine via purely local method calls to execute domain logic.

3. Serialize the modified object state and return it to the server, where the entity object is reconstituted and re-attached to the managed pool. This requires a gateway operation for uploading modified entity object state to the server.

It will be seen that this protocol implies a CRUD interface for the gateway, but it is at least, a coarse-grained CRUD interface. By analogy, rather than filling in the fields of a form with fine-grained method calls across the network for each field, instead the form is filled in at the client and then uploaded to the server. Indeed, this is exactly the model for client interaction in Web applications[13].

However, there is a very critical aspect of this protocol in the second step. In order to execute domain logic locally on the client, the implementation code for the entity objects (represented, for example, by the corresponding class files in Java and C#) must be relocated to the client. There is a major issue with this approach: protecting the client from malicious code downloaded from a server. This does not imply that the idea is out of the question. Browser plug-ins and mobile apps are now standard in Web and mobile phone applications, and both require that clients download and install code supplied by a party they may not necessarily have any familiarity with. Nevertheless, important security questions remain.

The current practice in enterprise systems is to side-step these security questions by not migrating entity domain logic to the client at all. Instead, the only information provided about entity objects is their interfaces, for example through a WSDL interface. The stubs generated from such an interface are guaranteed to not contain

---

[13]Modulo back-end Web service calls in RIA applications, which again should be coarse-grained.

executable code beyond that generated by the public IDL compiler for marshalling and unmarshalling data to be exchanged with the server. This necessarily means that all objects exchanged with the client are data transfer objects only, so this approach does not support DDD. It is largely the approach discussed in the next chapter.

Besides the security questions associated with mobile code, another issue to consider for the architecture in Fig. 5.16 is that of managing PDOs on the client. The default persistence model for JPA is based on *persistency by reachability:* if an object is persisted to the database, then all objects reachable from that object, provided they are not transient references, are also persisted [22]. This persistence model is broadly popular among application developers, as reflected by the fact that it is the default and also the only persistence model supported by JPA 2.0 (JPA does leave hooks for adding other, more discriminating, models of persistence in subsequent versions of JPA). Using JPA and its support for reachability, for example, the implementation of the gateway in Fig. 5.15 is straightforward, if not trivial: the gateway simply invokes the DAO methods for flushing updates to the database on the aggregate roots of the entity objects that have been retrieved. The DAO implementation is similarly simplified. For example, strategies such as lazy loading on demand of parts of the object graph are provided as part of the entity manager functionality, invoked on the basis of default strategies and meta-information supplied through program annotations. We saw an example of this in Fig. 5.9.

Once objects are detached from the managed pool, this management becomes the responsibility of the application, without run-time system support. The client must copy updated entity state back to the server, and the gateway must re-attach those objects to the managed pool before committing the updates. There is the very real danger of this re-attachment being done in an inconsistent manner so that some entity updates are persisted without the updates that should accompany them. For example, an update might involve the movement of a node from one place in the object graph to another. If not done consistently, persisting the updates might for example reflect the removal of the node but not its re-insertion elsewhere so, in effect, the node "disappears." Lazy loading of parts of the object graph is similarly left to the application, using callbacks to invoke the loading logic in a lazy fashion. There is a reason that enterprise application developers favor persistence frameworks.

We have seen that there are two problems associated with detaching domain objects and shipping them to client: security on the client side and management of persistence on both the client and the server. SOA avoids the client security problem, but is susceptible to the persistence-management problem. Rich internet applications are vulnerable to *both* problems. RIAs such as AJAX and Silverlight move the presentation logic, and potentially some part of the domain logic, to the client. Thus, this approach is vulnerable to the security problems of executing server code on the client. The database remains on the server, with Web service calls used to exchange data between the business logic on the client and the database on the server, again under application program control. Effectively, the server becomes the database in an otherwise conventional three-tier application. Because of loose coupling between client and server, the DAO and any managed pool must also exist on the server, so the persistence management problem also remains.

A final approach to supporting DDD in enterprise applications is provided in Fig. 5.17. This takes the RIA approach one extra step forward, back to *fat clients*. With this approach, the presentation logic, the domain logic, *and at least part of the server database* are moved to the client. With this approach, the gateway, DAO, and services are downloaded to the client. Under either an eager or a lazy loading strategy (e.g., a disk page at a time as requested by the application), the database is also downloaded and stored on the client disk. Queries to the database now go to the part of the database cached locally on the client. As the DAO and the database cache are both on the client, persistence management can be automated by the DAO. When the session transaction is committed, the database cache is flushed back to the server. If transactional semantics are not required, a background synchronizing process can periodically flush updates back to the server.

An example situation where such a framework is essential is in disconnected Web access, for example on mobile devices such as smartphones, where a continuous connection to the server may be neither possible nor desirable. Besides the obvious problem when a signal is lost, e.g., when a train enters a tunnel, there is also the issue that requiring continuous connection to a server over the radio network will quickly drain the batteries on a mobile device. Instead, the preferred strategy is to take advantage of periods of connectivity to synchronize an on-device database cache with the relevant part of the server database. The SQLite database management system has been a popular choice for implementors of client-side database caches, for example on the Android platform. IndexedDB is a standard API for client database caches in Web browsers, being developed under the auspices of W3C. Document-oriented databases such as CouchDB are another popular choice for caching portions of a database on a client.

An example application that runs on such a framework is mobile email. As mail quotas of several gigabytes are common, it is clearly impossible to cache the entirety of one's mail folders on the mobile device. Instead, as the user browses their mail folders, the relevant parts of the email archives are downloaded to the database

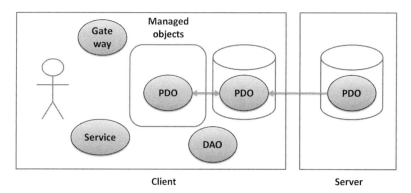

Figure 5.17   *Domain-driven architecture with fat client*

cache. The contents of the cache are periodically and automatically synchronized with the contents of the mail folders on the server. The level of synchronization is relatively small, as normally the email user is only editing a small number of messages, usually one at a time.

Client-side database caching is an enabling technology for fat client applications on Web client platform. An important issue is if clients will, or should, trust the suppliers of such apps. Similar comments apply to the deployment of domain-driven architectures as fat clients in an enterprise setting. Even if one cannot depend on a standard database infrastructure, such as SQLite or IndexedDB, such infrastructure can be dynamically deployed as plug-ins, where necessary. Beyond the negative associations with fat clients based on early experience with Web browsers, the key obstacle is the security issues raised by such deployments. We consider these implications in the sequel volume.

5.7 FURTHER READING

Evans [23] is the standard reference on DDD. Bien [1] proposes an architecture for DDD based on the gateway architecture; our discussion follows his approach.

Mernik et al. [11] provide a survey of DSLs, and approaches and methodologies for their realization. Van Deursen and Klint [10] report on the history and implementation of the Risla domain specific language. An interesting observation is that, at the time they were asked to consult on the language design and implementation, the ASD+SDF framework for automatically generating language frontends from BNF and algebraic semantics was becoming available. However, their clients balked at the idea of using this framework to implement the DSL. The idea of a DSL itself was revolutionary enough within their enterprise.

Peyton Jones et al. [12] report on the design and implementation of the Haskell Contracts language which arose from collaboration between Microsoft and one of its clients in the financial services industry[14]. There are numerous examples of embedded DSLs in functional languages such as Haskell and O'CAML. Perhaps the elegance of functional languages attracts DSL designers, or perhaps they are attracted by the economy of expression afforded by mechanisms such as list comprehensions, type inference, type classes, etc. A modern DSL that is popular in the financial engineering industry is F#, an official .NET language. It is essentially a functional language (in the same family as O'CAML) with a C# syntax. Of course Excel has provided a functional DSL for financial planning for several years.

REFERENCES

1. Bien A. Real World Java EE Patterns–Rethinking Best Practices. Adam Bien Press; 2009.

2. Dijkstra EW. The structure of the THE multiprogramming system. *Communications of the ACM* 1968; 11: 341–346.

---

[14]"Haskell Contracts" is our nomenclature. Peyton Jones et al. do not name their language.

3. Parnas D. On the criteria to be used in decomposing systems into modules. *Communications of the ACM* 1972; 15: 1053–1058.

4. Laribee D. Introduction to domain-driven design. *MSDN Magazine* February 2009.

5. Krogdahl S. The birth of simula. In: International Federation for Information Processing (IFIP), Vol. 174. Springer-Verlag; 2005: 261–265.

6. Bien A. Value object vs. data transfer object (vo vs. dto); August 2009. Available at: http://www.adam-bien.com/roller/abien/entry/value_object_vs_data_tr%ansfer.

7. Birrer A, Eggenschwiler T. Frameworks in the financial engineering domain: An experience report. In: European Conference on Object-Oriented Programming, Lecture Notes in Computer Science. Springer-Verlag; 1993.

8. Fayad M, Schmidt DC. Object-oriented application frameworks. *Communications of the ACM* 1997; 40.

9. Johnson R, Foote B. Designing reusable classes. *Journal of Object-Oriented Programming* 1988; 1: 22–35.

10. Mernik M, Heering J, Sloane AM. When and how to develop domain-specific languages. *ACM Computing Surveys* 2005; 37: 316–344.

11. Van Deursen A, Klint P. Little languages: Little maintenance? *Journal of Software Maintenance* 1997; 10: 10–75.

12. Peyton Jones S, Eber JM, Seward J. Composing contracts: an adventure in financial engineering. In: Proceedings of ACM International Conference on Functional Programming. ACM; 2000.

13. Ho T, Lee S. Term structure movements and pricing interest rate contingent claims. *Journal of Finance* 1986; 41: 1011–1028.

14. Krueger CW. Software reuse. *ACM Computing Surveys* 1992; 24: 131–183.

15. Bracha G. The Programming Language Jigsaw: Mmixins, Modularity and Multiple Inheritance. PhD thesis, University of Utah; 1992.

16. Bracha G, Cook W. Mixin-based inheritance. In: Proceedings of ACM Symposium on Object-Oriented Programming: Systems, Languages and Applications. ACM Press; 1990: 303–311. SIGPLAN Notices 25 (10).

17. Liang S, Hudak P, Jones M. Monad transformers and modular interpreters. In: *Proceedings of ACM Symposium on Principles of Programming Languages*. San Francisco: ACM Press; 1995, p. 333–343.

18. Duggan D. A mixin-based, semantics-based approach to reusing domain-specific programming languages. In: European Conference on Object-Oriented Programming, Lecture Notes in Computer Science. Cannes: Springer-Verlag; 2000.

19. Duggan D, Techaubol CC. Modular mixin-based inheritance for application frameworks. In: Proceedings of ACM Symposium on Object-Oriented Programming: Systems, Languages and Applications, Tampa: ACM Press; 2001.

20. Rosenberg D, Scott K. Use Case Driven Object Modeling with UML. Addison-Wesley; 2000.

21. Fowler M. Patterns of Enterprise Application Architecture. Addison-Wesley; 2002.

22. Atkinson M, Buneman P. Types and persistence in database programming languages. ACM Computing Surveys 1987; 19: 105–190.

23. Evans E. Domain-Driven Design: Tackling Complexity in the Heart of Software. Addison-Wesley; Boston, MA 2003.

6

Service-Oriented Architecture

If you google "SAP" and "Chuck Norris," the top site is SOA Facts.

—www.soafacts.org

6.1 SERVICES AND PROCEDURES

We saw in the previous chapter a domain-driven architecture that focuses on making persistent domain objects available to the application. The key part of this architecture is the gateway pattern that retrieves domain objects from storage and allows the application to manipulate these domain objects directly. Indeed, as the raison d'etre of DDD is to organize the domain logic around the domain entities, most of the application logic is in these domain objects themselves. A front-end service, the gateway service, is responsible for retrieving these objects and initiating processing, perhaps by spawning a user interface, but the main part of the logic is in the domain objects themselves. We saw in the previous section that accessing domain objects remotely does not scale with the fine-grained interactions that may be expected with many domain objects, leading to architectures that load the domain objects to the client, either as detached objects copied to the client or via a cached database on the client. In either case, the domain logic encapsulated in the domain objects executes directly on the client.

For SOA, the gateway pattern is an anti-pattern. Central to the notion of SOA is the encapsulation and abstraction of enterprise resources in the service of loose coupling and software reusability. We discuss these considerations in more detail in Sect. 6.6 and Sect. 6.8. As observed in Chapter 2, another significant motivation for SOA is the issue of heterogeneity in distributed enterprise software systems. SOA, a concept realized, albeit imperfectly, by Web services, seeks to control this

Enterprise Software Architecture and Design: Entities, Services, and Resources,
First Edition. Dominic Duggan.
© 2012 John Wiley & Sons, Inc. Published 2012 by John Wiley & Sons, Inc.

heterogeneity by using vendor-neutral open standards for communication and data exchange, and by abstracting the implementation details of the platforms joined by a SOA. The XML standards for exchanging data are only able to describe state, and not behavior. The unit of transfer now becomes, in middleware terms, a DATA TRANSFER OBJECT (DTO) rather than a persistent domain object. A DTO is an object that only carries data and has no executable methods beyond the defaults such as getter and setter methods for properties. In particular, there is no application logic associated with a DTO. In terms of the discussion of domain-driven architecture in Sect. 5.6, SOA follows the approach of detached PDOs illustrated in Fig. 5.16. If a persistence framework is used to manage entity objects exchanged with the database by a DAO, they must be detached before being transmitted to the client. As the DTOs carry no logic, there are no security issues associated with downloading them to a client. For example, for Web services, the client stubs and the formats for the DTOs are generated from WSDL interfaces; there is no opportunity for installing server code on the client.

Domain logic with this approach is no longer organized around domain objects, but is instead organized into services that are independent of individual objects. In terms of the robustness diagrams illustrated in Fig. 5.13, the controller logic stays with the service objects in the architecture derived from the requirements analysis and the entity objects remain as "dumb" database resources. Whereas the domain transfer object is an anti-pattern for DDD, it is central to SOA. SOA is, indeed, a procedural organization of the domain logic, as opposed to the object-oriented organization of the domain-driven architecture.

This distinction between the object-oriented and the procedural models is fundamental to understanding SOA, and it is worth spending some time understanding the point exactly. As noted in the previous chapter, the object-oriented programming model was developed to model real-world entities, each of which has an internal state that evolves over time. An object encapsulates the state of an entity as a collection of private variables and operations (methods) that operate on these variables. Method dispatch occurs on an object when it is sent a "message," at least abstractly consisting of the name of an operation to be performed and the arguments to that operation. There may be several different types of objects that share operations with overlapping names. The dispatch of a method, the choice of the operation to be performed, is therefore based on both the operation name and the type of the object.

The *procedural paradigm* decouples the operations from the data so that the "objects" become simple data values. Instead, the operations are organized into suites, sometimes referred to as *data algebras*, that exist separately from the objects that they operate upon. If objects organize the domain logic around the entities identified for that domain, then procedures organize the domain logic around the *use cases* from the requirements analysis. As an operation may be applied to several different types of data, the dispatch of the operation is based on both the operation name and the type of the value, as with the object-oriented approach.

A useful way to conceptualize the dispatch of operations on values is as a two-dimensional grid, organized around the operations that construct values and the

	Constructors of L	
Observation of L	empty	insert(n,L1)
isEmpty(L)	true	false
head(L)	_	n
tail(L)	_	L1
append(L,L2)	L2	insert(n,append(L1,L2))

Figure 6.1   *Constructors and observers for lists*

operations that compute with, or "observe", values [1–4]. This is illustrated for lists in Fig. 6.1. On one dimension, the columns say, we have the *constructors* that are used to build values. For example, for lists, a plausible set of constructors would be given by empty and insert. Starting from an empty list, constructed using the empty operation, we build up non-empty lists by inserting values using the insert operation. On the other dimension, the rows, in this case, we have the *observers* that access the values and compute over them. For example, for lists, a plausible set of observers would be given by head and tail operations, and a predicate isEmpty for checking for an empty list. The head operation returns the last item inserted into the list, while the tail operation returns the original list into which that item was inserted. Although definable in terms of these operations, it is useful for this example to consider the addition of a binary operation append for appending two lists together.

Object-oriented programming organizes this dispatch grid around the constructors. Each constructor represents a case in the building of a list value. In building a value, the constructor binds the data to the case of each observer operation for that data type. An example is provided in Fig. 6.2. We refer to this example as a *constructor-oriented representation*. The constructors are defined by the classes for building list values, Empty and Insert. Each class binds to the cases of each observer operation for that particular constructor. This is reflected in the interface for list objects, where each list object understands how to perform the isEmpty, head, tail, and append operations. For example, an Empty list object always throws an EmptyListExn exception when it receives the head or tail message.

Procedural languages organize the dispatch grid in Fig. 6.1 around the observers. For each observer operation, all of the cases for that operation are grouped in a single procedure. In turn, that procedure dispatches, by cases, to the appropriate observer pattern based on the data type of the argument. The example in Fig. 6.3 demonstrates this with a procedural implementation in Java, demonstrating that the programming style is not necessarily dictated by the language. The objects in this representation are DTOs, with no attached functionality. The run-time system type tags that Java attaches to objects are used in the observer procedures to decide which case of the operation should be dispatched. We refer to this as the *observer-oriented representation*. This is the organization that SOA requires for enterprise services, motivated by the need for loose coupling.

It will reasonably be argued that a service can, itself, be viewed as object-oriented. The service contract specifies an "object protocol." If the service is

```
public interface List {
  public boolean isEmpty();
  public int head() throws EmptyListExn;
  public int tail() throws EmptyListExn;
  public List append(List L2);
}
public class EmptyListExn extends Exception { }
public class Empty implements List {
  public Empty() { }
  public boolean isEmpty() { return true; }
  public int head() throws EmptyListExn { throw new EmptyListExn(); }
  public int tail() throws EmptyListExn { throw new EmptyListExn(); }
  public List append(List L2) { return L2; }
}
public class Insert implements List {
  private int n;
  private List L;
  public Insert(int n2, List L2) { this.n = n2; this.L = L2; }
  public boolean isEmpty() { return false; }
  public int head() throws EmptyListExn { return this.n; }
  public int tail() throws EmptyListExn { return this.L; }
  public List append(List L2) {
    return new Insert(this.n, this.L.append(L2));
  }
}
```

Figure 6.2   *Constructor-oriented representation of lists*

stateful, then that state is encapsulated by the contract, including access through the service binding. As a service can be identified with its endpoint URL, we can even treat a service as a "first-class" object in a program. The issue is the level at which one views the service. At the level of the domain model, where the focus is on the entities in the domain and the domain logic that governs them, we discussed in the previous chapter why loose coupling favors a procedural style of service definition, decoupling the domain logic from the domain objects. On the other hand, for the purposes of defining reusable service logic, there is reason to question if this procedural orientation is the correct one. At the level of services, one may consider issues of reusable services at a coarser grain, that of the business processes that services implement, rather than the domain entities and data values that they exchange and operate upon. This distinction between data and business processes is not a hard and fast one, since for example, a callback in an asynchronous service request is at the same level as the other data values passed as inputs to the request. The distinction is more one of granularity and one of the appropriate organizing paradigm based on the issue to be addressed. It does make a clear and necessary separation in the design of the software architecture between tightly-coupled local objects and loosely-coupled remote objects that implement services. The procedural view of SOA is useful for building loosely-coupled

```
public interface List { }
class Insert implements List {
  int n;
  List L;
  Insert(int n2, List L2) { this.n = n2; this.L = L2; }
}
class Empty implements List {
  Empty() { }
}
public class ListFactory {
  public static List empty() { return new Empty(); }
  public static List insert(int n, List l) {
    return new Insert(n,l);
  }
}
public class ListObservers {
  public boolean isEmpty(List lst) {
    return (lst instanceof Empty);
  }
  public int head(List lst) {
    if (lst instanceof Insert) return ((Insert)lst).n;
    else throw new EmptyListExn();
  }
  public List tail(List lst) {
    if (lst instanceof Insert) return ((Insert)lst).L;
    else throw new EmptyListExn();
  }
  public List append(List lst, List L2) {
    if (lst instanceof Insert) {
      Insert lstc = (Insert)lst;
      return new Insert (lstc.n, this.append (lstc.L, L2));
    } else {
      return L2;
    }
  }
}
```

Figure 6.3   *Observer-oriented representation of lists*

business processes across WANs. At a level above this, for reasoning about service reusability, there is good reason to believe that a different perspective, perhaps one that is more "object-oriented", may be a more useful perspective. We return to this point in the sequel volume.

6.2   SERVICE-ORIENTED ARCHITECTURE (SOA)

To contrast the perspectives of the service-oriented and domain-oriented architectures, Fig. 6.4 provides an example of a SOA organized into boundary, controller, and entity layers, analogous to that of Fig. 5.14. The central pattern in the

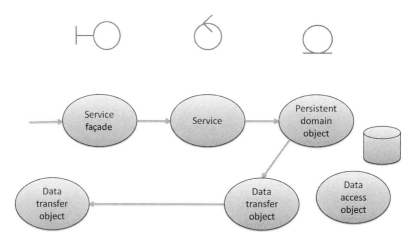

Figure 6.4   *Service-oriented architecture*

domain-driven approach is, as we have seen, that of the gateway pattern that is intended to expose domain objects to the application. Under the tenets of SOA, the gateway is an anti-pattern: SOA emphasizes encapsulating and abstracting resources, as discussed in this chapter. In the architecture in Fig. 6.4, by contrast, the gateway pattern is replaced with the SERVICE FACADE pattern. The service facade provides a set of procedures that encapsulate the underlying resources and domain logic, providing an external interface to clients that typically abstracts aspects of the these resources.

The service façade pattern provides a decoupling of the services provided by the application and the consumers of those services, facilitating the isolation of those consumers from subsequent modifications of the service logic. As described in Sect. 5.6, a service façade is a typical place where transaction management can be centralized. Each of the operations in a service façade implements the logic of a use case from the requirements analysis. When one of these opertions is invoked, a transaction is initiated, either explicitly by the operation, or implicitly by the container for the service façade based on meta-information associated with the implementation. The façade operation executes the logic for a use case, invoking back-end services, retrieving and operating on domain objects, and managing the synchronization of updates on those objects with back-end databases. Upon a successful completion of the operation, updates are committed to the database and transactional resources are freed up. A service façade should normally be a *project-specific* aggregation of more basic services. It serves to hide the complexity of the underlying collection of services, providing a higher-level API that may encapsulate logic for combined processing using lower level services, and isolating applications from the services that are not used. For example, an operation for transferring funds from one bank account to another, provided in a service façade, can make use of operations in lower level services for performing funds withdrawals from, and funds deposits to, bank accounts.

There are further refinements we can place on this notion of services:

1. *Entity services* or *basic services* are the definition of domain logic, now factored out of the domain objects, as we have seen. These are the essential building blocks for a SOA, providing modular, reusable service units that ultimately comprise the software inventory for the enterprise. Each of these services is identified with a business asset, i.e., an entity, with the expectation that it may be reused in several applications that reference that entity. As the building blocks for presumably multiple applications, it is important that such services be easily composable and schedulable across server clusters, so it is normally expected that such services be stateless. We discuss the meaning and implications of statelessness in Sect. 6.10.

2. *Task services* or *process services* are higher level units of business logic. Typically, these services are application-specific, only existing in the context of performing a particular end-function, and composing and orchestrating the activities of a collection of entity services. In contrast to stateless basic services, they may encapsulate stateful long-lived interaction with clients, perhaps expressed in a business processing language such as BPEL or BPMN. We consider service composition and orchestration more fully in Chapter 11 in the sequel volume.

3. *Utility services* provide cross-cutting, technology-specific functionality across domains and, as such, are not associated with specific business entities or applications. Examples include logging, transaction coordination, event notification, exception handling, and so on.

The layering of these forms of services into SERVICE LAYERS, with process services layered on top of entity and utility services, is a common pattern for service reusability. The lower a service is in this services "stack," the more important it is that it be defined for reusability, including context-agnostic operations, stateless semantics, etc.

Consider the example provided in Fig. 6.5, of an auction management service for sellers on an online auction site. There are two end-user services: an auction manager service for sellers and an auction closer service for buyers. The two services collaborate through a seller database service that keeps track of information for seller auctions that have closed. The seller's auction site account can be protected by only allowing the auction manager access to the auction site. Buyers interact with the auction closer service. Once payment has been made, the service forwards payment to the seller through a third party payment service, and arranges shipping through a shipping service.

In this example, both the auction manager and auction closer services can plausibly be regarded as "end-application" services, with little reuse in other contexts envisioned for them. We classify these as task services. As noted, such services are normally cognizant, rather than agnostic, of the context in which they are used, focused on a specific application and a specific class of clients, and not normally intended to be reused for other applications. On the other hand, an entity service

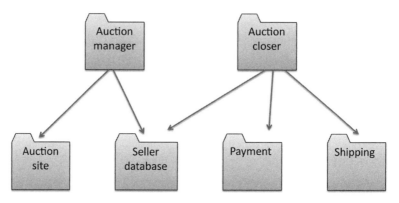

Figure 6.5   Auction services

such as the seller database service is intended to be a reusable asset in the definition of several services and applications.

Entity services are sometimes further classified into business logic and data services [5]. *Business logic* services essentially comprise business algorithms. For example, a financial institution in the business of granting mortgages to home buyers will have an algorithm for estimating how large a mortgage a prospective home buyer can afford to incur, given their income, career prospects, health, credit record, etc. While part of the back-end processing of mortgage applications makes use of this algorithm, it would be useful to also provide it to loan officers at local branches, to respond to consumer enquiries. Real estate brokers will also want access to this logic for evaluating which houses to show to a particular prospective homeowner. Consumers themselves may want access to this logic for their own evaluation purposes, for example to decide where to look for a house. As depicted in Fig. 6.6, SOA allows this logic to be factored into a standalone service, positioned in the software architecture where it can be invoked by back-end processing and by the branch loan officer while also being made accessible through the firewall to outsiders such as prospective home buyers and real estate brokers. Factoring it out of back-end processing, for example, avoids unnecessarily exposing the latter to network exploits, assuming that the back-end processing is in an enclave that prevents arbitrary egress from the rest of the network.

Data logic services constitute data sources in the enterprise, encapsulated behind a service interface. Figure 6.7 provides an example of the use of a data service. Fig. 6.7(**a**) shows two university departments, enrollment services and electronic classroom support, that track the students enrolled in courses. Enrollment tracks the students for billing and grading purposes, while classroom support tracks enrollment to restrict access to an electronic classroom to those students currently enrolled in the class. Periodic (e.g., nightly) batch jobs are used to reconcile the two departments' separate enrollment databases. Figure 6.7(**b**) shows an anti-pattern: the database is centralized in the enrollment service and is then accessed directly by the electronic classroom service. This violates the principle of loose coupling (discussed in Sect. 6.6), as the electronic classroom service is now tightly linked into

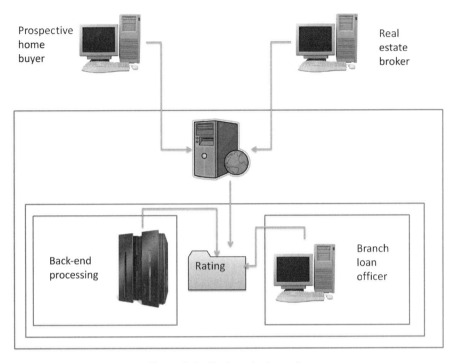

Figure 6.6 *Business logic service*

the implementation of the enrollment database. The preferred pattern of CONTRACT CENTRALIZATION disallows access to the functionality of a service unless that access is mediated by the service interface. Figure 6.7(**c**) demonstrates the correct way to structure this, according to the precepts of SOA: the duplicate databases are replaced by a single data service, with an interface tailored to the requirements of

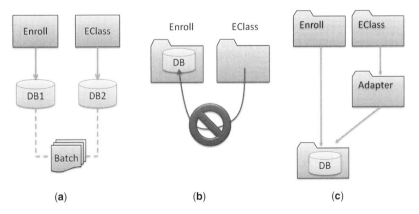

Figure 6.7 *Data logic service*

the enrollment service, and an adapter service mediates between this interface and the interface required by the electronic classroom service.

In the following sections, we consider SOA from the perspective of service design principles. In the process, we highlight some key design patterns that have emerged to support SOA. We begin with a summary of the principles.

6.3 SERVICE DESIGN PRINCIPLES

There have been many definitions of SOA through the years in which it has been advocated. Several principles are espoused in the SOA manifesto [6], some of which are:

1. *"Products and standards alone will neither give you SOA nor apply the service orientation paradigm for you ... SOA can be realized through a variety of technologies and standards."* This definition de-emphasizes the WS-* stack, perhaps reflecting some dissatisfaction with its complexity. At the same time, SOA advocates are arguing (not for the first time) that despite the failures of the technology, SOA is more than just Web services. The issue that gets closest to their point is that of SOA governance, which we discuss in Sect. 6.4.

2. *"Reduce implicit dependencies and publish all external dependencies to increase robustness and reduce the impact of change."* In the words of software components, strive for maximal cohesion within, and minimal coupling between, software services [7].

3. *"Recognize that SOA ultimately demands change on many levels ... Identify services through collaboration with business and technology stakeholders ... Verify that services satisfy business requirements and goals."* These principles place an emphasis on aligning SOA efforts with the goals and needs of the enterprise, rather than with the deployment of new IT infrastructure. There is a clear admonition to organize software services around the business processes of the enterprise, rather than around IT assets and processes.

4. *"At every level of abstraction, organize each service around a cohesive and manageable unit of functionality ... Evolve services and their organization in response to real use."* Do the previous step well.

5. *"The scope of SOA adoption can vary. Keep efforts manageable and within meaningful boundaries ... Establish a uniform set of enterprise standards and policies based on industry, de facto, and community standards."* Start small, and don't re-invent the wheel.

We consider some more specific principles in the remainder of this section. We draw on the set of principles identified by Erl [8] as a justification for a pattern language for SOA developed by the community [9]. These principles are broadly organized into two categories. First, there are the principles that introduce particular *design characteristics* of software services:

1. *Standardized service contract*: The service contract is a reiteration of the idea of an interface for a distributed service, the most important observation of the RPC technology. In turn, the notion of a component interface goes back to early work on component paradigms for software reuse [10].

2. *Service reusability*: Reusability is based on the notion of "context agnostic" services that can be used in a wide range of different application contexts. We have already seen an example of this in Fig. 6.6, with the business service for rating prospective home-buyers' purchasing power. In that example, the algorithm for determining the size of mortgage a customer can afford is reused in several different contexts, including back-end processing, at a local bank branch, as well as by customers themselves and by real estate brokers.

3. *Service autonomy*: This refers to the ability of a service to execute without its performance being degraded by the execution of other services. One way to achieve this is through replication, and this is a common strategy in server farms where a cluster of machines allows the load on a particular service to be spread across several server instances. We discuss this further below, including the use of virtualization to effectively manage resources.

4. *Service statelessness*: This property is an important property for the scalablility of Web services, as reflected by the fact that it is one of the most important properties of the REST architecture for the Web. We discuss statefulness in the context of design patterns such as partial state deferral, and we revisit this topic in the next chapter when we consider state management in RESTful Web services.

5. *Service discoverability*: We discuss the original vision of service discoverability for SOAP-based Web services and examine more recent ideas for global service discovery, as well as local service discovery as provided by frameworks such as Java EE and WCF.

Second, there are the design principles that *regulate the application* of the other principles:

1. *Service loose coupling*: This is a standard criterion for success for component languages. However, it is particularly important in wide-area enterprise applications, as we discuss below.

2. *Service abstraction*: Abstraction is a standard concept in computer science. In fact, one may argue that computer science is the science of abstraction, going back to early work in operating systems and programming languages [11–13]. We consider below what abstraction means for SOA.

3. *Service composability*: It should be possible to compose or orchestrate software services to perform a business task. We will defer a discussion of service composability until we discuss service composition and workflow languages in the sequel volume.

Figure 6.8 provides a summary of these principles and the related patterns. We consider each of these design principles in the sections that follow. Before

Principle	Pattern	Pg	Pattern	Pg
Standardized service contract	Schema centralization	224	Canonical Protocol	226
	Contract centralization	215	Dual Protocols	227
	Policy centralization	226	Canonical Expression	226
	Canonical schema	224	Canonical Versioning	231
	Compatible change	232	Data Model Transform	223
	Version identification	231	Partial Validation	224
	Message screening	223		
Service loose coupling	Service facade	212	Data Transfer Obj	208
	Contract denorm	223	Concurrent Contracts	243
	Proxy capability	299	Decoupled Contract	239
	Service callback	18		
Service abstraction	Inventory endpoint	278	Contract Centralization	215
	Exception shielding	263	Legacy Wrapper	244
Service reusability	Enterprise inventory	292	Entity Abstraction	295
	Domain inventory	293	Rules Centralization	298
	Logic centralization	294	Validation Abstraction	299
	Service layers	213	Agnostic Context	298
	Utility layer	295	Agnostic Capability	298
Service autonomy	Service normalization	293	Service Data Replicate	313
	Redundant implement	301		
Service statelessness	State repository	326	Stateful Service	324
	Partial state deferral	326	State Messaging	326
Service discoverability	Metadata centralization	342		
Service composability	Process abstraction	295	Non-Agnostic Context	298
	Reliable messaging	36	Protocol Bridging	229

Figure 6.8   Service and inventory design patterns

proceeding, however, we make reference to SOA governance, which is an important aspect of the practical implementation of SOA.

6.4   SERVICE-ORIENTED ARCHITECTURE (SOA) GOVERNANCE

SOA governance is a discipline growing out of IT governance. Interest in the latter has partly grown out of legislative requirements which, in turn, arose from lapses in corporate governance. For example, the Sarbanes-Oxley legislation in the US financial industry resulted from the collapse of firms such as Enron and Worldcom and the actions, at the time, of accounting firms, such as Arthur Anderson that were responsible for auditing these companies to protect shareholders' interests. The Health Insurance Portability and Accountability Act (HIPAA) legislation provisions governing patient privacy in the healthcare industry in the USA resulted, at least in part, from privacy breaches where, for example, sex offenders obtained contact information for patients from their records at hospitals where the offenders were employed. Interest in IT governance from a business perspective grew out of the "Year 2000" problem, when many resources were expended on upgrading software systems to handle the potential impact on legacy software at the turn of the millennium, due to the way that dates were represented, with controversy remaining about whether the problem was exaggerated.

Marks [14] makes the case for the *SOA Business model:* an enterprise is at all times attempting to optimize the utility of developing core competencies and assets internally, while "outsourcing" operations that are more efficiently implemented outside the enterprise. SOA is an enabling process and software architecture for supporting this business model, and the SOA business process is concerned with ensuring that IT operations are in alignment with business goals in furtherance of this business model. While much is made of service reusability as an end-goal of SOA, the emphasis here is on units of business logic or business processes, implemented as software services, rather than software libraries intended to support back-end IT operations. The focus is therefore not just on a coarse grain of software reuse, but also on businesss logic or processes as the reusable assets of interest. This is not incompatible with the focus of DDD, as we have seen in Chapter 5.

Weill and Ross [15] looked at IT governance in many successful enterprises and formulated a narrow definition of IT governance as:

Specifying the decision rights and accountability framework to encourage desirable behaviour in the use of IT.

They focused IT governance on five key IT decisions:

1. *IT principles* align IT decision making with the business goals of the enterprise.
2. *IT architecture* defines aspects such as technology standardization, and the overall enterprise architecture.
3. *Infrastructure requirements* define the IT assets required by the enterprise, such as networks, data centers, and computing needs.
4. *Business application needs* define the business need for internally-developed or commercial-off-the-shelf (COTS) applications.
5. *IT investment and prioritization* involves allocation of resources to programs and projects to meet the strategic enterprise goals.

As a point of interest, they also identify several archetypes for making these decisions in enterprises: (a) the *business monarchy* where decisions are made by top-level management; (b) *IT monarchies* where IT executives make decisions individually, or as a group; (c) *feudal*, where decisions are made at the level of an individual business unit, usually reflecting weak central control; (d) *federal*, where decisions are coordinated between regional or strategic centers and central management; and, (e) *IT duopoly* where decisions are made by two parties, typically IT leadership and top-level executives.

The key difference between governance and management is that the former emphasizes *stakeholder representation* in the decision-making process. These stakeholders include:

1. *business stakeholders*, focused on the business goals of the enterprise, are the consumers of IT resources and therefore of software services;
2. *IT stakeholders* typically act in the service provider role in the enterprise;
3. *service consumers* outside the enterprise may also be stakeholders in SOA decision-making, although typically SOA governance focuses on internal decision-making within the enterprise.

Stakeholder representation is important because of the ultimate business goal of SOA, to align the IT function with the business goals and operations of the enterprise. Business stakeholders must be involved so that IT decisions reflect business goals, while IT stakeholders must be involved so that business decisions are informed with respect to IT capabilities and the IT requirements that business decisions entail. While this is surely true of any modern enterprise, Marks [14] makes the case that it is particularly relevant for SOA because the SOA business model seeks to align the enterprise software architecture with the business processes of the enterprise. He therefore takes a broad view of SOA governance, going beyond the narrow definition of IT goverance provided by Weill and Ross [15], to incorporate SOA governance into overall enterprise strategic decision-making. He argues for a *SOA governance reference model* organized into different layers, which include:

1. *Enterprise and strategic governance*, with governance processes managed by top-level executives as part of an annual process and in tandem with decisions about budgets and resource allocations.
2. *Principles* that derive from the overall strategic goals and *policies* that are intended to ensure that these principles are adhered to in pursuit of SOA. Policies may be either business or IT-oriented; different forms of policies will require different procedures for their enforcement and for holding parties accountable for their adherence to these policies. An example of a business policy might be the "Chinese Wall" model from the financial services industry, where the same person cannot be on audit teams for two competing companies. An example of an IT policy would be the use of TLS to encrypt all enterprise communications at the transport level.
3. *Service development life cycle governance* may include aspects such as the management and use of the service inventory, which we discuss at length below. Other aspects include service registration and discovery, service versioning, etc.
4. *SOA governance-enabling technology* includes technical aspects of SOA governance, including the messaging infrastructure, metadata repositories, service design patterns, policy enforcement through WS-Policy, Web services management through run-time enforcement, etc.

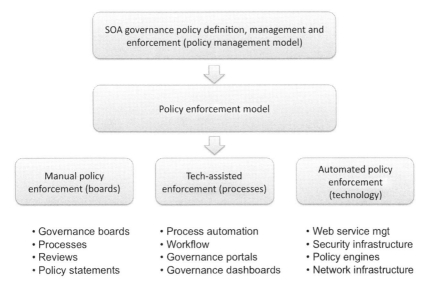

Figure 6.9 *Policy enforcement for SOA governance [14]*

Figure 6.9 provides a model for policy enforcement for SOA governance. This model reflects a policy enforcement framework that is part of a larger process of strategic SOA governance. The enforcement mechanism deriving from this will have both organizational and technical components. The organizational component will be intended to enforce business policies, and the typical mechanism for this is the use of SOA governance boards. The function of these boards is to ensure stakeholder buy-in for the policies being enforced. We will see examples of this when we discuss the software inventory. Perhaps the most important part of the functioning of such boards is to manage *exceptions* to the policies, as any agile enterprise must be able to recognize circumstances when adherence to policies should be relaxed.

The technical component of policy enforcement is reflected by several aspects of the WS-* protocol stack, particularly WS-Policy for annotating WSDL descriptions with policy requirements and then enforcing those policies at run-time. Between these two extremes, there may be opportunities for automated support for otherwise manual enforcement mechanisms, particularly through the use of tools for business process and workflow automation. Governance dashboards may also provide managers with rapid access to summary information about aspects of policy adherence, highlighting cases where exceptions have been provided, for example.

6.5 STANDARDIZED SERVICE CONTRACT

We have learned, from decades of experience in building software systems, of the importance of explicit and well-defined *contracts* or interfaces encapsulating the components of the system. Without such well-defined contracts, any enterprise software system is built on foundations of sand. Otherwise, incompatibilities and version mismatches creep into running systems as they evolve. Potentially, this will lead to catastrophic failure when an interface mismatch failure triggers a chain of application failures. As the experience of Mag.nolia demonstrates [16], any enterprise with an IT operation ignores modern software engineering practice at its peril. Even with well-defined interfaces, there is no guarantee of the absence of catastrophic failure. The Ariadne rocket failure, described earlier, occurred despite the application of sound engineering practices. The interface language was just not rich enough to describe the quality of service constraints that might have prevented the failure. If anything, this example only emphasizes that, without decent interface descriptions, any software system is doomed.

The primacy of the service contract is illustrated by the fact that the contract centralization pattern, discussed in Sect. 6.6 and illustrated in Fig. 6.7, dictates that all references to the resources of the service should be directed through the service contract. There should be no direct connections by service consumers to underlying resources such as databases or legacy applications. This pattern is motivated by the needs of loose coupling: consumers of a service should always bind to the service contract in order to access the service. Replacing or upgrading the service can be done by binding a new service to the contract without modifying binding between clients and the service contract. We discuss service versioning in more detail in Sect. 6.5.5.

Good interface design is a subtle and challenging art, and the only way to learn it is to spend some time studying well-designed interfaces. The principle of standardized service contracts provides some guidelines for organizing interface development by recommending policies and practices for the design of contracts. In general, a *service contract* will be composed of several parts: besides the specifications of the operations themselves, the contract will specify the data model for data that is exchanged by these operations, potentially quality of service aspects of the exchange, and some collection of specifications for how to bind to the service. We consider each of these aspects of the service contract in the following sections.

6.5.1 Operations Contract

A central aspect of a service contract is the description of the operations provided by the service. Perhaps surprisingly, this is a controversial claim for Web services. Although experience with operation-oriented service interfaces has been successful over LANs using RPC and RMI systems, the initial choice of an RPC style of interface for Web services has been an early failure. One reaction against this failure has been the RESTful or resource-oriented school of Web service development. This approach organizes Web services based on resources identified by URIs, and modified and queried by the verbs of the HTTP protocol. We consider this approach in more depth in Chapter 7. For now, we only comment that there should be no controversy about the need for a data model for the data being exchanged, and for a model for expressing quality of service properties, such as security policies for the data of the service invocation.

As we have seen, developing reusable units of business service logic is an important overall goal of SOA. This raises important issues of governance in terms of providing overall oversight to prevent separate departments and project teams from redundant duplication of efforts. Ultimately, the goal is to develop a *service inventory* of reusable software assets. The practice of CANONICAL EXPRESSION recommends a canonical naming scheme across projects for operation names in services, to facilitate discovery of appropriate reusable implementations.

As building and maintaining a service inventory on an enterprise-wide scale is unlikely to scale, it is recommended instead that the inventory strategy focus on developing domain inventories, discussed below. Ultimately, the goal is to develop services that are "agnostic" about the context of the project in which they are originally developed so they can be reused in other projects once they are inventoried. If the DDD practice of developing a domain-specific ubiquitous language is followed, then this can inform the choice of service and operation names in support of canonical expression. Further guidelines include a consistent choice of verbs and nouns, e.g., a consistent choice of CRUD verbs, using `get` for read operations, rather than `get`, `read`, `retrieve`, `report`, etc.

This can also aid with structuring services for CONTRACT DENORMALIZATION, where different operations may provide access to data at different levels of granularity. For example, a `getPatientRecord` operation may be provided for general access to a patient record, a `getPatientRecordAnonymized` operation for access to clinical information without violating a patient's privacy, a `getPatientRecordContactInfo` operation for patient information that does not reveal clinical information, and so on.[1]

6.5.2 Data Contract

At a minimum, a service contract should define a *data contract*, describing the data model that the parties must agree on for the data that is exchanged. Besides preventing run-time data format errors, input validation is also an important line of defense against network attacks by filtering out potentially malicious messages that do not match the expected input format (the MESSAGE SCREENING pattern). All operating systems perform input validation on arguments to system calls. Lack of precision in parsing Web site input is a source of many attacks, such as SQL injection and cross-site scripting attacks.

We have already seen (Fig. 4.10) the uses of XSLT between departments in the business tier, transforming data in transit between departments because of mismatches in the data models used by those departments. XQuery may be used between the business tier and the resource tier, mapping between the data model used by a business department and that used by a database or legacy application. This design pattern of DATA MODEL TRANSFORMATION is a common one in enterprise

---

[1]The REST advocate may have an alternative recommendation based on the pattern of these examples: a patient resource is identified by a resource—the specialized resources of that patient's anonymized information and contact information are provided as sub-resources by extending the URI for the patient resource.

software systems, unfortunately so because of the burden it places on computing resources and the cost in terms of processing delays. Some of these transformations may be unavoidable: the PARTIAL VALIDATION pattern refers to only performing validation on portions of an XML document: projecting out the part that has been validated and ignoring the rest. This can be used, for example, as a basis for filtering confidential information from data that is being made public, anonymizing patient health information or student grade information, or filtering confidential information and only leaving information that is viewable by the recipient of the data.

SCHEMA CENTRALIZATION refers to the recommended practice of developing an inventory of data models used by the enterprise. We refer to this inventory as the *schema inventory*. Organized on a domain basis, as suggested by the domain inventory pattern for services, the schema inventory corresponds to the data modeling part of the domain analysis done for DDD. Schema centralization enables the CANONICAL SCHEMA pattern that ensures canonical data models for domains shared by services, stored in the schema inventory and, perhaps, administered by a schema custodian. An obvious benefit of this is at least the potential for avoiding unnecessary data model transformations, as a result of disparities otherwise in the data models used by different departments or applications for common parts of the domain.

This sounds unobjectionable in theory, but obviously in practice there are governance issues that raise considerable challenges. Even done on a project-by-project basis, phasing in such a schema inventory over time, any project team will regard the centralized schema approach as unnecessary bureaucracy, jeopardizing the success of the project that the team is focused on. Therefore, a rational approach for the project team is to work to avoid the constraints of a centralized schema inventory.

Schema centralization should obviously be combined with canonical expression for service operations. The latter has the goal of standardizing operation signatures and the former has the goal of standardizing domain data models. This standardization is useful to avoid redundant effort as a result of different departments and project teams building data models for the same domains. This standardization of data models is necessary in order to provide some level of compatibility between organizational units that are ultimately expected to share and reuse each other's software assets.

Should subtyping between data contracts be allowed as it is with the lax versioning approach of WCF? This is a potentially controversial issue and one to which we return in Sect. 6.8.3.

6.5.3 Policy Contract

Besides the data contract, there are quality of service aspects of service invocation that need to be agreed upon. It will be essential, for example, to protect data being exchanged from malicious third parties by using cryptographic techniques, such as encryption and message authentication. State changes, as reflected by database updates, may be required to be transactional. In the WS-* stack, WS-Policy may be used to specify where security and transactions are required in the collaboration, as demonstrated in Sect. 4.4.3. Even outside the WS-* stack, security and transactional semantics are important for enterprise applications.

There are alternatives to the bureaucratic WS-Policy approach of annotating communication specifications with quality-of-service information. *Annotated types* are a well-known concept in programming languages, refining type specifications with additional information. We have seen examples of annotations on variable declarations as part of inversion of control and dependency injection. As another example, *security annotations* can provide information about confidentiality (who can read data) and integrity (who can modify data) that can guide the use of encryption and digital signing during transmission. End-to-end policies may be specified in terms of *information flow policies* [17]: Most simply stated, data is either "high" (private) or "low" (public), and information should never flow from high variables to low variables. In a distributed setting, matters are more complicated than "us" and "them." One possible approach to pursue here is to base information flow policies on access control policies. For example, in the approach of the *decentralized label model* [18], information flow policies, referred to as *security labels*, are based on sets of access control policies, Consider a healthcare example, where patients Jules and Jim may have provided Dr. Kildare with access to their health records for an AIDS clinic that they visit. The policies defined by Jules and Jim are named $Policy_1$ and $Policy_2$, respectively. Dr. Kildare performs a comparison of their responses to anti-retroviral treatments. The result of that comparison, based as it was on the access control policies $Policy_1$ and $Policy_2$, has a security label defined by the set of policies $\{Policy_1, Policy_2\}$. Dr. Kildare cannot provide the result of this comparison to Dr. Welby because the policies in the security label only provide Dr. Kildare access to the result. In fact, neither Jules nor Jim can see the result, although they each have access to their own health records. For Dr. Kildare to release the result of the comparison to Dr. Welby, he must first obtain the permission of Jules and Jim, effectively asking them to *declassify* their health records to Dr. Welby. Security policies like this can be enforced by programming language compilers during program static checking. There are several alternatives for mapping this to distributed systems: one may associate principals in security policies with cryptographic keys that are managed by an underlying public key infrastructure (PKI) [19], or one may make cryptographic keys explicit in policies by identifying them with principals [20, 21] similar to the Simple Distributed Security Infrastructure (SDSI) [22], for example.

This has only provided a sample of some of the alternatives that are available for modeling policies via annotated types. Indeed, despite its name, WS-Policy is a standard for specifying *mechanism* (e.g., secure HTTP or WS-Security for securing communication), rather than for specifying *policy*. A true specification of policy would describe the confidentiality and integrity properties required of the data. The actual mechanisms to enforce this policy would then form part of the concrete binding for a contract. WS-Policy provides the latter specification of mechanism, rather than a specification of the policy that this mechanism should be enforcing. The above disussion demonstrates how policy specifications may be incorporated into data models as type annotations. Unlike WS-Policy, policies may be specified independently of mechanism and of the WS-* protocol stack. Furthermore, policies may be specified at an arbitrary level of granularity in message contents, whereas the finest level of granularity in WS-Policy is at the level of an entire message. Where some of the security policy cannot be specified statically but is determined at run-time, this can be expressed by expressing the static part in terms of roles in access control lists and determining role membership dynamically.

The best practice of POLICY CENTRALIZATION recommends a central inventory of policy assertions. Policies are not necessarily domain-specific, but do reflect different forms of cross-cutting functionality that may be required of some domain services. The policy languages themselves, one language for each layer of cross-cutting functionality, are defined in the *policy inventory* and incorporated into service contracts where the particular cross-cutting functionality is specified. For example, specifying the use of WS-Security mechanisms in service contracts is specified in a WSDL binding using the language of WS-Policy for incorporating policy assertions. The assertions themselves are defined in the WS-SecurityPolicy language. The use of policy specifications assumes run-time system support for the enforcement of the corresponding policies, for example in an enterprise service bus, to ensure that applications are properly following the policy requirements.

6.5.4 Binding Contract

The *binding contract* specifies how clients connect to a service. It is specified in WSDL using the binding part of the Web service interface which specifies the transfer protocol that should be used to connect to the service. We have seen in Fig. 6.7 that the centralized contract pattern dictates that all consumers of a service should bind to the service contract and not access the underlying algorithms or resources directly. The CANONICAL PROTOCOL pattern dictates that, in addition, a single transfer protocol should be used to access the service. The intention is to avoid scenarios where, within an enterprise for example, services become connected through a proliferation of different proprietary transfer protocols. The result is a violation of the principle of loose coupling. By binding services in the service inventory to different protocols, this complicates the job of composing services from the inventory in an application. By binding a service to a particular protocol implementation, this complicates the task of later upgrading a service to a new, presumably improved, implementation that may not support the proprietary protocol of the original. Avoiding this form of tight coupling was a large part of the motivation for the original development of SOAP-based Web services, as explained in Sect. 2.6. The canonical protocol recommendation is intended to enshrine the principle that all services should be accessed via the Web services protocol stack.

In practice, life is more complicated. There is more than one choice of a Web services transfer protocol, even just over HTTP. Besides SOAP-based Web services over HTTP, there are RESTful, or native, HTTP Web service transfer protocols. These may exchange data as XML documents, but RESTful Web services are increasingly likely to exchange data in the JSON format. Interface languages, such as WSDL, and programming environments, such as Java EE and WCF, support the definition of both SOAP-based and RESTful bindings for the same Web service—each binding specifying a different endpoint. For example, the SOAP-based binding might be favored by the software architect mindful of integration issues with enterprise applications making use of upper layer support for security and transactions. On the other hand, the RESTful binding might be favored for more loosely-coupled applications, where the use of facilities such as transactional coordination is unfeasible across enterprise boundaries. However, the canonical protocol pattern recommends that just one transfer protocol should be used for all services. Perhaps we can say that the transfer protocol in both cases is HTTP, but this is weak. Although Java EE and WCF include support for specifying both SOAP-based and RESTful bindings for the same Web service, it is likely that the programming styles of the two forms of bindings will be quite different, with the SOAP-based service relying on the WS-* stack for quality of service guarantees such as security and reliability, while the RESTful service provides a more end-to-end implementation that explicitly handles aspects of quality of service.

Another complication is that the Web service protocol stacks are usually inappropriate for use *within* a server cluster. The protocol stack is either expensive and slow (SOAP/HTTP) because of the overhead of processing XML-based messages, or lacking in mechanisms for security and transactional execution (JSON/HTTP), or both (XML/HTTP). Within a server cluster, tightly-coupled RPC protocols may, instead, be favored for communication between services. These protocols will typically provide a more efficient use of server resources, and integrate well with local middleware mechanisms, such as domain-based authentication and transaction processing monitors. The DUAL PROTOCOLS pattern, recognizing that there may be a need for more than one protocol for binding to services, recommends the separation of multiple protocols into a primary protocol and secondary protocols. The deprecation of the latter protocols indicates that they should only be allowed under special extenuating circumstances, such as a significant performance improvement, or a protocol-specific functionality that is required within the server cluster. Typical candidate protocols for internal protocols within an enterprise middleware are CORBA IIOP or WCF `NetTcpBinding`.

An example of the definition of multiple bindings for a service is provided in Fig. 6.10(**a**), using the API for Java EE. As we have seen, the components for defining business logic in Java EE are EJBs. The default binding for these components is Java RMI over IIOP, with the application service automatically generating CORBA servant objects to act as server stubs for remote service requests. Clients bind to the service using client-side stubs, using the CORBA naming service to locate the EJB service. This binding may be appropriate for tightly-coupled clients in a server cluster.

Annotations are used in Java EE to specify aspects of the binding. In Fig. 6.10(**a**), the `@Remote` annotation on the `TaxCalculatorRemote` interface indicates that an implementation for this interface should be exported as a CORBA service.[2] A class

---

[2]The use of interfaces is not required by Java EE, but we use them for clarity.

that implements this interface provides a service implementation—in this case the TaxCalculatorBean class. The service implementation is defined as a *stateless session bean*, meaning that no assumptions should be made about the EJB object retaining state between client invocations.

Two other bindings are specified for the TaxCalculatorBean service.[3] Suppose another service within the cluster, e.g., a shopping cart service, is a client of the tax calculator, but is, in addition, running within the same application server as the tax calculator. As both services are on the same machine and within the same process address space, it would be much more efficient to invoke the operations of the tax calculator as a POJO, rather than going through the unnecessary, and not insignificant, expense of an RPC protocol stack. The @Local annotation on the TaxCalculatorLocal interface indicates that a service implementation binds to this interface as a POJO, and the service operations can be invoked directly as ordinary Java methods.

Finally, the TaxCalculatorWeb interface specifies a SOAP-based Web service interface, as indicated by the @WebService annotation, with its one Web service method identified by the @WebMethod annotation. The @WebService annotation uses the optional wsdlLocation attribute to specify the location, in the file system of the archive file from which the service is deployed, of a WSDL contract for the Web service. The endpointinterface attribute of the @WebService annotation on the EJB class links this as a service implementation for the Web service contract.

Figure 6.10(**b**) demonstrates how clients may bind to each of these possible bindings for the tax calculator service. A local client will be running within the same application server as the service. Dependency injection was introduced in Sect. 2.5 and in Sect. 5.5, where it was used to declaratively inject (JMS and JPA, respectively) resources into fields in EJBs. In Fig. 6.10(**b**), dependency injection is used to declaratively specify that the program variable calculator should be bound to a service (an EJB with local interface TaxCalculatorLocal) that is a POJO identified by the bean name "TaxCalculator". This is the bean name declared in the @Stateless annotation, that provides a name for the tax calculator implementation within the application.

Dependency injection is also used to resolve the binding for the remote EJB reference calculatorProxy. The annotation specifies that the reference should be bound to an EJB with remote interface TaxCalculatorRemote. Resolving this dependency binds the reference to a client stub or proxy for a CORBA server object. The client may be running in an application server or application client container that supports dependency injection. Java EE uses JNDI as an API that abstracts over various naming services, including the CORBA naming service (we discuss JNDI in Sect. 6.11.2). If the shopping cart bean is defined in the same application as the tax calculator service, then the beanName attribute of the @EJB annotation again links this variable to the class of the EJB to be injected. Notice here that the name attribute of the @EJB annotation identifies this *reference* to a tax calculator EJB and this, in turn, can be used by deployment descriptors to override the binding specified in the annotations. We consider various possibilities for resolving references

---

[3] A RESTful Web service interface binding can be specified using the techniques described in Sect. 7.5.

```
@Remote
public interface TaxCalculatorRemote {
  public real compute(real amt, String state);
}
@Local
public interface TaxCalculatorLocal {
  public real compute(real amt, String state);
}
@WebService(wsdlLocation="WEB-INF/wsdl/TaxCalculator.wsdl")
public interface TaxCalculatorWeb {
  @WebMethod
  public real compute(real amt, String state);
}
@WebService(endpointInterface="TaxCalculatorWeb")
@Stateless(name="TaxCalculator")
public class TaxCalculatorBean
  implements  TaxCalculatorRemote, TaxCalculatorLocal
{
  public real compute(real amt, String state) { … }
}
```

(**a**) Service declaration

```
// Local client, e.g., another EJB running in
// the same application server as the service
@EJB(beanName="TaxCalculator")
TaxCalculatorLocal calculator;
… calculator.compute(amount,state); …

// Remote CORBA client, e.g., application program running
// in an application client, on the same enterprise network
@EJB(name="ejb/TaxCalculator", beanName="TaxCalculator")
TaxCalculatorRemote calculatorProxy;
… calculatorProxy.compute(amount,state); …

// Web service client, with Service class generated from
// the WSDL service contract
@WebServiceRef(TaxCalculatorWebService.class)
TaxCalculatorWebPort calculatorPort;
… calculatorPort.compute(amount,state); …
```

(**b**) Service clients

Figure 6.10 *Binding contracts for an Enterprise Java Bean (EJB)*

to EJBs in Sect. 6.11.2. It should also be noted that all of the attributes in the @Stateless and @EJB annotations can be omitted, provided there is just one class implementing the TaxCalculatorLocal or TaxCalculatorRemote interface, the container can automatically resolve the EJB references in the client examples above using the type information alone.

Finally, the Web service reference is resolved in Fig. 6.10(**b**) by using a service class that is generated from the WSDL contract. This class includes client stubs for invoking the Web service programmatically, using the endpoint URL defined in the WSDL contract. The assumption is that the endpoint URL is defined in the WSDL service contract and then hard-coded into the service class. We demonstrate the use of the service class for simplicity. It is also possible to just generate the stubs at compile time and then resolve the server dynamically at run time, for example using an endpoint URL specified in a message, or using a discovery service.

With the use of secondary protocols to access services within a cluster, there may be interoperability issues, for example where a CORBA service needs to invoke a service implemented using WCF. This is surely a case where the two services should interoperate over the Web services stack. However, this may not be so clear. Although Web services were originally intended for this kind of interoperation, perhaps inevitably, incompatibilities have emerged in the implementations provided by different vendors. There are also third-party gateways for interoperability that may significantly out-perform the Web services stack. SOA adherents advocate for abstraction over performance whenever possible, but the careful architect may wish to at least evaluate the costs and benefits of employing proprietary protocol gateways versus using a Web services stack for inter-protocol interoperation. The evaluation should include consideration of long-term maintenance costs associated with proprietary gateways. The PROTOCOL BRIDGE pattern, depicted in Fig. 6.11 acknowledges that a proprietary gateway may be a useful way to bridge two protocols, but overuse of this approach should be considered as an anti-pattern.

It is worth repeating that, in the examples in this section, accesses to a service are limited to the service contract, as dictated by the centralized contract pattern. The examples only demonstrate how multiple binding contracts may be specified for a service contract. Accesses to the underlying resources are always through the service contract. Furthermore, the admonition to use a single canonical protocol for all services, or at least a primary protocol and deprecated secondary protocols for special circumstances, does not bear on the protocols used by the services to access the resources they encapsulate. For example, if a data logic service encapsulates a database, it will typically bind to that database using either the Distributed

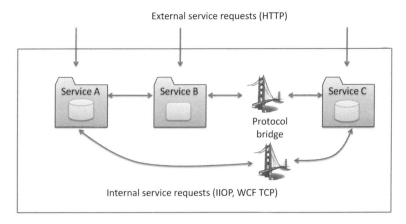

Figure 6.11   *Internal and external communications in a server cluster*

Relational Database Archicture (DRDA) protocol or the Remote Database Access (RDA) protocol. The use of these protocols should be encapsulated as part of the internal implementation of data logic services so that neither the canonical protocol pattern nor the dual protocols pattern bear on them.

6.5.5 Contract Versioning

Version control is a very important part of distributed services. If there is just one machine running with one user, software updates can be performed by stopping services, installing a new version of the service, and then restarting the machine. In a distributed environment, provided that there is centralized control of the IT environment, then systems administrators may be able to push out updates to machines overnight. If the enterprise operates on a 24-hour 7-day cycle with no scope for visible service interruption, there may be no choice but to perform "live" updates, updating services while they are in use by clients. Typically, this may involve deploying a new version of a service while the old version is still running, directing new clients (via DNS or IP routing) to the new version and taking the old version off-line as old clients complete their service. If services are long-lived, as they typically will be in B2B e-commerce, then it may ultimately be necessary, for business reasons, to update a service while it is processing client requests.

The traditional approach to version control in distributed services is the VERSION IDENTIFICATION pattern: contracts include information identifying their current version. The CANONICAL VERSIONING pattern recommends standards across a service inventory for describing the versions of the service contracts (with the usual governance issues for any pattern that uses the word "canonical"). Typically, version identifiers include major and minor version numbers, with the expectation that minor version updates are backward compatible with earlier versions with the same major version number. Another convention, used with XML namespaces, is to incorporate the date of a version release into its namespace. This may be used, for example, with major version updates, updating the namespace for the version contract.

Client service requests include the version of the contract that they have bound to, and a fault or exception is raised if this does not match the current major version of the service. If only the minor version has changed, the updated service may continue to support the earlier version of the contract in addition to the new one. This is an instance of the concurrent contracts pattern, described earlier in the context of concurrent binding contracts in Fig. 6.10. For example, a new tax calculator service might add an additional operation for computing the tax for a specified fiscal year (identified by a date in that year), while the original operation defaults to the current date:

```
@Remote
public interface TaxCalculatorByYearRemote
  extends TaxCalculatorRemote {
  public real computeByYear(real amt, String state, Date date);
}
```

```
@Stateless(name = "TaxCalculator")
public class TaxCalculatorByYearBean extends TaxCalculatorBean
       implements TaxCalculatorByYearRemote {
  @Override
  public real compute(real amt, String state) {
    this.computeByYear(amt,state,new Date());
  }
  public real computeByYear(real amt, String state, Date date) {
    ...
  }
}
```

For version control, a client should react to a version fault message by re-binding to the newer version of the contract. This may require generating or downloading new versions of the client stubs. Unless the new contract is backward compatible with the earlier version, as explained below, the client application will need to be modified and restarted. This is clearly an event that should happen infrequently; for mission-critical applications it should not happen at all except at well-understood update points in the application logic.

The COMPATIBLE CHANGE pattern recommends a practice of restricting updates so that consumers are able to continue functioning normally after the update, at least for minor version changes. To avoid service interruptions, it is worth considering what forms of updates allow for *backward compatibility* with older version contracts. The discussion of compatibility between schemas and their derivations in Sect. 3.4 highlights an important class of contract updates that provides this form of compatibility:

1. *Add additional operations to the service interface:* The client is free to ignore the additional operations. It is possible that some of the additional operations are specializations of existing operations that provide more efficient processing (e.g., return a patient's entire health record versus returning the most recent information about the patient). At least, the client has the freedom to decide if they are in a position to interrupt processing to update to the new contract.

2. *Remove operations from the client callback interface:* If results are returned through a callback service on the client, then operations may be *removed* from the callback interface without affecting the client as the service will simply no longer communicate with the client through the removed operations. The difference between this and the previous case is that it is the provider of the contract that is performing the update, and must therefore have updated its internal processing to bind to the new contract. The client can continue to function while being bound to the old contract. The point of this example is that the safety of adding or removing operations in a contract depends on the perspective of the party that has bound to the contract.

3. *Modifications to the data model that produce a compatible data model:* Examples of this are provided for XML schemas in Sect. 3.4, where the rules for deriving new complex types from existing complex types by

extension ensure the compatibility of the derived types with the original types. Such modifications in the data model for the service input are required to be *covariant*. Again, this is assuming that the data model is used to describe the *input* data for service operations.

4. For the case where the data model describes *output* data, such as in a client callback, the data model in the original contract must be backward compatible with that in the revised contract. This means that the client callback is compatible with the update because the service is *more* restricted by the update in the forms of result data it can return than it was before the update. Such modifications in the data model are required to be *contravariant*. We explain this notion of contravariance in Sect. 6.8.2.

5. If the same form of data may appear both as input to and output from a service request, then the model for that data cannot be modified by a contract update. Otherwise, the client must re-bind to the new service contract. Such modifications in the data model are required to be *invariant*. Web service contracts do provide an exception to this case (discussed below).

The discussion of version identifiers assumes that version updates for a contract are centralized. This is the point, for example, of standards organizations such as W3C and OASIS. Not only are versions distinguished, but it is easy to determine when one version is derived from another. For minor version changes, the latter enables the detection of when one version is backward compatible with another. Suppose, on the other hand, that version changes are not centralized and peer organizations, for example, are free to develop their own versions without going through a central approval process. This may be useful to allow an enterprise to develop its own local version of a data model, say for particular business documents for internal processing, while waiting for its business partners to accept the version change. A problem arises if another partner also develops its own update of the same original version. Without any central coordination, the two versions go from version k to version $k+1$, causing confusion because two different versions have the same version number. This is a problem with the representation of version identifiers as numbers. We can append the enterprise name to the version number to disambiguate version identifiers but then we lose the ability to determine the relationship between versions: is "Microsoft's Version 17" derived from "Oracle's Version 8" or vice versa, or are they incompatible? An alternative representation is as a version graph, that records a version as a sequence of unique version identifiers. A unique version identifier may be represented, for example, by pairing a URI for an organization with a sequence number generated by that organization, or it might be represented by a *globally unique identifier (guid)* that, with high probability, is unique. The sequence in the version graph lists all versions from which the current version is derived, from the original shared version to the current version. There are optimizations to this scheme that only record, for example, the current and previous version, but it is easy to construct examples where compatible versions are diagnosed as being unrelated (and therefore assumed to be in conflict), and where conflicting versions are recorded as being compatible. Another approach is to use *version vectors:* if there are N partner organizations, record versions as vectors of length N, where the ith element of the vector records the number of version updates for the data model performed by the ith partner organization. For example, if the partner organizations are Microsoft, Google, and Oracle, then a version vector (1,0,2) records a version with one update performed by Microsoft, zero updates performed by Google, and two updates performed by Oracle. Assuming that all updates follow the compatible change pattern, then data with version stamp (2,0,2) is backward compatible with the earlier version, as it extends the original version with an update by Microsoft. The version (1,1,2) is also backward compatible with the original version stamp, recording as it does an additional update, this time by Google. However, these two later versions are mutually incompatible and in conflict with each other as each of their histories include updates not seen by the other version stamp.[4] Version vectors are related to vector clocks (discussed in Appendix B). This scheme succeeds in correctly identifying conflicts, but requires more effort if the set of partner organizations is subject to change.

Most architectures for software update assume a centralized process [23, 24]: the provider of a service makes the change, and consumers of the service adapt as appropriate. Future systems will, no doubt, become more decentralized with organizations in collaborative enterprise partnerships not being willing to defer authority to perform updates (at least compatible updates) on shared service contracts and data models to their partners. Evans and Dickman [25] consider an architecture that supports decentralized software updates in a distributed environment. As depicted in Fig. 6.12, enterprises partition the network into *zones*, with contracts mediating the exchange of data between partner enterprises and, in particular, the versions of the data models used by the partners. Zones reflect regions where particular versions are in use. If an enterprise chooses to adopt its own local version, *change absorbers* are installed at the points where it exchanges data with partner enterprises to map between the different versions in a manner similar to the data model transformation pattern discussed earlier. The notion of zones provides a model for propagating version updates: as one enterprise accepts the version proposed by another enterprise, this acceptance is reflected by the modification of the contract mediating the exchange of data between the enterprises; the corresponding change absorber can then be removed.

This model makes no commitment to the semantics of change absorbers. Suppose a version update adds additional fields to a data transfer object. The transformation from new to old versions may simply delete the additional fields, while the transformation from old to new may add the fields with default values. This can cause problems with "round-trip" messages, where new version data is sent to a partner that is still using the old version data model. In the process of the data performing a round trip from the new version client to the old version service and back again, the additional fields in the original data have been transformed into default values. One might consider having the change absorber cache the values

---

[4]Version V$'$ is derived from version V if V $\leq$ V$'$. In general, if $V = (v_1, \ldots, v_k)$ and $V' = (v'_1, \ldots, v'_k)$, then $V \leq V'$ if $v_i \leq v'_i$ for all $i = 1, \ldots, k$. $V < V'$ if $V \leq V'$ and $V \neq V'$, i.e., $V \leq V'$ and $v_i < v'_i$ for some i in $1, \ldots, k$.

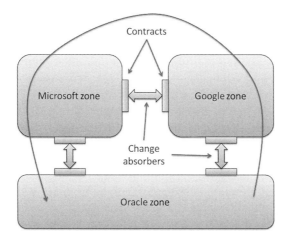

Figure 6.12 *Zones, change absorbers, and a round-trip message*

of the additional fields when removing them from the data object, and re-installing those values when that data object is returned from the old version zone to the new version zone; however, this is unlikely to scale. Potentially, a more scalable approach is to associate the inverse change absorber with the data object itself and execute this if the data crosses zone boundaries back into the new version zone. However, this only works for a simple roundtrip involving a request and response message. A more sophisticated data exchange might involve a data object from the Oracle zone being transmitted to the Google zone, then to the Microsoft zone, and, finally, to the Oracle zone. Simply attaching an inverse change absorber to the data object, to be applied when it is returned in a response message, does not help here in preventing information being lost as a result of the replacement of field values by default values. A final variant, if change absorbers are attached to data objects, is to apply change absorbers "lazily" when they are accessed, rather than "eagerly" when they cross zone boundaries [26]. Data objects accumulate compositions of change absorbers as they cross zone boundaries but the data itself is unchanged. Furthermore, examination of version stamps can reveal when application of change absorbers is unnecessary, for example when a message "round-trips" from Oracle to Google, then to Microsoft, then back again to Oracle. There are still some issues to be considered, for example caching of the results of applications of change absorbers, as well as trust issues if change absorbers can perform arbitary operations. These issues are resolved if version changes are restricted to, for example, the safe-type derivations allowed by XML Schemas. If data objects are mutable, intended to reflect updates contributed by the different parties that handle the data, then this raises other issues related to the handling of *view updates* in databases [27].

Consider, as an example, the support in WCF for versioning of service contracts. An updated service contract is compatible with the original if the change involves the addition of new service operations, without modifying or removing existing service operations, and changes to the data contract are compatible with the original data contract. Data contract versioning may be strict or lax. *Strict data versioning* is prescribed if clients may validate data exchanged with a Web service. Versions should be considered immutable under strict data versioning, so any version change requires the generation of a new contract with its own namespace, effectively a major version change.

Lax data versioning exploits the fact that many platforms do not validate XML data that is exchanged. As a result, both the addition and removal of fields in a data object are permitted in a data contract change. Additional fields are ignored by an old version receiver of data when de-serializing new version data to program data. Missing fields are replaced by default values during de-serialization, where callback operations may be specified to generate default values under application control. This is essentially the implicit application of a change absorber to the transmitted data during de-serialization, where the receiving process comprises a zone. Consider a scenario where an intermediate party, Julian, has updated a data contract by removing a field and acts as an application-level gateway between two other parties, Preston and Alan, using that data contract. If a data object is relayed from Preston to Alan via Julian, or if Julian returns to Alan a updated copy of a data object that Alan sends him, then Alan will only receive the default value of the field that Julian removed from his data contract.

Therefore, WCF versioning provides support for *forward-compatible data contracts*. If the program class for the data transfer object implements the `IExtensibleDataObject` interface, then an additional field is added to the transfer object, called `ExtensionData`. Any unrecognized (top-level) elements in the data are de-serialized to this field and, if the data object is transmitted, the value of this field is serialized back into the output data. The intention is to support round-tripping of data, where additional fields are ignored by the receiver, but returned with the modified transfer object if it is returned to the sender.[5] It is worth noting that XML Schemas may have an `any` content type that constitutes a wildcard for matching any content in a document. So, for example, the `<catalog>` element type from Fig. 3.23(**a**) may be modified to allow arbitary additional content, while still validating against the original schema:

```
<element name="catalog">
  <complexType>
    <sequence>
      <element ref="tns:content" maxoccurs="unbounded"/>
      <any/>
    </sequence>
  </complexType>
</element>
```

Changing data contracts by extending the set of subtypes of a type is not recommended for WCF, as this allows the possibility of an old version receiver not recognizing the additional cases provided by the new subtypes. In general, derived complex types that add subtypes are safe if consumers of values of the base type operate uniformly over all values of that base type and its derived types. Consider

---

[5]Round-tripping requires that the other party being communicated with does not perform validation on messages. Otherwise, this approach should not be used.

the example in Fig. 3.20 and Fig. 3.23. Provided a processor of a `<catalog>` element makes no assumptions about the content of the child elements beyond that specified by the `contentType`, it is safe to add additional subtypes for the content type and additional elements to the substitution group. The danger of run time type failure happens if, for example, an XQuery program uses the `typeswitch` construct to exhaustively test for all possible child elements in the catalog. This is the case where unrecognized child elements in the catalog will be discovered. If processing involves filtering a specific subset of the child elements, using an XQuery or XPath query, for example, then adding additional subtypes remains safe. Any additional otherwise-unrecognized child elements are simply ignored by the query. Unfortunately, if this filtering is only done on the data after de-serialization to a language such as C#, it may be too late, as de-serialization itself may fail on the unrecognized elements in the data.

6.6 SERVICE LOOSE COUPLING

We have discussed issues surrounding contract design at length because of its centrality to enterprise software systems. A large part of the motivation for explicit contracts is to provide decoupling of components in the software system, and we now turn to a discussion of the principle of *loose coupling of services*.

6.6.1 Motivation for Loose Coupling

There are several motivations for loose coupling. A motivation that is often cited by SOA advocates is that of *software maintenance and reuse*. If a software inventory can be organized as a collection of independent software units, with minimal coupling to other services, this will facilitate the reuse of those services. If an application is similarly composed from software services that are "agnostic" about the context in which they execute, then this will facilitate maintenance, allowing software services to be upgraded or replaced provided the underlying service contract is still honored. We discuss this motivation further in Sect. 6.8 when we consider the principle of Service Reusability.

A second motivation is that of *fault tolerance and scalable execution*. As stated in Sect. 2.1, the problem of implementing distributed software systems is the problem of independent failures. The challenge is to ensure that the system continues to function normally after some of the components in the system have failed. The more tightly coupled the components are in terms of their functional dependencies, the more vulnerable the system as a whole, or large parts of it, are to the failures of other components. This is not how distributed systems are intended to function.

There has been a great deal of research on constructing *highly available systems*. An example architecture for a highly available Web service was described in Fig. 2.10 in Sect. 2.3. However, the techniques that make this work do not scale to large numbers of parties or to large geographic distances. Instead, they are typically limited to use within a server cluster. For wide-area, intra- and inter-enterprise applications, the strategy is to limit the interactions and therefore the dependencies between diverse units.

A third motivation for loose coupling is that of *governance and trust*. Any tightly-coupled system that spans organizational boundaries, such as inter-department and inter-enterprise, raises governance issues in terms of who has control over what parts of that system. Consider just the ability to make a TCP connection to a machine: distributed denial of service (DDoS) attacks seek to overwhelm a target system by flooding it with TCP connection requests (so-called SYN floods), exhausting the buffer space in the TCP stack. This is an extreme example of the the vulnerabilities associated with exposing parts of the enterprise IT environment to outside parties. For this reason, enterprises install *firewalls* between the internal network and the wider internet, and typically only allow Web traffic through the firewall. Partner enterprises may seek to establish "trusted paths" that allow them to exchange information, such as opening ports in a firewall to enable virtual private networks, or using couriers to share USB drives or DVDs. Yet, as an example of trust violations, there are documented instances of consumer products installing rootkits[6] on the machines of consumers who purchased those products [28]. Perhaps the disincentives against such behavior are higher for enterprise partners than for consumers, as long as the partnership lasts. In any case, this is an indication of the risks associated with exposing any part of an enterprise's IT infrastructure to partners.[7]

A final motivation that is sometimes cited for loose coupling is *avoiding technological "lock-in"*. For example, a company may have built a business model on providing secure mobile enterprise e-mail services. At some point, consumers of these services develop a preference for more consumer-oriented smartphones, and a desire to combine this with their enterprise e-mail. If the original company has tied its e-mail services to its own proprietary hardware through various implementation assumptions, they risk losing market share to third parties who develop competing secure e-mail services, while they work to port their service to the newly popular consumer platform. Loose coupling aims to prevent this form of platform and technology dependence, at least insofar as it is possible. Some form of technology must eventually be used for communicating with clients.

This last example refers to the coupling of the service provider to a particular implementation technology. In the context of service contracts, it is sometimes stated that one of the goals of the service contract should be to prevent *clients* from coupling to the underlying service provider implementation. Thus, for example, a WSDL service contract, is in some sense, preferable to a CORBA IDL. This decoupling allows the service provider to change their implementation technology without being constrained by any coupling of service consumers to the preceding technology. For example, the provider may be able to switch between back-end

---

[6]A rootkit is software that seeks to hide its presence on a machine, while providing camouflaged administrator access. A worm that infects a machine typically installs a rootkit to cover its tracks while enabling later ingress.

[7]Even if one is inclined to sever all IT connections with the outside world, there still remains the largest risk for an enterprise: that of insider attacks.

database or middleware products if clients have not developed dependencies on the existing databases or middleware, such as the database query language, or the internal protocols used by the database or middleware. An opposing viewpoint, that of IT economics [29], suggests that clients *should* be tightly coupled to the service provider's technology, if this locks the clients into that technology and makes it difficult for them to transfer to competing service providers. Numerous examples of this exist, including competition among e-book reader technologies, where it is not in the interests of the competing service providers to support cross-platform e-books. Perhaps the sweet spot for such service providers is one where service consumers are tightly coupled to their implementation technology, while the providers themselves are not. In general, however, an installed customer base locked into a particular implementation technology also locks the service provider into that technology. This is the Faustian bargain made by all providers of services on proprietary platforms.

6.6.2 Contract Development

The role of a service contract in loose coupling is to minimize dependencies between the consumer and provider of a service by introducing a level of indirection between the two. This level of indirection is providing by requiring the consumer to couple to the service contract, rather than directly to the service itself. There are three possible scenarios for developing a service contract. The preferred and recommended approach, as depicted in Fig. 6.13(**a**), is to develop the service contract first and then develop the service implementation based on this contract. This is the *top-down* approach to developing a service contract. The difficulty with pursuing this approach, if pursued with Web service tools such as WSDL, is the perceived complexity of the WS-* protocol stack (including WSDL) and the baroque nature that the WS-*specification languages inherit from their XML origins. The examples of WSDL specifications provided in Sect. 4.4.2 give a flavor of the difficulty associated with defining and, perhaps more importantly, reading WSDL service contracts. The mechanics of what is being specified in these contracts is fairly straightforward but perhaps difficult to discern in the XML syntax. XML editing tools can ameliorate some of this complexity, with graphical editors for specifications that can shield the developer from the challenges of the syntax. An example of this is provided in Fig. 6.14.

The approach supported by most programming environments is, as depicted in Fig. 6.13(**b**) on the facing page, to generate the service implementation and subsequently the service contract from an implementation. This is the *bottom-up* approach to developing a service contract. It is generally regarded as an anti-pattern. The DECOUPLED CONTRACT pattern specifically dictates that a service contract should be decoupled from the underlying implementation technology of the service.

One may, and certainly should, avoid generating the contract from the implementation class. Instead, if pursuing the top-down approach, define an interface that is implemented by this class and generate the contract from the interface. This, at least, avoids having to unnecessarily regenerate the service contract if the internal

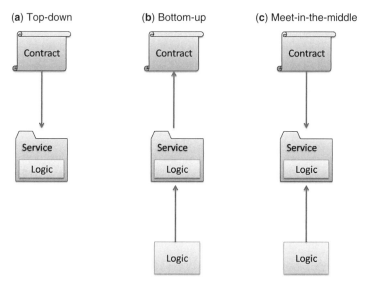

Figure 6.13   *Service contract development*

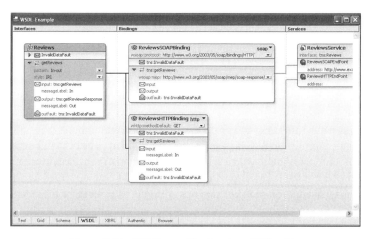

Figure 6.14   *WSDL specification in an XML editor*

implementation of the service is modified. It is also advisable to avoid those parts of the development API that involve proprietary extensions, such as WCF support for message round-tripping.

Ultimately, however, this strategy of generating contracts from implementa-tions is dangerous for the service developer. Service contracts generated from programming language-specific implementations or interfaces will inevitably, even deliberately, leak details about the language and the tools into the contract. The same is true of data contracts generated using proprietary tools from database schemas. Even if the tools generate service contracts that are in some sense inter-operable across platforms,[8] choices will be made by these tools that will be reflected in the documents they generate and that will be difficult to revise later once clients have bound to the contract.

Consider, for example, the following thought experiment: imagine defining a Web page in a rich text document editor, such as Microsoft Word or Open Office. Now, save this document as HTML and imagine the challenge of maintaining and modifying this HTML document over time. Alternatively, one may just try to edit the Web page in the document editor, saving a new HTML document every time a revised Web page must be published. Although the aesthetics of this process are questionable, it should at least get the job done: you will have succeeded in publishing the information you wished to on the Web.

This is essentially the approach promoted by popular development environments for Web services. The rationale is that the developer never has to read baroque WSDL specifications, but instead can develop and view service contracts in the same language in which the service logic is implemented. This is a seductive, but dangerous, strategy for developers. Pursuing it locks them into proprietary tools for service development. Even if there are no initial interoperability issues with clients connecting to the service, it will be difficult, if not impossible, for the service provider to later make a business or IT decision to switch to an alternative implementation technology. At that point, they will be locked in by the installed customer base that has bound to the contracts generated by the proprietary tools.

There is at least one scenario where the bottom-up approach is heavily used: that of refactoring legacy COBOL and CICS applications to make them available via Web interfaces instead of the traditional "green screen" VT-3270 terminal interaces. The amount of COBOL code in the world is still increasing, most of it no doubt as a result of XML filters and processors generated by proprietary refactoring tools.

The third route to contract development is, as depicted in Fig. 6.13(**c**), the *meet-in-the-middle* approach to contract development. This is the most complicated approach of all three alternatives, the least supported by existing tools and, there-fore, naturally a frequent scenario encountered by developers. Here, the situation is that an existing implementation must be exported as a service under a contract that has also already been developed. The existing service logic might be a legacy implementation that is now being exported as a service and the developer is fol-lowing best practice by not simply generating the contract using proprietary tools. Alternatively, this may be an existing service whose contract has been modified and now the service must be refactored to match the new service contract.

Solutions to this scenario were considered in Sect. 4.1.2. The obvious approach to this scenario (of defining in-memory transformations using, for example, XSLT) should be considered the approach of last resort, when other, more lightweight approaches are not feasible. As an example of a more lightweight approach, con-sider the JAXB XML marshalling API for Java. As demonstrated in Fig. 4.4,

---

[8]An example specification of what constitutes interoperability for Web services is provided by the profiles developed by the Web Services Interoperability Organization (WS-I).

this allows for annotations in schemas and classes to guide details of the translation. For more flexibility, tools such as Castor and JIBX support the definition of translations between program data and XML using external mapping rules, decoupling the structure of program data from its external representation in XML. These mapping rules form an important part of the service inventory. Some examples of mapping rules using JAXB and JIBX are provided in Sect. 4.1.2. The JIBX rules language includes support for extension hierarchies of mappings, supporting inheritance hierarchies that can mirror type inheritance hierarchies for schemas and program data.

6.6.3   Loose Coupling Patterns

We have already considered many of the patterns that are intended to support loose coupling. As observed at the beginning of this chapter, the service façade pattern is a key pattern for SOA. It is the controller of use cases for client applications. It provides access to underlying services, combining the facilities of other basic services, while abstracting away from the services in the composition that are not part of the service contract. The business logic of the service façade shields clients from the details of combining the lower level services, providing a layer of abstraction over these services. Besides the layered abstraction motivation, service façades play another important role in enterprise applications: they coarsen the grain of interaction between the client and the services. Assuming that the service façade runs, for example, in the same application server or at least the same server cluster as the basic services it invokes, communications between the services have low latency and high bandwidth. The service façade leverages this to provide an efficient execution of the composition logic, while using asynchronous communication with the client to compensate for high latency and discontinuous network connections.

Technically, a service façade has little internal logic of its own beyond that required to combine the use of other services. To be faithful to this definition, we should perhaps restrict the internal business logic of a service façade to, for example, the routing of service requests to its constituent services, overlaid with cross-cutting functionality, such as authentication and logging. Unless we make this distinction, we may be accused of allowing any composition of services to be called a service façade. However, we choose a broader definition. Another distinction that is sometimes made is between a service façade as a basic, or entity service, that is composed from other basic services, and a task or process service that is a potentially stateful business process composing other services. As we have seen earlier, the former is intended to be reusable software asset with wide applicability, whereas the latter is intended to be a an end-application with relatively little reusability. Again, we do not belabor this distinction when discussing service façades.

Figure 6.15 provides an example that includes service façades for a typical, successful business-to-consumer Web company. This operation may have started renting feature films online. At some point, they added a service that enabled users to provide reviews of films. These reviews are saved in a database, encapsulated

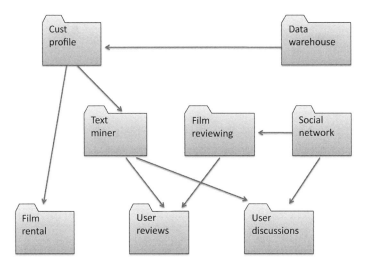

Figure 6.15 *Customer profiling services*

by another service to which only users registered as customers of the system have access. This film reviewing service eventually gets built out to a fully fledged social network, enabling public discussions between customers. This social network may have started as a commenting system for user reviews but eventually expanded into many different realms of discussion. The company realizes that there is business value in the databases that are gathering increasingly detailed information about their customers. A text mining service is developed to mine the text databases for users reviews and user discussions in the social networking system. A customer profiling service is built on top of this text mining service and the user rental records from the original rental service. Ultimately, a data warehouse service builds on top of the customer profiling system, building a treasure trove of consumer profile information. This data warehouse itself may become a data service made available, for a price, to third party enterprises, for example as a data resource for individualized marketing or election campaigns. At each level of this example, new services are built from the composition of existing services, encapsulating the lower level services and potentially adding new functionality.

Consider again the example of the auction service in Fig. 6.5. The seller database offers two service contracts: one to the auction manager service and another to the auction closer service. This is an example of the CONCURRENT CONTRACTS pattern where a service is coupled to several service contracts. We have seen another example of this pattern in the tax calculator service in Fig. 6.10. In the latter example, concurrent binding contracts were defined to support multiple protocols for accessing a service. The use of concurrent contracts in the seller database example has a different motivation: to avoid coupling two different classes of clients by requiring them to bind to a common contract that combines the different functionalities required by these clients. Instead, the contract is decomposed into two separate contracts, each specialized to the needs of the respective client class.

This avoids any client developing dependencies on parts of the contract tailored to the other class of clients. In the process, the service façades offered by the auction manager and auction closer services decouple clients of the auction management system from the seller database service. As long as the service contracts offered by the auction manager and closer services can be honored, the enterprise offering these services is free to modify the underlying database service.

LEGACY WRAPPERS are another pattern motivated by the principle of service loose coupling. Services avoid incurring an implementation coupling to any legacy systems by encapsulating those systems by wrapper services. The service contract for a wrapper, that should avoid implementation dependencies in the API, decouples other services from the underlying legacy system. We discussed legacy systems in Sect. 5.2 in the context of the anti-corruption layer, the name chosen in DDD for the legacy wrapper pattern. As described in Fig. 5.2, a legacy wrapper typically combines a façade pattern with an adapter pattern, the latter adapting the actual interface of the legacy system to an interface that is more useful for service consumers of the system and the former abstracting those parts of this service that are not of interest for the current application.

Figure 6.16(**a**) highlights one of the issues that can arise with wrappers for legacy systems. Consider the issue of services that use database back-ends. If an adapter is individually developed for each service for each form of back-end database that it may be deployed on, then there will be a proliferation and duplication of effort across services. A preferable solution is to abstract from the APIs provided by individual database vendors to develop a generic adapter type. Assuming that all services can couple to the generic database contract for this adapter, then each different vendor database only needs to be ported once by coupling it to the back-end database implementation. This is an example of the contract centralization pattern and is, indeed, exactly the motivation for the Java Connector Architecture (JCA). JCA defines both forward and backward contracts for an adapter that mediates between services running in a front-end application server and a legacy system such as a database that those services are coupling to via the adapter. At the front-end, the contract between client service and adapter is termed the Common Client Interface (CCI). Services couple to this contract by establishing a connection to the

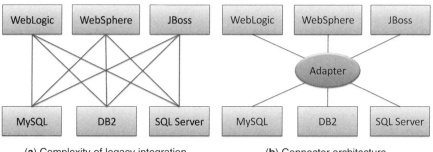

(**a**) Complexity of legacy integration   (**b**) Connector architecture

Figure 6.16 *Connector architecture for legacy integration*

adapter. In addition, the adapter defines system contracts with various managers in the application server. These contracts govern:

1. *Connection management*: Where the manager is responsible for managing connection pools to ensure the application server does not exhaust its resources;

2. *Transaction management*: Ensuring that operations on the legacy resource are transactional and integrated into other transactional operations as part of a service execution;

3. *Security management*: Managing user authentication and role-based authorization.

For integration with relational databases, a JDBC adapter is normally used, either Type 2 (for accessing a database on the same machine as the application server) or Type 4 (for accessing a database on another machine, using a protocol such as DRDA).

JCA is intended for other forms of legacy resources as well. Apart from relational databases, adapters have also been defined, for example for IMS, a hierarchical DBMS, and CICS, the transaction processing monitor that still powers most of the world's financial transactions. Figure 6.17(**a**) illustrates the use of a JCA adapter to provide access to legacy CICS applications. The intermediary may be a message

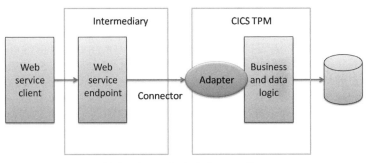

(**a**) Service endpoint in intermediary

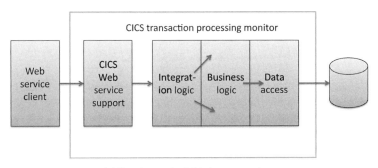

(**a**) Service endpoint in legacy system

Figure 6.17 *Wrapping legacy system as a service*

broker or an application server. In response to a Web service request, it establishes a connection to the adapter and through it interacts with the application. Interactions using JCA connectors are based on the transactional asynchronous exchange of messages with the legacy system.

For example, a legacy CICS application will have been engineered for transactional interactions with clients using "green screens" (3270 terminal screens). A re-engineering of this legacy application to interface with modern domain logic will make use of transactional message queues where the adapter simulates submitted screens using input messages and output messages are used to simulate screens for the next round of dialogue with the domain logic. Messages also keep track of the common area for dialogue-specific data which is stored by the legacy CICS system between exchanges. In this way, the integration between the domain logic and the legacy application is provided by a CICS adapter, with the domain client essentially co-routining with the pseudo-conversational logic of the CICS system. A service façade encapsulates this interaction, for example using callback objects to handle responses from the legacy system received as messages from JCA connectors.

Another approach to integrating a service with a legacy system is illustrated in Fig. 6.17(**b**). This approach makes use of the provision for defining a Web service directly in CICS. Application-specific integration logic provides the functionality of an adapter, mediating between the Web service API and the functionality of the legacy application. The integration logic will typically have been defined in COBOL, using language extensions to support XML processing and using proprietary tools to generate filters and transducers for XML data flows. This approach may be preferred if it is necessary to avoid the overhead of the intermediary approach. With this latter approach, the Web service connects directly to the legacy system. Nevertheless, while more efficient, it has all the dangers already cited of clients of the Web service developing implementation dependencies on the legacy system. For example, if the data is generated by proprietary tools, it may contain metadata to facilitate unmarshalling it back into COBOL.

6.6.4   Cost of Loose Coupling

It must be recognized that service loose coupling comes at a price. Part of the price is the extra layer of abstractions it usually imposes on top of the abstraction layers required for other design principles. Translating between these layers can incur significant overhead. In LANs, the performance bottleneck in network communication has been the cost of copying data between the layers in the protocol stack rather than the speed of network communication itself. Various approaches have been developed to overcome this bottleneck, such as safely sharing network buffers between layers in the protocol stack or allowing network device controllers to communicate directly (and safely) with application space. Techniques such as these are in widespread use in server clusters, where very fast network communication is essential.

Filter fusion [30] demonstrates one of several techniques that may be useful in reducing the overhead of layers of processing in SOA stacks. Rather than processing data by applying layer operations as the data is copied between layers, this approach combines the layer operations into a single combined operation and then applies that combined operation once. The advantage of this approach is the avoidance of the overhead of copying network data between buffers in the inter-mediate layers in the protocol stack. The key to the approach is the definition of a functional domain-specific language for defining filters and transducers for data flows in network protocol stacks. The design of this language ensures that filters are amenable to the optimizations that eliminate intermediate buffers. This is an instance of an optimization techique used in the implementation of functional programming languages and is known as *deforestation*.

Another downside of loose coupling is the lack of reliable failure handling in cross-network interactions. Failure handling inevitably involves separate nodes sharing state. The nodes might share a TCP transport connection, or they might share a custom RPC transport. Figure 6.18 illustrates some typical interactions over an RPC stack. The simplest interaction involves a request from the client followed by a reply from the server. The client then acknowledges the reply. The reason for this acknowledgement is shown in Fig. 6.18(**b**). The server's reply may be lost in transmission. For this reason, the protocol includes periodic Ping messages from the client to the request. If the server receives a ping after it has already replied, it responds by resending the reply message. The acknowledgement from the client then permits the server to discard the reply message and free up the buffer space. This buffer space, and the sequence counters that client and server must share in order to unambiguously identify request messages, are examples of the state the two parties are sharing in this tightly-coupled interaction. This form of tight coupling is considered too brittle as a basis for business interactions over WANs.

It may be possible to define a protocol that provides reliable communication while ensuring loose coupling between client and service. For example, an interface for reliably appending messages to a queue can provide two operations:

```
interface AddQ {
   int getRequestNum();
   void append(int reqNum, Object data);
}
```

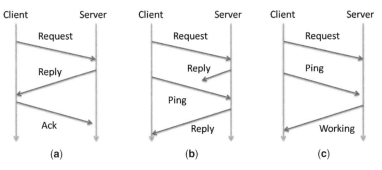

Figure 6.18 *Example interactions in an RPC stack*

The first operation is used by clients to request a sequence number for their next request. If we provide this operation with at-least-once semantics, the queuing service may generate several request numbers and the client simply ignores all but the one it eventually accepts. This sequence number is used in the append service call which, again, can be given at-least-once semantics, using timeouts and re-transmissions on the client side and acknowledgements on the service side. The service operation can ignore append requests if one with that sequence number has already been added to the queue. One issue with this approach is latency: the operation for obtaining a request number may request a sequence of numbers for several prospective requests to reduce latency. This protocol only deals with lost messages in a loosely-coupled fashion and does not completely handle service failures. Even if the service were to write a persistent commit record when it performed the operation, there is a race condition where the service might fail after performing the operation, but before writing the commit record.

In Sect. 2.3, we considered the problem of reliable failure detection in a distributed system based on non-receipt of heartbeast messages from neighboring processors. Failure detection protocols are, again, an example of tightly-coupled protocols that may be applicable in a cluster, but not among loosely-coupled processors.

6.7 SERVICE ABSTRACTION

Service abstraction is the necessary complement to the principle of the standardized service contract. If all coupling between a service provider and a service requester is mediated by the service contract, then service abstraction dictates that the client be isolated from aspects of the underlying service that are not relevant to their application. This is the well-known concept of *information hiding*. In some sense, this principle is a means to an end, where the end goals are loose coupling and service reusability. Abstracting service details is a necessary part of preventing a client from coupling to aspects such as the service implementation through the contract.

As noted earlier, abstraction is a concept that is central to the discipline of computer science. There are several different notions of abstraction that we review in the context of service orientation.

6.7.1 Platform Abstraction

Platform abstraction refers to the isolation of applications from the particular hardware and software platform that they run on. Historically, this has referred to hardware and operating system independence for applications. In the context of SOA, we must also consider dependence on the middleware stack. Historically, the solution to platform dependence has been to add another layer of abstraction above the platform. Examples abound, such as the Java write-once, run-anywhere model, intended to decouple applications from the Windows operating system. Similarly, the SOAP Web services stack was, at least in its inspiration, an attempt to abstract from proprietary and incompatable RPC stacks to support interoperability for B2B e-commerce.

The primary motivation for platform abstraction is implementation loose coupling, providing portability of services and applications across platforms, as discussed in Sect. 6.6.1. Another motivation is for security considerations. Although Kerckhoff's Principle [31] states that the security of a system should not depend on the obscurity of its security design, in practice network exploits such as buffer overflow attacks exploit vulnerabilities in protocol stacks and services that are usually platform-dependent. Therefore, in the context of defense in depth, there may be some benefit to not revealing implementation details, such as whether a Web server is Apache or Internet Information Services (IIS), when this is possible. An example design pattern for platform abstraction, one motivated by this rationale, is that of exception shielding, discussed below.

6.7.2 Protocol Abstraction

We have seen in Fig. 6.10 how in middleware environments the same service may have multipe binding contracts, each one defining a distinct protocol for using the service. In the earlier example, a service could be invoked as a local POJO, as an EJB (i.e., via the CORBA transfer protocol), or as a Web service. Similar facilities for multiple binding contracts are available in WCF. In this section, we consider support in WCF for protocol-independent service implementations. Besides the separation of service implementation from the underlying transfer protocol and data encoding, we also consider the relative flexibility of WCF and Java EE to adapt an interface to different programming styles. One can consider this a form of "application protocol abstraction".

Like WSDL, to which WCF interfaces are compiled, WCF distinguishes between abstract service definitions and their realization via concrete binding contracts. A *WCF binding* is a protocol stack for accessing a service. Some of the pre-defined bindings are:

1. `WsHttpBinding` is a reasonably full implementation for the protocol stack for WS-* SOAP-based Web services, including support for reliable messaging, security, and transactions. `WsDualHttpBinding` is a variant on this to support duplex communication using callbacks to return responses to clients.

2. `BasicHttpBinding` is a very basic SOAP/HTTP Web services protocol stack that essentially has enough functionality to move a SOAP message from point A to point B. It is provided for backward compatability with Web service implementations compiled to .asmx files in ASP.NET.

3. `WebHttpBinding` is the protocol stack for RESTful Web services.

4. `NetTcpBinding` is an optimized communication stack only suitable for use between WCF clients and services. `WsHttpBinding` uses the HTTP transfer protocol with text encoding for messages and the option of MTOM for binary attachments and WS-Security for message security. `NetTcpBinding` uses TCP for message delivery, binary message encoding to compress messages, and Windows Security for message security.

5. NetNamedPipeBinding provides access to the NamedPipe inter-process communication (IPC) protocol, for a WCF client and service running on the same (Windows) machine.

As with Java EE (Fig. 6.10), a service can be defined independently of the underlying binding.[9] In addition, WCF decouples the MEPs from the access patterns that services and clients use to provide and consume these services, respectively. There are three MEPs supported:

1. *Request-reply* is envisioned as the most common MEP: a request message is sent by a client and a response message is returned from the service.

2. *One-way* is provided for messages to be sent without requiring a correlated response message. In particular, if a fault happens with the sending of a message, there is no requirement that the sender be notified.

3. *Duplex* is provided for loosely-coupled duplex message exchanges. Whereas the other MEPs define a single service endpoint, with either "in-out" or "in-only" MEPs, the duplex WCF MEP defines two service endpoints, one for the service being invoked, the other a service endpoint for callbacks to the client. Both request and response messages are sent as one-way messages.

Figure 6.19 provides an example of a service definition in WCF that exemplifes two of these MEPs. The interface in Fig. 6.19(**a**) specifies a *service contract* for a shopping cart with interface IShoppingCart, using the ServiceContract attribute.[10] The service operations are identified using the OperationContract attributes. The ComputeTax operation is defined to use the default request-response MEP: the request message specifies a state in the USA and the response message returns the tax computed for the items in the shopping cart. The Add operation is a one-way operation that adds an item to the shopping cart where the arguments identify the item and the quantity to be added. The Checkout method initiates the checking out of the purchases in the shopping cart. It takes a purchase order number as an argument and returns the URL for tracking shipping once the goods are shipped.

An implementation of this service contract is provided in Fig. 6.19(**b**). In general *behaviors* in WCF are used to modify the run-time aspects of services and clients. The ServiceBehavior attribute in this case is used to define the *instancing* behavior of the service. There are three possibilities for the instancing of services in WCF:

1. *Single* instance: there is never more than one instance of that service running. This is useful for sharing state across multiple clients for a service, but obviously precludes replicating the service, which we consider in Sect. 6.9.1. The equivalent instancing specification is possible in Java EE with the @Singleton annotation for an EJB.

---

[9]There are some restrictions. For example, BasicHttpBinding does not support stateful Web services. We discuss stateful and stateless services in Sect. 6.10.

[10]In WCF, "attribute" is the terminology for "annotation" in Java EE, while "property" is the terminology in WCF for "attribute" in Java EE.

```
[ServiceContract(Namespace = "http://www.example.org/Shopping")]
public interface IShoppingCart {
  [OperationContract]
  public float ComputeTax (String state);

  [OperationContract(IsOneWay=true)]
  public void Add (String product, int amount);

  [OperationContract]
  public Uri Checkout (int purchOrder);
}
```

(**a**) Shopping cart interface

```
[ServiceBehavior
(InstanceContextMode = InstanceContextMode.PerSession)]
public class ShoppingCartService : IShoppingCart {
  float tax;
  public float ComputeTax (String state) {
    … return tax;
  }
  public void Add (String product, int amount) { … }
  public Uri Checkout (int purchOrder) {
    …    return shippingUri;
  }
}
```

(**b**) Shopping cart implementation

```
<system.serviceModel>
  <services>
    <service name="ShoppingCartService">
      <endpoint  address = "net.tcp://localhost:8090/Shopping"
                 binding = "netTcpBinding"
                 bindingConfiguration = ""
                 contract = "IShoppingCart" />
      <endpoint  address = "http://localhost:9000/Shopping"
                 binding = "wsHttpBinding"
                 bindingConfiguration = ""
                 contract = "IShoppingCart" />
    </service>
  </services>
</system.serviceModel>
```

(**c**) Shopping cart configuration

Figure 6.19   *WCF service definition*

2. *Per call* instance: a new instance is created for the service on every client invocation. This is obviously the best option for replicating the service. In practice, the server run-time might create a new service object on every service invocation, or it might maintain a pool of service instances to reduce latency. The equivalent instancing behavior is specified in Java EE with the @Stateless annotation for an EJB; this is also the instancing behavior required for Web services in Java EE.

3. *Per session* instance: the service instance retains its internal state across service calls with a single client. This is the correct instancing behavior for the shopping cart service, as the client will expect the contents of the shopping cart to be remembered by the service across service calls. There is more work to be done to support this behavior in WCF and we return to this in Sect. 6.10. The equivalent behavior in Java EE is obtained by specifying the @Stateful annotation for an EJB.

In the service definition in Fig. 6.19(**b**), the instancing behavior is specified to be per session. A client shares a session with a service instance created for that session. The proxy for the service instance is created using the InstanceContext class:

```
InstanceContext site = new InstanceContext();
ShoppingCartClient client = new ShoppingCartClient(site,"default");
client.Add("Enterprise Architecture", 39.95);
```

In the example in Fig. 6.19, two of the operations are request-reply, as they return results to the client. WCF makes a distinction between the service contract, which is purely a specification, and the client and server implementations. In particular, it is possible to define an asynchronous interface for an operation whose underlying MEP is synchronous, either for the client that invokes that operation or the service that implements that operation, or both. This is demonstrated in Fig. 6.20(**a**), where an asynchronous version of the CheckOut operation is offered to clients. For a synchronous operation F to be offered via an asynchronous API, the client contract provides two methods. BeginF is called by the client to initiate the service operation. This operation returns immediately with its result, a future that the client can use later to synchronize with the production of the result. The mechanics of synchronizing with the production of the final result are encapsulated in a second service method, the EndF method that returns the final result to the client. In the service contract in Fig. 6.20(**a**), the BeginCheckOut operation has an OperationContract attribute with its AsyncResult property set to be true. This identifies the operation as two parts of a synchronous service operation with an asynchronous API. The second part is the EndCheckOut operation that takes the future returned from the service operation initiation and synchronizes with the completion of the service operation. The client may register a (local) callback with the asynchronous service invocation, to notify it when the response is returned from the service provider.

It is also possible for an asynchronous API to be specified in the server-side contract, so that the server can implement the operation asynchronously. This can be a useful alternative to creating new threads for each service invocation, allowing the service to buffer pending requests while it waits for backend resource operations to complete. Fig. 6.20(**b**) provides an asynchronous implementation for the contract in Sect 6.20(a). The BeginCheckOut implementation creates a C# delegate for the operation implementation, CheckOut, that is assumed to be defined elsewhere in the service class. This initiates the asynchronous execution of the checking-out logic on a separate thread and the future resulting from this allows the service implementation to synchronize with the completion of the service request.

```
[ServiceContract(Namespace = "http://www.example.org/Shopping")]
public interface IShoppingCart {

  …
  [OperationContract(AsyncPattern=true)]
  IAsyncResult BeginCheckout (int purchOrder,
                              AsyncCallback cb, AsyncState s);
  Uri EndCheckout (IAsyncResult result);
}
```

(**a**) Shopping cart interface

```
public delegate Uri AsyncCheckOutCaller (int purchOrder);

[ServiceBehavior
(InstanceContextMode = InstanceContextMode.PerSession)]
public class ShoppingCartService : IShoppingCart {
  AsyncCheckOutCaller caller = new AsyncCheckOutCaller(this.CheckOut);

  …
  IAsyncResult BeginCheckout (int purchOrder,
                              AsyncCallback cb, AsyncState s) {
    IAsyncResult result = caller.BeginInvoke(3000, null, null);
    return result;
  }
  Uri EndCheckout (IAsyncResult result) {
    result.AsyncWaitHandle.WaitOne();
    return caller.EndInvoke(result);
  }
}
```

(**b**) Shopping cart implementation

Figure 6.20 *WCF service definition with asynchronous method implementation*

It should be noted that, in the case of either the client-side asynchronous service invocation or server-side asynchronous service implementation, the underlying MEP is exactly the same as it was with the earlier synchronous implementation in Fig. 6.19: a request message is sent from the client to initiate the service operation and a response message is eventually returned on the same transport connection as the request message was sent from the service back to the client. The difference is that the asynchronous API allows work to be performed, on the client or on the server, while the service operation is executed in parallel.

Another way of defining asynchronous communication in WCF is with the duplex MEP. In this case, the service contract defines two interfaces: an interface for clients to call into service operations and a callback interface that the service can use to call back to the client, e.g., with the result of a long-lived operation. Whereas the response message for asynchronous service invocation demonstrated in Fig. 6.20 is along the same transport connection as the original request message, in the case of a duplex operation the response message will be on a different transport connection (modulo TCP connection pooling). In effect, whereas the earlier synchronous operation implementation involved a single in-out WSDL MEP, in the case of the duplex WCF MEP, the operation involves two one-way WSDL MEPs, involving two separate WSDL interfaces: in-only and out-only. As no other

Web service impementation uses the out-only MEP, this makes the duplex MEP for WCF non-interoperable with other Web service stacks [32].

Among the properties specified in the service contract in Fig. 6.21(**a**), the Call-backContract property specifies an interface that clients are expected to implement in order to support callbacks from the service to the client. The callback interface, IShoppingCB, specifies a single one-way message for confirmation to the client when the purchased goods have shipped. The service operation for checking out is now specified as a one-way operation, with no return result. In a curious design decision for WCF, there is no correlation in the service contract between the service operations and the corresponding callback operations.

```
public interface IShoppingCB {
  [OperationContract(IsOneWay=true)]
  void Confirm (Uri tracking);
}

[ServiceContract(Namespace = "http://www.example.com/Shopping",
                 CallbackContract = typeof(IShoppingCB))]
public interface IShoppingCart {
  …
  [OperationContract(IsOneWay=true)]
  void Checkout (String shipToAddr);
}
```

(**a**) Shopping cart interface

```
[ServiceBehavior(InstanceContextMode = InstanceContextMode.PerSession)]
public class ShoppingCartService : IShoppingCart {
  IShoppingCB callback = null;
  public ShoppingCartService() {
    callback =
      OperationContext.Current.GetCallbackChannel<IShoppingCB>();
  }
  public void Checkout (String shipToAddr) {
    …    callback.Confirm(…);
  }
}
```

(**b**) Shopping cart implementation

```
<system.serviceModel>
  <services>
    <service name="ShoppingCartService">
      <endpoint  address = "http://localhost:9000/Shopping"
                 binding = "wsDualHttpBinding"
                 bindingConfiguration = ""
                 contract = "IShoppingCart" />
    </service>
  </services>
</system.serviceModel>
```

(**c**) Shopping cart configuration

Figure 6.21 *WCF service definition with duplex method*

Internally, the service implementation in Fig. 6.21(**b**) obtains a reference to a client callback service using a method in the `OperationContext` class. If a binding is the specification of a communication protocol stack, then a channel is a realization of this protocol stack. Remembering that an instance of this service will be created for the duration of a session with a client, the `OperationContext.Current.GetCallbackChannel` method allows the service to get a reference to the channel to the callback provided by the client for this session. This callback is used in the `Checkout` operation implementation to supply tracking information to the client as part of the confirmation of shipping. A client of this service now needs to provide an implementation for the callback interface:

```
public class ShoppingCB : IShoppingCB {
  public void Confirm (Uri shipping) { … }
}


InstanceContext site = new InstanceContext(new ShoppingCB());
ShoppingCartClient client = new ShoppingCartClient(site,"default");
client.Add("Enterprise Architecture", 39.95);
```

An example configuration for this duplex service is provided in Fig. 6.21(**c**). Because of the need for clients to provide a callback interface, either `WsDualHttp-Binding` or `NetTcpBinding` must be specified as bindings. The former specifies two HTTP transports for communication, the latter specifies a duplex TCP transport connection between two WCF parties.

Figure 6.22 demonstrates some of the choices in Java EE. The EJB (i.e., CORBA) interface in Fig. 6.22(**a**) allows the specification of some of the methods as asynchronous. For those asynchronous methods that return results, the result type must be a future. A client uses the blocking `get` method for a future to synchronize with the completion of the service operation:

```
Future<Url> result = shoppingCart.checkOut(…);
…
Url shippingUrl = result.get();
```

Within the service implementation, the mechanics of synchronization are hidden by the container. The implementation just has to be sure to return a future as its final result:

```
public class ShoppingCartBean implements ShoppingCartRemote {
  @Resource SessionContext ctx;
  public Future<Url> checkOut (int purchOrder) {
    … do some processing, generate url …
    if (ctx.wasCancelled) return null;
    else return new AsyncResult<Url>(url);
  }
}
```

As the future provides the client with the ability to cancel the operation asynchronously, the service implementation checks that this has not been done before

```
@Remote
public interface ShoppingCartRemote {
  public float computeTax (String state);

  @Asynchronous
  public void add (String product, int amount);

  @Asynchronous
  public Future<String> checkOut (int purchOrder);
}
```
(**a**) EJB interface

```
@WebService
public interface ShoppingCart {
  @WebMethod
  public float computeTax (String state);

  @WebMethod
  @OneWay
  public void add (String product, int amount);

  @WebMethod
  public String checkOut (int purchOrder);
}
```
(**b**) Web service interface

```
@WebService(name="ShoppingCart")
public interface ShoppingCart {
  @WebMethod
  @RequestWrapper(className="CheckOut")
  @ResponseWrapper(className="CheckOutResponse")
  public String checkOut (int purchOrder);
  ...
}
```
(**c**) Annotated Web service interface

Figure 6.22 *Asynchronous shopping cart operations in Java EE*

returning its result to the service container. The result is returned using the convenience class AsyncResult.

The Web service interface requires more effort.[11] The add method, that returns no result to the client but only modifies the service state, is easily made an asynchronous operation with the @OneWay annotation. However, asynchronous request-reply service invocation requires exposing more of the plumbing. Figure 6.22(**c**) provides a variation on the interface in Fig. 6.22(**b**) where we name the wrapper classes for the request and response message payloads, CheckOut and CheckOutResponse, respectively. The service class (i.e., client stub class) generated from the WSDL interface provides asynchronous versions FAsync for each synchronous

---

[11] The management of internal state for a Web service in Java EE is essentially non-existent. We consider issues of state in services in Sect. 6.10.

operation F, returning a future when invoked. We can use this to invoke the checkOut operation asynchronously and later poll the result for its completion:

```
ShoppingCartService service = new ShoppingCartService();
ShoppingCartPort port = service.getShoppingCartPort();
Response<CheckOutResponse> response = port.checkOutAsync(…);
while (!response.isDone()) { Thread.sleep(10); }
String uri = response.get();
```

Rather than polling the service until it completes, we can instead register a callback with the asynchronous invocation of the operation. The callback must implement the AsyncHandler interface, parameterized by the wrapper class for the response message, and provide an operation that processes a Response object:

```
public class CheckOutCallbackHandler
  implements AsyncHandler<CheckOutResponse> {
  public CheckOutResponse result;
  public void handleResponse (Response<CheckOutResponse> response) {
    result = response.get();
  }
}
```

The callback is then provided with the asynchronous invocation of the service operation. As the response handling operation has no return result, any saving of the result must be to a global variable or a field in the callback object that is accessible elsewhere in the program. In this case, the result is saved in the result field of the callback object. We invoke the operation as follows:

```
ShoppingCartService service = new ShoppingCartService();
ShoppingCartPort port = service.getShoppingCartPort();
CheckOutCallbackHandler cbh = new CheckOutCallbackHandler();
Future<?> response = port.checkOutAsync(…, cbh);
try {
  response.get(2000, TimeUnit.MILLISECONDS);
} catch (TimeoutException t) {
  response.cancel(true);
}
```

The asynchronous invocation returns a future of type Future<?>, i.e., the result type is opaque. This is used to synchronize with the completion of the service invocation, timing out and canceling the operation after a period of time (two seconds in this example). Assuming the operation is not cancelled and completes normally, the result is left in cbh.result.

A final example of an asynchronous Web service definition is provided in Fig. 6.23. This example uses annotations defined in WebLogic as extensions of the Java EE annotations, that allow an asynchronous Web service API to be automatically generated from an interface where some of the operations are request-reply. The @AsyncWebService annotation specifies that the Web service in Fig. 6.23(**a**) is composed of asynchronous operations. As before, the add operation is one-way and does not require a callback. The @CallbackMethod annotation is used to specify that the computeTax operation is synchronous. Finally, the interesting case is for

```
@WebService
@AsyncWebService
public interface ShoppingCart {
  @WebMethod
  @CallbackMethod(exclude="true")
  public float computeTax (String state);

  @WebMethod
  @OneWay
  public void add (String product, int amount);

  @WebMethod
  @CallbackMethod(name="confirm")
  public String checkOut (int purchOrder);
}
```

(**a**) Asynchronous Web service interface

```
@WebService(name="ShoppingCartResponse")
@Addressing(enabled=true, required=true)
public class ShoppingCartResponseImpl {
  @Resource
  private WebServiceContext wsContext;
  private static final
  AddressingVersion WS_ADDR_VER = AddressingVersion.W3C;

  @WebMethod
  @Oneway
  public void confirm (String shippingUrl) {
    // get messageId to correlate reply with request
    HeaderList headerList =
      (HeaderList)wsContext.getMessageContext()
      .get(JAXWSProperties.INBOUND_HEADER_LIST_PROPERTY);
    Header relatesToHeader =
        headerList.get(WS_ADDR_VER.relatesToTag, true);
    String relatesToMessageId =
        relatesToHeader.getStringContent();

  }
}
```

(**b**) Client callback implementation

Figure 6.23 *Asynchronous shopping cart operations in WebLogic*

the checkOut operation, where the @CallbackMethod annotation is used to specify that the callback method for this request operation is called confirm.

An implementation of the client callback is provided in Fig. 6.23(**b**). Surprisingly, there is no provision in WebLogic for associating a callback interface with the service interface, as there is to support duplex methods in WCF. The WebLogic callback service implements a single service operation, confirm. The key step in this message is to identify the request message to which this corresponds. The callback implementation requires the support of WS-Addressing for including correlation information in SOAP message headers, as reflected by the @Addressing annotation. The duplex MEP in WCF uses the latter's support for reliable sessions to correlate response messages with requests, with the mechanics of this automated by WCF.

The following code assumes that the client callback service has been bound to an endpoint URL and binds that endpoint URL in all request messes that are sent. When the service is invoked from this client, it calls back that endpoint URL when confirming shipment of goods purchased:

```
ShoppingCartService service = new ShoppingCartService();
ShoppingCart port = service.getShoppingCartPort();
WSBindingProvider wsbp = (WSBindingProvider)service;
WSEndpointReference replyTo =
    new WSEndpointReference("<callback url>", WS_ADDR_VER);
String uuid = "uuid:" + UUID.randomUUID();
wsbp.setOutboundHeaders(
    new StringHeader(WS_ADDR_VER.messageIDTag, uuid),
    replyTo.createHeader(WS_ADDR_VER.replyToTag));
```

Software component architecture SCA [33] is another iteration of various software component architectures that SOA descends from, with much of the same motivation as WCF. SCA defines *components* as the basic building blocks for software applications. Components may be assembled into molecular building blocks, referred to as *composites*. A composite may contain both components and other composites, allowing a basic hierarchical structuring of software components (as composites). A component runs inside a process; the components that make up a composite may run in a single process, or in separate processes running on the same machine or distributed across the network.[12] A *domain* defines a particular vendor-specific run-time system. Each host is assumed to be part of a single domain. Although a composite may be distrbuted across machines, it is assumed not to span domain boundaries. Communication within a composite may use domain-specific (i.e., vendor-specific) communication protocols, so-called *wires* that are specified in configuration files. Communication across domain boundaries, including the invocation of non-SCA services, is assumed to be based on Web services.

A component in SCA is composed of implementation code and a deployment descriptor described in an XML-based configuration language (SCDL). A component exports *properties* that can be used to configure it, as well as *services* that export functionality to clients of the components. Components themselves require certain functionalities to operate, such as access to databases—this is described using *references* that are injected into components by the run-time system. A software implementation encapsulated in a component is intended to be isolated from the underlying communication infrastructure, with the actual communication system specified using a *binding*, in a manner analogous to WCF. In fact, WCF is envisioned as just another layer abstracted by the SCA protocol stack. Communication may be further specified to be asynchronous, using either one-way communication or duplex communication using a callback interface. There is also a notion of

---

[12]Given its history, adoption of transparent distribution in SCA is somewhat surprising [34].

scopes associated with components to ensure that state is properly preserved across service calls. A similar idea appears in Java EE's context and dependency injection (CDI), which we consider in more detail in Sect. 6.10.1. Both SCA and CDI have been influenced in this regard by the Java Spring application framework [35].

A configuration file in SCA has a structure similar to a WSDL description of a Web service. Rather than providing an abstract service description, the configuration file includes a description of the components in terms of the implementation languages for the components and the language-specific modules that make up the components. The concrete part of the configuration file includes a description of bindings to communication platforms, a description of the services provided by a composite, and a policy description that may describe quality of service aspects, such as security and reliability. There is at least scope for interpreting policies in a domain-specific (i.e., vendor-specific) manner, although WS-Policy is the obvious choice for a policy language.

What we can learn from these examples? The first point is to acknowledge the commendable job that WCF has done of separating service interfaces and implementations from the protocol stacks that they run on, with the obvious caveat that certain functionality, such as security, stateful services, and duplex communication will place restrictions on the underlying protocol stack. Some of this modularity is enabled by the fact that all data is XML data with the data format defined by data contracts in the service definition. The Java EE interfaces offer either EJB (Java RMI over CORBA) or Web services. The former is a legacy transfer protocol, but still one better supported by Java EE than Web services, as evidenced by the clumsy support for asynchronous Web service invocations and the lack of support for stateful Web services.

The various means of invoking synchronous services in an asynchronous fashion are optimizations for clients of the services. These are essentially workarounds to deal with latency issues in request-response messaging patterns across WANs. For long-lived interactions that might last minutes, hours or days, this approach is clearly inadequate.[13] For these forms of applications, the WCF duplex MEP or the asynchronous Web service interface enabled by WebLogic are more appropriate. It is unfortunate that WCF duplex messaging is not interoperable with other Web service implementations, and that `@AsyncWebService` is a proprietary annotation and not part of Java EE. On the other hand, all of WCF is proprietary. Both the WCF and WebLogic approaches to defining asynchronous Web services are unsatisfactory. The WCF duplex MEP provides no correlation in the service contract between the request operation and the corresponding response callback operation (although they are correlated at run-time using reliable messaging support). At the service design level, what should be a long-lived request-reply interaction is broken into two one-way interactions, both at the implementation level and at the design level, as expressed by the service contract. The WebLogic approach has the interesting property that the connection between the request and response is retained in the design document (the Web service interface) where the operation is logically a request-reply pair. Only the `@AsyncWebService` annotation reveals that this

---

[13]Perhaps long-lived interactions should be thought of as situations of extreme latency.

is implemented as one-way interactions in both directions for performance reasons. On the other hand, there is no attempt to relate this specification to a corresponding client callback interface. The `@CallbackMethod` annotation names the callback method for a request-reply operation, but does not relate this to a specification of a client callback interface.

In the end, all platforms provide the ability to define message exchanges as one-way exchanges. That is not the point. The point is that the various platforms provide varying quality of support for expressing the business logic at a high level and then mapping this logic, not just to various transfer protocols, but also to specific application protocols, such as request-response, request-callback, and other forms of multi-message protocols. The fact that WebLogic comes closest to providing this level of abstraction may be a result of a desire of the Oracle designers to enable interoperability between Java components and components implemented in a workflow scripting language such as BPEL. Whereas saving an entire execution stack during the progress of a long-lived interaction may not appear feasible for Java (although it is more feasible with virtualization), it is plausible for a scripting language like BPEL. In the end, this may be the point of a workflow language like BPEL, which is an otherwise conventional language with message-passing primitives, transactional semantics and a very bad syntax.

6.7.3 Procedural Abstraction

Another notion of abstraction relevant to SOA is that of *procedural absraction*, referred to in discussions of SOA as *logic abstraction*. Procedural abstraction is an idea that is at least as old as Church's λ-calculus from the 1930s [36]. It is the concept of the subroutine, abstracting over a behavior and then reusing that abstraction by instantiating it as appropriate in different applications. It is a central organizing principle in all programming languages. Dynamic binding of method invocation in object-oriented languages is a further development of procedural abstraction [4], delaying the binding for the procedure that is instantiated from compile-time to run time. Function pointers in C provide a similar level of abstraction.

6.7.3.1 Exception Handling   There is one aspect of procedural abstraction that bears further discussion in the context of SOA because of its bearing on service contract design. A procedure's "contract" will be specified by the *signature* of that procedure: the types of the inputs to that procedure and the types of the results that it outputs. This contract requires that clients that invoke the procedure only provide inputs of the specified types. There are usually other *preconditions* and *post-conditions* that are harder to express precisely. For example, an operation for performing a withdrawal from a bank account may require that the withdrawal amount be less than current balance. A violation of this precondition is a violation of the service contract.

Who is responsible for dealing with this violation? It must be the responsibility of the client, who has caused the violation in the first place. The operation has failed because, under the conditions of the precondition violation, the service provider can no longer make progress. The way this is handled in modern programming languages is that the service raises an exception. An example of this was provided in Fig. 6.3. It is the responsiblity of the client to cope with the contract violation, by installing an exception handler in the calling context before invoking the service, as illustrated in Fig. 6.24. The purpose of the exception is to enable the client to roll back the computation to a point in its business logic where it can recover from the error and continue.

The standardized service contract pattern dictates that exceptions, insofar as they comprise an important part of the interaction between client and service provider, should be specified in the service contract. For example, an operation for retrieving a document might have the Java signature:

```
void download(String lDoc, String rDoc) throws DocNotFoundException;
```

The parameters lDoc and rDoc are bound during service invocation to names for the local and remote document files, respectively. The exception DocNotFoundException is raised by the download operation if the file is not found on the server.

Java distinguishes between *checked* and *unchecked* exceptions. A checked exception corresponds to a contract violation, while an unchecked exception corresponds to an error that is raised by the run-time system, e.g., NullPointerException. Only checked exceptions are required to be specified in a method signature. The C# language does not support exception declarations in method signatures at all [37]. Part of the rationale is that exception declarations are said to violate procedural abstraction, revealing implementation details that clients couple to because of the checked exceptions they are required to handle. If a new implementation raises a different set of exceptions, the service contract changes and clients must re-bind to the new operation. However, a counter-argument can be made that an implementation error should be related to a specific service contract violation. Thus, the exception that is raised should identify that contract violation (e.g., DocNotFoundException, as in the example above) rather than

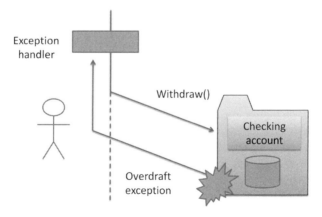

Figure 6.24   *Exception handling*

the implementation error it caused (e.g., `java.io.FileNotFoundException` or `java.sql.SQLException`). This philosophy requires that the service provider drill down into implementation exceptions to diagnose the source of the problem in the business logic before propagating the exception back to the client. If the failure is caused by contract violation, the server provider should then choose to raise a checked contract violation exception. The service provider may choose to raise an (implementation-neutral) unchecked run-time system error exception if the failure is outside of its control (e.g., the resource is currently unavailable, or a network failure occurred). The EXCEPTION SHIELDING pattern recommends this practice, independent of the issue of whether or not to declare exceptions, to protect against malicious attackers probing the service for platform vulnerabilities. There is a wider philosophical objection to checked exceptions in the C# language design: that clients have little interest in handling and recovering from exceptions. Instead, the preference is to shut down the program in an orderly fashion. This approach favors centralizing exception handling logic in one place. Where resources must be de-allocated under program control during the shut down, this can be done using the `try` ... `finally` construct.

6.7.3.2 *Effects and Resources*

The notion in Java, and other languages such as Mesa and Ada, of procedure signatures revealing the exceptions that may be raised in the execution of the procedure is an instance of a more general concept of *effect systems*. Consider, for example, a procedure that accepts an integer argument and returns an integer result. We can give this a procedure the abstract procedure type (`Integer`$\rightarrow$ `Integer`): a mapping from integers to integers. However, such a procedure may not only have an input and output behavior, but also have some form of side-effect that we wish to expose to clients of the procedure's interface. In the case of Java, the effects of interest are the exceptions that may be raised during the execution of the procedure. In other effect systems, the effects may record the use of resources in the procedure. An effect type for this procedure will have type (`Integer`$\xrightarrow{\varepsilon}$ `Integer`), where ε records the effect that results when this procedure is executed.

Figure 6.25 provides an example of the use of effects in the Cyclone language [38]. This is a C-like language with manual memory management and where effects are used to ensure the absence of memory leaks. The key idea is to allocate space in *regions* and use effects to statically ensure that there are no dangling references into a region when it is de-allocated. Every region has a region name `'r` and a capability `r`. Pointer types are generalized from `T*` in C to `T*'r` in Cyclone, where every pointer type records the region into which it points. Every region `'r` has a *capability* `r`, of region capability type `region_t<'r>`, that is used to allocate space in that region. The type system ensures that such a capability cannot outlive the lifetime of its region, so space cannot be allocated in a region once that region is de-allocated.

Regions are allocated within functions and effects associated with function names are used to scope the lifetimes of pointers into those regions. In the example in Fig. 6.25, there are two regions in the execution of the function `f`: the region `'r1` that is allocated by a client of `f`, and the region `'r2` that is allocated within `f`. Two

```
struct List<'r> {
  int head;
  struct List<'r> *'r tail;
};
int *'r g (region_t<'r> r, int ub) {
  List<'r> *r l = 0;
  for (int i = 0; i < ub; i++)
    l = rnew(r) List(i, l);
  return l;
}
int * 'r1 f ( region_t<'r1> r1 , int x) {
  { region r2;
    List<'r1> *r1 l1 = g (r1, ub);
    List<'r2> *r2 l2 = g (r2, ub);
    return l1;   /* cannot return l2 */
  }
}
```

Figure 6.25 *Region and effect based memory management in Cyclone*

lists of numbers are allocated by f, calling the function g to create each list. One list is allocated in region 'r1, the other in region 'r2. At the end of its execution, f returns the list allocated in region 'r1. Were we to attempt to return the list allocated in region 'r2, the type system would signal an error as no type reference to region 'r2 can exist outside of the declaration of that region. In this way, the analysis prevents a potential memory leak.

Another example of type and effect systems is provided in Deterministic Parallel Java (DPJ), where regions and effects are used to ensure the absence of interference between parallel threads [39]. A region-based type system ensures that every part of a data structure is allocated in a separate region. The key to this analysis is an effect system that records, for every method, the regions in the heap where that code modifies storage. The effect system ensures that pointers cannot be aliased, otherwise separate threads might follow aliased pointers to the same part of a data structure and interfere with each other during execution.

In Sect. 2.6, we observed that one of the challenges with SOA is the interference between services that access common resources (even if those resources are encapsulated as subsidiary services). As observed in component models for SOA, detecting this potential interference will require the declaration of those components' dependencies on those resources. Region and effect systems, as demonstrated in Cyclone and DPJ, are a general tool for performing modular analysis of resource usage that may have application in the analysis of software components and the specifications of their interfaces.

6.7.4 State Abstraction

State abstraction is the single most important principle underlying object-oriented programming. According to the precepts of DDD, "real world" entities are modeled

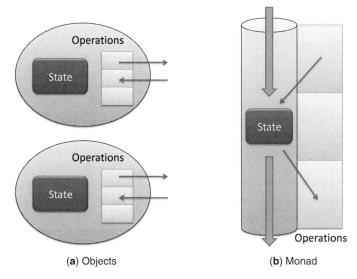

(**a**) Objects   (**b**) Monad

Figure 6.26 *State abstraction in constructor-oriented versus observer-oriented paradigms*

as objects that encapsulate internal state. An object defines a boundary around this internal state. As illustrated in Fig. 6.26(**a**), this internal state is only accessible to external clients indirectly, through an object protocol that mediates access to the object functionality. The object boundary also encapsulates the internal business logic of the object (the object methods). Abstractly, an object's interfaces define "messages" that it understands and each "message" corresponds to a part of the internal business logic. A message is "sent" with arguments to the object. As long as that message is included in the object's interface, it performs the corresponding business logic by invoking the method for that message on the arguments supplied with the message. In the purest manifestation of object-oriented programming, the internal state of the object is only accessible by the internal business logic and the interface provides a contract for providing clients with controlled access to that internal state. In practice, object-oriented languages provide direct access to this internal state, for example, by specifying `public` or `protected` access to fields in a class. However, this should be regarded as an optimization. For example, C# supports the specification of getter and setter methods for "properties", essentially virtual fields, and access to those properties is performed by clients using the same syntax as access to ordinary fields. It is this encapsulation of, and mediated access to, internal state that is the fundamental abstraction of object-oriented languages. We discuss this further in the context of data abstraction in Sect. 6.7.5. One can write object-oriented programs in assembly language as long as one correctly implements the abstraction of objects encapsulating internal state.[14]

---

[14] An object-oriented language that does not have inheritance and subtyping is sometimes referred to as *object-based*.

Typestate is a concept that extends the notion of the internal state of a program in order to support fine-grained reasoning about safe interactions with objects whose state changes over time. Typestate originated in the Hermes language of Strom and Yemini [40]. It corresponds to an enrichment of the normal notion of a type, to include the concept of types as states in a protocol for interacting with a program. This idea has been incorporated into object-oriented languages in a very natural way [41]: each object has a current typestate, and the interface offered by an object, in the sense of the methods that can currently be invoked on the object, are determined by its current typestate.

Consider, for example, a purchase ordering system where a purchase order is represented by an object, as in Fig. 6.27. We use hypothetical Java annotations to describe typestate in an object. The @Typestate annotation declares the typestates of the object. The @Pre annotation declares the preconditions for the execution of an operation: the typestates that must be satisfied. For example, a purchase order must be in the "Paid" state before the goods can be shipped. We interpret a collection of typestates in a precondition as a disjunction: the object must be in one of the specified typestates before the operation can be executed. For example, an order can be cancelled up until the point that it is shipped. Once it is shipped, it can no longer be cancelled (we do not consider a return policy). The @Post annotation specifies the post-conditions for an operation: the conditions that are guaranteed to be true when execution of the operation is completed. It is important to realize that

```
@Typestates("Open","Invoiced","Paid","Shipped","Cancelled")
public class PurchaseOrder {
  @Pre("Open","Invoiced","Paid")
  @Post("Cancelled")
  @NotAliased
  public void cancel() { … }

  @Pre("Open")
  @Post("Invoiced")
  @NotAliased
  public void invoice(…) { … }

  @Pre("Invoiced")
  @Post("Paid")
  @NotAliased
  public void pay(…) { … }

  @Pre("Paid")
  @Post("Shipped")
  @NotAliased
  public void ship() { … }

  public int status() { … }

  public float amount() { … }
}
```

Figure 6.27 *Purchase order with typestate interface*

these are *type* specifications of object state, and static checking includes verifying, before an operation is performed on an object, that the object is in one of the states described by the typestate precondition. The type of the object (the set of operations in the interface that it provides to clients) varies over time as object operations are invoked and the typestate is changed. For example, the `pay` and `ship` operations are not available in the initial typestate and the `pay` operation only becomes available in the interface after the `invoice` operation has completed. Typestate checking of the program is *flow-sensitive*, as it must account for the order in which the operations are performed.

As typestate is updated imperatively, it is important that aliasing of such objects be carefully controlled. Otherwise, the invocation of a method that changes the typestate of an object would leave an alias to that subject unchanged. This would essentially lead to a dangling reference, as the aliased reference would allow continued access to the old interface even though the change in typestate may make invocation of some of the methods in that interface an unsafe operation. The result would be a run-time error (essentially a typestate error) when clients with the aliased reference tried to invoke a now invalid method. For example, if `p1` and `p2` are two aliases to the same purchase order, and the purchase order is currently in the `"Paid"` typestate, then the following execution sequence may occur:

```
/* Assume Paid(p1), Paid(p2) */
p1.ship();
/* Shipped(p1), Paid(p2) */
p2.cancel();
/* Shipped(p1), Cancelled(p2) */
```

Therefore, the typestate preconditions include the `@NotAliased` annotation, which requires that there be no aliases to the object before the invocation of an operation that changes the typestate. For other operations, such as the query operations, no such restriction is necessary. Stork et al. [42] have demonstrated that a notion of *permissions*, based on the notion of capabilities for region-based memory management described above [43], can be used effectively to check the use of typestate and, in particular, the absence of aliasing in existing non-toy software systems. The challenge here is to ensure that such a capability is used in a linear or affine fashion, meaning that it is used exactly once or no more than once. However, this is a non-trivial undertaking. For example, näively storing a linear capability in a data structure also requires that data structure to be handled linearly. The approach of *focus and adoption* is one way of dealing with this, allowing a linear capability to be "adopted" by a data structure, with the capability used in a local context where there is a guarantee that there are no aliases to the capability [44]. We return to typestate in Sect. 7.6, when we consider a potential application in contract conformance for ROA.

As we have seen, in contrast with domain-driven architecture, we can regard SOA as essentially a procedural paradigm for organizing Web services. What is a suitable abstraction for state in procedural programming? The "pure" functional programming community, representing the procedural camp of programming languages,[15] has long wrestled with the right approach to abstract state. Pure functional languages such as Haskell, require that variables be immutable[16] for the purpose of referential transparency. A modification of state (e.g., an array update) at least abstractly generates a new, modified version of the original state. Imperative functional programs must then thread modified state into and out of procedures as extra arguments and return values. This must be restricted so that the use of the modified state is single-threaded, in order to allow updates to be done in place in the implementation. *Monads* are an abstraction that encapsulate this state-passing so that imperative programming can be combined with pure functional programming by masking the details of state-passing [45]. For example, here is an imperative Haskell program for a command line loop:

```
main :: IO ()
main =
do { line ← getLine      -- getLine :: IO Data
     processIt line       -- processIt :: Data → IO ()
     main                 -- main :: IO ()
}
```

The imperative computation runs inside the IO monad, that abstracts the passing of I/O state and ensures that it is used in a single-threaded fashion. This is illustrated in Fig. 6.26(**b**). Originating in the abstract mathematical field of category theory [46], a monad is an abstraction of a computation. There are two monad operations. First, the unit operation injects a value into a computation (it is analogous to a factory operation for creating computations). The getLine operation above uses the monad unit operation internally to inject a line of input (a value of type Data) into the IO monad. Second, the bind operation sequences one monadic computation to run after another, taking as its input the value computed by the first computation. In the example above, the use of bind is implicit in the "do" construct: the processIt operation takes a result of type Data and uses that result to build a monadic computation. The "do" construct sequences this processIt step to follow the getLine step, processing the line of input that is produced by getLine. Finally, the main step invokes itself tail-recursively. Again, the "do" construct implicitly uses the monadic bind operation to sequence this tail-recursive step to follow the processing of the line of input. We provide a more complete explanation of monads with further examples in Sect. A.3 (Appendix A).

With respect to SOA, monads are essentially a mechanism for abstracting cross-cutting functionality, such as logging, transactions, authentication, etc. Describing the compositions of these services in monadic terms, for example in a language for specifying business processes, enforces a protocol that requires all services to have certain *aspects*. Furthermore, the definitions of the monads describe how to relate

---

[15]For the purposes of this discussion, we draw the line between functional and object-oriented programming languages based on how the camps model state in programs.

[16]We consider functional languages in more depth in Appendix A, using Haskell as an example.

the processing of the aspects in each step, perhaps for example threading digital credentials through a chain of service invocations.

An interesting question is whether it is possible to allow a service to abstract over the monads or aspects it uses so that it can be reused in different contexts, based on the needs of the application. This abstraction over the underlying context in which a component computes, is a central concern in the SCA for component-based software reuse, described in Sect. 6.7.2. This abstraction over cross-cutting functionality can certainly be done with aspect-oriented programming. The issue here is specifying, and enforcing, a protocol of aspects that all services in a composition are required to satisfy. An example of this is provided in Sect. 6.10.1, using the framework of contexts and dependency injection which, among other things, provides some support for aspect-oriented programming in Java EE. There have been several investigations of this topic for monads, for example [47–49]. Monadic computations are inherently sequential, so its application to SOA is limited to single-threaded service compostions, e.g., in the single thread of control shared between a client and a server for the duration of a synchronous service invocation. The categorical concept of *arrows* has been used to generalize monads with applications in the semantics of data flow [50], i.e., in data-parallel computation. We consider an application of monads in RESTful hypermedia control in Sect. 7.6.

6.7.5 Data Abstraction

Data abstraction has been an important principle of software construction and maintenance for many decades, dating from early work on programming-in-the-large [7]. The motivation for data abstraction is *representation independence*: by decoupling clients from data representations in services, service providers have some freedom to modify or change that representation without disturbing client applications. This decomposition of client and server through the service contract that abstracts details about implementation and representation details is key to the maintenance of, and modular reasoning about, large software systems. We reviewed the relationship between object-oriented ("constructor-oriented") programming and procedural ("observer-oriented") programming in terms of how they organize a collection of operations around a collection of data types in 6.1. In this section, we continue this review by considering how these approaches support data abstraction and what form of data abstraction would be useful for SOA.

6.7.5.1 *Procedural Data Abstraction*   Figure 6.28 reviews the approaches to state abstraction taken by the constructor-oriented and the observer-oriented paradigms. The former approach, that of object-oriented programming, encapsulates the internal state and, therefore, also its representation type within a boundary defined by the object's interface. Of particular interest is that this interface becomes a protocol that enables interoperability among objects with different internal implementations. For example, we may define an alternative representation of the list object interface provided in Fig. 6.2. In this version, an internal array is maintained

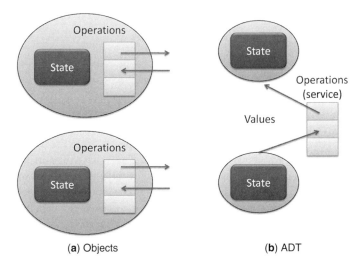

(a) Objects   (b) ADT

Figure 6.28   *Data abstraction in constructor-oriented versus observer-oriented paradigms*

to hold the front of the list, with a pointer to the remainder of the list whose representation type is abstracted by the list interface:

```
public class ArrayList implements List {
  private int top = 0;
  private int[] lst = new int[10];
  private List rest;
  public ArrayList(List l) { rest = l; }
  public ArrayList(int n, ArrayList A) {
    ArrayList(A.top, A.lst, A.rest);
    lst[top++] = n;
  }
  private ArrayList(int top2, int[] lst2, List rest2) {
    for (int i=0; i<top2; i++) lst[i] = lst2[i];
    top = top2; rest = rest2;
  }
  public boolean isEmpty() { return (top==0 && rest.isEmpty()); }
  public int head() throws EmptyListExn {
    if (top > 0) return lst[top-1]; else return rest.head();
  }
  public List tail() throws EmptyListExn {
    if (top > 0) return new ArrayList(top-1, this);
                 else return rest.head();
  }
  public List append (List L2) {
    return new ArrayList (this.top, rest.append(L2));
  }
}
```

A list built from this constructor and those defined in Fig. 6.2, will consist of a sequence of `Insert` and `ArrayList` nodes, with an `Empty` node at the end of the list. Other list implementations may be added, provided that they respect the protocol described by the List interface. This is the approach of *procedural data abstraction* (PDA).[17]

6.7.5.2 Abstract Data Types via Subtyping

As depicted in Fig. 6.28, the observer-oriented approach to data abstraction decouples the observer operations from the objects. They must therefore be provided "privileged" access to the underlying representation of the data values, while not themselves being encapsulated within the data values of methods. To clients of the service, the underlying representation for values is an abstract type, preventing abstraction violations by clients of the representation, while the service implementation has full access to the underlying representation in order to implement the service operations. This is the approach of *abstract data types* (ADTs).[18]

In this section, we consider one approach to providing abstract data types: the only approach that is supported by the WS-* Web services stack. We consider an alternative approach that has both advantages and disadvantages over this approach in the next subsection.

The approach we consider here is that of *subtyping*. We have already seen subtyping, or type inheritance, in Sect. 3.4. The approach of data abstraction via subtyping is to only expose a supertype of the representation type to clients and make use of the property of type substitutability to allow values of the representation type to be passed as arguments to, and results from, service operations, even while the service operations only make reference to the abstract supertype.

In the earlier example (Fig. 6.3) of an observer-oriented implementation, type opacity is achieved using subtyping. The only reference to the list representation type provided to clients is an abstract type (List) that is a supertype of the actual representation type. There are two concrete representations for list values, specified by the Empty and Insert classes in Fig. 6.3. The implementations of the observer operations need to check the type tags on list values and perform downcasts, as appropriate, on these values to their actual types. Although this successfully abstracts the underlying representation type, the downside is that it becomes a delicate matter to ensure the absence of type errors owing to a case in the representation for which an observer is unprepared. This is not a problem with the opaque-types approach to defining abstract data types that we discuss in the next subsection.

The example in Fig. 6.3 requires some care to provide data abstraction. A facility for exposing the underlying representation is necessary for the implementation of the observer operations, but some care must be taken to prevent clients from also

---

[17] As noted in Sect. 6.7.3, objects are an instance of procedural abstraction, where the methods of an object abstract over their arguments and, moreover, where the abstracted procedure implementation may not be bound until run-time. Although presented here in terms of objects, procedural data abstraction can also be implemented in a procedural language, e.g., using structs and function pointers in C. There is an admitted potential for confusion of terminology here, as we are contrasting the procedural style of SOA with the object-oriented style of domain-driven architecture. Therefore, we use the terminology of "constructor-oriented" and "observer-oriented", where appropriate, to avoid confusion.

[18] Historically, procedural data abstraction is associated with object-oriented languages, while abstract data types are associated with procedural languages.

exposing the representation. In Fig. 6.3, the constructors are, by default, only visible in the package in which they are declared. A factory class provides the constructor operations, avoiding the need to export the visibility of the constructor classes to clients. This approach works to provide abstract data types, provided client code is not defined elsewhere in the same namespace.

The approach in Fig. 6.3 allows the definition of further constructors by clients, by defining additional DTO classes that implement the List interface:

```
class ArrayList implements List { int n; int[] lst; List rest; }
public class ArrayListObservers extends ListObservers {
  public head(List lst) { if (lst instanceof ArrayList) … }
}
```

The observer operations must be carefully defined to handle the cases for these additional constructors. By default, the original observers are delegated to for the cases of the original constructors. The dangerous scenario to be avoided is one where, for example, an array list value is passed to one of the original observers. An example of where this might happen is in the recursive call in the original append operation in Fig. 6.3, if a list consists of an Insert node followed by an ArrayList node. If the methods in the original observer class are declared to be final, then original observer implementations bind too early to the fixed point of their recursive implementations. This is avoided by late binding for the observer operations in their recursive calls. We define a new implementation of the observers by extending their definitions using inheritance. In the process, inheritance re-binds recursive calls in the original observers to the new observer class where an observer operation understands how to process constructors in the extended data type:

```
/* In package declaring Empty and Insert classes. */
public class ListObservers implements IListObservers {
  public List append(List lst, List L2) {
    … new Insert (lstc.n, this.append (lstc.L, L2) ) …
  }
    …
}

/* In package declaring ArrayList class. */
public class ArrayListObservers extends ListObservers {
  public List append(List lst, List L2) {
    if (lst instanceof ArrayList) …; else super.append(lst,L2) ;
  }
    …
}
```

The boxed recursive call to this.append in ListObservers is to the final definition of append in whatever subclass of ListObservers this is eventually executed. The boxed call to super.append in the subclass delegates to the superclass implementation of append for the case where the list is not an ArrayList. By indirecting a recursive call to the append method through the this reference to the run-time suite of observer implementations, we dynamically re-bind recursive references to the `append` operation in the superclass implementation so that the extended implementation in the `ArrayListObservers` subclass is invoked. This is why `append` is defined as a dynamically dispatched method rather than as a static method in Fig. 6.3. Nevertheless, despite the use of inheritance, this is still essentially a procedural implementation of the list data type. Inheritance is not an intrinsically object-oriented mechanism.

There is a difficulty with this approach to extending the original data type. Operation dispatching is based on examining the tag of a data value to determine its constructor. If the tag is for a constructor for which no case is defined in the observer operation, then the latter will fail. The type system provides no guarantee that these kinds of unresolved failures will not happen at run-time. As systems grow in size and complexity, formed from the composition of subsidiary systems, these forms of failures become increasingly difficult to detect through manual means. These issues are largely avoided in the constructor-oriented (object-oriented) approach by encapsulating the observer operations with the data, so there is no possibility of failure to match a case in the form of the data.[19]

Subtyping is the only approach to data abstraction supported by XML schemas and therefore the only approach supported by the WS-* Web services stack. For example, we can define an abstract content type for a list and then define an abstract element based on it that can be the head of a substitution group:

```
<complextype name="listType" abstract="true"/>
<element name="list" type="listType" abstract="true"/>
```

The traditional approach in C, of using the `void*` type for an opaque type, is a primitive form of data-type abstraction using subtyping. The `void*` type merely forgets all information about the type of a value—beyond that it is a pointer. There is no safe way for a service implementation to ensure that a value of such a type does, indeed, match the expected representation type. Effectively, the type of such a value is opaque to *both* the service and the client, unless the service correctly "guesses" the right type.

6.7.5.3 *Abstract Data Types via Opaque Types*
As we have seen, the approach to providing abstract data types using subtyping may cause run-time failures as a result of a failure of an observer operation to have a case for dispatching that matches the format of the data. Such a failure, if it happens, will be caused by a violation of the principle of the standardized service contract. This violation may be unavoidable because of an inability of the current tools to express the constraint in such a way that it can be checked for safety. Nevertheless, in large software systems,

---

[19]There is an exception to this: the case of binary methods [51]. If an object takes another object of the same class as an argument to one of its methods and, if inheritance is allowed to specialize the type of this reference to the subclass, then interfaces for subclass objects will no longer be in the subtype relationship with interfaces for superclass objects. Fundamentally, the issue is with contravariant subtyping of subclass objects because of the "negative" reference in the method argument. We discuss contravariance further in Sect. 6.8.2.

running across WANs and potentially involving several collaborator enterprises, this may be an unacceptable risk.

An alternative approach to data abstraction by subtyping is to only use a single type definition for the representation type for both clients and service implementors. This single type definition is *transparent* to the service implementation, while it is *opaque* to clients. Such a facility has been provided by languages with mature module interconnection languages, such as Ada and Modula-3 [52–54].

Figure 6.29 demonstrates the approach of opaque types in a service interface, using the O'CAML language. In O'CAML, service implementations are referred to as *modules*, while a service interface is referred to as a *module type*. The interface in Fig. 6.29(**a**) specifies an abstract data type for lists. This interface declares an opaque representation type t for lists, an exception EmptyListExn, and both constructor and observer operations.

An implementation for this interface is provided by the module in Fig. 6.29(**b**). This implementation defines a concrete data type in O'CAML with two constructors: a constant Empty and a binary constructor Insert. This is an example of algebraic datatypes in functional languages; we provide more details using the Haskell language in Appendix A. Essentially, Empty and Insert define constructors for building data structures, and the match construct in O'CAML plays a similar role

```
module type LIST =
  sig
    type t
    exception EmptyListExn
    val empty : t
    val insert : e → t → t
    val isEmpty : t → bool
    val head : t → e
    val tail : t → t
    val append : t → t → t
  end
```

(**a**) ADT interface

```
module List : LIST =
  struct
    type t = Empty | Insert of int * t
    exception EmptyListExn
    let empty = Empty
    let insert n L = Insert(n, L)
    let isEmpty L =  match L with Empty → true
        | _ → false
    let head L = match L with Insert(n, _) → n
        | _ → raise EmptyListExn
    let tail L =  match L with Insert(_, Lst) → Lst
        | _ → raise EmptyListExn
    let append L L2 =  match L with Empty → L2
        | Insert(n, Lst) → Insert(n, (append Lst L2))
  end
```

(**b**) ADT implementation

Figure 6.29 *Abstract data types via opaque types in O'CAML*

to instanceof and checked downcasting in Java, to compute over such a data structure. The constructor operations empty and insert are defined in terms of the constructors (Empty and Insert) defined for this data type. The other operations use the match construct in O'CAML to examine and decompose a value of the representation type by pattern-matching against all possible ways that such a value could have been constructed. In contrast to the subtyping approach in Fig. 6.3, it is possible in all of these operations to ensure that they are exhaustive in their checking for possible data constructors. The type definition provides all of the cases to be considered.

Whereas the definition of the representation type is transparent within the module, it is opaque to clients of the module. The representation type is named relative to the module as List.t. The interface for the List module, LIST, makes this representation type opaque to clients of the module. Even if a client defines a type identical in structure to the representation type, the latter type has an abstract identity List.t that cannot match any other type. So, for example, we have:

```
let L = List.insert 3 (List.insert 17 List.empty));
let x = match L with Insert(y,_) → y | _ → 0
        (* fails to type-check *)
```

Matching the structure of the data representation fails outside the module, since a list has abstract type List.t.

6.7.5.4 *Partially Abstract Types*   Abstract data types via opaque types are also found in some object-oriented languages. An example is the Modula-3 language [55], an object-oriented language with opaque types that organizes programs into modules and provides each module with its own interface. The example program in Fig. 6.30 provides an interface called IBuffer. Different from interfaces in Java and C#, this is more akin to a "package type", which unfortunately Java does not have. This interface is the contract that the service supplier provides to clients in terms of types and implementations.

There are two types exported by this interface. The public type Buf provides an interface for buffer objects with an insert method exposed in this public interface. The implementation type for buffers is left opaque and revealed only as some subtype of Buf. The client knows no more about this abstract subclass and, in particular, a client cannot create new instances of this private type themselves. Instead, they must call the NewBuf operation that is provided by the service provider which can ensure that the buffer object is properly initialized before being returned to the client. The interface also provides an Append operation that creates a new buffer, that is the result of appending the two buffers that it is provided with as inputs.

The module Buffer implements the IBuffer interface. It "reveals" that the private type T is in fact a subclass inheriting from the public type Buf, adding in the process a private character buffer field that is not visible to clients. The NewBuf and Append operations, as they are defined in this implementation module, have privileged access to the internal representation of the buffer. In this way, clients are prevented from accessing the contents of a buffer in an unsafe fashion outside the Buffer module.

```
INTERFACE IBuffer;
  TYPE Buf = OBJECT METHODS insert(s:TEXT) END;
  TYPE T <: Buf;
  PROCEDURE NewBuf():T;
  PROCEDURE Append(b1,b2:T):T;
END IBuffer.

MODULE Buffer IMPLEMENTS IBuffer;
  REVEAL T = Buf BRANDED OBJECT buff:REF ARRAY OF TEXT;
            METHODS insert(s:TEXT) := Insert …
            END;
  PROCEDURE Insert(s:TEXT) = BEGIN … END Insert;
  PROCEDURE NewBuf():T = BEGIN … END NewBuf;
  PROCEDURE Append(b1,b2:T):T = BEGIN … END Append;
END Buffer.
```

Figure 6.30 *Partially abstract types in Modula-3*

6.7.5.5 *Abstract Data Types via Sealing*

The opacity in the example in Sect. 6.7.5.3 relies on the type system preventing the exposure of the representation type outside the service implementation by distinguishing the abstract type name List.t and its definition outside the implementation. In a distributed environment, malicious attackers seeking to subvert a system by modifying data in transit over the network will not typically respect the type system. Is there a way to define an abstract data type in such a way that values are protected from abstraction violations because of malicious activity?

Type sealing [56] is a technique that has been proposed to enforce abstraction boundaries at run-time. Consider, for example, the operations from Fig. 6.29 and, in particular, the insertion operation:

```
let insert n L = │ Insert(n, L) │
```

Within the module, the parameter L has the transparent type t, defined to be a data type for lists. The result of the insert operation crosses an abstraction boundary from the transparent internal type t to the opaque representation type List.t when it is returned:

```
let x : List.t = List.insert 3 List.empty
```

As the type is opaque, the client is unable to access the underlying representation, for example to access the value, 3, inserted into the list. To access the value at the head of the list, the client needs to call back into the module to one of the observer operations:

```
let y : int = List.head x
```

The argument to the head operation crosses the abstraction boundary from the opaque to the transparent when it is received by the operation:

```
let head L = match │ L │ with Insert(n, _) → n
   | _ → raise EmptyListExn
```

```
module List : LIST =
  struct
    type t = Empty | Insert of int * t
    let insert n L = │ seal Insert(n, L) with k │}
    ...
  end
```

```
                        Client 1 sends a sealed value:
                        let x : List.t = List.insert 3 List.empty
                        send (chan, x)

                        Client 2 receives the sealed value:
                        let y : List.t = receive(chan)
                        let z : int = List.head y
module List : LIST =
  struct
    type t = Empty | Insert of int * t
    let head L = match │ unseal L with k │ with Insert(n, _) → n
               | _ → raise EmptyListExn
    ...
  end
```

Figure 6.31 *Abstract data types via sealing in Not-O'CAML*

The idea of sealing is that these points where values cross abstraction boundaries should constitute points for the application of cryptographic operations: encrypting the result of a constructor (e.g., the result of insert) and decrypting an argument to an observer (e.g., the head operation). The encrypting is referred to as sealing, while decryption is referred to as unsealing. Using an O'CAML-like syntax, Fig. 6.31 describes an implementation of the List module using sealing at the abstraction boundary. The assumption is that two installations of this implementation at different network points can communicate securely by sealing and unsealing the abstract values using a secret encryption key that is negotiated as part of the establishment of a connection between the types; for example, it may be the result of Diffie-Helman key exchange. While it is unlikely that sealing will be realized in an actual language, it does demonstrate how data abstraction can be related to the use of cryptographic operations to protect data when transmitted over untrusted networks [20].

We conclude this discussion of data abstraction by summarizing some of the terminology we have been using:

Architecture	Unit of data	Programming paradigm	Data organization	Data abstraction
Domain driven	Persistent domain object (PDO)	Object oriented	Constructor oriented	Procedural data abstraction (PDA)
Service oriented	Data transfer object (DTO)	Procedural	Observer oriented	Abstract data types (ADT)

6.7.6 Endpoint Abstraction

A form of abstraction is provided by access control, preventing client access to proprietary or sensitive information in the service. Consider again the auction service example in Fig. 6.5. In this scenario, security considerations dictate that both seller and buyer access to the seller database should be restricted to the auction manager and auction closer services, respectively. Buyers should not have access to the seller database as it reveals information about other buyers. Similarly, a seller should not have access to information, such as the identity of buyers, from other sellers. This decoupling of sellers and buyers from the database is facilitated by the manager and closer services. Access may be restricted using standard forms of access control, such as role-based access control, digitally-signed access requests, and encrypted communication. However, the Internet is a dangerous space—Web sites are continually compromised by exploits such as buffer overflow attacks. Further protection for the database may be provided by placing the auction services behind a firewall. The firewall has open ports to allow access to the auction manager and closer services, but clients outside the firewall are not permitted to access the database service directly. For example, a proxying firewall may be used to forward communications between service requesters and providers, preventing direction communication between them and only offering proxies for the manager and closer services.

We can take this idea one step further and architect the system so that all service requests are directed through a single endpoint. An example implementation of this idea is a SOAP router, running in an application server, using the context root of the endpoint URL application server. Besides the original motivation of access control, this INVENTORY ENDPOINT pattern has another advantage: it abstracts from the internal configuration of services in the service inventory, allowing this configuration to be reorganized without affecting outside clients. Clients always connect to the same service endpoint; and the latter uses routing logic to forward service requests to the appropriate service implementation. Obviously, the service endpoint should actually be organized as a cluster, with the domain name for the service endpoint resolving to IP addresses for multiple load balancers, as exemplified by the architecture described in Fig. 2.10. This helps to ensure that the inventory endpoint does not become a performance bottleneck and a single point of failure.

6.8 SERVICE REUSABILITY

Krueger [57] cites four facets of software *reuse*. The most important facets are:

1. *Abstraction* is the fundamental facet of reuse. A reusable software asset must abstract from low-level details to a high-level description. This latter description provides enough information to be useful for clients of the abstractions, but elides the aspects of the asset that are not essential for clients to know.[20]

---

[20]The *Principle of Leaky Abstraction* states that all abstractions leak details of the underlying implementation, otherwise they are useless to clients.

For example, a sorting operation may abstract from the algorithm it uses (procedural abstraction), while a mapping from keys to values may abstract from the underlying data structure such as search trees or hash tables (data abstraction). Standards such as model-driven architecture (MDA) or SCA attempt to be abstract from aspects of the underlying deployment platforms. We have discussed abstraction at some length in Sect. 6.7.

2. *Specialization* is the mechanism for reusing assets once they are discovered. Examples include calling a procedure or instantiating a class to an object.

The remaining facets are rather secondary conceptually, although they may be critical for practical software reuse:

1. *Selection* refers to mechanisms for discovering reusable assets. For example, subtype hierarcies are a useful organizing principle in class libraries.

2. *Integration* refers to a mechanism for integrating reused assets into a software application, usually using some form of *module interconnection language* [58, 59].

We saw in Sect. 5.3 (Fig. 5.4) two approaches to instantiating application frameworks. The "white box" approach uses inheritance to specialize abstract classes in the framework with application functionality. The "black box" approach uses composition, integrating components that do not reveal internal implementation details beyond those exported in their interfaces. SOA originates in the latter school of *component-based reuse*, as opposed to the inheritance-based reuse of class libraries.

6.8.1 Parameterization and Bounded Polymorphism

Component-based reuse is a rather old and honorable tradition in software systems. It is essentially the approach of *abstract data types* [60], based on abstracting over supplier implementations (also known as modules or components) and building applications that are agnostic with respect to the internal implementation details of these components [61]. This is sometimes expressed by parameterizing the client implementation by the service implementation that it abstracts over.

Figure 6.32 provides an example of *parameterized modules* in O'CAML. We generalize the list interface from Fig. 6.29(**b**), by abstracting the list element type. Whereas the interface in Fig. 6.29(**a**) assumes that elements in a list are always integers, the interface in Fig. 6.32 abstracts this to an opaque type e.

In Fig. 6.32, we also provide an implementation of lists that abstracts over the element type of the list implementation to be created. The interface ORDSET defines an interface for an ordered type, where the requirement is that an inequality comparison operation leq must be provided for elements of the type. The ordered list implementation OrdList is defined as a module that parameterizes over this ordered type. The definition of the list type specifies that elements of the list have type O.t (in the type of the Insert constructor). The definition of the insert operation uses this in the case where the argument n is being inserted into a

```
module type LIST =
  sig
    type e
    type t
    exception EmptyListExn
    val empty : t
    val insert : e → t → t
    val isEmpty : t → bool
    val head : t → e
    val tail : t → t
  end

module type ORDSET =
  sig
    type t
    val leq : t → t → boolean
  end

module OrdList (O : ORDSET) : (LIST with type e = O.t) =
  struct
    type t = Empty | Insert of O.t * t
    exception EmptyListExn
    let empty = Empty
    let insert n L = match L with Empty → Insert(n, Empty)
        | Insert(n2, L2) → if O.leq n n2 then Insert(n, L)
                              else Insert(n2, insert n L2)
      …
  end
```

Figure 6.32 *Implementation reuse via parameterized modules in O'CAML*

non-empty list. The insertion operation checks if the value being inserted is less than the current head of the list, n2. This comparison is done with the comparison operation provided in the implementation of ordered sets that the list abstracts over. The result of this ordered list implementation is an implementation of the LIST interface where the list element type is revealed to be the same as the carrier type O.t for the ordered set implementation.

As an example of the use of these abstractions, we can instantiate the parameterized implementation in OrdList with the ordered set implementation OrdInt:

```
module OrdInt =
  struct
    type t = int
    let leq (x:int) y = (x <= y)
  end
module IList = OrdList(OrdInt)
let L = IList.insert 10 (IList.insert 3 (Ilist.insert 4 IList.empty))
```

In this example, we use the IList implementation to build ordered lists of integers. The OrdInt module provides an implementation of the ordered set defined by the type of integers, int, and the default comparison operation for integers. This implementation is used to instantiate the OrdList parameterized implementation, resulting in the implementation IList of ordered lists.

This form of parameterization is sometimes referred to as *parametric polymorphism*, as the parameterized module OrdList has abstracted over the element type for lists. As another example of parametric polymorphism in a procedural language, Haskell supports this form of genericity using *type classes*, as described in Sect. A.2, Appendix A. For example, we may define:

```
class Comparable a where leq :: a → a → Bool
instance Comparable Int where leq = intLeq
insert :: Comparable a ⇒ a → List(a) → List(a)
```

The type class Comparable groups overloaded operations defined over a type parameter a. Instances for this type class are defined for an instantiation of this type parameter. An instance of the type class Comparable for the type Int is defined using the integer comparison operation. The insertion operation is defined to be parametrically polymorphic in the list element type a:

```
insert :: … a → List(a) → List(a)
```

The elided type of the insertion includes an additional constraint: that any instantiation of the type parameter a should have an instance of the Comparable type class defined for it.

```
insert :: Comparable a ⇒ a → List(a) → List(a)
```

So, for example, the following operation is safe:

```
insert 6 [2,4,8]
```

On the other hand, the following fails to type-check because there is no instance of the type class Comparable defined for strings:

```
insert "Hiyo" ["Silver","Away!"]
```

Both Haskell type classes and O'CAML parameterized modules are providing similar approaches to software reuse. The difference is that Haskell uses type classes to constrain the possible instantiations of type parameters to have certain overloaded operations defined over them (the leq operation in the example above). O'CAML, on the other hand, requires that implementations of these required operations be explicitly provided in module instantiations. In the O'CAML example given in Fig. 6.32, the type parameter O.t to the OrdList parameterized module is unconstrained, but an implementation of the comparison operation for that type must be explicitly provided in any instantiation of the module.

The ML family of languages, including O'CAML, has tried to use parameterized modules as an organizing principle for a module interconnection language. With this approach, a client module C is defined as a module that is parameterized over the implementation it needs. This client module is linked to an implementation M of the service it requires by performing the application C(M). In practice, experience with this approach to system building has been negative: the linking code is fairly complex, difficult to understand and maintain, with a large number of nested instantiations. The approach of parameterized modules appears best suited to the reuse of generic data abstractions, as in Fig. 6.32, and in that realm its use (or that of type classes) can be considered *essential*.

To demonstrate this last point, the original Java language did not support parameterized (generic) types. Nevertheless, it is possible to specify the following:

```
void printList (Object[] list) { … }
String[] L = { "Hiyo", "Silver", "Away!" }
printList(L);
```

The actual argument—an array of strings—does not match the expected argument type, an array of objects. This application succeeds because Java has a type rule for subtyping of array types, that specifies:

If T_1 is a subtype of T_2, then $T_1[]$ is a subtype of $T_2[]$.

But this rule is unsafe! Consider, for example:

```
Integer[] X = { new Integer(3); }
Object[] Y = X;
Object Z = "Hello";
Y[0] = Z;
X[0].intValue() + 7;
```

The critical failure is in allowing the array of Integer objects (X) to be assigned to the variable Y that should only hold an array of generic objects. The problem is that this establishes Y as an unsafe alias to the array referenced by X. If we could not update an element of an array, this assignment would be safe. Allowing a value of type String[] to be coerced to a value of type Object[] would simply "forget" the actual element type of the array. The difficulty is that arrays do allow updates in place, therefore providing a back door for unsafe updates. In this case, allowing Y to reference the array of integers X allows an unsafe update of X by updating Y with a value that does not conform with the element type of X. This is performed by the update Y[0] = Z, assigning a string to Y, which by side-effect assigns a string to X, an array of Integer objects. If this assignment is allowed, the attempt to use the single element of X as an integer variable will now cause a run time type error.

In fact, the assignment Y[0] = Z is prevented, at run-time, by the Java Virtual Machine (JVM). The Java language runtime system performs a run time type check on every assignment to an array to ensure conformance with the element type of the array. This is obviously not conducive to either efficient or reliable execution. Fundamentally, the problem is with the unsafe assignment Y = X, which should not be allowed by the compiler but is allowed because originally Java did not have generics. As Java has subsequently been extended with generic types, the original motivating example can be defined properly by making the printList operation parametrically polymorphic in the element type of the array:

```
interface Printable { void print (OutputStream os); }
void print <A ≤ Printable> (A[] L) { … L[i].print(os) … }
class P implements Printable { … }
P[] X = { new P() };
printList(X);
```

In this definition, the `printList` procedure is parametrically polymorphic in the type parameter A. However, this type parameter is constrained by the constraint A ≤ `printAble`, so that it can only be instantiated to an object type A that implements the `Printable` interface, i.e., to a type that is a subtype of `Printable`. We can write the type of the `printList` function in a manner analogous to that of the Haskell `insert` function above:

```
printList :: (a ≤ Printable) ⇒ a[] → void -- pseudo-Haskell
```

This form of polymorphism is sometimes referred to as *bounded polymorphism* because the type parameter a has a type upper bound: any instantiation of a must be a subtype of `Printable`.

Qualified polymorphism is a more general term sometimes used to encompass both Java bounded polymorphism and Haskell type classes [62]. This term refers to a parametrically polymorphic type where the possible instantiations of the type parameters are constrained in the type:

1. In the type of `insert` in Haskell, the constraint is (`Comparable a`): any instantiation of the polymorphic type of `insert` is constrained to have an instance of the `Comparable` type class defined for it.

2. In the type of `printList` in Java, the constraint is (a ≤ `Printable`): any instantiation of the polymorphic type of `printList` is constrained to be a subtype of the `Printable` interface.

We have belabored the issues with parametric polymorphism, or genericity, and qualified polymorphism because, for all the concern in the SOA community about component-based software reuse, it is rather surprising that the frameworks developed for SOA, for example the WSDL interface definition language for Web services, make no provision for parametric or bounded polymorphism.

CDI is a framework for managing software components in Java applications that we describe in more detail in Sect. 6.10.1. The essence of CDI is the use of annotations to describe the configuration requirements for applications, with the application container performing the deploy-time and run-time configuration. This is a much more natural model for programming-in-the-large than the manual linking model originally considered for parameterized models. The nearest analogy with parameterization in functional languages is with Haskell type classes, where compile-time resolution implicitly selects and instantiates operations specified by overloaded names. As Haskell is a stateless language, it would appear that the configuration issues that type classes address are simpler than in the case of Java, given that the motivation for CDI is the management of interacting *stateful* components. Nevertheless, state can be incorporated into Haskell using monads, referenced using the type class mechanism as explained in Appendix A. In comparison, the major deficiency of the CDI framework is the lack of interfaces for components that reflect the dependencies that those components have on the environment in which they are deployed. Incompatibilities between components and their deployment environments are discovered by "debugging" deployment errors. The CDI framework certainly advances the practice of component deployment, including the replacement of name-based depencency injection with resolution based on type information. However, the "deployment contract" for a component is distributed around the code for the component. There is no decoupling of this contract from the component and the replacement of a component may have unforeseen consequences at deployment time.

6.8.2 Subtyping, Inheritance, and Contracts

Central to component-based reuse is the notion of the contract because of the decoupling it provides between service implementations. Consider the example in Fig. 6.33, a typical example used to explain subtyping and inheritance. In Fig. 6.33(**a**) we specify in Java an example of an interface for two-dimensional points, `Point`. Using this interface, we can, for example, provide two completely unrelated implementations of two-dimensional points, `CartPoint` and `PolarPoint`. Both implementations are required to satisfy the protocol that they expose operations for interrogating point objects for their X and Y coordinates in Cartesian coordinate space. Using this shared protocol, it is possible to define operations that work on objects of different underlying implementation by abstracting over the differences in their implementations:

```
void distance (Point p, Point q) {
  float dx = p.getX() - q.getX();
  float dy = p.getY() - q.getY();
  return Math.sqrt(dx * dx + dy * dy);
}
CartPoint p1 = new CartPoint (3.5, .89);
PolarPoint p2 = new PolarPoint (0.7, 60.0);
float d = distance (p1, p2);
```

Figure 6.33(**b**) continues this example by defining new implementations of color Cartesian points and color polar points from the implementations in Fig. 6.33(**a**), specializing the original implementations via inheritance. This example also specializes the interface for point objects to color point objects, providing a specialized object protocol for the interfaces.

Figure 6.33(**c**) illustrates the relationships involved in this example. There are several relationships between classes and interfaces involved in this example:

1. There is a type inheritance or subtyping relationship between `ColorPoint` and `Point`. An object of type `ColorPoint` can be substituted for an object of type `Point` by ignoring its color property. This is an example of *design reuse*.

2. There is an implementation inheritance relationship between `ColorCartPoint` and `CartPoint`, and between `ColorPolarPoint` and `PolarPoint`. This is an example of *implementation reuse*: the color point implementations

```
public interface Point {
  public float getX();
  public float getY();
}

class CartPoint
      implements Point {
  private float x, y;
  public float getX() { return x; }
  public float getY() { return y; }
}

class PolarPoint
      implements Point {
  private float rho, theta;
  public float getX() {
    return rho * Math.cos(theta);
  }
  public float getY() {
    return rho * Math.sin(theta);
  }
}
```

(**a**) Points

```
public interface ColorPoint
        extends Point {
  public Color getColor();
}

class ColorCartPoint
        extends CartPoint
        implements ColorPoint {
  private Color c;
  public float getColor() {
    return c;
  }
}

class ColorPolarPoint
        extends PolarPoint
        implements ColorPoint {
  private Color c;
  public float getColor() {
    return c;
  }
}
```

(**b**) Color points

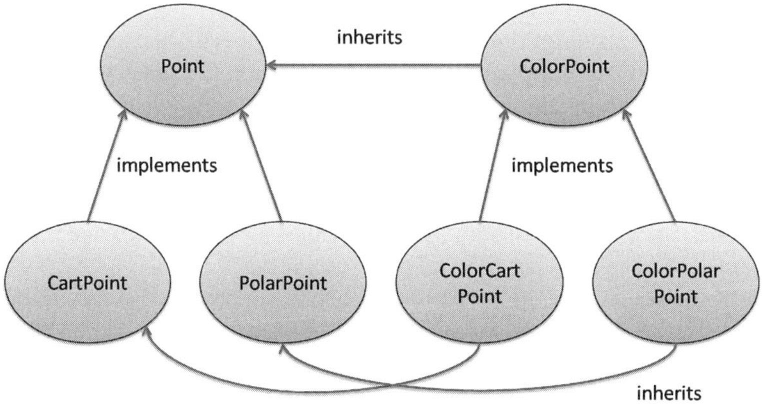

(**c**) Relationships

Figure 6.33 *Implementation and inheritance relationships*

are derived by reusing the original point implementations in a "white box" fashion.

3. There is also a third relationship: the implementation relationship between the classes and their interfaces. Thus, for example, both the CartPoint and the PolarPoint implementations are related by the "implements" relationship to the Point interface.

These are three different relationships here, reflecting that classes and interfaces are fundamentally different notions. An interface is a notion of *type*—a way of organizing descriptions of behavior whereas a class is a notion of *implementation*. The "implements" relationship relates these two notions. Historically, these two relationships have been confused in object-oriented languages, for example in Simula and C++. In these languages, there is no intrinsic notion of an interface. Instead, an interface is modeled as an abstract implementation. All three of the relationships in Fig. 6.33 are modeled using subclassing, a relationship between implementations. When we try to derive a new implementation via inheritance from an existing implementation, and at the same time relate it to an interface, this apparently requires the use of multiple implenentation inheritance, a notoriously difficult concept for which to provide a semantics or a reasonable implementation. The confusion this causes may explain some of the resistance to white box reuse in application frameworks. In the example of the ET++SwapsManager framework described in Sect. 5.3, the abstraction hierarchies, for example for financial instruments and calculator strategies in Fig. 5.5, are fundamental to the organization of the framework, but that should not constrain the implementations of these instruments. The implementor should be free to choose the implementation strategy that is most advantageous to them and the interface for that implementation should abstract over the details of that implementation and focus attention on the contract that the implementation honors. Much of the "controversy" about the choice of proper reuse mechanism stems from confusion caused by the poor abstraction mechanisms provided by modern tools and languages.

Some of the remaining criticism of "white box" reuse cites the fact that inheriting classes are exposed to implementation details of the parent classes. Again, this is an artifact of the poor abstraction mechanisms provided by languages such as C++, Java, and C#. In the Moby language [63], a parameterized module could abstract over a parent class and then within the parameterized module a subclass could be derived from that parent class via inheritance, effectively a form of mixin-based inheritance [64]. With sufficient abstraction mechanisms in one's language, inheritance becomes another form of black box reuse.

Subtyping has been used successfully in object-oriented languages to organize abstractions, as demonstrated for example in Fig. 5.5. In turn, this organization plays an important role in enabling software reuse by providing a way of cataloging the software inventory. If SOA is a procedural paradigm, is there an analogous notion of behavioral subtyping for procedure types so that service *operations* might similarly be organized into abstraction hierarchies? We can certainly organize services themselves into hierarchies based on interface containment (*width subtyping*), but there may be value in to also organizing services based on specialization hierarchies for operation types (*depth subtyping*).

In fact, it is possible to define subtyping for procedure types, but one must be careful when defining it. Consider, for example, procedure types of the form $(T_1 \rightarrow T_2)$, where the domain and range types are subsets of integers, and consider the examples of functions F, G and H in Fig. 6.34. We have already seen that, in the context of XML schemas, it is safe to assign a variable of a finite value

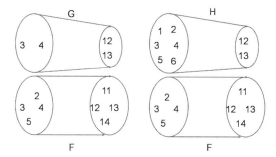

Figure 6.34 *Subtyping of service operation types*

type to a variable of another finite value type that includes the original type. For example:

```
// X has type {11,12,13,14}
// Y has type {12,13}
X = Y;  // safe
```

The assignment is safe because the assignment simply loses precision about the type of any value stored in Y. There are two possible choices for the vaue stored in Y, but there are four possible choices for the value stored in X. Since the two possible values for Y are included in the four possible values for X, a consumer of X will not be "surprised" by the value that X is bound to. The assignment just loses precision about the possible values, expanding the range of possibilities from two to four. Now consider another assignment:

```
// F has type {2,3,4,5} → {11,12,13,14}
// G has type {3,4} → {12,13}
F = G;  // Is it safe?
```

Is the type of G a subtype of the type of F? If it is, then the G function can be assigned to the F variable that holds a function value. It is promising that the range of G is included in the range of F. This means that any result we obtain by applying F after the assignment will still be contained in the original result type of F. However, there is a surprise with the domain types: the domain of G is included in the domain of F, but this turns out to be a problem, as there are input values that the original F could process that G may not be able to process. Consider, for example, F(5) after the assignment: the original F function could handle this input but once the G function is assigned to F, this value is outside the domain type of G.

On the other hand, the assignment of the H function to F is safe:

```
// F has type {2,3,4,5} → {11,12,13,14}
// H has type {1,2,3,4,5,6} → {12,13}
F = H; // Safe
```

In this case, the domain type of H includes the domain type of F. In addition, H can process other values that F cannot but, when assigning H to F, we simply forget this. The important issue for type safety is that H, when assigned to F, can handle all of the inputs that F could process. So, in summary, we say that a procedure subtyping $(T_1 \rightarrow T_2) \leq (T'_1 \text{ funtyop } T'_2)$ is safe if:

1. The subtyping is *covariant* in the range, i.e., $T_2 \leq T'_2$;
2. The subtyping is *contravariant* in the domain, i.e., $T'_1 \leq T_1$.

For example, one has the following:

1. The type (int $\rightarrow$ ColorPoint) is a subtype of (int $\rightarrow$ Point) because the subtyping is covariant in the range type.
2. The type (Point $\rightarrow$ int) is a subtype of (ColorPoint $\rightarrow$ int) because the subtyping is contravariant in the domain type.
3. On the other hand, the types (Point $\rightarrow$ Point) and (ColorPoint $\rightarrow$ Color-Point) are incomparable: neither one is a subtype of the other!

Indeed, we have seen exactly these rules in the requirements for safe updating of WCF data contracts in Sect. 6.5.5.

How are we to type a service operation that is polymorphic in its argument but at least requires some minimal fields in the supplied value and returns a result of that type?

```
Point proc(Point p) { print(p.getX()); return p; }
```

The type specification for proc is (Point $\rightarrow$ Point), but this type is too specific. It should be applicable to any subtype of Point, but with this specific type, we lose precision when we return a value of such a subtype. For example, if we apply the proc operation to a color point object cp, the result is a Point object; we have lost the original type in the result type. On the other hand, as we have seen, a type such as (ColorPoint $\rightarrow$ ColorPoint) is incomparable to the declared type of proc. The solution to retain precision is to use a bounded polymorphic type:

```
A proc <A ≤ Point> (A p) { print(p.getX()); return p; }
```

The corresponding Not-Haskell qualified polymorphic type for this is:

```
(a ≤ Point) ⇒ a  → a
```

This constrained polymorphic type can then be instantiated to each of the, otherwise incomparable, possible typings for proc.

We are now in a position to explain why the liberal Java subtype rule for arrays is unsafe. We can think abstractly of an array of type A[] as an object with getter and setter methods of type (int $\rightarrow$ A) and (int $\rightarrow$ A $\rightarrow$ void), respectively. Is it safe to say that (String[] $\leq$ Object[]), i.e., an array of strings is a subtype of an array of objects? This requires that the getter and setter methods are in the subtype relation. This is a safe assumption for getter methods because subtyping is covariant in the range type. On the other hand, subtyping fails for the setter because of contravariant subtyping. We would need to have:

```
(int  →  String  →  void) ≤ (int  →  Object  →  void).
```

However, because of contravariance, this requires that (Object ≤ String), which is clearly not true.

Obviously, XML does not have arrays, so it may be supposed that this is not an issue for Web services. On the other hand, Web service operations routinely include callbacks as part of their arguments which introduces negative references to types. We saw a reflection of this in subtype rules for WCF data contracts in Sect. 6.5.5. XML processing languages such as XQuery and XJ [65] include update operations as well as query operations and, for this to be safe, XML documents will need to include variance notations in their schemas where parts of the document can be updated. Where part of a document schema is marked mutable, the corresponding subtype rule for that part of the document type will need to be *invariant*.

6.8.3 Does Service-Oriented Architecture Require Subtyping?

Is it a good practice to organize services and data contracts into specialization hierarchies, as is commonly done with object-oriented languages (e.g., Fig. 5.5)? This is generally regarded as an anti-pattern for services, which appears surprising given the usefulness of such specialization hierarchies in the object-oriented world. There appear to be several factors at work here. First, there is concern about allowing multiple versions, for example for data contracts, and the resulting interoperability issues. While an over-proliferation of versions is certainly to be avoided, the real world is a messy place, and it is not clear if multiple versions can be avoided. This is particularly true in collaborative, distributed environments where organizations may work with their own versions internally and even arrange to share private versions with partner organizations while honoring standard versions to all other parties. Rather, the mechanisms should be in place for coping with decentralized version change on an organized basis. On the other hand, it is not clear that subtyping is the best model for versioning data.

Second, deriving new implementations by specialization is sometimes cited as violating service autonomy, as it makes one service implementation dependent on another. Here, the criticism is sometimes of "white-box" software reuse, making the client implementation dependent on details of the implementation it extends. However, as discussed above, this issue is an artifact of the extremely poor abstraction mechanisms provided in modern languages. There is no intrinsic reason that a subclass cannot abstract over the superclass that it inherits from. This provides a form of mixin-based inheritance [64], where new services can be defined in terms of the combination of "mixins." This can be useful in the procedural, as well as the object-oriented, style [66]. It is effectively a form of composition—one that is useful wherever one is combining recursively defined functionality.

Another criticism that is sometimes made is that this specialization leads to inflexibility, as it ties program structure to the derivation of the service implementation. This confuses design and implementation hierarchies; it is certainly understood by now that the type inheritance hierarchy can be largely independent of the implementation inheritance hierarchy, as demonstrated in Fig. 6.33. Furthermore, there is no intrinsic reason that subtype hierarchies must be declared by the designer. A more flexible alternative is to base such specialization hierarchies on structural interface containment. Then, the "history" of the inclusion hierarchies, i.e., what inclusions the designer chose to declare, become irrelevant since as the inclusion hierarchies are taken out of the programmer's hands. For example, with the following interface declarations, there is no reason that we should not allow the NotarizedDoc interface to be a subtype of both Document and Notarized:

```
interface Document {
  String getAuthor();
  String getAddress();
  String getContents();
}
interface Notarized {
  byte[] getSignature();
  String getNotary();
}
```

```
interface NotarizedDoc {
  String getAuthor();
  String getAddress();
  String getContents();
  byte[] getSignature();
  String getNotary();
}
```

Allowing this inclusion would require changing the subtyping relation in Java and C# from *nominal subtyping* (where the inclusion hierarchies are declared by the programmer) to *structural subtyping* (where the inclusion hierarchies are based on semantically sound structural inclusions of interfaces).

Nevertheless, do we need subtyping at all, at least for SOA? Figure 6.35 provides two examples of the uses of subtyping, both uses strictly defined for data transfer objects only, as is the case with SOA. The first example, in Fig. 6.35(**a**), is an example of observer-oriented data design, in this case the definition of a data type as the union of a set of constructors. In this example, there are constructors for undergraduate and for PhD students. This is the equivalent of a data type definition in O'CAML (as demonstrated in Fig. 6.29—the only difference being that common fields for all constructors are factored out into a base type). The Java/C# approach to defining constructors relies on subtyping to allow operations to be defined over the types. Each observer operation is defined for the base type and then uses type tag checking and downcasting to coerce the values to their actual concrete subclasses. Unlike with the object-oriented style, where data are bundled with the operations defined over those data, in the procedural style it is possible that an operation will fail because of a case of a data constructor that cannot happen. The type system cannot prevent these errors from happening, as discussed in Fig. 6.3. On the other hand, with the opaque-type approach to defining data types and operations on those types, exemplified by the O'CAML example in Fig. 6.29, all possible cases for the constructors are defined in the type definition. In this case, we can say that subtyping is a distinctly suboptimal way of defining data types if one is doing so in the observer-oriented (procedural), rather than

```
class Student {
  int CWID;
  String name;
  Faculty advisor;
}
class UG extends Student {
  String year;
  String major;
}
class PhD extends Student {
  String thesisTitle;
  List<Faculty> committee;
}
```

(a) Defining Union of Constructors

```
interface FacultyBase {
  int getCWID();
  String getName();
}
interface Advisor
extends FacultyBase {
  List<Student> getAdvisees();
}
interface Researcher
extends FacultyBase {
  List<Grant> getGrants();
}
interface Faculty
extends Advisor, Researcher { }
```

(b) Defining Union of Observations

Figure 6.35 Uses of subtyping

the constructor-oriented (object-oriented), fashion. XML Schemas support both the O'CAML approach (using choice elements, though without opaque types) and the Java/C# approach (using element substitution and subtype inclusion).

The second example, in Fig. 6.35(**b**), is an example of defining multiple views on a single underlying constructor, in this case that of a faculty member who both advises students and has research grants. Different observer operations may require different "views" of a faculty member record, hence the use of multiple *type* inheritance to combine these different views. However, in this case, there is just a single constructor for a faculty member's record.

If one thinks of the use of multiple type inheritance here as a form of mixin combination at the behavioral (type) level, there an interesting question of what would happen if one attempts to provide a similar form of mixin combination at the implementation level. The answer is: it depends. In one approach, that of *mixin modules* [67, 68], it is important that such "mixin interfaces" *not* support subtyping.[21] Other approaches based on *virtual types* do allow subtyping by relying on very precise typings using nominal dependent types, where the types of references to related entities are updated during inheritance by the use of dependent types [69, 70]. These approaches, on the other hand, are very much in the constructor-oriented camp of data organization.

We conclude therefore that:

1. Subtyping may be useful for allowing multiple versions of data, although there may be better, or more general, approaches.
2. Subtyping is useful for defining abstract data types, but there are better alternatives when data is organized in an observer-oriented fashion (as it is with SOA).

---

[21]The reason has to do with method-type specialization for mutually recursively-defined types, as the references in types to other types are in negative or contravariant position.

3. Subtyping may be useful for providing different views of data, although trying to extend this from type inheritance to implementation inheritance may (depending on how one does it) require that there *not* be subtyping of those views, for the sake of type safety.

4. For service interfaces themselves, subtyping based on interface containment is undeniably useful. It is, after all, the basis for the service façade pattern, eliding the service operations that are not exported to clients of the façade. On the other hand, it is possible that a coercion from the actual to the expected interface (or contract) of a service would be sufficient, as is done when matching module implementations to module interfaces in O'CAML.

6.8.4 Patterns for Service Reusability

The primary enemy of software reuse is the project team working on a deadline. Most of the patterns for service reusability propose to remove some level of design autonomy from project teams, and instead centralize it in enterprise-wide, or at least department-wide, support functions. While this sounds undeniably bureaucratic, it should be recalled that the concept of a bureaucracy, as originally termed by Weber [71], was a necessary and positive improvement over the patronage-ridden form of government that preceded it. With the rise of the modern industrial state, and the increasing involvement of government services in social and commercial life, Weber described the bureaucracy as a rational and goal-oriented enterprise staffed by career professionals designed to provide the effective and efficient delivery of these services. It can certainly be viewed as an improvement over the feudal systems that preceded it which focused as much on bestowing favors on political patrons as on deliverying services. There is certainly no shortage of modern examples of the failure of patronage-driven government services. Weber also saw the risk of the "iron cage" of an inflexible robotic application of bureaucratic control to social life. Therefore, he saw a role for the political system as a counter-vailing force in favor of the individual (as opposed to corporate) interest and the essential role of entrepeneurs in society. In modern organizations, the role of the *ombudsman* has become an important one in representing the interests of constituencies that are served by a bureaucracy, particularly in service organizations such as newspapers, whose business model critically relies on the trust of its constituencies. Perhaps such a mediating role will also be useful in enterprises that adopt some of the centralizing recommendations for SOA.

The ENTERPRISE INVENTORY pattern recommends a single global repository of reusable software assets. This inventory becomes the basis for reusing software as services. All design processes are required to provide consideration of existing services that may be reused in a project, as well as the services developed during a project that may be contributed to the inventory. Control of the inventory itself is centralized in a *service custodian*. There are many prerequisites to such a blue-sky ideal. At the minimum, it requires an IT infrastructure that supports interoperability among the services in the inventory, which presumably means a commitment to the WS-* protocol stack or RESTful Web services for intra-enterprise service development. Just achieving this level of buraucratization may be a challenge in many organizations, as evidenced by the disconnect between IT architects and service developers over relative preferences for SOAP-based versus REST-based Web services.

The DOMAIN INVENTORY pattern recognizes this tension, and recommends instead a more decentralized architecture for the service inventory, organized around individual departments. Presumably, a service inventory function located in a department will be more responsive to the needs of project teams working on deadines, as project failures may have negative repercussions on the department in which that inventory is located. Inevitably, this may lead to varying levels of application of the domain inventory pattern depending on the level of commitment within a department and the level of governance that can be applied to enforce the application of the pattern. There is also the risk of departmental fiefdoms developing, where resources are not shared across departmental boundaries. At the very least, there should be some enterprise-wide commitment to interoperability of services across department boundaries, perhaps using the WS-* stack or REST, even if departments may choose to use lighter-weight integration platforms internally. Web services then become an integration layer between these departments' services and those outside. The role of enterprise-wide management may be to offer incentives to departments to "build out" their inventories, making them available via a shared infrastructure to other departments.

It should still be recognizable that any laudable commitment to building an inventory of interoperable software services will eventually hit the reality of the lack of interoperability among the major platforms. This lack of interoperability is an economic inevitability as the incentives for the providers of the platforms mediate against it. Perhaps one may eventually see broad classes of assets in the inventory organized according to platforms, for example the Java EE and WCF service platforms, with protocol bridging provided as a necessary evil that is used at key contact points.

The SERVICE NORMALIZATION pattern is a basic criterion for the design of an inventory. It requires that services not overlap in the functionality that they provide because of the maintenance issues that this introduces. The analogy is with data normalization for relational database schemas, as discussed in Sect. 3.1.3. To review, consider the following database table:

Employee ID	Name	Dept	Supervisor
45345	Steve Dallas	IT	Bobbi Harlow
87452	Milo Bloom	Sales	Cutter John
87653	Michael Binkley	Sales	Cutter John
65349	Oliver W. Jones	IT	Bobbi Harlow

By repeating department-specific information for each employee, this schema causes maintenance issues, among other problems. For example, if the supervisor of a department changes, the records for all employees of that department must be updated. A more efficient schema factors out the department information to a separate table, referenced by a foreign key in the employee table:

Employee ID	Name	Dept ID
45345	Steve Dallas	786
87452	Milo Bloom	453
87653	Michael Binkley	453
65349	Oliver W. Jones	786

Dept ID	Name	Supervisor
453	Sales	Cutter John
786	IT	Bobbi Harlow

For example, a course-management system for on line teaching may rely on a tool for on line discussion fora for asynchronous interaction. This tool may include an on-line chat tool that allows posted discussions to become more interactive for parties that are signed on simultaneously. The course-management system may also rely on a video-conferencing tool for synchronous interaction, for example during office hours. The latter also includes a chat tool for students who do not have a microphone or would prefer text-based interaction. This provision of two chat tools is an example of overlapping functionality in two different services, and reflects a common phenomenon of two different tools developed independently. The chat tools will likely have different user interfaces, leading to "negative transfer" as users confuse the two interfaces. Their interfaces may even drift further apart over time. Effort is wasted on maintaining two separate tools that should have equivalent functionality. As further applications emerge for chat tools, such as in on-line 'Questions and Answers' sessions with prospective students, there is confusion about which tool to use. Service normalization dictates that the chat tool should be factored out into a separate tool, launched by the other client tools when necessary. An easier path may be to centralize the chat function in the video-conferencing tool. The discussion forum tool now becomes a service façade that includes both discussion forum and video-conferencing facilities, the latter launched from the former when necessary.

The LOGIC CENTRALIZATION pattern is intended to enforce the discipline required for the proper functioning of a service inventory. It requires that control of reusable software assets be centralized in the service inventory. The design process followed by project teams should require that any reusable services that are identified by that process be centralized in the service inventory. In particular, this pattern forbids the retrieval of a service from the inventory, its specialization, and then the incorporation of that specialized service into the final application. Such a practice is a recipe for a breakdown of the inventory, as more and more specialized instances of services are developed outside the inventory and eventually become a personal, reusable software base for development teams. Re-incorporating these specialized services back into the inventory, on the other hand, leads to a "de-normalized" service inventory, with overlapping functionality in different services owing to the independent development of service extensions by different project teams. Hence, the logic centralization pattern requires centralized control over such specialization, with that control located with the organizational unit with oversight over the inventory. What this means, in particular, is that if an existing service appears useful, but is missing functionality for an application, the project team depending on that extra functionality must defer to the controlling authority for the service inventory to manage the addition of the required extensions to the service. Not every project manager will be thrilled at this suggestion. Again, governance issues are critical.

Although there are good reasons for organizing the inventory on a domain by domain basis, there are still going to be services that can be reasonably considered as infrastructural support—cutting across both application and organizational boundaries. We have referred, at various times, to cross-cutting functionality, such as logging, authentication and authorization, transaction management, and so on. The UTILITY ABSTRACTION pattern recommends abstracting such common services to utility abstractions that become the basis for a UTILITY LAYER pattern that we described in Sect. 6.2 as the bottom layer in a generic SOA. *Transaction processing monitors* are a particularly important part of all middleware Support. Indeed, they are the most successful feature in modern middleware. We consider the subject of transactional computing and transaction-processing monitors in Chapter 9 in the sequel volume.

Security infrastructure is manifested by authentication services such as Kerberos and Security Assertion Markup Language (SAML), and authorization services such as eXtensible Access Control Markup Language (XACML), for role-based access control. We consider these in Chapter 15 in the sequel volume.

Some of these utility services will be wrappers for legacy services, for example the CICS transaction processing monitor. In addition to, or instead of, these utility services, applications will need to follow particular protocols, such as WS-Security or HTTPS for secure communication, and WS-Transaction or the XA API for transaction management. The CANONICAL RESOURCES pattern recommends this standardization of resources that are not encapsulated as services.

Layering is a general structuring concept for software systems. The example of layering of network protocol stacks was described in Sect. 2.2. More than simply the building of a composite system from simpler concepts, as with the service façade, SERVICE LAYERING builds a basic set of abstractons from lower-level services to be made available to upper-level services that may require these lower-level services for their inter-operation. The most basic form of layering is that of utility services, entity services, and process services described in Sect. 6.2, but further gradations are possible. For example, the layer of entity services may be further divided into *basic services* (business algorithms and databases) and *intermediate services* (service façades, technology gateways, etc.). As one supplier's service façade is another client's basic service, we have not emphasized this distinction. Just as the utility layer depends on identifying suitable utility abstractions to be encapsulated as services, so the ENTITY ABSTRACTION pattern recommends the identification of useful, stand-alone, and reusable business abstractions, for the definition of the entity layer. For example, useful business abstractions for insurance policy services would include quoting, billing and auditing services.

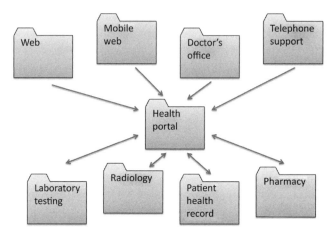

Figure 6.36 *Multi-channel health portal service*

Similarly, the PROCESS ABSTRACTION pattern recommends the identification of abstractions for potentially long-lived business processes. An interesting example of the application of this pattern is in the CHANNEL SWITCHING pattern [5]. Figure 6.36 provides an example of a health portal service, providing patients with access to view and manage their interactions with the healthcare systems. This makes use of several underlying services, such as laboratory testing, radiology, clinic and hospital out-patient services, etc. The patient has access to their personal health record and, through the portal, can also schedule tests and treatments and view the outcomes of tests and diagnoses. The patients themselves are, to some extent, being managed by this health portal. We might assume that the primary care physician can define a workflow for the tests, treatments, and consultations that a patient should follow during a course of treatment. The patient might be required to report their progress via the health portal. For example, AIDS patients would be reminded (via SMS) to take anti-retroviral drugs until they acknowledged doing so. Similarly, pregnant mothers could be reminded (again via SMS) to attend prenatal treatment at key points in the pregnancy. The physician is able to edit the workflow and may, for example, add decision logic based on threshold results from blood tests, or add logic for additional tests on the basis of what is learned from an initial test battery. Obviously, the physician is adding this logic through a form-based interface.

This is an example of the MULTI-CHANNEL ENDPOINT pattern, in the sense that it offers multiple entry points into the health portal. These include the obvious entry points via the Web and in a doctor's office (where privileged access may be provided to certain functions on the assumption of a more secure infrastructure, such as proper application of anti-computer-virus measures). In addition, there is both fixed network and mobile Web access. Finally, there is telephone support intended for clients who are having difficulty. Voice recognition software may be able to diagnose patient stress over a telephone. A cellphone camera may be used to measure a patient's heartbeat, based on micro-flushes in the patient's skin. If a client is exhibiting clinical symptoms with several possible diagnoses, it will useful for the support center to see the treatment workflow regime that the patient is currently under and perhaps move an appointment with a particular specialist earlier. The encapsulation of the patient's treatment as a workflow process facilitates this channel switching, as shown in Fig. 6.36.

Specific applications will make use of particular combinations of services at each layer. In particular, collaborative applications will need to agree on a "service stack" based on specific service layering. For example, services that require authenticated communication will require some form of *public key infrastructure* (PKI) to exchange trust. The parties will exchange documents digitally signed with their private cryptographic signing keys. Upon receipt of a document, the receiver uses the public authentication key of the sender to verify the signature for the document. For this scheme to work, the receiver must have some assurance that they have the correct authentication key for the sender. This infrastructure will typically consist of a *certification authority (CA)*, that issues certificates that certify the parties' public authentication keys. These certificates are, in turn, signed by the CA's private signing key—all parties trust the CA's signature. As private keys may be compromised, the CA provides a mechanism for revoking signatures. This can take two forms:

1. Signing key certificates may be revoked using a *certificate revocation list* (CRL) as depicted in Fig. 6.37(**a**). Such certificates are periodically issued by the CA, containing public authentication keys whose private signing keys have been revoked by signers. It is the responsibility of the party performing signature authentication to ensure that they have an up-to-date CRL.

2. Another alternative is to delegate the downloading of CRLs to a separate service, using an *online certificate status protocol* (OCSP) service as depicted in Fig. 6.37(**b**). This service is consulted whenever a signature is authenticated, to check the currency of the signing key corresponding to the signature.

In this example, the certificate authority, CRL directory, and OCSP service all comprise a service layer, along with protocol details such as the format of certificates and messages, and cryptographic algorithms, to support secure communication

(**a**) Certificate authority with certificate revocation lists (CRLs)

(**b**) Certificate authority with online certificate status protocol (OCSP)

Figure 6.37 *Certificate authority service layer*

between parties. Messages may, for example, use WS-Security to avail of this service layer in communication. WS-SecurityPolicy may be used to specify the use of WS-Security in the WSDL contract between the parties.

The SERVICE DECOMPOSITION pattern recommends decomposing services into the simplest basic services possible, to enhance both loose coupling and service reusability. The AGNOSTIC CONTEXT pattern recommends designing the basic services to be independent of the application context in which they execute. Again, this is important to facilitate reusability of the service. For example, in the health portal example above, the various basic processes that the patient workflow draws on should be defined to be independent of each other and of the overall patient-centered process to facilitate their use in other health-related applications. Laboratory services or pharmacies may be useful for epidemiologic purposes, revealing trends that indicate a particularly virulent flu outbreak. Services may still require the use of resources that would normally be provided as part of an application. For example, all of these services will require support for security and authentication. This dependency may be made explicit as part of the service contract, as suggested for example by service container applications that rely on runtime support from the container. This is not an implementation-dependent constraint, but an intrinsic part of the support that the service requires for its correct functioning. The AGNOSTIC CAPABILITY pattern recommends that this context-agnostic design approach be extended to the individual operations themselves in a service. The NON-AGNOSTIC CONTEXT pattern recommends that higher-level application logic be encapsulated as services—typically as process services. These then become part of the service inventory. Even though these services are not reusable per se, their encapsulation as services facilitates their composition with other services. For example, "mash-up" capabilities may be provided that allow clients to build customized portfolios of higher-level end-user services. We consider reuse of business process specifications in the sequel volume.

The *service inventory blueprint* is a document that outlines the structure and contents of the service inventory. It should identify both the agnostic and non-agnostic services in the inventory and their boundaries in such a way that ideally these boundaries do not overlap (i.e., the blueprint reflects a normalized design for the services in the inventory). The goal of logic centralization is to limit the choices for consumers of reusable services so that there is no ambiguity about which service to choose from the inventory. The contract centralization pattern then requires that all accesses to that service are with respect to the contract that it exports to clients. While logic centralization ensures exactly one candidate for a service, contract centralization ensures exactly one access point for that service.

We started this section by emphasizing the role of logic centralization in ensuring a normalized service inventory design. There is another pattern that centralizes business logic: the pattern of RULES CENTRALIZATION. Various workflows will give rise to data and control flows in the enterprise, and there will be business policies governing these flows. For example, there may be policies about not releasing certain documents classified at a particular confidentiality level without due authorization. HIPAA legislation governing patient health records places responsibilities on health providers to obtain patient permission before releasing their health records, for example to another provider. Financial reporting legislation, such as Sarbanes-Oxley, as well as historical archiving legislation for government bodies, will restrict the ability to dispose of certain documents, requiring that they be archived instead. It may be required to log all accesses to certain sensitive documents, i.e., to build audit trails in case of security breaches. There may be restrictions on the types of machines that data can be copied to. For example, data marked "top secret" cannot be stored on a machine that allows access to users with only "public" access, no matter the security measures on that machine. Rules centralization, as the name suggests, involves saving these forms of business logic in a rules engine—an architectural extension that reacts to events in the business by triggering a rule that executes the appropriate business logic. We consider this further, in the context of EDA, in Chapter 8 in the sequel volume.

The enterprise service bus is one particular manifestation of this pattern. The idea of the ESB is to provide a framework for flexible routing and data conversion logic for messages between parts of the enterprise. This routing logic is an example of the kind of business logic that may be centralized. Another form of logic that may be centralized is the validation of data exchanged between parts of the enterprise. The VALIDATION ABSTRACTION pattern abstracts the logic for validating data out of services and centralizes it, for example in the enterprise service bus. This achieves a form of loose coupling, allowing fine-grained changes in data contracts without unnecessarily affecting the services that are coupled by these data contracts. The data contract that is enforced by the services provides a coarse-grained specification of data—only revealing as much information as necessary for the service to be able to properly process the data.

6.9 SERVICE AUTONOMY

Service autonomy refers to the relative independence of services from each other. This has both a design-time and a run-time aspect to it. The design-time aspect is the pattern of service normalization, as discussed earlier: services should be designed to avoid overlapping functionality, as discussed in Sect. 6.8.4. However, the critical aspect of this principle is for run time: this principle dictates that a service implementation should have sufficient control over its run-time environment to be able to achieve quality-of-service guarantees for service clients, some of which may be formalized in service level agreements (SLAs).

For example, a financial accounting service provides operations for sales to, and payments from, customers. This is a critical resource for sales personnel and must be highly available and responsive at all times. Periodically, however, accounts must be reconciled during the normal accounting cycle; this reconciliation is an expensive operation in terms of the computing and network resources it requires. The DISTRIBUTED CAPABILITY pattern describes a design where the reconciliation operation is outsourced to a separate machine, in order not to interfere with the performance of the rest of the financial processing service. The PROXY CAPABILITY pattern describes an implementation of this design pattern, in terms of a client stub in the original service that invokes the actual reconciliation logic remotely. In Sect. 6.9.1, we consider support for the redundant implementation pattern, where a service implementation may be replicated across several (physical or virtual) machines.

We saw in Fig. 6.7 how data redundancy might be eliminated by encapsulating one of the data sources (the Enrollment and E-Classroom enrollment databases) as a single data service, perhaps "owned" by the Enrollment service, and then sharing it with the other service using an adapter. Although this removes the redundancy of two data stores in different services holding the same data, avoiding the danger of inconsistency and the overhead of synchronizing the two copies, it also makes the shared data store a performance bottleneck for the two services relying on it. In particular, the E-Classroom service that has given up "ownership" of the data store now may not have the control over the performance of the store that it requires to meet its own performance guarantees. Therefore, an appropriate configuration may be to cache the data at the second service by introducing a second data service that it controls and with the contents of that data service synchronized periodically with the Enrollment service data service. We consider caching in more detail in Sect. 6.9.4. Before then, we consider strategies for replicating services for high availability by replicating computation (Sect. 6.9.1) and by replicating state (Sect. 6.9.2). The latter of these strategies is related to the service data replication pattern, which we consider in Sect. 6.9.4.

6.9.1 Replicating Computation

Figure 2.10 in Sect. 2.3 provides a standard architecture for providing highly available services: a cluster of application servers run replicated versions of the service and a load balancer ensures that the load of client requests is uniformly distributed across the cluster. The load balancer itself is replicated, using *round-robin DNS*: the DNS service is used to inform clients about several possible endpoint addresses for a service, each one bound to by a load balancer. Clients attempt to bind to the services at the candidate IP addresses until they get a response. A key assumption underlying this architecture is that the services running in the cluster are stateless. This provides the load balancer with the freedom to direct each client request independently to the least loaded appliation server. If a service is engaged in a stateful dialogue with the client, then all of the requests from that client may need to be directed to the same application server instance: the one that has "affinity" with the client. There are ways of avoiding this inflexibility, using stateful services to factor the service state out of the application server. We discuss the principle of service statelessness in Sect. 6.10. Another obstacle to flexible load-balancing is *TCP connection pooling*: to reduce latency on the client, a TCP connection may be kept open (using the Keep-Alive field in HTTP headers) and reused over several Web requests in a HTTP session. Again, this ties the client to a particular server instance over time. Perhaps the logical approach to deal with this is to treat the open TCP connection on the server as part of the service state and allow it to be factored out to a state server in a similar manner to other forms of service deferral.

The recommended practice, however, is to keep the keep-alive period short, say starting at 30 seconds.

The REDUNDANT IMPLEMENTATION pattern is intended to build autonomous services by replicating their implementation, as in Fig. 2.10 in Sect. 2.3. There are several instances of the pattern in Fig. 2.10: the load balancer is replicated at different IP addresses, the application server running the service logic is replicated across the cluster, and, furthermore, the back-end database has a "hot standby" backup server, logging the updates of the primary database server and ready to take over if it fails.

Historically, service autonomy for replicated services has been realized by ensuring that each service instance is running alone on its own dedicated pool of machines in the server cluster, as illustrated in Fig. 6.38(**a**). For each service, there is a rack of servers in the cluster running just that service. The downside of this arrangement is the energy costs associated with such redundant implementation. Cooling costs are a significant part of the costs of hosting server farms. As a result, server architectures have moved to *virtualized platforms*, where several physical machines are consolidated onto one machine, as illustrated in Fig. 6.38(**b**). A software layer called the *hypervisor* mediates access to the underlying physical machine and provides the illusion of a "virtual machine" to each of the *guest servers* running on top of it. The benefit of this arrangement is that the enterprise does not need to allocate the maximum possible server resources across all types of servers. For "bursty" traffic for a particular service, resources can be diverted from lightly loaded parts of the cluster, subject to SLAs negotiated with the service providers. This is similar to the motivation for cloud computing, as discussed in Sect. 2.7.

The traditional approach to protection in operating systems is to make certain instructions *privileged*—accessible only to code executing in the operating system kernel. Each running application is isolated in its own process "address space"

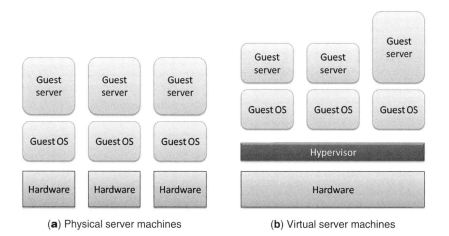

(**a**) Physical server machines   (**b**) Virtual server machines

Figure 6.38   *Redundant implementation: physical and virtual*

in memory, and access to hardware resources such as the disk and the network interface are similarly mediated by the operating system. The privileged access to certain instructions prevents applications from interfering with other applications by bypassing the kernel. Applications must call into the operating system for access to hardware resources. The challenge when virtualizing servers is that guest operating systems must similarly have restricted access to the hardware, so that access to the hardware (including memory) is mediated by the hypervisor. The first implementation technique used for virtualization (for the IBM VM/370 system) used *trap and emulate*. Guest machines run both user applications and the operating system in user mode on the physical hardware, although as far as the guest operating system is concerned, it is running in (guest) kernel mode, with privileged access to the hardware. Since it runs in actual user mode, an attempt by a guest operating system to use a privileged instruction traps to the hypervisor. The hypervisor must check that the guest machine was executing operating system code when it tried to execute a privileged instruction, so it is necessary for the hypervisor to keep track of the mode (guest user or guest kernel) of the guest machine. If the guest was running in guest kernel mode, then the hypervisor can emulate the privileged hardware instruction on behalf of the guest kernel, while ensuring that it does not interfere with other guest machines or the hypervisor data structures. However, this implementation method is too slow to be practical, requiring trapping to the hypervisor to emulate privileged hardware instructions. Furthermore, the x86 architecture, designed when virtualization was no longer considered relevant, has issues that do not make it amenable to trap and emulate for virtualization.[22]

Another implementation technique for virtualization is *binary translation*. The machine code for a running guest is dynamically translated by the hypervisor, rewriting it so that privileged instructions are replaced by calls to the hypervisor. This approach has the benefit that it works in the absence of hardware support. This was the original basis for VMWare's virtualization products on x86 architectures, and is the basis for emulators for mobile devices such as Android, where the instruction sets for the emulated and native machines are different.

Another implementation technique for virtualization, pioneered by the Xen hypervisor, is *paravirtualization*. A guest operating system is modified to call into hypervisor functions for privileged operations, instead of trying to access the hardware through privileged instructions. In effect the guest operating system becomes a client of the privileged hardware operations provided by the hypervisor. This approach requires modification of the guest kernel, though not of the applications that run on that guest kernel. It is considered the virtualization technique of choice for virtualizing high-performance I/O, and may be combined with other techniques such as interpretative execution for instruction emulation.

The preferred approach to implementing processor virtualization is hardware-assisted *interpretive execution*. The hardware distinguishes a guest mode and a

---

[22]There are x86 instructions that are *sensitive*, meaning that they expose aspects of the physical machine to the guest virtual machine, but they are *not privileged*, meaning that a guest will not trap to the hypervisor if it tries to execute the sensitive instruction [73].

hypervisor mode. The hypervisor executes in hypervisor mode, and uses a privileged hardware instruction to run guest machine code in guest mode. While running in guest mode, the privileged instructions are virtualized, in the sense that they are emulated on behalf of guest machines by the hardware. With trap-and-emulate, this emulation would be done in software by the hypervisor, relying on traps back to the hypervisor when the guest tries to execute privileged instructions. The advantage of the virtualized instruction approach is that it avoids these traps back to the hypervisor. Originally implemented in the System 370 Extended Architecture (370-XA) [72], interpretive execution is now supported on x86 platforms, and will eventually be available on mobile devices, such as smartphones and tablets. In the z/Architecture mainframe hardware, the instruction for executing code in guest mode is itself virtualized, allowing a hypervisor to launch another "child" hypervisor, referred to as a "second level" hypervisor.

A common technique for virtualizing I/O devices is to rely on a privileged process that performs I/O on behalf of guest machines. This is the approach taken by the Xen hypervisor. Because of the latency involved in transferring control from a guest to this privileged process, through the hypervisor, the KVM hypervisor combines the hypervisor and this privileged process, by embedding the hypervisor as a module in the Linux kernel. Guest machines then run as Linux processes, alongside normal Linux processes. The Linux kernel schedules I/O for guests, as it does for normal Linux processes, without attempting to provide "virtual" I/O devices. The advantage of this approach is the greater scalability of the virtualization. The KVM approach is now a standard part of the Linux kernel.

6.9.2   Replicating State

We have seen how stateless services may be distributed across a pool of application servers, running on a virtualized server rack. The distribution of services in this pool of application servers is greatly facilitated by the provision of stateless services. What if the services are in fact stateful? Such a service may be a state repository or back-end database to which application servers (implicitly or explicitly) connect to retrieve and update persistent state, or or it may be actual stateful services that keep state locally for performance reasons.

A peer-to-peer approach to replication allows a client to contact any of a pool of service replicas for its back-end operations. If one server in the pool fails, the client is unaffected as long as it can connect to another replica that is still available. The intention is that the servers in the replica pool cooperate to keep their shared state synchronized, so that a client has a consistent view of the replicated data, no matter which server instance it interacts with.

If the client is allowed to read from any replica in the pool, then any updates must be performed at all replicas to ensure that any subsequent reads by other clients see the results of those updates. If a single server fails, then no client can make progress with updates until that server recovers. This is not the definition of a highly available system. *Available copies* only requires that the client performs updates on the servers that are currently available, but issues still remain.

For example, if the network partitions into two separate partitions, perhaps because of a router failure on a subnet, then clients may make independent updates on two different replicas that are currently disconnected from each other. *Quorum consensus* prevents this pathology by requiring that an update can only be performed if a quorum of currently available replicas can be established. If such a quorum cannot be achieved, clients must wait until more server instances become available, for example when the isolated subnet rejoins the rest of the network, before they can do further updates.

Although clients can still make progress with failed servers as long as they can contact a quorum of available servers, there is still the issue that simply contacting any of the available servers to read the current state is insufficient to guarantee "fresh" data. The server that is contacted may have been down when the last update was performed and so has no record of the current value of the data. The rules of quorum consensus are formulated to ensure that, for every write *and for every read operation*, a client must attain a sufficient quorum of servers in order to make progress. Assuming N servers, the designer of a quorum consensus system must choose two quantities, a *read quorum* Q_R and a *write quorum* Q_W, such that the following two properties are satisfied:

1. $Q_R + Q_W > N$, i.e., any read quorum must overlap with any write quorum;
2. $Q_W + Q_W > N$, i.e., any write quorum must overlap with any other write quorum.

The rationale for these constraints is that a reader of service state must be guaranteed that it has read the service state on a sufficient number of replica servers so that at least one of the replicas is guaranteed to have the up-to-date value of the state. For example, with $N = 3$, we should set the read and write quora to two. This ensures that a client can still make progress with either a read or a write operation, even with the failure of one of the replicas.

With this scheme, we can still make progress despite the failure of any one server. We assume that some form of timestamp is placed on the state every time it is updated so we can always determine which value among those provided by the replicas is the most current. This is illustrated in Fig. 6.39(**a**), where Client A performs an update on Servers X and Y, but not Server Z, which is not available at the time of Client A's update. In Fig. 6.39(**b**), Client B is performing a read and must attain a read quorum of two. Client B successfully contacts Servers Y and Z. The value stored at Z is out of date as Server Z was down when Client A made its update. However, because of the rules on the size of the quora, the other server contacted by Client B (i.e., Server Y) must have an up-to-date copy of the state. Therefore, the protocol for performing a read of the service state is to obtain a read quorum of server replicas, and choose the copy of the state from the server replica in the read quorum that has the latest timestamp.

The overlapping of write quora prevents *concurrent updates*, for example two updates that are unrelated to each other and cannot be reconciled if they are being performed on the same part of the service state. As any client performing an update

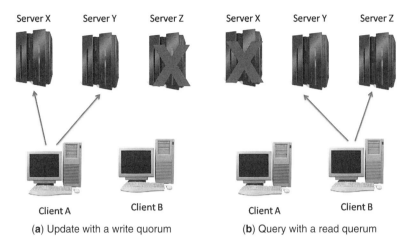

(a) Update with a write quorum   (b) Query with a read querum

Figure 6.39 *Quorum consensus*

must obtain a write quorum, if two clients attempt to perform their updates at the same time, there must be at least one server replica where their write quora overlap. Both updates will be done on this replica, and the order in which they are done on this replica determines the global order on those two update operations. In Fig. 6.39(**b**), if Client B is performing a write concurrently with Client A, their write quora overlap on Server Y; the order in which the update operations are performed on Server Y determines the global order for the two update operations.

The order of the update operations is critically important. It is vital to any form of replication scheme that the result of using replicated servers is indistinguishable from a single server, in terms of the underlying persistent state. The *active* or *state machine* approach to replication assumes that every replica is a deterministic state machine, meaning that every state change is completely deterministic: each machine will end up in exactly the same state, if they are in the same starting state and if they perform the same sequence of operations, with the same inputs, in the same order.[23] Therefore, the key to making sure that all replicas are consistent is to ensure that all see the update operations in the same order.

Although write quora ensure that two update operations are seen on at least one common replica (the one in the overlap of the write quora for those operations), there is still the possibility that two update operations will be performed on two different server replicas *in different orders*. Figure 6.40(a) demonstrates this with Clients A and B performing their updates on all three replicas. However, whereas Client A's update is done first on Server X, it is ordered after Client B's update on the other two servers. Suppose that Client A's update is to increment a bank account balance by $100, the result of a deposit, while Client B's update is to increment the bank account balance by 5%, the result of an interest payment. Because of the

---

[23] Actually achieving this deterministic semantics, with the asynchrony of I/O and multi-threaded execution, is a challenge, as evidenced by experience with the FT-CORBA model of replicated services [74].

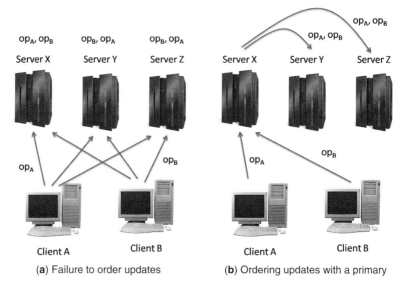

(**a**) Failure to order updates   (**b**) Ordering updates with a primary

Figure 6.40   *Ordered update*

order of the updates, Server X's copy of the bank account has a different bank balance from Servers Y and Z. The different replicas are inconsistent in the state they are replicating, which is disastrous for transparent replication and correct client functioning.

A peer-to-peer solution to this is to have a write quorum of replicas vote on a timestamp for the next update operation. Again, the use of a write quorum ensures that at least one replica in the quorum has seen the most recent updates, ensuring that the timestamp that is chosen for the update will be ordered after these previous updates. An example of this protocol is provided in Sect. B.3.2 in Appendix B. This is effectively a consensus protocol and is vulnerable to the impossibility results for consensus in asynchronous systems considered in Sect. 2.3. In the voting protocol in Sect. B.3.2, the impossibility result manifests itself in the fact that two clients competing to post their updates may loop infinitely often as they attempt to resolve their contention. We can say that with high probability, this behavior will not manifest itself and the protocol will terminate. However a more practical objection is that replicas must return copies of their logs to a client, so that the client can construct a view of the current state of the replicated object. Various optimization techniques, to reduce the amount of log information that is exchanged, do not fully alleviate this burden. This approach is mainly applicable when the operations simply overwrite existing values, so only the last operation in a log needs to be returned to the client. Even without failures, the performance of the active approach to replication degrades as the size of the system increases [75]. A more scalable approach is the *passive* or *primary copy* approach, where one server instance is designated as the primary [76, 77]. This primary replica then decides the order in which to perform the update operations, actually performs those update operations, and propagates the results of those updates to the available replicas. This is illustrated in Fig. 6.40(**b**). This approach has the advantage that, as the operations themselves are only performed on the primary, with updates propagated to the replicas, it is no longer necessary to ensure deterministic state machine semantics. A hybrid approach may have a primary choose the order of the updates and then distribute those updates to be re-executed on each replica. This approach may be preferable if state updates are large.

An obvious issue with the primary copy approach is: what happens if the primary server crashes? There must then be a protocol for failing over to another replica as the primary, preferably without affecting any client requests already in progress. The primary should wait to have its updates acknowledged from a quorum of the backups before responding back to the client, otherwise the primary might fail after responding to the client, and a subsequent primary might be unaware of the update. Note also that it is important that a process that is taking over as primary learn of any updates that it "missed" before it actually starts functioning as the primary by contacting a quorum of the replicas.

For performance reasons, the propagation of updates from the primary to the replicas might be done asynchronously in parallel with the response returned to the client. If the primary fails after notifying the client but before the update was recorded at the backups, the "lost" update will not be discovered until the recovery of the primary. In this case, updates done at the subsequent primary will need to be "reconciled" with the lost updates logged at the crashed primary but not propagated to replicas before failure. For example, a bank server might acknowledge a withdrawal of funds to an automated teller machine (ATM) before crashing. The customer's withdrawal is lost until the failed primary recovers. In the meantime the customer may make further withdrawals that, in combination with the lost update, put their account into overdraft. In this case, there may be protocols for resolving this inconsistency, for example by sending a letter to the customer asking them to deposit funds back into their bank account. The protocols described in Sect. B.3.2 avoid this pathology by waiting for a quorum of replicas to acknowledge an update before responding to the client. This guarantees that the update will survive a failure of a minority of the replicas.

The primary must be able to achieve a write quorum of replicas in order to complete the updates. The write quorum is to prevent more than one set of replicas choosing a primary and performing updates as a result of a network partition. In general, if up to f server failures are to be tolerated, then there must be at least $2f+1$ server replicas. Therefore, at least three replicas are necessary if a single failure is to be tolerated. Perhaps computer science and IT can learn from civil engineering [78]:

> [T]he major breakthrough [in engineering of railway bridges] was the concept of a margin of safety; engineers would enhance their designs by a factor of 3 to 6 to accommodate the unknown. The safety margin compensates for flaws in building material, construction mistakes, overloading, and even design errors. Since humans design, build, and use bridges, and since human errors are inevitable, the margin of safety is necessary. Also called the margin of ignorance, it allows safe structures

without having to know everything about the design, implementation, and future use of a structure. Despite use of supercomputers and mechanical CAD to design bridges [today], civil engineers still multiply the calculated load by a small integer to be safe.

In the *viewstamp* approach, each configuration of available server replicas is a *view* identified by an integer view identifier [79]. A crash of the primary causes a viewstamp change: the view identifier is incremented to choose the new primary, where the identity of the primary is taken to be the view identifier modulo N, the number of replicas. The read quorum is unnecessary as the client can contact the primary to access an up-to-date copy of the replicated state. All timestamps on updates are formed of a pair of the viewstamp (for the current primary) and an update count chosen by that primary. This ensures that there is no confusion between updates offered by different primaries during different views. We discuss this protol in more detail in Sect. B.3.2. We considered possible strategies to deal with the challenges of consensus in asynchronous systems in Sect. 2.3 and we consider some of these approaches in more detail in Chapter 10 in the sequel volume.

Some caveats should be offered. At least some of these approaches assume tightly-coupled protocols synchronizing updates to replicated data, and may only be applicable within a server cluster. Typically, the use of these approaches will be encapsulated behind a service contract with internal communication within the cluster using high performance, tightly-coupled communication protocols (i.e., not Web services). The quorum consensus approaches rely on ensuring that an update is successfully propagated to all (or at least enough) available replicas; this is an amazingly hard problem to solve, as evidenced by the FLP result described in Sect. 2.3. High-performance databases may not apply these heavyweight protocols on every update, but typically only attempt consensus between coordinated databases as part of the finalization of a client transaction—they then log those updates asynchronously to backups. As already mentioned, such asynchronous propagation of updates from a primary may eventually lead to a need for reconciliation, as recovering replicas reveal updates that were not propagated to the other replicas before they crashed. NoSQL data stores, discussed in the sequel volume, explicitly trade consistency for performance, allowing temporary data inconsistency to enable scalable database replication.

6.9.3 Sources of Errors and Rejuvenation

Why do services fail? Gray [80] famously blamed the software. He observed:

> Conventional well-managed transaction processing systems fail about once every two weeks [81, 82]. The ninety minute outage outlined above translates to 99.6% availability for such systems. 99.6% availability sounds wonderful, but hospital patients, steel mills, and electronic mail users do not share this view–a 1.5 hour outage every ten days is unacceptable. Especially since outages usually come at times of peak demand [82].

A large source of the failures are caused by operator errors. Gray noted that 42% of failures in a transaction processing system were caused by operator errors.

Patterson et al. [78] reported on a study that found that 59% of failures in a public, switched-telephone network, and 51% of failures among three anonymous Internet sites were caused by operator error. The smaller number of operator errors for public Internet sites is likely only caused by a higher number of software errors. Other major failures, such as the Three Mile Island incident and incidents involving fly-by-wire commercial airliners, are blamed on operator errors, usually after an investigation by the designers of the system that the operators were using [83]. *Autonomic computing* is a field of study that intends to make large software systems self-maintaining using approaches from machine learning [84]. Patterson et al. [78] report on the *automation irony* from human error research: as operator interfaces automate away the routine maintenance tasks, human users get less experience with the operation of the system, and then have less experience to draw on when dealing with rare but significant problems.

Gray splits software bugs into two categories: *Bohrbugs* and *Heisenbugs*. Bohrbugs are the forms of bugs that are deterministic and relatively easy to deal with. The developer allocated a certain amount of space for data, an array of a fixed size, and did not allow for the eventuality that the amount of input data exceeded this space. The software crashes, as a result of an array index being out of bounds when offered input data sets of a certain size. An interactive debugger allows the developer to reproduce this behavior as they step through the code.

Heisenbugs are far more subtle and difficult to diagnose. These bugs are typically not easily reproducible, making testing and debugging a challenge. Memory allocation failures, particularly dangling references, have historically been a source of many of these errors: a program module de-allocates a piece of storage because the logic dictates that it is no longer required, but a pointer is retained in some other part of the program to the storage. Some part of that memory is re-allocated to another program module. There are now two different parts of the application aliasing the same region of memory so that, for example, one module starts seeing its variables changing "by magic." Automatic memory management, using garbage collection, has eliminated many of these sources of error, but garbage collection has its limitations. For example, it does not scale over networks, except in extremely tightly-coupled applications. The approach is usually to provide a "lease" on a piece of storage to a client, and require the client to periodically renew the lease in order to keep the storage live. If the renewal message is delayed and the storage de-allocated, the client will eventually crash attempting to follow the dead pointer; however, this behavior is almost certainly preferable to unpredictable behavior caused by dangling references.

Race conditions are another common source of Heisenbugs. For example, two threads A and B may be incrementing the same integer variable X in parallel. If they do not synchronize, some increments will be overwritten and lost. Thread A may read the value of X, then thread B may read and modify the value with an increment. Thread A then overwrites this increment with its own incremented value. In large enterprise software systems with many moving parts, it is easy to make such synchronization mistakes. The over-cautious developer may start locking variables too aggressively, leading to increased deadlocking in applications. Software transactional memory is intended to automatically manage concurrent accesses to memory: access to memory is performed without synchronization, using transactional semantics and optimistic concurrency control. If interference is detected between two transactions as they attempt to commit, one of those transactions is aborted and rolled back.

Checkpointing, rollback, and recovery are techniques associated with server recovery from failures that could be combined with, for example, the primary copy approach described in the last section. A running application periodically saves a checkpoint of its state to disk. Such a checkpoint will include a copy of the variables for the application, as well as a "snapshot" that includes any messages in transit. Buffered file I/O will have been flushed to disk to ensure it survives a failure that loses all data in transient memory. Upon a failure, the application state is rolled back to the last snapshot, for example discarding any messages that are received that were originally sent after the snapshot was recorded. The in-transit messages that were saved, at least those exchanged internally between components of the applications, are re-sent from the saved snapshot. The values of the application variables are restored from the snapshot. Finally, the application itself is restarted from the recovered checkpoint.

The approach of *rejuvenation* is to pre-emptively roll an application back to a checkpoint and then restart the application [85]. In restarting the application, data structures may be "cleaned up", perhaps by re-initializing them altogether. Indeed, it may be possible to roll the application back to its original state. In general, there will be a cost to rejuvenation; this cost must be weighed against the benefit of reducing the probability of a future system failure. Presumably, the cost of a restart because of rejuvenation is less than the cost of recovering from failure. For example, system failures will typically fail at peak loads when an enterprise can least afford to have the system down (e.g., a television network's election coverage service fails on election night). Rejuvenation allows this downtime to be scheduled at a time that minimizes cost as a result of lost business.

The decision about when to rejuvenate is based on characteristics of the application. A model for reasoning about these characterisitics is provided in Fig. 6.41 [85]. In the model for making the decision about when to rejuvenate, it is assumed that there is a period at the start of execution of the application when its probability of failure is close to zero. This period is termed the application's *base longevity interval*. At some point, a threshold is passed at which the probability of failure

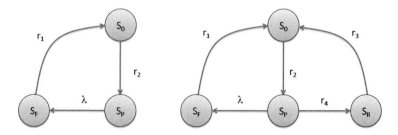

Figure 6.41 *State transitions with and without rejuvenation*

begins to increase significantly and the application transitions from the safe state S_0 to the failure-probable state S_P. The length of the base longevity interval is assumed to be exponentially distributed, with a probabilistic mean rate of r_1. In other words, r_1 is the inverse of the expected time that the system takes to transition to the failure-probable state. The system eventually transitions to a failed state S_F, with probabilistic mean rate λ. Finally, the system is recovered back to the initial safe state, with the recovery period again exponentially distributed with probabilistic repair rate r_2. Letting p_0, p_p, and p_f denote the steady state probabilities of being in states S_0, S_P, and S_F, respectively, we can derive closed form solutions for these probabilities using the flow equations $p_0 \cdot r_1 = p_p \cdot \lambda$ and $p_p \cdot \lambda = p_F \cdot r_2$, and $p_0 + p_p + p_f = 1$.

Rejuvenation introduces a new state, the rejuvenation state S_R, with a steady state probability of being in that state of p_r. The repair rate for transitioning from the rejuvenation state to the safe state is r_3, reflecting the possibility that recovering from rejuventation, a planned shutdown and restart, will take less time than recovering from an unanticipated fault. If the rejuvenation period is set to be t time units, the system transitions to the rejuvenation state with probability or rejuventaton rate $r_4 = \frac{1}{t}$. Solving the flow equations for this modified system, we obtain the probabilities:

$$p_p = \frac{1}{1 + \frac{\lambda}{r_1} + \frac{r_4}{r_3} + \frac{\lambda + r_4}{r_2}}$$

$$p_f = \frac{\lambda}{r_1} \cdot p_p$$

$$p_r = \frac{r_4}{r_3} \cdot p_p$$

$$p_0 = \frac{\lambda + r_4}{r_2} \cdot p_p$$

Then, for an interval of length L time units, and costs c_f and c_r associated with being in the failure and rejuvenation states, respectively, we have the expected down-time and expected down time cost:

$$DownTime(L) = (p_f + p_r) \cdot L$$

$$Cost(L) = (p_f \cdot c_f + p_r \cdot c_r) \cdot L$$

The result of the analysis, differentiating with respect to r_4, demonstrates that r_4 does not affect the decision to use rejuvenation. Rejuvenation should be used not at all, or used as soon as the system enters the failure probable state. Whether or not to use rejuvenation depends on the cost of rejuvenation, and whether or not it is sufficiently dominated by the cost of failure.

Example 1. The mean time between failures (MTBF) is 12 months, so $\lambda = \frac{1}{(12 \cdot 30 \cdot 24)}$. The recovery time from an unexpected error is 30 minutes, so $r_1 = 2$, assuming the time units are hours. The base longevity interval is estimated to be seven days, so $r_2 = \frac{1}{7 \cdot 24}$. The mean repair time after rejuvenation is estimated to be 20 minutes, so $r_3 = 3$. Finally, the average cost of unscheduled downtime caused by failure, c_f, is \$1000 per hour, while the average cost of scheduled downtime owing to rejuvenation, c_r, is \$40 per hour. Then, we have the following results:

	No rejuvenation $(r_4 = 0)$	Every three weeks $(r_4 = \frac{1}{2 \cdot 7 \cdot 24})$	Every two weeks $(r_4 = \frac{1}{1 \cdot 7 \cdot 24})$
Hours of downtime	0.490	5.965	8.727
Cost of downtime	490	554	586

In this case, the benefit of rejuvenation does not justify its use. One may as well let the system fail, and then plan to recover from unanticipated failure.

Example 2. The MTBF is shorter than before (three months), so $\lambda = \frac{1}{(3 \cdot 30 \cdot 24)}$. The recovery time from an unexpected error is 30 minutes, as before. The base longevity interval is estimated to be three days, so $r_2 = \frac{1}{3 \cdot 24}$. The mean repair time after rejuvenation is estimated to be 10 minutes, so $r_3 = 6$. Finally, the average cost of unscheduled downtime caused by failure, c_f, is \$5000 per hour, while the average cost of scheduled downtime owing to rejuvenation, c_r, is \$50 per hour. This scenario is much more conducive to rejuvenation and we have the following results:

	No rejuvenation $(r_4 = 0)$	Every two weeks $(r_4 = \frac{1}{11 \cdot 24})$	Every week $(r_4 = \frac{1}{4 \cdot 24})$
Hours of downtime	1.94	5.70	9.52
Cost of downtime	9675.25	7672.43	5643.31

In this example, rejuvenation is beneficial. Indeed, although down-time increases when the rejuvenation rate r_4 is increased, the cost of down time decreases. As long as cost is the deciding factor, one should perform rejuvenation as frequently as possible.

Example 3. For this example, the parameters are as before, except that the base longevity interval is 10 days (so $r_2 = \frac{1}{10 \cdot 24}$). Also, the time to recover from unanticipated failure is 2 hours, so $r_2 = 0.5$. In this case, both down-time and the cost owing to down-time are reduced when the rejuvenation rate is increased:

	No rejuvenation $(r_4 = 0)$	Every month $(r_4 = \frac{1}{(30-10) \cdot 24})$	Every two weeks $(r_4 = \frac{1}{(14-10) \cdot 24})$
Hours of downtime	7.19	6.83	6.36
Cost of downtime	3600	2480	1110

6.9.4 Caching

The final aspect of service autonomy that we will consider is the use of *caching*. A cache is a temporary data store placed between a storage system (referred to as the *backing store*) and clients of that storage system, temporarily saving data that has been retrieved from the backing store in case the client attempts to retrieve the same data from the storage system again. Examples of caching in computer systems abound. Both Web browsers and Internet service providers use Web proxies to cache data retrieved from the Web, to cut down on Web traffic.

The SERVICE DATA REPLICATION pattern is intended for situations where a service is using a backing store of some kind, typically a relational database, and caches some of that content locally at the service network node. Many Web sites use Memcached, a distributed in-memory data cache where database content is cached in the memory of cache servers that act as proxies for the database. NoSQL data stores weaken the relational data model in order to better support database replication, among other reasons, to provide regional caches of database content. The motivation is largely to reduce the latency on data accesses from the backing store and, in the context of service autonomy, to decouple the service from any heavy loads experienced by the back-end. If the service is running in a cluster of application servers, there are several issues:

1. The cache may be used to store client-specific information for the duration of a client session. This means that a load balancer must always be used to redirect that client's requests to the same application server. In turn, this mediates against transparent load-balancing of client requests across the available application servers, hence the admonition by middleware systems that developers implement services as stateless services as much as possible. We consider state in Web services in more detail in Sect. 6.10.

2. If database updates are being performed on the service cache, then there is the danger that updates will be lost if that application server fails. An even worse situation may arise if some of the updates have been posted back to the database (but not all of them) when the application server fails. The typical solution to this is to use transactional semantics to ensure that either all of the changes are made permanent, or they are all discarded.

6.9.4.1 Tightly-Coupled Caching   If the cache is tightly coupled to the backing store, then the important issue is when updates on cached data are flushed to the backing store. The NFS architecture is a reasonable example to use when discussing some of these issues [86]. The original intent of NFS was to provide *sequential semantics* for files, in the sense that any update made to a file on the server is viewed by any clients that subsequently read the file. This is the semantics of local file accesses—sequential semantics seeks to provide the same semantics for files accessed on the server as files accessed locally. File contents are retrieved at the granularity of a disk block at a time and, for performance, the NFS client caches these disk blocks locally, actually using the block buffer cache of the client

file system. Disk blocks that are modified on the client are marked "dirty", to be written back to the server eventually.

An interesting, although overstated, issue with NFS is the simultaneous sharing of a cached file by multiple clients when the updates made by a client are made visible to other clients.[24] There are several possible semantics for the handling of updates on cached data. *Write-through caching* flushes an update to the server immediately. On the other hand, other clients may not become aware of this update immediately, unless the server keeps track of the clients that have the file open and notifies them when the updates are flushed. This has not been the case with NFS which, as we saw in Sect. 2.4, was originally designed to be a stateless server. Clients are configured to periodically poll the server to see if file blocks that they have retrieved have been modified by other clients. The longer this interval, the wider the window for clients to work with stale data. However, shorter intervals place extra load on the network, with polling traffic. Write-through caching is not part of the NFS default semantics because of its poor performance for the client. It results in high latencies on every write operation. Write-through caching may be configured for database applications that require prompt notification of client updates.

Delayed-write caching propagates updates to the server "lazily" and asynchronously with the updates being performed locally on the client. This will typically be implemented by regular scans of the cache and the flushing of dirty disk blocks to the server. For performance reasons, this strategy is much more widely used. Client applications do not experience high latency waiting for write operations to complete on the server. However, it can be a source of low reliability. For example, if a client crashes, it is non-deterministic which of the client updates were flushed to the server, leading to the possibility of inconsistent data. The Microsoft Common Internet File System (CIFS), aka Server Message Block (SMB), uses *opportunistic locks* to grant permission to a client to use delayed-write caching. If another client requests an "OpLock" on a file, the first client is sent a message by the server requiring it to release its OpLock and flush its updates back to the server. Opportunistic locks are only for caching behavior, not for synchronization.

Write-on-close semantics is "required" by NFS semantics, but can be disabled in a client. This semantics requires that a client flush its updates to the server when a file is closed—any other client that subsequently opens the file will see the first client's updates. This semantics is also used by the Andrew File System (AFS), although AFS also requires the server to notify clients that have the file open when updates are flushed to give them the opportunity to refresh their copy of the file.

There are subtle interactions between client-side and server-side caching, as illustrated in Fig. 6.42. If the client issues a close operation that flushes its updates

---

[24]In practice, files that are shared are usually programs, and therefore modified infrequently, usually by periodic software updates. If a client is updating a file, it is probably their own file, not shared with other clients. If two clients are in the special case of sharing a file that they are updating simultaneously, then numerous solutions exist to support this, for example, collaborative editors such as Lotus Notes or Google Docs, database servers, or file version-management tools such as subversion and git.

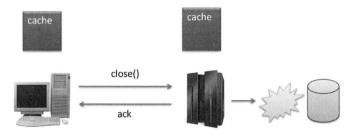

Figure 6.42 *Failure to commit client updates on an NFS server*

to the server, then when does the server acknowledge receipt of the updates? A typical behavior is to acknowledge receipt of the updates once they are received in the server block buffer cache in memory. The client-side `close` operation returns to the client application, which now believes its changes have been made permanent on the server. However, the updates are only cached in memory on the server. If the server crashes, the updates are lost, which may confuse the client when they try to read their updates in a subsequent session. The obvious solution, to have the client wait until the updates in the server cache are written to disk, would introduce too much latency on the server. Since NFS v3, an *asynchronous COMMIT* operation is provided for flushing updates from client to server; the client is required to buffer the updates until the COMMIT is acknowledged.

The choice of the update propagation semantics has a bearing on, and is heavily influenced by, the *cache consistency policy*, i.e., the level of sharing consistency experienced by clients. As we have seen, *sequential sharing semantics* requires that every update on a file is immediately visible to all other clients: a read of a disk block by a client returns the result of the last write, even if that write was done by another client. As can be seen, this is a very expensive semantics to support: not only does it require write-through caching, but any other clients with access to the file must be immediately notified of the update.

A second form of cache consistency is *session semantics*: updates by a client are only made visible when the client closed the file. AFS uses this update policy: when a file is opened, a copy of the entire file is transmitted to the client. When the client closes the file, the updated file is transmitted back to the server. The server keeps track of all clients that have the file open, and notifies them when a client flushes an updated version of the file. These other clients then have the option of retrieving a more up-to-date version of the file from the server. If an AFS server crashes, then its recovery protocol includes contacting clients to find out what files are being cached by clients. The NFS semantics, using *close-to-open*, is not quite session semantics, as it allows updates to be flushed to the server before the file is closed. Also, NFS does not require the server to notify other clients of this update, as the server does not maintain this state information for clients. NFS v4 does support *delegation on open*: if a file is being updated by a single client, then the server may delegate opening, closing, and locking operations to the client. The advantage is that these operations are done locally at the client, so periodic cache consistency checks are unnecessary. Delegation is lease-based: when the lease expires, or another client opens the file for update, the server revokes the delegation via a callback to the client.

A third semantics is *immutable files*: files cannot be modified—any modifications result in a new file. This leads to a very simple sharing semantics: there is no sharing of updates and clients that require shared updates should avail of other solutions, as mentioned above. A final option is *transactional semantics*: the updates on a file by a client are grouped into a transaction—transactional semantics prevents other clients from seeing those updates unless, and until, the transaction commits.

6.9.4.2 Loosely-Coupled Caching   Loosely-coupled caches are useful for mobile clients. This is the motivation for the IndexedDB Web standard (under development by W3C) to enable platform-neutral database caching on Web clients. We discuss ways of replicating data in a loosely-coupled fashion, for caching purposes. Such replication may be done in a client-server fashion, or the replication may be done peer-to-peer, for example synchronizing data between devices across a Bluetooth connection instead of synchronizing through the cloud. In what follows, we focus on replication with a central data resource, which may or may not be in the cloud.

We saw that a key design decision in tightly-coupled caching schemes is the cache consistency property that the system is designed to provide to clients. The Grapevine replicated email system [87] provided *best effort consistency*. Experience with the system was that replicas failed to converge to consistent copies of the shared data (mail folders). The causes included updates performed in different orders on replicas. Therefore, it is important for some notion of consistency for updates be ordered, as we saw in Sect. 6.9.2 for replicated databases in a cluster. For mobile data sharing, consistency is normally specified as *eventual consistency*, which has two properties:

1. *Total propagation*: all updates are eventually propagated to all replicas.
2. *Consistent ordering*: the ordering of the updates on the replicas is, in some sense, "consistent." One notion of consistency is total ordering: the updates are seen in the same order at all replicas. A weaker notion of ordering is causal ordering: an ordering is only specified between two updates if there is a causal chain of updates from one update to the other. We review these notions in Sect. B.2 (Appendix B).

Another question is what to do with out-of-order updates received on replicas. The approach suggested in Fig. 6.40(**b**) (with more details in Appendix B) is to delay delivery of an out-of-order update to the application at the replica; instead, the update is buffered in the middleware until the logically preceding updates are received. For loosely-connected operation, such as in mobile systems, this is impractical. Update delivery may be delayed indefinitely, buffered in the middleware and unavailable to applications, while waiting for the propagation of preceding updates. The alternative approach with loosely-connected operations is to perform *tentative update*: an update U_2 is performed as soon as it is received at a replica but, upon receipt of an update U_1 that logically preceded it, the update U_2 must be rolled back, the update U_1 applied, and the update U_2 then re-applied to the replica. For this to scale, it is critical to have an API for specifying when operations are *commutative*. This will allow a later update to be permuted with an earlier update that is received after it, instead of having to undo the later update to apply the earlier update.

Other notions of consistency may be layered on eventual consistency. *Bounded consistency* may require that, for example, data be no more than one hour old, although this puts bounds on the level of disconnectivity that can be tolerated [88]. *Hybrid consistency* may have dual notions of consistency, based on the level of connectedness. For example, strong consistency may be required while the device is connected via WiFi or 3G/4G, while only local access to the data is allowed while the device is disconnected. In general, the approach of remote versus local access is related to the consistency of the data versus the latency of accessing a remote copy. So, even if connected, weak consistency may still be allowed if the connection has low bandwidth or high latency.

We have seen that session semantics are the most viable for tightly-coupled caching that supports concurrent updates. Several notions of session consistency are available when working with local replicated data [89]. These consistency semantics can again be layered over the global consistency requirements such as strong or eventual consistency. The client should pick the session semantics that is most suitable for its application. The first two session semantics, illustrated in Fig. 6.43, concern client reads performed in a session:

1. *Read Your Writes* [Fig. 6.43(**a**)]: This provides a sequential semantics *within a session*. A read issued after a write by the client in the same session returns the result of the last write. To understand why this is not trivial, consider that the server to which the client is connected for data may be replicated, therefore it may be accessing different replicas for the write followed by the read.

2. *Monotonic Reads* [Fig. 6.43(**b**)]: As the client issues successive reads, the results of successive reads should be consistent with the results of earlier reads. In the example in Fig. 6.43(**b**), other clients may be posting to a calendar, that is replicated. The client issuing successive reads continues to see the calendar entry added by the first poster as it reads the calendar entry added by the second poster.

In the previous two session semantics, both forms of semantics only concerned the consistency provided for a single client performing reads within a session. In the write session semantics illustrated in Fig. 6.44, the consistency guarantee concerns the view that other clients have of this client's updates.

1. *Writes Follow Reads* [Fig. 6.44(**a**)]: With the Writes Follow Reads semantics, if a client issues a write operation after a read operation, then that write

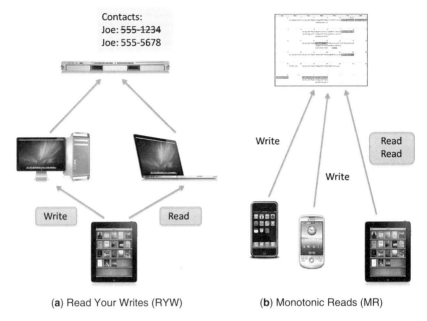

(**a**) Read Your Writes (RYW)   (**b**) Monotonic Reads (MR)

Figure 6.43   *Read session semantics*

operation is ordered after the read operation in any view that other clients have of the data. In the example given in Fig. 6.44(**a**), the client responds to a blog post and that blog response is ordered after the original blog post in any view that other clients have of the blog.

The Writes Follow Reads semantics actually splits into two semantics; some applications may only require one of these.

(a) *Ordering of Write Propagation* [Fig. 6.44(**b**)]: The first of these two semantics, Ordering of Write Propagation, concerns the order of writes *where those writes are viewed by other clients*. As shown by the example in Fig. 6.44(**b**), on those sites where the blog response is viewed, it is viewed as following the original blog post. However, there is no guarantee that the response will be viewed on the second replica.

(b) *Global Ordering of Writes* [Fig. 6.44(**c**)]: The second component of Writes Follow Reads concerns the extent of propagation of the client writes. In the example given in Fig. 6.44(**c**), the client is only concerned with ensuring that all other clients see its update of a weather posting. It is not concerned that clients be able to see the original weather posting that was updated. In fact, the original weather posting may never be seen at the second replica.

2. *Monotonic Writes* [Fig. 6.44(**d**)]: the inverse of Monotonic Reads, this semantics guarantees that clients' views of the updates by a client in a session are monotonic. In the example in Fig. 6.44(**d**), as the client is posting its

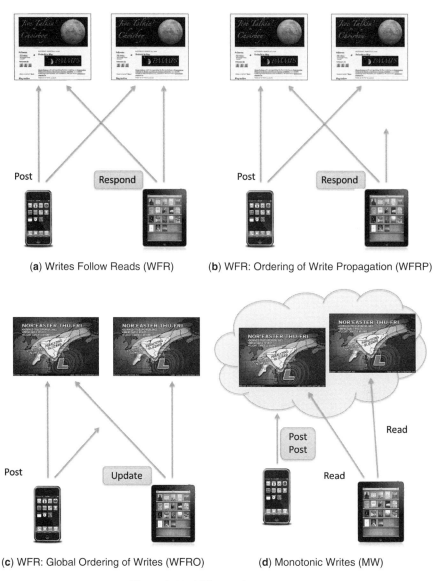

(a) Writes Follow Reads (WFR)   (b) WFR: Ordering of Write Propagation (WFRP)

(c) WFR: Global Ordering of Writes (WFRO)   (d) Monotonic Writes (MW)

Figure 6.44 *Write session semantics*

weather forecasts in the same session, clients viewing these posts continue to see the old weather posts as the new posts appear.

To illustrate the relationships between these consistency guarantees, consider the Monotonic Writes session guarantee: as a client issues multiple writes within a session, other clients see the accumulation of those writes, rather than the second write in isolation from the first write. If the system supports Read Your Writes, then the client will be able to read the results of their writes (postings). Suppose the client posts an update of a posting [Fig. 6.45(**b**)] after reading the original posting [Fig. 6.45(**a**)]. If the system also supports Write Follows Read session semantics, then other clients should then see the posting that the client read before it posted the update. Therefore, it appears that the combination of Read Your Writes (RYW) and Writes Follow Reads (WFR) provides the equivalent of Monotonic Writes. However, this is not quite the case. As illustrated in Fig. 6.45(**c**), an intervening posting, by a client that does not read the original client's updates, breaks the Write Follows Read connection between the two posts by the original client. Therefore, a subsequent (third) client may read the original client post, then later read the client's update of that post without being able to see the original post. On the other hand, Monotonic Writes would require that the third client should be still able to see the first post by the first client, after seeing that client's update.

There are two broad approaches to communicate updates. *Log-based replication* [Fig. 6.46(**a**)] maintains a log of the updates performed on a replica while it is disconnected. Upon re-connection to the original data server, the replica log replays the operations in its log on the server. Part of the replay process will include detecting conflicting updates performed by other clients on the server, and

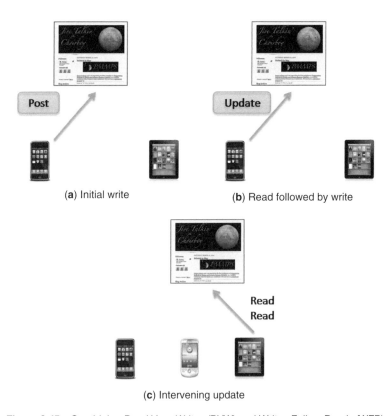

Figure 6.45   *Combining Read Your Writes (RYW) and Writes Follow Reads (WFR)*

automatic conflict resolution strategies that attempt to resolve the issues. Manual intervention may be necessary if automatic conflict resolution fails. When another client re-connects to the server, the server determines which part of the data or file system replicated on that client has been affected by updates on other replicas, and updates that client's copy of the data. For log-based replication, the replicas will converge to a consistent state provided each replica receives and applies all of the update operations or updated data, the (non-commutative) operations are applied in the same order on all replicas, and, finally, provided that the operations have a deterministic semantics.

State-based replication [Fig. 6.46(**b**)] does not maintain an update log. Instead, replicas exchange copies of data items that have been modified. This is closer to the form of data sharing we saw when discussing tightly-coupled caching. With this approach, some form of meta-data is associated with the data items (i.e., the shared files), such as a modified bit, an update timestamp or a version number. This meta-data is used to identify the most up-to-date version of a data item during synchronization. One issue with this approach is *create-delete ambiguity*: An update may be received for a data item that has already been deleted. Some form of record of the previous existence of deleted items is normally kept to cope with this (referred to as a *tombstone* or *death certificate*), i.e., a deleted bit for the item is kept rather than removing all evidence of it altogether. When a client re-connects to the server, it uploads the timestamps of the data it has cached to the server. The server determines what data is stale on the replica and updates the replica accordingly. The client uploads the data that was modified while disconected to the server, to update the server's copy of the data.

We discussed approaches to version conflict detection in Sect. 6.5.5 in the context of discussing contract versioning. More generally, with values modified by programmer-defined operations that are logged, an *operation conflict table* may be used to define when two operations conflict. Allowing operations to commute will often be critical to avoiding version conflicts when reconciling updates done by different clients on shared data. A complication with the operation conflict table is that determining if two operations conflict may depend on the values of some of the arguments to the operations, which in general may require recursive checks for conflicts among the arguments.

Conflict detection may be combined with transactional execution. Gray et al. [75] suggest a two-tier scheme for transactions where databases may be replicated on mobile devices. In particular, a transaction that executes on a mobile replica only completes tentatively. When the replica re-connects with the database server, conflict detection is combined with optimistic concurrency control to determine if it is safe to complete the transaction. The transaction will have accessed parts of the database, reflected by the read-set and write-set recorded with the transaction in optimistic concurrency control. Upon re-connecting, concurrency control checks if any of the database variables in these sets have been modified by another client. If so, the transaction performed on the mobile device may be rolled back, with a notification and explanation provided to the device owner. The analogy is with the owner of a checking account writing a check with insufficient funds in their bank account, and then having the check returned by the bank for insufficient funds. The bank cannot prevent the writing of the check, but they can roll back the financial transaction that it was part of. This is also related to snapshot isolation, which we discuss in Chapter 9 in the sequel volume.

Integrity constraints in back-end databases may also be combined with conflict detection. Integrity constraints may be used to express application logic, such as that no employee in a department should earn more than the manager of that department (if there is such a rule). Integrity constraints can express high-level constraints for conflict detection in replicated systems, such as limits on total withdrawals of funds from certain accounts in a time period that cannot be expessed in terms of single operations alone.

An important class of applications that require local caching are collaborative text editors, for example Google Docs, that allow multiple clients to edit the same documents simultaneously. In this case, conflicting operations are allowed to be performed simultaneously on separate copies of the same document. The key to this approach is that the parties share the conflicting operations, for example through a collaboration server, and, in the process, conflicting operations are transformed to remove the conflict. In the example shown in Fig. 6.47, the two parties apply conflicting updates to the edit buffer. A deletion operation is performed on the left, shortening the buffer, while an append operation on the right adds data to end of the buffer. The conflicts between these two updates are removed by transforming the latter insertion operation, changing the position to where it is applied to reflect the deletion in the first operation. In general, where there are n operations, this approach will require $O(n^2)$ rules for reconciling conflicting updates

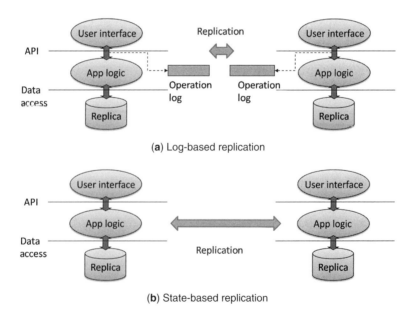

(a) Log-based replication

(b) State-based replication

Figure 6.46   *Communicating updates*

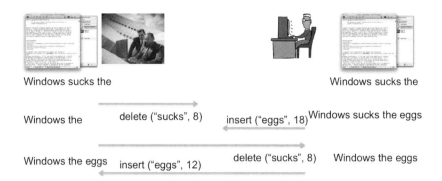

Windows sucks the

Windows the   delete ("sucks", 8)   insert ("eggs", 18) Windows sucks the eggs

Windows sucks the

Windows the eggs   insert ("eggs", 12)   delete ("sucks", 8)   Windows the eggs

Figure 6.47   *Collaborative editing based on operation transformations*

by transforming one, or both, of the updates. A related notion of virtual time is discussed in Sect. B.4 (Appendix B).

6.10 SERVICE STATELESSNESS

We have already considered some of the reasons why *stateless service* implementations are preferred and are, if anything, essential for low level services. To summarize:

1. A stateless implementation enables the transparent replication and distribution of the service in a server cluster. This enables the load from multiple client requests to be distributed transparently across a pool of server instances (Fig. 2.10). As long as services are stateless and have no "affinity" with clients (i.e., have no memory of their previous client interactions in the current session), then load balancers are free to direct client requests to service instances in such a way that the load is evenly shared among all such instances. This also allows a load balancer to automatically redirect client requests to a different service instance if the service instance that originally handled the client request is no longer responding.

   The architecture in Fig. 2.10 relies on an assumption that most business logic can be executed without involving the back-end database server. For example, most business-to-consumer e-commerce consists of customers browsing the vendor Web site and exploring their inventory. As long as the Web site does not attempt to keep the Web inventory tightly synchronized with the actual inventory in the vendor database, the database server only becomes involved when items are added to the shopping cart, or when the customer eventually checks out. Therefore, the focus is on replicating the execution of the stateless logic, while pursuing a less aggressive replication strategy for the database.

2. As there is no state in the service instance, the update protocols for replicated state considered in Sect. 6.9.2 are unnecessary. On the other hand, the architecture in Fig. 2.10 pushes the issue of synchronizing updates on replicated

data to the database, but there the scale of the replication and therefore the difficulty of the challenge may be smaller.

3. Failure-handling for a stateless service is simple. An (old) NFS server can be restarted by recycling the server machine. Restarting of a stateful process requires rolling the state back to the last stable checkpoint before restarting. If some server state was only held in transient memory, this state will have to be recovered as part of failure recovery, perhaps by interrogating clients, as happens with AFS. If failure is handled by rolling over to a hot standby server, there are many issues to be considered: ensuring that only one primary is running after the rollover, carrying over state from the primary, redirecting client requests, etc.

4. The interaction of stateless services with transactional semantics is simple. Business logic implemented in Java EE is not permitted to use the default Java I/O library, `java.io`, because all operations in an EJB are potentially transactional and therefore may need to be rolled back if the transaction aborts. The developer who wishes to save data in a file will need to buy, or implement, a transactional file system.

5. Reusability of services is enhanced if they are stateless. There are no protocols to be followed in the usage of the service, such as when they can be reset to an initial state. The space usage of such services is predictable, as they are memory-less and can reset memory usage after every invocation.

Despite the fact that most of the application state is stored on back-end database servers, there are still three forms of application state that may be present in a service. The first form of state, *session state*, records information about a current session involving a client and a service. A session may be identified by *correlation identifiers* in the HTTP or SOAP headers of the messages exchanged in a Web service interaction. The first time a Web site is visited in a session, the server creates a session and stores a session identifier in a cookie on the client. On subsequent visits from the client, to this or other Web pages on the site, the client browser returns the session identifier to the server. This can be used to direct client requests to the same application server in a cluster, if that server has affinity with the client requests. The session identifier is available to server-side processing code, for example as the page property `SessionID` in ASP.NET.

A second form of service state, *context state*, refers to control state that goes beyond correlation identifiers for messages. For example, the ASP.NET API provides *session variables*, a per-session associative memory for Web applications. This allows applications to manage context state on the server side, by saving the values of variables across Web service calls. The default implementation of session variables saves this context state on the Web server where the ASP.NET engine resides; other choices that can be configured are a back-end database or (preferably) a separate state server that is shared by all Web servers in the cluster. Storing the state on a separate session state server is an example of the STATEFUL SERVICE pattern, intended to support the off-loading of state maintenance from services to a separate state service. This is also an example of *state delegation*, as the example delegates state management to a separate process. If the context state is stored on the Web server, the correlation identifers in the HTTP headers can be used to redirect all postbacks of a Web page back to the original server instance in a cluster, where the context state is stored. Obviously, this may not be desirable for load balancing in a cluster. In any case, the context state is accessed by server-side code as properties of a class called Session. For example, server-side processing of a client login can save information, including the authenticated user ID (in this example, the Web control property Userid.userid) as the value of a session variable:

```
public partial class Login : System.Web.UI.Page {
  protected void LoginButton_Click(object sender, EventArgs e) {
    … Session["userid"] = Userid.userid; …
  }
}
```

It is still possible for malicious parties to "sniff" the session identifier and hijack the Web session. Hence, the safest alternative is to pass HTTP connections over a secure SSL or TLS socket transport (i.e., use https rather than http for the protocol specification in the URLs). Besides saving the user ID of the user who has logged in, the context state in the server can also be used to cache parts of the user profile, for example the user name for a friendly user interface, user preferences for the presentation logic, etc.[25]

For Web services, context state may include information about, for example a transaction that is coordinating the interactions of several Web service calls. The WS-Coordination and WS-Transaction standards describe the context information that is passed between parties collaborating in a Web service transaction, including the header blocks that are stored in the SOAP messages. Other examples include contextual security information used to authenticate clients (WS-Security) and to authorize access to resources. The WS-Addressing standard defines a way of identifying the two endpoints in a Web service interaction that is independent of the underlying transfer protocol via the wsa:ReplyTo field that identifies the sender of a Web service request. The OASIS WS-Context standard defines a framework for general, structured, context information passed in the headers of SOAP messages.

The third form of state in a service is *business state*—state that is an integral property of the business logic. Server-side processing logic in ASP.NET will typically require application state beyond that stored as properties of a Web page it is processing. For example, the state might be the contents of a shopping cart to which the client is adding items as they browse an on-line catalog. This application state is not saved on the Web server between postbacks of the Web form. Rather, ASP.NET saves this state information in the client browser using the mechanism of *viewstate*: application state is encoded (using base64 encoding) in a hidden field in a Web page that is returned to the client browser and then returned with that Web page when it is posted back to the server for further processing:

---

[25] ASP.NET provides a caching service for application-controlled caching of parts of the database on the server. The context state should only be used to cache control information for the applications.

```
<form name="form1" method="post" action="Default.aspx" id="form1">
  <div>
    <input  type="hidden" name="__VIEWSTATE" id="__VIEWSTATE"
            value="view state value" />
  </div>
  … Rendered output of inner Web controls …
</form>
```

Encryption can be used to prevent tampering by a malicious client of this form data, using a secret key (the `Machine Key`) stored only on the server.

Viewstate is an example of the STATE MESSAGING pattern, explicitly passing part of the service state in messages. It is also an example of the partial state deferral pattern, temporarily deferring some portion of the service state to a separate process, as discussed below. In this case, the application state is deferred to the client browser.

The viewstate mechanism is not without controversy. As the amount of application state grows, the size of the viewstate can impede client processing. For example, the `GridView` data control stores the entire result of a database query in its state, even if only a small part of the result is displayed at a time. Rendered as part of the viewstate in a page, this may result in a large amount of hidden data that is passed between the server and the browser. ASP.NET installations may disable viewstate altogether to prevent these problems. Deployments may use *control state* in this case, to save critical state information that the Web application requires to function, bypassing the disablement of viewstate.

The alternative to client-side application data storage choices, such as viewstate, is to store intermediate service state on the server side. This may, for example, result from caching the results of database queries. As long as application servers are organized into a cluster, this storage is best organized separately from the application servers. It may be cached on the back-end database itself, or in a caching state provider in the application server cluster. This latter provides a useful trade-off between the cost of retrieving the state from the back-end and the inflexibility and resource cost of storing it on the application server itself. The practice of deferring state to another part of the architecture, be it storing on the client or the server side, is an example of the PARTIAL STATE DEFERRAL pattern. The use of a separate caching server to store this deferred state is an example of the STATE REPOSITORY pattern. This is distinguished from the stateful service pattern by the fact that the latter manages service state, providing an API for services to explicitly retrieve and update state that is stored on their behalf, while the state repository acts as a cache for service state while it is idle. In addition to, or instead of, the store provider for application state, the application servers may have in-memory databases that cache the results of queries to the database, as described in Figs. 4.15 and Sect. 6.48.

Stateful Service in WCF. WCF stateful services require that service and client share a session for the duration of their interaction. In Fig. 6.49, we provide a modification of the shopping cart service contract from Fig. 6.19(**a**). In Fig. 6.49(**a**) the service contract specifies that any client of the service must be able to maintain a session

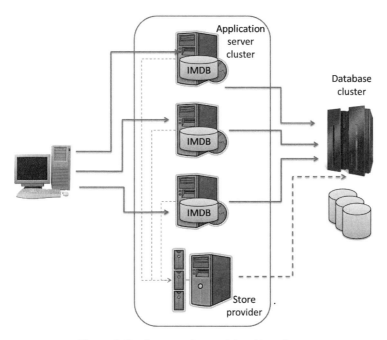

Figure 6.48 *Sources of state deferral in a cluster*

with the service provider. The default is that a service will allow a session with a client, but not require it. Certain bindings, such as `BasicHttpBinding`, do not support sessions.

If sessions are supported by the binding, the current session is available via the property `OperationContext.Current.SessionId`. This may be used, for example, as a key to retrieve the shopping cart contents from a database. With `PerSession` activation mode set, this is unnecessary. With sessions enabled, this mode maintains the same in-memory service instance across service calls by the client so the service state can be kept in the service instance memory. The session is initiated on the first service call by the client to the service. The session is terminated when the client invokes the `checkOut` operation because its `IsTerminating` property is set. In the service configuration in Fig. 6.49(**b**), both the `NetTcpBinding` and the `WsHttp-Binding` sessions are set to time out after 10 seconds of inactivity by the client.

There are some caveats to offer about this support for stateful services. The WCF notion of a session is different from session state in ASP.NET and, in particular, the instance state is not persisted across application servers, as is possible with ASP.NET session variables. The implementation of sessions relies on the WCF implementation of the WS-ReliableMessaging standard, a standard for end-to-end message security for Web services that may not be supported on all platforms.

Stateful Service in Java EE. Figure 6.50(**a**) provides an implementation of the shopping cart as a stateful session bean in Java EE. There are several forms of session beans in Java EE:

```
[ServiceContract(Namespace = "http://www.example.com/Shopping",
                 SessionMmode=SessionMode.Required)]
public interface IShoppingCart {
  [OperationContract]
  public float ComputeTax (String state);

  [OperationContract(IsOneWay=true)]
  void Add (String product, int amount);

  [OperationContract(IsTerminating=true)]
  Uri Checkout (int purchOrder);
}

[ServiceBehavior
(InstanceContextMode=InstanceContextMode.PerSession)]
public class ShoppingCartService : IShoppingCart {
  List<CartItem> cart;

  …
}
```

(**a**) Interface and implementaton

```
<System.serviceModel>
  <bindings>
    <netTcpBinding>
      <binding name="tcpBinding" receiveTimeout="00:00:10" />
    </netTcpBinding>
    <wsHttpBinding>
      <binding name="wsBinding" receiveTimeout="00:00:10" />
    </wsHttpBinding>
  </bindings>
</System.serviceModel>
```

(**b**) Configuration

Figure 6.49   *Stateful services in WCF*

1. *Stateless session beans* are marked with the `@Stateless` annotation. Such beans can be used to implement stateless EJBs and Web services, as we saw in Fig. 6.10(**a**).

2. *Stateful session beans* are marked with the `@Stateful` annotation. Such beans have a similar session semantics as per-session service instances in WCF: a stateful bean maintains state across a session with a client. The `@Remove` annotation identifies the `checkout` method as a terminating operation similar to the `IsTerminating` property set in the WCF interface.

3. *Singleton session beans* are marked with the `@Singleton` annotation. The container ensures that there is a single instance of this bean, shared by all clients. Such a bean might be useful, for example, in implementing an in-memory data cache, shared by all instances.

4. *Message-driven beans* are used by JMS to associate callbacks with message queues, executed upon receipt of a message on that queue. We consider

```
@Stateful(name = "ShoppingCart")
public class ShoppingCartBean implements ShoppingCartRemote {
  List<CartItem> cart;
  public void add (String item, int qty) {
    cart.add (new CartItem (item, qty));
  }
  public float computeTax (String state) { … }

  @Remove
  public String checkOut (int purchOrder) { … }
}
```

(**a**) Java EE EJB shopping cart

```
@WebService(endpointinterface = "ShoppingCartWeb")
@Stateless
public class ShoppingCartBean {
  @Resource WebServiceContext wsContext;
  @PersistenceContext EntityManager em;
  …
  @WebMethod
  @OneWay
  public void add (String item, int qty) {
    MessageContext mc = wsContext.getMessageContext()
    HttpSession session = ((HttpServletRequest)
      mc.get(MessageContext.SERVLET_REQUEST)).getSession();
    CartEntity cart =
      em.find (CartEntity.class, session.getId());
    if (cart==null) { …; em.persist(cart); }
    cart.add (new CartItem (item, qty));
  }
  …
}
```

(**b**) Java EE Web service shopping cart

Figure 6.50   *Stateful services in Java EE*

message-driven beans in the context of event-driven architecture in Chapter 8 in the sequel volume.

Both stateless and stateful session beans have associated lifecycle callback methods associated with them. For example, the @PostConstruct annotation may be used to identify a callback method to be invoked by the container after the default initialization of a session and before it services clients requests. The @PreDestroy annotation may be used to identify a method to be called before a session bean is finalized. These methods may be used, for example, to open files or database connections on initialization, and close those connections on shutdown. Logically, a stateless session bean's lifetime does not last beyond the client service call, although in reality, the container may manage a pool of such beans to avoid latency on bean creation. A stateful session bean exists in memory for the duration of the session with the client, across service calls and until the client removes the bean, or the container times out and terminates the session. Such stateful beans, suspended in memory and awaiting client requests, may have an impact on server performance [90]. To mitigate this, if a stateful bean is inactive for a period of time, the container may choose to *passivate* the bean by serializing its state to disk and de-allocating it from memory. Upon a subsequent client request, the container re-activates the bean by de-serializing its state from disk and re-initializing a copy of the bean in memory. Lifecycle methods may be annotated with @PrePassivate and @PostActivate to denote that they should be invoked before passivation of the bean and disk, and after reactivation, respectively.

The Java EE API allows more than one instance of a stateful bean to be associated with a client. Each bean represents a distinct session, and the multiple instances do not share state:

```
InitialContext initCtx = new InitialContext();
Context ctx = (Context)initCtx.lookup("java:comp/env");
ShoppingCartRemote cart1 =
                (ShoppingCartRemote) ctx.lookup("ejb/CartBean");
ShoppingCartRemote cart2 =
                (ShoppingCartRemote) ctx.lookup("ejb/CartBean");
cart1.add("SOA With Java Web Services", 1);
cart2.add("A Fistful of Dollars", 1);
```

In this example, the application is maintaining separate shopping carts for professional and for personal purchases.

Figure 6.50(**b**) provides an example of a Java EE Web service implementation of the shopping cart. As Java Web services are required to be stateless, we need to save the contents of the shopping cart in a persistent storage across client calls. As we cannot use the file system,[26] we store the information in a back-end database. Dependency injection injects a reference to an entity manager for the persistence context. We still need some way of identifying the shopping cart for a particular context. We use the identifier for the current HTTP session as a primary key for storing the contents of the shopping cart in the database. The latter should be obtainable from the Web service context, also injected via dependency injection. We assume an entity bean class CartEntity has been declared for the shopping cart stored in the database, and the database record for the shopping cart contents is created on the first add service request in this session. This approach requires that the client agrees to maintain a HTTP session with the service; methods to do this include storing a cookie on the client or rewriting URLs to include a session identifier in the query string:

```
ShoppingCartService service = new ShoppingCartService();
ShoppingCart port = service.getShoppingCartPort();
Map requestCtx = ((BindingProvider)port).getRequestContext();
requestCtx.put (BindingProvider.SESSION_MAINTAIN_PROPERTY, true);
```

---

[26]Recall that all file I/O must be transactional for a session bean, and may also need to be shared among server instances in a cluster.

6.10.1 Contexts and Dependency Injection

Dependency injection was described as an example of inversion of control in Sect. 5.5: a component declaratively specifies the resources and support that it requires in the environment where it is deployed, and the container provides that support for the component. This decoupling of the component from its environment enhances modularity, reusability, and maintenance. However, there are typically many more aspects of the use of a component than injecting an instance:

1. That component has a lifecycle during which it is created, accessed, and invoked by clients, perhaps passivated and re-activated, and eventually destructed. Although lifecycle methods provide hooks for allowing the component to interact with the container during its lifetime, these do not address the issue of when the resource should be destructed. At the systems level, *garbage collection* has been successfully used for resource management at the systems level, albeit with limited success in distributed systems. Nevertheless, judging component lifetimes is an application-level, rather than a system-level, issue. For example, an application server manages a pool of connections for queue and database connections, and it is important for performance that applications release such connections when they are done with them. This is an application-level rather than a system-level resource-management issue. Requiring the client of a component to manage that lifecycle is a form of tight coupling. The avoidance of this form of lifecycle management by clients is part of the motivation for loose coupling in Web services and SOA. Stateless session beans are an example of the benefits to be derived from stateless services: invocations of the bean are memory-less and can be treated as unrelated—initialization and termination can be completely managed by the container. In contrast, a stateful session bean requires the client to manage its lifecyle, with the invocations of the bean by the client related by its internal state and using a method specified by the `@Remove` annotation to determine when the stateful bean can be terminated.

2. The use of a component by a client may require customization of that component by the client. One way to perform this customization is to perform it in a "white box" fashion, as explained in 5.3, inheriting from an implementation class. However, better modularity is achieved if the client abstracts over the component implementation, requiring some mechanism for "black box" customization of the component.

3. We review name-based discovery using JNDI in Sect. 6.11.2, although we have already seen several examples, including Fig. 6.10(**b**) and in the previous section. For injecting an EJB that is defined in the same application, a client may specify the instance required by specifying the bean name for the implementation class, for example:

```
@EJB TaxCalculatorLocal calculator1;
@EJB(beanName="TaxCalculator") TaxCalculatorLocal calculator2;
```

However, there is no type information associated with the name. Without an explicit specification of the bean name, it defaults to the class name without any package qualifier; however, this is just a convention that may be overriden in an application (and must be overridden if there is more than one class implementing the interface). This introduces the possibility of a run-time error if the container attempts to inject a component of an incompatible type into the field or variable.

As discussed at the end of Sect. 6.8.1, contexts and dependency injection provide a framework for managing components that addresses these issues. Components in this framework are generically referred to as *beans* and include both sessions beans, as well as *managed beans*[27] and other forms of Java objects. *Contextual lifecycle management* delegates the management of the lifecycles of stateful, as well as stateless, components to the container, by specifying the *scopes* of the components. Several scopes are pre-defined and can be specified using annotations, including @ApplicationScoped, @SessionScoped (for the duration of a HTTP session), and @RequestScoped (for the duration of a service call). For example, a stateful shopping cart that is automatically created at the beginning of a HTTP session and destructed at the end of that session, can be declared by:

```
public @SessionScoped
class ShoppingCartImpl implements IShoppingCart {…}
```

A bean has one or more types,[28] and one of these types may be used to specify the bean instance that should be injected in a client component. If there is ambiguity, *qualifiers* may be used to provide further information to uniquely identify the bean. We discuss qualifiers in more detail in Sect. 6.11.2. For now, we note that one qualifier that is provided allows the bean to be identified by name:

```
public @SessionScoped @Named("ShoppingCart")
class ShoppingCartImpl implements IShoppingCart {…}
```

An instance is injected into a client using the @Inject annotation:

```
@Inject @Named("ShoppingCart") IShoppingCart cart;
```

The @Named annotation is directly analogous to the beanName attribute for the @EJB annotation, but its use is deprecated in the specification for CDI [91]. Instead, a qualifier should be defined that includes the type of bean to be injected, as well as any other attributes that uniquely identify it. We return to this in Sect. 6.11.2.

Producer methods may be used to define methods in factory beans that produce values when injections are performed that specify the class of the producer method:

---

[27] In CDI, a managed bean is a particular form of Java concrete class (or decorator) that defines objects whose lifecycle may be managed by the container. They are required not to be defined as EJBs, i.e., session beans, to distinguish them from the additional semantics associated with sessions beans.

[28] A remote interface for an EJB, i.e., a class or interface annotated with @Stateful or @Stateless, is excluded from the bean types for the EJB for the purposes of CDI because of the semantics associated with that interface.

```
public @ApplicationScoped class RandGenerator {
  private Random rand = new Random(System.currentTimeMillis());
  @Produces @Named @Random int getRand() {
    return random.nextInt(100);
  }
}
```

The annotation @Random is an application-defined qualifier that identifies a resource to be injected. Its presence at both the production and injection points connects the two together. The following injects a random number into a field called rand in a client:

```
@Inject @Random int rand;
```

Clients in the same scope may share an instance of a bean whose scope encompasses the scopes of those clients. For example, a bean marked as @Application-Scoped is essentially a singleton bean, as a single instance of that bean is created for the duration of an application execution. The difference between an application-scoped bean and a true singleton bean is that clients of the latter obtain an actual reference to the bean instance. In the former case, clients obtain a proxy object for the actual instance. This extra decoupling is necessary to prevent the actual bean instance that is injected from being serialized if the client component is passivated. Furthermore, scopes may be mixed, with a session-scoped resource used in the context of a request-scoped execution. A resource cannot be used in a scope that extends beyond its own scope (as otherwise the resource may be destructed before the client is finished with it); however, the scope of a resource may be defined to be dependent on that of a bean into which it is injected. This is done by annotating a bean with the @Dependent pseudo-scope annotation; this is the default scope annotation when one is not specified. Furthermore, the @New qualifier may be used at an injection point to specify that the bean instance that is injected has a scope depedent on that of the client, no matter what the original bean scope is defined to be.

Producer methods may be combined with dependency injection to inject several types of bean instances, all with the same interface, into the method (as parameters), and then have the method use run-time decision logic to choose one of these instances. For example, we may have an interface CalcStrategy for performing calculation strategies for financial instruments, with implementations for money market funds, futures, and swaps. We define qualifiers @MoneyMarketStrategy, @FutureStrategy and @SwapStrategy to specify the various calculation strategies. The following producer performs the decision logic to select one of the injected instances:

```
public class StrategyGenerator {
  @Produces @SessionScoped ICalcStrategy getStrategy (
      @New @MoneyMarketStrategy ICalcStrategy mm,
      @New @FutureStrategy ICalcStrategy f,
      @New @SwapStrategy ICalcStrategy s) {
    switch (chooseStrategy()) {
```

```
      case MONEY_MARKET: return mm;
      case FUTURE: return f;
      case SWAP: return s;
      default: return null;
    }
  }
}
```

The `@New` annotation is used to specify that the scopes of injected strategies should be the same as the client of the producer method (and *not* that of the bean containing the producer method).

Rather than defining separate qualifiers for alternative choices, we can define a single qualifier with values that distinguish the different alternatives:

```
public enum Calc { MONEY_MARKET,FUTURE,SWAP }
@Qualifier @Retention(RUNTIME) @Target({METHOD,FIELD,PARAMETER,TYPE})
public @interface CalcStrategy {
 Calc value();
}
```

This is the definition of a value-carrying annotation. The example above is modified to specify the alternatives using the single qualifier `@CalcStrategy`:

```
@Produces @SessionScoped ICalcStrategy getStrategy (
     @New @CalcStrategy(Calc.MONEY_MARKET) ICalcStrategy mm,
     @New @CalcStrategy(Calc.FUTURE) ICalcStrategy f,
     @New @CalcStrategy(Calc.SWAP) ICalcStrategy s) { … }
```

For beans that require manual finalization, the producer method can have an associated *disposer method* that is invoked when the context for the bean ends:

```
@Produces @RequestScoped Connection open(…) {…}
void close (@Disposes Connection connection) {
 connection.close();
}
```

In addition to lifecycle management, another aspect of managing components is the addition of cross-cutting functionality, such as logging and transaction management. *Interceptors* allow such "interception" of the invocation of a method in a component, basically a form of aspect-oriented programming where additional "aspects" are woven into method invocations. In order to define this interception, an application defines a qualifier to identify those points where it should be injected. This qualifier is defined using the `@InterceptorBinding` annotation. For example, the following defines an interceptor type for specifying that business methods should have transactional semantics:

```
@InterceptorBinding @Target({METHOD,TYPE}) @Retention(RUNTIME)
public @interface Transactional { … }
```

If necessary, attributes can be associated with the @Transactional annotation. Having defined an interceptor type, the following uses this type with the @Interceptor annotation to define an actual interceptor for business methods that wraps invocations of those methods with transactional semantics:

```
@Transactional @Interceptor
public class TransactionInterceptor {
   @Resource UserTransaction transaction;
   @AroundInvoke
   public Object manageTransaction
                  (InvocationContext ctx) throws Exception { … }
}
```

The @Transactional annotation can then be used to associate transactional semantics with business methods, or with all of the business methods in a bean:

```
@Transactional public class ShoppingCart { … }
```

Interceptors may be combined. For example, a @Secure interceptor type may be defined that requires secure communication and business methods can be annotated with both @Transactional and @Secure in order to wrap them with secure transactional semantics.

Interceptors are generic across all business methods that they wrap as they add cross-cutting functionality. *Decorators* are intended to support separation of concerns, allowing certain business concerns to be expressed as beans that wrap the functionality of another bean. Both the original bean and the decorator bean are required to implement the same interface. While interceptors are agnostic about the business logic that they wrap, decorators are specific to the business interface that they decorate. This limits their generality with respect to interceptors, but they have the ability to interact with the business logic that they extend, for example delegating to that logic where they need to. Decorators can be considered as a form of *mixins* that are combined to produce the logic for several concerns that are combined in the overall business logic. For example, a decorator may be defined for shopping carts that logs large purchases for special review:

```
@Decorator
public abstract class CartLogger implements IShoppingCart {
   @Inject @Delegate @Any IShoppingCart cart;
   public void checkout () { … }
}
```

The decorator includes a *delegate injection point*, that injects a reference to the bean instance that the decorator's logic wraps. The qualifiers on the decorator must match the qualifiers on this delegate injection point as the two beans are combined via decoration. Where necessary, the methods of the decorator may call into the methods of this delegate to invoke the business logic that it wraps. Where the decorator does not wrap a particular business method, that method may be declared abstract in the decorator, with automatic delegation to the decorated bean's method. This is the only instance where a bean may be an abstract class.

This framework for depencency injection can be viewed as furthering the concept of canonical expression. Rather than specifying resources and services for injection using long names that encode the criteria for their selection, simple names (such as a type name) are used instead, and qualifiers then used as "adjectives" to refine the specification of the resource to be injected.

6.11   SERVICE DISCOVERABILITY

6.11.1   Global Discovery

Service discoverability is considered a core part of SOA, as evidenced by its elevation to a core principle. Early conceptualizations of discoverability for Web services were ambitious, assuming that global services would be automatically discoverable across the entire Internet. In supply chain management, for example, a company might automatically identify suppliers, shippers, and brokering services using searches for Web services. At least some envisioned a world where software agents used service discoverability to identify services to satisfy client needs, and used artificial intelligence (AI) planning techniques to automatically synthesize compositions of discovered services into higher-level services based on specifications of the latter.

Unfortunately the world, and the World Wide Web, is a messier place than these early dot-com era visions imagined. Many of the companies with an "online" presence are fake, front companies, with various motivations. For example, some are "scraper sites" that copy text wholesale from legitimate sites and establish themselves as clones of these sites, albeit with different domain and company names. The motivation for these sites is to collect advertising revenue from page clicks. As search engines penalize Web sites whose content is largely duplicated from other Web sites, some scraper sites employ low-wage writers to generate content for them, to maintain some measure of apparent legitimacy. Even without considering pornography sites that harvest credit card numbers for organized crime, the Web is not quite the open and cooperative space that it was perhaps perceived to be at the end of the 20th century.

UDDI was conceived as a core service in the WS-* protocol stack. The UDDI specification includes both a data model for service descriptions, and SOAP-based protocols for registry search. The data model comprises three layers:

1. *businessEntity* records (white pages) provide information about the enterprise offering services through a UDDI registry;
2. *businessService* records (yellow pages) provide information about particular families of technical services;
3. *bindingTemplate* records (green pages) provide technical information about service entry points and implementation specifications. A particularly important part of this description are *t-Model* records, referenced by

bindingTemplates, that provide specifications for services, including WSDL contracts for services.

To facilitate domain-specific searching based on taxonomies, in addition UDDI supports the use of multiple taxonomies for organizing entities, such as the United Nations Standard Products and Services Code (UNSPSC) and the North American Industry Classification System (NAICS). The original UDDI specification envisioned a global centralized UDDI repository, the UDDI Business Registry (UBR), analogous to the root service name resolution service for the DNS. Revisions to the specification envisioned more decentralized, peer-to-peer arrangements of registries, related by various forms of *registry affiliation*. The various forms of registries included private enterprise registries, only available behind the enterprise firewall, public UBRs "in the cloud", and affiliated registries that might enforce restricted access to industry partners. Various forms of affiliation were envisaged, including replication of public UBR content (for the same reason that DNS root servers are replicated), publication of private registry content to public UBRs for services exported outside the enterprise, and peer-to-peer subscriptions to service publications between registries in affiliated enterprises.

The UDDI vision has not materialized, and support for the standard is receding among various Web service platforms. Some consider it too ambitious, while some consider it not ambitious enough. For example, should UDDI have considered tagging records with semantic ontological content, for knowledge-based service discovery [92]? In any case, an investigation of "live" Web services in 2008 revealed a great deal of Web services that are in the public domain but not published in any kind of UBR [93]. Several reasons are offered for the failure of UDDI: the limited single-criterion search function, the lack of support for quality-of-service specifications, service pricing or Web service lifecycle management, and the lack of support for managing registry consistency. The central criticism made of UDDI is its *push* model for service registration which can lead to the ultimate consistency problem: an empty registry. Instead, the authors of the study recommend a *pull* model for service registration, modeled after modern Web search engines, and based on Web crawlers performing specialized structured searches of service descriptions. The results of this constant Web crawling are cataloged and provided through a global service search engine [94]. However, both this and the original UDDI specification may be missing the most critical issue in a scheme for global service discovery: how do you know whom it is safe to do business with? In any case, at the end of this section we consider a layered naming scheme for Internet services that is compatible with the notion of global search engines for service discovery.

6.11.2 Local Discovery

The traditional approach to service discovery is to perform a name-based look-up for a service using a naming and discovery service, such as the Windows Active Directory or the CORBA Common Object Service (COS). JNDI is a layer used in Java applications to unify the various APIs for these different naming services, so that Java applications can access these services uniformly. In JNDI terminology, a *context* is a set of name-to-object bindings, such as the binding of a file path to a file on a disk, or the binding of a DNS domain name to an IP address. All of the bindings in a context follow a particular naming convention, such as Active Directory or COS. Contexts may be nested, for example, a file directory may contain other directories, or a DNS domain may contain subdomains. A *naming system* is a connected set of contexts with the same naming convention; a *namespace* is the set of names in a naming system. Naming services may also support *directory services* that bind names to collections of *attributes* for the associated objects. This enables content-based searching for objects based on attributes rather than object names.

The standard naming and directory service for the Internet is the Lightweight Directory Access Protocol (LDAP) [95]. LDAP organizes directories into a tree, where objects in the tree may represent bindings for organizations or individuals, effectively combining naming contexts with containers for attributes. For example, the LDAP entry cn=Irving Thalberg,o=MGM,c=US identifies the context cn=Irving Thalberg as a subcontext of o=MGM, which, in turn, is a subcontext of c=US. An LDAP naming system might map an enterprise name to a namespace for the departments in that enterprise, map each department name to a namespace for the employees in that department, and map each employee to further information about that employee, including their credentials for access control decisions.

JNDI provides an API for accessing these various naming systems, including the InitialContext class for bootstrapping access to the different namespaces. One can obtain an instance of this bootstrapping class easily enough, but some configuration is necessary if something other than the default naming services are required. For example, if a CORBA client, perhaps running in an application client container, and probably running in the same enterprise network, requires access to the CORBA naming service on a different machine, it can obtain access as follows. We assume that the nameserver runs on a local machine called "nameserver", which is resolved to an IP address by doing a DNS lookup. The name service listens on the standard TCP port 3700 on this machine for client requests

```
import javax.naming.*;
Hashtable env = new Hashtable();
env.put (Context.INITIAL_CONTEXT_FACTORY,
        "com.sun.jndi.cosnaming.CNCtxFactory");
env.put (Context.PROVIDER_URL, "iiop://nameserver:3700");
env.put ("org.omg.CORBA.ORBClass",
        "com.sun.corba.se.internal.POA.POAORB");
env.put ("org.omg.CORBA.ORBSingletonClass",
        "com.sun.corba.se.internal.corba.ORBSingleton");
Context ctxt = new InitialContext(env);
```

JNDI provides a "local" namespace for a Java component, into which bindings from various other namespaces are copied. These namespaces include EJBs (CORBA namespace), JMS connection factories and destinations, data sources and other forms of JCA resources, as well as initial values for parameters that can be used to configure components. The actual values for the parameters are set in deployment descriptors, from which bindings are created in the JNDI initial context. The JNDI can be looked up by specifying the component namespace ("java:comp/env") in a look-up from the initial context:

```
InitialContext ctxt = new InitialContext();
Object v = ctxt.lookup("java:comp/env/encname");
```

Alternatively, dependency injection can be used to inject instances of resources based on their ENC names. The local context allows clients of resources to be decoupled from how references to these resources are recorded in the namespace; deployment descriptors can be used to bind a local context name to the object bound to a corresponding global JNDI name.

Portable JNDI names are specified using three different forms of names: "java:global/*name*", "java:app/*name*" and "java:module/*name*". These specify names that should be accessible in the global JNDI namespace, the application namespace (defined by an enterprise archive file) and the module namespace (defined by a Java archive file), respectively.[29] Default JNDI names are defined for Java EE components, but applications may, in addition, define their own portable JNDI names using these conventions. Applications may use annotations to bind resources to JNDI names and to reference those resources by their JNDI names where they are used. However, it is better practice, if less convenient, to reference resources by their local context names, injected by dependency injection, while *deployment descriptors* are used to connect those local logical names to JNDI names. We explain this point with some examples below.

Dependency injection was discussed in Sect. 6.10.1 with examples of dependency injection provided in Sect. 2.5, Sect. 5.5 and Sect. 6.5.4. The JMS example used the local (ENC) context name "jms/RequestMessages" to reference the queue:

```
@Resource(name = "jms/RequestMessages")
Queue requests;
```

The binding of that local context name to the object bound to a global JNDI name can be specified in the sun-ejb-jar.xml deployment descriptor, for example:

```
<ejb>
  <ejb-name>SalesBean</ejb-name>
  <resource-ref>
    <res-ref-name>jms/RequestMessages</res-ref-name>
    <jndi-name>jms/email/sales/updates</jndi-name>
  </resource-ref>
</ejb>
```

The name of the bean that is a client for this queue resource, SalesBean, identifies the component in whose local JNDI context this logical reference is defined. This

---

[29] A *Java EE Module* is defined as a collection of classes packaged in the same Java archive (jar) file. An *application* is defined as a collection of classes whose jar files are packaged in the same enterprise archive (EAR) file. An EAR typically contains a jar file for the business logic, a Web archive (WAR) file for the presentation logic, and a resource archive (RAR) file for any resource connector implementations.

is the "portable" way of specifying the global JNDI name for a resource, in a deployment descriptor. A non-portable way of specifying the latter name, without using a deployment descriptor, is to use the `mappedName` attribute instead of the `name` attribute in the `@Resource` annotation. The `mappedName` attribute specifies a global name for the resource in a vendor-dependent namespace. Alternatively, a portable JNDI name may be specified in the `name` attribute for the `@Resource` annotation, using the syntax for portable JNDI names described above. Specifying a JNDI name, in a portable fashion using the `name` attribute or a non-portable fashion using the `mappedName` attribute, avoids the need to use deployment descriptors. As a matter of taste, most developers prefer to avoid the use of descriptors. However, binding resources to JNDI names specified in the code embeds configuration information for applications within the specification of core business logic, requiring re-compilation when configurations change. Presumably, the optimal approach would be to specify configuration information in deployment descriptors separate from the source code, and have program editors be sufficiently sophisticated to present that configuration information to developers in the form of annotations in the source code, without physically embedding configuration information in the source.

As another example, the shopping cart bean in Figure 6.50(**a**) may require a reference to an instance of the tax calculator service defined in Fig. 6.10(**a**), for example of the form:

```
@EJB(name = "ejb/TaxCalculator", beanName = "TaxCalculator")
TaxCalculatorRemote calculatorProxy;
```

If the tax calculator service is provided by a bean in the same application as the shopping cart bean, then the latter can use the `beanName` attribute to identify the class of the instance to be injected as we have seen. For a non-local reference to the tax calculator service, where the tax calculator service and shopping cart bean are defined in separate applications, the service must be referenced through its JNDI name. The reference above provides a local logical name for the tax calculator service, `"ejb/TaxCalculator"`, in the local context (ENC) for the shopping cart component. The EJB descriptor (`ejb-jar.xml`), can be used to specify a binding that should be added to the shopping cart ENC by the container. For example, the following descriptor specifies that the logical name `"ejb/TaxCalculator"` for the tax calculator reference in the shopping cart component should be bound to the object referenced by the portable global JNDI name `"java:global/ejb/TaxCalculator/2010"`:

```
<session>
  <ejb-name>ShoppingCartBean</ejb-name>
  <ejb-local-ref>
    <ejb-ref-name>ejb/TaxCalculator</ejb-ref-name>
    <ejb-ref-type>Session</ejb-ref-type>
    <lookup-name>java:global/ejb/TaxCalculator/2010</lookup-name>
  </ejb-local-ref>
</session>
```

The global JNDI name for the tax calculator service (as opposed to the client reference) can be specified in the `sun-ejb-jar.xml` deployment descriptor:

```
<ejb>
  <ejb-name>TaxCalculator</ejb-name>
  <jndi-name>java:global/ejb/TaxCalculator/2010</jndi-name>
  …
</ejb>
```

Alternatively, the global JNDI name may be specified directly in the code. The JNDI name for the tax calculator implementation may be specified using the `name` attribute for an `@EJB` annotation for the class definition, using the portable JNDI syntax for the name. The JNDI name may also be specified in the client `@EJB` annotation referencing the resource, using the `lookup` attribute, or (in a non-portable fashion) using the `mappedName` attribute. As with the JMS example above, there are maintenance reasons for preferring the specification of the JNDI names in deployment descriptors, with reference to these resources made indirectly through components' local JNDI contexts.

We saw in Sect. 6.10.1 that contexts and dependency injection supports delegating resource management to the environment by associating "scopes" with the resources. Producer methods provide a form of dynamic polymorphism in the injection of resources, allowing run-time decision logic to choose the actual resources to be injected, where necessary. Another aspect of CDI is the ability to ensure that injection is type-safe. In addition to producer methods in a generator bean, *producer fields* can be defined to hold references to beans that are injected. CDI allows such a producer method or field to be defined as a *resource*, using an annotation that also associates a name (such as a persistence unit name or a JNDI name) with the resource reference:

```
@Produces @PersistentContext(unitName="PatientDB")
@PatientDB EntityManager patientDBPersistenceContext;

@Produces @EJB(lookup="java:global/ejb/ShoppingCart")
IShoppingCart shoppingCart;
```

These producer fields (or producer methods) encapsulate the logic for performing a look-up in the environment for a resource. Every injection of such a resource is based on type and qualifier information, that must match that specified in the producer field:

```
@Inject @PatientDB EntityManager patientDB;

@Inject IShoppingCart shoppingCart;
```

As the `@Named` qualifier is deprecated for dependency injection, the resolution for injections should be based only on type information and other qualifiers. These qualifiers refine the selection based on type information, to disambiguate the resource that is being injected. With named resources encapsulated in producer code, type failure during an injection is at least isolated to that producer code.

The METADATA CENTRALIZATION pattern recommends a private registration service for recording metadata about the contents of a service inventory, to facilitate discovery of the available services by development teams. This should be distinguished from the form of deploy-time discovery discussed here, where services bind to resources they require in the context in which they execute. Nevertheless, the qualifiers specified for contexts and dependency injection may provide a useful basis for cataloging and indexing services in the service inventory.

A related model of service discovery is provided by the Jini architecture [96]. The latter was developed by Sun Microsystems as a platform for modular composition of distributed systems, particularly over a LAN. The Jini analogy is with installing a consumer electronics device: when the consumer installs such a device at home, it is seamlessly connected to the residential electrical network and, through that, to the power grid. The Jini vision was to make the installation of network software components equally simple and modular when a software component is installed, it uses the Jini discovery protocol to find the services that it needs. This protocol involves a boot-strapping process where a multicast IP signal is broadcast over the LAN to find the Jini look-up service. Once the component has discovered the look-up service, it can use that service to locate other services that it requres on the network. For example, a Web client might require a printing service. The component can also register itself with the look-up service if it is, in turn, providing a network service to other components. The implementation technology for Jini is Java: service specifications are provided by Java interfaces, and location transparency is provided using proxies for remote services. This is similar to Java RMI, with some important differences: the discovery protocol for boot-strapping the location of the service registry, interface-based service identification, and the use of explicit client leases to manage resources across the network. RMI uses garbage collection based on reference counting, with leases given to clients that expire if regular heartbeat messages are not received from clients. Jini makes this leasing mechanism (and the management of leases) explicit in service implementations. Finally, RMI requires network errors to be exposed to the application as exceptions of type `RemoteException`, whereas Jini relies instead on a transactional semantics for remote operations.

WCF builds its discovery mechanism on the WS-Discovery standard for Web service discovery, which has some similarities to the Jini approach. WS-Discovery provides specifications for two forms of service discovery. *Adhoc service discovery* uses a protocol related to the Jini discovery protocol for boot-strapping service look-up and registration, providing a UDP-based multicast IP-based local discovery process. A client that is seeking a service broadcasts a query on a designated multicast IP address. The discovery process includes the use of search criteria, such as the service interface being sought, to filter the set of available services that the searching process is interested in. Other criteria include, for example, an LDAP "scope", quality of service criteria, etc.

Services that are joining the network "announce" themselves via a UDP discovery endpoint, broadcasting via multicast IP; clients can be configured to listen for such broadcasts to learn of new services. Services also announce their departure from the network so clients can use these announcements to keep track of which services are currently available. Multicast IP is limited to service discovery over the LAN, which limits its scope. It also will not scale to a large number of services. It should be understood, as with the Jini multicast IP-based discovery protocol, as a boot-strapping protocol for locating critical services, such as a service registry.

The second form of service discovery, *managed service discovery*, is a more scalable form of discovery. It uses a service registry (called a *discovery proxy service* in WCF) to keep track of the services that have announced their availability on the network. Clients can be configured to use ad hoc discovery to initially discover services and thereafter be directed by a service registry to communicate directly with it for future service discovery. The discovery proxy is so-called because in most cases it should substitute for the ad hoc multicast protocol for service discovery.

Figure 6.51 provides an example of an ad-hoc service discovery in WCF. Figure 6.51(**a**) provides a configuration file that exposes two endpoints for the ShoppingCart service. There is an endpoint for clients to connect to when invoking the service, using WsHttpBinding. There is also a second endpoint, which the service uses to "announce" itself to clients, via periodic broadcasts on a multicast IP address. The service is identified by the interface IShoppingCart that it is providing. The second configuration point of interest in Fig. 6.51(**a**) is in the service behaviors for the ShoppingCart, where service discovery is enabled as a behavior on the service endpoint. This makes the shopping cart discoverable, by configuring it to respond to service probes from clients broadcasting queries via multicast IP on the local network.

Figure 6.51(**b**) provides an example of a client performing ad hoc discovery to locate the shopping cart service. It instantiates a discovery client with an endpoint for listening to UDP service broadcasts. It then performs a search for a service, broadcasting a query via multicast IP for a service implementing the IShoppingCart interface. In general, search will return a list (array) of endpoints discovered as a result of this search—the client chooses the first in the list of endpoints that are returned. The client program then creates a client stub for the shopping cart service, setting its endpoint address to the endpoint address resulting from discovery.

In order to use managed discovery, an application needs to provide an implementation of a discovery proxy service. WCF provides an abstract class for a discovery proxy that automates many aspects of a discovery service. The methods to be implemented, to complete the definition of the discovery proxy service, are callbacks for three kinds of events:

1. The event of a service announcing its availability as it joins the network.
2. The event of a service announcing its end of availability as it leaves the network.
3. The event of a probe from a client searching for a service.

For example, an instantiation of the default implementation abstract base class might look as follows:

```
<system.serviceModel>
  <services>
    <service name="ShoppingCart">
      <endpoint binding="wsHttpBinding"
                contract="IShoppingCart" />
      <endpoint name="udpDiscovery"
                kind="udpDiscoveryEndpoint"/>
    </service>
  </services>
  <behaviors>
    <serviceBehaviors>
      <behavior>
          <serviceDiscovery/>
      </behavior>
    </serviceBehaviors>
  </behaviors>
</system.serviceModel>
```

(**a**) Enabling ad hoc discovery

```
// Find service endpoints in the specified scope
DiscoveryClient discoveryClient =
  new DiscoveryClient(new UdpDiscoveryEndpoint());
FindCriteria findCriteria = new FindCriteria(typeof(IShoppingCart));
FindResponse findResponse = discoveryClient.Find(findCriteria);
EndpointAddress address = findResponse.Endpoints[0].Address;

// Connect to discovered endpoint
ShoppingCartClient client =
  new ShoppingCartClient("shoppingCartEndpoint");
client.Endpoint.Address = address;
client.Add("The Good, The Bad and The Ugly", 1);
```

(**b**) Discovery Client

Figure 6.51   *Ad hoc discovery in WCF*

```
[ServiceBehavior(InstanceContextMode = InstanceContextMode.Single,
                 ConcurrencyMode = ConcurrencyMode.Multiple)]
public class MyDiscoveryProxy : DiscoveryProxyBase {
  // Repository to store EndpointDiscoveryMetadata.
  Dictionary<EndpointAddress, EndpointDiscoveryMetadata>
     onlineServices;
  ...
}
```

The properties of the service behavior attribute indicate that there should just be a single instance of this object on the network. Consider, for example, what would happen if there were more than one instance of the discovery proxy running on the network. A service might register for discovery with one discovery proxy instance, while a client might probe another discovery proxy instance searching for that service. On the other hand, a single instance represents a single point of failure and a target for a denial of service attack, unless the methods of Sect. 6.9.2

are used to make it highly available. The other property of the discovery proxy that is set is to enable multi-threaded access, to support high performance through concurrent execution of the callback methods. The proxy implementation must be careful to properly manage synchronization of concurrent accesses.

The internal state of the discovery proxy is a record of the metadata for each service that has registered on the network, indexed by the endpoint addresses for the services. As this discovery service is intended for discovery at deployment time, it is not the same as the private metadata registry advocated by metadata centralization. This latter is intended to provide a private registry for the service inventory and, indeed, a discovery service may use such a registry to obtain further metadata about the services that are currently deployed. In the implementation above, an in-memory dictionary data structure is used. The use of an in-memory data structure means that the contents of the service registry will not survive a recycling of the discovery proxy; an alternative implementation might save the registry to file or database periodically. The in-memory data structure is also the reason that there must be a single instance of the discovery proxy. The in-memory data structure must be shared by all clients calls (multicast or unicast) into the managed discovery service.

Figure 6.52(**a**) provides an example of code to register the discovery proxy; the registration is in two parts. The discovery proxy must listen for probes by clients looking for service registrations. The proxy binds to the unicast address at TCP port 8001 on the current machine, using the NetTcpBinding. *Clients* seeking to discover services will connect at this unicast address instead of multicasting searches for services on the network. The discovery proxy must also listen for announcements by services of their joining and leaving the network. For this, it binds to another unicast endpoint, this time at TCP port 8081, again using the NetTcpBinding. This is the endpoint at which *services* will connect via unicast, to announce their joining and leaving the network. As with service clients, the services on the network will no longer need to multicast their announcements on the network. All such announcements will be unicast to the discovery proxy.

Figure 6.52(**b**) provides the code for registering the shopping cart service with the discovery proxy. The shopping cart service first binds to its own service end-point. Again, the service uses the NetTcpBinding, binding at TCP port 9001, with a globally unique identifier (guid) specific to this registration to ensure that clients can distinguish different versions of the service. A service host is a concept from the Windows operating system: many system services are compiled as Dynamic Link Libraries (DLLs), and then run inside a service host process, corresponding to an execution of the svchost Windows program. In Fig. 6.52(**b**), the start-up code for the shopping cart service initializes a service host with the shopping cart code, and then binds it to a NetTcpBinding service endpoint at TCP port 9001, exporting the IShoppingCart service contract.

The shopping cart service still needs to register with the discovery proxy. It does this by creating a unicast announcement endpoint, to which it will send announcements when it joins and leaves the network. These unicast messages will be sent to the endpoint URL "net.tcp://localhost:8081/Announcement", which is the

```
Uri probeEndpointAddress = new Uri("net.tcp://localhost:8001/Probe");
DiscoveryEndpoint discoveryEndpoint = …
discoveryEndpoint.IsSystemEndpoint = false;
ServiceHost proxyServiceHost =
 new ServiceHost(new MyDiscoveryProxy());
proxyServiceHost.AddServiceEndpoint(discoveryEndpoint);

Uri announcementEndpointAddress =
  new Uri("net.tcp://localhost:8081/Announcement");
AnnouncementEndpoint announcementEndpoint = …
proxyServiceHost.AddServiceEndpoint(announcementEndpoint);
proxyServiceHost.Open();
// Discovery service now running.
```
(a) Announce the discovery service

```
Uri baseAddress =
  new Uri("net.tcp://localhost:9001/ShoppingCart/"
  + Guid.NewGuid().ToString());
ServiceHost serviceHost =
  new ServiceHost(typeof(ShoppingCart), baseAddress);
ServiceEndpoint netTcpEndpoint = serviceHost.AddServiceEndpoint(
  typeof(IShopping), new NetTcpBinding(), string.Empty);

// Create an announcement endpoint pointing
// to the hosted proxy service.
Uri announcementEndpointAddress =
  new Uri("net.tcp://localhost:8081/Announcement");
AnnouncementEndpoint announcementEndpoint = …
ServiceDiscoveryBehavior serviceDiscoveryBehavior =
  new ServiceDiscoveryBehavior();
serviceDiscoveryBehavior
  .AnnouncementEndpoints.Add(announcementEndpoint);
serviceHost.Description.Behaviors.Add(serviceDiscoveryBehavior);
serviceHost.Open();
```
(b) Announce the shopping cart service

```
// Discovery endpoint for the discovery service.
Uri probeEndpointAddress = new Uri("net.tcp://localhost:8001/Probe");
DiscoveryEndpoint discoveryEndpoint = …
DiscoveryClient discoveryClient =
 new DiscoveryClient(discoveryEndpoint);
FindResponse findResponse = discoveryClient.Find(
  new FindCriteria(typeof(IShoppingCart)));
```
(c) Discovery Client

Figure 6.52 *WCF managed discovery*

address at which the discovery proxy is listening for such announcements. Having
created the announcement endpoint for the shopping cart service, the start-up code
adds a service behavior to enable service discovery. This modification of behavior
programmatically achieves what was achieved using the <serviceDiscovery> element, in the configuration description for ad hoc service discovery in Fig. 6.51(**a**).

Once the service host is opened, it announces it presence to the discovery proxy, which will then inform clients on the network about its availability.

Figure 6.52(**c**) provides the code for a client program, using the discovery proxy to locate the shopping cart service. Whereas the cart service connected to the discovery proxy at its announcement endpoint, the client program connects to the proxy at its service probe endpoint, at the endpoint URL `"http://localhost:8001/Probe"`. The program creates a discovery client that will send unicast discovery messages to the discovery proxy at this probe endpoint. The `Find` operation is invoked on the discovery client to do exactly this, specifying the `IShoppingCart` interface as the search criteria. The remainder of the client protocol is as in Fig. 6.51(**b**): a shopping cart client is created, and its address set to the endpoint address or addresses resulting from discovery. This then serves as a proxy for the shopping cart service.

6.11.3 Layered Naming

We have seen that the push-based model for wide area service discovery exemplified by UDDI has failed, and that some have advocated for a pull-based model based on structured Web crawlers that find Web services and feed this information to search engines. In this section, we consider how wide-area service discovery is currently done and we also consider an architecture for a future Internet naming scheme, that has been proposed to be a better match with this reality than the current Internet structure.

To the extent that it is done, global service discovery today is based on text search engines. Yet, below this initial layer of searching, there are several other mediating layers before a client binds to a particular service instance:

1. At the first level of service discovery, a search string is provided to a search engine. This search string might be of the form "Widget suppliers who can deliver within 24 hours in the greater New York City area, including Saturday deliveries", or "Auction sniping services that are highly rated by their users for reliability".

2. A search engine delivers a series of URLs for potential service suppliers. The URLs for these providers are, in turn, based on domain names, where a domain name should identify the supplier of the service. The WHOIS service is available to identify the owner of a domain, although the owner may have elected to register a domain privately.

3. Invoking a service is not necessarily just a case of looking up the IP address based on the domain name. There are ways in which a service provider can redirect clients to particular servers. For example, if one visits the provider's main Web page to get links to the services that they provide, the provider can determine the approximate location of the client from their IP address and rewrite the links in the Web page to direct the client to the geographically closest server farm. As we saw in Sect. 2.8, there are other "tricks" that can be played with the DNS system itself to redirect client requests into a parallel routing network, such as the Akamai caching network. Service providers may

also use mechanisms such as Dynamic DNS to re-bind domain names to IP addresses; this latter binds a static DNS address to IP addresses obtained, for example, through Dynamic Host Configuration Protocol (DHCP), updating DNS entries as services bind to new IP addresses.

4. Once one has translated the domain name to an IP address, the IP routing infrastructure delivers service requests to an eventual destination determined by routing tables in the network and routing protocols such as Border Gateway Protocol (BGP) and Open Shortest Path First (OSPF). Within a server farm, as we have seen, various strategies may be used to determine the server instance to which the request is directed: load-balancing across replicated servers, affinity for stateful services, etc.

Mobility complicates this picture even further. Mobility comes in many forms: data and services become mobile as Web sites become re-organized, breaking old Web links. Clients bind to location-specific versions of services, such as to particular server farms chosen to minimize latency for service consumers, and to minimize the cost of network traffic for the service provders. Clients, in the form of laptops, cellphones, and tablets, move around so that their bindings to location-specific services has to change over time. The routes between clients and service providers may need to change dynamically, during data transfer, as the devices physically move.

What we can see is that the Internet, as noted by Balakrishnan et al. [97], is a network that was largely frozen in the mid-1990s, and now creaks with the twists and turns that network and service providers have taken to adapt it to modern needs for which it was never designed. The reliance on host names to identify data and services leads to the problems of broken links and ad hoc service resolution described above. Once a data communication path is established between client and service provider, the IP addresses (and TCP port numbers) of the parties become the identifying information for this data path. However, if devices are mobile during data transfer, this binding to network addresses is premature as the network address of the mobile host changes as it moves across networks.[30] These situations are depicted in Figure 6.53. A device uses a search function to locate a service, as a URL with a domain name. The domain name resolves to different hosts as the device moves. Some of the re-binding can be done by the device reconnecting to services after it has moved, as depicted by the solid request links, although movement during data transfer may require the ability of a service provider to dynamically re-route data to the mobile host's new location.

The solution to the latter problem, of dynamically re-routing data transfer paths, is *Mobile IP* [98]. Mobile IP is an example of the classical aphorism that "there is no problem that Computer Science cannot solve with an extra level of indirection". In this case, Mobile IP solves the problem that a mobile device cannot retain its IP address while it moves across networks, by indirecting communications to that device through a *home agent* that remains on its home network. The

---

[30]Using the same IP address in different networks is not a scalable solution as IP addresses identify the physical subnet as part of the address.

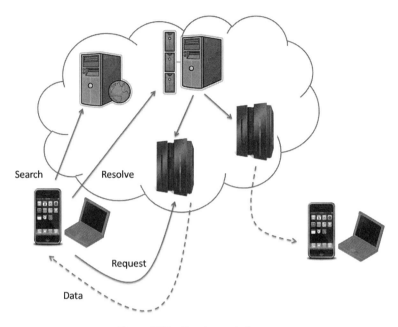

Figure 6.53 *Naming and discovery*

mobile host, when it arrives at the network it is visiting, uses a discovery protocol to find a *foreign agent* on the network. The foreign agent broadcasts periodic
"agent advertisements" on the foreign network, and the mobile host listens for
these advertisements. From such an advertisement, the mobile host obtains a *care-
of address* (COA). It connects back to the home agent, through the foreign agent,
to provide the COA and establish a tunnel[31] from the home agent to the foreign
agent. When a party wishes to establish a data connection to the mobile host, the
home agent intercepts communications to the mobile host on the home network,
using the proxy Address Resolution Protocol (ARP) protocol. Communications are
forwarded through the aforesaid tunnel to the mobile host. Various optimizations
can be considered. The mobile host may establish a direct route to a party it is
communicating with, as re-routing through the home agent is only necessary for the
device that has moved while retaining its IP address. On the other hand, firewalls
may require that data connections back to connecting sites go through the home
network, to prevent denial of service attacks based on spoofing source addresses.
Parties that connect to mobile hosts may be informed by the home agent of their
actual address on the foreign network, although this complicates handover when
the device moves between foreign networks; there are also security issues with
trusting the information about the current location of the mobile host. The major
problem with Mobile IP is, not surprisingly, the issue of how the home network
knows to trust the foreign network. Therefore, it is mainly seeing application in

---

[31]Tunnelling was explained in Sect. 2.2.

mobile telephone networks, for transfer among the regional networks of a single service provider, rather than across the networks of rival service providers.

For the purposes of service discovery and invocation, we are not yet at the point where services are hosted on mobile devices.[32] Dynamic DNS is too slow for dynamic re-routing of data transfers for in transit devices and, in any case, such data transfer connections are identified by their endpoint IP addresses. However, Dynamic DNS may be sufficient to allow mobile hosts to rebind to a new IP address once they reach a foreign network. Mobile IP is unlikely to be a general solution across different network providers, because of the trust issues associated with it.

The more relevant issues for service discovery are in the upper layers, specifically the issues of mobile services and mobile data. Here, the issue is that binding to a service using a URL is premature, as the URL that the service binds to may change over time. The problem is with using the host name to provide a long-term identifier for the service. The context root may also change over time, as enterprises re-organize the namespace for ther services.

Balakrishnan et al. [97] propose an alternative layered architecture for naming in the Internet to address these issues. While the chances of this architecture replacing the multi-billion dollar investment in the current Internet are approximately zero, it can still provide some useful suggestions for organizing service discovery where the investment can be justified. At the upper layers, the proposal is to use a *session identifier* (SID) to identify a service in a host-independent manner. Discovery of the session identifier for a service is outside of the framework and could be via a search engine, DNS, UDDI, or whatever search facility is proposed for finding services. The service identifier provides a persistent identifer for a particular service, one that survives across changes in the host that provides the service.

When establishing a connection to the service, clients bind to an *endpoint identifier* (EID). This is a location-independent host name. The purpose of EIDs is to identify the ends of a transport connection between client and service provider, without binding to IP addresses, which would be considered a premature binding. The framework envisions a look-up service between a session layer and a transport layer that resolves session identifiers to endpoint identifiers, and between the transport and the network layers, that resolves endpoint identifiers to IP addresses. So, IP addresses are only resolved when data is being routed over the network, avoiding the need for the forwarding mechanism of Mobile IP. The relationship between the current DNS/IP approach, Mobile IP, and the layered naming scheme of SIDs and EIDs, is summarized in Fig. 6.54.

The look-up service between the layers is envisioned as a *distributed hash table* (DHT), a fast, wide-area indexing service intended for applications such as finding content in large peer-to-peer file-sharing networks. DHTs are optimized to provide

---

[32]However, it is entirely plausible that mobile devices will host services made available locally by broadcasting over Bluetooth or WiFi networks, perhaps to avoid monitoring in the cloud.

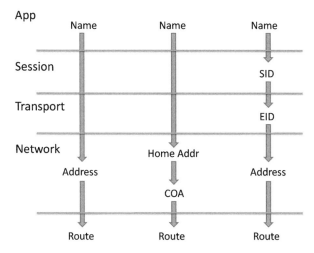

Figure 6.54 *Naming and discovery*

$O(\log(N))$ search time, where N is the number of nodes in the network, while surviving a high degree of "churn" in the network. We consider DHTs in more detail in Chapter 10 in the sequel volume.

One may wonder how feasible it is to perform a DHT look-up on the IP address of the recipient node every time a packet is being sent. However, for service discovery, dynamically re-routing data transfers is not as important as providing a stable service identifier. Here, the decoupling of a service name from the host it is provided on, using a session identifier, seems to be a plausible halfway approach. Unlike EIDs, the infrastructure (a global DHT) for resolving SIDs to endpoint addresses (EIDs or IP addresses), can be deployed atop the current Internet infrastructure, and may provide a more stable infrastructure than the current "tricks" that service providers play with DNS.

6.12 FURTHER PATTERNS

There are some major gaps in our discussion so far. We have not considered the principle of service composability. Some of the patterns we have considered, such as reliable messaging and protocol bridging, are intended to support service composability. However, a fuller discussion of this principle must also consider issues of availability and failure recovery. Although we have considered examples of replication and caching, there are still important issues of distributed agreement to consider, particularly in light of the results summarized in Sect. 2.3. Consideration of recovery requires a deeper discussion of transactional computing models. Also, in discussing service loose coupling, there are several aspects of asynchronous messaging that we have not considered, such as intermediate routing and event-driven messaging. These are particularly important for EDA, that complements SOA. We defer discussion of these issues to the sequel volume.

6.13 FURTHER READING

The distinction between DDA and SOA, based on object-oriented versus procedural paradigms, is due to Bien [99]. The conceptual framework provided by service principles, and the patterns language for SOA underlying the discussion here, are due to Erl et al. [8, 9].

Procedural data abstraction originated with Parnas' seminal work on programming modules for programming in the large [7], while the notion of abstract data types originated with the CLU language [59]. Reynolds [1] provided an early contrast between procedural data abstraction and abstract data types, with updates by Cook [3, 4]. The work of Cook et al. highlighted the semantic distinction between inheritance (implementation reuse) and subtyping (behavior reuse) [100, 101].

We have touched on many aspects of type systems from programming languages because they are at the heart of many of the software engineering issues raised by SOA. The definitive reference on the theory of modern type systems is Pierce [102].

Many fine tutorials exist on WCF and Java EE, for example Löwy [103] and Goncalves [104]. Cachin et al. [105] consider protocols and algorithms for building reliable distributed systems in detail. Charron-Bost et al. [106] provide a collection of advanced essays on issues and approaches to replication for highly available systems. Terry [107] surveys data management in mobile computing, where replication is obviously essential.

REFERENCES

1. Reynolds J. User-defined data types and procedural data structures as complementary approaches to data abstraction. In: New Advances in Algorithmic Theory. INRIA; 1975.

2. Abelson H, Sussman G, Sussman J. *Structure and Interpretation of Computer Programs*. Cambridge: MIT Press; 1985.

3. Cook WR. Object-oriented programming versus abstract data types. In: de Bakker JW, de Roever WP, Rozenberg G, editors. Foundations of Object-Oriented Languages, REX School/Workshop, Noordwijkerhout, The Netherlands, May/June 1990, 489 of Lecture Notes in Computer Science, p. 151–178. New York; Springer-Verlag; 1991.

4. Cook W. On understanding data abstraction, revisited. In: Proceedings of ACM Symposium on Object-Oriented Programming: Systems, Languages and Applications. ACM; 2009.

5. Krafzig D, Banke K, Slama D. Enterprise SOA: *Service-Oriented Architecture Best Practices*. Prentice-Hall; New York 2005.

6. Arsanjani A, Booch G, Boubez T, Brown PC, Chappell D, deVadoss J, Erl T, Josuttis N, Krafzig D, Little M, et al. The SOA manifesto. Available at: http://www.soa-manifesto.org; 2009.

7. Parnas D. On the criteria to be used in decomposing systems into modules. *Communications of the ACM* 1972; 15:1053–1058.

8. Erl T. SOA: Principles of Service Design. Prentice-Hall, New York 2008.

9. Erl T, et al. SOA Design Patterns. Prentice-Hall; New York 2009.

10. David Parnas. A technique for software module specification. *Communications of the ACM*, 1972; 15:330–336.

11. Backus JW, Beeber RJ, Best S, Goldberg R, Haibt LM, Herrick HL, Nelson RA, Sayre D, Sheridan PB, Stern H, et al. The FORTRAN automatic coding system. In: Proceedings of the IRE-AIEE-ACM '57 (Western) Papers presented at the Western Joint Computer Conference: Techniques for Reliability. ACM; 1957.

12. McCarthy J. Recursive functions of symbolic expressions and their computation by machine, Part I. *Communications of the ACM* 1960; 3:184–195.

13. Dijkstra EW. The structure of the THE multiprogramming system. Communications of the ACM: 1968; 11(5):341–346.

14. Marks E. Service-Oriented Architecture (SOA) Governance for the Services Driven Enterprise. Wiley; Hoboken, NJ 2008.

15. Weill P, Ross JW. IT Governance: How Top Performers Manage IT Decision Rights for Superior Results. Boston: Harvard Business School Press; 2004.

16. Calore M. Ma.gnolia suffers major data loss, site taken offline. Wired Magazine, January 30, 2009. Available at: http://www.wired.com/epicenter/2009/01/magnolia-suffer/.

17. Sabelfeld A, Myers AC. Language-Based Information-Flow Security. *IEEE Journal on Selected Areas in Communications* 2003; 21:5–19.

18. Myers AC, Liskov B. Protecting privacy using the decentralized label model. *ACM Transactions on Software Engineering and Methodology* 2000; 9:410–442.

19. Liu J, George MD, Vikram K, Qi X, Waye L, Myers AC. Fabric: a platform for secure distributed computation and storage. In: *SOSP '09: Proceedings of the ACM SIGOPS 22nd symposium on Operating systems principles*, Big Sky, MT New York: ACM; 2009, p. 321–334.

20. Duggan D. Type-based cryptographic operations. *Journal of Computer Security*, 2003; 12(3–4)485–550.

21. Chothia T, Duggan D, Vitek J. Type-based distributed access control. In: Computer Security Foundations Workshop, Asilomar: IEEE; 2003.

22. Abadi M. On SDSI's linked local name spaces. *Journal of Computer Security* 1998; 6:3–21.

23. Hicks M, Moore J, Nettles S. Dynamic software updating. In: Proceedings of ACM SIGPLAN Conference on Programming Language Design and Implementation Snow Bird, UT ACM. 2001.

24. Neamtiu I, Hicks M, Stoyle G, Oriol M. Practical dynamic software updating for c. In: Proceedings of ACM SIGPLAN Conference on Programming Language Design and Implementation. ACM Press; 2006.

25. Evans H, Dickman P. Zones, contracts and absorbing change: An approach to software evolution. In: Proceedings of ACM Symposium on Object-Oriented Programming: Systems, Languages and Applications. Denver, CO: ACM Press; 1999, p. 415–434.

26. Duggan D. Type-based hot swapping of running modules. *Acta Informatica* 2005; 181–220.

27. Cosmadakis S, Papadimitriou C. Updates of relational views. *Journal of the ACM* 1984 31:742–760.

28. Halderman JA, Felten EW. Lessons from the Sony CD DRM episode. In: Proceedings of the 15th Conference on USENIX Security Symposium. Baltimore, MD USENIX Association; 2006.

29. Shapiro C, Varian HR. Information Rules: A Strategic Guide to the Network Economy. Boston: Harvard Business Press; 1998.

30. Proebsting T, Watterson S, Filter fusion. In: Proceedings of ACM Symposium on Principles of Programming Languages. 1996, p. 119–130.

31. Kerckhoff A. La cryptographie militaire. *Journal des Science Militaires* 1883; 83:161–191 [in French]

32. Carr H. Metro interoperates with .NET wsDualHttpBinding; 2009. Available at: http://weblogs.java.net/blog/haroldcarr/archive/2009/04/metro_interoper%.html.

33. Marino J, Rowley M. Understanding SCA (Service Component Architecture). Addison-Wesley; Boston, MA 2009.

34. Waldo J, Wyant G, Wollrath A, Kendall, S. A note on distributed computing. Technical report. Sun Microsystems Laboratories; 1994.

35. Walls C. Spring in Action, 3rd edn Manning; Shelter Island, NY 2010.

36. Church A. *The Calculi of Lambda Conversion*. Princeton: Princeton University Press; 1941 Reprinted by University Microfilms Inc., Ann Arbor, 1963.

37. Eckel B, Venners B. The trouble with checked exceptions: A conversation with Anders Hejlsberg, part ii. Artima Developer, 18 August 2003. Available at: http://www.artima.com/intv/handcuffsP.html.

38. Jim T, Morrisett JG, Grossman D, Hicks MW, Cheney J, and Wang Y. Cyclone: A safe dialect of C. In: USENIX Annual Technical Conference Berkeley: USENIX Association; 2002, p. 275–288.

39. Bocchino Jr. RL, Adve VS, Adve DDSV, Heumann S, Komuravelli R, Overbey J, Simmons P, Sung H, and Vakilian M. A type and effect system for Deterministic Parallel Java. In: Proceedings of ACM Symposium on Object-Oriented Programming: Systems, Languages and Applications. 2009.

40. Strom RE, Yemini S. Typestate: A programming language concept for enhancing software reliability. *IEEE Transactions on Software Engineering* 1986; 12:157–171.

41. Deline R, Fähndrich M. Typestates for objects. In: Proceedings of the 18th European Conference on Object-Oriented Programming (ECOOP). Oslo, Norway. Springer: 2004, p. 465–490.

42. Stork S, Marques P, Aldrich J. Concurrency by default: using permissions to express dataflow in stateful programs. In: Proceeding of the 24th ACM SIGPLAN conference companion on Object oriented programming systems languages and applications, OOPSLA '09. New York: ACM; 2009, p. 933–940.

43. Walker D, Crary K, Morrisett G. Typed memory management in a calculus of capabilities. *ACM Transactions on Programming Languages and Systems* 2000; 22:701–771.

44. Fahndrich M, DeLine R. Adoption and focus: practical linear types for imperative programming. In: PLDI '02: Proceedings of the ACM SIGPLAN 2002 Conference on Programming language design and implementation. New YorkACM Press; 2002, p. 13–24.

45. Peyton-Jones S, Wadler, P. Imperative functional programming. In: Proceedings of ACM Symposium on Principles of Programming Languages. Charleston: ACM; Press 1993, p. 71–84.

46. Pierce BC. Basic Category Theory for Computer Scientists. Cambridge: MIT Press; 1991.

47. Steele G. Building interpreters by composing monads. In: *Proceedings of ACM Symposium on Principles of Programming Languages* ACM; 1994, San Francisco, CA p. 472–492.

48. Liang S, Hudak P, and Jones MP. Monad transformers and modular interpreters. In: *ACM Symposium on Principles of Programming Languages (POPL)*. San Francisco, CA ACM; 1995.

49. Duggan D. A mixin-based, semantics-based approach to reusing domain-specific programming languages. In: European Conference on Object-Oriented Programming (ECOOP). Lecture Notes in Computer Science Cannes: Springer-Verlag; 2000.

50. Hughes J. Generalising monads to arrows. *Science of Computer Programming* 2000; 37:67–111.

51. Cook W, Hill W, Canning P. Inheritance is not subtyping. In: Gunter CA, Mitchell JC, editors. Theoretical Aspects of Object-Oriented Programming. Cambridge: The MIT Press; 1994.

52. Ichbiach JD, Barnes JPG, Firth RJ, Woodger M. Rationale for the design of the Ada programming language. *SIGPLAN Notices* 1979; New York, NY 14.

53. Intermetrics, Cambridge. *Ada-95 Reference Manual*, 1995. International standard ISO/IEC 8652:1995(E).

54. Cardelli L, Donanue J, Jordan M, Kalsow B, Nelson G. The Modula-3 type system. In: Proceedings of ACM Symposium on Principles of Programming Languages. Austin: ACM Press; 1989, p. 202–212.

55. Brown MR Nelson G. IO Streams: Abstract types, real programs. Technical report. Palo Alto: DEC Systems Research Center; 1989. Available at: ftp://gatekeeper.research.com paq.com/pub/DEC/SRC/research-reports/abstr%acts/src-rr-053.html.

56. Morris Jr JH. Protection in programming languages. *Communications of the ACM* 1973. 16(1):15–21.

57. Krueger CW. Software reuse. *ACM Computing Surveys* 1992; 24:131–183.

58. DeRemer F, Kron HH. Programming-in-the-large versus programming-in-the-small. *IEEE Transactions on Software Engineering* 1976; 2:80–86.

59. Neighbors JM. Draco: A method for engineering reusable software systems. In: Biggerstaff TJ, Perlis AJ, editor Software Reusability: Voume 1–Concepts and Models. ACM Press; Waltham, MA 1989, p. 295–319.

60. Liskov B, Snyder A, Atkinson R, Schaffert C. Abstraction mechanisms in CLU. *Communications of the ACM* 1977: 20; 564–576.

61. Goguen JA. Parameterized programming. *IEEE Transactions on Software Engineering* 1984; 10:528–543.

62. Jones M. Qualified Types: Theory and Practice. Cambridge: Cambridge University Press; 1994.

63. Fisher K, Reppy J. The design of a class mechanism for Moby. In: Proceedings of ACM SIGPLAN Conference on Programming Language Design and Implementation. Atlanta: ACM Press; 1999, p. 37–49.

64. Bracha G Cook W. Mixin-based inheritance. In: Proceedings of ACM Symposium on Object-Oriented Programming: Systems, Languages and Applications, ACM Press; 1990, p. 303–311. SIGPLAN Notices;25(10).

65. Harren M, Raghavachari M, Shmueli O, Burke MG, Bordawekar R, Pechtchanski I Sarkar V. XJ: Facilitating XML processing in Java. In: World Wide Web (WWW) Conference, May Chiba, Japan 2005.

66. Duggan D, Sourelis C. Mixin modules. In: Proceedings of ACM International Conference on Functional Programming; 1996, 262–273.

67. Bracha G. *The Programming Language Jigsaw: Mmixins, Modularity and Multiple Inheritance*. PhD thesis, University of Utah; 1992.

68. Duggan D, Techaubol CC. Modular mixin-based inheritance for application frameworks. In: Proceedings of ACM Symposium on Object-Oriented Programming: Systems, Languages and Applications. Tampa: ACM Press; 2001.

69. Ernst E. gbeta—a Language with Virtual Attributes, Block Structure, and Propagating, Dynamic Inheritance. PhD thesis. Department of Computer Science, University of Aarhus, Århus; 1999.

70. Odersky M, Cremet V, Röckl C, Zenger M. A nominal theory of objects with dependent types. In: *Proceedings of European Conference on Object-Oriented Programming (ECOOP). Darmstadt, Germany*. Springer LNCS; 2003.

71. Weber M. The Theory of Social and Economic Organization. London: Collier Macmillan Publishers; 1947. Translated by A.M. Henderson and Talcott Parsons.

72. Gum PH. System/370 extended architecture: Facilities for virtual machines. *IBM Journal of Research and Development* 1983; 27:530–544.

73. Popek GJ, Goldberg RP. Formal requirements for virtualizable third generation architectures. *Communications of the ACM* 1974; 17:412–421.

74. Felber P, Narasimhan P. Experiences, strategies and challenges in building fault-tolerant CORBA systems. *IEEE Transactions on Computers* 2004; 53:497–511.

75. Gray J, Helland P, O'Neil P, Shasha D. The dangers of replication and a solution. In: Proceedings of the 1996 SIGMOD Conference; 1996.

76. Alsberg P, Day J. A principle for resilient sharing of distributed resources. In: Proceedings of the Second International Conference on Software Engineering; 1976, p. 627–644.

77. Budhiraja N, Marzullo K, Schneider F, Toueg S. The primary-backup approach. In: Mullender S, editor. Distributed Systems. ACM Press; Waltham, MA 1993.

78. Patterson D, Brown A, Broadwell P, Candea G, George C, Chen M, Cutler J, Enriquez P, Fox A, et al Recovery oriented computing (roc): Motivation, definition, techniques, and case studies. Technical report. UCB//CSD-02-1175 Berkeley Computer Science, 2002.

79. Oki B, Liskov B. Viewstamped replication: A new primary copy method to support highly-available distributed systems. In: Proceedings of ACM Symposium on Principles of Distributed Computing; 1988, p. 8–17.

80. Gray J. Why do computers stop and what can be done about it? In: Symposium on reliability in distributed software and database systems. Los Angeles, CA. IEEE Computer Society Press. 1986, 3–12.

81. Burman M. Aspects of a high volume production online banking system. In: *Proceedings of the International* Workshop on High Performance Transaction Systems; 1985.

82. Mourad S, Andrews D. The reliability of the IBM/XA operating system. In: Digest of 15th Annual International Symposium on Fault-Tolerant Computing. Ann Arbor, MI. IEEE Computer Society Press; 1985.

83. Perrow C. *Normal Accidents: Living with High Risk Technologies*. Perseus Books; New York, NY 1990.

84. Kephart JO, and Chess DM. The vision of autonomic computing. *IEEE Computer* 2003; 36:41–50.

85. Huang Y, Kintala C, Kolettis N, Fulton ND. Software rejuvenation: analysis, module and applications. In: *Twenty-Fifth International Symposium on Fault-Tolerant Computing (FTCS)*. IEEE; 1995, p. 381–390.

86. Lirch O. Why NFS sucks. In: Proceedings of the Linux Symposium. USENIX; 2006.

87. Birrell A, Levin R, Needham R, Schroeder M. Grapevine: An exercise in distributed computing. *Communications of the ACM* 1982; 25:260–274.

88. Alonso R, Barbara D, Garcia-Molina H, Abad S. Quasi-copies: Efficient data sharing for information retrievel systems. Venice, Italy In: *International Conference on Extending Database Technology (EDBT)*, number 303 in Lecture Notes in Computer Science. Springer-Verlag; Berlin 1988, p. 443–468.

89. Terry DB, Demers AJ, Petersen K, Spreitzer MJ, Theimer MM, Welch BB. Session guarantees for weakly consistent replicated data. In: Proceedings of the Third International Conference on Parallel and Distributed Information Systems (PIDS '94) IEEE Computer Society Press; 1994, p. 140–150.

90. Hauser C, Jacobi C, Theimer M, Welch B, Weiser M. Using threads in interactive systems: A case study. In: Proceedings of the Fourteenth ACM Symposium on Operating Systems Principles. 1993, p. 94–105.

91. King G, JSR 299: Contexts and dependency injection for the Java EE platform. Technical report. Java Community Process; 2009. Available at: http://www.jcp.org/en/jsr/summary?id=299.

92. Hartman F, Reynolds H. Was the universal service registry a dream? *Web Services Journal* 2004.

93. Al-Masri E, Mahmoud QH. Investigating web services on the world wide web. In: World Wide Web Conference (WWW); 2008.

94. Al-Masri E, Mahmoud QH. A broker for universal access to web services. In: Proceedings of the 2009 Seventh Annual Communication Networks and Services Research Conference (CNSR '09). IEEE Press; 2009.

95. Zeilenga K. Lightweight directory access protocol (LDAP): Technical specification road map. Technical Report 4510, Internet Engineering Task Force (IETF), June 2006.

96. Arnold K, O'Sullivan B, Scheifler R, Waldo J, Wollrath A. *The Jini Specification*. Addison-Wesley; Boston, MA 1999.

97. Balakrishnan H, Lakshminarayanan K, Ratnasamy S, Shenker S, Stoica I, Walfish M. A layered naming architecture for the internet. In: ACM SIGCOMM, 2004.

98. Perkins C. Mobile IP. *IEEE Communications* 1997; 35(5):84–99.

99. Bien A. Real World Java EE Patterns–Rethinking Best Practices. Adam Bien Press; 2009.

100. Canning P, Cook W, Hill W, Olthoff W, Mitchell J. F-bounded polymorphism for object-oriented programming. In: *Proceedings of ACM Symposium on Functional Programming and Computer Architecture*. ACM Press; 1989, p. 273–280.

101. Cook W, Hill W, Canning P. Inheritance is not subtyping. In: Proceedings of ACM Symposium on Principles of Programming Languages, 1990: 125–135.

102. Pierce BC. Types and programming languages. Cambridge: MIT Press; 2002.

103. Löwy J. Programming WCF Services: Mastering WCF and the Azure AppFabric Service Bus, 3rd edn; 2010.

104. Goncalves A. Beginning Java EE 6 Platform with Glassfish 3. Apress; New York, NY 2009.

105. Cachin C, Guerraoui R, Rodrigue L. Introduction to Reliable and Secure Distributed Programming. Springer-Verlag; 2011.

106. Charron-Bost B, Pedone F, Schiper A, editors. Replication: Theory and Practice. Lecture Notes in Computer Science. Springer-Verlag; Berlin 2010.

107. Terry D. Replicated Data Management in Mobile Computing. Morgan & Claypool; San Rafael, CA 2007.

7

Resource-Oriented Architecture

"If you have Microsoft saying 'Well, the best approach is to make this elaborate infrastructure we've spent billions of dollars building out optional, then the debate is over'."

Rob Sayre

"I am amused by the people who are valiantly trying to decipher Roy."

Sam Ruby

7.1 REPRESENTATIONAL STATE TRANSFER

(REST) was developed by Roy Fielding [1] in a widely cited PhD thesis describing a software architecture for the Web. RESTful Web services emerged largely in opposition to SOAP-based Web services, although the concept of REST dates back to the design of HTTP and the Web itself. REST is not a difficult concept to understand, but it has some subtlety. Part of the challenge with appreciating the subtleties of REST is undoubtedly because of "interference" from pre-existing conceptions about enterprise and distributed applications. Some of the REST philosophy questions the appropriateness of RPC for inter-enterprise applications, advocating for a more loosely-coupled approach based on communication through updatable resources that have real-life analogues in the business documents that are exchanged as part of normal business collaborations. There are layers that can be discerned in the application of the REST principles; any architect or developer should carefully consider the level of application of REST principles that is most appropriate their situation. Perhaps the greatest benefit to be derived from an excursion into RESTful thinking is that of questioning fundamental assumptions, so that

Enterprise Software Architecture and Design: Entities, Services, and Resources,
First Edition. Dominic Duggan.
© 2012 John Wiley & Sons, Inc. Published 2012 by John Wiley & Sons, Inc.

design decisions are based on careful reasoning, rather than blind application of an existing knowledge and experience base.

REST was developed to fill a very real need for a conceptual architecture for the Web, where the semantics of extensions such as shared caches needed to be better understood, both for developers and for users. The Web could be understood as a stateless, client-server system, with optional client-side caching, but this picture was too simple for the more sophisticated architectures being implemented. The central idea of REST is to view Web browsing as the navigation of a hypermedia space, where the space is made up of a collection of *resources* that are connected by hyperlinks. Unlike hypertext networks, the values associated with these resources may be time-varying. Resources are identified by URIs, that include uniform resource locators and uniform resource names. These identifiers do not change as the value of resource changes over time.

The internal representation of a resource is not important as clients of a resource only see a representation of that resource, downloaded upon request from a server. Using HTTP, for example, the user obtains a *representation* for a resource, specified by a URI, as a document or other form of data element. Clients update resources or create new resources by uploading representations to a server. In the terminology of HTTP, the representations that are downloaded to the client or uploaded to the server are referred to as *entity bodies*, not to be confused with domain entities in DDD. A resource may have more than one URI, but it must have at least one URI. *Addressability* is the defining property of a resource. Before the Web, remote files were available for download using the File Tranfer Protocol (FTP) and the Gopher protocol. The FTP protocol required that one log into a site e.g., `ftp.example.com`, navigate to a directory (e.g., `/bib/aids`), and then download the file of interest (e.g., `aidsint.ps`). With addressability, this resource is given a single URI: `ftp://ftp.example.com/bib/aids/aidsint.ps`. This suffices to reference it from any applications, as long as the file's location and access permissions do not change. A piece of downloadable software may have one URI for the latest version of that software, and another URI for the specific version of the software. These are two different resources as they are conceptually two different things: the specific version of the software does not change once released, but the latest version is changed with each new software release. A resource may have several URIs but, in order not to dilute the communicativeness of the URI, there should, ideally, be one canonical URI for the resource. The `Content-Location:` response header in HTTP may be used to report the canonical URI for a resource, when a non-canonical URI is used to reference it. Although names in REST are usually assumed to be synonymous with URIs, the use of URIs for persistent names sometimes has issues, which we considered when we considered an alternative naming scheme for resources on the Internet in Sect. 6.11.3. The difficulty with a URI is that it can be intended to represent both a name, that should be immutable, and an address (the location of a resource on the Internet). We consider this issue further when we consider the principles of ROA in Sect. 7.3.

Another distinguishing feature of the REST style is the *uniform interface* that all resources provide via the use of HTTP to exchange uniform representations. HTTP provides a basic, coarse-grained API for accessing Web resources:

1. A resource should be created using the PUT operation, which identifies the resource to be created by a URI. A representation for the state of the new resource is uploaded as part of the HTTP message.

2. GET is the read operation for retrieving a resource. The resource to be retrieved is identified by the URI, with additional *scoping information* in the query string. The result of the GET is the downloading of a resource representation (e.g., HTML document, JPEG image, etc). The Web architecture dictates that the GET command should not result in a change of state of the Web site being queried.

3. The POST operation results in the update of the specified resource. Here, we need to distinguish between an update that "adds to" a resource, in the sense of, for example, appending to a list, and an update operation that completely replaces the resource. The PUT operation is intended for the latter replacement, while POST is intended for the former "append" semantics.

4. The PATCH operation is used to upgrade a resource to a newer version. This operation expects a recipe to be supplied for how the update should be performed.

5. HTTP specifies a DELETE operation for deleting a resource, again identified by a URI.

6. The HEAD method retrieves just the metadata for a resource from a server, without requiring the retrievel of a representation for the entire resource.

7. The OPTIONS method can be used to discover what Web methods may be applied to a resource. The Accept: response header may be used to report to a client the operations that can be performed on a resource. For example, a response of Accept: GET, HEAD signifies that a resource is read-only and cannot be updated or deleted. In the Amazon S3 system discussed in the next section, the permitted operations on a resource will depend on the identity and access permissions of the client, where the former is specified in the Authorization: request header, and the latter is specified in an access control list and policy specification provided in the metadata for the resource.

A resource representation may also have associated representation metadata (such as the media type, or the time it was last modified), as well as resource metadata (e.g., the source link) and control data (HTTP headers such as if-modified-since:, for a conditional GET, which we explain below).

A client in the Web is conceptualized in the REST model as a state machine. Downloading the representation of a resource corresponds to a state transition of this machine, tracing the arc in the transition graph that brings the state machine to the point where it has received that resource representation. *Statelessness* is a critical aspect of the REST architecture: all evolving state in the Web is in the client, updated as it traverses links in the hypermedia Web, while the server remains stateless with respect to its interactions with clients. Although many Web sites use cookies stored on a client browser to identify session state on the server, this is in violation of the REST principle. All state is held by the client. If the server is to have stateful memory of its session with the client then, according to REST, this state may be saved on the client and uploaded from the client to the server on each interaction. Alternatively, if there is session state associated with an interaction between client and server, then this session state is a resource that should be identified by a URI, with the client explicitly identifying this session state in its interaction with the Web service. We provide examples of this in Sect. 7.5.

The typical resource representation contains a collection of links to other resources. This *connectedness* is, again, a central aspect of the Web according to REST, since it defines the hypermedia space that the Web client navigates. Assuming the client keeps going forward, it will next follow one of the links leading from the resource representation, leading to another state transition as another resource representation is downloaded. We consider an example of programming environment support for this notion of connectedness and hypermedia programming in Sect. 7.6.

Figure 7.1 provides an example contrasting the RESTful form of a Web service interaction with a RPC-based interaction exemplified by the SOAP approach to Web services.[1] Figure 7.1(**a**) describes a hypothetical SOAP-based interaction with a Web service that enables train reservations. The Web server on the service side of the interaction includes a SOAP router; all service requests for train reservations identify this SOAP router as their destination by specifying its endpoint URL in the HTTP request headers. In a typical scenario, a service request message is provided as the payload for the HTTP POST message, and the response from the Web service is provided as in the HTTP response. Each SOAP request message contains information, such as the root element of the message body, to identify the operation being invoked, and the SOAP router dispatches to the appropriate service operation based on this information. An example request message might be:

```
<soap:envelope xmlns:soap=...
            xmlns:tr="http://www.example.org/schemas/train/soap">
  <soap:body>
    <tr:ScheduleRequest>
      <tr:departure>tr:NYP</tr:departure>
      <tr:destination>tr:WAS</tr:destination>
      <tr:date>05-02-2011</tr:date>
    </tr:ScheduleRequest>
  </soap:body>
</soap:envelope>
```

An example response provides a list of possible trains to select from on the specified date:

```
<soap:envelope xmlns:soap=...
            xmlns:tr="http://www.example.org/schemas/train/soap">
```

---

[1]This is independent of the distinction made in SOAP between RPC style and document style interaction, where this latter restriction only refers to the encoding of request messages in SOAP message bodies.

POST /train/soap

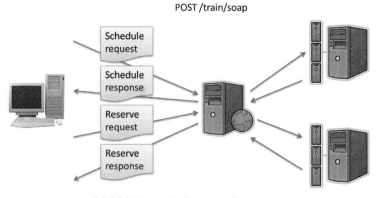

(a) SOAP-based train reservation service

GET /train/rest/schedule?src=NYP&dst=WAS&date=05-02-2011

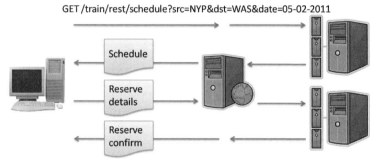

POST /train/rest/train/2107

(b) REST-based train reservation service

Figure 7.1 *SOAP versus REST Web services*

```
<soap:body>
  <tr:ScheduleResponse>
    <tr:train>
      <tr:tid>2103</tr:tid>
      <tr:time>0600</tr:time>
    </tr:train>
    <tr:train>
      <tr:tid>2107</tr:tid>
      <tr:time>0700</tr:time>
    </tr:train>
    <tr:train>
      <tr:tid>183</tr:tid>
      <tr:time>0717</tr:time>
    </tr:train>
    <tr:train>
      <tr:tid>2109</tr:tid>
      <tr:time>0800</tr:time>
    </tr:train>
    …
  </tr:ScheduleResponse>
```

```
  </soap:body>
</soap:envelope>
```

A reservation request message then picks from one of the trains in the schedule and includes passenger and payment information, presumably encrypted using TLS or WS-Security, or both. The same SOAP router dispatches to the service for processing reservation requests.

Figure 7.1(**b**) provides the REST architecture for a similar service for booking trains. SOAP completely disappears as part of a RESTful Web service. Rather than performing service requests on a remote server, the metaphor in this application is one of querying and updating resources at the server. The initial resource that is queried is the list of all trains for the specified route, for a particular date. This resource is identified by a URI, including the domain of the reservation service (www.example.org) and scoping information that specifies the departure and destination cities (and date) of the form:

```
/train/rest/schedule?src=NYP&dst=WAS&date=05-02-2011
```

An alternative specification of the schedule would include the parameters identifying the schedule as part of the URI:

```
/train/rest/schedule/NYP/WAS/05-02-2011
```

However, although programming frameworks, such as JAX-RS, certainly support this form of path parameters in a URI, the use of such path parameters should be used judiciously, as we discuss in the next section.

According to the proper usage of HTTP, this query should be specified using the GET verb. There is no payload uploaded to the service; additional scoping information (e.g., for business or first class service) can be provided in the query string if needed. The HTTP response may be an XML or JSON document that provides a list of train departures for the specified route on the specified date. The SOAP response contains a list of train codes, whose meaning is known only to the service. To obtain further information, or to make a reservation, the client will have to send another SOAP request to the service, specifying the train by its code in the schedule. In contrast, the RESTful Web service response to the initial schedule query includes URIs to identify each of the trains in the schedule. Again, this follows the REST model, reflecting the principle of connectedness where each resource is uniquely identified by a URI:

```
<tr:Schedule xmlns:tr="http://www.example.org/schemas/train/rest">
  <tr:train>
    <tr:uri>
      http://www.example.org/train/rest/train/2103
    </tr:uri>
    <tr:time>0600</tr:time>
  </tr:train>
  <tr:train>
    <tr:uri>
      http://www.example.org/train/rest/train/2107
```

```
    </tr:uri>
    <tr:time>0700</tr:time>
    </tr:train>
    <tr:train>
    <tr:uri>
       http://www.example.org/train/rest/train/183
    </tr:uri>
    <tr:time>0717</tr:time>
  </tr:train>
  <tr:train>
    <tr:uri>
       http://www.example.org/train/rest/train/2109
    </tr:uri>
    <tr:time>0800</tr:time>
  </tr:train>
  …
</tr:Schedule>
```

A reservation request is made by operating on the resource for the particular train being chosen. The HTTP POST method is used to update an existing resource; this is appropriate as we are updating an existing train with a new reservation. The payload for the HTTP POST may provide customer identification and payment information. For services that require user authentication, this may be provided by a request message authentication code, signed by a client private key, in the HTTP request headers. This is how Amazon S3, for example, authenticates accesses to client files.

A framework sometimes used to categorize approaches to RESTful Web services is a REST maturity model originally proposed by Richardon [2]:

1. The simplest level of RESTful Web services, the so-called "zero-th" level, is that of *plain old XML* (POX) services. In this approach, a "RESTful" Web service simply eschews the use of the SOAP/WSDL stack but otherwise communicates data in XML (or JSON) form over HTTP. Many Web services that support Web applications, including Amazon Web Services and the Flickr API, are of this form.

2. The first "real" level of RESTful Web services is one that takes the notion of resources seriously by identifying the resources that are acted upon through the use of URIs. In the train reservation example, the use of URIs to iden-tify train and reservation resources demonstrates this result. The difference between this and the previous level may not be as great as it at first appears, if the design of the system principally relies on the use of URIs to encode parameters to an underlying RPC-like Web service. We elaborate on this in the next section.

3. The second level of enlightenment is one that adopts the RESTful notion of the uniform interface, for example through proper use of the HTTP verbs. Although sometimes a source of heated debates about the correct use of the HTTP verbs, it is worth emphasizing that REST is not the same thing as HTTP. HTTP is just a particularly good example of a REST

protocol. Similarly, a uniform interface does not necessarily mean the HTTP methods. Rather, it entails *some* uniform vocabulary for acting on resources.

4. In this maturity model, the final level of enlightenment for the REST model is one where applications take seriously the notion of application execution as navigation of a hypermedia network. Recall that this is, indeed, the central concept of the REST architectural style—that of the client as a state machine navigating a hypermedia network defined by resources, and the links between them. This is sometimes referred to using another acronym, *Hypermedia As The Engine Of Application State* (HATEOAS). We consider support for hypermedia programming in 7.5.

In the next section, we consider examples of Web services, and consider to what extent they realize the principles of REST. Some services realize the principles of REST better than others, although this is not meant to pass judgement, as there may be situations where a partial application of REST principles is more than enough. This leads us to a deeper discussion of some of the ramifications of the REST architectural style. We consider programming environment support for REST in the subsequent sections. Before proceeding, it is worth considering the HTTP protocol in more detail, given its centrality to RESTful Web services.

HTTP is layered over the TCP protocol, assuming a duplex reliable data stream between the sender and the receiver. The sender supplies a request as a series of lines, separated by newlines (carriage-return-linefeeds): a *request line*, containing the HTTP verb and context root; the request headers; and a blank line followed by the message payload, where appropriate. The Host: request header, required for all requests, identifies the domain name under which the underlying IP address is being addressed, to support *virtual hosting* where a single server may host several different domains, each a different service. The response message consists of: a *status line*, which includes a numeric status code and a textual reason phrase; the response headers; and a blank line followed by the response payload, where appropriate. Latency can be reduced by re-using the same TCP transport connection for multiple HTTP requests, using the Keep-Alive: request header to specify how long the connection should be left open. Where enabled, *HTTP pipelining* may be used to send several HTTP requests in parallel, without waiting for the responses to each message. A sample client request is given by:

```
GET /index.html HTTP/1.1
Host: www.example.org
```

A sample response is given by:

```
HTTP/1.1 200 OK
Date: Mon, 1 May 2011 21:38:14 GMT
Server: Apache/1.3.34 (Debian) mod_ssl/2.8.25 OpenSSL/0.9.8c …
Last-Modified: Wed, 25 Nov 2009 12:27:01 GMT
```

```
ETag: "7496a6-a0c-4b0d2295"
Accept-Ranges: bytes
Content-Length: 2572
Content-Type: text/html
Via: 1.1 www.example.org
Vary: Accept-Encoding
...
```

Clients download a representation of a resource on each state transition as they navigate the hypermedia Web. There may be several different representations for a resource. For example, a client may be prepared to accept a response document either as XML or as JSON data. There are MIME types to describe either of these: `application/xml` and `application/json`, respectively. The `Accept:` request header supports *content negotiation*, allowing the client to specify the response document types it can support. The `Content-Type:` response header informs the client of the type of the response returned by the service. Many MIME types are available for request and response documents, including:

1. ATOM (`application/atom+xml`), a widely understood format for publishing Web feeds that supports addressability.

2. RDF (`application/rdf+xml`), a standard encoding format for "facts" in semantic content, that may be used by inference engines such as may be employed by software agents. We consider RDF in Chapter 14 in the sequel volume.

3. XHTML (`application/xhtml+xml`), favored by some RESTful Web services despite the fact that it is intended for presentation logic.

4. Form-encoded key-value pairs (`application/x-www-form-urlencoded`), originally intended to encode the values of the input fields in a Web form as key-value pairs, and often used to encode the actual arguments in a RPC-like Web service as key-value pairs.

The client may specify content encodings (i.e., compression algorithms) that it can support via the `Accept-Encoding:` header. The `Content-Encoding:` response header informs the client of any compression performed on the response document. The `Content-type:` response header may also specify a character set encoding for the document data, e.g., UTF-8, US-ASCII, UTF-EBCDIC or UTF-16 (16-bit Unicode encoding). This is dangerous, as it may override a different character set encoding specified in an XML document, and should be avoided.

Various headers support caching. The *conditional GET* is supported by request and response headers headers that allow the client to specify when it will accept data already cached at the client side. The `Last-modified:` response header specifies the time of last modification of a resource (though with low precision). A client request can specify via the `If-Last-Modified:` request header that a representation of the resource should only be returned if it has been modified since the date specified in the request header. A resource that has not been modified is indicated by a status code of 304 ("Not modified") rather than the default 200 ("OK"). The

Etag: ("entity tag") response header returns a hash of the metadata for a resource. A subsequent If-None-Match: request header can specify that a representation of the resource only be returned if its metadata hash no longer matches the specified hashes. The Cache-Control: response header provides some service control over client-side caching, including specifying how long a representation can be safely cached for, or when it should not be cached at all.

The Authorization: request header specifies application-defined authorization information for authorizing access to a resource. For example, it is used by the Amazon S3 cloud storage system to authorize access to files. The WWW-Authenticate: response header is used with a status code of 401 ("Unauthorized") to notify the client that they need to authenticate to access the resource, including information about how they should authenticate. Authentication techniques include basic and digest techniques. *Basic authentication* incorporates a user name and password, encoded using base64 encoding, and should only be transmitted over an encrypted (SSL or TLS) transport. *Digest authentication* hashes the user credentials to protect them during transmission. The client first contacts the service for a challenge, a nonce ("number used once") from the service, provided in the WWW-Authenticate: response header. The client generates its own nonce and then hashes a response that includes both the server and client nonces, and the user credentials, to assure the service that this is not a replay attack. A disadvantage of this approach is that the password must be stored in cleartext on the server, a violation of best practices for password storage. Amazon S3 uses a custom digital signing protocol, using a private signing key on the client to sign a hash of an access request and placing that hash with the signature in the Authorization: request header. The server uses its own copy of the key to authenticate client accesses. Enterprise solutions to authenticating RESTful service requests include protocols such as OAuth and SAML. We consider authentication and authorization in Web services further in Chapter 15 in the sequel volume.

Cookies are transmitted using the non-standard Cookie: request header to transmit cookies from the client to the server, and the Set-Cookie: response header to save a cookie on the client. Presumably, these should have much less relevance for Web services than for business-to-consumer purposes. They are one possible basis for HTTP sessions, storing session state or just a session identifier on the client, although their use for the latter is frowned upon for RESTful services. We consider this further in Sect. 7.5. The *same origin policy* for cookies provides a service with access to all cookies stored under the domain for that service. Among many security issues introduced by cookies, so-called *secure cookies* are intended to only be transmitted over SSL or TLS; however, HTTP does not provide information to a Web service about whether or not the transport is secure. Suppose a site has used secure communication using HTTPS to save secure cookies on a client, for example from https://www.google.com/accounts. A man-in-the-middle attack allows a malicious third party to add Set-Cookie: response headers into a subsequent cleartext response from the same domain, for example from http://www.google.com, allowing the attacker to overwrite the values of the cookies. So, whereas secure cookies may ensure *confidentiality* of the information they contain during transmission, they do not ensure *integrity*.

The Upgrade: response header is a, so far, little-used method for the service to indicate that it wishes the client to change to a different protocol. For example, it might be provided in response to a cleartext connection request, to request an upgrade to a secure (SSL or TLS) connection. One use case for the Upgrade: header is in the WebSocket draft protocol standard [3] that allows a stream connection, such as a TCP connection, to be tunnelled through firewalls in a HTTP connection.

The HTTP response codes are an important part of the interaction between clients and services. There are several classes of response codes:

1. The 1XX codes are used for negotiation with the Web server. The 101 code ("Switching protocols") may be used in conjunction with the Upgrade: header to inform the client that the server is switching to a different protocol.

2. The 2XX codes are used to signal success to clients. Besides the obvious success code of 200 ("OK"), the response code of 201 ("Created") can be used to inform the client that a request has been created. The Location: response header provides the canonical URI for the newly created resource.

3. The 3XX codes provide redirection information to clients. The 303 code ("See Other") directs clients to another resource that represents a response, without requiring them to download a representation for that resource. It may be used, for example, to provide the canonical URI for a resource, perhaps at the conclusion of an update operation. The 307 code ("Temporary Redirect") directs a client to another URI for a resource, without processing a request that might update or delete that resource. In both cases, the Location: response header specifies the URI to which the client is directed.

4. The 4XX codes indicate client-side errors, including the famous 404 ("Not Found"). The 400 response code ("Bad Request") signals a malformed request, while 409 ("Conflict") can be used to signal a client-side logic error. The 401 ("Unauthorized") response code can be used in conjunction with the WWW-Authenticate: response header to provide clients with information about how they should authenticate. The 403 ("Forbidden") response code signals that the service has chosen not to execute the service request; perhaps the request is not allowed from the client IP address.

5. The 5XX codes signal server-side errors. The 500 response code ("Internal Server Error") is raised when an un-caught exception is raised by server-side processing.

7.2 RESTFUL WEB SERVICES

What are the principles of software architectures that are faithful to the principles of REST? When is a divergence from these principles a reasonable compromise, and when is a divergence so fundamental that the service should no longer be classified as RESTful? Clearly, RESTful applications are organized around resources, that are on the Web and may be manipulated by the HTTP methods. These resources are identified by immutable URIs, and clients download and upload representations of these resources as documents and various forms of data elements.

Many widely-used RESTful Web services are simple "plain old XML" services and do not incorporate this focus on resources identified by URIs. Consider some of the API calls in the popular Flickr Web service, provided in Fig. 7.2. The URI is the same in all cases: `http://api.flickr.com/services/rest`. Photographs and galleries are identified as extra parameters referenced in query strings. There is nothing particularly resource-oriented about the API in the sense of emphasizing resources identified by URIs. The lack of addressability of resources betrays this as a POX-style, RPC-style Web service in common with most of the well-known business-to-consumer Web services, despite the use of the word "rest" in the URL for the API. Flickr does, indeed, have a SOAP alternative to the "RESTful" service interface at the endpoint URL `http://api.flickr.com/services/soap/`. A sample SOAP request message is of the form:

```
<env:Envelope xmls:env="http://www.w3.org/2003/05/soap-envelope">
  <env:Body>
    <flickr:FlickrRequest xmlns:flickr="urn:flickr">
      <method>flickr.photos.delete</method>

      …
    </flickr:FlickrRequest>
  </env:Body>
</env:Envelope>
```

Even though this is not technically an "RPC-style" SOAP request, Flickr is following a convention with this "document-style" interaction, where the name of the operation being invoked at the service site is specified by the `<method>` sub-element of the root element of the SOAP body. Both the SOAP and the "RESTful" Flickr Web service APIs are RPC-based, in the general sense of the term. Neither follows the precepts of REST. This is not to say that the Flickr API is badly-designed: it is a perfectly fine RPC interface, but it is not REST.

Another REST principle is that of the uniform interface. In the Flickr API, some of the operations use the GET HTTP verb, while others use POST. However, as with the SOAP API, each service request contains a designated argument (the method parameter) that identifies an operation to be performed.

What of the use of GET and POST as the verbs for the operations? Two particularly important properties of some Web methods are safety and idempotence. *Safety* refers to the fact that a method, when invoked, does not have any discernable side effect on the server. The operations for querying resources (GET and HEAD) are examples of safe operations. A server may log method invocations for auditing purposes, but that does not change the fact that the query operations do not have side effects at the application level. A Web site that updates application data as a result of a GET request is in violation of the specification of HTTP and the REST principles.

Idempotence refers to the fact that an operation has the same effect if it is performed once or many times; it must be performed at least once. We have encountered idempotence for service operations already in Sect. 2.4. For example,

Purpose	API calls
| Get list of photos in a gallery | ```
GET http://api.flickr.com/services/rest/?
  method=flickr.galleries.getPhotos
  &api_key=b
  &gallery_id=b
  &api_sig=b
``` |
| Add a photo to a gallery | ```
POST http://api.flickr.com/services/rest/?
  method=flickr.galleries.addPhoto
  &api_key=b
  &gallery_id=b
  &photo_id=b
  &api_sig=b
``` |
| Create a gallery | ```
POST http://api.flickr.com/services/rest/?
  method=flickr.galleries.create
  &api_key=b
  &title=b
  &description=b
  &api_sig=b
``` |
| Delete a photo | ```
POST http://api.flickr.com/services/rest/?
  method=flickr.photos.delete
  &api_key=b
  &photo_id=b
  &api_sig=b
``` |

Figure 7.2 *Flickr API*

overwriting a record in a file or a database table is idempotent. No matter how many times the operation is performed, as long as it is performed at least once, the result is the same. On the other hand, incrementing an integer counter, or appending to a list, are examples of operations that are not idempotent. For the latter, the number of times an operation is invoked to add to the list will be reflected in the number of additional items added. In HTTP, PUT and DELETE are operations that are intended to be idempotent. The PUT operation is intended to write data, rather than append it. No matter how many times it is performed, as long as it is performed at least once, the result is the same: the resource has been created or replaced. Similarly, no matter how many times a resource is deleted, as long as it is deleted at least once, the end result is the same: the resource has been deleted. The discussion of RPC failures in Sect. 2.4 demonstrates the usefulness of distinguishing idempotent from non-idempotent update operations. For idempotent operations, at-least-once semantics is equivalent to exactly-once semantics, while exactly-once semantics is, in general, impossible to implement in an asynchronous system.

To what end the POST method, so ubiquitous in RPC-style Web services? POST is defined according to the HTTP standard as an operation for creating "subordinate data". Examples of this include appending to a database or posting a message to a bulletin board. For example, a logging operation, responsible for maintaining an audit trail for accountability, might append a record to a log file whenever a significant event is observed. A logging operation obviously does not care about the name or key for the record it adds to the log file. The latter will later be read sequentially by applications looking for interesting events or patterns in the log. So, in a sense a log record is "subordinate" to the log file it is appended to and, in this case, the POST method is the appropriate way to add the log record. The response from this operation may return a URI for the new subordinate resource that has been added. This might be used, for example, for posting to a bulletin board or adding a contact to a contacts database, where the bulletin board or database has a URI of the form http://hostname/context-root and each posting in the bulletin board or contact in the database has a URL of the form http://hostname/context-root/*pid* for some integer posting identifier *pid*. The latter URI is returned as a result of the successful completion of the POST in the Location: response header for clients that want to keep track of the results of their actions.

In adding a record to a database, the primary key for the record might be defined by the application, for example using a campus-wide identifier for a student record, or generated internally by the database when the record is added. The PUT verb would be appropriate for the former case, while POST would be appropriate for the latter case. In the former case, the client is first creating the resource and then directing it to be stored in the database table where the argument URI identifies the record. In the latter case, the argument URI identifies the database that is being extended and the URI for the newly created record can be returned in the Location: response header. So why is POST used so ubiquitously for RPC-style Web services? The RFC for HTTP [4] specifies another use for POST: "providing a block of data, such as the result of submitting a form, to a data-handling process". What constitutes a data-handling process? The phrase is deliberately broad to allow its use in situations that fall outside the scope of standardization, as long as it is used for stateful update.

In the Flickr interface, the GET method is used for operations that retrieve resources without changing the state of resources, while the POST method is used for all operations that change the state of resources. This is a general pattern for "tunnelling" RPC commands through the HTTP stack. Such tunneling may sometimes be done for the HTTP methods themselves when tunneling them through client HTTP stacks that only support GET and POST. Such APIs may be designed for the implementation of Web browsers, as GET and POST are the only verbs required for Web forms. The WSDL 2.0 specification allows for a similar specification for HTTP verbs for tunnelling SOAP requests through the HTTP stack: using POST as the default verb, but using GET in the case where an operation is declared to be safe. Such a declaration can be done by specifying wsdlx:safe="true" for an operation that does not discernibly change the state of the resources acted upon.

Amazon S3 is a cloud-based storage system, with both SOAP-based and resource-oriented APIs. The storage system for a user of Amazon S3 is made up of *buckets* and *objects*. The former correspond to folders; the latter to files. Buckets may not be nested; however, the "/" character may be used in object names ("keys"), and a subset of the objects in a bucket may be chosen in a query by specifying a prefix of the names of the desired objects in the query.

Using the "virtual hosting" method, a bucket named `jeddak` is identified by the URI `http://jeddak.s3.amazonaws.com`. Amazon adds the `Authorization:` HTTP header that includes a digital signature identifying the party making the access request. A bucket might be named `www.example.org`, so that its URI is `http://www.example.org.s3.amazonaws.com`. That bucket might then be aliased in DNS to the domain `www.example.org`, so that the use of a cloud provider is not revealed in the Web services provided to clients.

As far as S3 is concerned, an object is an opaque data object contained within a bucket. The object also has metadata, specified as a collection of name-value pairs. An object is specified by a triple of bucket, object key, and object version; the latter defaults to the most recent version. Object names may contain "/" so, for example, the bucket `http://jeddak.s3.amazonaws.com` might contain the objects:

```
docs/manual.pdf
docs/security.pdf
talks/snt.pdf
```

Retrieving one of these objects is done using the `GET` method:[2]

```
GET http://jeddak.s3.amazonaws.com/docs/manual.pdf
```

The two objects with names starting with `docs` can be retrieved by:

```
GET http://jeddak.s3.amazonaws.com/docs
```

Amazon S3 therefore exhibits addressability, by virtue of the fact that buckets and objects are all addressable using URIs.

Amazon S3 also provides a good example of the use of a uniform interface for accessing and updating resources, providing a CRUD interface for accessing buckets and objects using the HTTP verbs:

Method	Bucket list	Bucket	Object
`GET`	List buckets	List bucket objects objects	Get value and metadata
`HEAD`			Get metadata
`PUT`		Create bucket	Set object value and metadata
`DELETE`		Delete bucket	Delete object

[2]More preciesely, this is specified using the HTTP headers:

```
GET /docs/manual.pdf HTTP/1.1
Host: jeddak.s3.amazonaws.com
Date: …
Authorization: …
```

In S3, queries for lists of buckets, contents of buckets, and contents of objects (including metadata) are performed using the GET method, as may be expected. The HEAD method is used to obtain metadata for an object, and DELETE is used to delete a bucket or an object. Finally, the PUT method is used to create new buckets and to add new objects to buckets. It is quite possible for multiple clients to perform PUT on the same object simultaneously. S3 does not provide object locking, but does ensure that the writing of an object is an atomic operation. Therefore, the result of simultaneous PUT operations on the same object is that the copy with the newest time stamp is the one that is the result of the updates.

In the case where an object does not already exist, the PUT method both creates that resource and also updates the bucket into which it is inserted. In this case, there is a defensible case for using POST rather than PUT to perform the initial creation of a object in a bucket, with the URI for the newly created resource returned in the Location: header. The reason that S3 does not follow this course is because of the structure it imposes on URIs: The URI for an object, for example http://jeddak.s3.amazon.com/docs/manual.pdf reflects the fact that this resource is subordinate to a parent resource—the bucket identified by http://jeddak.s3.amazon.com. A similar hierarchical structure could be used in the train schedule and reservation example in the previous section, where a reservation could have a URI that identifies it as a sub-resource of a particular train. In that case, POST would operate on a train resource to create a reservation as a sub-resource, returning the URI for the reservation as part of the result.

However, assuming a structure to the URIs that reflects a hierarchical structuring of resources is also a violation of REST principles. The most important underlying motivation for the REST architectural style, the motivation for some of the principles, is that of *loose coupling* between clients and servers. Resources are intended to be abstract entities to clients. The only coupling between clients and resources is intended to be that provided by the verbs that can be applied to those resources, the content type for the resource representations that are exchanged, and the connectedness provided by URL links in a resource representation that is provided to a client when they "get" a resource. The hierarchical structure of the S3 API, considered as an alternative for the train reservation example, imposes additional structure on the resources beyond that specified in the RESTful compact and, as such, reflects a violation of REST principles.

The train reservation example demonstrates another aspect of this violation. An alternative form of the URI for a schedule that was considered was composed from the source and destination train stations and the date of travel:

```
/train/rest/schedule/NYP/WAS/05-02-2011
```

Frameworks for designing and implementing RESTful Web services, including Web Application Description Language (WADL) and JAX-RS, support the passing of parameters to a Web service as components of the URI. This feature should be used judiciously, as it may lead to the practice of *URI tunnelling*—tunnelling parameters to an RPC call through a URI that should only be concerned with identifying a resource. URI parameters used in this way again place a structure on resource identifiers that violates the REST principle of loose coupling. If the train reservation service at some point decides to change the way it identifies particular trains, then this will invalidate the interface with existing clients. Even the passage of the parameters as a query string would be preferable, since the order of the parameters is not important, and services can be extended to accept additional parameters without invalidating existing clients. The more RESTful API for the train reservation system that is provided includes a top-level URI for an entry search service for train schedules. The parameters for the search are specified as query string parameters—the result of the search is a representation for a train schedule matching the search request. A client should be able to cache this URI and use it in the future (perhaps years in the future) to retrieve a representation of the up-to-date state of the schedule resource. When abused, URI tunneling amounts to a particularly clumsy form of POX-based Web services. URI tunneling is a deprecated practice because of the unnecessary tight coupling it introduces between client and service.

The HTTP methods are not the only possible choice of verbs that might be chosen as the basis for ROA services. Various extensions have been developed over time, proposing richer basic vocabularies without resorting to the RPC-oriented style of defining new operations on an application-specific basis. For example, WWW Distributed Authoring and Versioning (WEBDAV) extends the HTTP methods with eight additional methods for collaborative Web-based file management:

1. PROPFIND retrieves the properties of a resource or the directory structure of a remote file system.
2. PROPPATCH performs atomic update and deletion of multiple properties on a resource.
3. MKCOL creates a directory (collection).
4. COPY copies a resource from one URI to another.
5. MOVE moves a resource from one URI to another.
6. LOCK places a lock on a resource.
7. UNLOCK removes a lock from a resource.

The difference between these operations and those of S3 is that the latter explicitly makes no attempt to support collaborative file editing. Thus, S3 has no locking/unlocking operations. While an object can be moved by deleting it and recreating under a new URI, this cannot be made an atomic operation in S3, and it cannot be done using the REST operations as CRUD operations without copying the object through the client. The REST perspective is that this extended interface is unnecessary, as the same can be accomplished by providing resources representing the desired atomic actions. The mistake of the WEBDAV interface is to only consider the use of the HTTP verbs for a CRUD interface for a Web-based file system.

Recall that the model of computation assumed by REST is one of a stateful *client* abstract machine transitioning between states as a result of resource representations downloaded from the server. This is the basis for the principle of statelessness in RESTful Web services. Here, we need to be careful to distinguish between *application state* and *resource state*. Any form of service providing data logic will have some form of resource state as it is providing a storage service. Amazon S3 provides a data storage service in the cloud—obviously any uploads or updates of data are semi-permanent, lasting until the resource is updated again by a client application. These are global data changes, visible across client applications. Besides content data, a service such as Amazon S3 will also store metadata for objects, including content type (Content-Type:) and access control information. However, according to the principles of ROA, there should be no notion of session state between a client and a server.

As we have seen, a great deal of emphasis in the original REST model is placed on connectedness—the fact that the Web is a hypertext network that clients navigate by downloading resource representations. Each new document that is encountered provides a collection of hyperlinks, all related to the resource whose representation the client has just downloaded. The next state the client will progress to will depend on which of these links they choose to follow. A classic example of this is the Web search result, which provides a collection of links related to the original search term. An example was provided in the train example in Fig. 7.1(**b**), where an initial query for a train schedule between two endpoints on a given date provides in its result a document with links to all of the possible trains that could be taken between those endpoints on that date. The next state to be transitioned to will depend on which of the possible trains the client chooses from this list of possibilities. This linking of related resources is regarded in the REST model as a fundamental part of the cognitive model that explains the success of the Web.

In this respect, Amazon S3 fails this particular principle of resource orientation completely. Querying a bucket for a list of the objects, or a particular subset of the objects, in that bucket returns a result such as the following:

```
HTTP/1.1 200 OK
x-amz-id-2: …
x-amz-request-id: …
Date: …
Content-Type: application/xml Content-Length: …
Connection: close
Server: AmazonS3

<?xml version="1.0" encoding="UTF-8"?>
<ListBucketResult xmlns="http://s3.amazonaws.com/doc/2006-03-01">
    <Name>jeddak</Name>
    <Prefix>docs/</Prefix>
    <IsTruncated>false</IsTruncated>
    <Contents>
      <Key>docs/manual.pdf</Key>
      <LastModified>2006-01-01T12:00:00.000Z</LastModified>
      <ETag>&quot;…&quot;</ETag>
```

```
        <Size>20356</Size>
        <StorageClass>STANDARD</StorageClass>
        <Owner>… </Owner>
    </Contents>
</ListBucketResult>
```

The result does not provide hyperlinks to the related resources linked to from the bucket. The consumer of this resource representation must understand how to build a URI for each object in the bucket from the bucket name and the key. This information is application-specific, in this case specific to the protocols and document formats used by S3. This result is reminiscent of the result of the SOAP-based query for available trains in Fig. 7.1(**a**).

What of the train reservation service and connectedness? In fact, this service also violates the REST principle of connectedness. The content type that is returned from a query for a train schedule has MIME-type `application/xml`, reflecting general XML data for application processing. XML itself has no notion of hyperlinks. In the example given in Fig. 7.1(**b**), each `<train>` element in a schedule has a `<uri>` child element that identifies a hyperlink for that train resource. However, that is not reflected in the MIME type for the resource representation and again reflects implicit coupling between the client and the server not otherwise reflected in the resource interface.

To remove this implicit coupling, we can make it explicit with a description of the protocol that is encoded in the links provided by resource representations returned to clients. The specification of this protocol includes:

1. The format of the data (resource representations) exchanged in the protocol.
2. A delineation of where the links to other resources can be found in the representation of a resource.
3. For each link, a specification of the semantic role that link represents in the workflow represented by the linking of resources.

This specification can be defined by a domain-specific media type, that describes such a *domain application protocol* (DAP). In this case, we define an XML Schema for the document representations of resources, as well as a schema for the links that are included in those representations. The Atom format for publishing feeds includes a generic framework for describing resources (entries) and links. However, this is specific to publishing authored data on the Web and is not a general solution for specifying domain application protocols, where we expect to be able to perform conformance checking on programs that participate in such protocols. XHTML is another well-known markup language that includes a notion of hyperlinks, but it is designed for presentation logic and is a poor choice for machine-to-machine Web service interactions. *Microformats* represent an approach to adding domain-specific structure to XHTML documents, using the `class` attribute on document elements to annotate the document with application semantics. However, the current focus of microformats is on human readability rather than automated conformance checking.

In the case of the train schedule, a sample schedule of media type `application/vnd.trains+xml` is as follows:

```
<tr:Schedule xmlns:tr="http://www.example.org/schemas/train"
             xmlns:dap="http://www.example.org/schemas/train/dap">
  <tr:train>
    <dap:link
      url="http://www.example.org/train/rest/train/2103"
      rel="http://www.example.org/train/rest/relations/reserve"
      mediaType="application/vnd.trains+xml"/>
    <tr:time>0600</tr:time>
  </tr:train>
  <tr:train>
    <dap:link
      url="http://www.example.org/train/rest/train/2107"
      rel="http://www.example.org/train/rest/relations/reserve"
      mediaType="application/vnd.trains+xml"/>
    <tr:time>0700</tr:time>
  </tr:train>
  <tr:train>
    <dap:link
      url="http://www.example.org/train/rest/train/183"
      rel="http://www.example.org/train/rest/relations/reserve"
      mediaType="application/vnd.trains+xml"/>
    <tr:time>0717</tr:time>
  </tr:train>
  <tr:train>
    <dap:link
      url="http://www.example.org/train/rest/train/2109"
      rel="http://www.example.org/train/rest/relations/reservation"
      mediaType="application/vnd.trains+xml"/>
    <tr:time>0800</tr:time>
  </tr:train>
  ...
</tr:Schedule>
```

The content for the links connecting the resources is given by the `<dap:link>` element. In these links, the actual link itself is given by the `url` attribute. The `rel` attribute provides a URI that provides semantic information about the relationship of that link to the overall DAP. In this example, each link is to make a reservation on the train resource that is linked. The `mediaType` attribute identifies the content type of any elements that must be provided when traversing the links. In this case, the media type is `application/vnd.trains+xml` as payment information will need to be transferred when traversing any of the reservation links.

Richardson and Ruby [5] define four principles for ROA in order to differentiate RESTful Web services from POX Web services:

1. Statelessness (which we have discussed at length in Sect. 6.10).
2. Addressability (data elements are organized into resources that are named).
3. Uniform interface (the ROA equivalent of canonical expression).
4. Connectedness (the hypermedia of the Web).

The first of these principles really reflects the fact that all application states should reside on the client, while only the resource state resides on the server. However, as we wil see in Sect. 7.5, some application state may be made into resource state. The remaining three principles reflect the three levels of Richardson's maturity hierarchy for the application of REST principles. In the next section, we consider a refinement of these principles that reflects the use of REST principles in designing and implementing enterprise applications.

7.3 RESOURCE-ORIENTED ARCHITECTURE (ROA)

In this section, we consider an application that demonstrates the application of REST principles in an enterprise application. We then consider these principles in more detail.

We considered an example of a purchase order service with a usage protocol in 6.7.4 (Fig. 6.27): the purchase order is invoiced, paid, and shipped, in that order. At any point before the order is shipped, it may be cancelled. We can describe this protocol again in RESTful terms, using a domain-specific media type with links that contain semantic information about their role in the protocol. The workflow would begin with a POST operation to a URI for making a purchasing request, providing a purchase order as an entity body that is an input to the POST operation. The result of this purchasing operation is a representation of an invoice, such as the following:

```
<po:invoice
    xmlns:po="http://www.example.com/schemas/purchases"
    xmlns:dap="http://www.example.com/schemas/purchases/dap">
  <po:invoice-num>12345</po:invoice-num>
  <po:purch-order-num>67890</po:purch-order-num>
  <po:amount>39.95</po:amount>
  <dap:link
    url="http://www.example.org/purchases/rest/invoice/12345"
    rel="http://www.example.org/purchases/rest/relations/pay"
    mediaType="application/vnd.purchases+xml"/>
  <dap:link
    url="http://www.example.org/purchases/rest/purchase/12345"
    rel="http://www.example.org/purchases/rest/relations/update"/>
    mediaType="application/vnd.purchases+xml"/>
  <dap:link
    url="http://www.example.org/purchases/rest/purchase/12345"
    rel="http://www.example.org/purchases/rest/relations/cancel"/>
</po:invoice>
```

The first link in the document is to the invoice resource. The semantic information associated with the link reveals it to be a link for payment. The client uses the POST verb to complete payment for the purchase. The media type associated with this link specifies the same XML namespace as that of the invoice. There are two links in the invoice document to the purchase resource, identified by a URI that includes the invoice number:

```
http://www.example.org/purchases/rest/purchase/12345
```

The semantic information associated with these links reveals their different purposes: the first link is to update the purchase, for example by deleting items or
adding items to the purchase. This update should be done using the PATCH operation. The second link to the purchase resource allows the purchase to be cancelled.
The DELETE verb is appropriate for cancelling the purchase. In this case, there is
no input entity body associated with the operation (although there would be if we
required a statement of the reason for the cancellation), so there is no statement of
a media type for the link

 If the client follows the payment link and submits payment, using the POST verb,
then they obtain a receipt document:

```
<po:receipt
    xmlns:po="http://www.example.com/schemas/purchases"
    xmlns:dap="http://www.example.com/schemas/purchases/dap">
  <po:invoice-num>12345</po:invoice-num>
  <po:purch-order-num>67890</po:purch-order-num>
  <po:amount>39.95</po:amount>
  <dap:link
    url="http://www.example.org/purchases/rest/purchase/12345"
    rel="http://www.example.org/purchases/rest/relations/ship"
    mediaType="application/vnd.purchases+xml"/>
  <dap:link
    url="http://www.example.org/purchases/rest/purchase/12345"
    rel="http://www.example.org/purchases/rest/relations/cancel"/>
</po:receipt>
```

 This resource representation has two links: the client can still cancel the order, or
they can contact the shipping department in order to arrange shipment of the item.
Once shipment has been arranged, the client is provided with a resource that has
no DAP links to other resources, reflecting the terminal state in the workflow logic:

```
<po:shipping-receipt
    xmlns:po="http://www.example.com/schemas/purchases"
    xmlns:dap="http://www.example.com/schemas/purchases/dap>"
  <po:invoice-num>12345</po:invoice-num>
  <po:purch-order-num>67890</po:purch-order-num>
  <po:shippingUri>…</po:shippingUri>
</po:shipping-receipt>
```

 With this illustrative example as a guide, what should be the principles for ROA?
We follow the outline suggested by Richardson and Ruby [5], with some further
clarification suggested by the above example.

Loose coupling via explicit state. Statelessness is not an end in itself for Web
services. Rather, it serves the end goal of decoupling a client from a Web service,
facilitating caching, load balancing and failure recovery. Consider as an example
the shopping cart provided by a Web service to a client in Sect. 7.5. The classic
approach to supporting this shared state between client and server is to use a session

identifier to record a location in the server database where the state of the cart is saved. Each client request includes this session identifier, typically in a cookie or, alternatively, as a query string parameter. The server uses the session identifier to retrieve the contents of the cart from the database. The REST philosophy is that this state, if it is stored on the server, should be identified as a resource, and therefore have an identifying URI that the client provides on any stateful request. Alternatively, the state may be stored on the client, to be re-sent on each request. Provided the state is not overly large, this may be a preferable approach to sharing state between client and server, as it off-loads state management from the server in the service of scalability. In either case, the important point is that the REST computational model centers application state on the state machine in the client. Any application state on the server must be made explicit as resources. This information may be used by load balancers when routing client requests, but there should be no implicit shared state between client and service. In the shopping cart example, the cart (that might otherwise be an implicit application state shared between the client and server) can instead be made into a resource by giving it a URI. This URI is explicitly specified by the client as part of their interactions with the server, removing the tight coupling resulting from shared session state between client and server.

Data abstraction via addressable resources. Resources are fundamentally a form of data abstraction, again motivated by the needs of loose coupling. In this case, the motivation is maintainability of long-lived systems. Part of the success of the Web for sharing information is that clients are decoupled from server-side representations of resources, particularly if URLs do not identify the file type of the resources (e.g., `html`, `php`, or `aspx`). This latter point raises a further issue that needs clarification: *resource identifiers should also be abstract*. Web service interfaces that encode parameters to service calls as URL parameters violate this abstraction, and introduce tight coupling between client and service that makes clients vulnerable to API changes. Indeed, the notion of session identifiers discussed in Sect. 6.11.3 is the appropriate notion of naming for RESTful Web services: names should be treated as atomic quantities by clients. The use of a URL of the form:

```
http://www.example.org/purchases/rest/purchase/12345
```

only reflects the fact that the internal logic of the service uses the invoice number for a purchase to build a URI for each invoice resource. If this is changed to a different format, for example using globally unique identifiers, then clients should be unaffected by this internal implementation detail.

A common way that this name abstraction is broken on the Web is when the domain name system of a Web service, or the file system on a Web server, is re-organized, causing Web links to "break". The layered naming scheme discussed in Sect. 6.11.3 is intended to address this by providing a mapping infrastructure based on distributed hash tables to perform a look-up from an atomic name to the actual location of the resource. If the location of a resource is changed, its mapping in the DHT is changed so that clients can continue to access the resource in its new location. The advantage of the use of a DHT for performing the mapping is that the abstraction of the name is preserved, ensuring that clients of a service are unaffected by re-organization of the Web service using that name. Similarly, the Atom markup language for publishing content via feeds on the Web makes a distinction between the identity of a link (the `<atom:id>` element, which is intended to be immutable) and the address of a link (the `<atom:link>` element, which may change over time).

The other aspect of data abstraction is the contract between client and server regarding the resource representations that may be exchanged. Just as service contracts provide an interface between service providers and clients of that service, the media types provided with resource representations provide an interface between resource producers and consumers of those representations. Standard MIME types, as defined by the Internet Assigned Numbers Authority (IANA) standardization, such as `application/xml` and `application/json`, while appropriate for user-oriented Web applications, are too coarse-grained for automated Web services. One may think of a XHTML or a PDF document, or a MPEG video, as a program that specifies processing in the browser. For example, XHTML is a markup language that is interpreted by the rendering engine in a browser as the declarative specification of a presentation logic. This level of granularity is sufficient when the result of rendering is interpreted by a human, with their own notion of an application semantics to superimpose on the presentation. When the result of processing is to be interpreted by an automated Web service client, as in the case of B2B e-commerce, then finer-grained specifications of the contracts between clients and resource providers are required. The vendor-specific media types mentioned in the examples in this and the previous section (`application/vnd.purchases+xml` and `application/vnd.trains+sml`, respectively) are examples of such media types. There are obvious shortcomings with these media type specifications. A domain-specific media type is assumed to include all of the document types used by applications in that domain, but only a specific subset of those document types should be encountered on traversal of a link. For example, purchase orders and invoices are two different forms of resources in this application, yet representations for both share the media type `application/vnd.purchases+xml`. The Atom format includes a `type` attribute for `<link>` elements, that allows content type to be documented for hyperlinks provided in an Atom feed. The DAP protocol type already includes a `mediaType` attribute to describe the domain media type; this could be augmented with a `type` annotation that described the expected domain-specific content type, such as `application/vnd.purchases+xml;type=Invoice`. There is nothing in the media type that restricts the HTTP verbs that may be used to access a resource; the information provided by the "relationship" attribute `rel` may only be documentation for humans, rather than machine-processable descriptions for interpreters and conformance verifiers. Another attribute might be added to a DAP link, for example an `op` attribute, that specifies the HTTP verb to be used in following that link. We consider an approach to providing a tighter specification of these REST-based business protocols at the end of this section; we consider another approach based on typestate in 7.6.

Canonical expression via a Uniform Interface. At the simplest level, the uniform interface for RESTful services is interpreted as a CRUD interface for creating, reading, and updating resources. A representation of a resource is retrieved from a server using GET, updated locally by the client, and then uploaded to the server using PUT, replacing the original content of the resource. In other operations, a resource is partially updated in some way using POST or PATCH, a new resource is created using PUT, and a resource is deleted using DELETE. In the background, on the server, these operations on resources trigger business activities that may synthesize resource representations from database lookups or interactions with background services.

However, as the supply chain management example above demonstrates, the idea of a uniform interface is more general than a CRUD interface for persistent resources. A successful application of REST requires that one consider application protocols in terms of networks of linked resources. Clients participate in these protocols by operating on these resources using the uniform interface. Transitions in these protocols are expressed abstractly in terms of verbs of the uniform interface. This perspective is certainly appropriate for inter-enterprise applications, where collaborations are expressed in terms of a document trail reflecting communications between the parties. A resource may represent one of these documents that is exchanged as a part of a business protocol, or it may represent a persistent record of part of the state of the protocol itself. For example, a purchase order may contain the current status of an order (placed, invoiced, paid, shipped, etc.), and parties will sometimes need to poll the resource in order to be notified of progress in parts of the protocol in which they are not directly involved. We have not considered a publish-subscribe framework for RESTful Web services; we consider this in Chapter 8 in the sequel volume, when we consider EDA.

Workflow logic via hypermedia networks. As we have seen, a full realization of REST involves the use of hypermedia networks as the driver for business protocols, based on navigation of a linked network of resources. Loose coupling of clients from services is based on factors such as the absence of implicit shared state (pace cookies and session state), and the data abstraction provided by resources. Services reveal just enough information about resources in the representations that they provide to clients, in order to allow clients to consume or produce resources.

For an automated client of a Web service, we need to know more of a resource beyond the representations that it may provide or accept. As interacting with that resource will typically involve traversing hyperlinks that represent transitions in a business protocol, there should be a specification of that protocol to guide the construction of the client logic. How might we describe a "behavioral" contract for a RESTful Web service, where interaction with the service is based on navigating a hypermedia network? One approach to doing this is to describe the contract as an "abstract program", and use this specification to check the conformance of an application program with the protocol specification. If an automated client needs to navigate a hypermedia network, it needs to know a priori what the structure of this network will be so that it can handle all possible cases. Where the presence of some cases is uncertain, dynamic testing can be used to check for these cases in a way that is completely understood in modern typed programming. Backward compatible extensions of the hypermedia network may be defined that do not affect old version clients. Where changes to the hypermedia network may invalidate assumptions made by old version clients, this can be signaled to those clients by notifying them that there has been a major version change and that they need to re-bind to the new version of the hypermedia network. However, the presence of a model of the hypermedia network, as a description of business protocols that clients are expected to follow, is essential for conformance checking of clients and isolation of the failure points that they will need to deal with.

Traditional service-oriented computing emphasizes an interface of operations that clients invoke to perform stateful operations. A client performs a service operation, with all of the arguments provided up front, and eventually the remote service returns a result. This form of distributed computing is deliberately designed by analogy with procedure call or method invocation in local computing. Instead, RESTful programming emphasizes an interaction model based on clients navigating a hypermedia network of linked resources where clients may provide entity bodies as arguments to services in the course of an interaction, and receive entity bodies as resource representations from services. An analogous idea is that of *session types* [6–8], particularly in its application to object-oriented programming [9]. Session types describe protocols for parties that communicate over private session channels, where these types are described as abstract programs that application programs must conform to. The point of communication over a private sessional channel is to prevent interference from outside processes. In practice, this privacy might be achieved using cryptographic techniques. These abstract programs will need to make non-deterministic choices at key points in the decision logic, as the session type abstracts over the details (such as run-time values) of how branching is resolved in a program. For example, a session type for the payment protocol considered above can be roughly described as follows:

```
Client  › Vendor : purchase order.
Vendor → Client :
          { invoice : Loop.
          [] out_of_stock : Client → Vendor :
                                      {  confirm.
                                         Loop.
                                      [] cancel.
                                         end
                                      }
     }
Loop =
  Client → Vendor :
  { payment : Vendor → Client : receipt.
             Client → Shipper : address.
             Shipper → Client : shipping info.
             end
  [] update : Vendor → Client : invoice.
```

```
          loop.
[] cancel :   end
}
```

This is a specification of the global protocol that the parties must follow. At various points, there are branches in the global decision logic, where different parties have control over which branch is taken in the decision logic. From this global protocol description, we may project the protocol that the parties must follow in the role of client, vendor, and shipper. For example, the protocol to be followed by the client assumes a communication channel ch_{vendor} shared with the vendor, and a channel $ch_{shipper}$ shared with the shipper. The notation for sending a value of type T on a channel ch is denoted by $ch!T$, while the notation for receiving a value of type T on a channel ch is denoted by $ch?T$. The session type ignores the actual values that are exchanged, although we do assume some form of run time type tagging to identify the type of a value that is communicated, for example, using XML element tags or object type tags. Then, the protocol to be followed by the client is as follows:

```
ch_vendor !purchase  order.        client  loop =
&{ ch_vendor ?invoice.             ⊕{ch_vendor !payment.
client  loop.                      ch_vendor ?receipt.
[]  ch_vendor ?out_of_stock.       ch_shipper !address.
⊕{ ch_vendor !confirm.             ch_shipper ?shipping_info.
client  loop.                      end
[]  ch_vendor !cancel.             []  ch_vendor !update.
end                                ch_vendor ?invoice.
}                                  client  loop.
}                                  []  ch_vendor !cancel.
                                   end
                                   }
```

The operator & denotes an *external choice*, i.e., a branching in the logic controlled by the other party, the vendor. In this case, the vendor sends either an invoice or out_of_stock message to the client after receiving the purchase order sent by the client. If the vendor sends an out_of_stock message, then the client chooses to confirm the original purchase order (waiting for inventory to be replenished), or they cancel the order. This client choice is represented by the ⊕ operator for *internal choice*, i.e., a branching in the logic controlled by the local party, the client. Another internal branching point is in the logic for the client main loop, where the client chooses based on internal logic whether to make payment, update the purchase, or cancel the purchase completely. It is worth emphasizing that this is a *type*, expressed as an abstract program and, hence, the non-determinism in the internal client decision logic. The type only describes the communication patterns between the parties without attempting to describe the internal details of their decision logic.

The vendor has a session type that is dual to that of the client, where message sends and receives are interchanged, as are internal and external decision points. The symbol ch_{client} denotes the vendor side of the communication channel between the vendor and the client. The interactions between the client and the shipper are not included in this vendor part of the protocol:

```
ch_client ?purchase  order.            vendor  loop =
     ⊕{ ch_client !invoice.                &{ ch_client ?payment.
         vendor  loop.                          ch_client !receipt.
     [] ch_client !out_of_stock.          end
         &{ ch_client ?confirm.               [] ch_client ?update.
         vendor  loop.                    ch_client !invoice.
             [] ch_client ?cancel.        vendor  loop.
         end                                  [] ch_client ?cancel.
     }                                    end
     }                                }
```

These session types are abstract concurrent processes, with apparent non-deterministic choices where internal and external choice are specified. In practice, as the protocol is single-threaded, the execution is completely deterministic. Internal choices are based on conditional branching; each party in the session has just one end of the shared communication channel so there is no non-deterministic contention for access to the channel.

In an amalgamation of session types with an object-oriented language [9], the arguments of a method signature are replaced by a duplex communication channel, private between a client and a service, and allocated at the beginning of a session. The dual session types for the client and service describe the protocol that they should follow to exchange data in order to avoid run-time type errors because of a mismatch in the expectations of the party. If there is an analogy between service-oriented computing and procedure call, then there is a similar analogy between resource-oriented computing and the computing model underlying session types, although the granularity of RESTful Web services is much coarser than that normally assumed for session types.

A distinction sometimes made between service-oriented and resource-oriented computing is that of a *control-oriented* computing paradigm as opposed to a *data-oriented* one. Service-oriented computing is essentially an algorithmic point of view for distributed computing, as reflected by the state machine or active replica model for highly available systems. Resource-oriented computing emphasizes a model of "lazy loading" of distributed data in a hypermedia network of linked resources. The session types perspective, based on message passing, does not contradict this data-oriented model of resource-oriented computing. Kahn networks [10], the original model of data flow computation, provide a low-level model of processes communicating via asynchronous message-passing, with demand-driven data flow computation as the execution model realized by these communicating processes. In this case, the data flow model provides the perspective for reasoning about the global behavior of a system composed from such processes. Similarly, the data-oriented perspective provides a semantic view of the execution of a collection of collaborating RESTful processes.

7.4   INTERFACE DESCRIPTION LANGUAGES

We saw in Chapter 2 that one of the most critical developements in distributed systems was the notion of the service contract. Without contracts to mediate between service consumers and service requesters, any sizeable enterprise software system is built on pillars of sand. We consider two alternatives for defining service contracts for RESTful Web services: extensions to support REST in WSDL 2.0, and an alternative interface definition language, the WADL, designed specifically for RESTful services.

7.4.1   Web Services Description Language (WSDL)

We considered WSDL v2.0 in Sect. 4.4.2. As we saw, WSDL separates an abstract service description from its concrete definition, i.e., the transfer protocol defined by the binding, and the endpoint specified in the service definition. Figure 7.3 provides part of the WSDL specification for a train reservation service. The schema in this WSDL specification provides the declarations of two elements: <checkAvail> for requesting information about availability of trains on a given date between two cities, and <checkAvailResponse> for the result of that query (a list of pairs of train codes and the corresponding train's departure times).

Figure 7.4 provides the interface for the train reservation service and two bindings. The service has a single operation: checkAvailability. The WSDL MEP for this operation (In-Out) specifies that it expects a request message from clients and returns a response message. The style of this operation is iri, which means that ther input parameters for the service operation are restricted in type so they may be encoded as name-value pairs in the query string part of a URL. The reason for this becomes clear when we consider the REST binding for the service.

There are two bindings for this service. The reservationSOAPBinding is a SOAP binding such as we have seen already, as defined by the binding type http://www.w3.org/ns/wsdl/soap. The SOAP transfer protocol is defined to be HTTP, and the SOAP MEP is response, meaning that the HTTP verb for the service invocation is chosen to be GET; no SOAP is sent for the service invocation. Instead, the arguments are encoded as name-value pairs in the query string in the HTTP headers. The endpoint URL for this SOAP service is http://www.example.org/train/soap.

The second binding for this service is reservationRESTBinding. This has binding type http://www.w3.org/2006/01/wsdl/http, signifying that this is a native HTTP binding with no SOAP messages. Instead, message payloads are sent over the native HTTP transfer protocol. The arguments are, again, passed as name-value pairs in the query string for the endpoint URL, with a default HTTP verb of GET declared. The endpoint URL is http://www.example.org/train/rest/schedule.

Is this a RESTful binding for the Web service? There is certainly no SOAP messaging but all requests are directed to the same endpoint URL. One of the important REST principles is addressability—the notion that every resource has a URI that

```xml
<?xml version="1.0" encoding="utf-8" ?>
<description
    xmlns = "http://www.w3.org/ns/wsdl"
    targetNamespace = "http://www.example.org/wsdl/schedule"
    xmlns:tns = "http://www.example.org/wsdl/train"
    xmlns:tr = "http://www.example.org/schemas/train/soap"
    xmlns:whttp= "http://www.w3.org/2006/01/wsdl/http"
    xmlns:wsoap= "http://www.w3.org/ns/wsdl/soap"
    xmlns:soap="http://www.w3.org/2003/05/soap-envelope"
    xmlns:wsdlx= "http://www.w3.org/ns/wsdl-extensions">
  <types>
    <xs:schema
        xmlns:xs = "http://www.w3.org/2001/XMLSchema"
        targetNamespace = "http://www.example.org/schemas/schedule"
        xmlns = "http://www.example.org/schemas/train/soap">
      <xs:element name="checkAvail" type="checkAvailType"/>
      <xs:complexType name="checkAvailType">
        <xs:sequence>
          <xs:element name="start" type="xs:string"/>
          <xs:element name="end" type="xs:string"/>
          <xs:element name="travdate" type="xs:date"/>
        </xs:sequence>
      </xs:complexType>
      <xs:element name="checkAvailResponse"
                  type="checkAvailResponseType"/>
       <xs:complexType name="checkAvailResponseType">
         <xs:sequence minoccurs="0" maxoccurs="unbounded">
           <xs:element name="departure">
             <xs:sequence>
               <xs:element name="code" type="xs:integer"/>
               <xs:element name="time" type="xs:time"/>
             </xs:sequence>
           </xs:element>
         </xs:sequence>
       </xs:complexType>
       <xs:element name="invalidDataError" type="xs:string"/>
    </xs:schema>
  </types>
```

Figure 7.3   *Train reservation service: type definitions*

identifies it. A RESTful binding may, for example, identify train reservations for a date by a URI and query those reservations using GET. WSDL 2.0 supports this by allowing the incorporation of the parameters for the service into the endpoint URI, for example as follows:

```xml
<binding name="reservationRESTBinding" ...>
  <operation ref="tns:checkvailability"
            whttp:location="{start}/{end}/{travdate}" />
</binding>
```

```
<interface name="reservationInterface">
  <fault name="invalidDataFault" element="tr:invalidDataError"/>
  <operation name="checkAvailability"
      pattern = "http://www.w3.org/ns/wsdl/in-out"
      style = "http://www.w3.org/ns/wsdl/style/iri"
      wsdlx:safe = "true">
    <input messageLabel="In" element="tr:checkAvail" />
    <output messageLabel="Out" element="tr:checkAvailResponse" />
    <outfault ref="tns:invalidDataFault" messageLabel="Out"/>
  </operation>
</interface>

<binding name="reservationSOAPBinding"
    interface="tns:reservationInterface"
    type="http://www.w3.org/ns/wsdl/soap"
    wsoap:protocol="http://www.w3.org/2003/05/soap/bindings/HTTP/">
  <operation ref="tns:CheckAvailability"
    wsoap:mep="http://www.w3.org/2003/05/soap/mep/soap-response"/>
  <fault ref="tns:invalidDataFault" wsoap:code="soap:Sender"/>
</binding>
<service name="reservationService"
    interface="tns:reservationInterface">
  <endpoint name="reservationEndpoint"
    binding="tns:reservationSOAPBinding"
    address="http://www.example.org/train/soap"/>
</service>

<binding name="reservationRESTBinding"
    interface="tns:reservationInterface"
    type="http://www.w3.org/2006/01/wsdl/http"
    whttp:methodDefault="GET">
  <operation ref="tns:checkAvailability" />
</binding>
<service name="reservationService"
    interface="tns:reservationInterface">
  <endpoint name="reservationEndpoint"
    binding="tns:reservationHTTPBinding"
    address="http://www.example.org/train/rest/schedule"/>
</service>
</description>
```

Figure 7.4   *Train reservation interface: interface and bindings*

The `whttp:location` attribute specifies additional context to be added to the context root in the endpoint URL to refer to the specific day and start and end points, for which train availability is being queried. Therefore, some of the request parameters are passed as part of the URI, rather than in the payload of a request message, or in query string parameters.

By now, it should be clear that WSDL is a weak choice for an interface description language for RESTful Web services. It provides no support for hypermedia programming, which is at the heart of RESTful Web services. It provides support for passing some parameters to Web services as URI parameters and for a "POX" message format; however, it is only sufficient for defining RESTful Web services at the lowest levels of the maturity hierarchy. It is tempting to believe that WSDL can be used to provide both SOAP-based and RESTful Web bindings for the same Web service so that it can serve as a unifying IDL for both forms of service. However, this point of view misses the critical fact that the architecture of SOAP-based Web services is, in general, very different from that of REST-based Web services. SOAP-based Web services are control-oriented, focused on external clients performing updates on a black-box state machine. Coordination between the client and the service, or a collection of services in the case of a composed service, is intended to be achieved on the basis of end-to-end protocols such as WS-ReliableMessaging, WS-Transaction and WS-Security. The RESTful approach eschews these forms of coordination protocols, viewing them as entailing tight coupling across enterprise application boundaries. The RESTful approach replaces this tightly-coupled control-oriented service interface with a loosely-coupled data-oriented service interface based on navigating a hypermedia network of linked resources. For example, rather than relying on a "black-box" atomic commitment protocol for completing a distributed transaction, as is assumed by WS-Transaction, the RESTful approach would, instead, be to incorporate an application-level commitment protocol that may involve the client accumulating state as it traversed the protocol state machine, with scope in the protocol for explicit rollback (represented by hypermedia links) if the response codes from some operations signaled application errors. In a truly RESTful Web service, the "abstract" API should reflect this different logical structuring of the client interaction from a SOAP-based interaction—a difference that a provision for different concrete bindings does not begin to address.

7.4.2   Web Application Description Language (WADL)

WADL [11] was developed as an alternative to WSDL for providing formal descriptions for RESTful Web services. The focus of a WADL description is on the resources, identified by URIs, rather than on operations organized into interfaces. Resources have a notion of methods, but those describe the HTTP verbs that may be applied to a resource and the input and output representations for these actions. The description of the operations includes parameters that may be provided in HTTP headers as part of the context root of the URL, or in the URL pattern, i.e., the query string. The description of a representation may optionally contain the description of links in the representation, in support of the principle of connectedness.

Figure 7.5 provides a WADL description of the RESTful train reservation service. The <grammars> element provides specifications for the structure of the data, in this case an XML schema for train schedule and reservation information. WADL can incorporate type information described in XML Schemas and Relax NG, unlike WSDL which is committed to XML Schemas. The <resources> element provides information about the two forms of resources described by the specification. The base URI is shared by all resources. In this case, there are three forms of URI:

```
http://www.example.org/train/rest/schedule?
                        src=NYP&dst=WAS&date=05-02-2011
http://www.example.org/train/rest/train/2107?class=business
http://www.example.org/train/rest/reservation/12345
```

The first of these is used for a query for the train schedule for a specified date. The second of these is used for a reservation request for a particular train, with an optional specification of the class of travel (coach, business, or first class). The third of these is used to identify an individual reservation on a train.

The first resource specification in Fig. 7.5, the first <resource> element, specifies a URI for the root schedule resource. A query on this resource using the GET verb specifies the starting location, destination, and the date of travel, and returns a representation for a new resource: the schedule for all trains matching the search parameters. The location of this new resource can be provided in the Location: response header—entries in the schedule could contain parent links to this schedule resource. The second <resource> element defines the URI for a specific train in the schedule identified by the path variable for the train identifier tid. The third <resource> element defines the URI for a reservation on a specific train identified by the path variable for the reservation identifier rid.

Each of these resources have business logic associated with them: getSchedule for querying a train schedule resource, makeReservation for updating a train resource with a reservation, and getReservation for querying a train reservation

```
<?xml version="1.0"?>
<application xmlns:xsi="http://www.w3.org/2001/XMLSchema-instance"
    xsi:schemaLocation="http://wadl.dev.java.net/2009/02 wadl.xsd"
    xmlns:xsd="http://www.w3.org/2001/XMLSchema"
    xmlns:tns="http://www.example.org/train/rest/wadl"
    xmlns:tw="http://www.example.org/train/rest/wadl"
    xmlns:tr="http://www.example.org/schemas/train"
    xmlns:dap="http://www.example.org/schemas/train/dap"
    xmlns="http://wadl.dev.java.net/2009/02">
  <grammars>
    <include href="Train.xsd"/>
  </grammars>

  <resources base="http://www.example.org/train/rest">
    <resource path="/schedule" type="scheduleType"/>
    <resource path="/train/{tid}" type="trainType">
      <param name="tid" style="template" type="xsd:int"/>
    </resource>
    <resource path="/reservation/{rid}" type="reservationType">
      <param name="rid" style="template" type="xsd:int"/>
    </resource>
  </resources>
  ...
</application>
```

Figure 7.5 *WADL example: resources*

```
<resource_type id="scheduleType">
  <method href="#getSchedule"/>
</resource_type>

<method name="GET" id="getSchedule">
  <request>
    <param name="src" style="query" type="xsd:string"/>
    <param name="dst" style="query" type="xsd:string"/>
    <param name="travdate" style="query" type="xsd:date"
        default="today"/>
  </request>
  <response status="200">
    <representation mediaType="application/vnd.trains+xml"
                    element="tr:schedule">
      <param name="train" style="plain" type="xsd:anyURI"
             path="/tr:schedule/tr:train/dap:link/@url">
        <link resource_type="#trainType"/>
      </param>
    </representation>
  </response>
  <response status="400">
    <representation mediaType="application/vnd.trains+xml"
                    element="tr:error"/>
  </response>
</method>
```

Figure 7.6   *WADL example: get train schedule*

resource. These are specified in the WADL resource type specifications in Fig. 7.6 and Fig. 7.7. Figure 7.6 provides the interface specification for the getSchedule business logic, which defines one way of operating on a train schedule resource. Here, the getSchedule identifier is used only to identify the corresponding <method> element. The actual operation is the HTTP GET verb. As the GET verb allows no input entity body, the parameters to the schedule search are defined in a query string, with parameters named src, dst and date, respectively.

There are two possible responses to this operation, distinguished by their representations and their status codes. A correct response is represented by a <tr:schedule> element, with a HTTP status code of 200. The specification of this response includes an output hyperlink parameter identified by a path in the <tr:schedule> element. This path identifies the URIs for all of the train trips listed in the query result. The <link> child element provides the description of the resources identified by these links. These linked resources each have the resource type <trainType> specified in Fig. 7.7. This latter resource type has a single method defined for it defined by the method reference makeReservation. An incorrect response to a train schedule query is specified by a return element of <tr:error> and a status code of 400.

The makeReservation method definition is specified in Fig. 7.7, and uses the POST HTTP method. This operation has an optional input query parameter that can take one of three possible values: coach, business, or first. In this case, the

```
<resource_type id="trainType">
  <method href="#makeReservation"/>
</resource_type>

<resource_type id="reservationType">
  <method href="#getReservation"/>
</resource_type>

<method name="POST" id="makeReservation">
  <request>
    <param name="class" style="query" default="coach">
      <option value="coach"/>
      <option value="business"/>
      <option value="first"/>
    </param>
    <representation mediaType="application/vnd.trains+xml"
          element="tr:reserveInfo">

      <param name="name" style="plain" type="xsd:string"
            path="/tr:reserveInfo/tr:payment/tr:name"/>
      <param name="ccardNum" style="plain" type="xsd:string"
            path="/tr:reserveInfo/tr:payment/tr:ccardNum"/>
      <param name="expDate" style="plain" type="xsd:date"
            path="/tr:reserveInfo/tr:payment/tr:expDate"/>
    </representation>
  </request>
  <response status="200">
    <representation mediaType="application/vnd.trains+xml"
                  element="tr:reservation">
      <param name="reservation" style="plain" type="xsd:anyURI"
            path="/tr:reservation/tr:details/dap:link/@url">
        <link resource_type="#getReservation"/>
      </param>
    </representation>
  </response>
  <response status="400">
    <representation mediaType="application/vnd.trains+xml"
                  element="tr:error"/>
  </response>
</method>
```

Figure 7.7   *WADL example: make train reservation*

operation takes an input entity body, as specified by the element `<tr:reserveInfo>`. The parameter declarations specify three fields expected of the element for purchaser name, credit card number, and expiration date. The response entity body includes a link to the reservation resource that is created by this operation. A GET on this resource can provide details about the reservation. Other logic that could be supported would include DELETE (to cancel the reservation) and PUT (to update the reservation—perhaps upgrading the class of travel).

WADL has some curious aspects as a service description language. It is not clear what the point of specifying parameters in resource representation descriptions is, if those representations already have descriptions in XML Schema. Presumably, the motivation is that the representation may be in a different format than XML, such as JSON, or may not have a description in XML Schema or Relax NG. One of the alternatives to providing input parameters as an XML element would be the media type `application/x-www-form-urlencoded`, defined for the list of name-value pairs representing the encoding of a HTML form submission:

```
<method name="POST" id="makeReservation">
  <request> …
    <representation mediaType="application/x-www-form-urlencoded>"
      <param name="name" style="query" type="xsd:string"/>
      <param name="ccardNum" style="query" type="xsd:string"/>
      <param name="expDate" style="plain" type="xsd:date"/>
    </representation>
  </request>
  …
</method>
```

However, the programming environment support for checking that client and service implementations honor this contract is weak. Although sometimes clumsy, the XML representation of input and output entity bodies at least ensures some automated conformance checking.

If input and output representations are XML documents, then the parameter specifications may be omitted from the representation descriptions, and conformance checking can be performed as part of the marshalling and unmarshalling between XML and program data. Defining XML schemas for the data also allows validation checking at gateways between domains, delimited by XML firewalls, for example. The result is essentially a stripped-down version of WSDL, where interface and operation descriptions are omitted and a single message transfer protocol is used. Still, there is, at least, a superficial similarity between the support in WADL and WSDL 2.0 for defining RESTful Web services:[3]

WADL	WSDL 2.0
application	interface
method	operation
representation	message

The major conceptual gap between WADL and the RESTful WSDL binding is the absence of a notion of resources in the WSDL service-oriented specification. This absence begins to take on significance when we consider a notion of

---

[3]Presumably, this explains why WADL is viewed with some suspicion in parts of the REST community.

parameters in resource representations that is a crucial element of WADL. These parameters identify URIs for resources, particularly in response representations. In the train reservation example, the result of the getSchedule business logic contains URIs for the individual trains in the schedule, each of which supports the makeReservation business logic. Performing the latter operation on a train results in a resource representation with a URI providing the details of the reservation. This begins to resemble a workflow specification interlaced with the specification of the message exchange protocol. WSDL has some provision for specifying these protocols, with the allowance for specifying other MEPs beyond the standards, such as In-Only and In-Out. However, this is clearly much more clumsy and heavyweight than the way this is done in WADL, following the connectedness principle of REST. Instead, the SOAP/WSDL framework depends on workflow languages such as WS-BPEL and BPMN to specify these workflows. These are defined independently of the interface descriptions but, at least in the case of BPEL, use the WSDL descriptions to describe the contracts between the parties in workflow interactions.

Some of the controversy surrounding WADL arises from a school of thought in some REST quarters that interface contracts are not relevant for RESTful Web services. The poor support for typeful programming of RESTful Web services may reflect some of this attitude. Certainly in distributed systems, any conformance check of a client against a service contract only provides a temporary guarantee against contract mismatches, as, eventually, the service will be upgraded to the point where it can no longer maintain backward compatibility. The proper approach to dealing with this is to establish a strategy for notifying clients and migrating them in a safe fashion when a major version change of this form occurs. For example, an attempt to use a service that has been upgraded to a new major version can result in an error response returned to the client, with information in that response about how to access the new version of the service. Well-known techniques, including in the field of session types, can provide flexibility in interface matching, so that services can be extended while retaining backward compatibility with older clients. The point of conformance checking is to determine when a change breaks the contract with old clients, so that provision must be made for them to re-bind to a new contract. This is one aspect of distributed systems where the Web is a poor guide, given the prevalence of broken Web links.

Any developer implementing a Web service provider or consumer must have a protocol that they are implementing, even if parts of that protocol are dynamic. If they do not, then by definition they do not know what they are doing. The challenge for tools such as protocol description languages (including type systems) and conformance checkers is to be sufficiently rich to be able to capture these protocols, including their dynamic parts, and to be able to deal with situations where the rules underlying the static checking no longer hold. We consider an example and a very preliminary approach to doing this in Sect. 7.6.

7.5 AN EXAMPLE APPLICATION PROGRAM INTERFACE (API) FOR RESOURCE-ORIENTED WEB SERVICES

In this section, we consider an API for RESTful programming: the JAX-RS API for Java. As the name suggests, JAX-RS is part of the Java EE suite for developing enterprise systems, offered as a RESTful alternative to the JAX-WS framework for developing SOAP-based Web services. Much of the JAX-RS API is reminiscent of WADL. For the Jersey implementation of JAX-RS, a WADL description of a service is available via the URL `http://hostname/context-root?application.wadl`.

In JAX-RS, resources are implemented using classes and methods. An application class specifies the base context root for the RESTful service and the classes that provide the resource implementations. A resource class is defined using a `@PATH` annotation that specifies an extension of the base context root. Methods of the resource class provide access to the resource using the HTTP verbs. Sub-resources may be implemented as methods of this root resource class with `@PATH` annotations that specify extensions of the context root for the resource class. Methods are annotated to specify the HTTP verb that should be used for their realization as a Web service: `@GET`, `@PUT`, `@POST`, `@DELETE`, `@HEAD`, and `@OPTIONS`. Methods can specify the MIME types for entity bodies that they produce as output, using the `@PRODUCES` annotation. Methods that expect input entity bodies can specify the MIME types for those inputs via the `@CONSUMES` annotation. Methods can extract parameters from various sources: `@PathParam` extracts parameters from the URL path; `@MatrixParam` from comma-separated or semicolon-separated parts of matrix URIs; `@QueryParam` from query parameters; `@CookieParam` from cookies; and `@HeaderParam` from HTTP request headers. The `@FormParam` annotation is reserved for a parameter specified for a representation, as it is used to extract a parameter in the encoding of a HTML form (content type `application/x-www-form-urlencoded`). Finally, a method may be specified with a `@PATH` annotation, but without a HTTP verb annotation. In this case, the method returns an instance of a resource, allowing more than one path to a resource in the Web service interface.

Here is a simple example—the ubiquitous "Hello, World" example as a resource class:

```
@Path("/HelloService")
public class HelloResource {
  @GET
  @Produces("text/plain")
  public String sayHello ( @QueryParam("name") String name ) {
    return "Hello, " + name;
  }
}
```

This service is invoked using a command of the form:

```
GET http://host/HelloService?name=Joe
```

It responds with a plain text response containing the string: `"Hello, Joe"`.

Figure 7.8 contains part of the specification of the train schedule and reservation service. The @Application annotation identifies TrainApp as the class for the application. This defines the base context root, "/train/rest", and the classes for the resources that make up the application. Figure 7.8 also defines the class for schedule resources, ScheduleResource. This defines a resource path ("/schedule") that is appended to the base context root for the application. The resource defines a single operation, getSchedule, which is defined using the GET verb. Three parameters to this operation (start, destination and travelDate) are specified as query string parameters, as there is no input entity body for the GET verb. The @Default-Value annotation for this last parameter specifies a default value to be injected if the parameter is not defined in the query string. Therefore, the general form for the query for a train schedule has the form:

```
GET http://host/train/rest/schedule?src=src&dest=dest&date=travelDate
```

The definition of the ScheduleResource class includes the dependency injection of two other resources into the resource instance when it is created. A service bean is injected that provides the business logic associated with train schedules,

```java
@ApplicationPath("/train/rest")
public class TrainApp extends Application {
  public Set<Class<?>> getClasses() {
    Set<Class<?>> s = new HashSet<Class<?>>();
    s.add(ScheduleResource.class);
    s.add(TrainResource.class);
    return s;
  }
}

@Path("/schedule")
public class ScheduleResource {

  @Context UriInfo uriInfo;

  @EJB(beanName = "ScheduleService") ISchedule scheduleService;

  @GET
  @Produces("application/vnd.trains+xml")
  public Response getSchedule (@QueryParam("src") String start,
                               @QueryParam("dst") String destination,
                               @DefaultValue("today")
                               @QueryParam("date") String travelDate)
  {
    ScheduleRepresentation schedule =
        scheduleService.get(start, destination, travelDate, uriInfo);
    return Response.ok().entity(schedule).build();
  }
}
```

Figure 7.8   *Train schedule resource*

including the logic for searching for a train schedule. The definition also injects information about the URI for the class, using the @Context annotation. Various forms of contextual information may be injected into a resource, for use in the definition of the resource operations by combining this annotation with the appropriate field type. For example, annotating a field of type SecurityInfo with @Context injects security information about the Web service request, including whether it was performed over a secure transport and what security roles are specified for the requestor, etc.

The business logic for searching for a train schedule is defined in the EJB in Fig. 7.9. This is defined as a local POJO object in the same application server as the resource implementation. Dependency injection is used to inject an entity manager for performing a database query for all records for trains satisfying the search criteria. The base URI is extracted from the URI information and used to construct the URI for each train using the primary key from the train database. This is done in the logic for the schedule representation that is returned as a result of the query.

The representation of a schedule is provided in Fig. 7.10. Following Webber et al. [12], we define a base class for representations that defines the namespaces and URIs used when serializing representatons as XML data. The RELATIONS string is the prefix for all relation URIs used in DAP links and, for example, RELATIONS_RESERVE is the URI for DAP links that should be traversed to make

```
@Local
public interface ISchedule {
  public ScheduleRepresentation get (
        String start, String destination, String travelDate,
        UriInfo ui ) {
}

@Stateless(name = "ScheduleService")
public class ScheduleBean implements ISchedule {
  @PersistenceContext(unitName="TrainsPU")
  EntityManager em;

  public ScheduleRepresentation get (
        String start, String destination, String travelDate,
        UriInfo ui ) {
    Query query = em.createNamedQuery("findTrain")
                  .setParameter("start", start)
                  .setParameter("destination", destination)
                  .setParameter("travelDate", travelDate);
    List<Train> trains = (List<Train>) query.getResultList();
    UriBuilder ub = ui.getBaseUriBuilder();
    ub = ub.path("train").path("{tid}");
    return new ScheduleRepresentation (trains, ub);
  }
}
```

Figure 7.9 *Train schedule service*

```java
public abstract class Representation {
  public static final String
         RELATIONS = "http://www.example.org/train/rest/relations/";
  public state final String
         RELATION_RESERVE = RELATIONS + "reserve";
  public static final String
         NAMESPACE = "http://www.example.org/schemas/train";
  public static final String
         DAP_NAMESPACE = NAMESPACE + "/dap";
  public static final String
         MEDIA_TYPE = "application/vnd.trains+xml";
  public abstract List<Link> getLinks();
}

@XmlRootElement(name="Schedule", namespace=NAMESPACE)
public class ScheduleRepresentation extends Representation {
  public List<TrainEntry> trains;
  public ScheduleRepresentation(List<Train> ts, UriBuilder ub) {
    trains = new ArrayList<TrainEntry>();
    for (Train t : ts) trains.add(new TrainEntry(t,ub));
  }
  public List<Link> getLinks() {
    List links = new ArrayList();
    for (TrainEntry t : trains) links.add(t.link);
    return links;
  }
}

@XmlElement(name="train", namespace=NAMESPACE)
public class TrainEntry {
  @XmlElement(name="link", namespace=DAP_NAMESPACE)
  public Link link;
  @XmlElement(name="time", namespace=NAMESPACE)
  public String time;
  public TrainEntry (Train t, UriBuilder ub) {
    this.link = new Link (ub.build(t.getTid()),
                          RELATION_RESERVE, MEDIA_TYPE);
    this.time = t.getTime());
  }
}
```

Figure 7.10   *Train schedule representation*

train reservations. There are two namespaces: NAMESPACE for XML data and
DAP_NAMESPACE for DAP links that may be embedded in the XML data. This
abstract base class defines an abstract method for getting a list of all DAP links in
a representation.

The Schedule Representation class inherits from this base class, to define a
representation for schedules. A field is defined to hold a list of the trains in the
schedule, and the implementaton of the method for extracting DAP links retrieves
the links from this list of trains in the schedule. A TrainEntry object copies any
relevant information from the corresponding Train object and, in addition, defines

a DAP link for each train. The semantic information associated with each such link specifies that the link should be traversed in order to make a reservation. We omit the details of the Train and Link classes. The Train class is an entity class for storing train information in the database. The Link class stores the pieces of information associated with a DAP link: URL, media type, and semantic information.

Figure 7.11 provides the specification of a train resource. A train is updated with a new reservation when a POST operation is done on the corresponding resource using the request form:

```
POST http://host/train/rest/train/tid?class=class]
```

The train identifier in the URI uniquely identifies the train, including the date of travel. The class of travel is specified as an optional query parameter (with a default value of business class). Payment information (customer name, credit card number and expiration date) is provided as an entity body that must be an instance of the media type specified for this domain. In fact, the input should obviously be an XML element that provides reservation information, such as the customer identification and payment information. Another alternative would be to provide this information using URL-encoded form parameters but this prevents the provision of a specification of the expected content type, separate from the signature of the method implementing this resource operation. Alternatively, a system may require registration of user accounts for billing purposes; an Authorization: request header could provide a digital signature for the request. Then, the @HeaderParam annotation could be used to extract the value of this request header and pass it as an argument to the operation.

The makeReservation operation injects an EJB implementing the services for train operations, including the operation for updating a train with a new passenger reservation. We omit the details—the result that is returned has an empty response message (hence the absence of a @Produces clause), but uses the Location: response header to specify the location of information about the reservation. It does this using a Response object as a result, with a status code of 201 (created).

The getReservation business logic, defined as the implementation of the GET method for a reservation resource, uses an injected reservation service to perform a look-up for that representation in the database and returns a representation for the corresponding reservation. We omit the details.

Figure 7.12 provides an implementation of a shopping cart service using JAX-RS. By default, JAX-RS Web services are stateless, and a new instance of a resource is created for each service request. However, JAX-RS allows Web services to be annotated with @Singleton or @PerSession. The former ensures that there is a single instance of the resource for all Web service requests, while the latter ensures that there is a single instance for each Web session. Note that this is the same choice of semantics for EJB CORBA services (@Stateless, @Stateful and @Singleton), but for JAX-WS-based SOAP-based Web services, only stateless services are available (with the option of the application explicitly

```
@Path("/train")
public class TrainResource {

@Context UriInfo uriInfo;

  @EJB(beanName = "TrainService") ITrain trainService;

  @POST
  @Path("/{tid}")
  @Consumes("application/x-www-form-urlencoded")
  @Consumes("application/vnd.trains+xml")
  public Response makeReservation (
                    @PathParam("tid") String tid,
                    @PathParam("travdate") String travdate,
                    @DefaultValue("business")
                    @QueryParam("class") String _class,
        {   String reserveInfo)
      URI reserveURI =
        trainService.reserve(tid, _class, uriInfo, reserveInfo);
      return Response.created(reserveURI).build();
  }
}

@Path("/reservation")
public class ReservationResource {

  @Context UriInfo uriInfo;

  @EJB(beanName = "ReservationService")
  IReservation reservationService;

  @GET
  @PATH("/{rid}")
  @Produces("application/vnd.trains+xml")
  public ReservationRepresentation getReservation (
                                @PathParam("rid") String rid )
  {
    ReservationRepresentation reservation =
      reservationService.get(rid, uriInfo);
    return reservation;
  }
}
```

Figure 7.11 *Train and reservation resources*

managing session state). In the example given in Fig. 7.12, the state of the shopping cart is held in a field in the resource instance. The PUT verb is used to initialize the cart, the DELETE verb to remove the cart, and GET to query the contents of the cart. Any attempt to access the cart before it is initialized (or after it is removed) results in the return of a 404 status ("Not Found"). The exception

```java
@PerSession
@Path("/rest/shoppingcart")
public class ShoppingCartResource {
  List<CartItem> cart = null;

  @PUT
  public void newCart () {
    cart = new ArrayList<CartItem>();
  }

  @GET
  @Produces("application/xml", "application/json")
  public CartRepresentation getCart () {
    if (cart == null) throw new NotFoundException();
    return new CartRepresentation(cart);
  }

  @DELETE
  public void deleteCart () {
    if (cart == null) throw new NotFoundException();
    cart = null;
  }

  @POST @Path("add")
  @Consumes("application/x-www-form-urlencoded")
  public void add (@FormParam("product") String product,
                   @FormParam("amount") String amount) {
    if (cart == null) throw NotFoundException();
    cart.add(new CartItem(product,amount));
  }
  @POST @Path("checkout")
  @Consumes("application/x-www-form-urlencoded")
  public Response checkout (
        @FormParam("name") String name,
        @FormParam("ccardNum ") String ccardNum,
        @FormParam("expDate ") String expDate) {
    if (cart == null) throw NotFoundException();
    … URI shippingUri = …
    return Response.created(shippingUri).build();
  }
}
```

Figure 7.12   *Stateful shopping cart*

`NotFoundException` extends the `WebApplicationException` class, which defines exceptions that are mapped to Web service responses that reflect Web application errors. This exception is defined as follows:

```java
public class NotFoundException extends WebApplicationException {
    public NotFoundException() { super(Response.Status.NOT_FOUND); }
}
```

The operations for adding an item to the shopping cart and checking out the contents of the cart are defined as sub-resources of the shopping cart.

```
@Path("/rest/shoppingcart/{cartId}")
public class ShoppingCartResource {
  @PathParam("cartId") String cartId;

  @PersistenceContext(unitName="ShoppingCartPU")
  EntityManager em;

  @PUT
  public Response newCart () {
    CartEntity cart = em.find(CartEntity.class, cartId);
    if (cart != null)
      throw new WebApplicationException(Response.Status.FORBIDDEN);
    cart = new CartEntity(cartId);
    em.persist(cart);
    return Response.status(Response.Status.CREATED);
  }

  @GET
  @Produces("application/xml", "application/json")
  public CartRepresentation getCart () {
    CartEntity cart = em.find(CartEntity.class, cartId);
    if (cart == null) throw new NotFoundException();
    return new CartRepresentation(cart);
   }

  @DELETE
  public Response deleteCart () {
    CartEntity cart = em.find(CartEntity.class, cartId);
    if (cart == null) throw new NotFoundException();
    em.remove(cart);
    return Response.ok();
  }

  …

}
```

Figure 7.13   *RESTful shopping cart*

The provision of session semantics for JAX-RS services differentiates it from JAX-WS (which only supports stateless services). However, the session semantics is a violation of the loose coupling principle for RESTful Web services. Figure 7.13 provides an alternative implementation that is stateless, at least according to the precepts of REST. This example represents the shopping cart as a persistent resource, albeit one with a state that varies over time. The state of the shopping cart is stored in a database on the server and an entity manager is injected into the server by the application container to provide access to the database. A key is needed to retrieve the cart from the database; this key is therefore made part of the shopping cart URI and a path parameter for the service methods. This key might be a User ID that requires clients to register with the system before they obtain a shopping cart. Alternatively, another resource may be provided for allocating a shopping cart identifier; the response from allocating the cart identifier would include links to cart operations whose URIs identified the new cart.

Why is the example in Fig. 7.13 "more stateless" than the example in Fig. 7.12? There is certainly state in both cases; however, the session state in the first shopping cart example is only shared between the client and the server, effectively forming a tight coupling between the two. It is this form of tight coupling that violates the statelessness principle of REST, as it inhibits scalability of applications over the Web. For example, a typical implementation method for the session state representation of the shopping cart in Fig. 7.12 will hold the state of the shopping cart in memory as the state of the resource instance object. Such objects can have performance implications for servers, as they hold memory resources, unless a framework of passivation and re-activation, such as supported by CORBA and described in 6.10, is provided for such instances. There is then the issue of such state being held on a particular server machine inhibiting load balancing in a cluster. Perhaps the serialized service object state may be stored on a back-end database server or session server, to be retrieved by the next server that is designated to execute that service object. Without relying on speculative run-time system support such as this, the service can be implemented as in Fig. 7.13, i.e., as a stateless service with the shopping cart state stored in a database and the URI identifying the state saved on the back-end database.

JAX-RS v1.1 does not specify a client API, but one is provided by the Jersey reference implementation. This API is intended to wrap earlier client APIs, such as HttpURLConnection and Apache HTTP client, and provide a higher level interface for clients of RESTful Web services. The following is an example of an interaction with the RESTful shopping cart service in Fig. 7.13:

```
Client c = Client.create();
UriBuilder uriBase =
  UriBuilder.fromURI("http://www.example.org/rest/shoppingcart/joe");
URI cartUri = uriBase.build();
WebResource cart = c.resource(cartUri);
cart.put();
Form f1 = new Form();
f1.add("product","Lawrence of Arabia");
f1.add("amount","24.95");
URI addUri = uriBase.path("add").build();
WebResource cartAdder = c.resource(addUri);
cartAdder.post(f1);
Form f2 = new Form();
f2.add("product","A Fistful of Dollars");
f2.add("amount","19.95");
cartAdder.post(f2);
cart = cart.accept(MediaType.APPLICATION_JSON_TYPE);
CartRepresentation cartRep = cart.get(CartRepresentation.class);
```

The final operation in this example retrieves the state of the shopping cart from the server. The original server specification shown, in Fig. 7.13, declares that it can produce content of MIME media type either `application/xml` or `application/json`. The request header specifies that the client can accept content of media type `application/json`—this is how the data is transmitted. This is an example of the negotiation of content type between the client and the server—by now standard in interactions between Web browsers and servers.

In all of the Web service requests, the client does not check the resulting response for errors. In this case, any error will be raised as an exception of type `UniformInterfaceException`. This exception may be caught, and the corresponding response extracted:

```
CartRepresentation cartRep = null;
try {
  cartRep = cart.get(CartRepresentation.class);
} catch (UniformInterfaceException e) {
  ClientResponse response = e.getResponse();
}
```

Alternatively, the response may be obtained directly as a result of type `ClientResponse` from which information such as the status code, entity tag, and entity content can be retrieved:

```
ClientResponse addResp = cartAdder.post (ClientResponse.class, f2);
if (addResp.getClientResponseStatus() == Response.Status.NO_CONTENT) {
  ClientResponse getResp = cart.get (ClientResponse.class);
  if (getResp.getClientResponseStatus() == Response.Status.OK) {
    CartRepresentation cartRep =
    getResp.getEntity(CartRepresentation.class);
    ...
  }
}
```

In general, in order to support the marshalling and unmarshalling of Java types to and from various entity content types, JAX-RS requires the definition of *entity providers* at the server and client side. Several standard entity providers are predefined for the following types:

1. For byte arrays, strings, input streams and readers, files, and data sources (`javax.activation.DataSource`). All types take the default media type `*/*`.
2. For XML transformation sources (`javax.xml.transform.Source`) with XML media types (`text/xml`, `application/xml` and `application/*+xml`). This enables XML data to be filtered and transformed in the course of processing it with a RESTful Web service.
3. For the JAXB representaton type for XML elements (`JAXBElement<*>`) and any application-supplied JAXB classes with the same XML media types as in the previous case. Entity providers for these types are used when an object is passed to JAXB for marshalling whose class does not contain JAXB annotations. A subtlety with JAXB-annotated classes is that if a class C does

not have the XmlRootElement annotation (which does not propagate to child classes), then values of that class must be marshalled and unmarshalled as values of type JAXBElement<C>.

4. For a multi-valued mapping, MultivaluedMap<String,String>, representing the encoding of the completed fields in a form with media type application/x-www-form-urlencoded.

5. For StreamingOutput type of media type */*. This is a callback interface that JAX-RS defines for raw stream output and is useful for asynchronous responses, where the client reads the response stream potentially on a different thread from the original request.

Most implementations of JAX-RS v1.1 include support for interoperability between XML and JSON, using the techniques and encodings described in Sect. 4.5.

Extended support for RESTful Web services figures prominently in plans for Java EE7. In the next section, we consider an experimental extension of JAX-RS that may influence the design of Java EE7. We conclude with an illustrative example of the application of some of the techniques described in Sect. 6.7.4, to ensure conformance of RESTful Web services with a hypermedia business protocol.

7.6   HYPERMEDIA CONTROL AND CONTRACT CONFORMANCE

We considered an example of a purchase order service with a usage protocol in Sect. 7.3: the purchase order is first invoiced, then paid and, finally, shipped (in that order). At any point before the order is shipped, it may be cancelled. We considered in Sect. 6.7.4 (Fig. 6.27) the use of typestate to statically ensure that the underlying protocol was followed by users of the service—a standard application of typestate in constructing reliable software. Typestate provides a way of enforcing this protocol in the type system, with the order service not offering the payment operation in its interface, for example, until the order has been invoiced.

The hypermedia control experimental extension in Jersey provides a similar notion of state-based control of the possible operations provided by a resource, but using a conventional state machine control implementation with run-time checking raising an exception if an operation is invoked in a state where it is not enabled. On the client side, a proxy for the server-side controller can perform these run-time checks for invalid operation invocation before communicating with the server. Server-side checking is obviously also still necessary. Presumably, client-side checking catches protocol errors earlier, although this motivation is less compelling than that for typestate. The motivation for typestate is to eliminate such errors completely through careful analysis of the client code with respect to a resource usage protocol.

Figure 7.14 provides an example of a server-side hypermedia controller for purchase order resources. This follows the MODEL-VIEW-CONTROLLER (MVC) pattern: the model is the data state of the resource, the controller is the service encapsulating

```
@Path("/orders/{orderId}")
@HypermediaController(model=Order.class,
                      linkType=LinkType.LINK_HEADERS)
public class OrderResource {
  @PathParam("orderId") String orderId;

  private Order order;

  @POST @Action("invoice") @Path("invoice")
  @Produces("application/xml")
  public Invoice invoice (@QueryParam("invNum") String invNum) {
    … order.setStatus(INVOICED);
  }

  @POST @Action("pay") @Path("pay")
  @Consumes("application/x-www-form-urlencoded")
  @Produces("application/xml")
  public Receipt pay (@FormParam("ccardNum") String ccardNum) {
    … order.setStatus(PAID);
  }

  @POST @Action("ship") @Path("ship")
  public void ship (@QueryParam("method") String method) {
    … order.setStatus(SHIPPED);
  }

  @POST @Action("cancel") @Path("cancel")
  @Consumes("application/x-www-form-urlencoded")
  public void cancel (@FormParam("reason") String reason) {
    … order.setStatus(CANCELLED);
  }

  @GET
  @Produces("application/xml")
  public Order getOrder () { return order; }

  @ContextualActionSet
  public Set<String> getContextualActionSet() { … }
}
```

Figure 7.14   *Server-side hypermedia controller*

the control state for the resource, and the view is the client side of the interaction. The `@HypermediaController` annotation identifies the `OrderResource` class in Fig. 7.14 as the controller for a service, with the data state provided by an instance of the `Order` class. Each purchase order is distinguished as a resource by the order identifier, specified as a path parameter in the URI. Each operation is identified as a sub-resource by an extension of the purchase order's URI. In addition, each operation provided to clients has an `@Action` annotation. This annotation logically connects a remote operation provided by the resource to an operation invoked on the client proxy.

```
@HypermediaController(model=Order.class,
                      linkType=LinkType.LINK_HEADERS)
public interface OrderController {

  private Order getModel();

  @Action("invoice")
  public Invoice invoice (@Name("invoiceNum") String invoiceNum);

  @Action("pay")
  public Receipt pay (@Name("ccardNum") String ccardNum);

  @Action("ship")
  public void ship (@Name("method") String method);

  @Action("cancel")
  public void cancel (@Name("reason") String reason);
}
```

Figure 7.15 *Client-side hypermedia controller interface*

The interface for the client-side controller proxy is provided in Fig. 7.15. The proxy for the controller encapsulates the details of the resource, including the URIs for the service operations on that resource and the HTTP verbs used to access the resource. The @Action annotations on the proxy methods relate them to the corresponding service operations. The proxy also provides an operation for returning the model—the data state for the purchase order resource. This resource will contain links to other resources, such as the customer resource and the resources for the products being ordered.

So far, this is a service façade, which we recall encapsulates one or more services and abstracts some of the details of interaction for clients. The elision of the details of the underlying network communication is similar to the abstraction provided by a client stub. For the purposes of hypermedia control, the critical part of the service implementation is a local method, getContextualActionSet(), whose details are omitted in Fig. 7.14. An order description is assumed to contain a property (status) that records the control state of the service. Each of the operations in Fig. 7.14 updates this status at the completion of the operation. A "contextual action set" relates this control state for the service to the set of operations ("action set") that this service is currently enabled to perform. The actual definition of the control logic is provided by the getContextualActionSet() operation. This operation is annotated with @ContextualActionSet to denote that it returns the current set of enabled operations as a set of action names. This operation can be defined as follows:

```
@ContextualAction
public Set<String> getContextualActionSet() {
  Set<String> enabledOps = new HashSet<String>();
  switch (order.getStatus()) {
    case OPEN:
```

```
        enabledOps.add("invoice");
        enabledOps.add "cancel");
        break;
      case INVOICED:
        enabledOps.add("pay");
        enabledOps.add("cancel");
        break;
      case PAID:
        enabledOps.add("ship");
        enabledOps.add("cancel");
        break;
      case SHIPPED:
      case CANCELLED:
        break;
  }
  return enabledOps;
}
```

The actions are associated with sub-resources for the service operations via the action names in the @Action annotations. The service controller is therefore able to associate the currently-enabled service operations, as sub-resources, with the current control state. This enables automated protocol compliance checking based on raising an exception if an operation is invoked in a state where it is not enabled.

The final ingredient is the communication of the enabled operations and other information regarding their calling pattern to the client. In the example shown in Sect. 7.3, we adopted the approach of Webber et al. [12] and assumed a designated element, always a child of the root element, that contains the DAP links in a resource representation. An alternative approach is to store these DAP links in the HTTP response headers using Link: headers [13]. For example, after successful invocation of the invoice operation, the response headers may include:

```
Link: https://.../orders/rest/12345/pay;rel=review;op=POST
Link: https://.../orders/rest/12345/cancel;rel=review;op=DELETE
```

These links may, in turn, be extracted from a WADL description of the service from link specifications on the representations.

Actions and contextual actions sets are used to describe protocols that clients should follow, but no attempt is made to prevent run-time failure because of a client's failure to conform to the protocol. The client-side proxy for the hypermedia controller enables the server to perform some "remote controlling" of the client, for example changing the protocol by changing the Link: headers that are returned to the client. However, this is only used to capture protocol errors on the client side instead of, or as well as, on the server side. The conformance-checking guarantees are so weak that the benefit of this approach for dealing with dynamic protocol updates is correspondingly weak. In the remainder of this section, we consider a more ambitious scheme where we extend hypermedia control with a notion of typestate. We describe this in the Haskell language, for reasons that will become clear. Further details of the Haskell language are provided in Appendix A.

We describe the type of an order as a parameterized type, (Order S), where S represents the current typestate of an order. Typestates are represented by type constants Open, Invoiced, Paid, Shipped, and Cancelled. The interface for the order service is provided by these operations:

```
invoice :: String → (Order Open) → (Int, Order Invoiced)
pay     :: String → (Order Invoiced) → (Int, Order Paid)
ship    :: String → (Order Shipped) → (Int, Order Shipped)
cancel  :: (Cancellable a) ⇒
                String → (Order a) → (Int, Order Cancelled)
```

The cancel operation is defined for several cases, each corresponding to one of the allowable preconditions. We give cancel a parametrically polymorphic type to ascribe it a template type and we then adapt type classes to constrain the possible instantiations. This is a hypothetical extension of type classes for typestates, where no operations are defined—we only provide enough details of such a hypothetical extension to motivate the example. Cancellable is defined as a type class of one parameter with instances:

```
Cancellable Open
Cancellable Invoiced
Cancellable Paid
```

With these instances, there are three possible instantiations for the cancel operation:

```
cancel :: String → (Order Open) → (Int, Order Cancelled)
cancel :: String → (Order Invoiced) → (Int, Order Cancelled)
cancel :: String → (Order Paid) → (Int, Order Cancelled)
```

We also need some operations to begin, and to complete, each run of the protocol:

```
getOrder :: (Order None) › (Int, Order None)
commit   :: (Order Shipped) → ((), Order None)
abort    :: (Order Cancelled) → ((), Order None)
```

The getOrder operation obtains a new purchase order and must not be invoked during a run of the protocol. Depending on branching in the decision logic, a purchase order may be shipped or cancelled; the commit and abort operations bring these two branches in the logic together at the end. The typestates enforce the use of safe protocols for interacting with the order service, for example:

```
o1 :: Order Open
let o2 = invoice "56789" o1
…
let o3 = pay "76348" o2
…
let o4 = ship "express" o3
```

However, this representation does not prevent aliasing, which allows the static checking to be subverted. For example, in the following o4 and o5 are aliases to the same order, one with the order shipped and the other with the order cancelled:

```
o3 :: Order Paid
let o4 = ship "express" o3
let o5 = cancel "I changed my mind" o3
```

There are a number of ways to handle this. As mentioned in Sect. 6.7.4, we could associate type-based "capabilities" or "permissions" with the use of a purchase order. The type system then ensures that the capability is used in a linear or affine fashion. In particular, such a capability, associated with a purchase order of type (Order Paid), ensures that it can only be used once in a program. A simpler alternative is to encapsulate the state of the purchase order in a monad. Threading this state through a monad enforces the discipline that is necessary to ensure the protocol is followed by a client, without the use of exoticisms such as linear or affine types. Instead of a purchase order parameterized type, we now define a monad type (OrderM T S_1 S_2), where T is the type of the value computed in a monad and S_1 and S_2 represent the typestate pre- and post-condition, respectively, of the underlying computation control logic. We refer to this monad type as a *typestate monad*, essentially a form of state monad, and define it as follows:

OrderM T S_1 S_2 = (Order S_1) → (T, Order S_2)

In other words, a monad abstracts a computation that takes a purchase order control state S_1 as its input and returns a new control state S_2 paired with a return value of type T. Recall that the point of a monad is to encapsulate the use of the control state in order to ensure that it is handled linearly without resorting to approaches such as linear types.

The following operation injects a value into the monad:

```
initialM :: a → (OrderM a s s)
initialM x s = (x, s)
```

The most important operation in the monad is that for composing the steps in a computation. We define the following general composition operation:

```
seqM :: (OrderM a s1 s) → (a → (OrderM b s s2)) → (OrderM b s1 s2)
seqM m f s = let { (x, s1) = m s } in f x s1
```

We also define a lifting of operations on control states to operations on the monad. The primitive operations on control state should only be invoked from these lifted operations to ensure single-threaded or linear handling of the control state:

```
lift :: (a → (Order s1) → (b, Order s2)) → (a → (Order b s1 s2))
lift f s x = f x s
```

We have one more operation to define that calls the getOrder operation to generate a new purchase order. This operation should be the only place where getOrder is invoked:

```
getOrder' :: a → (Order None) → (Int, Order Open)
getOrder' x s = getOrder s
```

We can then complete the definition of the monad by instantiating the generic composition operation with the various operations on the control state:

```
getM :: a → (OrderM Int None Open)
getM = lift getOrder'

invoiceM :: String → (OrderM Int Open Invoiced)
invoiceM = lift invoice

payM :: String → (OrderM Int Invoiced Paid)
payM = lift pay

shipM :: String → (OrderM Int Paid Shipped)
shipM = lift ship

cancelM :: (Cancellable s) ⇒ a → (OrderM a s Cancelled)
cancelM = lift cancel

commitM :: a → (OrderM a Shipped None)
commitM = lift commit

abortM :: a → (OrderM a Cancelled None)
abortM = lift abort
```

The following script defines a procedure whose body is executed in the monad, starting in typestate None and ending in the same typestate. As the control state is never manipulated explicitly, it is impossible to violate the protocol using aliasing:

```
proc :: (OrderM Int None None)
proc =
   do { getM 0;                    -- Open
        x ← invoiceM "56789";      -- Invoiced
        y ← payM "76348";          -- Paid
        z ← shipM "express";       -- Shipped
        commitM z;                 -- None
   }
```

This has been a very simple example illustrating the application of concepts from functional programming to checking conformance of clients with resource update protocols. In general, the RESTful notion of making all state explicit as resources, identified by URIs that are not shared by any other resources, is strongly reminiscent of the principles of functional programming. Others have already made this observation [14], and this is a topic that we expect will see further developments as the field evolves.

7.7 CONCLUDING REMARKS

The "rise of REST" as a basis for Web services is heralded by some REST advocates as the "death of RPC". It is important to understand that this refers to REST in the wider conceptualization of the term, as HTTP is, after all, fundamentally a RPC protocol. Beyond its rejection of the WS-* protocol stack, the important divergence between REST and SOAP-based Web services is the notion of client execution driven by the navigation of a hypermedia network of linked resources. Without this notion of hypermedia programming, so-called RESTful services reduce to POX services, or services with coarse-grained CRUD APIs. The traditional RPC-oriented approach to services emphasizes a control-oriented approach to interaction with remote services, whereas the REST approach emphasizes a more loosely coupled data-oriented interaction based on asychronous exchange of business documents (resource representations). Although we have considered support for asynchronous communication in the previous chapter, the support for asynchrony that is truly envisioned for B2B interactions over the Web would involve asychronous exchange of messages, where the immediate response may be no more than the acknowledgement of receipt of a message. Many examples of RESTful programming still emphasize business-to-consumer interactions, thus, for example relying on polling, rather than callbacks, for delayed responses, as most consumers do not run Web servers to receive responses from Web services. Nevertheless, callbacks are common in business-to-consumer business interactions, using e-mail rather than the Web to provide follow-up to customers (such as shipping notification) after the initial Web interaction. Both RESTful and SOAP-based Web services will need to evolve further to properly support this truly loosely-coupled form of interaction, especially in the presence of failures and security threats.

Even in the realm of business-to-consumer services, the interactions are rapidly evolving beyond simple two-party interactions. A purchase on the Web may nowadays involve at least three parties: the consumer, the vendor, and the third-party payment service. The challenges in this arena have been demonstrated by the discovery of vulnerabilities in underlying payment protocols [15]. These vulnerabilities would allow malicious parties to purchase goods without providing payment. This e-commerce example is a demonstration of the importance of distributed agreement and a failure of Web protocols to ensure agreement among the three parties (client, vendor and payment service) in a Web purchase. Yet, traditional approaches to reaching such agreement, as reflected in the WS-Transaction standard for SOAP-based Web services, reflect the form of tight coupling that few believe is scalable for B2B interaction over the Web. The conclusion is that important challenges still remain in the development of platforms and frameworks for inter-enterprise applications over the Internet and the Web.

Much of the opposition to WS-* has been caused by the size and complexity of the protocol stack—but what is the alternative for enterprise applications? This is not a rhetorical question; support for asynchronous RESTful Web services plays a prominent role in the plans for Java EE 7. Reliable message queues, rather than synchronous or even asynchronous RPC, have been the basis for enterprise B2B e-commerce for many years. It appears plausible that RESTful Web services will play a role in new programming models; however, it remains to be seen what the higher levels of this protocol stack will look like. Java EE and WCF have largely failed to achieve the original goal of SOAP-based Web services: providing interoperability between different middlewares in support of inter-enterprise collaboration. REST may be the basis for loosely-coupled B2B interactions in the future, based on the exchange of documents as resource representations, with "interfaces" based on media content types and, hopefully, higher-level specifications of business protocols underlying hypermedia programming. Presumably, transactional middleware will still have a role to play within enterprises, performing the background processing in support of RESTful state transitions. However, the problems with payment protocols demonstrate that distributed agreement remains a critical issue for services, and one that loosely-coupled applications need to deal with themselves, rather than relying on protocols provided by an underlying middleware. End-to-end arguments will also presumably figure prominently in future designs for inter-enterprise applications.

If new programming models do emerge, will they be based on paradigms such as functional programming, or will new programming paradigms emerge? Presumably, software architectures for enterprise applications will increasingly reflect a synthesis of concepts and ideas from some of the architectural principles considered here, as well as the principles of EDA that we consider in Chapter 8 in the sequel volume. Will genuinely new architectures emerge that properly address the challenges of building reliable and secure, yet loosely coupled, inter-enterprise applications of the future? It is at least interesting that there is so much uncertainty regarding these questions, as it signals an opportunity for innovative approaches to addressing some of these issues.

7.8 FURTHER READING

Fielding's thesis still constitutes an important reference on the principles of REST. Richardson and Ruby [5] describe ROA, a strict interpretation of the REST principles that attempts to remove some of the ambiguity around their application to Web services; our notion of ROA refines the principles that they espouse. Webber et al. [12] demonstrate the use of hypermedia programming to describe business protocols. The approach of domain application protocols, including domain-specific media types, and DAP links in the train schedule and purchasing examples, is influenced by their approach.

REFERENCES

1. Fielding R. Architectural Styles and the Design of Network-based Software Architectures. PhD thesis. Irvine: University of California; 2000.

2. Richardson R. Justice will take us millions of intricate moves. In: QCon Conference San Francisco: InfoQ; 2008. Available at: http://www.crummy.com/writing/speaking/2008-QCon.

3. Fette I. The WebSocket protocol. Technical report. Internet Engineering Task Force (IETF), June 2011. Available at: http://tools.ietf.org/html/draft-ietf-hybi-thewebsocket-protocol-09.

4. Fielding R, Gettys J, Mogul J, Frystyk H, Masinter L, Leach P, Berners-Lee T. RFC 2616: Hypertext Transfer Protocol—HTTP/1.1. Technical report. Internet Engineering Task Force (IETF), 1999. Available at: http://tools.ietf.org/html/rfc2616.

5. Richardson L, Ruby S. RESTful Web Services. O'Reilly; Sebastopol, CA, 2007.

6. Dezani-Ciancaglini M, De'Liguoro U. Sessions and session types: an overview. In: Proceedings of the 6th International Conference on Web Services and Formal Methods, WS-FM'09. Bologna, Italy, Springer-Verlag; 2010, p. 1–28.

7. Vasconcelos V, Ravara A, Gay S. Session types for functional multithreading. In: *CONCUR'04*. Springer-Verlag; 2004, p. 497–511.

8. Dezani-Ciancaglini M, Mostrous D, Yoshida N, Drossopoulou S. Session types for object-oriented languages. In: *ECOOP'06*. Springer; 2006, p. 328–352.

9. Capecchi S, Coppo M, Dezani-Ciancaglini M, Drossopoulou S, Giachino E. Amalgamating sessions and methods in object-oriented languages with generics. Theoretical Computer Science 2009; 410: 142–167.

10. Kahn G. The semantics of a simple language for parallel programming. In: Information Processing 74: Proceedings of the IFIP Congress. Stockholm, Sweden: North-Holland; 1974, p. 471–475.

11. Hadley M. Web Application Description Language, August 2009. Available at: http://www.w3.org/Submission/wadl/.

12. Webber J, Parastatidis S, Robinson I. REST in Practice. O'Reilly; Sebastopol, CA, 2010.

13. Nottingham M. Web linking. Technical report. Internet Engineering Task Force (IETF), 2010. Available at: http://www.ietf.org/rfc/rfc5988.txt.

14. Vinoski S. Welcome to "the functional web". *IEEE Internet Computing*, 2009. 13(2): 104, 102–103.

15. Wang R, Chen S, Wang XF, Qadeer S. How to shop for free online–security analysis of cashier-as-a-service based web stores. In: IEEE Symposium on Security and Privacy. Oakland: IEEE Press; 2011.

Introduction to Haskell

> Haskell was made by some really smart guys (with PhDs).
> **_Miran Lipovaca [1]_**

A.1 TYPES AND FUNCTIONS

We have used the functional language Haskell in several examples. In this appendix, we review some of the salient concepts of Haskell that are used in the text.

Haskell is an example of a "pure" functional language. Therefore, as one may expect, functions play a central role in the language. Haskell was introduced in Sect. 5.4 and we repeat the introduction provided there of the basic ideas of the language syntax:

> The declaration e :: T specifies that the expression e is a program expression with type T. If that expression is evaluated as a program, then if the evaluation completes it will result in a value of type T. If e :: T_1 → T_2, then e is a function from the domain T_1 to the range T_2. If e :: T_1 → T_2 → T_3, then e is a function of two parameters from the domain T_1 and the domain T_2 to the range T_3. The application of a function f to arguments e_1 and e_2 is written simply using juxtaposition, i.e., as (f e_1 e_2). Parentheses are only used to remove syntactic ambiguity.

There are several features that one may or may not expect to see in a functional language. One feature that is often cited is the provision of *first class functions*. This means that a function or procedure may be passed as an argument to another function, or returned as a result from a function. Consider the following example:

Enterprise Software Architecture and Design: Entities, Services, and Resources,
First Edition. Dominic Duggan.
© 2012 John Wiley & Sons, Inc. Published 2012 by John Wiley & Sons, Inc.

```
let F = (let x = 3; f y = (x+y) in f)
let x = "hello";
F(3);
```

Here, we use the `let` construct to bind functions in the top level command line interface. In the definition of F, a `let` clause is used to locally bind the variable x to 3, and then to locally bind the function f. This is different from previous uses of `let`, such as for F and x in this example, which have been used to bind variables in the top-level command line interface. The function F is bound to the value of the locally defined function f. This binding "remembers" the local binding of x to 3 and is not subsequently confused when F is applied in a context where another x variable has been bound (perhaps to a value of a different type than the original x). The function f closes up its nonlocal bindings (such as that for the variable x) so they are not confused by later bindings; f is then referred to as a *closure*. A language that does this is said to be *statically scoped*.

Javascript is another language that has first class functions. ECMAScript v3 had dynamic scoping but, because of problems reasoning about programs (for security purposes), ECMAScript v5 has static scoping. You should only use ECMAScript v5. One can think of an object as a closure where the scaffolding is made explicit in the sense that one must explicitly bundle the bindings for the nonlocal variables (object fields) in with the shared closure for the methods of the object. Java provides anonymous classes in order to make it easier to define "closures" as objects, while minimizing the bureaucracy. C# provides *delegates* as a form of closure in an object-oriented language—in this case a function pointer to a method that is registered as an event handler. More recently, Java has added support for "lambda abstraction", to support the definition of closures, and function types. Scala has had closures since its inception.

We are now in a position to provide further clarification on the syntax of types, described above. If we type:

```
let g x y = (x+y);     -- g :: Int → Int → Int
let h y = g 3 y        -- h :: Int → Int
```

We can see that g is a function of two integer arguments[1] and returns an integer result. The h function specializes the first argument of g, returning a new unary function that, as with the definition of f above, "remembers" the binding of x to 3. Now the arrow type is right-associative, so we can, in fact, write the type of g as:

```
g :: Int → (Int → Int)
```

So, we see that g, in fact, takes its first argument (the value for x) and returns a new function that then takes its second argument. The definition of g is said to be *curried*[2]. Then, an alternative definition of h is given by:

---

[1]We are over-simplifying for the sake of exposition.
[2]The name is a reference to the logician Haskell B. Curry, after whom the Haskell language is also named.

```
let h = g 3
```

Another feature that is often cited for so-called "pure" functional languages is *referential transparency*. This means that the values of variables cannot be mutated, as they can be in languages with assignment. The motivation for this draconian restriction is that it greatly simplifies reasoning about program equality, as one can substitute equals for equals in performing calculations about the value of program expressions. Referential transparency also simplifies the implementation of parallel programming, as it is easier to identify data parallelism once state is made explicit.

There are languages that have referential transparency but not first class functions, and there are languages that have closures but allow variables to be mutated. Alice [2] is an early functional language that is an example of the former, while Javascript and O'CAML are examples of the latter. The term *applicative language* may be reserved for languages with referential transparency but not first class functions.

Another aspect often found in functional languages is *algebraic datatypes*. We saw examples of such datatype definitions when considering type definitions in O'CAML, in Fig. 6.29(**b**):

```
type t = Empty | Insert of int * t
```

Algebraic datatypes provide the main form of data structuring in functional languages. Data structures are finite or infinite labelled trees. A datatype definition provides the specification of such a labelled tree type, as a set of labels (`Empty` and `Insert` in the example above), and the type of data associated with each label in the tree (no data for the `Empty` label and a pair of an integer and a subtree for the `Insert` label). A datatype declaration also introduces *data constructors*, one for each case in the possible node types in a tree. In Haskell, the O'CAML type above is defined as:

```
data t = Empty | Insert Int t
```

This introduces two data constructors: `Empty`, for defining an empty list, and `Insert` for inserting an element into a list. The following are example data structures built using these data constructors:

```
Empty
Insert 1 Empty
Insert 1 (Insert 2 (Insert 3 Empty))
```

The first example denotes an empty list, the second denotes a singleton list containing one, and the third example denotes a list of three elements. As another example, the following defines a type of binary trees where integer values are stored at the leaf nodes:

```
data Tree = Leaf Int | Branch Tree Tree
```

Then, a binary tree can be represented in Haskell as:

```
Branch (Branch (Leaf 1) (Leaf 2)) (Branch (Leaf 3) (Leaf 4))
```

Lists are so important in functional programming that they are pre-defined with their own syntax in Haskell:

1. [T] for the type of lists of elements taken from the type T.
2. [] for the empty list.
3. x:xs for the insertion of an element x into a list xs.
4. $[x_1,...,x_k]$ is shorthand for the list $x_1:x_2:...:x_k:[]$.
5. *List comprehensions* provide a convenient shorthand for defining new lists that filter existing lists. For example, the following comprehension builds a list of all elements of xs that are not divisible by 2: [x | x ← xs, x 'mod' 2 > 0].

Therefore, the above examples can be instead expressed as [], 1:[] (or just [1]), and 1:2:3:[] (or just [1,2,3]). The operation for inserting an element into a list (denoted by :) should not be confused with the operation for concatenating two lists (denoted by ++). For example, 1:[2,3] = [1,2,3], while [1,2]++[3,4] = [1,2,3,4]. On the other hand, [1,2]:[3,4] and 1++[2,3] are not well-formed expressions, and will be rejected by the compiler.

Algebraic datatypes are usually used to define *inductive types*. By this, we mean a recursive type definition that has a monotonic structure, where each case in the definition of the type adds elements to the definition of the type without removing elements. The meaning of an inductive type definition can then be defined as the least fixed point of a monotonic set-valued function constructed from the type definition. For example, for a given list element type t, we can define an inductive definition of the type [T], the set of lists whose elements are from the type T, as follows:

1. [T] contains [], the empty list.
2. If x is an element of the element type T, and xs is an element of [T], then (x:xs) is an element of [T].

To provide a semantics for this inductively defined type, define the function F_T as follows:

$$F_T(X) = \{[]\} \cup \{(x : xs) \mid x \in T, xs \in X\}$$

Define the k-fold application of this function by:

$$F_T^0(X) = F_T(X)$$

$$F_T^{k+1}(X) = F_T^k(F_T(X))$$

Then:

$$F_T^k(\{\}) = \{[x_1, \ldots, x_j] \mid 0 \leq j \leq k \text{ and } x_1, \ldots, x_j \in T\}$$

That is, the kth iteration of F_T contains all lists of length less than or equal to k. Define the least fixed point operation by:

$$lfp(F) = \bigcup_{i=0}^{\infty} F^i(\{\})$$

Then $lfp(F_T)$ contains all *finite length* lists whose elements are taken from the element type T.

When is a type not inductively defined? Here is an example:

```
data U = Lambda (U → U)
apply :: U → (U → U)
apply (Lambda f) = f
```

This odd datatype defines a type U that is isomorphic to its own function space[3], i.e., $U \cong U{\to}U$. This is the definition of the so-called "untyped lambda calculus" [3]. The lambda calculus is the theoretical basis for functional languages, such as Haskell, and for programming languages generally [4]. It is a very small kernel language with unary functions[4] $\lambda x.e$ and applications $(e_1\ e_2)$. The untyped lambda calculus obviously does have a type: the universal type U which is isomorphic to its own (continuous) function space via the isomorphisms given by Lambda and apply. The negative occurrence of U in its recursive definition means that it is not clear that this definition is well-defined. Providing a semantics for such definitions that underlie any functional or object-oriented language, where functions may be part of values, has been one of the contributions of the field of domain theory.

To compute with lists, Haskell provides a case construct but, more typically, one defines a function over a list using *pattern matching*. For example, here is a function that computes the length of a list:

```
length :: [T] → Int
length [] = 0
length (x:xs) = 1 + length xs
```

The intention is that functional programs look suggestively similar to the way one defines mathematical functions. Recursive function definitions are important in functional programming because they are the only way to define loops in programs. The definition of length runs in linear time, as one might expect, but it also runs

---

[3]For cardinality reasons, we restrict the function space to *continuous* functions, where any finite part of the output depends only on a finite part of the input.

[4]There is a perhaps aprocryphal story that the use of lambda arose as a result of a typesetting accident. In the original manuscript describing the calculus, unary functions were simply denoted $\hat{x}.e$. The "hat" on the parameter was translated by the typesetter to a capital lambda Λ, and abstraction subsequently became $\lambda x.e$.

in linear space. The reason for this latter is that, on every recursive call, the fact that the result of the recursive call must be incremented has to be saved on the call stack. This is a very inefficient way of doing things. In an imperative language, such as Java, one might instead say:

```
int len = 0;
while (!empty(xs)) { xs = tail(xs); len += 1; }
```

One can always write a loop like this as a *tail-recursive* function by adding *accumulating parameters* for the variables that accumulate the result of the loop, such as len above. The original function calls the tail-recursive function with accumulating parameters:

```
lengthTr :: [T] → Int
lengthTr xs = lengthAux xs 0
lengthAux :: [T] → Int → Int
lengthAux [] N = N
lengthAux (x:xs) N = lengthAux xs (N+1)
```

Comparing the execution of the two length functions, we have:

```
length [1,2,3]                  lengthAux [1,2,3] 0
= 1 + (length [2,3])            = lengthAux [2,3] 1
= 1 + 1 + (length [3])         = lengthAux [3] 2
= 1 + 1 + 1 + (length [])     = lengthAux [] 3
= 1 + 1 + 1 + 0               = 3
= 1 + 1 + 1
= 1 + 2
= 3
```

By accumulating its result in the extra parameter, the lengthAux function runs in constant space, as any Haskell implementation is required to execute a tail-recursive function in constant space, re-using the stack space from the previous iteration on the next iteration. Another example of a tail-recursive function is one for reversing a list:

```
reverse :: [T] → [T]
reverse xs = rev xs []
rev :: [T] → [T] → [T]
rev [] acc = acc
rev (x:xs) acc = rev xs (x:acc)
```

So, for example:

```
reverse [1,2,3] = rev [1,2,3] []
               = rev [2,3] [1]
               = rev [3] [2,1]
               = rev [] [3,2,1]
               = [3,2,1]
```

Certain forms of loops are so common that Haskell, and any functional language, provide pre-defined functions for defining such loops. First, there is the form of loop that transforms one form of list into another form of list. For example, the following transforms a list of lists into a list of lengths for the original lists:

```
lengths :: [[T]] → [Int]
lengths [[1,2,3],[4,5],[6,7,8,9]] = [3,2,4]
```

We can define this function, and others of its ilk, using the map operation that transforms a list into another list element-wise:

```
map :: (T₁ → T₂) → [T₁] → [T₂]
map f [] = []
map f (x:xs) = (f x):(map f xs)
```

Then, the lengths function can be defined as:

```
lengths xs = map length xs
```

Or, more succinctly, using partial application as:

```
lengths = map length
```

Note that the individual transformation steps in the definition of map are independent of each other and could be performed in parallel. This is the motivation for the MapReduce parallel programming framework for cloud computing [5]. The idea itself has been known for some time in the parallel functional programming community. Another operation that is useful is to combine the elements of a list using a binary composition operation ⊗ with a unit a:

```
foldl ⊗ a [x₁,…,xₖ] = (… ((a ⊗ x₁) ⊗ x₂) ⋯ ⊗ xₖ)
```

This operation is similar to the reduce operation in MapReduce, although the latter is a modified version of the reduce operation commonly found in functional programming. The foldl operation can be defined in a tail-recursive manner:

```
foldl :: (T₂ → I₁ → T₂) → T₂ → [T₁] → T₂
foldl f a []     = a
foldl f a (x:xs) = foldl f (f a x) xs
```

Another operation that is very useful is a filtering operation for lists:

```
filter :: (a → Bool) → [a] → [a]
filter p [] = []
filter p (x:xs) =  if p x then x : filter p xs else filter p xs
```

As examples of these two operations, we have:

```
                                test x = (x 'mod' 2) > 0
foldl (+) 0 [3,4,5,6]           filter test [3,4,5,6]
= foldl (+) 3 [4,5,6]           = 3 : filter test [4,5,6]
= foldl (+) 12 [5,6]            = 3 : filter test [5,6]
= foldl (+) 60 [6]             = 3 : 5 : filter test [6]
```

```
= foldl (+) 360 []              = 3 : 5 : filter test []
= 360                           = 3 : 5 : []
```

It is not hard to see that `filter` can be defined in terms of `foldl`:

```
filter p = foldl step []
           where step b a = if p a then a:b else b
```

The `where` clause in a function definition allows the specification of auxiliary functions in that definiion. However, this definiion of `filter` is wrong! It reverses the order of the elements in the filtered list—the proper definition requires a right-associative version of the folding operation:

```
foldr :: (T₁ → T₂ → T₂) → T₂ → [T₁] → T₂
-- foldr ⊗ a [x₁,…,xₖ] = (x₁⊗ (x₂ ⊗ ⋯ (xₖ⊗ a)…))
foldr f a []     = a
foldr f a (x:xs) = f x (foldr f a xs)
```

Define the step functions:

```
stepl b a = if (a 'mod' 2) > 0 then a:b else b
stepr a b = if (a 'mod' 2) > 0 then a:b else b
```

Then, we have:

```
foldl stepl [] [3,4,5,6]        foldr stepr [] [3,4,5,6]
= foldl stepl [3] [4,5,6]       = 3 : (foldr stepr [] [4,5,6])
= foldl stepl [3] [5,6]         = 3 : (foldr stepr [] [5,6])
= foldl stepl [5,3] [6]         = 3 : 5 : (foldr stepr [] [6])
= foldl stepl [5,3] []          = 3 : 5 : (foldr stepr [] [])
= [5,3]                         = 3 : 5 : []
```

To reason about programs that compute over such inductively defined types, functional programmers can resort to *structural induction* over the list type or, equivalently, by induction over the fixed point construction used to define the semantics of that list type. To provide an example of this, we consider one more definition. Haskell provides an operation for composing functions, `_._`, so `(f.g)(x)` `= f(g(x))`. The following is a useful property relating nested mappings and composition:

$$\forall xs \in [T], \mathsf{map}\ f\ (\mathsf{map}\ g\ xs)\ =\ \mathsf{map}\ (f.g)\ xs$$

This property is useful for optimizing network protocol stacks, for example by composing the transformations at several layers in the stack into a single transforomation. The benefit is that the intermediate list is not required with the combined operation. We verify this result by induction on the inductively defined structure of lists. Recall that there are two cases in the definition of the list type: one for the empty list and the other for non-empty lists:

1. Case xs = []: Then:

   ```
   map f (map g []) = map f [] = [] = map (f.g) []
   ```

2. Case xs = y:ys: Then:

   ```
   map f (map g (y:ys)= map f ((g y):(map g ys))
                      = (f (g y)):(map f (map g ys))
                      = (f (g y)):(map (f.g) ys) by induction hypothesis
                      = ((f.g) y):(map (f.g) ys) by definition of f.g
                      = map (f.g) (y:ys)
   ```

We have performed this simple verification to demonstrate the simplicity that comes with reasoning about functional programs. There is another aspect of functional programming languages that is perhaps a bit more controversial in the design space—the use of *lazy evaluation*. Consider the following definition:

```
ones = 1:ones
```

What does this mean? Strictly speaking, ones is not a list because there is no base case: it is an infinite list of ones, 1:1:1:.... Haskell does not actually go into an infinite loop computing this list because evaluation is suspended until a consumer of this data structure asks for another one. We call ones a *stream* to distinguish it from a finite list; a stream is the infinite analogue of finite lists and computation with streams is *demand-driven* in the sense that values are computed as required by consumers of those values, rather than the producer-driven computation associated with lists [6]. In turn, streams are used as the "glue" for composing software modules, streaming the output of one component into the input of another. Streams are one basis for defining stateful computation in a functional language: representing the different states that a variable may be in over time as an infinite sequence of values. Consider, for example, a pseudo-random number generator. A stateful definition of such a generator in an imperative language encapsulates the mutable state of the generator in a closure—each generation of a new random number also updates the internal state with this new seed via a side-effect. A functional representation models the random number generator as a process that generates an infinite sequence of random numbers on demand by clients:

```
data RandStream = Rands Float RandStream
randGen :: Float → RandStream
randGen seed = Rands n (randGen n)
               where n = rand seed
```

Here, we assume that rand is a function that generates a new random number given a seed value. The generating function produces an infinite sequence of such random numbers, feeding in the last random number generated as the new seed for the next iteration. We define the type for the stream of random numbers as a *co-inductive type*. Note that there is no base case in the definition of this type, so reasoning by induction is not possible for programs that process such infinite data structures.

Alternative proof techniques, such as fixed-point induction or co-induction, are available to reason about such programs.

As another example, here is a perspicuous implementation of the Sieve of Eratosthenes in Haskell:[5]

```
primes = sieve [2..]
sieve (p:xs) = p : sieve [x | x ← xs, x 'mod' p > 0]
```

The `sieve` stream filter generates an infinite stream of prime numbers from a stream of all of the natural numbers starting at 2. On each recursive call, `sieve` adds the next prime number p to the output stream and then filters the remaining numbers that are not divisible by the prime numbers generated so far. This effectively defines a pipeline of processes with each stage in the pipeline defined by the stream comprehension `[x | x ← xs, x 'mod' p > 0]` that removes numbers divisible by a prime p.

Haskell has chosen a demand-driven computation strategy based on lazy evaluation, where an expression is only evaluated when its value is required in the program. This design choice has some controversy associated with it because of the run-time cost incurred in supporting lazy evaluation when it is mostly not needed. Where lazy evaluation is useful, it could be supported by defining lazy data constructors in a language that otherwise defaulted to eager evaluation (as in Java and C#, for example). Instead, the Haskell strategy is to make lazy evaluation the default and to require annotations by programmers to signal when evaluation should be strict. One school of thought regards this as faithful to the referential transparency of functional languages. Another school regards it as ill-advised and unnecessary: ill-advised, because Haskell compilers must perform heroic analyses and optimizations to obtain reasonable performance (with the resulting compiler footprint perhaps discouraging language adoptors), and unnecessary because the use of streams could be obtained by explicitly declaring some data constructors as lazy, without requiring ubiquitous lazy evaluation in the language.

A.2 TYPE CLASSES AND FUNCTORS

Another aspect of most functional languages is their support for implicit typing and parametric polymorphism. We avoided discussing this in the previous session but it was implicit in many of the examples. Consider for example:

```
S f g x = f x (g x)
```

What is the type of `S`? Even without a type declaration, the Haskell compiler is able to compute a type for this, using *type inference*. It can reason that the formal

---

[5]Although elegant in its simplicity, this implementation is much less efficient than the equivalent imperative implementation. An efficient implementation is possible in Haskell using priority queues [7]. The example demonstrates that there is no "magic" and, even in declarative languages, software developers must be careful to write sensible code.

parameters f and g are functions, whose domains are both the same as the type of the third parameter x:

S :: (T_x → ?) → (T_x → ?) → T_x → ?

As f x is applied to the result of g x, and the result of this is the overall result of S, we can furthermore reason that S has type:

S :: (T_x → T_1 → T_2) → (T_x → T_1) → T_x → T_2

What of the remaining types, T_1, T_2, and T_x? These types are completely uncon-strained, so we are free to choose any types we wish for them. The Haskell strategy is to parameterize over all possible choices for these types and, in the process, generalize the type of S to a template or polymorphic type:

S :: (a → b → c) → (a → b) → a → c

This is an example of a parametrically polymorphic type, as discussed in Sect. 6.8.1 Each instantiation of this procedure includes the instantiations of the type parameters a, b, and c. Several of the functions defined in the previous section have parametric polymorphic types as their most general types:

```
length :: [a] → Int
map :: (a → b) → [a] → [b]
foldl :: (b → a → b) → b → [a] → b
```

This allows us, for example, to apply length to lists of integers, lists of strings, lists of lists of integers, and so on, by choosing different instantiations of its type at each use.

Polymorphic types are only useful in conjunction with parameterized types, i.e., types that contain one or more type parameters. We have already seen two forms of parameterized types in Haskell: the function type _→_ and the list type [_]. Algebraic datatypes may be defined as parameterized types:

```
data list(a) = Empty | Insert a (List a)
```

So, for example (Insert 3 Empty) has type List(Int), while (Insert "hello" Empty) has type List(String). As another example, the following defines the parameterized type of binary trees:

```
data Tree(a) = Leaf a | Branch (Tree a) (Tree a)
```

The following function "flattens" such a binary tree to a list:

```
flatten :: Tree(a) → [a]
flatten (Leaf x) = [x]
flatten (Branch left right) = (flatten left) ++ (flatten right)
```

Now consider the following example:

```
double x = x + x
```

What is the proper type for `double`? It is not simply (a → a), as the type can only be instantiated to type parameters for which the overloaded + operation is defined. As explained in Sect. 6.8.1, Haskell uses type classes to support definitions such as this. A type class is a collection of operations indexed by a type parameter:

```
class Num a where + :: a → a → a
```

The type of `double` reflects in its "qualified" polymorphic type that the type parameter must have an instance of the `Num` class defined for it:

```
double :: (Num a) ⇒ a → a
```

Such instances may be defined for numeric types, such as `Int`, but they may also be defined for collection types such as lists:

```
instance Num Int where …
instance Num a ⇒ Num [a] where
    [] + [] = []
    (x:xs) + (y:ys) = (x+y) : (xs+ys)
```

The instance for lists requires an instance defined for the element type of the lists. With these instances, the + operation is defined for arguments of type `Int`, `[Int]`, `[[Int]]`, etc.

Another example of an operation that it is useful to overload is the equality operation. For example, a dictionary maps from a domain key type to a range value type. The key type must have equality defined for it in order for searching to be performed based on the key. Assuming we have defined a type (`Dictionary` T_1 T_2) for dictionary, we can define a look-up operation:

```
data Maybe a = Nothing | Just a
lookup :: Eq a ⇒ Dictionary a b → a → Maybe b
```

The `Maybe` datatype is used for the return type because there may be no binding for a key value in the dictionary. The `Eq` class is defined to contain boolean operations for checking for equality and inequality. Haskell does not assume these operations are defined for all values. For example, extensional equality for functions cannot be tested in finite time and, unlike object-oriented languages, there is no notion of pointer equality to provide an intensional notion of equality[6]. Instead, one must define implementations of equality as instances of the `Eq` type class. In most cases, one can add a `deriving` clause to the definition of a datatype and Haskell will generate boilerplate implementations of equality for instances of the datatype:

```
class Eq a where ==, /= :: a → a → Bool
instance Eq Int where (==) = eqInt …
instance Eq a ⇒ Eq [a] where (x:xs) == (y:ys) = (x==y) && (xs==ys) …
```

---

[6]*Extensional equality* of functions is based on observable behavior, the results that a function returns when it is applied to different arguments, without considering the internal details of the function. *Intensional equality* would be based on aspects of the definition of the functions themselves, e.g., the address in memory of the code for the function.

One can think of types such as lists ([]), trees (Tree), and options (Maybe) as *contexts* for component values. Type classes provide a way to define functions that operate uniformly over contexts, provided certain operations are defined for the elements of those contexts. But what of defining uniform functions that require certain operations defined over the contexts themselves? For example, map is a useful operation for transforming a list of one type to a list of another type, but similar operations may be useful for other forms of contexts. Mapping operations are so important that Haskell defines a standard type class for this operation:

```
class Functor f where fmap :: (a → b) → f(a) → f(b)
```

The name *functor* comes from category theory. A category can be thought of as a collection of types ("objects") and functions between those types ("arrows" or "morphisms"). We write $f:A{\to}B$ when f is a morphism from object A to object B. The only operation defined for morphisms is composition,[7] written $f.g$, which is required to be associative: $f.(g.h) = (f.g).h$. For every object A and B, there are identity morphisms id_A and id_B such that if $f: A{\to}B$, then $f.id_A = id_B.f = f$.

A functor is a mapping between categories. Hence, a functor F maps objects from a domain category to objects of a range category. For our purposes, a functor can be considered as a way of injecting values into a context. A functor also maps morphisms of the domain category to morphisms of the range category such that if $f: A{\to}B$ in the domain category, then $F(f):F(A){\to}F(B)$ in the range category. The functor must also commute with the composition of morphisms: $F(f.g) = F(f).F(g)$, where the first composition is in the domain category and the second composition is in the range category. Finally, a functor is required to map identity morphisms to identity morphisms: $F(id_A) = id_{F(A)}$. It is the programmer's responsibility to verify these latter two properties for instances of the Functor type class, where the fmap instance defines the mapping of morphisms in the functor, as the compiler is only able to verify the type of the functor mapping.

Type constructors such as the list and binary tree type constructors provided in this review are examples of functors: the type *contructor* itself (i.e., [], List or Tree) maps from element types T to context types (i.e., [T], List(T) and Tree(T), respectively). The Functor type class defines the mapping of morphisms: an instance of fmap lifts mappings between component types to mappings between context types. Whereas, for example, an instance of Eq for lists is defined for list types [a], that include the element type a—an instance of Functor is defined for the list type *constructor*, []. For example, we may define instances of the functor class for the Haskell list type constructor, as well as for Maybe, List, and Tree:

```
instance Functor [] where
    fmap = map
instance Functor Maybe where
    fmap f Nothing = Nothing
    fmap f (Just x) = Just (f x)
```

---

[7]Category theory is intended as an alternative to set theory for formalizing mathematical and logical concepts, taking functions rather than sets as the primitive notion.

```
instance Functor List where
    fmap f Empty = Empty
    fmap f (Insert x xs) = Insert (f x) (fmap f xs)
instance Functor Tree where
    fmap f (Leaf x) = Leaf (f x)
    fmap f (Branch left right) = Branch (fmap f left) (fmap f right)
```

These definitions provide instances for `fmap` of types:

$$(a \rightarrow b) \rightarrow ([a] \rightarrow [b])$$
$$(a \rightarrow b) \rightarrow (\text{Maybe } a \rightarrow \text{Maybe } b)$$
$$(a \rightarrow b) \rightarrow (\text{List } a \rightarrow \text{List } b)$$
$$(a \rightarrow b) \rightarrow (\text{Tree } a \rightarrow \text{Tree } b)$$

These types reflect that an instance of the functor class lifts a mapping over element types to a mapping over corresponding context types. So, if `f` has type $(T_1 \rightarrow T_2)$, then `fmap(f)` is the result of "lifting" this to type $(F(T_1) \rightarrow F(T_2))$, where F is the context type constructor for which the instance of `fmap` is defined.

There is a computational way of viewing these context types. For a context type such as $[T]$, or `Maybe(T)`, one can view the component type `T` as the result type of an underlying computation. A context type enriches this underlying computation. For example, `Maybe(T)` enriches the underlying computation with the possibility of no result value. This corresponds to adding a special error result if something goes wrong in the underlying computation. The functor lifts an evaluation in the underlying error-free computation into the error-handling context. The list type $[T]$ enriches the underlying computation with several possible result values. This corresponds to enriching the underlying computation with non-deterministic computation, where several possible execution paths may be followed and the results of each of these executions is returned in a list that collects those results. The functor lifts an evaluation in the underlying computation, with a single execution path, into the non-deterministic evaluation context.

What if the evaluation to be performed, rather than defined at the component level, is already defined in the context? For example, we may compute a value and an operation to be applied to that value, both in the error-handling context:

operation :: Maybe $(T_1 \rightarrow T_2)$
value :: Maybe T_1

Rather than applying an evaluation to a value in the context, the need here is to apply an evaluation, already defined in the context, to a value that is also in the context. Haskell defines the *applicative functor* type class for this purpose:

```
class (Functor f) ⇒ Applicative f where
    pure :: a → f a
    (<*>) :: f (a → b) → f a → f b
```

The operation of interest in this class is the infix operation `<*>`. Consider the type of the operation for applying a function to an argument:

```
($) :: (a → b) → a → b
f $ x = f(x)
```

The infix `<*>` operation is similarly an application operation, with the difference that both the function it is applying, and the value that function is being applied to, are in an underlying context, as given by the type constructor `f`. The `pure` operation provides a way for injecting a value into the context. For example, here is an instance of the applicative functor type class for optional, or error-handling, computation:

```
instance Applicative Maybe where
   pure x = Just x
   None <*> _ = None
   _ <*> None = None
   (Just f) <*> (Just x) = Just (f x)
```

In other words, the application operation returns an error value if either the computation to be applied or the argument it is being applied to is an error value. Otherwise, the underlying computation is applied and the result tagged as a non-error value. The injection operation `pure` simply tags its argument as a non-error value. As another example, here is an instance of the applicative functor type class for lists:

```
instance Applicative [] where
   pure x = [x]
   fs <*> xs = [f x | f ← fs, x ← xs]
```

The context enriches values to lists of values that can be interpreted as collecting the results from following several different possible execution paths. So, instead of applying a single function to a single value, in the enriched context we need to apply a list of functions to a list of values; this is performed using a list comprehenesion that returns the $m \cdot n$ possible results of applying m functions to n values. The injection operation simply injects a value into a singleton list.

Functors and applicative functors may be combined. For example, + is a Curried function of two integer arguments. We may use the `fmap` functor operation to inject it into a context on its first argument, then use the `<*>` functor operation to apply the partially-applied function to its second argument:

```
fadd :: (Functor f, Applicative f) ⇒ (f Int) → (f Int) → (f Int)
fadd x y = (fmap(+) x) <*> y
```

Instantiating this function on the list type, we obtain the result:

```
fadd [1,2,3] [4,5,6] = [5,6,7,6,7,8,7,8,9]
```

The application of `fadd` to lists instantiates the `f` type parameter to the list type constructor, `[]`; the `Functor` and `Applicative` type classes are resolved to the instances for lists. The application (`fmap(+) [1,2,3]`) then results in the list of functions $[add_1, add_2, add_3]$, where $add_x(y) = x + y$. This list of functions has type `[Int → Int]`, so this represents an operation "in the context". The infix `<*>`

operation then applies this list of functions to the argument [4,5,6], that is also in the context.

A.3 MONADS

Referential transparency is often cited as an important aspect of functional programming, supporting the simple form of equational reasoning described in Sect. A.1. However, stateful computation is still a useful idiom for many applications. We saw in Sect. A.1 how state could be modelled in functional languages as an infinite stream of values. In practice, it would clearly be unreasonable to explicitly construct these streams of values for every stateful variable. Instead, one would want to store the current value of the variable in a single location and overwrite that location each time the value is updated. The problem is that, because of the stream-based representation of a variable's states, the compiler must by default assume that such values are persistent, in the sense that the implementation maintains a complete history of the variable's past states, because the application may make backwards reference to these earlier values. Removing this default assumption will require a careful analysis by the compiler that the variable is being used in a single-threaded fashion, where no reference is made to the variable's previous values. The handling of state explicitly by the program also makes for a clumsy programming style, where the state must be provided as an explicit input to a side-effecting expression, and the updated state returned as part of the result of that expression. For example, a function that logs its actions must take the log state as an explicit argument, and return the updated log state in its output:

```
f :: Int → Log → (Int, Log)
f x log = let newLog = logappend log "I did something"
              result = …
          in (result, newLog)
```

Here, we are returning two values as a tuple—a convenient way of combining values with different types into a single value. In this case, the return tuple contains both a result value and an updated log. The problem is that there is no way to prevent a reference to the original value of the log, even after this function is called, so the log must be stored in a persistent manner where reference can still be made to earlier versions.

A monad is a structuring mechanism for effectful computations that retains referential transparency while enforcing the discipline that ensures that side-effected values are used in a single-threaded fashion. Monads are so critical to Haskell that it provides a special syntax for monadic computation and, using this (with the appropriate form of monad LogM), the above computation may be expressed as:

```
f :: Int → LogM Int
f x = do logappend "I did something"
         result ← …
         return result
```

A monad can be viewed as a generalization of the functors and applicatives considered in the previous section. Functors provide a way for injecting computations into a context, such as the Maybe context for error-handling and the list context for nondeterministic computation. Applicatives provide a way for applying a function already in a context to values in the same context. A monad provides a way of *sequencing* computations in a context; this is particularly important for side-effecting operations where the order in which the operations are performed is significant for application semantics. As with functor and applicative functors, monads can be defined as instances of a type class:

```
class Monad m where
   return :: a → m a
   >>= :: m a → (a → m b) → m b
   ...
```

The return operation is, like the pure operation for applicatives, a way to inject values into a context. The other operation of interest is the "bind" operation, >>= . One can consider it as a kind of sequential composition, sequencing its right operand as a computation to be executed after its left operand computation is finished. The right computation, sometimes referred to as the "continuation" of the left computation, takes the result value of the left computation as an input. There is also a variant on the >>= operator that ignores the result value from the left computation:

```
>> :: m a → m b → m b
```

As with functors, monads provide a context around a computation. It is the inability of computations to escape that context that provides the discipline for ensuring the correct single-threaded handling of state.

A standard example of a monad for these purposes is the state monad. We define a representation of a stateful computation as a mapping from an input state to a pair of a result value and an updated state:[8]

```
data State s a = State (s → (a,s))
```

Then we can define an instance of the Monad class for the State(s) type, polymorphic in the actual underlying representation of state, s:

```
instance Monad (State s) where
   return x = State skip where skip s = (x, s)
   left >>= right = State run
                    where runs = let State runLeft = left
                                     (x, s') = runLeft s
                                     State runRight = right x
                                 in runRight s'
```

---

[8]Technically, Haskell defines this type as a newtype—a special form of algebraic datatype where there is only a single data constructor. The compiler uses this fact about newtype to avoid the overhead of tagging and untagging values associated with algebraic datatypes.

The composition operator builds a new computation that, given an input state, runs the left computation to produce a result value and updated state, then runs the right computation on this result and updated state.

The do syntax for Haskell is defined in terms of this type class, where statements in a do-block are assumed to be composed using the >>= or >> operators, and values are implicitly injected into statements using the return operator. The particular instances of >>= , >>, and return are resolved based on the monad representation type. For example, we can define the representation for the state of a pseudo-random number generator simply as a floating point value. We can then define an operation for accessing this state in the monad:

```
randGen :: (State Float) Float
randGen = State run
          where run s = let n = rand s
                         in (n, n)
```

The state is treated as the seed for the next random number that is generated. The randGen function returns the new random number as the updated seed and as the next random number for the application:

```
appl :: (State Float) String
appl = do n1 ← randGen
          n2 ← randGen
          return "Done"
```

The bindings of n1 and n2 correspond to implicit uses of the >>= operation to compose computations. A stateful computation is run by providing an initial seed value for the state and extracting the final result value at the end:

```
exec :: (State s a) → s → a
exec monad init =  let State run = monad
                        (x, last) = run init
                    in  x
```

Input-output is organized in a similar fashion, with the provision of the IO monad and operations for reading and writing "in the monad":

```
putStrLn :: String → IO ()
getLine :: IO String
main = putStrLn "What's your name?"
       name ← getLine
       putStrLn "Hello, " ++ name
```

The IO monad is defined as a variant on the state monad, effectively:

```
data IO a = IO (World → (a, World))
```

where World is an abstract type representing the state of the world and only accessible through the operations of the IO monad. The main program should be a function of type IO(T), for some T, and the Haskell run-time system initializes the monad appropriately.

The list [] and Maybe type constructors also define monads. Rather than show this directly, we show how functors and applicatives can be defined in terms of monads. First, we quickly note that there is a suggestive similarity between the type of the monadic binding operation and the types of the map and apply operations for functors and applicatives, respectively, where =<< is the same as >>= but with the order of the parameters reversed:

```
fmap  :: (Functor f) ⇒ (a → b) → f a → f b
(<*>) :: (Applicative f) ⇒ f (a → b) → f a → f b
(=<<) :: (Monad m) ⇒ (a → m b) → m a → m b
```

The monadic equivalent of the functorial mapping operation is defined as a lifting operation, lifting "pure" functions into a monad:

```
liftM :: (Monad m) ⇒ (a → b) → m a → m b
liftM f run = do  x ← run
                  return (f x)
```

The monadic equivalent of the applicative operation for applying a computation "reifies" the underlying pure function into the base computation:

```
ap :: (Monad m) ⇒ m (a → b) → m a → m b
ap runf run = do f ← runf
                 x ← run
                 return (f x)
```

The monadic composition operation is more useful than the applicative operation because the former allows new computations to be defined in terms of the results of preceding computations, whereas the latter just allows the definition of the operation as a pure function that is then lifted into the monad.

Returning to the example of logging mentioned at the beginning of this section, we can define a monad for logging as follows:

```
data LogM a = LogM a [String]
instance Monad LogM where
   return x = LogM x []
   left >>= right = let LogM x logLeft = left
                        LogM y logRight = right x
                    in  LogM y (logLeft ++ logRight)

logappend :: String → LogM ()
logappend x = LogM () [x]
```

We could have structured this as a state monad, as suggested by the explicit log passing in the example at the beginning of this section. For variety, we have instead structured it as a monad where log entries are implicitly returned as part of inter-mediate results, and appended where computations are composed. The list append operation results in an inefficient implementation of logging. A more efficient alter-native would use a state monad and extend logs by inserting log entries at the front of the log. Nevertheless, this form of log serves to illustrate a further generalization: rather than assuming that the log is a list of strings, we can generalize it to an arbitrary monoid.[9] This can be specified using another standard type class:

```
class Monoid m where
    mempty m :: m
    mappend :: m → m → m
    mconcat :: [m] → m
    mconcat = foldr mappend mempty
```

The list type is easily seen to define a monoid:

```
instance Monoid [a] where
    mempty = []
    mappend x y = x ++ y
```

Haskell defines a Writer monad for logging, that allows the log to be any monoid:

```
data Writer w a = Writer w a
instance Monoid w ⇒ Monad (Writer w) where
    return x = Writer mempty x
    left >>= right =  let Writer leftLog x = left
                          Writer rightLog y = right x
                      in  Writer (mappend leftLog rightLog) y

logappend :: Monoid (m a) ⇒ a → Writer (m a) ()
logappend x = Writer (mconcat [x]) ()
```

Finally, just as functors and applicatives must satisfy certain laws that the programmer should verify, an instance of the Monad type class should satisfy the following properties:

$$(\text{return } v) \gg= f = f(v)$$

$$f \gg= F = f \text{ where } F(x) = (\text{return } x)$$

$$(f \gg= g) \gg= h = f \gg= F$$

$$\text{where } F(x) = (g(x) \gg= h)$$

These laws state that the return operator defines the left and right identities for monadic computation, and that composition of monadic computations is associative. The reader will note that this is the third time that we have seen this set of properties specified in this appendix.

---

[9]A monoid is a concept from abstract algebra. It consists of a set of values, the *carrier set*, and a binary operation ($\cdot$) satisfying the following properties:

1. The operation is associative: $a \cdot (b \cdot c) = (a \cdot b) \cdot c$.
2. There is an operation id that is the identity for the operation: $id \cdot a = a \cdot id = a$ for any a.

A.4 FURTHER READING

The Haskell Web site `http://www.haskell.org` contains a wealth of materials on Haskell, including open source implementations, such as the Glasgow Haskell compiler (GHC), online tutorials, and pointers to books on Haskell.

REFERENCES

1. Lipovaca M. Learn you a Haskell for great good! No Starch Press; 2011.
2. Darlington J. and Reeve MJ. ALICE: A Multiple-Processor Reduction Machine for the Parallel Evaluation of Applicative Languages. In *Functional Programming and Computer Architecture (FPCA)*, Arvind and Dennis J (editors). ACM, New York, NY, pages 65–76, 1981.
3. Church A. The Calculi of Lambda Conversion. Princeton: Princeton University Press; 1941. Reprinted by University Microfilms Inc., Ann Arbor MI, 1963.
4. Landin PJ. The correspondence between Algol 60 and Church's lambda notation. *Communications of the ACM* 1965; 8: 89–101, 158–165.
5. Dean J, Ghemawat S. Mapreduce: Simplified data processing on large clusters. In: Operating Systems Design and Implementation (OSDI). 2004.
6. Burge WH. Stream processing functions. *IBM Journal of Research and Development* 1975: 12–25.
7. O'Neill M. The genuine sieve of eratosthenes. *Journal of Functional Programming* 2008.

Time in Distributed Systems

> Jim Gray once told me that he had heard two different opinions of this paper: that it's trivial and that it's brilliant. I can't argue with the former, and I am disinclined to argue with the latter.
>
> **Leslie Lamport**

B.1 WHAT TIME IS IT?

Any algorithm or protocol for distributed systems requires coordination between the parties that make up that system, including agreement on the points at which critical actions must be taken in the protocol. Time is also a critical aspect of resource usage in an enterprise network, where client reservation of resources on servers is based on leases that expire if they are not renewed with "dirty" messages within the expiration period of the lease. Time is also important for security, for example forming the basis for expiration of authorization certificates such as Kerberos tickets, and preventing replay attacks based on the resending of old protocol messages. Some notion of time is critical to any form of distributed coordination.

In philosophy, there are two views on time. From one point of view, the one we consider in this section, time is a measurable dimension of the physical universe, the so-called "fourth dimension", as popularized by H. G. Wells [1]. It is useful to distinguish two different notions of the correctness of the measurement of time:

1. *Accuracy* refers to degree of divergence of a "correct" clock from an external clock that provides the "true" time. This latter might be Coordinated

Enterprise Software Architecture and Design: Entities, Services, and Resources,
First Edition. Dominic Duggan.
© 2012 John Wiley & Sons, Inc. Published 2012 by John Wiley & Sons, Inc.

Universal Time (UTC), International Atomic Time (TAI) or Global Positioning System (GPS) Time, explained below.

2. *Precision* characterizes the *skew* or difference in time measurements between two devices whose clock readings are sampled at the same instant. Skew may be as a result of the clocks having been initialized with different starting times, or it may be because of differences in the oscillation frequencies of quartz resonators underlying the clocks (*clock drift*), for example.

Accuracy may be the predominant concern in applications such as financial markets, where high-frequency trading relies on microsecond-level timing of transactions. In other applications, such as sensors and actuators, relative agreement on time, and therefore precision, may be more useful than accuracy.

In general, there are three approaches to real-time applications in distributed systems [2]:

1. *Message-based systems* exchange messages across LANs, with timestamps based on the time of message receipt. These timestamps convey information about the state of the system, but latencies in network communication and communication stacks reduce the usefulness of the time information. Historically, enterprise networks have suffered from significant clock skew among the machines on the network, where just variations in heating and cooling may have significant impact on the accuracy of local machine clocks. The Network Time Protocol (NTP), described below, provides support for synchronizing time on a network, but it is, again, subject to variable network latency. Its main application appears to be in timestamping transactions in a distributed system.

2. *Time-slotted systems* constrain application functions to execute to completion in well-defined time slots—effectively a synchronous system where time is divided into time slots that may be fixed or variable in length. Each slot is given a sequence number and events given a timestamp based on the sequence number of the slot in which they occur. Such an approach may be used for control systems in hard, real-time systems, for example in avionics and industrial automation.

3. *Time-based systems* establish a global time scale for all processes in the system based on synchronizing the clocks of the system using a protocol. Typically, a master clock is chosen for the system, to which the other slave clocks synchronize their times. Precision Time Protocol (PTP), also known as IEEE 1588, is an example standard protocol for this purpose.

Today, time is measured precisely using atomic clocks. The international definition of a second of time, the SI second, is based on the time taken for a cesium atom to transition between two ground states. This transition is associated with a photon of frequency 9,192,631,770 Hz (cycles per second). Time in an atomic clock is measured by exciting cesium atoms with radio frequency (RF) signal and measuring the number of atoms that change state to determine the current frequency.

This provides a current accuracy of ± 1 second of drift every 100 million years. More recently, optical clocks based on quantum logic have been able to achieve accuracy in the range of ± 1 second every 3.7 billion years [3]. By comparison, a typical quartz oscillator has an accuracy of about $\pm \frac{1}{2}$ second every day, although techniques are available to reduce this error to one second per year [4]. TAI is a coordinated measurement of atomic time based on taking the average of about 200 atomic clocks around the planet, compared using GPS and high-precision time transfer protocols. The time measurements from the clocks are adjusted to make them correspond to time measurements at mean sea level (the Earth's geoid). This is done to account for relativistic effects from clocks at different altitudes and reflects the fine accuracy of the time measurements involved. The international standard for time, UTC, is a compromise between the precise measurement of time provided by atomic clocks and the imprecise measure of time based on the Earth's rotation (the latter is subject to significant speed-ups and slow-downs). The two are reconciled by basing the definition of time on the cesium atom, but incorporating leap seconds periodically to reconcile the atomic definition of time with Earth time (Greenwich Mean Time).

UTC time is not available in real time, so applications requiring a precise measurement of time will instead rely on systems that are periodically calibrated with respect to this global notion of time. A popular choice is GPS. The design of the latter requires at least 24 satellites in space orbit, such that at any given time four satellites are in range of an Earth-bound device (provided there are no physical obstacles such as tall buildings). In practice, there is now sufficient redundancy in the system to ensure 6–12 satellites are in line of sight at any given time for GPS devices. Each satellite carries atomic clocks for precise time measurement, with these clocks periodically calibrated to TAI via signals from ground stations. For historical reasons, GPS time differs from TAI by 19 seconds. A satellite broadcasts a signal with a timestamp. Upon receiving this signal, a receiver can compare the timestamp with its own time and thereby compute its position on the surface of a sphere radiating from the satellite. Knowing the positions of the satellites at the time they broadcast their signals, and intersecting the spheres radiating from at least three satellites, the receiver can determine their own location in three dimensions. In practice, most mobile devices do not yet come equipped with atomic clocks, so errors in time measurement on the receiver must be accounted for. The error on the receiver introduces an extra unknown quantity, hence the need for a fourth satellite. There is further uncertainty owing to frequency-dependent delay in signal propagation in the ionosphere. This is factored out for military applications by transmitting high bandwidth encrypted signals on two different frequencies and measuring the differences. As satellites can be obscured in urban environments, Assisted GPS (AGPS) requires at least one satellite in line of sight; the cellular phone network provides the additional information, obtained from other satellites, to determine the position of a mobile telephone. Differential GPS systems such as Maritime GPS and the Wide Area Augmentation System (WAAS) use information from stationary ground positions (e.g., lighthouses) to improve the accuracy and reliability of the GPS navigational data, correcting for errors in GPS data by comparing it with known location information for the ground stations. The GPS measurement of UTC time is accurate to within about 14 nanoseconds (with corrections for UTC time provided as part of the GPS signal) [4]. However, it takes considerably longer to retrieve that time information from the GPS receiver. Nevertheless, times with accuracy counted in microseconds are possible on stock hardware and software, while specialized GPS receivers can report UTC time with an accuracy of about 50 nanoseconds.

GPS provides a global measure of time that may be incorporated into distributed systems by placing a host with a GPS receiver on a local network. Other protocols are available for obtaining measurements of the current time over the network. The NTP [5] is a protocol and network service for estimating the current time based on measurements with confidence intervals gathered from several sources; so-called stratum 1 sources are connected to *reference clocks* (atomic clocks and GPS receivers). The protocol on a stratum $n+1$ server polls several stratum n time sources, obtaining time estimates with confidence intervals based on statistical sampling of the time source and comparison with other sources. These estimates define confidence intervals for the current time that may not all overlap. The underlying algorithm for the protocol computes the best estimate of the time to be the one with the smallest confidence interval, consistent with the largest number of sources, filtering out sources that are clearly out of sync (i.e., seconds, or, in one case, years out of sync with the actual time). It can achieve accuracy in the milliseconds (up to 100ms) range over the Internet and in the microseconds-to-hundreds of microseconds range in a LAN under ideal conditions. Clearly, these estimates are highly dependent on factors such as network load and latency.

The PTP (IEEE 1588) is a protocol intended to achieve sub-microsecond time accuracy in a LAN [2]. There are several kinds of clocks in the system: *grandmaster clocks* determine the time that the other clocks calibrate to. Typically, such a clock is connected to a local GPS receiver and is selected by the "best master clock" algorithm in the protocol. The PTP protocol organizes the nodes in a LAN into a minimum spanning tree, as depicted in Fig. B.1, with the grandmaster clock at the root of the tree and *ordinary clocks* at the leaves of the tree. The intermediate clocks in the spanning tree are referred to as *boundary clocks*.

Any communication link in the spanning tree is a unicast or multicast link with a master (e.g., the grandmaster at the root) and one or more slaves (e.g., an ordinary clock at a leaf). The slave devices synchronize their clocks with that of the master. A boundary clock has one slave link (along the path to the grandmaster clock at the root of the spanning tree) and one or more master links to clocks who synchronize their time with that boundary. The boundary clocks are central to the PTP design; they are intended to ensure predictable latency between clocks so they may be typically implemented as part of switches that multiplex ports between normal and time-message traffic. In addition, *transparent clocks* may modify time messages in transit to adjust for communication delays on long communication paths on the network. Because of the tight accuracy required, timestamp generation and detection is best implemented low in the communications stack, perhaps in Ethernet link controllers. Nevertheless, PTP may be implemented high in the

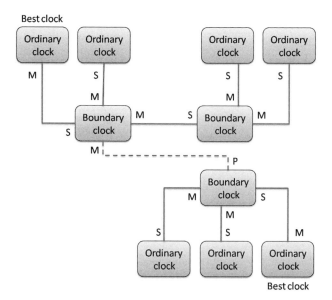

Figure B.1   *PTP spanning tree*

stack, although queueing, scheduling, and interrupt handling introduce variability in latency.

If there is more than one grandmaster clock, i.e., more than one clock connected to a GPS receiver, PTP partitions the spanning tree into multiple trees with distinct grandmaster roots. This is obviously a problem if a grandmaster clock or a communication link in the tree fails. The protocol does not yet consider failure redundancy, either in communication links or in a primary-backup arrangement for the grandmaster clock. The Flooding Time Synchronization Protocol (FTSP) is a high precision time protocol for wireless networks [6] that handles link and node failures by flooding a network with timestamps from a root time server.

All of these protocols for obtaining the time over the network rely on the client receiving an estimate of the current time from a time server. Obviously the actual time will depend not just on the timestamp for the response received from the server, but also the delay in relaying that response from the server back to the client. In general, there are four sources of delay in this communication: *send time* (the time taken for the sender to construct the request message); *access time* (the time taken to access the network, e.g. on a broadcast network such as Ethernet or 802.11); *propagation time* (the time taken for the message to propagate through the network to the time server); and *receive time* (the time taken for the receiver to unmarshall the request message). Furthermore, there may be random *jitter* associated with these quantities, such as the effects of interrupt handling on the network stack; some of this jitter may be in the order of hundreds of milliseconds. Jitter may be accounted for by placing timestamps on the messages at the medium access control (MAC) layer, at both the sending and receiving sides, when messages are put on the network and when they are taken off the network [7]. A least squares linear regression analysis may be used to account for clock drift on the local machine clocks to provide high precision on these timestamps. There remains the propagation delay to account for in estimating the actual time based on a time message received from a reference time server. A typical approach is for the nodes to organize themselves into a spanning tree, with nodes requesting the current time from their parent node. Figure B.2 illustrates the traditional *sender-receiver* protocol: a client contacts a parent node in this spanning tree and uses various time stamps to compute the time based on the response from the root node. Let θ denote the clock offset between the nodes, (the difference between the clocks at the two sites), and let δ denote the propagation delay. If a client sends a time request at time t_1, then it is received at the parent node at time $t_2 = t_1 + \theta + \delta$. If the parent node sends its response at time t_3, it is received at the client at time $t_4 = t_3 - \theta + \delta$. Then, the client can compute:

$$\delta = \frac{(t_4 - t_1) - (t_3 - t_2)}{2}$$

$$\theta = \frac{(t_2 - t_1 + \delta) - (t_3 - t_4 + \delta)}{2} = \frac{(t_2 - t_1) + (t_4 - t_3)}{2}.$$

These calculations assume that the uplink and downlink delays are the same. However, there may be (and typically is) *path asymmetry* along the communication path between client and server, such that the "uplink" and "downlink" speeds are different, as suggested in Fig. B.2. The NTP protocol assumes that path asymmetry is not significant enough to cause noticeable problems. The PTP protocol includes a message exchange to measure these uplink and downlink speeds between slave and master. However, without information about the clock offset between the two device, there is not enough information to solve for these quantities. Therefore the default assumption is that the two delays are the same. Calibration of a carefully

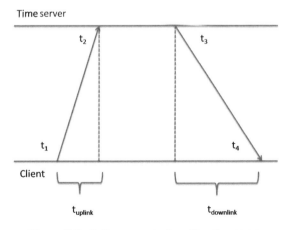

Figure B.2 *Path asymmetry in polling time server*

engineered network may adjust for actual uplink and downlink speeds, although it is also possible that the delays may vary over time.

An alternative to polling the time server and computing the phase offset from the response, is to have a single time source broadcast a timestamp to all clients [8, 9]. With this *reference beacon* approach, clients compute their own difference from this central time source by recording the difference between their own local time and the server time. Two clients that are communicating peer-to-peer can then determine their phase offset relative to each other by comparing their relative differences from the server.

Once a node has received an accurate time measurement from a time source, it cannot simply set its local clock time to that measurement as that may set the clock back on the system. This would certainly be beneficial for attackers trying to stage replay attacks, for example, but would otherwise be undesirable. Even discontinuous jumps forward in time can confuse application programs. Instead, assuming that the rate of clock drift is constant, which may not be an unreasonable assumption over a short period of time, clocks can be adjusted gradually using a compensating clock drift. For example, if a node detects a clock drift of 100 ms in the last minute, it can adjust with a compensating clock drift of −200 ms for the next minute to align its clock with the master clock [10].

B.2   TIME AND CAUSALITY

In the previous section, we considered Newtonian time in distributed systems. This view assumes that space and time are absolute quantities that can be measured using the techniques previously described. Leibniz [11], to some extent anticipating Einstein's Special Theory of Relativity, argued against Newton's view of absolute space and time. Instead, he argued for these as "imaginary" concepts that the mind creates in order to organize observations of the physical universe. Thus, the absolute position in space of an object is not important because space does not "really" exist in the absence of objects occupying that space. Instead, what is important is the position of the object as perceived by an observer. Similarly, the time at which an event occurs is not important, rather what is important is the relative order of events with respect to each other. Nor did Leibniz consider causation as anything more than an imaginary concept, emphasizing instead the "pre-established harmony" between substances (Leibniz's "monads"). Kant argued for time and space as "transcendent ideals", as ways that the mind organized the physical world but, in contrast to Leibniz, he does not agree that notions of space and time are simply imaginary concepts of the mind. It is impossible for the human mind to make sense of physical observations without a priori notions of space and time to organize those observations, for example via notions of simultaneity and of events occurring before other events. It is not possible to understand the objects of the "real world" independent of spatiotemporal experience. However, this experience is not simply an artifact of the mind. Rather, this spatiotemporal context is part of the forms of the empirical objects and, indeed, it is the only way that the mind can experience these objects.

The "relativistic" notion of time has an honored tradition in distributed systems. In particular, notions of time based on causation have played an important role in the design and implementation of distributed systems, for example, in debugging, replication, and version control. The fundamental concept underlying these notions of time is the *happened-before relation*. Before explaining this relation, we review some basic definitions. An *ordering* is a pair $(A, \leq_A)$ where A is a set of elements and $\leq_A$ is a binary relation over A, i.e., $\leq_A$ is a subset of $A \times A$. We write $a \leq_A b$ if $(a, b) \in \leq_A$. The ordering is *total* if it satisfies the following properties:

1. *(Antisymmetry)* If $a \leq_A b$ and $b \leq_A a$, then $a = b$.
2. *(Totality)* For all $a, b \in A$, either $a \leq_A b$ or $b \leq_A a$.
3. *(Transitivity)* If $a \leq_A b$ and $b \leq_A c$ then $a \leq_A c$ for all $a, b, c \in A$.

An ordering is *partial* if it is transitive and reflexive, i.e., $a \leq_A a$ for all $a \in A$. Reflexivity weakens totality, so any total ordering is also a partial ordering, but not vice versa. A relation is a *pre-order* or irreflexive partial order if it is transitive but not reflexive and therefore asymmetric. We often denote the underlying pre-order for a partial order $\leq_A$, obtained by removing reflexivity, as $<_A$.

We assume a collection of n sequential processes, executing in parallel and communicating via message-passing. There is a notion of events within a process occurring on a sequential timeline so that an event at a process is preceded in time by all the events that have already happened before that event occurs. In addition, if one of the events that precedes an event e corresponded to the receipt of a message, then e is preceded by all the events that occurred at the sender up to, and including, the sending of the message itself. Formally, we define the relation of "a happened before b", denoted a⇝b for events a and b, as follows:

1. *(Local ordering)* If event a occurs immediately before event b on the timeline for the same sequential process, then a⇝b.
2. *(Distributed ordering)* If a is the event of a message m being sent and b is the event of that message being received at the destination where we assume that messages are uniquely identified, then a⇝b.
3. *(Transitivity)* Finally, if a⇝b and b⇝c, then a⇝c.

If a does not happen before b, nor does b happen before a, denoted a⇝̸b and b⇝̸a, then we say that these two events are *concurrent*, denoted a∥b. The happened-before relation obviously defines a pre-order over events.

Figure B.3 provides an example timeline involving four processes, X, Y, Z, and W. On the timeline for the Z process, for example, we have G⇝H, H⇝I, I⇝J, J⇝K and K⇝L. By transitivity, we have G⇝L. In addition, we have A⇝C and D⇝G as a result of the messages sent from X to Y and from Y to Z, respectively. By transitivity again, we have A⇝G, and then again by transitivity we have A⇝L. This reflects a causal chain from the sending of the message at event A to the sending of a message back to X at event L. Notice, on the other hand, that L⇝̸F and F⇝̸L, as neither of these events causally precedes the other. We certainly have

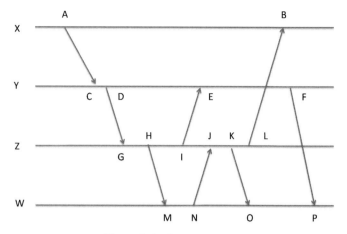

Figure B.3 *Example timeline*

a common causal ancestor for these two message-passing events. Event I, where process Z sends a message to Y, causally precedes the sending of the message at event F (which succeeds the sending of the message at I), so I⤳F. As it happens on the same internal timeline as event L, event I also precedes event L, where process Z sends a message to X, so I⤳L. However, there is no causal relationship between F and L, so these are concurrent events, F ‖ L.

We seek an implementation of this happened-before relation based on mapping events to timestamps that are ordered according to the relation. Let TIME denote the timestamp assigned by this algorithm to event e, then we may require the following properties:

1. *(Completeness)* If a⤳b, then TIME(a)<TIME(b).
2. *(Accuracy)* If TIME(a)<TIME(b), then a⤳b.

An implementation of clocks that satisfies completeness is said to satisfy the *Clock Condition*. An implementation of clocks that satisfies both completeness and accuracy is said to satisfy the *Strong Clock Condition*.

The first algorithm we consider is the *logical time* protocol introduced by Lamport [12]. The idea of this protocol is to represent time at a process as a count of the number of events that have happened at that process. We are only considering message send and receive events, but internal events might also be included. As some processes may be more active in message exchanges than others, some processes' local clocks may fall behind over time. Once a "slow" process receives a communication from another process whose clock has advanced beyond their own clock, the clock of the slow process is advanced up to that of the faster process before its clock is incremented to record the message receipt event.

A description of this protocol is provided in Fig. B.4. "Clocks" are simply (double precision) integer counters, with one counter per process. Each process is identified by a process identifier, an internal variable `pid` that is initialized when

```
public class LClock {
   private long counter = 0;
   public long tick() { counter++; return counter; }
   public void advance(long timestamp) {
      counter = max(counter,timestamp);
   }
}
public class Message {
   public int pid; // sender pid
   public long timestamp;
   public String payload;
   public Message (int p, long ts, String s) {
      pid = pid; timestamp = ts; payload = s;
   }
}
public class Process {
   private int pid;
   private LClock clock = new LClock();
   public Process (int pid) { this.pid = pid; }
   public void sendMessage(String payload) {
      long timestamp = clock.tick();
      Message message = new Message(pid, timestamp, payload);
      … send the message …
   }
public String receiveMessage() {
   Message message = … receive the message …
   clock.advance(message.timestamp);
   clock.tick();
   return message.payload;
   }
}
```

Figure B.4   *Logical clocks protocol*

a process is created. Messages have timestamps associated with them and are uniquely identified by their timestamp and the process ID of the sending process. The operation for sending a message increments the logical clock for the sending process and adds the resulting clock value as the timestamp associated with the message. The operation for receiving a message first updates the local clock on the receiver in case its clock has fallen behind that of the sender. The receiver's clock is then incremented.

Figure B.5 provides an example of the application of the protocol in Fig. B.4 to the example in Fig. B.3. At various points in the algorithm, the clock at a process is advanced upon receipt of a message from another process whose logical clock is further ahead. For example, when process X eventually receives a reply back from Z (event B), its local clock still just records the initial sending of a message to Y (event A); process X has been oblivious to the messages being exchanged between the other processes. Therefore, the protocol advances the logical clock of X from 1 to the timestamp on the message (10, reflecting the logical time at the sending process Z when the message was sent); the clock at X is then incremented to record the message receipt event.

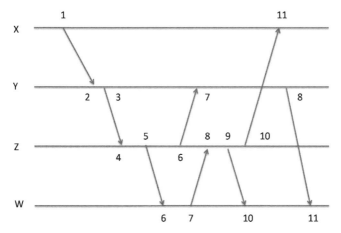

Figure B.5   *Logical time example*

Let $LT(e)$ denote the logical time computed for an event e according to the protocol. It is not hard to verify that the protocol is a complete representation of the happened-before relation: if a↝b, then $LT(a) < LT(b)$. We verify this by induction on the proof that a↝b. The cases for local and distributed ordering are easy to verify ($LT(a) < LT(b)$ in both cases after the algorithm has been executed); the case for transitivity follows using induction.

On the other hand, logical time does not satisfy the strong clock condition: logical time is a complete representation of causality, but may not be accurate. Consider, for example, events L and F in Fig. B.3. These two events have a common causal ancestor, event I: $LT(I) = 5 < 8 = LT(F)$ and $LT(I) = 5 < 10 = LT(L)$. However, we also have $LT(F) = 8 < 10 = LT(L)$ but, as we have seen, these two events are concurrent: F ∥ L. The ordering on the integers is a total ordering and, in particular, for any two integers m and n, either $m \le n$ or $n \le m$. However, the causal ordering on events is a pre-order and, in particular, there is no ordering defined between concurrent events. Therefore, the representation of time in the logical clocks protocol means that the algorithm does not provide an accurate representation of happened-before. Instead, it is representing *potential causality* between events. This is the result of a deliberate decision in the design of logical time to impose a total ordering on what are otherwise partially-ordered events (the reflexive closure of the happened-before pre-order). This total ordering is critical for certain applications that involve ordering messages by timestamp, as we see in the next section. In other applications, this ordering may induce unnecessary delays, as we also explain in the next section.

Another version of algorithmic clocks provides an accurate measure of causality. This is the notion of *vector time* [13–15]. The idea is to represent "time" as a vector of n elements—one element for each process. For a given time, the ith element of the vector records the events at the ith process that have occurred by that time. So, we have a vector of sets of events. This is clearly going to be a very large timestamp, but there is a simple optimization. We do not need to record all of the events that have occurred at each process: it suffices to record the *number* of events at each process in the timestamp. The timestamp now becomes a vector of integers, that records for an event exactly how many events have transpired at each process before this event happened. This provides a complete and accurate characterization of the causal history of an event. Let $VT(e)$ denote the vector time associated with the event e, where e is an event at the ith process. Then we have the following interpretation of the components of this vector timestamp:

1. If $VT(e)[i] = k$, then e is the kth event to occur at the ith process.
2. If $VT(e)[j] = k$, where $i \neq j$, then the event e is causally preceded by k events at the jth process.

Figure B.6 provides the protocol for vector timestamps, modeled after the logical timestamps protocol in Fig. B.4. The clock in each process, and the timestamp on each message, is generalized from a single integer counter to an array of counters. When a message is sent, the `tick` method for vector clocks increments the counter component for the current process, reflecting that the ith component of any such timestamp reflects the number of events at the ith process; therefore, it is only the ith process that increments the ith component of the timestamp. As in the logical clocks protocol, receipt of a message causes the receiver to advance each component of its vector clock up to that reflected in the timestamp in the message. Again, this reflects the situation where some parts of the vector clock have fallen behind because the receiver is not aware of some of the communications between other processes. Note that, unlike the logical clock protocol, the vector clock is not incremented on receipt of a message, so the vector clocks only count "send" events. This is not an essential aspect of vector clocks, but reflects the kinds of applications one sees for them, as explained in the next section. It is relatively easy to verify that the vector clock protocol is a complete and accurate implementation of the happened-before relation. For completeness, as for logical time, the verification is by induction on the derivation of a⤳b. For accuracy, the verification is by induction on the steps in the execution of the processes.

An example of the application of the vector clock protocol is provided in Fig. B.7. As we are not counting message receive events (only send events) in this protocol, the only change of the vector clock on the receipt of a message is based on advancing the vector clock to reflect components of the clock that had fallen behind that of the sender. We need to also define the notion of the ordering on vector times:

Assume $VT(a)$ and $VT(b)$ are both vector timestamps of length n. Then $VT(a) \leq VT(b)$ if, for all $0 \leq i < n$, $VT(a)[i] \leq VT(b)[i]$. Furthermore, $VT(a) < VT(b)$ if $VT(a) \leq VT(b)$ and $VT(a) \neq VT(b)$. Equivalently, $VT(a) < VT(b)$ if $VT(a) \leq VT(b)$ and $VT(a)[i] < VT(b)[i]$ for some $0 \leq i < n$.

For example, $(1,1,0) < (1,2,0)$ since $1 < 2$, and $(0,1,0) < (1,2,2)$, but $(0,1,2)$ and $(1,2,0)$ are incomparable: the former is smaller on the first and second components

```
public class VClock {
   private int pid, nProcs;
   private long[] counter;
   public VClock (int p, int n) {
      pid = p; nProcs = n; counter = new long[n];
      for (int i=0; i<n; i++) counter[i] = 0;
   }
   public long[] tick() {
      counter[pid]++; return counter;
   }
   public void advance(long[] timestamp) {
      for (int i=0; i++; i< nProcs)
         counter[i] = max(counter[i], timestamp[i]);
   }
}
public class Message {
   public int pid; // sender pid
   public long[] timestamp;
   public String payload;
   public Message (int p, long[] ts, String s) {
      pid = pid; timestamp = ts; payload = s;
   }
}
public class Process {
   private int pid;
   private VClock clock;
   public Process (int n, int p) {
      clock = new VClock(nProcs); pid = p;
   }
   public void sendMessage(String payload) {
      long[] timestamp = clock.tick();
      Message message = new Message(pid, timestamp, payload);
      … send the message …
   }
   public String receiveMessage() {
      Message message = … receive the message …
      clock.advance(message.timestamp);
      clock.tick();
      return message.payload;
   }
}
```

Figure B.6   *Vector clocks protocol*

of the vector timestamp, but the latter is smaller on the third component of the vector timestamp In other words, the ordering $\leq$ on vector timestamps is a partial order, not a total order. In the example in Fig. B.7, we see that $VT(L) \not< VT(F)$ and $VT(F) \not< VT(L)$, since $1<2$ on the second component of the timestamp, but $2<4$ on the third component. This incomparability between the vector timestamps is entirely to be expected, as the underlying events are concurrent and incomparable under causal ordering.

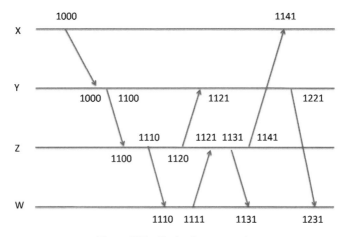

Figure B.7 *Vector time example*

B.3 APPLICATIONS OF LOGICAL AND VECTOR TIME

B.3.1 Mutual Exclusion

The first application that was originally considered for logical time was distributed mutual exclusion, ensuring that no more than one process at a time is using a shared resource. A key condition for the mutual exclusion algorithm is that requests to gain access to the resource are granted in the order in which they are made. As there is no assumption of physical time, the order of requests is based on logical timestamps associated with requests. As it is possible for two different processes to issue requests with the same logical timestamp, process identifiers are used to break these ties, so timestamps on requests are pairs (k,p), where k is a logical timestamp and p a process ID. The ordering on timestamps is defined as: $(k,p) < (m,q)$ if $k < m$, or if $k = m$ and $p < q$. The process IDs in the timestamps are only used to break ties.

Each process maintains, in addition to its logical clock, a local queue of requests, ordered by timestamp. Each process also maintains an array of timestamps, where the ith element of the array is the logical time on the last message received from the ith process. Implicitly in what follows, a process sets the ith value of this array to k, when it receives a message with timestamp k from process i. We assume first in, first out (FIFO) channels between all processes.

1. To request the resource, a process increments its logical clock and then broadcasts a request message to every other process. It adds its request to its own local request queue.
2. A process acknowledges a request message when it is received, including its own logical time with the acknowledgement.
3. When a process has its own request for the resource at the front of its request queue, ordered by request timestamp, and when that process has

received messages from all other processes with timestamps greater than the timestamp on its request, then that process decides that it has mutually exclusive access to the resource.

4. A process releases the resource by sending release messages to every other process and removing its own request from the request queue. The other processes similarly remove the request from their request queue when they receive the release message.

Note that this protocol requires a totally ordered notion of time for sorting the request queue; this is why logical time imposes a total ordering on the happened-before relation. Assuming FIFO delivery of messages along communication channels, a process that has received a message from every other process with a timestamp greater than its current request is guaranteed that there will never be a request with a smaller timestamp. If another process had made a request with a larger timestamp, it will have contacted this process for an acknowledgement, and the FIFO property of the channels ensures that the request of this process will be delivered ahead of the acknowledgement of this process at that process. Therefore, the other process will not attempt to access the shared resource until this process sends it a release message.

B.3.2 Quorum Consensus

Some of the issues with replicating stateful services were considered in Sect. 6.9.2. The "active" approach is to ensure that each service is a deterministic state machine, and that all replicas see the updates in the same order. The replicas may cooperate in a voting protocol to choose the order of the updates. In this section, we consider a protocol to achieve this cooperation [16–18]. Another approach, the "passive" approach, is to have a primary server choose the order of the update operations. We describe a protocol for this strategy at the end of this section.

Figure B.8 provides an example of a voting protocol for active replication. There are three server replicas p, q, and r. These servers replicate a queue that supports Insert and Remove operations. Other operations, such as for example a read-only Peek operation, for viewing the first element of the queue without removing it, may also be provided. We show two clients c_1 and c_2, competing to commit the next operation on the replicated queue. Each of the replicas has logs reflecting the operations that have been committed at those servers in the past. Each log entry has a version number associated with it. We assume the logs in this example have the following contents:

Log of p	Log of q	Log of r
1:Insert(a)	1:Insert(a)	
2:Insert(b)		2:Insert(b)
	3:Insert(c)	3:Insert(c)

The logs reflect that value a was inserted into the queue using a quorum that consisted of p and q, that value b was inserted using a quorum of p and r, and that c was inserted using a quorum of q and r. As a result, none of the replicas has enough information to know what the full state of the queue is. In Fig. B.8, clients c_1 and c_2 (or more precisely frontends for those clients, perhaps distributed as client stubs by the enterprise IT) wish to retrieve the element at the front of the queue, removing that element from the queue in the process. This is supported by an operation called Remove. The clients attempt to contact the servers in order to obtain the current state of the replicated queue, from which items may have been removed by other clients.

We assume that server q has crashed and does not respond to the requests from c_1 and c_2. If we further assume that the read quorum is two, then the clients can still proceed with just the responses from p and r. By merging the logs from p and r, the clients may reconstruct the full state of the queue as:

Merged Log
```
1: Insert(a)
2: Insert(b)
3: Insert(c)
```

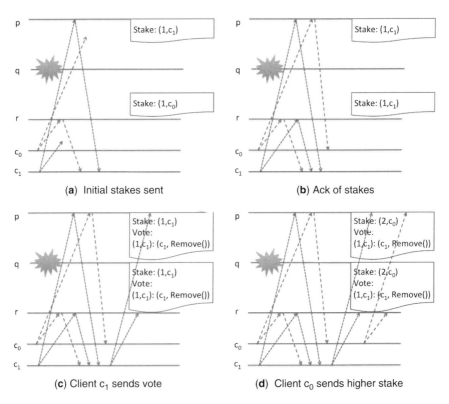

Figure B.8   Ordered updates based on Voting Protocol

Because the client has received logs from a read quorum of servers, it is guaranteed that the write quorum for every update that has been performed on the queue intersects with this quorum. Therefore every update that has been performed on the queue is reflected in the result of merging these logs. From this, the clients are able to determine the value returned by the Remove operation, the element at the front of the queue.

We still have to deal with the issue that both clients are contending to perform distinct Remove() operations on the queue. The contention is resolved in two stages. First, each client proposes a *stake*, a logical timestamp that it proposes for the time of the next update to the queue. The use of logical clocks here is just for a run of the protocol for performing a single update on the shared data, so the clock may be reset for each run of the protocol. The timestamps are different from, and have nothing to do with, the version numbers for the individual updates, which provide a total ordering on the updates that are performed. As different clients may offer the same clock value for requests (because all logical clocks are local), the stake combines the logical timestamp with the client's process id, to break any ties, with stakes ordered lexicographically. When clients contend, the client with the largest stake "wins" the competition for whose update should be voted on next. If a client "loses" this competition, it increments its logical clock and tries again with another stake. There are indeed pathological situations where clients may continually propose higher stakes, by incrementing their logical timestamps, so that no client eventually gets to propose its own update. Some form of non-termination is inevitable, given the proven impossibility of consensus in an asynchronous system. However we can at least say that, with very high probability, one of the clients eventually proceeds to ask for a quorum of the servers to vote for its update as the next update to be performed. Once some of the servers have voted to perform a particular update next, the other contending clients will cooperate to have that update committed, before attempting to have their own update performed after it (by starting again with a new run of the stake protocol).

In Fig. B.8(**a**), clients c_0 and c_1 have proposed stakes $(1,c_0)$ and $(1,c_1)$ at servers r and p, respectively. In Fig. B.8(**b**), the stakes proposed by c_0 and c_1 are received at p and r, respectively. Server p remains committed to c_1's stake, while server r increments the stake it is committed to, to that of c_1. Client c_1 will receive a positive reply for a quorum of p and r, that have accepted its stake, while client c_0 must try again with a larger stake.

In Fig. B.8(**c**), client c_1 enters the second, "voting" phase, where it seeks to get a quorum of the servers to vote for its own Remove() update (paired with the client's id to distinguish it from c_0's update). Once a quorum of the servers have voted for c_1's update, that becomes the committed operation that defines the next version of the queue. In Fig. B.8(**d**), client c_0 restarts the first phase of the protocol with a larger stake. It has the largest stake at this point, but it learns that some servers have already voted for c_1's update. Therefore c_0 will go ahead and perform the voting phase, but it will ask the servers to vote for c_1's update. Once this is done, c_0 will start another run of the protocol, attempting once more to get a quorum of the servers to commit its own operation, but this time it will try to commit for the next version of the queue.

Why does c_0 go ahead and ask the servers to vote for c_1's update, once it has learned that some of the servers in the quorum have voted for c_1's update? The issue is that c_1 itself may fail before the update is committed at all servers in the quorum. Therefore another client that tries to commit its own update will learn of c_1's update, partially committed, and finalize the commitment of that operation, before trying again to commit its own operation.

We have already considered in Sect. 6.9.2 some of the issues with this approach, in particular the overhead of sending logs to the client to reconstruct the current state of the replicated data object. Figure B.9 demonstrates another protocol for choosing the order of updates, based on a primary server [19]. Each server has an identifying process identifier—the current primary is based on the current view identifier. Figure B.9(a) demonstrates the protocol for performing a client update. The client contacts the primary for the current view. In this case, the current view is view number 2 and the update operation is U_1. The primary chooses a timestamp for this update, based on an internal counter, and combines the current view number and timestamp into a *viewstamp* that uniquely identifies that operation. It then tells the other servers to *prepare* to perform the update with that viewstamp. In this

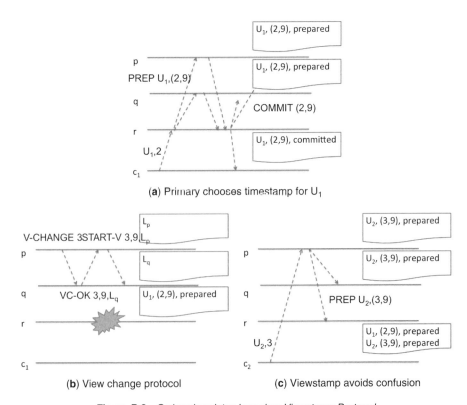

(a) Primary chooses timestamp for U_1

(b) View change protocol

(c) Viewstamp avoids confusion

Figure B.9 *Ordered updates based on Viewstamp Protocol* case, update U_1 is sent to the other servers with viewstamp (2,9). Each server that receives the preparation message, as well as the primary, records the update as one it is prepared to perform in its log once its log contains all the operations that precede the operation being proposed. Once the primary has heard from a quorum of the servers, it is guaranteed that any other quorum will also contain at least one server that is aware of this update. At that point, the primary can write this as a committed operation in its log, respond immediately to the client with the success of the operation, and notify the other replicas that they should also *commit* the operation.[1] Commitment of an operation means that its updates are committed to the state of the replica, or that the operation is performed on the replica, depending on whether replication is active or passive. If we assume that a majority of servers survive failures (in other words, if up to f servers can fail, then there are at least $2f+1$ servers), then the update is guaranteed to survive the failure of some of the servers.

Figure B.9(**b**) gives an example of a *view change* in response to the failure of the primary. When replicas detect the failure of the primary, they initiate the view change protocol, sending their logs to the next primary based on the current view identifier. In this case, p will be the new primary after the failure of node r. It sends a "view change" message to all other servers, in this case proposing the new view identifier of 3. Each replica, on receiving this message, responds with an acknowledgement that, at least abstractly, includes all of the operations that it has in its log.[2] The reason for this log in the reply is that potentially only the old primary knew of all the operations that were performed in the previous view. However, every operation that was committed had a majority vote, so every committed operation is at least prepared among the replicas that respond to the view change message. The new primary must wait for a response from a quorum (including itself) of the replicas, at which point it selects the log that is the longest among its own log and those sent with acknowledgements. This log will have the most recent operations, which the new primary sends back to the other replicas as it notifies them of the view change.

Figure B.9(**c**) demonstrates why the view identifier is included in the unique identifier for every message. This example continues the example in Fig. B.9(**b**), after node p has taken over as the primary. Another client request, for update U_2, is sent to the primary, which then proposes this update to the other servers. Server r is among the replicas, but did not participate in the view change. Furthermore, r has a prepared operation in its log that the other servers were not aware of, with the same timestamp as that chosen by primary p. The view identifier in the viewstamp distinguishes these two update operations in the logs of the servers. As the later operation uses the same logical timestamp as the earlier operation, the earlier prepared operation is not recorded in the new view. Therefore, it can be discarded by process r once it learns of the later operation with the same timestamp.

---

[1]This is not the same as atomic commitment. We explain the difference between consensus and atomic commitment in Sect. 2.3.

[2]More realistically, the replica that responds can include a hash of its log and, if the new primary detects a difference between this hash and its own, the primary and replica can run a separate protocol to determine which operations should be forwarded to the new primary.

This protocol does not require that log entries be written during the sending and acknowledgement of messages during normal processing. A replica that fails can recover its state from the other replicas during a recovery protocol. It broadcasts its current view to the other replicas and waits for the current primary to send it a log that informs it of the operations that it failed to learn of while crashed. This recovery protocol requires that the recovering replica records its current view in non-volatile storage on disk during view changes. This requirement can be removed with a more expensive recovery protocol where the recovering replica polls a majority of the other replicas to learn of the most recent view known among the working replicas. This protocol also requires a "pre-phase" in the view change protocol, where a majority of the replicas agree on the new view identifier before the view change protocol is executed.

The primary-backup protocol considered here assumes reliable failure detection. Without this, it is entirely possible for a process to continue to function as a primary after some of the other replicas have elected a different primary, giving rise to the so-called "split brain" problem where two primaries run simultaneously, with potentially catastrophic results for the correctness of the system. Approaches to dealing with leader election with unreliable failure detection have the same property as the voting protocol considered earlier in this section, that processes may in pathological circumstances contend indefinitely. They are considered in the sequel volume.

B.3.3   Distributed Logging

Our next example involves an application of logical and vector time in distributed logging. Consider the example in Fig. B.10(**a**). Four processes (p, q, r, and s) are logging their events to a monitor process p_0—this latter process is building a log of the execution of the system. The solid lines between processes correspond to application messages that are exchanged, while the dotted lines correspond to notifications of events sent by the processes to the monitor process that is building a debug log. The difficulty is that, because of network delays, some of the notifications arrive at the monitor process out of order. There are two places where log messages are delivered in the wrong order to the monitor:

1. Event B precedes event C at process q, but the notification of C arrives at the monitor before the notification of B. Both notifications are sent by the same process so, in this case, it is relatively easy to ensure that the notifications arrive in the correct order by ensuring a FIFO channel between q and the monitor. This can be done by using a TCP/IP connection for the communication channel, or else using a lighter-weight protocol where sequence numbers are attached to the notifications sent by q.

2. Event E precedes event F, but the notification of F arrives at the monitor before the notification of E. This situation is more problematic because the two notifications are coming from separate processes. Therefore, a FIFO channel such as TCP/IP does not suffice to ensure the correct order of delivery of the notifications. Furthermore, it is important that the notifications be added

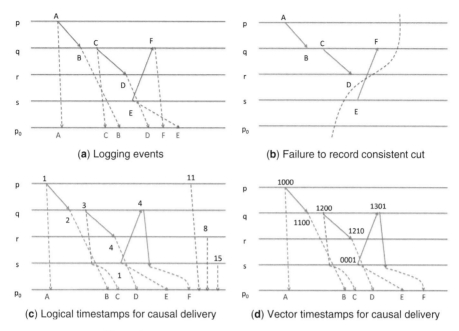

Figure B.10 *Logging distributed events for debugging*

to the log in the correct order as E corresponds to the sending of a message from process s and F corresponds to receipt of that message at process q. By logging the F event before the E event, the monitor is building a *causally inconsistent* log of the system—one where receipt of a message is logged before the sending of the message.

A *cut* is any prefix of the execution histories of the processes being monitored. A *consistent cut* is one that is causally consistent, in the sense that if an event e is in the cut, then any event upon which e causally depends is also in the cut. As shown in Fig. B.10(**b**), if the occurrence of event F is recorded without a record of its causal predecessor E, then the log will contain an inconsistent cut of the system. In this case, this corresponds to a message receipt event F without any record of the message having been sent. In order to ensure that the log always records a consistent cut, we should delay the addition of F to the log until a notification of its causal predecessor is received. This would correspond to shifting the curve for the cut in Fig. B.10(**b**) left to exclude F.

Figure B.10(**c**) shows how this can be done using logical timestamps. The events are given logical timestamps using the algorithm given in Fig. B.4. Now the question is: when is it safe to add a notification message to the log? In general, we only want to add an event notification to the log when we are guaranteed that no causal predecessors will appear later to invalidate the addition of that notification to the log. How do we know that there are no such causal predecessors still possibly in transit? We know that any causal predecessors a of an event e will have logicial clocks $LT(a) < LT(e)$. Furthermore, if we assume FIFO channels between any of the monitored processes and the monitor building the log, then the logical timestamps on the notifications received on each channel are monotonically increasing in value. Therefore, we know it is safe to add event e to the log once we have received event notifications with logical timestamps at least as great as $LT(e)$ on all communications channels. This is depicted in Fig. B.10(**c**), where we know it is safe to add the notification of F to the log once we have received logs of events for events that occur in the "logical future" of F. In fact, it is safe to add event F to the log once we receive the notification of E, but there is no way to tell this from the logical timestamps alone. Instead, we have to wait as depicted in Fig. B.10(**c**).

The problem is that, having received notification of F and then of E, with $LT(E) < LT(F)$, where $LT(E) = 1$ and $LT(F) = 4$, we cannot tell if there are other events in the causal gap between E and F that we do not yet know about. Matters are improved considerably by using vector clocks, which completely characterize causality among the events. Fig. B.10(**d**) provides the same example with vector timestamps on the events. Note that we compute timestamps for both send and receive events, as both are being logged at the monitor process. At the time that the notification of F is received, assume that we have logged events A, B, C, and D. The timestamp on the F event, an event at process q, is $VT(F) = (1, 3, 0, 1)$. The following table summarizes what the process monitor "knows" when it receives the notification of F with this timestamp:

Process	# of preds	Logged events
p	1	A
q	2	B, C
r	0	D
s	1	

The monitor has already logged the causal precessors of F that occurred at p and q. The monitor has logged event D that occurred at process r, although F has no causal precessors at r—this is okay because D is concurrent with F. On the other hand, the vector timestamp records an event at process s that causally precedes F that has not yet been logged. Therefore, the addition of the event F to the log should be delayed until the notification of that event at s has been received. Once sufficient events have been logged from all processes, as specified by the vector timestamp, and with all those events ordering by their vector timestamps, i.e., by their causal histories, we know at that point that it is safe to add the notification to the log. There is no danger of a causally inconsistent log.

B.3.4   Causal Message Delivery

In this section we consider message delivery beyond the logging motivation of the previous subsection. Figure B.11(**a**) describes a scenario where FIFO delivery

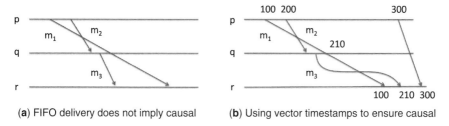

(a) FIFO delivery does not imply causal   **(b)** Using vector timestamps to ensure causal

Figure B.11   *Causal message delivery*

does not ensure causal delivery of messages. Process p sends message m_1 and then message m_2, so m_1 causally precedes m_2. In response to receipt of m_2 at process q, message m_3 is sent. As a result of network delays, this is received at process r before process m_1. This means message delivery will not be causal, as m_3 is received before one of its causal predecessors, m_1, is received. As m_1 and m_3 are sent by separate processes, FIFO channels do not prevent this problem.

Figure B.11(**b**) shows how this problem can be fixed with vector timestamps. Each send event is given a vector timestamp using the algorithm in Fig. B.6. When the message m_3 is received, its vector timestamp is $(2,1,0)$, reflecting that it is causally dependent on two events at process p. However, because we are only considering unicast communication, it is possible that not all of these messages were sent to the current process. Indeed, this is the case: one of the causal predecessors to m_3, the sending of m_2, was directed to process q rather than process r.

Figure B.12(**a**) describes the problems that can arise with using vector times-tamps to ensure causal unicast message ordering. Again, the protocol is only computing vector timestamps for message send events. When the message sent by q is received at s, the vector timestamp records two send events at p, on which it causally depends. One of these message send events was directed at s, the other was not. Therefore, delivery of the message from q is delayed until another message from p is received at s. Figure B.12(**b**) demonstrates a dual situation laid on top of this, where delivery of a message from r to p is delayed until a second message is sent from s to p, for exactly the same reason as before. At this point, p and s are deadlocked, waiting for the other to send another message so they can unblock delivery of messages causally dependent on earlier messages sent by them, but not to each other.

There are two options for dealing with this deadlock. One is to recognize that the problem is with imprecise characterization of causal dependences among messages, and therefore to generalize vector clocks to matrix clocks. Clearly, the space overhead for this will be significant. An alternative is to generalize the communication paradigm from unicast to multicast. Now, whenever a process sends a message, that message is seen by all other processes. This is depicted in Fig. B.12(**c**). The process p multicasts its two messages to all processes. Although the multicast from q with timestamp $(2,1,0,0)$ is currently held waiting for a second message from p, its delivery will no longer be delayed once the multicast with timestamp $(2,0,0,0)$ is received.

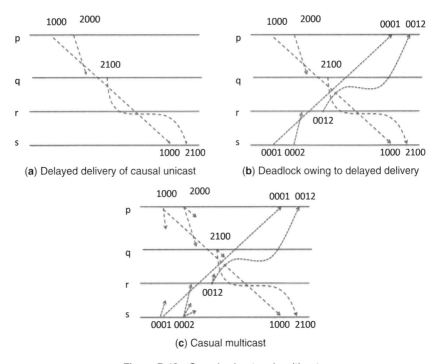

Figure B.12   *Causal unicast and multicast*

Obviously, there will be a problem if a multicast message is lost; therefore, it is important that every process receive all multicasts. *Reliable multicast* can be achieved in several ways. It is important that multicast be reliable, even when the original sending process crashes, because of the causal dependencies that can hold up delivery of a multicast if not all of its causal predecessors are available. Every process can buffer all multicasts that they receive. In this way, any process that sends a multicast message has buffered copies of all of the causal predecessors of that multicast. It docs not matter if some of the senders of those causal precessors have crashed. When a process receives a multicast that causally depends on multicasts that the receiver has not seen, the receiver can "negatively acknowledge" the multicast back to the sender, asking for the causal predecessors it has not seen. The remaining issue is when is it safe to free up buffer space by deleting a saved multicast message? One avenue is to have every process re-broadcast a multicast when it receives it. A process knows it can delete its copy of the multicast when it has received a copy from the $n-1$ other processes. This is an expensive protocol, with $O(n^2)$ messages for every multicast. Another alternative is to maintain a "causal frontier" reflecting the vector clocks seen at other processes, based on the vector timestamps on the messages received from those processes. If a process sends a multicast with a particular vector timestamp then, by definition, it will have seen all of the causal predecessors of that message, as reflected by the timestamp.

Therefore, once a message comes inside the causal frontier, in the sense that it has come within the causal history of every process, processes no longer need to maintain a buffered record of that message for possible re-transmission. This primitive is a particularly good fit with processes that are sharing copies of the same replicated data and need to multicast updates of the data to each other with some message delivery guarantees.

We have seen in Sect. 6.9.2 that ordered delivery of update requests to all copies of a replicated database, or at least to a quorum of the replicas, is essential to maintain the relative consistency of the databases: all replicas must perform the update operations in the same order. We saw a protocol for doing this in Sect. B.3.2 based on a voting protocol using logical timestamps. This protocol provides a *total order* on request delivery. This is a strictly stronger message delivery order than causal order, as demonstrated in Fig. B.13. Figure B.13(**a**) demonstrates two multicasts (m_1 and m_2) that are delivered in different orders at different replicas. For example, the multicasts are delivered in different orders at processes q and r. Nevertheless, the delivery of the multicasts in this example is causal as there is no causal relationship between the two multicasts! The send events for these multicasts are concurrent. Total ordering provides a stronger guarantee: even in the absence of a causal relationship between send events, total ordering requires that the multicasts (including concurrent multicasts) be delivered in the same order, including at the sender processes. This is demonstated in Fig. B.13(**b**), where message m_1 is delivered before m_2 at all processes. This requires delaying delivery of m_2 at process r until m_1 is received, and also at process s—the process that sends message m_2.

Why is causal delivery useful? For application programming purposes, causal multicast can be viewed as a generalization of FIFO delivery. The FIFO delivery rule can be stated in terms of the happened-before relation, where we again assume that messages are uniquely identified; $send(m)$ *on* i denotes the send event for the sending of m on process i and $deliver(m)$ *on* i denotes the event of the message m being delivered by the middleware to the application on process i (perhaps some time after it is received):

Delivery of messages is *FIFO* if, when $(send(m_1)$ *on* $i) \rightsquigarrow (send(m_2)$ *on* $i)$, then $(deliver(m_1)$ *on* $k) \rightsquigarrow (deliver(m_2)$ *on* $k)$.

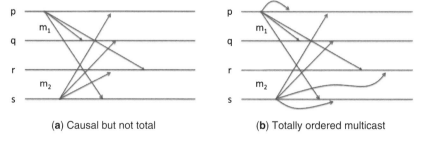

    (**a**) Causal but not total   (**b**) Totally ordered multicast

Figure B.13 *Causal and total multicast*

Causal message order generalizes this definition by allowing causal relationships between send events *on different processes*:

Delivery of messages is *causal* if, when $(send(m_1)$ *on* $i) \rightsquigarrow (send(m_2)$ *on* $j)$, then $(deliver(m_1)$ *on* $k) \rightsquigarrow (deliver(m_2)$ *on* $k)$.

Figure B.14(**a**) demonstrates a situation where there is a single process where all updates are done. This process then notifies the other processes, holding copies of replicated data, of each update. Assuming FIFO message delivery between this single source process X and the other processes, it is easy to guarantee that each recipient sees the update operations in the same order. For example, this can be ensured by using TCP/IP channels. As every update is sent by X, and each such update is received before any subsequent updates sent by X, every process sees the updates in the same order.

Figure B.14(**b**) provides an example where updates originate at different senders, in this case X and Z. However, in some sense this is similar to the case of a single process sending all updates. In Fig. B.14(**b**), the intention is that there is a *single thread of control*, indicated by the dashed line. This thread of control originates at process X then, via a service request, moves to process Z. This single thread of control performs an update at X, then a second update at Z. Although the updates originate at different processes, they originate at the same "virtual" sender: the thread of control. Therefore, delivery of these update notifications should be ordered at all recipients so that the first update is always delivered first. This is done at process W, where the delay of delivery of the first update causes the second update to be buffered until the first update is delivered. This is the approach of *causally ordered* update operations. Causal message order ensures that these update messages are seen in the same order at all replicas, with lower overhead than would be required of a protocol for total ordering.

One aspect of both logical and vector timestamps that should be noted is that both protocols are based on tracking the causal ordering between events at the communication level. For example, the local ordering clause in the definition of the happened-before relation relates any event in a process timeline to all the events that occurred before it on the same process timeline. There may be no

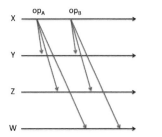
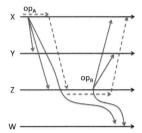

(**a**) FIFO delivery form a single sender   (**b**) Causal delivery from a single thread

Figure B.14   *FIFO and causal order*

causal relationship in the application logic between two events on a timeline of a process, so tracking these dependencies at the communication level may introduce "false causalities" between the events. This is part of the basis for Cheriton and Skeen's argument for tracking these dependencies at the application rather than the communication level, applying the end-to-end argument to reason against the use of communication middleware to track causal dependencies [20].

B.3.5 Distributed Snapshots

As a final application of logical and vector time, we consider an important algorithm for distributed systems that is also an example of the derivation of an algorithm using notions of time. The goal is to build a *snapshot* of a distributed system, a record of the states of the different processes in the network at a "moment" in time, where time is, again, assumed to be relativistic.

Figure B.15 suggests the challenge with obtaining a snapshot of a running distributed system. In Fig. B.15(**a**), processes q and r report back to the initiator of the protocol, which might, in this instance, be process r. The q process has sent a message to p requesting access to a resource that p controls; the r process has sent a message to q requesting access to a resource that q controls. Figure B.15(**a**) illustrates the point in the timelines for q and r where the snapshot has been taken. Figure B.15(**b**) illustrates a later point in time, where process p has reported its state back to the protocol initiator. By the time it reports, p has sent a message to q granting its resource request and is now itself blocked waiting for r to release a resource that it controls. The problem is that the snapshot is not instantaneous and, by taking a snapshot of the state of p at a different "time" than q and r, an incorrect snapshot has been constructed. In this case, the snapshot signals that the system is deadlocked because of a cycle in the "wait-for" graph for resource requests. In fact, there is no deadlock! Process p has granted its resource to q, so process will

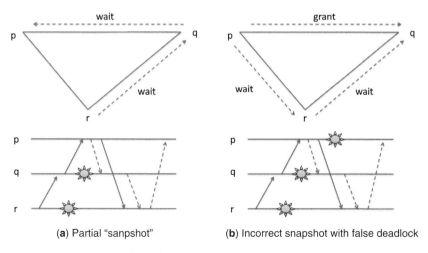

(**a**) Partial "sanpshot" (**b**) Incorrect snapshot with false deadlock

Figure B.15 *Problems with snapshots*

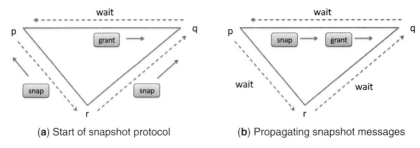

(**a**) Start of snapshot protocol   (**b**) Propagating snapshot messages

Figure B.16   *Snapshot protocol*

be able to continue processing and eventually grant its resource to r. Resource r will, in turn, eventually be able to release its resource to p. However, because the snapshot has been taken at different points in time at the different processes, the original release by p of its resource to r has been missed.

Assuming we had a global real-time clock, synchronized among the processes, we could use this to ensure that processes computed their snapshots at the same instant. In fact, this is the basis for the first algorithm for computing snapshots and is an example of a general strategy for deriving distributed algorithms: define an algorithm assuming that there is a global clock and then provide an implementation of clocks that provides the properties of the imaginary global clock that the processes require. One complication is that the internal states of the process alone are not sufficient, as it is possible that, for example, the message from p to q granting the latter access to p's resource is in transit at that point in time. Here, the algorithm makes an additional assumption: it is assumed that communication channels between processes are FIFO. This assumption provides a strategy for recording messages in transit as part of the snapshot. We assume that every message contains a timestamp, recording when it is sent. The protocol is as follows:

1. The process initiating the protocol sends a message to all other processes, requesting them to run the protocol at a time t. This time is chosen far enough in the future that every process will be able to receive the request message by time t.

2. At time t, each process records its current state as part of the snapshot. Before sending any other message, each process also sends a null message, timestamped with time t, or any $t' \geq t$, on all output channels and begins recording messages that are received on input channels.

3. When a process receives a message with timestamp $t' \geq t$, the FIFO property of the channels ensures that no earlier messages will be received on that channel. Therefore the process stops recording input messages on that channel and saves the recorded messages as part of the snapshot.

4. When a process has received messages on all input channels with timestamps $t' \geq t$, it knows that there are no more input messages to be received that were sent before the snapshot time instant. That process returns the snapshot of its state that it has created to the protocol initiatior.

Note the requirement that every process send a null message on all output channels at the beginning of the protocol. This is necessary in order to know when the protocol has terminated. Unlike the mutual exclusion algorithm, this protocol makes weak assumptions about the communication topology of the network. The protocol initiator must somehow communicate with all processes by time t, so that everyone is ready to start the protocol by that time t. Thereafter, the algorithm only assumes FIFO one-way channels between processes, where some processes may need to route their messages to some destinations through other processes. A duplex channel is represented by two one-way channels.

The next version of the protocol removes the need for synchronized physical clocks by replacing them with logical clocks.

1. The process initiating the protocol advances its logical clock to a value t that is larger than current logical clock value of any process. It records its own current state as part of the snapshot and then sends a special "snap" message to all other processes. This snap message requests these processes to run the protocol at logical time t, which immediately becomes the current logical time at the recipient.

2. When a process first receives the snap message, it advances its logical clock to the timestamp on that message as usual. As the time has now become the time at which the protocol is intended to run, the recipient immediately records its current state as part of the snapshot it has started recording and relays the snap message on all of its output channels. The process also begins recording in the snapshot any input messages that are received on the remaining input channels.

3. When a process receives a message with logical timestamp $t' \geq t$, the FIFO property of the channels ensures that no earlier messages will be received on that channel. Therefore, the process stops recording input messages on that channel and saves the recorded messages as part of the snapshot.

4. When a process has received messages on all input channels with logical timestamps $t' \geq t$, it knows that there are no more input messages to be received that were sent before the snapshot time instant t. That process returns the snapshot of its state that it has created to the protocol initiatior.

Figure B.16 illustrates the operation of this protocol on the example from Fig. B.15. In Fig. B.16(**a**), process r sends snap messages to p and q. When process p receives the message, it records its internal state, relays the message on all outgoing channels, and begins recording on any remaining input channels. In Fig. B.16(**b**), process p has relayed the snap message to q; this message is now behind the resource grant message in the FIFO channel from p to q. There are two possible scenarios:

1. If the grant message arrives at q before the snap message from r, then the state of q is changed to no longer be blocked, waiting for p to grant the resource. At this point, it does not matter which of the snap messages arrives

at q first as the snapshot will not record its state as blocked and no false deadlock will be detected.

2. If the snap message from r arrives at q first, then q will record its current state, relay the snap message to p, and begin recording incoming messages on the input channel from p. The grant message from p is then recorded as part of the snapshot at q. Processes p and q complete the protocol when they receive each other's snap messages and r completes the protocol when it receives snap messages from both p and q.

The final versin of the protocol is based on the observation that, with the special snap messages, explicit timestamps are no longer needed. Every process begins the protocol as soon as it receives the first snap message. The timestamps on the messages are used to determine when a process can stop recording messages on an input channels but, in fact, the first message to be received with timestamp $t' \geq t$ on an input channel, where t is the logical time for running the protocol, will be the snap message. This message will either be echoed by a downstream process or sent by another process on a parallel path from the original snap message received. The actual distributed snapshot protocol is finally:

1. The process initiating the protocol records its own current state as part of the snapshot and then sends a special "snap" message to all other processes. This snap message requests these processes to run the protocol as soon as they receive it.

2. When a process first receives the snap message, it immediately records its current state as part of the snapshot it has started recording and relays the snap message on all of its output channels. The process also begins recording in the snapshot any input messages that are received on the remaining input channels.

3. When a process receives the snap message on an input channel, the FIFO property of the channels ensures that no earlier messages will be received on that channel. Therefore, the process stops recording input messages on that channel and saves the recorded messages as part of the snapshot.

4. When a process has received the snap message on all input channels, it knows that there are no more input messages to be received that were sent before the snapshot protocol started. That process returns the snapshot of its state that it has created to the protocol initiatior, via the process from which it received the first "snap" message.

The protocol assumes that messages are delivered reliably and in order. More seriously, it is vulnerable to process failures, which are outside the scope of the basic protocol. We consider resilient solutions to process failures in Chapter 10 in the sequel volume. The algorithm also has a curious property: the snapshot state that is recorded may not correspond to any actual state that the system transitions through. Consider the example in Fig. B.17: there are two processes. The first process starts in state p and may, at any time, send message m_1 and transition to

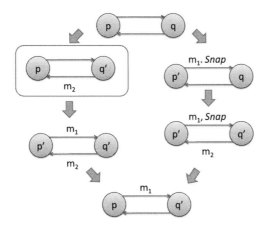

Figure B.17 *State transitions and snapshot state*

state p'. It will transition back to state p when it receives message m_2. The other process starts in state q and may, at any time, send message m_2 and transition to state q'. It will transition back to state q when it receives message m_1. We describe the state of the system by a triple:

(state of first process, messages in transit, state of second process)

The system in Fig. B.17 starts in overall state $(p, \{\}, q)$: the first process sends the snap message, recording its own state as p. The first process then emits the m_1 message and the system transitions to the $(p', \{m_1\}, q)$ state. The second process emits the m_2 message and the system transitions to the $(p', \{m_1, m_2\}, q')$ state. The m_2 message is received by the first process and it records this message as part of the snapshot while transitioning back to the p state (and finishing its recording of its input channels). The snap message finally arrives at the second process. It records its state as q' and immediately completes, as it received the snap message on its single input channel. The state, at this point, is $(p, \{m_1\}, q')$. However, there is an interesting observation: the actual recorded snapshot state, $(p, \{m_2\}, q')$, was never an actual state of the system during the recording of the snapshot.

Nevertheless, the snapshot state is reachable from the starting state (by the emission by the second state of the m_2 message). Once in the snapshot state, the first process cannot receive the m_2 message until it emits its own m_1 message—at that point the first process can receive the m_2 message and transition back to the p state. The result is that the system, had it entered the snapshot state, could have transitioned to the actual state of the system after the execution of the snapshot protocol.

There is a particular class of properties for which the protocol provides a useful result. A *stable property* of system states is one such that, once it holds for a system state, it then continues to hold for all successors of that state. Examples of such stable properties are if the system has terminated, if it has deadlocked, or if a resource is no longer in use and can be retrieved by the system. If we evaluate a stable predicate for the snapshot state and find that property true for that state, then it will continue to be true for any successors of the state, including the state that the system actually eventually enters that is a successor of the snapshot state.

B.4   VIRTUAL TIME

In the protocols for ordered message delivery in Sect. B.3.2 and Sect. B.3.4, the assumption was that delivery of messages could be delayed until agreement could be reached on order of delivery and a message's precedessors can be delivered to the application in order, before the message itself. This is a pessimistic model of concurrency control. We consider optimistic methods for concurrency control in distributed databases in Chapter 9 in the sequel volume. In this section, we consider a notion of *virtual time* that is a basis for a class of optimistic concurrency control mechanisms in distributed systems [21].

If the notion of logical time is to fit a measure of time to the actual execution of the system, the notion of virtual time is to fit the execution of the system to a logical notion of time. Time may be a real quantity number in this case, so there is no attempt to determine if all messages in the interval between two timestamps have been received. Instead, the notion of time is assumed to be totally ordered; this is used to determine the order in which mesages are delivered. However, in this case, the determination is performed retroactively and, if it is determined that messages were delivered prematurely before some of their predecessors, then the execution of the application is rolled back to before the receipt of the prematurely-delivered message.

Figure B.18(**a**) provides an example. Process p sends message m_1 to q and then sends message m_2 to r. Process q sends m_3 to process r after receiving m_2, so m_3 is a causal successor to the sending of m_1. Nevertheless, m_3 is delivered immediately to process r which, in turn, sends a message m_4 to process s. When message m_1, which has been delayed in the network, finally arrives at process r, its timestamp reveals that it should have been delivered before m_3. At this point, the execution of the application at r is rolled back to the most recent checkpoint before receipt of m_3. Rolling back the execution of the application includes undoing any messages

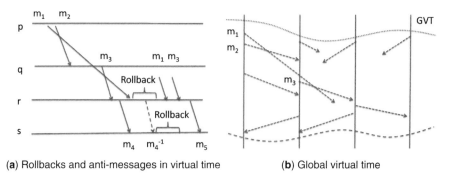

(**a**) Rollbacks and anti-messages in virtual time   (**b**) Global virtual time

Figure B.18   *Virtual time*

that were sent during this execution. This undoing involves the sending of *anti-messages* to the destinations of the original messages. An anti-message is exactly like the original message, except for a single bit that identifies the "sign" of the message. If a message is in a receipt queue and a message with the opposite sign is received, then the two messages cancel out and the original message is deleted from the queue. If a message has already been processed when its "negative" is received, then the process where the message has been received must be rolled back past the point of receipt. In Fig. B.18(**a**), the rollback of process r after receiving m_1 causes the anti-message m_4^{-1} to be sent to s to cancel the message m_4 that was sent. If s has already processed m_4, then its execution must be rolled back past the point where m_4 was received. At process r, once the rollback is finished, the messages m_1 and m_3 are delivered to the application in the correct order. It may subsequently send another message to process s, perhaps replacing the message m_4 that was sent in the previous execution—perhaps even the same as m_4. Clearly, some facility for specifying that certain messages commute is an important part of improving the scalability of the approach. For example, if m_1 and m_3 commute, then receipt of m_1 after receipt of m_3 would not require the rollback of process r, even though m_1 has a smaller timestamp.

Rollback requires the buffering of messages, in case anti-messages need to be sent or messages need to be re-delivered. What is the limit on the extent of this buffering? The notion of *global virtual time* (GVT) is used to determine when messages (and process checkpoints) no longer need to be buffered. GVT is defined, at a moment in physical time, as the minimum of (1) the local clocks (local virtual times) at the processes, and (2) the timestamps of the messages that have been sent but not yet processed (including messages in transit). Figure B.18(**b**) illustrates this, where the lower curve reflects the frontier of the executions of the processes and the upper curve reflects global virtual time defined, in this case, by messages sent by the processes that have not yet been processed. Once any of these messages are received, say with a timestamp t, they may trigger the rollback of the receiver process past virtual time t, so all processes must retain state (including messages sent) for the minimum of these virtual times. The global virtual time is not something the processes will, in general, know with certainty, but it can be approximated at a process by broadcasting a request to the other processes for their current local clock values, as well as timestamps of messages sent but not acknowledged, and messages received but not yet processed. This assumes reliable FIFO message transmission.

In general, some form of optimistic, possibly premature, message delivery appears essential in mobile systems, where messages may be delayed for arbitrary periods, perhaps forever, depending on the state and connectivity of mobile devices. It remains to be seen if process state can be check-pointed and reliably rolled back and re-started, at least in any scalable fashion. Certainly, there is application in the state of content databases for mobile devices, where updates on the content need to be ordered, and delay on updates would lead to owners of devices not being able to "see" updates yet, because not all predecessors of those updates have been received at the device yet. Instead, updates are performed immediately when they are received, then rolled back and reapplied when earlier conflicting updates are subsequently received.

B.5 FURTHER READING

Cachin et al. [22] consider, in detail, protocols and algorithms for building reliable distributed systems. Charron-Bost et al. [23] provide a collection of advanced essays on issues and approaches to replication for highly available systems. Terry [24] surveys data management in mobile computing, where replication is obviously essential.

REFERENCES

1. Wells HG. The Time Machine. William Heinemann; London, 1895.
2. Eidson JC. Measurement, Control and Communication Using IEEE 1588. Springer; Berlin, 2006.
3. Ghose T. Ultra-precise quantum-logic clock trumps old atomic clock. Wired Magazine, February 2010. Available at: http://www.wired.com/wiredscience/2010/02/quantum-logic-atomic-clock/.
4. Allan DW, Ashby N, Hodge CC. The science of timekeeping. Technical Report Application Note 1289. Hewlett Packard; 1997.
5. Mills D. Internet time synchronization: The Network Time Protocol. *IEEE Transactions on Communications* 1991;39:1482–1493.
6. Maroti M, Kusy B, Simon G, Ledeczi A. The flooding time synchronization protocol. In: Proceedings of the 2nd ACM Conference on Embedded Networked Sensor Systems (SenSys). 2004, p. 39–49.
7. Ganeriwal S, Kumar R, Srivastava MB. Timing-sync protocol for sensor networks. In: Proceedings of the 1st ACM Conference on Embedded Networked Sensor Systems (SenSys). 2003, p. 138–149.
8. Verissimo P, Rodrigues L, Casimiro A. CesiumSpray: a precise and accurate global time service for large-scale systems. *Journal of Real-Time Systems* 1997;12:243–294.
9. Elson J, Estrin D. Fine-grained network time synchronization using reference broadcast. In: Fifth Symposium on Operating Systems Design and Implementation (OSDI). 2002, p. 147–163.
10. Srikanth TK, Toueg S. Optimal clock synchronization. *Journal of the ACM* 1987; 34:626–645.
11. Mates B. The Philosophy of Leibniz: Metaphysics and Language. Oxford: Oxford University Press; 1989.
12. Lamport L. Time, clocks and the ordering of events in a distributed system. *Communications of the ACM* 1978;21:558–565.
13. Mattern F. Virtual time and global states of distributed systems. In: Corsnard M editors. Proceedings of the International Workshop on Parallel and Distributed Algorithms. Elsevier; London, 1988. Pages 215–226.
14. Fidge CJ. Timestamps in message-passing systems that preserve the partial ordering. In: Raymond K, editor. Proceedings of the 11th Australian Computer Science Conference (ACSC'88). 1988, p. 50–66.

15. Schwarz R, Mattern F. Detecting causal relationships in distributed computations: In search of the Holy Grail. Technical Report SFB124-15/92. Kaiserslautern: Department of Computer Science, University of Kaiserslautern; 1992.

16. El Abbadi A, Skeen D, Cristian F. An efficient fault-tolerant protocol for replicated data management. In: Proceedings of the 4th ACM Symposium on Principles of Database Systems, 1985, p. 215–229.

17. Herlihy M. A quorum consensus replication method for abstract data types. *Transactions on Computer Systems* 1986;4:32–53.

18. Van Renesse R, Guerraoui R. Replication Techniques for Availability. In: Replication: Theory and Practice, Charron-Bost B, Pedone F, Schiper A (eds). Lecture Notes in Computer Science. Springer-Verlag, 2010.

19. Oki B, Liskov B. Viewstamped replication: A new primary copy method to support highly-available distributed systems. In: *Proceedings of ACM Symposium on Principles of Distributed Computing*. 1988, p. 8–17.

20. Cheriton DR, Skeen S. Understanding the limitations of causally and totally ordered communication. *SIGOPS Operating Systems Reviews* 1993;27:44–57.

21. Jefferson D. Virtual time. *ACM Transactions on Programming Languages and Systems*, 1985;7:404–420.

22. Cachin C, Guerraoui R, Rodrigue L. Introduction to Reliable and Secure Distributed Programming, 2nd edn. Springer-Verlag; Berlin, 2011.

23. Charron-Bost B, Pedone F, Schiper A, editors. Replication: Theory and Practice. Lecture Notes in Computer Science. Springer-Verlag; April 2010.

24. Terry D. Replicated Data Management in Mobile Computing. Morgan & Claypool; San Rafael, California, 2007.

Index

Enterprise Software Architecture and Design: Entities, Services, and Resources,
First Edition. Dominic Duggan.
© 2012 John Wiley & Sons, Inc. Published 2012 by John Wiley & Sons, Inc.